T0271233

COMPETITION POLICY AND PATENT LAW UNDER UNCERTAINTY

The regulation of innovation and the optimal design of legal institutions in an environment of uncertainty are two of the most important policy challenges of the twenty-first century. Innovation is critical to economic growth. Regulatory design decisions and, in particular, competition policy and intellectual property regimes can have profound consequences for economic growth. However, remarkably little is known about the relationship between innovation, competition, and regulatory policy. Any legal regime must attempt to assess the trade-offs associated with rules that will affect incentives to innovate and allocate efficiency, competition, and freedom of economic actors to commercialize the fruits of their innovative labors. The chapters in this book approach this critical set of problems from an economic perspective, relying on the tools of microeconomics, quantitative analysis, and comparative institutional analysis to explore and begin to provide answers to the myriad of challenges facing policy makers.

Geoffrey A. Manne is the founder and Executive Director of the International Center for Law and Economics (ICLE) in Portland, Oregon. He is also a Lecturer in Law at Lewis & Clark Law School in Portland. Prior to founding ICLE, Professor Manne was Director of Global Public Policy at LECG and directed Microsoft's legal and economics academic outreach program. Earlier, Professor Manne was a law professor specializing in antitrust law and economics, intellectual property law, corporate governance, and international economic regulation, all topics on which he has written. His publications have appeared in journals including the *Journal of Competition Law and Economics, Harvard Journal of Law and Public Policy, Wisconsin Law Review, Alabama Law Review*, and *Arizona Law Review*. He is an expert in the economic analysis of law, drawing on degrees from the University of Chicago as well as work for Judge Richard Posner, private practice, and brief service at the Federal Trade Commission. Professor Manne has practiced antitrust law at Latham & Watkins, has served as a Bigelow Fellow at the University of Chicago Law School and an Olin Fellow at the University of Virginia School of Law, and has clerked for Judge Morris S. Arnold on the 8th Circuit Court of Appeals. Professor Manne is a co-founder of the Microsoft / George Mason Annual Conference on the Law and Economics of Innovation (with Joshua D. Wright). He blogs at Truth on the Market.

Joshua D. Wright is an Associate Professor of Law at George Mason University School of Law, Arlington, Virginia, and the Director of Research of the International Center for Law and Economics. Professor Wright was appointed as the inaugural Scholar in Residence at the Federal Trade Commission Bureau of Competition, where he served until fall 2008. Professor Wright was a Visiting Professor at the University of Texas School of Law and a Visiting Fellow at the Searle Center at the Northwestern University School of Law during the 2008–2009 academic year. Professor Wright's areas of expertise include antitrust law and economics, intellectual property law, consumer protection, empirical law and economics, and economics of contracts. His publications have appeared in leading academic journals, including the *Journal of Law and Economics, Antitrust Law Journal, Competition Policy International, Supreme Court Economic Review, Yale Journal on Regulation, Journal of Competition Law and Economics, Review of Law and Economics*, and *UCLA Law Review*. Prior to joining the faculty at George Mason, Professor Wright clerked for the Honorable James V. Selna of the Central District of California and taught law and economics at the Pepperdine University Graduate School of Public Policy. He blogs at Truth on the Market.

Competition Policy and Patent Law under Uncertainty

Regulating Innovation

Edited by

GEOFFREY A. MANNE

International Center for Law and Economics

Lewis & Clark Law School

JOSHUA D. WRIGHT

George Mason University School of Law

International Center for Law and Economics

CAMBRIDGE
UNIVERSITY PRESS

CAMBRIDGE
UNIVERSITY PRESS

32 Avenue of the Americas, New York NY 10013-2473, USA

Cambridge University Press is part of the University of Cambridge.

It furthers the University's mission by disseminating knowledge in the pursuit of
education, learning and research at the highest international levels of excellence.

www.cambridge.org
Information on this title: www.cambridge.org/9780521766746

© Cambridge University Press 2011

First published 2011

A catalogue record for this publication is available from the British Library

Library of Congress Cataloguing in Publication data

Competition policy and patent law under uncertainty : regulating
innovation / [edited by] Geoffrey A. Manne, Joshua D.Wright.
p.   cm.
Includes index.
ISBN 978-0-521-76674-6 (hardback)
1. Patent laws and legislation.   2. Competition, Unfair.   3. Technological innovations –
Law and legislation.   4. Antitrust law.   I. Manne, Geoffrey A.   II. Wright, Joshua D.
K1575.C66   2011
346.04'86 – dc22   2010054599

ISBN 978-0-521-76674-6 Hardback

Contents

Contributors

Robert D. Cooter University of California Berkeley School of Law

Vincenzo Denicolò University of Bologna

Richard A. Epstein University of Chicago School of Law

Luigi Alberto Franzoni University of Bologna

Damien Geradin Tilburg University

Keith N. Hylton Boston University School of Law

Marco Iansiti Harvard University Business School

F. Scott Kieff George Washington University School of Law

Bruce H. Kobayashi George Mason University School of Law

Anne Layne-Farrar LECG, LLC

Mark A. Lemley Stanford Law School

Douglas G. Lichtman University of California Los Angeles School of Law

Stan J. Liebowitz University of Texas at Dallas

Haizhen Lin Indiana University

Gerard Llobet Centre for Monetary and Financial Studies

Geoffrey A. Manne Lewis & Clark Law School

Stephen E. Margolis North Carolina State University

Michael Meurer Boston University School of Law

Adam Mossoff George Mason University School of Law

Jorge Padilla LECG, LLC

Gregory L. Richards Keystone Strategy

Henry E. Smith Harvard Law School

Daniel F. Spulber Northwestern University

David J. Teece University of California Berkeley

Joshua D. Wright George Mason University School of Law

Introduction

Innovation is critical to economic growth. While it is well understood that legal institutions play an important role in fostering an environment conducive to innovation and its commercialization, much less is known about the optimal design of specific institutions. Regulatory design decisions, and in particular competition policy and intellectual property regimes, can have profoundly positive or negative consequences for economic growth and welfare. However, the ratio of what is known to what is unknown with respect to the relationship between innovation, competition, and regulatory policy is staggeringly low. In addition to this uncertainty concerning the relationships between regulation, innovation, and economic growth, the process of innovation itself is not well understood.

The regulation of innovation and the optimal design of legal institutions in this environment of uncertainty are two of the most important policy challenges of the twenty-first century. The chapters in this book approach this critical set of problems from an economic perspective, relying on the tools of microeconomics, quantitative analysis, and comparative institutional analysis to explore and begin to provide answers to the myriad of challenges facing policy-makers. Any legal regime, after all, must attempt to assess the trade-offs associated with rules that will affect incentives to take risks, allocative efficiency, competition, and freedom of economic actors to commercialize the fruits of their innovative labors and foster economic growth.

The strength of this analysis – often described as the New Institutional Economic approach – is in its recognition that understanding economic performance requires not only economic modeling of narrow behavior, but also an understanding of that behavior in its legal, economic, social, and political institutional contexts. New Institutional Economics employs the tools of

1

economics to rigorously analyze these institutions and relationships.[1] In the context of innovation, the New Institutional Economics approach requires rigorous thought about questions of institutional design and its potential impact on technological change. As Joskow notes, technological change has always been understood as an important component of economic growth,[2] but

> the theoretical and empirical foundation for understanding the rate and direction of innovation and how they are influenced by microeconomic, macroeconomic, institutional and policy considerations was poorly understood. Economic growth was driven by changes in capital and labor inputs, exogenous technological change, and poorly understood differences between countries over time and space.

In the tradition of Coase, North, Williamson, Klein, Alchian, Demsetz, and other key contributors to the development of the New Institutional Economic approach, the chapters in this volume apply economic insights to the challenging questions associated with regulating innovation, contributing a more rigorous theoretical and empirical understanding to the policy debate of how particular legal institutions are likely to impact innovation and growth. The application of this robust framework to the economics of innovation suggests several fruitful paths for scholarly inquiry that are explored throughout the book, including, at least, the economics of innovation, the relationship between innovation and competition policy, the patent system itself, the nature of property rights and theoretical perspectives on patent law, and the appropriate antitrust regulation of standard-setting organizations. However, each of these issues is related to the much broader and unifying theme of regulating competition in a dynamic and innovative market setting.

We have entitled our book *Competition Policy and Patent Law under Uncertainty: Regulating Innovation* because we believe any coherent regulatory framework must take into account the low level of empirical knowledge surrounding the complex relationship between regulation –through both competition policy and patent law – and innovation, and the corresponding uncertainty caused by this absence of knowledge. The relationship between regulation and innovation has posed a significant challenge to antitrust economists at least since Joseph Schumpeter's,[3] suggestion that dynamic

---

[1] Joskow, P. "Regulation of Natural Monopoly." In Handbook of law and economics. Amsterdam: Elsevier, 2007.

[2] *Id.*

[3] Schumpeter, Joseph Alois. Capitalism, socialism, and democracy. 3d ed. New York: Harper, 1950.

competition would result in "creative destruction," leading to a competitive process where one monopolist would replace another sequentially as new entrants developed a superior product.

Schumpeter's argument is often relied on in support of the proposition that antitrust enforcers should be reluctant to intervene in product markets because short-run welfare gains are likely to be swamped by a reduction in dynamic efficiencies associated with less innovation. The Schumpeterian argument naturally has limits, and it need not be the case that all welfare trade-offs between static product market competition and dynamic efficiencies everywhere tilt in favor of the latter. The central, elusive issue at the heart of the patent system, however, is the trade-off between the *ex ante* incentive to create and the *ex post*, dynamic consequences of patent policy that may impede sequential innovation to incentivize a priori creation.[4] Unsettled is the question of the magnitude of this trade-off and the long-run economic consequences of specific elements of the patent system aimed at promoting development on either side of this trade-off.

In the domain of competition, the well-known and oft-discussed tensions between monopoly, innovation, and product market competition have generated a substantial body of literature concerning the appropriate role of antitrust enforcement in the regulation of innovation.[5,6,7] This debate has prompted numerous proposals from commentators seeking to identify the most desirable approach to incorporating innovation into antitrust analysis, including the development of the "innovation market" concept,[8] or a more precise and rigorous approach to accounting for the likely costs and benefits of innovation in merger analysis.[9] Federal agency officials, particularly at the Department of Justice, have also recently demonstrated a concern for antitrust policy that overreaches by attempting to increase short-run

---

[4] Scotchmer, Suzanne. Innovation and incentives . Cambridge, Mass.: MIT Press, 2004.
[5] Baker, J. *Beyond Schumpeter vs. Arrow: How Antitrust Fosters Innovation*, 74 ANTITRUST L.J. 575 (2007).
[6] Gilbert, Richard. "Holding Innovation to Antitrust Standard." Competition Policy International 3, no. 1 (2007).
[7] Evans, David and Keith Hylton. "The Lawful Acquisition and Exercise of Monopoly Powers and the Implications for the Objectives of Antitrust." Competition Policy International 4, no. 2 (2008).
[8] Gilbert, Richard and Steven Sunshine. "Incorporating Dynamic Efficiency Concerns in Merger Analysis: The use of Innovation Markets." Antitrust Law Journal 63 (1995).
[9] Katz, Michael and Howard Shelanski. "Merger Policy and Innovation: Must Enforcement Change to Account for Technological Change." In Innovation Policy and the Economy Volume 6. Cambridge: MIT Press, 2006.

product market competition at the expense of dynamic efficiencies created by innovation.[10,11]

Taken collectively, the above are a welcome departure from a regime that myopically presumed a static market analysis would generate desirable outcomes, especially when that analysis is undertaken without sufficient sensitivity to the institutional settings in which enforcement occurs costlessly and omniscient enforcers act on the basis of perfect economic models and full information. Until Easterbrook's seminal insights about the relationship between the social costs of erroneous antitrust enforcement and optimal liability rules, the long-term economic consequences of imperfect intervention (or non-intervention, for that matter) had been an oft-ignored but fundamental aspect of proper competition policy.[12] The more recent recognition of the importance and difficulty of dynamic economic analysis is part and parcel of this trend. Both reflect the influence of New Institutional Economics.

These ongoing policy discussions are even more acute in the debate over whether reform of the antitrust laws is required to make them coherent in a "new economy" in which innovation, intellectual property, and technological change are essential components of the competitive process.[13] The emerging consensus appears to be that economic analysis and learning are a sufficient basis to conclude that antitrust *should* incorporate dynamic efficiencies into the current framework by accounting for the impact of competition to engage in research and development for new or improved goods, services, or processes. For example, the Antitrust Modernization Committee Report and Recommendations optimally declares:[14]

[C]urrent antitrust analysis has a sufficient grounding in economics and is sufficiently flexible to reach appropriate conclusions in matters involving industries in which innovation, intellectual property, and technological change are central features.

---

[10] Masoudi, Gerald F. Deputy Assistant Attorney General, Antitrust Division, Intellectual Property and Competition: Four Principles for Encouraging Innovation (April 11, 2006), available at http://www.usdoj.gov/atr/public/speeches/215645.htm.

[11] Barnett, T., Assistant Attorney General, Antitrust Division, The Gales of Creative Destruction: The Need for Clear and Objective Standards in Enforcing Section 2 of the Sherman Act (June 20, 2006), available at http://www.ftc.gov/os/sectiontwohearings/docs/Barnett-statement.pdf.

[12] Easterbrook, Frank. "The Limits of Antitrust." Texas Law Review 63, no. 1 (1984).

[13] Posner, Richard. "Antitrust and the New Economy." Antitrust Law Journal 68 (2001).

[14] Antitrust Modernization Commission Report and Recommendations, 2007, *found at* http://govinfo.library.unt.edu/amc/report_recommendation/toc.htm.

Slowly, the center of the policy debate appears to have shifted from whether regulatory efforts should account for the relationships between competition, property rights, innovation, and economic welfare to how regulators should incorporate theoretical and empirical knowledge of these relationships into sensible policy. These developments have the potential to improve antitrust analysis and benefit consumers. Regulatory regimes ignoring dynamic competition and efficiencies are as unlikely to improve welfare as those that are so paralyzed by fear of deterring innovation that they fail to make appropriate interventions in product markets where consumers are threatened by anticompetitive conduct.

In patent policy the debate is no less acute, although there may be a better appreciation for the limits of both our knowledge and our regulatory institutions. There is a strong, recent push in the courts, in the commentary, and in Congress to limit the extent of the property rights protected by patents. In the courts, a string of recent decisions culminating in the Federal Circuit's 2008 *Bilski* decision has weakened the scope and strength of patent protection, particularly for the sorts of algorithmic innovations at the heart of the "new economy." Commentators have similarly mounted a scathing campaign against the present U.S. patent system. While some of this has been essentially ideological, "antiproperty" rhetoric,[15] more recent economic analysis has been built on far stronger foundations.[16] Along the same lines, the push for patent reform in Congress has reached a frenzied pitch, with passage of some sort of legislation almost inevitable in the coming years.

Much of the economic literature on the patent system is inherently built on an institutional foundation where elements of the patent-granting and enforcement systems are subjected to close scrutiny. Nevertheless, there remains a dearth of rigorous economic literature seriously addressing the role of property rights and institutions in facilitating competition, innovation, and economic growth. Certainly work remains to be done to rigorously incorporate the potential impact of antitrust and patent law on innovation and dynamic efficiency. The fundamental challenge is identifying a sound analytical framework to guide policy-makers, courts, and agencies in designing policies that achieve the desired goals of encouraging innovation and growth while satisfying the constraint that the social gains obtained through intervention still outweigh the sum of administrative and error costs.

---

[15] Stallman, Richard. Free software, free society: selected essays of Richard M. Stallman. Boston, MA: Free Software Foundation, 2002.

[16] Bessen, James, and Michael James Meurer. Patent failure: How judges, bureaucrats, and lawyers put innovators at risk. Princeton: Princeton University Press, 2008.

Meeting the demands of this challenge is easier said than done. Our economic knowledge regarding innovation itself, conduct affecting innovation, and how economists and regulators should assess competitive outcomes involving trade-offs between product market competition and innovation is far less impressive than our knowledge in a purely static setting. The error-cost approach to antitrust policy[17] teaches that regulators' decision-making process must be informed by the relatively high costs of false positives that lead to a chilling of pro-competitive innovation. The error-cost framework has been applied fruitfully to resolve debates over the optimal antitrust liability rules for predatory pricing, bundling, tying, and other contractual practices.[18,19,20,21] Over the past several decades, industrial organization economists have collected a small but ever-growing body of empirical evidence concerning the likely competitive effects of various business practices that have attracted antitrust scrutiny, such as vertical contractual restraints.[22] This empirical evidence informs both our perceptions of the likelihood that any given practice is pro-competitive and our expected frequency of false positives. Where the conduct at issue involves innovation, the key to economic growth, the social costs associated with false positives are no doubt high. It is therefore critical to assess the state of our economic learning related to antitrust analysis of competitive effects in markets where innovation is an important component of the competitive process. A key policy question is whether existing economic theory and empirical knowledge provide a sufficient basis for identifying those instances of innovation or conduct affecting innovation that will reduce welfare and produce social gains that outweigh administrative and error costs.

While the emerging consensus appears to answer this question in the affirmative, the incorporation of innovation considerations into competition policy and patent law is a more difficult enterprise than has generally been appreciated. Many scholars have recognized that our empirical knowledge of the relationship between market structure and innovation, as well as between market structure and consumer welfare, is limited relative to

[17] Easterbrook 1984, ibid.
[18] Cooper, James, Luke Froeb, Dan O'Brien, and Michael Vita. "Vertical Antitrust Policy as a Problem of Inference." International of Industrial Organization 23, no. 7–8 (2005).
[19] Evans, David, and A. Jorge Padilla. "Designing Antitrust Rules for Assessing Unilateral Practices: A Neo-Chicago Approach." University of Chicago Law Review 72 (2005).
[20] Beckner, C. Frederick, and Steven Salop. "Decision Theory and Antitrust Rules." Antitrust Law Journal 67, no. 1 (1999).
[21] Hylton, Keith and Michael Salinger. "Tying Law and Policy: A Decision-Theoretic Approach." Antitrust Law Journal 69 (2001).
[22] Froeb et al., ibid.

our understanding of static price effects in conventional product markets. The limits of our empirical knowledge are just one important constraint on the ability of regulators to confidently intervene in markets on behalf of consumers.

A second such constraint is the multidimensional nature of competition. "Competition" involves a remarkably heterogeneous set of activities. The competitive process requires various forms of rivalry that occur on multiple dimensions: output, price, quality, and innovation. The key point for would-be regulators, highlighted by Demsetz,[23] among others, is that these forms of competitive rivalry are frequently inversely correlated. The critical point is that the relevant question for competition policy authorities is whether they have a reliable basis on which to determine which mixture of competitive activities, including innovation, will maximize welfare.

The Demsetzian view was that the multiplicity of competitive activities undermined, perhaps completely, the ability of "scholars, lawyers, judges, and politicians" to confidently "agree that a policy has increased (or decreased) the general level of competitive intensity." Even when there was consensus that a particular rule change or change in the mix of competitive activities was for the better, Demsetz argued that the consensus was likely the product of "our heavy reliance on perfect competition, monopoly, and oligopoly models, all of which focus only on imitative output competition." While today's competition and innovation policy communities may not publicly express Demsetz's skepticism concerning the promise of antitrust rules in improving the mix of competitive activities, the spirit of the underlying skepticism illustrates the heart of the question motivating a significant portion of modern competition policy debates: Is the economic or empirical basis of rules and proposed policies providing incentives to alter the mix of competitive activities sufficient to justify confidence that the policy changes will do more good than harm?

Where these forms of competitive rivalry are negatively correlated, such as static price competition and innovation, evaluating the benefits of these alternative bundles in terms of consumer welfare requires knowing the marginal rates of technical substitution between competitive forms to convert different forms into common units of consumer welfare. What empirical evidence do we have about these rates of substitution? Others[24] have documented this extensive literature in greater detail than is required for

[23] Demsetz, Harold. 100 Years of Antitrust: Should We Celebrate?, Brent T. Upson Memorial Lecture, George Mason University School of Law, Law and Economics Center (1991).
[24] Gilbert 2007; Baker, 2007, ibid.

our purposes, but we briefly survey the existing theoretical and empirical knowledge of the relationship between product market competition, consumer welfare, innovation, and market structure.

It is useful to begin with an understanding of some well-established economic principles of the relationship between competition and innovation that have emerged from this literature. The first principle is that competitive rivalry associated with innovation is a form of competition itself. In other words, competition encourages innovation by providing an incentive for each competitor to win the "prize" associated with appropriating the gains from the innovation. The second principle is that product market competition encourages competitors to innovate to face less competition and earn greater profits. The converse can also hold: A firm that does not face substantial product market competition might have less incentive to innovate. This effect is at the heart of John Hicks's observation that the "best of all monopoly profits is a quiet life," and has been referred to as the "escape-the-competition" effect.[25] The third principle is related to the second and posits that firms that face greater product market competition post-innovation will have less incentive to engage in research and development. The fourth principle is often referred to as the "pre-emption effect," which illustrates that a firm may have an additional marginal incentive to innovate if the innovation will discourage rivals and potential entrants from investing in research and development themselves.

By themselves, these non–mutually exclusive and sometimes conflicting economic principles do not tell us what role competition policy and patent law should play in innovative industries. For example, the maxim that innovation is a form of competition offers little guidance for antitrust policy. All agree that innovative activity is an essential part of the competitive process. The *antitrust-relevant* questions, however, are not whether competition that spurs innovation and consumer benefits should be encouraged or whether attempts to reduce such competition should violate the antitrust laws. Rather, the antitrust-relevant policy question is whether antitrust agencies and judges can confidently predict when antitrust policy might increase or decrease innovative activity in a way that net increases consumer welfare. If firms are engaging in an endogenously determined mixture of competitive activities and an antitrust policy designed to encourage innovation is successfully introduced, we can expect the new mixture of competitive forms to involve more innovation and less of other forms of competition. But it is unclear that the first principle tells us anything more about the

[25] Hicks, John. "Annual Survey of Economic Theory: The Theory of Monopoly." Econometrica 3, no. 1 (1935).

likely consumer welfare effects of the policy. The key policy challenge is to identify the conditions under which antitrust agencies and courts can test a sufficient economic and empirical basis to find out if a specific intervention is going to improve welfare.

The same logic applies, of course, to patent law reform. Competition might be encouraged by the strengthening of property rights, with firms competing for a more-substantial reward; or it might be deterred, where strong rights and inefficient institutions impede future competition and innovation or induce inefficient rent-seeking. Again, regardless, the first principle does little to enable any informed or rigorous analysis of specific policy proposals. The second and third principles do not offer better policy guidance on their own. Leaving aside the methodological issue of how one measures competition in these models, these principles teach that product market competition might increase or decrease the incentive to innovate under different conditions. Finally, the fourth principle, the "pre-emption effect," teaches that dominant firms might have a greater incentive to innovate to reduce the innovation incentives of rivals and potential entrants. The pre-emption effect applies not only to "sham" innovations but also innovations that offer consumers immediate and tangible benefits such as offering a new product or increasing product quality.

The theoretical literature relating to competition and innovation is by itself insufficient to instill any great confidence in our – or regulators' – ability to determine what antitrust policies will encourage innovation and result in net consumer welfare gains. Specifically, our ability to apply antitrust standards depends on our ability to predict how a rule will impact the *mixture* of competitive forms that will exist after the policy is implemented and to rank these mixtures on consumer welfare or efficiency criteria. At this point, economic theory does not appear to provide a reliable method of making such a determination. Gilbert notes that "economic theory supports neither the view that market power generally threatens innovation by lowering the return to innovative efforts nor the Schumpeterian view that concentrated markets generally promote innovation."[26]

There are several reasons for this uncertainty. First, as discussed previously, our theoretical knowledge cannot yet confidently predict the direction of the impact of additional product market competition on innovation, much less the magnitude. Additionally, the multi-dimensional nature of competition implies that the magnitude of these impacts will be important as innovation and other forms of competition will frequently be inversely correlated as they relate to consumer welfare. Thus, weighing

---

[26] Gilbert, *supra* note 5.

the magnitudes of opposing effects will be essential to most policy decisions relating to innovation. Again, at this stage, economic theory does not provide a reliable basis for predicting the conditions under which welfare gains associated with greater product market competition resulting from some regulatory intervention will outweigh losses associated with reduced innovation.

But regulators, policy-makers, and judges need not rely only on this theoretical literature alone to guide policy. Rather, one expects policy-makers to turn to our empirical knowledge of the relationship between competition, innovation, and consumer welfare. There are at least three empirical relationships that are relevant to policy-making in this area. The first is the relationship between product market competition and innovative activity, the second is the link between firm size and research and development, and the third is the connection between patent activity and innovation or economic growth.

Unfortunately, here, too, we believe that the available evidence, given the current state of the empirical literature, is an insufficient basis on which to ground policy decisions. Early studies of the link between product market competition and innovation supported the Schumpeterian hypothesis by finding an inverted-U relationship: Innovative activity is at its maximum at intermediate levels of market concentration and decreases as concentration approaches monopoly or more atomistic structures.[27,28,29] But the failure of these early studies to account for differences between industries, and the endogeneity in the relationship between market structure and innovation, undermine their value. A recent study by Philippe Aghion et al.,[30] suggests that the link between market structure and markups of price over average costs might indeed have an inverted-U shape, though commentators have noted that the study does not provide a basis for policy decisions regarding the role of innovation in well-defined markets because the analysis only controls for industry effects at the two-digit SIC code level. Other studies have examined the impact of changes in market structure within a single industry over time to analyze the relationship between product market competition and productivity or innovation with mixed results.[31] And others[32]

[27] Baker, J. "Beyond Schumpeter vs. Arrow: How Antitrust Fosters Innovation." 74 Antitrust Law Journal 575 (2007).

[28] Katz, M. and Shelanski, H.: "Mergers and Innovation." 74 Antitrust Law Journal 1 (2007).

[29] Gilbert, Richard. "Holding Innovation to an Antitrust Standard." 3 Competition Policy International 47 (2007).

[30] Aghion, P., *Competition and Innovation: An Inverted U Relationship*, 120 Q.J. Econ. 701 (2005).

[31] Hylton, Keith and Fei Deng. "Antitrust Around the World: An Empirical Analysis of the Scope of the Competition Laws and Their Effects." Antitrust Law Journal 74, no. 2 (2007).

[32] Hylton and Deng, 2007, ibid.

have examined whether competition policy enforcement is associated with greater competition or productivity, again with mixed results.

Another strand of empirical literature examines the relationship between firm size and research and development. Gilbert[33] summarizes the findings in this literature as consistent with the theory that the effects of firm size and competition on innovation should be greater for processes than product innovations. Gilbert's careful examination of the empirical record concludes that the existing body of theoretical and empirical literature on the relationship between competition and innovation "fails to provide general support for the Schumpeterian hypothesis that monopoly promotes either investment in research and development or the output of innovation" and that "the theoretical and empirical evidence also does not support a strong conclusion that competition is uniformly a stimulus to innovation."

Finally, another expansive vein of literature has explored the relationship between patent activity and innovation or other determinants of economic growth.[34] Perhaps the most compelling of these studies is Moser.[35] Again, the conclusions and policy implications that can be drawn from this literature are unclear. Measuring complex relationships and controlling for confounding variables are significant problems, and little of the "evidence" supporting the role of patents in promoting economic growth in a given patent system is very strong. This means, however, that claims regarding the costs or benefits of tweaking marginal aspects of the patent system are also weak. In sum, the theoretical and empirical literature reveals an undeniably complex interaction between product market competition, patent rules, innovation, and consumer welfare. While these complexities are well understood, their implications for the debate about the appropriate scale and form of regulation of innovation are not.

The implication of this uncertainty is not necessarily that economically coherent regulation of innovation is hopeless, however. To the contrary, economists are developing tools to generate more precise and reliable understandings of these relationships. There are indeed some well-supported institutional, political, and microeconomic relationships that can and do inform our thinking about shaping these regulatory institutions – we are not completely powerless or ignorant, but nor can we be secure in our judgments. In the meantime, scholars and regulators in the fields of competition

---

[33] Gilbert, *supra* note 5.

[34] Maskus, Keith and Mohamed Lahouel. "Competition Policy and Intellectual Property Rights in Developing Countries: Interests in Unilateral Initiatives and a WTO Agreement." World Economy 23, no. 4 (2000).

[35] Moser, Petra. "How Do Patent Laws Influence Innovation? Evidence from Nineteenth-Century World Fairs," The American Economic Review, 95, no. 4, (2005).

policy and patent law must do their best to grapple with uncertainty, problems of operationalizing useful theory, and, perhaps most important, the social losses associated with error costs. It is our hope that the chapters compiled in this volume will begin a fruitful inquiry into how to design legal institutions that are mindful of the complexities of the relationships between regulation, innovation, and welfare.

The Chapters

The Institutions of Growth
The first two chapters in this volume, presented as keynote addresses at the first two George Mason Law School/Microsoft conferences, present some important institutional background for understanding the narrower chapters that follow. In the first, Robert Cooter sets out to describe some of the problems of targeting industrial policy to achieve economic growth – arguably the ultimate goal of the regulation of innovation – in states with poorly defined markets and laws. The basic intuition is that sustained growth occurs in developing nations through improvements in markets and organizations, rather than through laws aimed at protecting or challenging specific business practices. Entrepreneurial innovation resembles biological mutation in that it is unpredictable before it occurs and understandable afterward. It is unpredictable because it begins with an innovator who acquires private information and earns extraordinary profits. It is understandable because its ends with the public figuring out the innovation and subsequent investors earning ordinary profits. According to Cooter, these characteristics of innovation have important consequences for law and policy to foster economic growth. Government officials who rely on public information cannot predict which firms or industries will experience rapid growth. Consequently, industrial policies that promote growth are unlikely to succeed. In contrast, secure property and contract rights and effective business law (especially the laws regulating financial markets) create conditions under which competition naturally produces entrepreneurial innovation and nations become rich. The main obstacle to sustained economic growth in poor countries today is ineffective civil and business law.

The implications of these insights are quite substantial. First, Cooter highlights the information problems that plague even well-meaning regulations aimed directly at encouraging growth – a problem perhaps magnified in developing nations but one that is not ameliorated in economically successful ones. Second, Cooter's normative claim – that governments can and should provide background commercial and civil laws that allow innovation to occur – suggests that there is a role for law and regulation in encouraging growth. This claim nevertheless requires us to take seriously institutional limitations in identifying where and how to use the law to do so.

Richard Epstein's chapter develops further the case against targeted regulatory efforts to stimulate innovation in intellectual property. In particular, Epstein develops a framework for understanding basic property rights and property laws to help to explain how the basic rules governing the assignment and alienation of property rights work to facilitate innovation and growth. He uses this framework to critique modern IP ("intellectual property") cases that impose limits on the terms of private licenses and that restrict the property-rights scope of intellectual property in the name of encouraging innovation. Epstein's conclusion, like Cooter's, is that the underpinnings of innovation are to be found in the basic rules of law, not targeted at correcting a perceived imperfection but rather aimed at ensuring ample space for entrepreneurship, innovation, and contracting activity that spurs economic growth.

These chapters lay the groundwork for the chapters that follow, all of which lend some support to the institutionalist view espoused in these keynotes. The essence of the chapters is found in the notion that economics, and in particular a clear understanding of the economics of institutions, can inform our understanding of the optimality of regulation in this complex arena. Although we do not have a clear answer to the question of what regulations best promote innovation in an economy, we do have the rudiments of a better understanding of the question.

The Economics of Innovation

The first set of chapters considers the *processes* of innovation and attempts to assess the extent to which management of the process may be successful and necessary, or misguided. The first chapter, by Stan Liebowitz and Steve Margolis, considers the prevalence of bundling in product innovation. Liebowitz and Margolis note that in a number of distinct product markets, regulators have acted against the bundling of product features or services, but it is not clear that the regulators understand the role of bundling in these technologies. A clearer understanding of the process leads to important policy implications. Among others, for example, there has been regulatory opposition to patent pools, cable television programming, software products, hardware–software combinations, and telephone service. But Liebowitz and Margolis note that these arrangements often appear to be attractive ways of marketing information goods. In many of these cases, bundling solves a pricing problem regarding nonrival goods; in others it offers production or service cost advantages. As Liebowitz and Margolis note, political or legal opposition to bundling often originates with competitors who wish to sell individual components of a bundle, or from consumers who wish to buy one component of a bundle, usually at some a pro-rata price. It is difficult, however, to discover legitimate anticompetitive instances of bundling. The chapter considers why bundling arrangements arise in the marketplace, particularly in the context of new technological innovations. The chapter then uses this framework to assess some of the claims that are used to support regulations imposing unbundling and finds them wanting. Without knowing (because we can't) in specific circumstances whether bundling might be anticompetitive, Liebowitz and Margolis give us strong insight into the general justifications and prevalence of bundling – which in turn helps to reshape our assessment of the desirability of regulatory "solutions."

Like bundling, networks are a pervasive feature of many modern technological innovations, and platform development has proved to be a machine of economic growth. Nevertheless, many economists and legal scholars argue that the presence of network effects creates a form of market failure known as "network externalities." Based on this alleged market failure, advocates recommend new forms of antitrust and regulation targeted at particular firms in the communications and information technology industries. The debate over network effects has had major consequences for these industries, with effects comparable to landmark antitrust cases involving IBM, AT&T, and Microsoft. Dan Spulber's chapter builds on both his own earlier work as well as Liebowitz and Margolis to demonstrate that many supposedly deleterious aspects of technology "lock-in" and network effects applied in antitrust discussions are based on an incorrect economic analysis. The chapter begins with a comprehensive examination of the nature of technology lock-in and its relationship to network effects. Following on the technological analysis, the chapter considers whether market institutions are capable of adjusting to address network effects or whether market failure leads to "network externalities." The chapter finds and details three powerful mechanisms that exist to mitigate the presumed extent of network externalities, and these essential processes are, in fact, an important part of the value of networks. The chapter then proceeds to examine how network effects arguments call forth various types of antitrust policy. In the end, Spulber's chapter presents some fundamental but novel thinking about the intentional structure of networks and shows that while network effects are an important economic phenomenon, market institutions are fully capable of addressing their problematic consequences. Technology lock-in does not constitute a major market failure, and antitrust policy based on ameliorating it is likely to have adverse impacts on both competition and innovation.

The final chapter in this part, by Marco Iansiti and Greg Richards, examines the innovation life cycle and its implications for competition and public policy. Again the focus is on the dynamics of certain market structures and the process of innovation. Here, Iansiti and Richards illustrate the workings of technological "assimilation": how technological innovations that were once marketed as individual products become integrated into broader platforms, which in turn provide the building blocks of further innovation. Here both bundling and networks come into play, with different stages of platform development displaying different characteristics of bundles and networks. Relying on the findings of recent patent citation studies, the chapter finds that certain "core" innovations serve as a broad foundation for future generations of innovative products, shaping the evolution of sometimes-vast ecosystems of beneficiaries. The implications are important for regulatory policy, which does not generally take into account product life cycle and the development (or disintegration) of bundles and networks, but rather neglects these more dynamic characteristics of much new technology. As the authors suggest, any regulatory intervention at a single point in time may not fully account for the follow-on development that may justify narrow restrictions of competition in the short run.

In sum, the chapters in this part consider that the form of innovation – whether through bundling, networks, or assimilation – has important implications for the propriety of the regulatory response. Here the authors have presented simple (as in the opposite of complex, not the opposite of difficult) explanations for the processes of innovation, shedding important light on the relevance of these processes for the innovations themselves. In turn, these analyses illuminate the (in)applicability of regulations that insufficiently consider the underlying dynamics of the innovation process.

Innovation and Competition Policy

The next part deals directly with the application of antitrust rules to organizations, with particular attention to the role of innovation in assessing the proper role for antitrust. These chapters again build on the previous chapters, highlighting the problems of ensuring that competition policy promotes innovation given the informational and dynamic problems of complex and innovative markets.

The first chapter, from David Teece' carries over the discussion from the previous part, highlighting the problem of optimal regulatory policies in a world where innovation occurs in markets with rapid technological change, including through platform development, bundling, and product life cycle development. Building on the core insight that the benefits of economic activity should be weighed over a broader range than is customary in both time and space, the chapter asks how competition policy should be shaped if it were to favor Schumpeterian (dynamic) competition over neoclassical (static) competition. Schumpeterian competition is the kind of competition that is engendered by product and process innovation – the sort encompassed in particular in Iansiti and Richards concept of assimilation. According to Teece, such competition not only brings price competition – it tends to overturn the existing order. A framework that favors dynamic over static competition would put less weight on market share and concentration in the assessment of market power and more weight on assessing potential competition and enterprise-level capabilities. By embedding recent developments in evolutionary economics and the behavioral theory of the firm into antitrust analysis, the chapter begins to develop a more robust framework for antitrust economics. As other chapters in this volume discuss, this framework is likely to lead to less confidence in the standard methodologies of antitrust economics when the business environment is associated with rapid technological change.

Joshua Wright's chapter also highlights the complexities of markets and the constrained ability of targeted regulations to maximize innovation. Harold Demsetz once claimed that "economics has no antitrust relevant theory of competition." Demsetz offered this provocative statement as an introduction to an economic concept with critical implications for the antitrust enterprise: the multidimensional nature of competition. Competition does not take place on a single margin, such as price competition, but several dimensions that are often inversely correlated: A liability rule that deters one form of competition will often result in more of another. This insight has important implications for the current policy debate concerning how to design antitrust liability standards for conduct involving both static product market competition and dynamic innovative activity. Wright's chapter revisits Demsetz's broader challenge to antitrust regulation in the context of the frequently discussed trade-offs between innovation and price competition. The chapter summarizes recent developments in our knowledge of the relationship between competition and innovation, highlighting the sorts of deficiencies described in previous chapters in this volume – deficiencies that significantly constrain antitrust enforcers' abilities to confidently calculate inevitable welfare trade-offs. Highlighting the fact that neither economic theory nor empirical evidence provides guidelines that allow enforcers to accurately identify conduct in markets where innovation is an important dimension of competition, Wright argues that antitrust enforcement should be held to a high standard of proof and evidence to minimize the significant social costs associated with false positives in this context.

Keith Hylton and Haizhen Lin's chapter turns specifically to the problem most implicated in the application of antitrust law to innovative industries: monopolization law. In particular, Hylton and Lin compare American and European monopolization law to begin to identify and measure the extent to which monopolization law as applied contributes to or detracts from economic growth. As the authors note, American courts have taken a relatively conservative approach toward monopolization law insomuch as courts have shown reluctance to penalize a monopolist absent proof of anticompetitive conduct and that they have, at least at the doctrinal level, permitted a wide consideration of "efficiency defenses." Europe, in comparison, has taken an interventionist approach. Given the problems of information and a dynamic economy, the authors conclude that error-cost analysis provides a justification for the American approach.

Taken together, these chapters present a coherent argument for humility in the application of antitrust laws, particularly in environments characterized by significant innovation and change. The institutional limitations of those called on to enforce antitrust laws, the complex processes of innovative markets, and the probability as well as the cost of Type II errors lead these authors to counsel caution.

The Patent System
The next set of chapters applies a similar critical analysis to the operation of national patent systems – the other pillar of regulation most relevant to the operation of innovative markets. Again, the central problem of uncertainty and the error costs of overly restrictive limits on rewards to innovation are the central themes animating the conclusions in these chapters.

The first chapter, by Vincenzo Denicolò and Luigi Franzoni, asks what rights should be assigned to a party that has discovered a new idea or a new technology given the dynamic process of innovation and the inherent limitations in granting long-term rights in the absence of information about the future. Should the first innovator be able to exclude potential rivals, or should property rights be mitigated so as to allow for some degree of imitation and competition? Denicolò and Franzoni address some basic issues pertaining to the optimal nature of the exclusion rights of successful innovators with respect to parties that might arrive at the discovery at a later time.

Further, the authors develop a test for the patentability of innovations able to capture the difficult trade-off between the goals of fostering innovation and promoting its diffusion.

Denicolò and Franzoni argue that *fully exclusive rights* represent the efficient way of rewarding innovation when competition in the product market is weak, the innovation is "big," and research entails little spillovers. The chapter's essential insight is that incentives to invest in research (particularly where spillovers from others' research are small) and thus to make important innovations are dependent on the size of the *ex post* reward. As a result, even where granting a relatively expansive right might seem to restrict the further exploitation of an innovation (an assumption not necessarily warranted, although not discussed in the chapter), the authors suggest it may still be efficient to induce efficient investment in innovation. This insight suggests, among other things, that an independent inventor defense may be quite counterproductive in some environments, that closed industry standards may be preferable to open ones, and that patent breadth should perhaps be large. Moreover, the authors suggest that the application of antitrust laws to claimed exclusionary behavior involving patents is likely undesirable – again because of the risk of under-incentivizing innovation research expenditures.

Next, Doug Lichtman and Mark Lemley apply a close institutional analysis of the U.S. Patent and Trademark Office (USPTO) to assess the scope and cost of a particular (and important) type of error, deriving implications for patent reform from their findings. As the authors note, the USPTO is charged with the Herculean task of reading and assessing all patent applications, pursued subject to enormous informational and budgetary constraints. Nonetheless, under current law, courts are largely bound to defer to the Patent Office's decisions regarding patent validity. As the authors point out, such deference to previous decision-makers is appropriate in instances where those previous decisions have a high likelihood of accuracy, and the patent system should endeavor to create processes that fit this mold. Granting significant deference to the *initial* process of patent review, however, is indefensible and counterproductive. The informational constraints inherent in the system should render patents vulnerable to challenge until and unless they are significantly evaluated in an information-rich environment. The effect of facilitating such challenges – challenges impaired by the law's automatic presumption of patent validity – would be to give patent applicants better incentives to file for genuine inventions but leave their more obvious and incremental accomplishments outside the patent system's purview. Counterintuitively, Lichtman and Lemley find that the costs of gathering and assessing information counsel for weaker, rather than stronger, property rights in patents. Nevertheless, the approach reaffirms the analytical framework that precedes – information and institutional capacity limitations are important elements in assessing the error costs of particular regulatory approaches.

Michael Meurer echoes this assessment in his chapter, focusing on the exacerbation of information problems caused by the "fuzziness" of patent boundaries. Meurer's chapter surveys the mechanism design approach to patent design and comments on whether the key results are robust to the inclusion of fuzzy patent boundaries in the models, and what sort of future research is needed to incorporate a serious treatment of patent notice failure into models of patent design. According to Meurer, a failing of the current patent system is that the grand bargain – exclusive rights in exchange for full disclosure enabling subsequent innovation – may not be functioning effectively in some subject areas.

Property Rights and the Theory of Patent Law

The chapters in this part take up the question of the role of the institution of property set out by Epstein in his chapter with particular reference to the patent system. These chapters are concerned with the broader, more philosophical question of the importance of property rights in encouraging and facilitating innovation – and thus they also take up the mantle of Cooter's chapter by illuminating the importance of well-defined background rules and the concepts that imbue them.

Adam Mossoff's chapter finds the origins of exclusive property rights in the basic concept of information costs. According to Mossoff, innovation is central to the American patent system, but current economic theories of patent law cannot account for the role it plays in shaping patent doctrine. Instead, Mossoff suggests that the patent system promotes innovation by creating a default presumption that secures maximum liberty to a patentee in using its invention. Accordingly, patentees may engage in a broad array of exclusive licensing practices that reflect the fundamental use and alienation rights long secured to them as central patent entitlements under the normative policy of securing to patentees the fruits of their inventive labors. Where other theories of patents view the monopoly profits secured by patentees as simply the necessary evil in promoting inventive activity and receiving disclosure of these inventions through the patent systems quid pro quo, Mossoff sees patent exclusivity as a feature of a system plagued by uncertainty. According to the chapter, the reward, prospect, and commercialization theories of patents have all failed to explain the array of exclusive licensing practices long secured to patentees and the wide latitude given to patentees under the patent exhaustion doctrine, although the Denicolò and Franzoni chapter in this volume does offer some explanation. In contrast, Mossoff's chapter attempts to explain why expansive licensure rights were secured to patentees as a fundamental design principle of the patent system: the fundamental *ex ante* unpredictability of innovation. Inventors require substantial liberty in the free use and alienation of their property rights to adapt to the path of innovation. Although Mossoff does not draw economic conclusions, the implications are not only philosophical or historical: Maximizing incentives for innovation requires the flexibility afforded by exclusive rights.

Henry Smith's chapter focuses on a similar theme, again finding the roots of patent doctrine and theory in the fundamental uncertainty of the innovative process. The chapter extends recent work on modularity in organization theory to explain how delineation strategies from property serve to manage information costs in intellectual property. For information cost reasons, it makes sense in property law to deal with a wide range of problems using an exclusion strategy in which decision-making over discrete things is delegated to owners whose authority is protected by relatively simple on/off signals – like boundary crossings in the case of real property. By defining a right to exclude from a thing, many potential uses by the owner and various contractual partners can be protected without separate delineation. Only when use conflicts become large and private ordering is likely to fail can a system of governance rules be cost-justified, whether by regulations, contracts, or tort law. The basic presumption in property law, the right to exclude, serves to economize on information costs.

Smith's chapter explains that, in effect, the exclusion strategy allows the system to manage complexity with *modularity*, with much information hidden in property modules and interactions governed by simple rules. As organizational theorists have increasingly emphasized, modularity helps to manage complexity in team production. By specifying interface conditions, a wide range of activities can occur in one module, making the system easier to use, more robust, and more flexible. Intellectual property, like property and organizational law, can be seen as a second-best solution of a complex coordination problem of attributing outputs to inputs. Seen in this way, the granting of alienable, well-defined, exclusive rights permits coordination at minimum cost and facilitates exactly the sort of valuable flexibility in the allocation of initial entitlements proposed by Epstein.

Finally, Scott Kieff addresses the same issues of information and coordination costs and likewise finds exclusive rights to be a solution. As Kieff notes, property rule treatment of intellectual property is sometimes said to cause a myriad of problems, including "excessive" transaction costs, thickets, anticommons, hold-ups, hold-outs, and trolls, unduly taxing and retarding innovation, competition, and economic growth. As Meurer and Lemley and Lichtman (in this volume) and others have suggested, such problems counsel for a shift toward some limited use of weaker liability rule treatment to facilitate transactions in those special cases where the bargaining problems are at their worst and where escape hatches are most needed. Kieff's chapter, by contrast, suggests that over just the past few years, the patent system has been re-shaped from a system having several major, and helpful, liability-rule-pressure-release-valves into a system that is almost devoid of significant property rule characteristics. The chapter then explores some harmful effects of this shift, focusing on the ways liability rule treatment can seriously impede the beneficial deal-making mechanisms that facilitate innovation and competition. According to Kieff, the basic intuition behind this deleterious effect of liability rules is that they seriously frustrate the ability of a market-challenging patentee to attract and hold the constructive attention of a potential contracting party while preserving the option to terminate the negotiations in favor of striking a deal with a different party. In other words, property rules not only promote the incentives to create highlighted by Mossoff and ameliorate the cost of coordinating inputs outlined by Smith, but also enable an inventor to commercialize innovations. Such a regime thereby facilitates the relatively inexpensive reallocation of rights to more valuable uses.

Intellectual Property and Antitrust: The Regulation of Standard-Setting Organizations

The final part of this volume operates as a sort of case study of the interactions of patent and antitrust rules in perhaps their most contentious setting: standard-setting organizations (SSOs). Current controversies over patent policy place SSOs on a collision course with antitrust law. Recent theoretical research, particularly by Lemley and Shapiro,[36] asserts that in an SSO, patent owners can "hold-up" patent users by demanding high royalties for a patented input after the SSO has adopted the patented technology as an industry standard and manufacturers within the SSO have incurred sunk costs to design end products that incorporate that standard. Various solutions to the purported problem have been proposed, implicating, generally, either weaker property rights or more antitrust enforcement. The SSO

---

[36] Lemley, Mark and Carl Shapiro. "Patent Holdup and Royalty Stacking." Texas Law Review 85, no. 7 (2007).

problem is necessarily complicated, not easily amenable to neat or elegant solutions, and, as some of the chapters in this part suggest, may not be a problem at all. While this volume does not seek to address the underlying normative question of the desirability of SSOs per se, the chapters in this part offer by implication some important justifications for SSOs. In keeping with the chapters throughout this volume, SSOs are viewed here as solutions to information or coordination problems, and the rules governing what may and may not be done within the institution are scrutinized based on how well they likely facilitate the institution's purpose. This is an important backdrop, and an essential lesson of this volume: Market institutions governed by simple rules that take seriously the difficulties of prescribing innovative behavior should not be interfered with lightly. Presumed problems must be evaluated against the effect of tinkering with institutional objectives.

Over the past few years, there has been an unprecedented degree of interest among competition authorities, scholars, SSOs, and trade associations with respect to the level of royalties that are charged by holders of intellectual property rights. In April 2007, the Department of Justice and the Federal Trade Commission jointly released a report on "Antitrust Enforcement and Intellectual Property Rights," while the European Commission (EC) is currently investigating the compatibility of certain licensing regimes and conduct within SSOs against EC competition law. Reflecting the debate at the policy level, scholars have produced a large body of legal and economic literature on intellectual property rights (IPR) and standardization issues, including patent hold-up and royalty stacking.[37]

The first chapter in this part, by Anne Layne-Farrar, Gerard Llobet, and Jorge Padilla, examines the proposed imposition of "incremental value" caps on licensing fees for patents. The chapter first surveys the literature surrounding SSOs and licensing on "reasonable and nondiscriminatory" (RAND) terms and explains how the proposed valuation of patents by incremental value seeks to operationalize RAND rates by limiting potential licensing fees for adopted technologies. Layne-Farrar, Llobet, and Padilla find, however, that this approach rests on a flawed conflation of *ex post* and *ex ante* expectations from innovations. In keeping with the observations made in other parts of this book, when all decisions are made *ex ante* with regard to the innovation, a proposed incremental value cap on royalty payments should reduce research and development investments and, as a consequence, innovation both within and across firms. This rule, like many

---

[37] Wright, Joshua and Bruce Kobayashi. "Federalism, Substantive Preemption, and Limits on Antitrust: An Application to Patent Holdup." *Journal of Competition Law and Economics* 5, no. 3 (2009).

regulatory price ceilings, would reduce both participation in SSOs as well as SSO participants' earnings.

Damien Geradin looks at the institutional arrangement of SSOs to assess the quality of claims that SSO's royalty-setting practices are problematic. The chapter first looks at a number of concrete scenarios where firms holding IPRs seek to obtain a return on their patent portfolios by licensing them. As the chapter suggests, the behavior of these firms depends on whether they are vertically integrated or non–vertically integrated. Vertically integrated firms engage in research and development (R&D) activities, patenting at least some of their inventions, and also manufacturing products based on their own innovations and the innovations produced by others. Non–vertically integrated firms, in contrast, specialize in one or the other layers of production. Pure upstream firms conduct R&D activities and patent their innovations, but they do not engage in manufacturing. Downstream firms specialize in manufacturing, but do not engage in R&D.

Considering, again, the SSO as a solution to an information and coordination problem, Geradin offers additional insight into the sorts of problems and solutions imbued within SSOs by distinguishing types of firms – with different problems to solve. As it turns out, according to Geradin, the potential problems caused by strong patent rights and weak antitrust enforcement are mitigated by the dynamics of integrated firms.

Finally, Bruce Kobayashi and Joshua Wright look at the legal landscape governing SSOs, assessing the relative competency of different institutions and different laws to promote the efficient objectives of SSOs. Kobayashi and Wright begin by considering *Credit Suisse v. Billing*, a recent Supreme Court case in which the Court held that securities law implicitly precluded the application of the antitrust laws to the conduct alleged in that case. In that case, the Court considered several factors, including the availability and competence of other laws to regulate unwanted behavior, and the potential that application of the antitrust laws would result in "unusually serious mistakes." Relying on the Supreme Court's recent antitrust jurisprudence appearing to adopt error-cost analyses that are sensitive to the costs of false positives, Kobayashi and Wright extend and apply Easterbrook's[38,39] seminal analyses of two of the most significant limitations on antitrust enforcement: error costs and federalism. The chapter examines whether the considerations raised in *Credit Suisse* suggest restraint when applying the antitrust laws to conduct that is regulated by state contract laws and other

---

[38] Easterbrook, Frank. "Antitrust and the Economics of Federalism." Journal of Law and Economics 23 (1983).

[39] Easterbrook 1984, ibid.

federal laws. In particular, Kobayashi and Wright emphasize the availability of robust contract and patent remedies for SSO members who are the victims of contractual opportunism and the limited benefits of additional deterrence of SSO hold-up afforded by antitrust remedies. While, as noted previously, some have suggested that the conduct associated with patent hold-up illustrates a gap in the current enforcement of the antitrust laws, Kobayashi and Wright conclude that contract and patent law offer superior substantive doctrine for identifying patent hold-up and distinguishing it from simple contract modification, and are likely to provide optimal deterrence without imposing serious risks of false positives.

PART I

THE INSTITUTIONS OF GROWTH

Legalize Freedom

A Chapter on Law and Policy for Innovation and Growth

Robert D. Cooter

Introduction

Sustained growth occurs in developing nations through improvements in markets and organizations. Entrepreneurial innovation resembles a biological mutation that is unpredictable before it occurs and understandable afterward. It is unpredictable because it begins with an innovator who earns extraordinary profits from private information. It is understandable because its ends with the dissemination of the innovation, so everyone earns ordinary profits from public information. These characteristics of innovation have important consequences for law and policy to foster economic growth. Government officials who rely on public information cannot predict which firms or industries will experience rapid growth. Consequently, industrial policies are unlikely to succeed in promoting growth by picking firms or industries to receive tax advantages, subsidies, or tariff protection. Proponents of such industrial policies today make the same mistake as the mercantilists whose interventions Adam Smith attacked as a cause of national poverty. Instead of industrial policy, developing countries should secure property and contract rights, and create effective business law (especially the laws regulating financial markets). When the state legalizes entrepreneurial freedom, innovators create, and nations become rich.

I. Legalize Freedom[1]

In the last two centuries, the wealth of the richest countries has risen above the poorest like Mount Everest rising above the Ganges Plain. The gap

---

[1] The chapter draws on portions of Robert Cooter and Hans-Bernd Schaefer's book, *Solomon's Knot: How Law Can End the Poverty of Nations* (Princeton University Press, forthcoming).

opened because the richest countries grew richer, not because the poorer countries grew poorer. Most poor countries today are somewhat richer relative to their past and much poorer relative to rich contemporary countries. One scholar estimated income per capita for fifty-six countries in 1820.[2] He found that the richest countries in the sample had income per capita of approximately $1,800, and the poorest countries had approximately $400, for a ratio of 4:1. Repeat the same exercise for 2003 and you find that the richest countries had income per capita of approximately $25,000 and the poorest countries had approximately $500, for a ratio of approximately 50:1. Such is the difference between roughly 2 percent and .1 percent annual growth over two centuries.

This chapter discusses how law and policy affect innovation and growth. In recent decades, dramatic events demarked new eras in economic history: the creation and expansion of the European Union since 1950, decolonization in Africa in the 1950s and 1960s, the creation and dissolution of communes and the restoration of private business in China after 1980, the dismantling of central planning in India beginning in the 1980s, the collapse of communism in Eastern Europe after 1989, and privatization and liberalization in Latin America in the 1990s. These events caused seismic changes in economic law and policy. Changes in law and policy affect the protection of property, the enforcement of contracts, and the effectiveness of business law. Much statistical and qualitative evidence suggests that large changes in these laws have large consequences for growth, and small changes often have measurable consequences.

This chapter explains how such changes in law and public policy affect economic growth in developing nations by changing the rate of innovation.

II. Markets and Organizations

In every country, sustained growth occurs through innovation, but its form differs across nations. Innovations in Silicon Valley usually have a technological basis, such as new computer chips or programs that were previously unknown to the world. Technological innovation often requires research universities and similar institutions. Their relative weakness in developing countries at this point in history limits the scope for technological innovation. Technology mostly flows from developed countries to developing countries through international trade, investments, and educational

---

[2] Angus Maddison, *Monitoring the World Economy 1820–1992*, OECD, Paris 1995. . . . He used 1990 dollars as the base.

exchanges. The flow hastened in the last century when major wars ended, communism collapsed, and tariffs and transportation costs fell.

Instead of improving technology, many innovations improve organizations and markets. To illustrate, Philip Knight, co-founder of the Nike Corporation, began by selling running shoes out of the trunk of his car in 1972. In 2006 the company reported $15 billion in worldwide sales of sports equipment and clothing. Knight obviously discovered something new, but what was it?

His company does not manufacture anything. Its main facility in Beaverton, Oregon, is a "campus," not a factory. Instead of manufacturing, it contracts with foreign companies to make all of the goods that it sells. The business of Nike is research and marketing. It thinks up new products, contracts with other firms to make them, and then markets them through extensive advertising. This new organizational form has spread dramatically in America as more and more companies "outsource" manufacturing and focus on research and marketing. Other examples of recent innovations in markets and organizations in the United States include debit cards, hostile takeovers, venture capitalists, and team production (imported from Japan).

With technological innovation limited, innovation in developing countries mostly takes the form of improving organizations and finding new markets. To illustrate, people who buy edible oil for cooking need assurance of its quality. African consumers smell and taste it to assure that it is fresh, which requires open containers. Closed containers, however, have many advantages, including lower shipping and storage costs. Bhimji Depar Shah figured out how to sell oil in closed containers and retain the trust of African consumers. He started an edible oil company in Thika, Kenya, in 1991 that developed into a business empire. The company's homepage reads: "Integrity is what all our people value and uphold ruthlessly, which enables trust leading to empowerment." Selecting reliable salespeople and trustworthy workers dispersed around Africa required innovation in organization much like outsourcing by the Nike Corporation.

Entrepreneurs in developing countries often adapt organizations and markets that originate in developed countries to local conditions. Adaptations in markets and organizations often introduce new kinds of contracts. According to Easterly, two such innovations were crucial to developing the textile business in Bangladesh: bonded warehouses and back-to-back letters of credit.[3] Bonded warehouses protect producers against theft or fraud in

---

[3] Easterly, William. *The Elusive Quest for Growth: Economists' Adventures and Misadventures in the Tropics* (MIT Press, 2001).

the chain of distribution, and letters of credit protect buyers against theft or fraud at the point of sale.

In business, adaptation is creative and risky. The adapter has an idea that is new to a developing country. Proving its worth in the market place requires investments that may fail. Instead of adaptation, some people imagine that developing countries can grow by imitation, which is mechanical and safe. If growth were this simple, poor countries would already be rich. In poor and rich countries alike, new ideas in business mostly fail and the investors lose their money, whereas a few succeed spectacularly and drive growth. Picking out the adaptation that will succeed in Africa is just as hard as picking out the invention that will succeed in Silicon Valley.

For organizational adaptations, development imbeds an idea in a new kind of organization for the place in question. Developing a new kind of organization is risky, whether in Sichuan or Silicon Valley. The innovator must trust the investor not to steal his organization, and the investor must trust the innovator not to steal his money. If the adaptation succeeds, it attracts competitors, who diffuse the idea and reduce the innovator's profits. Thus adaptation in developing countries faces the same obstacles as invention in developed countries.

III. Mutations and Innovations

We have explained that growth in developing countries especially comes from innovations in markets and organizations, which are risky. Next we explain how risk limits the success of laws and policies on growth. Viruses generally mutate in search of a weakness in the host's immune system, and hosts change their immunities to resist viruses. Today's science cannot reliably predict the moves and countermoves. Thus scientists did not predict the appearance of the SARS virus (severe acute respiratory syndrome) in China in 2003 or its spread around the world.

Similarly, economists did not predict the invention of the "personal computer" by International Business Machines ("IBM") in 1981, the explosive growth of this industry, or IBM's domination of it for a decade. As the industry matured, IBM lost its leadership and finally sold its personal computer business to the Chinese company Lenovo in 2005.

Just as American officials did not foresee the success of IBM and the personal computer, Japanese planners did not predict the surge of its automobile manufacturing after 1960, and Indian planners did not predict the surge of computer firms in Bangalore after 2000. In general, economists and officials cannot predict the cycle of innovation in an industry before it occurs.

Unlike the virus-host example, scientific progress cannot solve the problem of predicting business innovation, even in principle. People invest in innovative ideas in order to earn extraordinary profits. To earn them, they must keep much information private. This is true for innovations in technology, organizations, and markets. Technological innovators will protect unpatentable inventions as trade secrets, or disclose patentable ideas only after a patent is issued. Innovative organizations will try to keep competitors from learning their operating practices. Firms that discover new markets will try to disguise the source of their profits. Predicting business innovation, consequently, is a problem of strategy, not a problem of science. Business strategy is no more predictable by science than strategy in Saturday afternoon football games.

Although scientists did not predict the appearance of the SARS virus, they quickly understood its origins and path of transmission. With this knowledge, they could suppress its spread and assist natural recovery by its victims. Similarly, economic innovation resembles a biological mutation that is unpredictable before it occurs and understandable afterward. It is unpredictable because it begins with an innovator having private information. It is understandable because its ends with competitors figuring out what the innovator knows, which causes private information to become public information.

IV. More Is Less: Failed State Leadership

No matter how good science becomes, the path of business development will surprise people who rely on public information. Those who rely on public information to make decisions about the economy include most administrators and state officials, including economists. To illustrate, administrators and officials did not foresee or plan the emergence of Silicon Valley in California or the technology business in Bangalore, India. The unpredictability of business innovation before it occurs, and the understandability of it afterward, is decisive for promoting growth by laws and policies. We will explain why, beginning with the problem of official overreaching.

In the eighteenth century, physicians thought that an imbalance in the blood caused disease. To restore the balance, doctors put leaches on patients to suck their blood, which hastened the death of people already weakened by illness, including Mozart. Similarly, economic development is plagued by false theories whose application sucks the vitality from economies. In the last half of the twentieth century many poor countries pursued industrial policies that favored manufacturing over agriculture, heavy industry over light industry, dirty industry over clean industry, fishing and cutting wood over sustainable production, and import substitution over exports. Most economists now view these policies as mistakes that retarded economic growth. With some exceptions, public officials have performed dismally in channeling investments to enhance growth. Like leeches on the sick, these manipulations strain already weak economies.

The unpredictability of business innovation limits the way laws and policies can foster economic growth. State officials seldom identify in advance the firms and industries that will soar and sink. However, officials routinely pursue public policies that cross-subsidize industries in the hope of accelerating growth rates. In many countries, public officials proclaim the goal of economic growth and manipulate markets to achieve it, using tax breaks, subsidies, tariffs, licenses, and regulations. These officials overreach their abilities.

The failure of state policies to lead economic growth has two causes. The first cause is deficient information. Even if officials were motivated to make wealth for the nation, they do not have the information to guide industrial development by picking the winners among industries and firms. The life cycle of innovation explains their lack of information. In the first phase of the life cycle, an innovator has a new idea. When combined with capital, the new idea causes a spurt in growth and profitability. By financing innovation in its early stages, investors increase the rate of the economy's growth. In the private sector, investment bankers use private information to finance innovations that earn extraordinary profits.

The innovator guards its secrets to prolong its extraordinary profits. Or else the innovator patents its secrets and makes them public. In either case, officials using public information know little about the early stages of an innovation's development. As time passes, trade secrets are leaked and competitors work around patents. The innovative idea eventually becomes public and the innovator's rapid growth ceases. Consequently, people who rely on public information understand innovations when they cease to be new and lose their extraordinary value.

After information, the second cause of the failure of officials to lead economic growth is motivation. Many people have convinced themselves that politicians and officials will invest other people's money better than private investors can invest their own money. This is a delusion and a snare. The motivation of public officials to make wealth is weak because they cannot keep it. In contrast, public officials keep their salaries and bribes. By leading economic development, officials increase their responsibilities, which justifies higher salaries and increases their opportunities for bribes.

Industrial policy is rife with political favoritism, chicanery, cronyism, and corruption.

Failure's second cause (motivation) lies behind its first cause (information). Specifically, the corruptibility of public officials explains why they should base law and policy on public information, not private information. Although officials talk about economic growth, politicians mostly want to build loyalty by directing public money to their supporters. State officials can easily divert secret state investments to their cronies. Conversely, requiring officials to explain and justify their policies in public creates a basis for accountability. Public discussion, debate, and criticism dampen nepotism, favoritism, chicanery, and corruption. Consequently, citizens in most democracies expect officials to base economic policies on public information. In this respect, officials deciding economic policy should act like judges deciding cases, not like diplomats conducting foreign policy.

We have explained that allowing state officials to use private information for public investments is dangerous. However, officials who base economic policies on public information suffer a decisive disadvantage relative to private investors: They are not privy to business secrets and strategies. Public officials have less information about which firms and industries will soar and sink than the executives in the firms. Private investors with private and public information can predict the surge of a particular firm or industry better than public officials with only public information. Consequently, diverting funds from private investors to public officials and allowing them to choose among firms and industries will retard growth on average.

V. Asymmetrical Information versus Efficient Markets

Our proposition that private investors are better than state officials at picking winners and losers among firms depends on private investors having more information than public investors – the *asymmetrical information hypothesis*. Some economists, however, go much further and proclaim the *efficient market hypothesis*. This hypothesis asserts that stock market prices efficiently capture all relevant information about the future prospects of firms.

To illustrate, assume that a firm's stock is actively bought and sold. If the firm innovates and enjoys extraordinary profits, people with private information will quickly buy the firm's stock and bid up its price. By the time the public knows about the innovation, the stock's price has risen sufficiently so that it is no longer a bargain.

According to the efficient market hypothesis, stock markets work like garage sales: Informed buyers arrive early and find bargains, whereas later customers find none. Similarly, investors with private information buy rising stocks early at bargain prices, whereas investors who rely on public information buy stocks after they reach prices that are not bargains.

Consistent with the efficient market hypothesis, empirical studies in finance often conclude that investors who possess only public information cannot earn extraordinary profits in the stock market except by chance. Indeed, some recent studies suggest that people who trade in stocks based on public information do worse than chance because they lose money to people who trade based on private information.[4]

In spite of some evidence supporting the efficient market hypothesis, confidence in it among scholars collapsed with stock prices in the United States during the crash of 2008. Early in 2008, many financial institutions in the United States held mortgage-backed securities that were overpriced relative to the real risk of default on the underlying loans. Many people in the industry knew, or should have known, about the riskiness of these securities for several years. Contrary to the efficient market hypothesis, the information was not leaked to the public. If it had, the stock prices of financial institutions holding mortgage-backed assets would have fallen gradually as their portfolios accumulated more risky securities. Instead, the information become public abruptly, which triggered a collapse in stock prices and confounded public officials. For many economists, events refuted the efficient market hypothesis and confirmed the asymmetrical information hypothesis.

VI. East Asian Exceptionalism?

We asserted that private investors pick winners and losers among firms better than public officials. This is true to the extent that private investors have more information than public officials. In East Asia, however, pubic officials allegedly have – or had – more of the relevant information than private investors. In the second half of the twentieth century, political and administrative practices in Japan and Korea allowed public officials to obtain much private information about private firms. The best and brightest officials at Japan's Ministry of International Trade and Investment (MITI) and Korea's Ministry of Finance had the power to extract private information from firms and the confidence to use it. In the 1950s and 1960s, they directed capital to selected industries for expansion and actively manipulated markets.

---

[4] Thus, using complete records from trades on the Taiwan stock exchange from 1995 to 2000, Barber et al. found that individuals lost more than 3% of the value of their portfolios through day trading and the winners were mostly institutional investors with better information." Barber, B. M., Y.-T. Lee, et al. (2007). "Just How Much Do Individual Investors Lose by Trading?" Berkeley Law and Economics Workshop.

Short of leading, public officials in East Asia sometimes coordinate private firms. For example, MITI officials allegedly enjoy mutual understanding and trust with private firms, which allows them to pressure Japanese companies into sharing technological innovations with each other through cross-licensing.[5]

Japan and Korea enjoyed rapid economic growth in the 1960s. Perhaps Japan's MITI stimulated growth by directing investment or requiring private firms to share information with each other.[6] Or perhaps not. A recent article argues that MITI did not have a political mandate to direct growth in Japan and it never did so. MITI participated in the rapid growth of the Japanese economy without contributing to it. Claims to the contrary, according to this article, were made by self-interested officials and Marxist social scientists who did not understood markets. Experts disagree about whether state officials *caused* rapid growth in Japan and Korea.

The experience of the two Chinas differs dramatically from Japan and Korea. Taiwan has grown faster than Japan and comparably to Korea since 1990.Taiwan, however, has no equivalent of Japan's MITI or Korea's Ministry of Finance. Growth proceeded spectacularly in Taiwan without state leadership.

In the case of mainland China, the cultural revolution in the decade roughly from 1966 to 1976 destroyed the institutions of property and contract more thoroughly than in most communist countries. In the 1980s, the process reversed: China quickly improved its property protection and contract enforcement to develop a free-market sector of the economy. The results have been spectacular. China's double-digit growth rates since the 1980s are without historical precedent in lifting large numbers of people out of poverty.

China describes itself as a "socialist market economy." The private, unplanned sectors of the economy like textiles and light manufacturing are the contemporary engine of growth, not the heavy industries that continue to operate with much government involvement. In China's market socialism, the market sector supplies growth and the socialist sector consumes subsidies.

---

[5] Yishiro, M. and J. M. Ramseyer (2002). "Capitalist Politicians, Socialist Bureaucrats? Legends of Government Planning from Japan." Harvard Law and Economics Discussion Paper No. 385. In contrast, Aoki argued that the Japanese state enhanced markets in the first few decades of the post-war period by allowing for "cooperation-contingent rents."

[6] Milhaupt, C. and K. Pistor (2008). "Law & Capitalism: What Corporate Crises Reveal About Legal Systems and Economic Development Around the World." The University of Chicago Press.

VII. Quantity, Quality, and Creativity

State-led growth ended in Japan and Korea, and retreated in China. One possible reason is a natural progression in production. An industrializing country tends to favor the mass production of relatively simple, homogeneous goods. Examples include manufacturing textiles, forging steel, growing rice, and mining coal. As industrialization proceeds, emphasis shifts toward producing high-quality, differentiated goods and services. Examples include automobiles, electronic gadgets, fine clothes, and services such as boutique banks and specialized insurance. Beyond quality, the economy may eventually produce creative, innovative goods, such as computer software, pharmaceuticals, medical devices, and designer clothes.

We have described a progression from handicraft to quantity production, from quantity to quality, and from quality to creativity. All three types of production co-exist in a developed economy, but emphasis shifts as development proceeds. Progression in this direction changes what firms need from their workers. Mass production requires disciplined workers to perform repetitive tasks by using machines and following orders. Quality production requires teams of skilled workers to exercise their judgment. Creativity requires workers with internal motivation to seek novelty relentlessly. As a developing economy adds more quality and creativity to the production mix, workers need fewer orders and more discretion. The art of management shifts from authority to incentives.

Centralized control is possible for quantity production, difficult for quality production, and impossible for creativity. Thus the task of public officials who want to lead the economy becomes harder as the economy develops. MITI's development plan for Japan roughly followed the first two steps of the progression: First develop relatively basic manufacturing industries (e.g., textiles, steel), and then proceed to more complex goods (e.g., cars, electronics). In the 1980s, production in Japan completed the shift in emphasis from quantity to quality. Going forward, quality and creativity were the central themes of economic development. MITI significantly reduced its intervention and guidance of the economy in the 1980s and has never resumed its former role. Perhaps MITI withdrew its guidance of the Japanese economy because it could no longer identify firms and industries that should grow fast.

In principle, public officials who acquire private information can succeed in leading or coordinating economic growth. Perhaps Japanese and Korean officials did so in the 1950s and 1960s. However, allowing public officials to influence private investment in secret aggravates the risk of corruption. For each example of secret public investment that succeeds, there are many counterexamples where officials use secrecy to siphon wealth to their political cronies.

When a trust is created, it often pays commissions to the trustees for managing its portfolio, which involves buying and selling securities. The law requires the trustees to manage the trust's portfolio in the best interests of its beneficiaries. However, the trustees sometimes "churn" the trust by excessive trading to earn commissions, even though the trades fail to increase the value of the trust's portfolio.[7] Churning a trust resembles public officials trying to redirect capital to growth industries. Their efforts mostly waste resources without increasing growth rates. The waste comes from using taxes to pay public officials to perform unproductive activities. The waste also comes from unproductive expenditures on political influence and bribery of state officials. The more detailed and intricate the manipulations by officials, the more they distort investment and weaken the economy.

Officials prosper by trying to direct the economy. Overreaching in economic matters creates more jobs with higher pay for public employees and nonprofit organizations. Material advantages apparently generate self-serving ideology for all people everywhere. It has taken a particular form with public officials. In past centuries, the higher castes in India and aristocrats from Europe to Japan despised people in business who made wealth. For aristocrats, "tradesman" or "bourgeois" was a pejorative term. In the twentieth century, this hostility to business transferred from aristocrats to leftist intellectuals, especially those employed by the state and nonprofit organizations. The selection of people for these jobs relies heavily on academic performance, where intellectuals excel. People who excel in school easily imagine that they could excel in running the economy. Intellectuals who work for the state or nonprofit organizations often view themselves as understanding capitalism better than businessmen, while being morally superior by holding less material values.

VIII. Legalize Freedom, Again

As with viruses, no magic pill cures are underdevelopment, but social science can diagnose impediments to economic growth. The right diagnosis can

---

[7] In the United States, a legal revolution has changed the definition of churning in trust management. In the past, state laws applied the "prudent man" rule, which required trustees to choose a portfolio from an enumerated list of "safe securities." Recently, many states switched to a "prudent investor" rule, which allows the trustees to hold a diverse portfolio in which risks counterbalance each other. See Schanzenbach, M. M. and R. H. Sitkoff (2006). "Did Reform of Prudent Trust Investment Laws Change Trust Portfolio Allocation?" Berkeley Law and Economics Workshop.

guide state policies to promote development. State officials do not have the information to pick winners among industries and firms in the growth race, and they should not try. Specifically, they should not try to accelerate growth by choosing firms and industries to receive subsidies and other privileges.

Instead of leading growth directly, the state should take the indirect approach. By the indirect approach, state officials create a framework for competition among businesses and let it decide which firms will soar and which ones will sink. According to this prescription, the state's first role in economic development is to build the legal foundations for markets where competition will flourish.

To illustrate historically, in the nineteenth century the United States became the largest zone in the world for free trade in goods and free mobility of capital and labor. Subsequently the United States became the dominant economic power of the twentieth century. The former substantially caused the latter. In the second half of the twentieth century, the European Union (EU) became the world's largest zone for free trade, and it steadily moved toward free mobility of capital and labor. Consequently, its economic production surpassed the United States. In the first half of the twenty-first century, China has created a free trade zone encompassing more people than the United States and the EU combined. China is apparently moving toward free mobility of capital and labor. If existing trends continue, its production will surpass the United States in 2014.[8]

Competition over a large area, including free mobility of capital and labor, requires centralized institutions of government to provide infrastructure and legal uniformity. Examples are the U.S. federal government, the government of the European Union, and China's communist party. Whereas a centralized government creates a free market economy, a fractionalized government creates a flea market economy – tiny firms produce and sell products without liability, guarantees, or the use of credit.

With free trade and free mobility of capital and labor, many can compete for wealth. Freedom and competition release the energies of entrepreneurs and send innovation on its creative, unpredictable path. Like biological mutations, spectacular successes in entrepreneurial innovation drive

---

[8] This prediction was made by C. J. Dahlman, Luce Professor of International Affairs and Information of Georgetown University, in remarks to the Chinese Reform Summit, National Development and Reform Commission (NDRC), Beijing Diaoyutai State Guesthouse, July 12th-13th, 2005. Dahlman extended existing trends, allowed for a modest slowing of Chinese growth rates, and used the purchasing power parity method of comparison. Since China's population is 4 to 5 times greater than the U.S., China's income per capita in 2014 will still be 1/4 to 1/5th that of the U.S.

change, but failures outnumber successes. To get results, entrepreneurs need freedom to experiment with organizations and markets. The basic principle of law for innovation is economic liberty for the many.

Freedom requires law, not its absence – hence the title of our chapter, "Legalize Freedom." Recent history suggests that when a country removes legal restrictions on economic liberty ("liberalizes"), growth results when the state has effective property, contracts, and business law, but not otherwise.[9] Specifically, economic freedom requires effective laws for property, contracts, and business law.

Each body of law performs an essential role. Property law ideally enables the people who create wealth to keep much of it. When the makers of wealth can keep much of it, greed overcomes fear and entrepreneurs take the risk of innovating. With effective contract law, people can commit to doing what they say. The power to commit enables people to coordinate and cooperate. However, contracts for innovative activities are necessarily incomplete and imperfect. Part of the fix comes from business law, which includes business organizations, finance, and bankruptcy. These laws help people to overcome incomplete contracts in organizations and markets. Business organizations provide a framework for repeated interaction that decreases the need for detailed contracts. Finance and bankruptcy laws provide specialized rules to fill gaps in business contracts.

Legalizing freedom requires effective law, not merely written law. Effective law requires deterring law-breakers by sanctions. Deterrence comes from state sanctions such as liability, injunctions, fines, or imprisonment. State institutions must impose state sanctions, such as police, courts, regulators, and autocrats. Deterrence also comes from nonstate institutions such as political parties, professional clubs, religious organizations, and extended families. Nonstate sanctions include loss of reputation, refusal to deal, and exclusion from an exchange. Drafting a law is so easy compared to enforcing it that written law vastly exceeds effective law.

The enemy of economic liberty is monopoly, which only permits a few to seek wealth. Thus, many countries restrict entry to industries by licenses, charters, and regulations. With restrictive laws, state officials can enrich their friends and extract bribes by choosing who is allowed to do business. To sustain monopoly, public officials crowd out private law with public law. When regulations prevent creators from keeping much of what they make, entrepreneurs have little incentive to take the risks required to

---

[9] Cooter, Robert and Hans-Bernd Schaefer, *Solomon's Knot: How law can end the poverty of nations* (Princeton University Press, forthcoming).

innovate. When regulations systematically override contractual obligations, entrepreneurs cannot make the commitments that they need to coordinate their behavior. When courts fail to enforce loan agreements, businessmen have trouble borrowing.

IX. Other State Activities

We have stressed the state's role in developing a legal framework for competition and innovation. In addition, the state must support economic growth through a variety of other activities. The state must stabilize money and banking. A reliable supply of money lubricates almost all economic transactions. Conversely, rapid inflation or currency fluctuations burden almost all economic transactions. To control the timing of investment and consumption, people need to store wealth securely in banks. Banks should invest these savings in productive businesses. Conversely, an unstable banking system causes people to store wealth in real goods such as jewels, furniture, and real estate. The economy grows faster when wealth is invested instead of being stored.

The state must also provide infrastructure: roads, water, electricity, telephone lines, airports, harbors, industrial parks, and so forth. Some forms of infrastructure are "natural monopolies." For example, most towns do best with a single grid of electricity wires, a unified road system, and a few cable systems for Internet and television. By supplying infrastructure, the state channels the expansion of business, without picking which firms or industries will succeed or fail. Unlike innovation, public officials can make most infrastructure decisions by using public information, which technical experts collect and the citizens debate.

Natural monopoly, especially for infrastructure, often requires state participation as regulator or owner. Infrastructure developments sometimes face obstacles that only the state can overcome. In particular, developing infrastructure often requires assembling large tracts of land from fragmented private owners. Thus, a proposed road may cross land owned by many different people. Voluntary purchase of land to construct the road encounters a fatal problem: Owners who hold out by refusing to sell their land can command a higher price. To avoid holdouts, most legal systems allow the state to compel owners of land to sell it (the power of "eminent domain").

In addition to money, banking, and infrastructure, the state must regulate or supply such public goods as defense, education, public health, social security, poverty relief, and environmental protection.

X. Conclusion

We have explained that sustained growth occurs in developing nations through innovations in markets and organizations. These innovations resemble biological mutations that are unpredictable before they occur and understandable afterward. Growth is unpredictable because it begins with an innovator who acquires private information and earns extraordinary profits. It is understandable because its ends with the public figuring out the innovation and all investors earning ordinary profits.

These characteristics of innovation are decisive for using law and policy to foster economic growth. Government officials who rely on public information cannot predict which firms or industries will experience rapid growth. Consequently, industrial policies are unlikely to succeed in promoting growth by picking firms or industries to receive tax advantages, subsidies, or tariff protection. Proponents of such industrial policies today make the same mistake as the mercantilists whose interventions Adam Smith attacked as a cause of national poverty.

In contrast, secure property and contract rights, and effective business law, create conditions under which competition naturally produces entrepreneurial innovation and nations become rich. The main obstacle to sustained economic growth in poor countries today is ineffective civil and business law.

Responding to these facts, rich countries rely mostly on the private sector as the engine of growth. The state supports growth indirectly by supplying legal and physical infrastructure. Developing countries should do the same. If this diagnosis is right, then, contrary to popular belief, developing countries do *not* need more planning and less markets than developed countries. State officials can accomplish more by doing less to influence growth directly. The state should provide a framework for competition through effective property, contract, and business laws. The state legalizes freedom so entrepreneurs can grow the economy.

2

What Is So Special About Intangible Property?

The Case for Intelligent Carryovers

Richard A. Epstein

One of the major controversies in modern patent law is the extent to which property right conceptions developed in connection with land or other forms of tangible property can be carried over to different forms of property, such as rights in the spectrum or in patents and copyrights. This chapter defends the thesis that, once the differences in the optimal duration of patents and copyrights is taken into account, the carryover of basic property conceptions from tangible to intangible property should be much encouraged. In some instances, the property right concepts applicable to land work even better because some of the difficulties in designing a land based system disappear. The short life of patents, for example, obviates the need to create rules dealing with restraints on alienation over time. In addition, this chapter critiques the recent developments that limit the use of injunctions to protect exclusive rights of patent use, in *eBay v. Merc-Exchange*. In a similar fashion, it notes that the limitations on rights of alienation in spectrum also create major social losses, as does the use of the patent exhaustion rule in the licensing of intellectual property, as applied by the Supreme Court in *Quanta v. LG Electronics*.

My original keynote address at the Third Conference on the Law and Economics of Innovation, sponsored by George Mason Law School and Microsoft, was given under the title *The Disintegration of Intellectual Property*. That speech has morphed into a much larger project that was published in the *Stanford Law Review* under the title *The Disintegration of Intellectual Property? A Classical Liberal Response to a Premature Obituary*, STANFORD L. REV. (2010). In the present chapter, I deal with other aspects of the relationship between tangible and intangible property, and include references to events that took place after the conference. I shall make references to that larger work as appropriate.

Introduction: Points of Differences
and Points of Similarity

The purpose of this chapter is to explore anew the much contested relationship between property in tangible and intangible resources. For these purposes, I consciously use the term "intangible property" because it embraces not only all forms of intellectual property but also other nonphysical forms of property, including, most critically, the airwaves and the Internet. It should be apparent from the outset that there is a tremendous diversity of resources by type on both sides of this line. What is less commonly accepted are the powerful similarities that span the tangible/intangible divide. Indeed, on this last point, some version of the separationist theory – that we should be quite wary of drawing analogies from tangible to nonphysical property – is now taken almost as a point of conventional wisdom in academic[1] and judicial[2] writings. The physical descriptions that dominate the one area are said to create misleading metaphors that leave us ill-equipped to deal with the complexities of the other.

There is no doubt that significant differences exist between tangible and intangible property. But that point has to be put into perspective. There are equally significant differences between various branches of the law of tangible property, such that the principles that govern land, water, minerals, oil and gas, and air rights vary immensely. There are also significant variations within the different classes of intellectual property.[3] But before we celebrate the culture of irreducible differences, it is important to glance at the opposite side of the coin, which shows that, on many key points, there are tight logical and functional resemblances among the various forms of tangible and intangible property. I shall stress these points of connection to give a more systematic understanding of the organization of a wide range of property rights systems.

In Section I, therefore, I give a thumbnail sketch of the basic arrangements used to deal with tangible property. I stress the basic common features and ignore all the fine points of difference that crop up within the law of any given jurisdiction and across the laws of jurisdictions. However important

---

[1] See, e.g., Dan Hunter, *Cyberspace as Place and the Tragedy of the Digital Anticommons*, 91 CAL. L. REV. 439 (2003); Dan L. Burk, *The Trouble with Trespass*, 4 J. SMALL & EMERGING BUS. L. 27 (2000). For the opposite view, see David McGowan, *The Trespass Trouble and the Metaphor Muddle*, 1 J.L. ECON. & POL'Y 109 (2005); Richard A. Epstein, Intel v. Hamidi: *The Role of Self-Help in Cyberspace?*, 1 J.L. ECON. & POL'Y 147 (2005).

[2] See, e.g., *Intel Corp. v. Hamidi*, 71 P. 3d 296, 309–11, 310 n.7 (Cal. 2003) (Werdegar, J.).

[3] I have discussed many of these issues in Richard A. Epstein, *Intellectual Property: Old Boundaries and New Frontiers: Addison C. Harris Lecture*, 76 IND. L.J. 803 (2001).

these are for dealing with individual cases that are selected for litigation, they have little systemic importance for assessing the overall desirability of various property rights regimes.

In Section II, I identify what I think to be the salient differences between some forms of intangible and tangible property with an effort to cash out the differences between them. In this regard, it is critical to remember that different systems of intangible rights take on different forms, such that these differences will play out in separate, but predictable, ways as we go across different areas. In working through these examples, we must remember that the movement from tangible to intangible property actually has two opposing effects. In some instances, the shift increases the complexity of organizing a property rights system. In other cases, however, the shift to intangible property actually works a welcome *simplification* of legal doctrine.

In Section III, I apply this framework to a number of key issues that deal with the protection and transfer of property rights to show that the mis-understanding of the similarities between the two systems leads to serious intellectual confusions and social losses that could have been avoided by a more careful analysis of the overall situation. The first of these examples concerns the use of the highway analogy in cyberspace, most notably, in *Intel Corp. v. Hamidi.*[4] The second deals with the right to exclude and the rise of forced transactions under *eBay Inc. v. MercExchange L.L.C.*[5] and its progeny. A third example deals with the ability to sell or to license intellectual property, which is put in stark form by the recent decision in *Quanta Computer, Inc. v. LG Electronics, Inc.*[6]

I. Property Rights in Physical Resources

Every legal system has to devise a system of property rights to establish entitlements to both natural and intellectual resources. In dealing with this question, the issue of natural resources came first. The Roman law system of Justinian set the framework for both the civil and common-law developments for tangible property in the United States. Its initial distinction was between common and private property.[7] Common property

---

[4] 71 P.3d 296 (Cal. 2003).
[5] 547 U.S. 388 (2006).
[6] 128 S. Ct. 2109 (2008).
[7] J. INST. 2.1 (J.B. Moyle trans., 5th ed. 1913) (With respect to Things, "some admit of private ownership, while others, it is held, cannot belong to individuals: for some things are by natural law common to all, some are public, some belong to a society or corporation, and some belong to no one.").

covers those resources that all individuals may use but that none may occupy exclusively, which in classical times included the air, the water, and, to a limited extent, the beach.[8] On top of that system, individuals were entitled to acquire, by first possession, outright ownership of land, animals, and chattels, which they could then hold and use in exclusion of all others.[9] On this model, land could therefore be held in perpetuity, and animals and chattels could be held until they were consumed, used up, or destroyed. For none of these resources did the law impose an artificial limitation on the time period that its owner enjoyed its exclusive use.

This simple division between common and private property made good sense. By keeping waterways in the commons, for example, the law facilitated transportation between owners of different parcels of private property. To allow any person to privatize a river would disrupt these valuable forms of interactions, which would then paradoxically reduce the value of all private properties that lie along the commons. The basic judgment here does not take any deep empirical insight. Water from a river in a barrel is worth a lot less to everyone than the water in a river where it can support transportation, recreation, and plant and animal life. That some water could be taken out of the commons for private use was always recognized. At the same time, however, it was always subject to limitations as part of a crude effort to make sure that, at the margin, the last drop of water taken for private consumptive use had an equal value with the last drop of water left in the river for common uses. The case for limiting withdrawal was so compelling that all customary systems everywhere have recognized the mix of collective and private uses, at least in those riparian jurisdictions where both types of uses are feasible. However, these open access systems are, unfortunately, always vulnerable to political override. That destructive tendency was clearly realized with the construction of multiple castles along the Rhine River, each of which charged tolls to the commerce that passed along its banks.[10] That noncooperative behavior allowed for the erection of

---

[8] The beach is the middle case because individual occupation often makes sense as when people build huts to take refuge from storms. This involves more intensive use by one individual than others, where there is a high utility to shift. But at the same time, the private interest so created is strictly limited in time. Once the storm has passed, the shelter has to come down and the beach is returned to the commons.

[9] J. INST. 2.1.12; G. INST. 2.66.

[10] See, for discussion, MICHAEL HELLER, THE GRIDLOCK ECONOMY: HOW TOO MUCH OWN-ERSHIP WRECKS MARKETS, STOPS INNOVATION, AND COSTS LIVES 3 (2008). Heller gets the right description of the problem to which he supplies the wrong diagnosis. The castles along the Rhine represented mini sovereigns before the unification of Germany. The river was one reopened for commerce by the Treaty of Westphalia, which explicitly prohibited

blockades along the river that cut sharply into its value for transportation and communication. The whole incident thus became a symbol of what happens when certain forms of property are privatized in ways that run against the common-law tradition. Yet the danger of state involvement is not limited to cases of this sort. The dominant characteristic of American water law shows the identical weakness that stems from the ability of the U.S. government to unilaterally override the sharing arrangements for common property that were developed under customary law. Thus, the creation of the federal "navigation servitude"[11] has allowed the federal government, free from any obligation to compensate, to destroy existing mills or block access to rivers by its own public projects.[12]

The river and the ocean are said to be held in common "by nature" because no human action was needed to either create or preserve these waterways. The need for communication and transportation is, however, so powerful that within societies it is necessary to create, by condemnation if necessary, other long, thin, and continuous common resources that help link individuals together. In rough historical order, state action was needed to organize highways, railroads, telecommunications, electricity, pipelines, airplanes, and the Internet, all of which share the same long and thin characteristics of rivers and coastlines, which makes them mesh only awkwardly with the squarish tracts of land used for agriculture, manufacture, and retail. So long as each of these skinny network elements represents the only way to get from point A to point B, they will exhibit some of the open access elements of common property. But since they are not networks created by nature, some conscious human action is needed to construct and maintain them. These requirements make it impossible for these systems to operate as open networks at zero price as they did under customary regimes. Accordingly,

tolls in two sections and called for a return to the customary regimes of open access. Treaty of Westphalia, Holy Rom. Emp.- Fr., art. LXIX, LXXXIX (Oct. 14, 1648), available at http://avalon.law.yale.edu/17th_century/westphal.asp. This illustrates the perils of too much government, not too little. For further discussion see Richard A. Epstein, *Heller's Gridlock Economy in Perspective: Why There is Too-Little, Not Too-Much Private Property* (forthcoming).

[11] The navigation servitude is defined as "An easement allowing the federal government to regulate commerce on navigable water without having to pay compensation for interference with private ownership rights" or as "An easement, based on the state police power or public-trust doctrine, that allows a state to regulate commerce on navigable water and provide limited compensation for interference with private ownership rights." BLACK'S LAW DICTIONARY 1400 (8th ed. 2004).

[12] See, e.g., *United States v. Willow River Power Co.*, 324 U.S. 499 (1945) (invoking the navigation servitude to deny compensation to a power company whose ability to generate electricity was diminished when the water levels were raised after the government constructed a dam across a navigable river).

these networks require some collective expenditures for their creation and upkeep, which has to be funded by some combination of general revenues and user fees. The entire area of rate regulation is, in effect, held hostage by the need to organize these common networks.[13] To be sure, this need for common access changes when technological advances allow for the creation of competing networks, as with modern cable and telecommunications systems, that can operate in competition with each other so long as there are some appropriate interconnection rules. But until very recently, the model of the commons as a regulated network industry fit the technical realities of what is sometimes called a "natural monopoly," – that is, industries where, over the relevant range of outputs, a single supplier could satisfy the market at diminishing marginal costs.

Yet, by the same token, the historical development of a private-property side for other resources has proven presumptively efficient. Neither land that is used for production, nor animals, nor chattels can be put to their highest value use if they are left in the commons. No one will invest in clearing land if he knows that someone else thereafter may plant crops on it. No one will take care of animals that others may take or kill. No one will plant crops on land if he knows that some interloper may harvest them with impunity. A system that grants exclusive rights in these assets *over time* therefore offers the most convenient baseline for incentivizing investment in natural resources. It is commonly said, therefore, that a system of private property depends on the right to exclude.[14] That point is true as far as it goes, but it does not go far enough.

The right to exclude in and of itself is without value, for it does not even give the stripped-down owner of the property any rights to enter, possess, use, or dispose of the property in question. All mature systems of private property rights, which regulate disputes between neighbors, assume that these "incidents" are part of the bundle of rights that we call property rights. All owners of land, for example, must have unimpeded access to the network elements of the property system, which means that they must have the right to both enter and exit their lands. In addition, they have to have the

---

[13] For the most recent Supreme Court pronouncements on the problem, see *Duquesne Light Co. v. Barasch*, 488 U.S. 299 (1989) (allowing alternative rate base methodologies) and, *Verizon Communs., Inc. v. FCC*, 535 U.S. 467 (2002) (using deferential approach in construing Telecommunications Act of 1996).

[14] Indeed it is the preoccupation with exclusion, without regard to use, development, and sale, that makes hash out of modern takings law in land. On this point, contrast the near per se rule of compensation that protects land from invasion in *Kaiser Aetna v. United States*, 444 U.S. 164 (1979), with the squishy protection for regulatory takings in *Penn Central Transp. Co v. City of New York*, 438 U.S. 104 (1978).

right to use that land and to develop it in ways that are consistent with the like rights of their neighbors, which usually imposes some restrictions on use typically embodied in the law of trespass and nuisance.[15] The protection of use rights in land normally implies the recognition of development rights, including the right to construct improvements, subject to the same nuisance constraints. Within very broad limits (which are usually applicable to family interests) ownership also carries with it the right to dispose of the land, in whole or in part, to one or more individuals on whatever terms and conditions one sees fit. It is this possibility of alienation, when combined with labor contracts, that allows property owners to take advantage of gains from trade and specialization. Similar rules apply with respect to animals and chattels, although obviously the notion of perpetual ownership now means ownership only for so long as the asset continues to exist.

To be sure, this basic system is subject to some key limitations that also play a key role with intangible forms of property. The first deals with the rules of acquisition and relates to the problem of excessive hunting and fishing in the commons, with the consequent creation of a commons problem leading to the premature extinction of species that are of value to man.[16] There is no sensible way, of course, to abandon or tinker with the first possession rule as the way to establish ownership over these animals. So long as those rules are efficient to decide conflicts between two claimants to a given resource, they should be left in place. But, it is, in the analogy to the use of rivers, possible to limit, through an *independent* system of regulation, the amount of wildlife or fish that can be gotten from the commons in order to avoid this problem. The exact form of limitation is critical, and the ability to allow the transfer of rights to catch, which allows these rights to be assigned for cash to those parties who can better utilize them, thereby simultaneously reduces the costs of capture and increases overall yield.

The important lesson that comes from this simple exercise is that it shows us the importance of the *partition* of different regulatory systems with different purposes. The worst way to fix the common pool problems is to tinker with the rules that deal with the capture of wild animals. There is no point in creating such inefficiency when independent means can be used to address the overconsumption problem. That partition shows how it can be efficient to keep old rules in their limited office when new problems

---

[15] I will not to trace out these elements here, but I have developed them at length in Richard A. Epstein, *Nuisance Law: Corrective Justice and Its Utilitarian Constraints*, 8 J. LEGAL STUD. 49 (1979).

[16] For an account of how well-designed responses can improve net yields from common pool resources, see R. Quentin Grafton et al., *Private Property and Economic Efficiency: A Study of a Common-Pool Resource*, 43 J.L. & ECON. 679 (2000).

arise. There is no reason, as we shall see, that similar approaches cannot be used to deal with intangible forms of property.

The second limitation that attaches to the basic system of property rights deals with the ability to use contractual devices for the purposes of exchange or cooperation. Exchange and cooperation normally increase the size of the pie and thus are welcome. But there are always counterexamples. Every modern system of property rights profits from the articulation of some antitrust law that is intended, broadly speaking, to prevent various kinds of contractual arrangements that operate in restraint of trade. Thus, the cooperation among individuals does not carry with it the right to fix prices or to divide territories or take other steps to convert the exclusive ownership of property into a cartel-like form. In addition, a second set of more difficult rules is directed toward unilateral practices that can also work to raise prices and reduce output. In practice, the most powerful application for these antitrust laws is to an exclusive provider of services who would normally be subject to common carrier regulations of universal service in virtue of its monopoly position. Yet, owing to the peculiar nature of the business, the hookups to end users are done most efficiently at a zero price, which is often the appropriate rule for Internet connections.[17]

The third limitation deals with the risk of holdout that may arise in cases of imminent danger of loss of life or destruction of property.[18] These natural perils, such as storms, radically restrict the set of alternatives that are available to outsiders. No longer is it possible for a boat owner to choose to use any one of a number of docks to land. It is either this dock or serious danger to person or property. The privilege of necessity allows the outsider, in such cases, to take or use the property for the duration of the risk, subject normally to a duty of compensation when the risk has passed.[19] This set of rules can apply to individuals who need to clamber to safety in times of personal peril or to the destruction of goods at sea whose loss is then regulated by the law of general average contribution.[20] The point in all of these cases is to recognize that when competitive markets no longer

---

[17] I develop this theme at greater length in RICHARD A. EPSTEIN, ANTITRUST CONSENT DECREES IN THEORY AND PRACTICE: WHY LESS IS MORE 74–76 (2007).

[18] See, e.g., *Ploof v. Putnam*, 71 A. 188 (Vt. 1908); *Vincent v. Lake Eric Transp. Co.*, 124 N.W. 221 (Minn. 1910).

[19] *See, e.g., Vincent*, 124 N.W. at 222.

[20] For the early development, see *Mouse's Case*, 66 Eng. Rep. 1341 (K.B. 1609) (holding that in order to save a ship, some cargo may be thrown over, but the loss must be split equally amongst all parties). For longer discussion of the efficiency characteristics of the rule of general average contribution, see William M. Landes and Richard A. Posner, *Salvors, Finders, Good Samaritans, and Other Rescuers: An Economic Study of Law and Altruism*, 7 J. LEGAL STUD. 83, 106–08 (1978).

work, duties to allow entry, similar to those imposed on common carriers,[21] emerge.

This theme of holdout and necessity also carries over to cases where the excessive fragmentation of interests prevents the productive deployment of resources. That common problem arises, for example, when there is need for land assembly for an extensive project like a railroad or a hospital. It is best coped with by the creation of an eminent domain power that can be exercised either by the state or private authorities acting under state power. This enduring solution gives the state entity the power to take private property for public use, but only if it pays compensation to the owner that leaves him at least as well off as he was before the taking took place. The requirement for compensation counteracts the risk of excessive condemnation. The limitation of such compensation to market value stops the holdout problem on the other side and permits the needed land use assembly to take place. Needless to say, condemnation powers are often exercised in connection with network industries, as in the acquisition of land, or rights of way over land, for railroads, highways, power lines, and gas mains. It can also be used to deal with the assembly problem for large tracts of land for public purposes such as schools and hospitals.

In basic outline, then, mature systems of property in tangible assets have rules that demarcate common from private property and specify how private property may be acquired, used, and transferred. It also has three sets of limitations: rules to deal with common pool problems for all forms of wildlife, antitrust laws to deal with contracts in restraint of trade, and rules governing necessity and condemnation to deal with fragmentation and holdout problems.

II. The Transition from Tangible to Intangible Property

How does this system transfer to the world of intangible property? In many instances, very well. One element of similarity that arises in both physical space and cyberspace is the separation of elements into common and private. The analogy to physical resources open to all is, of course, ordinary language, ideas, laws of nature, and other natural occurring phenomena, none of which are located within the sphere of private property.[22] On the other

---

[21] A common carrier is a "commercial enterprise that holds itself out to the public as offering to transport freight or passengers for a fee. A common carrier is generally required by law to transport freight or passengers or freight, without refusal, if the approved fare or charge is paid." BLACK'S LAW DICTIONARY 226 (8th ed. 2004).

[22] For discussion, see *Diamond v. Chakrabarty*, 447 U.S. 303 (1980).

hand, there are two key differences between private property in physical things and in intellectual property. One is that the demarcation of the scope of property rights in some forms of intellectual property, for example, patents, is sometimes more difficult than it is for physical property, even though both systems divide themselves up conveniently into private and common resources. That difference of specification is less critical in areas like copyright and trademarks, where the distinctiveness of the claim is easier to establish. In large measure, this explains why the recordation systems for these two forms of intellectual property more closely resemble the ministerial systems that are used to record titles to land and automobiles, while the registration of patent rights involves a far more complex system of public examination prior to registration. Even then, the state imprimatur receives only presumptive validity,[23] which can be challenged in judicial proceedings.

The second difference is, of course, that for patents and copyrights the ease of nonrivalrous use militates strongly against any system of perpetual rights, which in turn suggests that patents and copyrights should both be limited to a fixed term of years. When that term expires, they fall into the public domain, where they can be treated like general ideas or laws of nature. That regime would be suicidal for land, whose value necessarily falls if it is designated as common property. Why precipitate a second race for first possession, which is costly in its own right and needlessly disrupts the planning options and incentives of the prior possessor of the land?

Thus far, these differences have pointed to the greater complexity of various forms of intellectual property. But there are other ways in which intellectual property is in fact *simpler* to organize than physical property. In particular, at least three problems tend to disappear as we cross systems. The first is that the shorter duration of property interests for patents and for copyrights (which have become far too long under the Copyright Term Extension Act[24]) results in a massive simplification of intellectual property law relative to the law of land. The infinite duration of private land ownership leads to its division over time between separate persons. In the Roman system, this differentiation was limited to a single temporal form, the usufruct, which, roughly speaking, gave an inalienable life estate in possession, with access to both use and fruits, with a remainder interest to

---

[23] See, e.g., 35 U.S.C. § 282 ("A patent shall be presumed valid.").

[24] Sonny Bono Copyright Term Extension Act, Pub. L. No. 105–298, 112 Stat. 2827 (1998) (codified at 17 U.S.C. §§ 302–05) (increasing the length of copyright term from 75 to 95 years).

the "bare proprietor" of the land.[25] Even that one simple division requires the articulation of an elaborate body of law that governs what goes to the usufructuary and what is reserved to the bare proprietor. Nevertheless, that Roman division is far simpler than the common-law doctrines of estates that allow for the proliferation of multiple life estates in the same property coupled with a bewildering array of future interests, including contingent remainders and executory interests.[26] In part, these interests in land proliferate because the real estate and many forms of personal property are treated as part of family settlements, which make it sensible to tie property interest to the life or death of key players. On the other hand, patents and copyrights are purely commercial interests, so that the life estates, contingent remainders, and executory interests tend to fall away. Given the short duration of these interests, especially for patents, patent law has no use for doctrines intended to clean up the title to land, including the rule in *Shelley's Case*,[27] the doctrine of worthier title,[28] and the rule against perpetuities,[29] all of which are functionally obsolete now that tangible assets can be held in trust.[30] The elimination of future interests in property also reduces the pressure on the doctrine of waste, in which the guiding principle is that the tenant for life must not use or consume the land, or the fruits thereon, in ways that diminish the value of the remainder interest.[31]

The second point of simplification of intellectual property is that it does not have to develop a body of nuisance law to deal with nontrespassory invasions of property that nonetheless impinge on the reasonable use and

---

[25] For a discussion of the usufruct, see BARRY NICHOLAS, AN INTRODUCTION TO ROMAN LAW 144–45 (1962).

[26] A contingent remainder is "A remainder that is either given to an unascertained person or made subject to a condition precedent." BLACK'S LAW DICTIONARY 1317 (8th ed. 2004). An executory interest is "A future interest, held by a third person, that either cuts off another's interest or begins after the natural termination of a preceding estate." BLACK'S LAW DICTIONARY 611 (8th ed. 2004).

[27] 1 Co. Rep. 936 (1581).

[28] For discussion, see *Doctor v. Hughes*, 225 N.E. 221 (N.Y. 1919).

[29] The rule against perpetuities is a "common-law rule prohibiting a grant of an estate unless the interest must vest, if at all, no later than 21 years (plus a period of gestation to cover a posthumous birth) after the death of some person alive when the interest was created. The purpose of the rule was to limit the time that title to property could be suspended out of commerce because there was no owner who had title to the property and who could sell it or exercise other aspects of ownership. If the terms of the contract or gift exceeded the time limits of the rule, the gift or transaction was void." BLACK'S LAW DICTIONARY 1357 (8th ed. 2004).

[30] For a discussion of the rise and fall of these doctrines, see Richard A. Epstein, *Past and Future: The Temporal Dimension in the Law of Property*, 64 WASH. U. L.Q. 667 (1986). I shall not speak about the particulars here.

[31] See, e.g., *Brokaw v. Fairchild*, 237 N.Y.S. 6 (N.Y. Sup. Ct. 1929). Parallel doctrines existed in Roman Law on the duties placed upon the usufructuary.

enjoyment of one's property. The law of nuisance thus draws a rough distinction between largish invasions that are in general actionable and minimal invasions, such as sounds and cooking smells, which are wiped off the slate by a comprehensive doctrine of live and let live.[32] The problem is in fact so acute that oftentimes the law of nuisance is not capable of handling it, such that, for example, in planned unit developments, an elaborate set of covenants is used to *increase* the restrictions placed on land use in ways that tend to maximize the overall value of the land in question, by governing exterior design, size, setbacks, green spaces, and the like. The question of nuisance under the Internet is small, as the use of photon packets avoid that problem and leave only congestion issues to be dealt with. This congestion is far less acute than on physical highways, for whatever we may think of spam jams, they are far more benign than traffic jams. For its part, intellectual property is a one-dimensional asset that has none of these physical spillover effects like noise and pollution. The only operative tort therefore is infringement, which is subject to boundary-crossing rules that bear close resemblance to the trespass rules on entry for real property.

Third, intangible property is not subject to the risks of exhaustion through the common pool that occurs with physical property. Excessive consumption is an issue of excluding spam or charging for it. It is not a question of the exhaustion of protons that prevent the next generation from sending desirable messages. Likewise, it is thought desirable for older inventions and writings to fall into the public domain where all can use them, as none can destroy the invention or writing in question. Trade names, on the other hand, to the extent that they remain exclusive identifiers, should never go into the public domain, or they could no longer serve their intended (reputational) function of giving consumers brand assurance when they make individual purchases. The only problem that remains, therefore, with copyrights and patents is the anticommons, or an excessive fragmentation issue that also arises in the physical space.

Fourth, in general, the class of needed privileges with intangible forms of property is, if anything, smaller than with physical property. The cases of necessity are sharply limited, for no one needs to use someone else's patent to escape from a storm. To be sure, there is the possibility of the need to have government march-in rights[33] to take over patents for key drugs to deal with epidemics, but placing a large order would almost always be preferred to taking over the drug in question. The key privileges that do exist often

---

[32] See *Bamford v. Turnley*, 122 Eng. Rep. 27, 33 (Ex. 1862); Restatement (Second) of Torts § 822 cmt. g.

[33] See 35 U.S.C. § 203 (allowing for federal revocation of patents under extreme circumstances.

arise with protection from defamation suits by persons who give references on request[34] or the privilege of fair comment on artistic works and the like.[35] Other key privileges, such as the fair use privilege for the copyrighted works of others,[36] should generally be narrowly limited so as to avoid the danger that the original work will not be produced at all.[37] So long as a viable market can be created for the resale of copyrighted works, the fair use privilege should not be invoked, for the increased dissemination comes at too a high a cost in the lost creation of new works for which insufficient compensation would be provided.

These quick outlines of the various property type systems set the stage for a consideration of some of the various rules in particular instances. In this context, the basic approach is as follows: Make as *few* shifts between the different systems as is necessary to respond to the key differences in type. This approach is just another application of the rules that are used to control catch limits for common pool resources, where the trick was, as noted, to leave the rules on first possession in place and then to introduce an independent set of rules that deals explicitly with the problems of overconsumption. The point here is that there is no reason to tie the cure of one problem to the creation of inefficiencies in those portions of the system that work well. The same principle applies to intangible property. Carry over the basic rules from various forms of tangible property to intangible property to the extent possible. I shall look at this problem insofar as it relates to both the right to exclude and the right to dispose.

III. The Application of Tangible Property Rules to Intangible Property

A. The Right to Exclude

It is commonly agreed that that all forms of private property must necessarily include some right to exclude, without which they would necessarily be

---

[34] "In the context of employment recommendations, the law generally recognizes a qualified privilege between former and prospective employers as long as the statements are made in good faith and for a legitimate purpose." *Lewis v. Equitable Life Assurance Society*, 389 N.W.2d 876, 889 (Minn. 1986) (citing *Stuempges v. Parke, Davis & Co.*, 297 N.W.2d 252, 257 (Minn. 1980)).

[35] See, e.g., *Magnusson v. New York Times Co.*, 98 P.3d 1070, 1074–75 (Okla. 2004) ("The common law fair comment privilege extends to fair expressions . . . encompassing expressions of opinion on all matters of public opinion.")

[36] See 17 U.S.C. § 107.

[37] See, e.g., The Copyright Act of 1976, Pub. L. No. 94–553, 90 Stat. 2541 (1976) (codified as 17 U.S.C. § 107(4)) (requiring consideration of "the effect of the use upon the potential market for or value of the copyrighted work" in determining whether a particular use is fair).

forms of common property. But the next question asks what form of remedy should be given in the event that a defendant has entered or used the plaintiff's property or threatens to do so for some purposes of his own. The three available remedies, which can be mixed and matched, are self-help, damages, and injunctions. Self-help and injunctions are intended to either stop or reverse the invasion or infringement, as the case may be, while damages compensate for past losses and may, if set at a high enough level, induce a defendant to either forswear or cease any use or infringement of the plaintiff's property. The coordination among these three remedies has been organized around two key cases, *Intel v. Hamidi* and *eBay v. MercExchange*, both of which require some separate attention.

B. Intel and the Internet

In *Intel v. Hamidi*, the question was whether Intel, as the owner of its own computer system, could exclude Hamidi from making unauthorized use of it to send disturbing e-mail messages to Intel employees that caused a good deal of confusion and disarray within the firm. The remedy sought, injunctive relief under the law of trespass to chattels, was rejected on the ground that the common law of chattels allowed the unlimited use of self-help to keep the outsider off, but denied the use of injunctive relief in the absence of proof of actual damages.[38]

That argument seems wrong for a number of reasons.[39] The first deals with the nature of the protected interest. The normal law of trespass to land and chattels allows the plaintiff to recover either actual damages, as measured by the tort law, or restitution damages, which represent the benefit obtained by the defendant from the use of the plaintiff's property. Thus, the defendant trespasser who takes his own goods across the plaintiff's land can be forced to disgorge the benefit obtained from the shorter journey even if there is no actual harm to the plaintiff.[40] In *Intel*, it is hard to quantify the damages that were caused to Intel, although they must have exceeded, at least in their mind, the resources that they were prepared to commit to stop the

---

[38] See RESTATEMENT (SECOND) OF TORTS § 218, cmt. e; *Intel Corp. v. Hamidi*, 71 P.3d 296, 302–03 (Cal. 2003).

[39] See my brief for The California Employment Law Council et al. as Amici Curiae Supporting Petitioners, *Intel Corp. v. Hamidi*, 71 P.3d 296 (Cal. 2003) (No. S103781), 2002 CA S. Ct. Briefs LEXIS 39.

[40] See, e.g., *Raven Red Ash Coal Co. v. Ball*, 39 S.E.2d 231 (Va. 1946) (allowing action for the benefit conferred on the defendant trespasser on the theory of an implied promise); *Jacque v. Steenberg Homes*, Inc., 563 N.W.2d 154 (Wis. 1997) (defendant liable for nominal and punitive damages for crossing plaintiff's land without permission to deliver a mobile home to a customer, even in the absence of actual damages).

intrusion. It is also difficult to quantify the nonpecuniary gains to Hamidi, although it surely must have exceeded the costs that he incurred to get the messages through. The difficulty of estimating damages in most instances is an argument for allowing the injunction to issue, because it restores the status quo ante without putting the burden on courts to calculate numbers that are likely to be both large, on the one hand, and subject to significant disagreement, on the other. Self-help has exactly that same characteristic. It can also be used without the need to calculate tort damages by reference to the plaintiff's harm or restitution damages by reference to the defendant's gain.

The question then arises as to the proper relationship between self-help and injunctive relief. The answer, I believe, is the same as it is for the rule of damages, which allows a plaintiff in trespass cases to elect to use for the greater of either the defendant's gain or the plaintiff's loss. Here the plaintiff should be allowed the same option. If self-help does the job, it will generally be preferred because it is cheap. But if it is unable to do the job, leave the plaintiff the option of picking injunctive relief when the additional costs are less than the additional benefits.

There is nothing whatsoever in the *Intel* opinion that addresses this issue. What the court did do was to reject my argument that the entire trespass to chattels model was not quite right given that cyberspace was organized by direct analogy to physical space, with the same mix of common and separate elements.[41] The use of such terms as Internet addresses and Internet highway survive precisely because they render an accurate description of the relevant relationships. Of course there is no demarcated highway as with land, but the same is usually true with respect to travel by sea and air, where there are at most a few markings of where boats and planes are allowed or required to go. Rather, there are a set of enforced conventions that guide boats and planes in their designated lanes to avoid the risk of collision and to allow them to reach any given point from any point of departure. The Internet in this regard is easier than the physical world because there are many different ways to go from one point to another, so that the key function of interconnectivity is easier to preserve. At this point, the right rule is that no one can use self-help, damages, or injunctions to block the use of the common elements of the system, but anyone can keep other persons from making unauthorized use of their private space on the other side of the Internet device. In *Intel*, this means that the electrons can go where they

---

[41] For the court's discussion of my amicus brief, see *Intel Corp. v. Hamidi*, 71 P.3d 296, 309–10 (Cal. 2003).

will so long as the messages do not pop up on computers located within the Intel complex. Judge Werdegar resisted this conclusion by quoting from Lawrence Lessig for the proposition that "to the extent that individual sites begin to impose their own rules of exclusion, the value of the network declines. If machines must negotiate before entering any individual site, then the costs of using the network climb."[42]

Unfortunately, Lessig's passage contains two separate ideas, both wrong. The first is the claim that the use of site exclusion techniques reduces the value of the Internet. But sites do exactly this all the time when they impose rules on who can enter a particular site and the purposes for which they can use it. Passwords are the ultimate in exclusion, and they are part of every known wireless system. The ability to exclude from individual sites is no more a danger to the integrity of the Internet than the use of gates and locks in private homes is a danger to the integrity of public highways. Quite the opposite. The ability of site owners to select who enters and who does not is the key inducement to connect building sites with public roads. That power to select means that the individual site owner can interact only with that portion of the public traffic he chooses, without having to deal with all unwanted actors, spammers included. That ability to select *increases* the willingness to join the network. We know about the general efficiency of this distribution between public and private elements because behind the initial gate often lies other networks that are organized internally with the same distribution of common and private elements – which again increases connectivity by encouraging people to organize networks behind gates that allow them to exclude the rest of the world, just as they do in gated communities.

Nor is Lessig correct to think that the costs of running the network will climb because of the arduous difficulties in negotiating entrance. The key point here is that all networks set default options. For ordinary individuated communications, admission is the presumption. Intel embraced that default option, because, even when it was firmly in place, all Intel needed was the right to give explicit notice to Hamidi that his use of the network was not desired. Indeed, Intel had (and has) no general desire to set the default in the opposite direction because that would increase its costs of getting new business from strangers. Even endless amounts of spam do not alter the basic equation, because spam filters, however imperfect, offer the best line of defense. If Intel, and most everyone else, could enjoin specific persons

---

[42] Lawrence Lessig, The Future of Ideas: The Fate of the Commons in a Connected World 171 (2002), quoted in Intel, 71 P.3d at 310–11.

and organizations from sending spam, that would offer a highly useful complement to these self-help filters, which suffer from both standard forms of errors, too much junk gets through, and some desired email gets blocked and lost.

The overall point should be clear. There are superficial differences between cyberspace and real space, which indicate how networks are constructed. But the basic rules on the mix between exclusions and licenses survive quite nicely as one moves from rules that govern access to private homes from the public street to Internet interconnections. It is only if the switch between systems somehow mandates weird shifts in orientation, such as a reversal of the usual default rule on contact, that the supposed inefficiencies of a property rights regime appear. Cleanse them from the system, and the carryover is evident.

C. *eBay v. MercExchange*

The battle over the scope of the right to exclude shifted to patent law in the Supreme Court's critical, if misguided, decision in *eBay*.[43] At war in that case were two specific conceptions of the right to exclude. The first, which represented the position in the Federal Circuit, was that injunctions were remedies of course in patent cases, which could be denied only in well-defined circumstances. Many of the cases denying injunction relate to the behavior of the plaintiff in prosecuting or sitting on a patent claim, thereby invoking such doctrines as laches, waivers, and estoppels. These doctrines are always critical in individual disputes where some delay of the plaintiff in the enforcement of rights may well have set up powerful expectations in the defendant of his freedom to use a particular patented technology. However, these cases pose no system-wide risk, for the injunction cure is always available to the diligent patent owner who gives notice and prosecutes cases in which interlopers seek to take advantage of his position.

The hard issues therefore arise only in those cases in which nothing that the plaintiff has done disentitles him to any relief that is otherwise available. The standard rule for the injunction is based on many of the concerns that are in play in *Hamidi*. Damages for improper use are difficult to estimate, even when large. The injunctive relief forces cessation of the practice, which in turn reduces the likelihood of its occurrence in the first place. A strong injunctive relief system also drives potential infringers to seek voluntary licenses from a patent holder, which in turn expedites the

---

[43] 547 U.S. 388 (2006).

flow of commerce. In light of these considerations, the level of discretion in equitable relief, I believe, should be exercised largely in those cases where the alleged infringement takes place with respect to a complex device of which the plaintiff's patent constitutes only a small part. Here the damages should be calculated to reflect the patented part's level of functionality in the composite apparatus. In most of these cases, delaying the injunction should be sufficient to allow the defendant to make an easy fix of the technical problem that avoids future infringing activity.

The strength of this approach is reflected in the recent decision of the Federal Circuit in *Lucent Technologies, Inc. v. Gateway, Inc.,*[44] which took basically this line with respect to a small component of Microsoft Outlook Calendar that was found to infringe a Lucent patent. The District Court affirmed the jury award of $358 million, which was presumably influenced by the plaintiff's expert who advocated for an 8 percent royalty on the entire sales price of the object for the one component thereof – a "date-picker" in the calendar function,[45] which was "but a tiny feature of one part of a much larger software program."[46] The actual award worked out to more than $3 per each of the more than 110 million delivered units of Outlook.[47] That damage figure seems preposterous on its face, for if a dozen of the components of this complex program infringed patents, the total damage award would equal or exceed the entire revenue stream for the program. Microsoft's ability to invent around or to remove the offending component was taken as a given. There should be no difficulty in issuing an injunction against the future incorporation of this patented component into Outlook, say thirty days after judgment, which would create little or no disruption of the market. The damages should be cut severely, perhaps not to the $6.5 million that Microsoft had urged,[48] or about $0.06 per unit, but close.[49] Note that in this case, no one would urge an injunction for units already sold to third persons, so that royalties are the only remedy for past damages,

---

[44] Nos. 2008–1485, 2008–1487, 2008–1495, 2009 WL 2902044 (Fed. Cir. Sept. 11, 2009), *aff'g in part and vacating in part,* 580 F. Supp. 2d 1016 (S.D. Cal. 2008). Lucent first sued the relevant manufacturers, but Microsoft later intervened. See also Brent Kendall, *2nd UPDATE: Appeals Court Throws Out $358M Verdict Vs Microsoft,* WALL STREET JOURNAL ONLINE, Sept. 11, 2009, http://online.wsj.com/article/BT-CO-20090911-709923.html.

[45] 580 F. Supp. 2d at 1042.

[46] 2009 WL 2902044, at *25.

[47] *Id.* at *16.

[48] *Id.* at *17.

[49] For the complications of valuing specific components that are only sold as part of a larger device, see Solomon supra note at 25–36, noting the tendency to overvalue a patent when it is "the basis for the demand" for the composite product, and undervaluing it when it is. The patents at issue in *Lucent* are not demand drivers.

indicating that injunctive relief may be second best in this case. *Lucent* offers a sober warning that high damages sought by a patentee that bides its time is a risk worth watching even when no injunctive relief is in the picture.

There is, then, little reason to think that the traditional levels of equitable discretion are not sufficient to handle a case in which the injunctive relief looks most unattractive. The question is whether one need go beyond these rules to adopt the fourfold test that the Supreme Court championed in *eBay*, which made the issuance of an injunction turn on four related factors:

1) that [Plaintiff] has suffered an irreparable injury; (2) that remedies available at law, such as monetary damages, are inadequate to compensate for that injury; (3) that, considering the balance of hardships between the plaintiff and defendant, a remedy in equity is warranted; and (4) that the public interest would not be disserved by a permanent injunction.[50]

This approach is a mistake.[51] The first and second of these factors are mirror images of each other. The question, therefore, is what is added by the third and fourth factors, which take the inquiry far afield from the particulars of the individual case without giving any instruction as to how hardships are to be balanced and the public interest to be determined. If the system of damages and delayed injunctions just mentioned s applied to the tiny component case, the rest of the exercise looks odd. On the public interest, there is little reason to believe that the infringement of any minor patent will disrupt the use of the larger program by third parties who are already protected by the rule that denies the injunction against the end user. Furthermore, given the ease with which the small glitch can be fixed, it is hard to see why an individuated inquiry into the balance of hardships works better than the delayed injunction rule. One of the real risks of the *eBay* rule is that it calls into question, at least in the eyes of some, the ability of either the patentee, who does not practice a patent, or its nonexclusive licensees to obtain injunctive relief. That result is a serious mistake because it means that any effort to license to an industry carries with it the risk that no one will be able to prevent some potential licensees to avoid the system conditional on their willingness to pay damages. The net effect is that these practices will undermine the system of voluntary licensing.[52]

---

[50] *eBay*, 547 U.S. at 391.

[51] For a more detailed critique, see Richard A. Epstein, *The Disintegration of Intellectual Property? A Classical Liberal Response to a Premature Obituary*, 62 Stan. L. Rev. XX, 132–42 (forthcoming 2009–2010), available at http://papers.ssrn.com/sol3/papers.cfm?abstract_id=1236273.

[52] For the suggestion that courts "should grant injunctions to patent owners who participate in the market, whether by selling the patented invention, exclusively licensing it to someone

The point here should be clear. The adoption of a weak rule on injunctive relief generates two sources of social loss. The first is that it eliminates the ability of patentees to decide which firm or firms should be licensees. Any relaxation of the *eBay* rule would permit, for example, a nonlicensee to establish a pattern of use before a licensing agreement is complete, and thus will necessarily undermine the system. It would also make it impossible, for example, for patent licensors to develop territorial limitations on licenses to have their licensees better support their products by supplying the ancillary services needed for effective product promotion. Second, compulsory damage awards contain no ancillary provisions, which further makes it impossible to spur cooperative behavior between licensors and licensees. The overall efficiency losses from a soft *eBay* rule come from the bypass of the licensing function, with its normal gains from trade. The situation becomes graver when poor judicial decisions themselves impair the efficacy of licensing arrangements, a topic to which I now turn.

D. The Right to Disposition

The ability to dispose of property is yet another key element that carries over without a hitch from tangible to intangible property. The key virtue of dispositional rights is that they facilitate the cooperation between any two or more parties by allowing for the division of property rights and a coordination of labor on whatever terms and conditions they deem fit. This gain from trade depends only on human ingenuity and not on the nature of the underlying resource in question. The government limitations on how these dispositional rights can be exercised make a huge difference, as demonstrated by the following two examples, one from telecommunications and one from patent and copyright law.

E. Spectrum Licenses

The organization of the telecommunications spectrum could employ either a top-down or a bottom-up strategy. For our purposes, the vital difference between the strategies is how the property rights are acquired, and how that

else who sells it, or selling a product not covered by the patent but which competes with the infringing product," see Brief Amici Curiae Of 52 Intellectual Property Professors in Support of Petitioners at 9, *eBay, Inc. v. MercExchange, L.L.C.*, 547 U.S. 388 (2006) (No. 05–130). For a response, see Brief of Various Law & Economics Professors as Amici Curiae in Support of Respondent, *eBay, Inc. v. MercExchange, L.L.C.*, 547 U.S. 388 (2006) (No. 05–130), which I coauthored with F. Scott Kieff and R. Polk Wagner.

influences the way in which they can be used. Historically, the use of top-down licenses in telecommunications meant that the government could determine, in its capacity as owner, which kinds of restrictions could be placed on licenses. Unfortunately, in the grand spirit of the New Deal, that determination never utilized an auction option that would create permanent private licenses subject only to an anti-interference restraint, a limitation that works to maximize resource value just like an auction of condominium units. Instead, Congress decided that the Federal Communications Commission ("FCC") allocation decisions were to be permissible so long as they conformed to the "public interest, convenience and necessity."[53] The difficulty here lies not solely in the incurable vagueness of a standard whose ambition surely exceeds its content; rather, it lies in the mental frame of Justices like Felix Frankfurter, who broadly construed the mandate beyond the interference concerns whose analogies carry over so easily from other forms of trespass. In a self-conscious repudiation of the land model, he stated that the broad standard "puts upon the Commission the burden of determining the composition of that traffic."[54] But just how that is to be done, he never says. It turns out that there are many stations and many demands on their use. The government's effort to develop a centralized standard test for desirable frequencies came up empty handed.[55] One problem is that large stations tend to gravitate to the median viewer, which in turn reduces the ability of fringe players to gain air time. One private effort to combat this tendency was undertaken by the Cosmopolitan Broadcasting Corporation, whose simple idea was to issue sublicensees for the use of station WHDI to group representatives of various nationalities. That downstream decision allowed for the partition of the license into smaller units, each closer to the public at large, and it put people who knew something of the preferences of the groups that they wish to serve in charge of actual programming. There was much market acceptance of this program. However, the reward for such innovation was the termination of a license at the demand of the FCC, on the ground that the licensee impermissibly delegated its oversight authority to its sublicensees, who determined the content of their own broadcasts.[56]

---

[53] See *Nat'l Broad. Sys. v. United States*, 319 U.S. 190, 215 (1943) ("The criterion governing the exercise of the Commission's licensing power is the 'public interest, convenience, or necessity.'") (referring to authority under the Communications Act of 1934, §§ 307(a)(d), 309(a), 310, 312, 48 Stat. 1064).

[54] *Id.* at 216.

[55] See, for the initial critique, R. H. Coase, *The Federal Communications Commission*, 2 J. L. & Econ. 1 (1959).

[56] *Cosmopolitan Broad. Corp. v. Fed. Commc'n Comm'n*, 581 F.2d 917 (D.C. Cir. 1978) (Bazelon, J.). For my critique, see Richard A. Epstein, *What Broadcast Licenses Tell Us about*

The allocative losses from this heavy-handed approach are, if anything, greater than the limitations on sublicensees in other contexts. With landlord–tenant relationships, where the sublease of a part could create negative feedback on the retained space, the protection often justifies some restriction on the further disposition of the property in question. However, the adjacencies between radio slots are likely to be small, and are in all likelihood fully taken into account by the licensee's own decision. There is no discernible interest in the government as the ultimate spectrum owner to interfere in such cases, except for the twisted statutory mandate that drove the final decision in *National Broadcasting*.

The loss of the power of disposition comes with a high price. That cost is even higher than appears at first because alienation or division of broadcast licenses can take place along multiple dimensions, none of which pose serious threats to the public interest. Thus, when technology improves, the subdivision of a license by bandwidth makes good sense. Any such subdivision must abide by the interference constraint with respect to third persons, which is ever easier to do as technology improves. A subdivision must also account for the physical and marketing adjacencies of the new users of the various portions. However, that task is one to which the license owner (if he is so endowed) will handle privately for the same reason that condominium associations do well imposing covenants and restrictions on their potential unit buyers. All the net gains and losses are reflected in the total revenues received from all sales and licenses, coupled with any impact on any retained interest. Yet those are precisely the costs that any licensing procedure will adopt. Recognizing full rights of disposition also facilitates switches in frequency uses from broadcast, say, to mobile phones, or the reverse. Those use changes in turn can alleviate the huge current imbalances in spectrum utilization that stand as mute testimony to the inefficiency of a distinct system of licensing rules.[57] The bold claim that the distinctive nature of the resource requires its own unique rules falls hallow once the legal system assigns frequencies to particular owners. The unique physical feature of spectrum use is static across frequency lines. Once those boundary lines are established, it is easy to transplant the rules that govern trespass, assignment, and subdivision. The situation, moreover, is

---

Net Neutrality: Cosmopolitan Broadcasting Corporation v. FCC, in NEW DIRECTIONS IN COMMUNICATIONS POLICY 85 (Randolph May, ed., 2009). The lesson for net neutrality is to back off from the control of broadcast licenses unless one of the usual grounds for interference with freedom of contract applies, most notably, monopoly power.

[57] For vivid illustration of the differential levels of spectrum use, see Thomas W. Hazlett, *Spectrum Tragedies*, 22 YALE J. ON REG. 242, 248 fig.1 & n. note 28 (2005).

one that becomes easier, not more difficult, over time because the improved technology allows for a narrower width for each transmission, allowing far more separate signals to be carried by individual owners.

F. Patent and Copyright Licensing

This basic pattern of argumentation carries over, again without a hitch, to the difficult area of patent and copyright licensing. I use the word "licensing" in this context only because the usual pattern of disposition for most forms of intellectual property are licenses due to the difficulty of pricing outright sales. The range of license terms is itself a worthy topic for an extended treatise, because there is no dimension of patent or copyright use over which the parties cannot negotiate, if allowed, for their mutual gain. Consistent with our major thesis, the basic antitrust concern about license pools is whether they will be used to facilitate horizontal price-fixing arrangements, which is effectively countered by a rule that allows complementary but not substitute patents to be included in the same pool.[58]

The instructive question is whether it is possible to find some independent normative justification for the impositions on the power of disposition above, beyond those that belong in a sound antitrust system applying to all sorts of endeavors.[59] Consistent with my core carryover thesis, I think that the set of possible rules is empty. One major challenge to this thesis arises in the patent law under the rubric of the doctrine of "patent exhaustion" and under the law of copyright in connection with the "first sale" doctrine. The purport of both these doctrines is to say that the ability of a patentee or copyright holder to charge royalties is limited to their initial licensees. In a version of the old "privity" requirement, the patent or copyright monopoly reaches only the initial licensee, not further downstream users.

Both these doctrines exhibit the following logic. The positive law has created a monopoly in the patentee or the copyright holder for the express purpose of inducing innovative behavior. The scope of the grant should be limited to that initial purpose, from which it follows that the patentee or licensee should be entitled to one, and only one, royalty with respect to the product in question, after which the patented or copyrighted product passes into the stream of commerce free of any further claim of the original owner.

---

[58] For discussion, see Herbert Hovenkamp, THE ANTITRUST ENTERPRISE: PRINCIPLE AND EXECUTION 265–67 & 277–78 (2006).

[59] For further discussion, see Epstein, *Disintegration, supra* note 51, at 142–60.

One common articulation of this doctrine is found in *Keeler v. Standard Folding Bed Co.*,[60] which put the doctrine as follows:

[When a patentee] has himself constructed a machine, and sold it without any conditions, or authorized another to construct, sell, and deliver it, or to construct, use, and operate it, without any conditions, and the consideration has been paid to him for the thing patented, the rule is well established that the patentee must be understood to have parted to that extent with all his exclusive right, and that he ceases to have any interest whatever in the patented machine so sold and delivered or authorized to be constructed and operated.[61]

The obvious question about this particular rule is whether it should be treated as an "inherent" restraint that is embodied in the law of patents and copyrights, or whether it should be treated as though it were a default provision that was attached to the normal sale of a patented or copyrighted article, which could be reversed by clear notice of the patentee to all down-stream parties. The manifest parallels between the default and mandatory rules in *Intel v. Hamidi* seem clear, as does the proper resolution. The key distinction is the source of the restraint on alienation, be it by sale or license or some combination thereof. Thus the government restrictions in the FCC license cases may look legitimate because the state was the first owner of the property. However, it is instructive to note that the bottom-up approach to spectrum acquisition would have denied the government that option by creating perpetual ownership in particular frequencies. The acceptance of government ownership of the spectrum makes it impossible to say that the license conditions are outside its province. The objection to government policy thus rests solely on the dissipation of social wealth through its ill-advised licensing procedures.

With intellectual property, the first set of objections, which ask whether these restraints should be classified as either default or mandatory, bite because a patentee or copyright holder is not a mere licensee of the government. Rather, it receives a full-fledged property interest. Under these circumstances it is a mistake to treat the first sale and patent exhaustion doctrines as mandatory terms, and better to treat them as sensible default subject to explicit variation by the parties subject only to the standard limitations on contracts embodied in the antitrust laws. The argument here proceeds identically as it did with broadcast licenses. There is perfect internalization of all future gains and losses when the patentee or copyright holder issues one, or more, licenses with respect to a protected work.

---

[60] 157 U.S. 659 (1895).
[61] *Id.* at 663.

Therefore, the rule should let them decide what terms, what conditions, and what parties to involve.

In many of these cases, it turns out that the exhaustion rule makes good sense. If a patentee sells a product to one person for resale to a second, the total amount of royalties that can be captured from the subpurchaser is strictly limited by the value of the patent to the end user.[62] That price can be collected in one of two ways. The first is to put a single tariff on the immediate purchaser and to extract none from any other. The obvious advantage to all parties is the ease with which this tariff could be determined and collected. It need not be separately stated, but could be included in the price of the article sold. Alternatively, if the initial transaction is a license to manufacture goods, a single royalty eases the burdens of collection and reduces the transactional burdens on third parties. It seems clear that the correct default rule in these cases is to charge but a single fee for the use of the patented technology or the products from which it derives. So limited, the exhaustion rule thus has a firm economic base.

The sense of this economic logic is evident from one of the early cases that inspired its use. Thus, in *Adams v. Burke*,[63] a third party had the exclusive rights to make, use, and sell patented coffin lids within a 10-mile radius with Boston at its center. That assignee sold a patented item "without condition or restriction" to the defendant, who then used it outside that original territory, only to be sued by the assignee of the patent outside that region. In these circumstances, the rule makes perfectly good sense. There is no way that the original seller of the coffin lid can determine the final resting place for the coffin. Yet it is very difficult to create a two-part tariff to deal with this situation, and pointless as well, given that many people who purchase the coffin lids outside the smaller territory might use them within that territory. It would be truly grotesque if every movement of the coffin lid across territories generated another fee. If the original owner wants to impose restrictions on use, the original deal is the place to do it. Since the sale was without further restriction or restraint, its territorial limitations should not denigrate from the value of the patent, for to do so is to reduce the net royalties from patent use all over. The Court was right to conclude that "when the patentee, or the person having his rights, sells a machine or instrument whose sole value is in its use, he receives the

---

[62] For discussion, see Anne Layne-Farrar, Gerard Llobet, A. Jorge Padilla, *A Chicago School Take on Patent Licensing: Understanding the Economics of the Patent Exhaustion Doctrine* 22–27 (working paper), available at http://www.cemfi.es/~llobet/Patent%20Exhaustion. pdf.

[63] 84 U.S. 453 (1873).

consideration for its use and he parts with the right to restrict that use."[64] Goods that move quickly in commerce should not, unannounced, be subject to multiple royalty claims, as it is just too difficult to make the necessary price adjustments among all the parties in the chain of distribution.

The patterns of distribution and use, however, are sufficiently varied that it is dangerous to convert the commonplace into the necessary. To see how differences in product distribution and use can matter, it is instructive to examine the much-mooted case of *Mallinckrodt v. Medipart*,[65] which various consumer groups have wrongly attacked as a dangerous repudiation of the patent exhaustion rule.[66] Mallinckrodt brought suits, one for patent infringement and a second for the inducement of a breach of contract, against two defendants who used or arranged for the use of the plaintiff's "UltraVent" patented device for generating, collecting, and analyzing radioactive materials that are inhaled and exhaled from the lungs.[67] When sold to the hospitals, the device contained a clear legend that conspicuously stated the sale was for "single-use only." With full knowledge of the restriction, Medipart entered into an agreement with hospitals whereby it serviced these devices to refurbish them for further use in violation of that original agreement. The work involved was quite exacting; its improper performance carried with it the risk of infection and other adverse medical consequences. I see no reason why the actions for both patent infringement and inducement of breach should not be allowed. Indeed, the latter is exceptionally important because of the difficulty and expense of chasing after individual hospitals, all of which have relations with Medipart, the breach inducer.

To begin the analysis, it is clear that the original sale price, negotiated on the assumption that the restraints on alienation were valid, doubtless reflected the obligation to return the device to Mallinckrodt for additional

---

[64] *Id.* at 456.

[65] 976 F.2d 700 (Fed. Cir. 1992).

[66] Brief Amici Curiae of Consumers Union (CU), Electronic Frontier Foundation (EFF), and Public Knowledge in Support of the Petitioner, *Quanta Computer, Inc. v. LG Electronics, Inc.*, 128 S. Ct. 2109 (2007) (No. 06–937) [hereinafter CU, EFF and PK Amicus Brief] (prepared by Mark N. Bernstein, Fred von Lohmann and Jason Schultz).

[67] The Court's full description of the UltraVent reads as follows: a unitary kit that consists of a "nebulizer" which generates a mist of the radioactive material or the prescribed drug, a "manifold" that directs the flow of oxygen or air and the active material, a filter, tubing, a mouthpiece, and a nose clip. In use, the radioactive material or drug is placed in the nebulizer, is atomized, and the patient inhales and exhales through the closed system. The device traps and retains any radioactive or other toxic material in the exhalate. The device fits into a lead-shielded container that is provided by Mallinckrodt to minimize exposure to radiation and for safe disposal after use. *Mallinckrodt*, 976 F.2d at 702.

servicing and use. These provisions served at least two sensible functions. The first is that it allowed for some price discrimination among potential buyers based on the intensity of their use, which has the positive effect of allowing low demanders into the market. The inability to keep this restriction in place would necessarily entail charging a higher single price that would not be able to capture the differential demand – surely not an issue in *Adams v. Burke*, where we can be quite confident that each coffin had one, and only one, use. Second, medical devices are vulnerable to tort liability. Divided control could always leave open complex questions as to whether Mallinckrodt or Medipart was responsible for any failure by others who at one time or other were in the same chain of custody. Single control over the manufacture and servicing obligation does not eliminate the possibility of erroneous use at the hospital level, but the elimination of even one element of concern surely counts as a positive. Furthermore, we know that these conditions do not raise any antitrust concerns, given the correct decision in *Illinois Tool Works Inc. v. Independent Ink, Inc.*,[68] which rejected the proposition that the ownership of a patented product created a presumption of market power sufficient to trigger further scrutiny under the antitrust laws. Quite simply, so long as other vendors sold, or licensed, other combinations of the device and the additional service, competition at the first level – that involving the patented device itself – would take into account the full costs of routine servicing in the aftermarket. It follows, therefore, that it hardly matters whether we call the original transaction between Mallinckrodt and its hospitals a sale or a license. The key issue is not the location of the title, to which the patent exhaustion doctrine gives great weight, but the economic logic of the basic transaction.[69] In effect, the Federal Circuit took the position that for these tripartite arrangements freedom of contract was the norm between the parties: "Unless the condition violates some other law or policy (in the patent field, notably the misuse or antitrust law), private parties retain the freedom to contract concerning conditions of sale."[70]

---

[68] 547 U.S. 28, 31 (2006).

[69] For a rejection of the proposition that the location of title counts for antitrust purposes, see *Continental T.V., Inc. v. GTE Sylvania Inc.*, 433 U.S. 36, 57–59 (1977) (making antitrust liability depend on "demonstrable economic effect," rather than "formalistic line drawing" on questions of legal title). *Sylvania* overruled the prior decision of the Supreme Court in *United States v. Arnold, Schwinn & Co.*, 388 U.S. 365 (1967) (treating vertical restraints as per se illegal).

[70] *Mallinckrodt*, 976 F.2d at 708 (citation omitted). Judge Newman cited *United States v. Univis Lens. Co.*, 316 U.S. 241 (1942), as an instance in which the patent exhaustion doctrine was justified under the antitrust law, which at that time had a per se rule against resale price maintenance; see *Dr. Miles Medical Co. v. John D. Park & Sons Co.*, 220 U.S. 373 (1911), which meant that it was not possible at that time to disentangle the two rules. After the Court's decision in *Leegin Creative Leather Products, Inc. v. PSKS, Inc.*, 551 U.S. 877 (2007),

Accordingly, "[a]s was said in *United States v. General Electric Co.*, the patentee may grant a license 'upon any condition the performance of which is reasonably within the reward which the patentee by the grant of the patent is entitled to secure.'"[71] This conclusion in turn justified the use of the tort of inducement of breach of contract against the third party and the application of patent remedies that specifically reach inducers.[72] The key point here is that the entire process of reuse within the closed community gave this case a context to which the exhaustion rule did not apply, even though it explicitly kept to one side all cases that involve products "in the ordinary channels of trade,"[73] – those sold to third persons with whom neither the original patentee nor its first buyer have ongoing relations.

The strong freedom of contract spin in *Mallinckrodt* was not evident in the recent Supreme Court decision in *Quanta Computer, Inc. v. LG Electronics, Inc.*,[74] which applied the patent exhaustion doctrine in cases that once again did not involve sales to the trade in the ordinary course of business. At issue in *Quanta* was a contract settlement between LG Electronics (LGE) and its customer, Intel, who agreed to give notice to its customers, including Quanta, that any sale of products that embedded LGE's products would be subject to a potential royalty to LGE. That notice provision is a cheap and effective way to put the potential buyer in a position to calibrate the initial royalty to allow for the second. Indeed, there is good evidence of its transaction utility. There is evidence that LGE did not want Intel to charge a uniform royalty to all potential buyers.[75] It appears that some of those

resale price maintenance was no longer per se unlawful. For the resurrection of the patent exhaustion doctrine as an independent constraint, see the discussion of *Quanta Computer, Inc. v. LG Electronics, Inc., infra.*

[71] *Mallinckrodt v. Medipart*, 976 F.2d 700, 704–05 (Fed. Cir. 1992) (quoting *United States v. General Electric Co.*, 272 U.S. 476, 489 (1926)).

[72] 35 U.S.C. § 271 (b) ("Whoever actively induces infringement of a patent shall be liable as an infringer."). The force of the word "actively" is unclear, but surely reaches all parties, like Medipart, that initiated the business transaction.

[73] *Mallinckrodt*, 976 F.2d at 705.

[74] 128 S. Ct. 2109 (2008). For my extended critique, see Epstein, *Disintegration, supra* note 51, at 154–56.

[75] Robert W. Gomulkiewicz, *The Federal Circuit's Licensing Law Jurisprudence: Its Nature and Influence*, 84 WASH. L. REV. 199, 233 (2009), noting that the exception in the Intel license "is good news for computer-system manufacturers who have a patent portfolio cross license with LG Electronics. These companies already paid for the patent rights. They do not want to pay again as part of the price of Intel's microprocessors. For those manufacturers who do not have such a license, however, Intel cannot serve as a "reseller' of LB Electronics' patent rights. These manufacturers must purchase their patent rights directly from the patentee, LG Electronics." My thanks to Rochelle Dreyfus for pointing out this article, which fills a big hole in the business back story of the case. For the concern that *Quanta* "downstream resellers need to be accommodated in the one-time sale with the licensee," precluding price discrimination, see Neal E. Solomon, What is a Reasonable

potential buyers had already acquired blanket licenses from LGE for the use of all its products, while others had not. Any uniform charge by Intel would not distinguish between these two types of buyers. The notice position does, for it allows those buyers who have paid for blanket licenses to avoid any further negotiations with LGE, which can deal independently with those who have not obtained those licenses. These negotiations, moreover, need not be done after taking title to LGE products from Intel, at which point a holdup problem could arise. The notice provision has the great advantage of allowing the potential buyer from Intel to negotiate with LGE *before* entering into a contract of purchase to avoid just that risk. The price of that second license will of course depend on the nature of the substitutes available in the market. Described in this fashion, there is no reason to think that the transactions at issue in *Quanta* raised any distinct antitrust concerns. However, the Court nonetheless held that the patent exhaustion rule blocked the transaction, despite offering no functional explanation as to why there is any reason to do more than apply the antitrust restraints that everyone agrees are inapplicable here.

The fact pattern in *Quanta* is clearly distinguished from that in *Mallinckrodt* in that the latter case involved key issues of product reuse that posed serious risks of tort liability, while *Quanta* was simply a commercial dispute over royalties without these overtones. Accordingly, it is not surprising that the Supreme Court at no point discussed *Mallinckrodt* in ways that could cast its narrow rational into question. Nonetheless, the Amicus Brief filed by the Consumers Union, the Electronic Frontier Foundation, and Public Knowledge (CU/EFF/PK)[76] sought to draw the explicit connection between the two cases, by treating *Mallinckrodt's* broad statements in defense of freedom of contract as a total repudiation of the patent exhaustion doctrine. In and of itself, such an interpretation would have been a welcome development because the increase in licensing freedom acts as an indirect spur to innovation. Nonetheless, the CU/EFF/PK position predicted a massive loss in consumer welfare from the upset of long-time settled expectations resting on the exhaustion rule.[77] That position is odd for two reasons. First, there is nothing whatsoever in *Mallinckrodt* (or *Quanta*) that is meant to displace the default rule that works so well in the downstream distribution of ordinary consumer products through ordinary commercial channels. Second, it is hard to detect any change in general practices in the two decades that *Mallinckrodt* has been in effect. Quite to the contrary, efforts to use clear

Royalty? A Comparative Assessment of Patent Damages Methodologies at 42 (mss on file with author).

[76] CU, EFF and PK Amicus Brief, *supra* note 66.
[77] *Id.* at 5–6.

notice to prevent the unwanted resale of books and records have become ever more common. Law casebooks that are given to teachers as complimentary samples now have emblazoned on their front covers signs that say they are for professor use only and not for resale. The reason seems clear enough. It is an effort to reduce the price of allowing professors to sample books for free by preventing their resale to students who would otherwise buy from the publisher. The effort to prevent the resale of stripped-down demonstration records that are distributed to key figures in the music industry has the same purpose.[78] There are of course difficulties with the enforcement mechanism, but that is hardly a reason to say that the effort to so limit the initial distribution should be illegal. The entire system of notice, through recordation, of restrictive covenants has been widely accepted since the landmark decision in *Tulk v. Moxhay*.[79] So long as the notice in question is given only to protect valid claims, it is hard to see any reason why techniques that make sense with chattels (where their legality is not certain) and are common with land should be regarded as presumptively unwise with patents and copyrights.

Yet just that position was taken in the Amicus Brief of CU/EFF/PK. Their effort was commendable insofar as it sought to ground the attack on these contractual restrictions in functional explanations. However, the explanations offered for attacking the restrictions at play in *Mallinckrodt*, and through it the restrictions at issue in *Quanta*, are wholly unpersuasive. They allege that the results of removing the patent exhaustion doctrine include

- Increased information costs when trying to ascertain restrictions on patented goods
- Erosion of the well-established right to repair patented goods
- Interference with the functioning of vibrant secondary markets (such as eBay and Craigslist) enabled by new technologies
- Diminished opportunities for "user innovation"
- Expanded use of inefficient and unfair price discrimination in connection with patented goods.[80]

As to the first, the information costs are trivial if notice is attached to the goods in question as it clearly is in all the relevant cases where the

---

[78] See, e.g., *UMG Recordings, Inc. v. Augusto*, 558 F. Supp. 2d 1055 (C.D. Cal. 2008). The case involved the resale of demo CDs given in the music industry which bore a legend prohibiting resale. For a detailed critique of its particulars, see Epstein, *Disintegration*, *supra* note 51, at n.177 and accompanying text.

[79] *Tulk v. Moxhay*, (1848) 41 Eng. Rep. 1143, 1144 (Ch.). I discuss the connections between real and personal covenants in greater detail in Epstein, *Disintegration*, *supra* note 51, at n.47 and accompanying text.

[80] CU, EFF and PK Amicus Brief, *supra* note 66, at 3.

defendant admits full and clear knowledge of the restriction that is attached to the patented object, as in the cases they instance in their brief.[81] All the burdens on information costs are borne by the patentee, which takes the risk if notice is not communicated. In those cases of common goods for sale in the ordinary course of business, the costs are never incurred because the restrictions are never imposed.

Second, the erosion of the right to repair patented goods is no different from the rights to repair those goods that are not under patent. Normally, a patentee does have an interest in stopping reconstruction that violates patents because those devices are sold in competition with those of its own manufacture.[82] However, repairs present a different issue. The imposition of an unnecessary restraint on purchasers could easily reduce initial sales. Unless there is some efficiency advantage to tying repair services to the product, the seller of the patented product has no interest in the repair process and will not seek to impose the condition. On the other hand, in cases like *Mallinckrodt*, where the risk of tort liability is serious, that condition is often imposed. Similarly, in other contexts, the consumer may gain the right to repair only if he is prepared to forfeit the product warranties that are otherwise attached to the goods. The risk of poor repairs increases the cost of the original warranty in ways that are hard to price. There is thus no reason to think that this condition would be invalidated, for there is always the risk that poor repairs by an independent party could increase the risk of tort liability of the original product supplier.

Third, it is not creditable to argue that the *Mallinckrodt* rule could interfere with the emergence of efficient secondary markets. *Mallinckrodt* was decided in 1990, and none of the web-based markets emerged until close to

---

[81]   See CU, EFF and PK Amicus Brief, *supra* note 66, at 2–3 (citing *Ariz. Cartridge Remfrs. Ass'n v. Lexmark Int'l, Inc.*, 421 F.3d 981, 983–84 (9th Cir. 2005) ("single use only" restrictions for toner cartridges"); *Jazz Photo Corp. v. Int'l Trade Comm.*, 264 F.3d 1094, 1107–08 (Fed. Cir. 2001) ("single use only" restrictions in camera instructions); *Hewlett-Packard Co. v. Repeat-O-Type Stencil Mfg. Corp.*, 123 F.3d 1445, 1453 (Fed. Cir. 1997) ("single use only" for inject printer cartridges)). These cases are subject to multiple interpretations because in *Jazz Photo* the court did not read the instructions as a license limitation, and held that there was no infringement. *Hewlitt-Packard* contained no clear notice restriction.

[82]   Judge Newman wrote in *Mallinckrodt*:

Even an unconditioned sale of a patented device is subject to the prohibition against "reconstruction" of the thing patented. A purchaser's right to use a patented device does not extend to reconstructing it, for reconstruction is deemed analogous to construction of a new device. However, repair is permissible. Although the rule is straightforward its implementation is less so, for it is not always clear where the boundary lies: how much "repair" is fair before the device is deemed reconstructed.

976 F.2d at 709 (citations omitted).

a decade later. Clearly the rule had no effect for the simple reason that there is no overlap. The kinds of ordinary consumer goods that get sold in these markets are those to which the general default provision applies. The rapid growth of these markets is proof positive that *Mallinckrodt* does not exert any destructive secret influence on these markets.

Fourth, any claim of diminished user options raises the question of the relative importance of downstream and upstream innovation, and the possible coordination between them. Initially, nothing stops the upstream person from offering payments to individuals who improve their products or discover new applications for them. In addition, the downstream user could easily obtain an improvement patent that gives some leverage for negotiation with the holder of the original patent. Furthermore, where there is a direct conflict between the upstream and downstream users, the possibility remains that user innovation will come at the expense of manufacturer innovation that could prove to be of greater value. It is now widely know that the United States does not offer any explicit exemption for the users of research tools,[83] but by the same token it is highly unlikely that any patentee will crack down on downstream innovators of *complementary* products that only increase the sale potential of the patented goods.

Fifth, the economics of price discrimination are without question difficult, for there is no a priori way to rule out the possibility that some marketing practice increases monopoly power for the seller. But don't count on it, for in many cases price discrimination (which requires a prohibition against resale that could defeat the differential tariff) allows sellers to *reduce* the licensee fees for some class of potential consumers, which thus increases consumer welfare. Furthermore, even if there are cases that do raise legitimate antitrust concerns, the antitrust law remains there to deal with it. As Herbert Hovenkamp has remarked in connection with the so-called patent misuse doctrine, there is no need for patent-specific rules in this area.[84] Here is a classic case where the imposition of two systems of liability is worse than one.

At this point, the key issue over *Quanta* is not whether it is sound, but whether the damage can be contained to the small subset of cases that look

---

[83] *Madey v. Duke University*, 307 F.3d 1351, 1362 (Fed. Cir. 2002) (finding no experimental use defense to infringement if "act is in furtherance of the alleged infringer's legitimate business and is not solely for amusement, to satisfy idle curiosity, or for strictly philosophical inquiry").

[84] HOVENKAMP, *supra* note 58, at 272 ("'[I]f 'misuse' means the same thing as an antitrust violation, then why bother having a separate concept of 'misuse'?" In the same vein he writes, id at 273 ("[T]he Federal Circuit's position seems incredible to someone familiar with the expansive body of antitrust doctrine," given that "§2 [of the Sherman Act] reaches every act that monopolizes or dangerously threatens to do so.").

like it. Only the future can answer the positive inquiry, but the normative issues do seem clear. The carryover thesis that works well with rules on exclusion works equally well with rules for the license or sale of patents and copyrights. Once again, the effort to create a unique set of rules for a special legal environment has come up empty.

IV. Conclusion: The Case for Carryover

In this chapter I have pressed forward with the long-term project of showing how the law of intangible property can be integrated with the property law that governs various forms of natural resources. In undertaking this inquiry, I do not seek to prove that there are no critical differences in the law that governs these intangible interests. Quite the opposite, any full accounting of the overall property system requires a systematic explanation of differences as well as similarities. However, I do wish to contest strongly the proposition that each area of law is to some extent "special," such that it needs special consideration.[85] In too many areas claims for special rules have led to the introduction of price controls in agriculture and rent control in residential real estate markets. The background presumption should be against ad hoc claims of uniqueness. The differences that are inevitably found as the law moves from field to field are, at best, of little consequence and, at worst, can lead analysts far astray. With that mission in mind I have shown ways in which the law of intangible property avoids many of the difficulties that are found with tangible property – ways that afford full respect to the basic axioms of exclusion and disposition that do (or at least should) work in connection with such vital resources as land and chattels. The illustrations that I have chosen come from the law as it relates to the Internet, the spectrum, copyright, and patents for all different kinds of goods and products. I have sought to document the mischief that arises when courts introduce ad hoc rules in connection with these issues that ignore the fundamental gains from systems that make the right distinctions between private and common property. The long-term agenda is to return the law as it relates to all of these areas to its sound theoretical foundations. The payoff is a system-wide improvement in the rules governing property that work for the benefit of us all in both the long and the short run.

[85] I have pushed hard on this point in virtually every area in which I write. See, e.g., Richard A. Epstein, *Why is Health Care Special?*, 40 U. KAN. L. REV. 307 (1992).

PART II

THE ECONOMICS OF INNOVATION

3

Bundling and Unbundling in New Technology Markets

Seven Easy Pieces: The Ideal Is the Enemy of the Efficient

Stan J. Liebowitz and Stephen E. Margolis

Bundling and tie-in sales are well-worked topics in both economics and law. Economists have largely answered the claim that tying the purchase of a monopolized good to a variable quantity of some other good does not readily provide the owner of the first monopoly with rents from a second monopoly. Only under very limited circumstances can a tie-in create a new monopoly. Beyond that, economists have hatched some clever theories that explain why firms might nevertheless engage in tie-in sales. Some of these explanations find that tie-ins can be socially harmless, harmful, or beneficial but nevertheless not monopolizing. Economists have also turned their attention to bundling. Most of these examinations try to explain conditions whereby bundles might increase profits.

In law, tie-in sales were made illegal under section 3 of the Clayton Act in instances where they would tend to create a monopoly. Since then, doctrines developed in case law now extend the provisions of the Sherman Act to tie-in sales, expanding awards and easing the burden of proof by making tie-in sales a per se violation of the law once certain threshold conditions are met.[1] Tie-ins and bundles have also long been addressed by patent abuse doctrines, and most recently they are under attack under telecommunications regulation.

Much of the economics literature on tie-ins and bundling is predicated on the assumption of either a simple monopoly or a dominant firm. Market foreclosure theories, which are the basis for what limited support there is for a rule against tie-in sales, require that the dominant firm's sales of tied goods could capture a very large share of that industry. We will have more to say on this later.

---

[1] *Jefferson Parrish Hospital District v. Hyde*, 466 U.S. 2 (1984).

Lately, though, some economists have called attention to the important fact that a great deal of actual tying takes place in industries in which there is competition of one sort or another.[2] In fact, a great majority of bundling can be found in markets that are either an adequate approximation of the economist's theoretical model of competition, or at least that exhibit the sort of rivalry that common usage and common sense would call competition, even if some economists wouldn't. That bundling occurs in competitive markets is evidence that the practices have efficiency explanations, for otherwise the practice would be competed away. In turn, if bundling is efficient when practiced by competitors, it may well have similar properties when practiced by a monopolist. Finally, although it may well be efficient, bundling always restricts choice to some extent, and therefore consumers interested in that choice may express frustration and unhappiness with a welfare-enhancing process that is nevertheless not ideal. In this case the ideal is the enemy of the efficient.

This chapter considers some of the economics and law of tie-in sales with particular attention to innovation. Markets affected by innovation will involve invention, creative works, other new goods, and new ways of producing or delivering goods. Typically these are markets in intellectual property or markets that are fundamentally affected by intellectual property. Many of the contemporary controversies over bundling and tie-ins involve these markets, and many innovation markets seem to collide with a regulatory disposition that is antagonistic to bundling. While regulators' antagonism to bundling is widely noted, we will also observe that in important cases, regulators or would-be regulators have been hostile to unbundling. We will return to that later.

This chapter offers support for three general claims. First, bundling is pervasive for reasons that have to do with efficiencies of a simple and obvious nature. Most goods are bundles. Second, the conditions required for tying or bundling to create monopoly power for reasons other than product improvement are very restrictive, so restrictive that such episodes are a vanishingly small fraction of all tie-ins or bundles. Most bundles have the potential to foreclose sales by others in an equally simple and

[2] *See* Kobayashi, Bruce H. 2006. "Two Tales of Bundling: Implications for the Application of Antitrust Law to Bundled Discounts." In *Antitrust Policy and Vertical Restraint*. Edited by Robert Hahn, pp. 10–37. Washington, DC: AEI–Brookings Joint Center for Regulatory Studies; Hazlett, Thomas W. 2006. "Shedding Tiers for A-La-Carte? An Economic Analysis of Cable TV Pricing." George Mason University Law and Economics Research Paper Series; Evans, David S. and Michael Salinger. 2005. "Why do Firms Bundle and Tie? Evidence form Competitive Markets and Implications for Tying Law." *Yale Journal on Regulation* 22, no. 4.

obvious way. Houses with kitchens will reduce the demand for restaurants. But most bundling has nothing to do with monopoly power in any sense. Third, in light of the first two, tying and bundling should not be illegal per se in antitrust law, that is all cases should require a demonstration of a high likelihood of actual exclusion and the absence of an efficiency defense. Equivalently, the presumption in telecommunications regulation that bundling is harmful should be reversed.

We begin by offering some clarifications of terminology and a general discussion of tying, bundling, and its alternatives. After that, we review some of the competing explanations of bundling and tie-ins, with particular attention to markets in intellectual property. We follow that with a list of new-technology bundling-related practices that currently encounter regulatory scrutiny and then begin a more detailed case-by-case discussion of these markets. We examine actual bundling practices to see how they relate to the proffered explanations, how they are regulated, and what problems they solve. Finally, we consider briefly the legal treatment of tie-in sales, noting recent progress, in the anti-trust world at least, away from a per se doctrine against bundling and tie-ins.

I. The General Framework

The terminology in this literature is getting clumsy. We will use "tying" or "tie-in sale" throughout to refer to any arrangement in which a buyer's access to one good (the tying good) is conditioned on his consenting to purchase a variable amount of one or more other (tied) goods from the seller. Typically, this takes the form of an "all requirements" clause, by which the buyer of a tying good agrees to satisfy all requirements for some other good through purchases from the seller of the tying good. We will refer to *virtual ties* when firms try to reach this type of arrangement without actual contracts. We will use *bundling* where fixed quantities of items are sold together. *Pure bundling* refers to the circumstance in which goods are only sold in bundles and *mixed bundling* occurs when a seller offers both bundles and one or both of the individual goods.

We will take up some space here to elaborate on this terminology because there is a risk that useful distinctions will become lost, and our vocabulary less useful, much like the terms *externality* and *public good* have become muddled, with numerous and inconsistent definitions in circulation.[3]

---

[3] Carlton, Denis W. and Michael Waldman. 2006. "Why Tie an Essential Good?" In *Antitrust Policy and Vertical Restraint*. Edited by Robert Hahn, pp. 10–37. Washington, DC: AEI–Brookings Joint Center for Regulatory Studies. It appears as if some writers are beginning

Tie-in sales have a history going back to shoe machinery, IBM and Hollerith cards, and canning machines using tin-plate. The key feature of tie-ins was a contract based on a promise to purchase the secondary good from the seller of the primary product. This led to a *variable* relationship between the quantities of the two goods.

Bundles, on the other hand, are just what the name implies – fixed amounts of multiple units or multiple products. The interest within the profession has been with bundles containing more than one product due to the antitrust issues involved. Stigler's 1963 example of movies being sold to theaters was an example of bundling different items.[4] One of the more recent bundles of interest was Microsoft's inclusion of, first Internet Explorer and then, later, Media Player, in Windows. Cable and satellite television packages sold to consumers consisting of numerous stations also appear to be bundles. Only if the goods are used in fixed proportions would ties and bundles be the same.

But there are other combinations of products that are neither ties nor bundles. Go into a buffet restaurant and what you are offered is neither a tie nor a fixed bundle. The food items are consumed in variable proportions, but there no tie in the normal sense. You are given access to a bundle of goods, but the bundle is larger than what you can consume, and what is consumed varies for each consumer. The price you pay is an entrance fee and is not a function of use – customers can eat as much or as little as they want. We refer to this as *all-you-can-eat pricing*. The cable TV example is an example of this type of good as opposed to a traditional bundle.

Finally, the antithesis of a bundle is complete a-la-carte pricing. This is a case whereby consumers pay for the amount of an item that they consume. Every penny's worth of gasoline, every portion of a kilowatt hour of electricity, and every hundredth of a pound of filet mignon represents a-la-carte pricing. Bundling is incompatible with a-la-carte pricing. There is nothing about tie-in sales, however, that precludes a-la-carte pricing.

Economists live in an a-la-carte world.[5] We do not mean, by this, that our physical world is a-la-carte – if it were, we would have nothing to write

   to equate pure bundling with tie-in sales, which seems wrongheaded to us. Hahn states on page 2 that "so-called pure bundling is equivalent to tying." Evans states on page 68 that "pure bundling necessarily involves a tie."

[4] Stigler, G. J. (1963). United States v. Loew's, Inc.: A note on block-booking. Supreme Court Review, 1963, 152

[5] Recent discussions of a-la-carte include Liebowitz, Stan. 1983. "Tie-in Sales, Risk Reduction and Price Discrimination," Economic Inquiry, pp. 387–399; Hazlett, Thomas W. 2006. "Shedding Tiers for A-La-Carte? An Economic Analysis of Cable TV Pricing." George Mason University Law and Economics Research Paper Series.

about in this chapter – but that our models of markets are of the a-la-carte variety. In the idealized markets that we use to illustrate supply and demand, there is a perfectly homogeneous good sold in individual units. Consumers might purchase more than one unit of a good, but there is no point in selling anything other than individual units. Transaction costs are swept under the rug so there is no extra cost in purchasing ten individual units or five groups of two.

Efficiency arguments come easily in this a-la-carte world. Goods are produced at a positive marginal cost, and consumers will chose, on their own, to purchase only those goods for which their evaluation exceeds that marginal cost, no more, no less. Any more, or any less, would be inefficient. A-la-carte sales provide the right incentives to consumers and no unnecessary constraints. We don't observe leftover amounts since no one orders any more than they want, or, for that matter, any or less.

A-la-carte also appears to provide maximum consumer sovereignty. Not only do consumers purchase the exact amounts of goods that they want, they also purchase the exact goods that they want. When we pump gas, the amount we pay is directly related to the amount we purchase, measured to the last hundredth of a penny. This corresponds directly to our a-la-carte models. We do not purchase more gasoline than we want, nor do we purchase less. We purchase just the right amount. We could achieve similar results for goods that are not easily broken into smaller pieces by renting the good instead of selling it (although robust resale markets might help to achieve the same goal).

But this is not how most markets actually function. As we will see, deviations from this ideal do not imply inefficiency, merely that some costs are left out of our convenient fairy tale.

When you go to a restaurant, you might order rice as a part of your meal. You do not specify the numbers of kernels of rice that you wish to have put on your plate. Nor does MacDonald's sell individual French fries. Food is almost always sold in bundles. But so is almost everything else. Unless you go to stores with unpackaged ingredients sold by weight, you buy packages: paint, tape, nails, golf balls, and blank CDs, for example. Automobiles are not usually sold by the miles traveled, nor are homes sold by the hours used, although there are rental markets for each.

The reason for these bundles is simple. Although physical packages may be too big or too small compared to the ideal for each consumer, the cost of having someone to measure out an amount exactly equal to the customers' wishes is greater than the potential welfare losses from packages that are not the ideal size for each individual consumer. The time cost of counting or measuring the kernels of corn, and the cost of pricing such variable amounts, would be greater than the benefits from perfect consumption levels. Otherwise vendors who provided exact measurements would have survived and packaged goods would not have come to dominate the markets. In the case of food, there is also a sanitary benefit to packaging it at the factory.

For similar reasons, complex items like refrigerators, which contain numerous component parts, come prepackaged and not sold as separate components. A few tinkerers who enjoy building refrigerators might benefit from being able to pick and choose parts, but the rest of us prefer to have the package assembled at the factory. The cost savings are very large in having a factory assemble the good as opposed to individual craftsmen. Think Henry Ford here. Customization is an expensive way around standard bundles. Information costs play a role here too: Refrigerators are not often rented because the costs of tracking usage and misuse are too high relative to whatever small benefits might occur from the "ideal" a-la-carte type of usage.

Although the reason for these bundles is fairly obvious, we will get some nonideal consumption with bundles compared to an idealized a-la-carte world. But we all know that the benefits of such bundles, in the real world, outweigh the costs and thus we lose no sleep over a theoretical loss from these types of bundles that are so commonplace that it is almost impossible to think of any manufactured consumer product that is not a bundle of components.

Services are usually bundles as well. When you get your hair cut you not only use the services of the haircutter, but also the tools used to cut your hair, the mirrors, the shop they work in, the floor cleaning equipment, and so forth. The consumer could provide these additional materials and merely hire the hairdresser, but it is much more convenient to hire the bundle. The same is true of doctors, dentists, plumbers, and most other services.

Although bundles violate the a-la-carte model, the true opposite of a-la-carte is "all-you-can-eat." In all-you-can-eat markets consumers pay an entrance fee that allows them to consume as much as they want of the product or products being sold. This more completely eviscerates the linkage between the quantities consumed and the price paid than does bundling, which can still provide a fairly close linkage if bundles contain small quantities of each the items being bundled. All-you-can-eat brings up different problems than normal bundling. If the product being consumed has a positive marginal cost, an all-you-can-eat model appears to be inefficient since consumers will overconsume the product in question. Bundles may be too big or too small, but all-you-can-eat pushes consumers to the point where marginal value equals zero, which is always too much, unless the marginal costs are zero. Nevertheless, all-you-can-eat can make sense when there are high costs in measuring usage, where tastes, or capacities to consume, are not too different, and where marginal cost is low.If all-you-can-eat models existed in concentrated markets the way they exist in fragmented markets like restaurants, we suspect there would be many economic models describing the inefficiencies of such a scheme.[6]

It is possible to have both bundles and tie-in sales for single goods, although there is no possibility of monopolizing a "second" market when bundles involve just a single good. When eggs are sold in packs of six or twelve, that is a bundle. When a book publisher sells his publishing services to an author and puts a "right of first refusal" into the contract, that is a tie-in sale of early publishing services with later publishing services. Consumers may be unhappy when they go to Costco and find a colossal 128-ounce jar of peanut butter at an attractive price, but they generally don't believe that the seller is trying to monopolize their consumption of peanut butter for the rest of their lives.

How do bundles differ when the items in the bundle are actually different products sold in different markets? When McDonald's sells a hamburger *and* French fries *and* a toy together in a Happy Meal, it has created a bundle made of separate products. McDonald's practices mixed bundling, however, meaning that you can also buy the food items separately. No one seems to object to the bundle, although some nanny-wannabes object to the food.

Your ordinary restaurant, however, is not likely to be so accommodating. There you may order a dish that comes with a vegetable, a starch, and a salad. Although some restaurants have been known to allow users to mix onion rings with French fries, you most often will not be allowed to put a plate together from various sides unless you offer extra money on the side. Sometimes you may not be allowed any mixing and matching of various dishes, as the Jack Nicholson character found out in *Five Easy Pieces*. As the Nicholson character amply demonstrated, however, bundling can make consumers mad, because they lose the choice available in a-la-carte. Fortunately he did not go to the antitrust authorities to for help, but instead proposed a novel rebundling to obtain a plain omelet with wheat toast. Unfortunately, there were prohibitive transactions costs.

---

[6] Nahata, Babu, Krzysztof Ostaszewski, and Prasanna Sahoo. 1999. "Buffet Pricing." *Journal of Business*, 72, p. 2.

II. Theories of Bundling/Tie-Ins

A. A Theory, of Sorts, of Pervasive Bundling

As should be clear from our earlier discussion, bundling is so common that its main purpose should be abundantly clear. Very simply, lots of things are bundled, and bundles often include lots of components because there are enormous efficiencies in bundling. Efficiencies commonly arise on the production side, where building and shipping a multifunction device may be cheaper than building and shipping several single-function devices; think combined radios and CD players and multifunction pocket knives. The economies can also originate on the consumer side – kits for making a cake or repairing a toilet.

The automobile often serves as an illustration of bundling that occurs in competitive markets. Several writers note that standard equipment for automobiles has changed over time. Heaters, air conditioners, rust proofing, and sound systems that once were optional have become standard equipment. Each of these once supported active aftermarkets.

In fact, in the early days of the automobile, the "name" manufacturer often supplied only the chassis, the drivetrain, and the instrument panel, which were typically sent off as a unit to a coachworks for the addition of the car body itself. There clearly were viable markets for chasses without bodies and for bodies without chasses, so that by today's *Jefferson Parrish* standard, a basic car is two goods, a running chassis and a body. An automobile manufacturer that offered only complete automobiles would be practicing a tie-in sale.

So, while the automobile example seems almost trivial, even silly – of course people want to buy a complete automobile – it does present one important lesson with regard to innovation: What passes for two goods at one moment in time may be understood to be a single good not many years later. As automobiles became more common, more utilitarian devices and less luxury items that were afforded only by the very rich, integrated packages of what were once understood as distinct goods, became the norm. Series production and integration came with mass production to make automobiles available to the masses.

The automobile example also usefully illustrates the importance of economies of coordinating multiple components in a package and of marketing, shipping, and assembling many disparate components in a single package. Heaters and air conditioners have become standard equipment on most cars because there are economies in engineering a car with all those things included and integrated into the automobile itself. Tires and wheels are sold with a car, in spite of an active aftermarket, because most people want them that way and because it is awkward to deliver cars without them.

To illustrate this further we propose an economic experiment, one you can do at home. It's actually more of a demonstration than an experiment, but it's one of those learning by doing exercises that are done in chemistry classes and increasingly in economics classes. Here it is. When you go home today, go out in your garage and disassemble your car. Start off by removing the hood. (Loosen the hinge bolts on one side, then get a friend to hold that side while you loosen the bolts on the other side. You probably will need to disconnect some wiring and possibly some windshield washer hoses before you start unbolting things.) Now find a place to put the hood down so that it rests on something soft, otherwise you will chip it or scratch it. The trunk lid is a good thing to do next. Use the same technique, and again be careful where you put it down. Next unbolt all the doors and find a place for them. With the doors out of the way, it will be pretty easy to take out the seats. Careful though, there's often a lot of wiring to the seats that you will need to disconnect before you try to lift the seats out. All that stuff comes off pretty quickly and you will have a good sense that you are making progress. The rest of the process, as we say, is left to the reader. And, as they say in the repair manuals, to assemble, reverse the disassembly.

This demonstration teaches two lessons. The first you might well assume. There's more to a car than parts. Assembly is costly, difficult, and takes specialized knowledge and tools. The second will have occurred to you about the time you were removing the seats: An automobile is an efficient way to package, protect, store, and ship car parts.

It is sometimes observed that the sum of the prices of all the parts in a car is a fairly large multiple of the price of an entire car. The observation is sometimes offered to show monopoly power in the parts market. But for many kinds of parts there is a competitive aftermarket. And the prices of those parts, while less expensive than "factory" parts, also seem to be quite high, relative to their "share" of the automobile itself. A nicely equipped Honda Accord sells for something less than seven dollars a pound. But there are few individual parts for a Honda that could be purchased, even in the competitive aftermarket, for seven dollars a pound. Figure three times that for a fender, delivered. Many components will have per pound prices much higher than that. Much of that cost differential has to do with the high costs of maintaining inventories of thousands of separate items, arranging supply channels, packaging and shipping individual items, and handling the transactions. Bundling often provides important economies regarding these costs.

No sensible person would expect that car parts should be priced as the price per pound of the car multiplied by the weight of the part. But such pricing will come up again, in modified form, when we discuss some examples of regulatory unbundling.

B. Some Theories of Bundling and Ties Other Than Humdrum Efficiency

Tie-ins are less common than bundling and their purpose is less obvious. Thus it is understandable that economists and courts would try to determine their purpose. At the same time, bundles have also come under regulatory scrutiny and consequently have prompted economists to develop theories that explain them.

The theories of tie-in sales and bundling that follow all have some currency among economists; they are regarded as being plausible explanations of why a seller would ever tie or bundle two or more goods together. That is not to say that there is agreement about the empirical relevance or applicability of these explanations.

Before getting started, we take note of one theory of tie-in sales that is no longer accepted by economists, what is now commonly called *leverage.* A simple explanation of tie-in sales, too simple, it turns out, is as follows. A monopolist in good A would, of course, charge a monopoly price for good A. In addition, if he chose to, he could compel his customers to purchase a second good that is otherwise available competitively. The monopolist would charge his customers a monopoly price on that good as well. The tie-in, therefore, would give the monopolist a second monopoly in good B, and two monopolies are better than one. It is now widely understood that two monopolies are not necessarily better than one when the second monopoly is imposed as a cost of using the first monopoly product. Users of the first product will decrease their demand for the first product as they are required to pay an above-market price for the second product.

In the fixed proportion case, elevation of the price of B above the competitive price has the same effect on sales of A as an increase in the price of A, and so the full benefit of the monopoly can be attained through the standard monopoly pricing of A, and without the complication of a tie-in contract. If the second market is competitive, then life is easy for the good-A monopolist, who makes maximum profits just by charging the monopoly markup for A. It has long been understood, however, that if the market for some complementary good B is not competitive, then the monopolist in A will either have to collaborate with producers of B or the joint profits of the two goods will not be maximized if the producers of both goods charge ordinary monopoly prices.

C. Market Foreclosure

Market foreclosure is basically the last man standing in defense of antitrust provisions against tie-in sales. Some of the other explanations of tie-ins presented later also involve monopolies, and some allow a seller to capture more of the consumer surplus than he otherwise would, but none of them can be said to create a new monopoly or to have clear negative welfare implications. There is a parallel in antitrust law, as recent key cases regarding tie-in sales have emphasized the market foreclosure argument.[7]

The market foreclosure theory as presented in Whinston[8] involves a firm that is a monopolist in good A also requiring its customers to purchase good B as a condition of purchasing good A. By tying B to A, the monopolist crowds out potential rivals in the market for B. Production of B is assumed, in this model, to be subject to increasing returns to scale such that a firm producing B can survive only if it acquires a substantial share of the B market. For example, suppose the minimum efficient scale for a producer of B was 25 percent of the B market. If users of good A constitute more than 75 percent of the market for B, then a tie of B to A will foreclose the B market to any competitor, yielding a new monopoly to the good-A monopolist. Of course, raising the price of B charged to the monopolist's A customers may not do the monopolist a lot of good, since he is already extracting the monopoly rent from them and if he goes beyond that level his customers will abandon him for the potential entrant in B who then enters. Elevating the price of good B will only lower the price that the monopolist can extract from selling A. But the good-A monopolist now can extract rents from a new

---

[7] For example, see *Jefferson Parrish Hospital District v. Hyde*, 466 U.S. 2, 16 (1984). "Of course, as a threshold matter there must be a substantial potential for impact on competition in order to justify per se condemnation. If only a single purchaser were 'forced' with respect to the purchase of a tied item, the resultant impact on competition would not be sufficient to warrant the concern of antitrust law. It is for this reason that we have refused to condemn tying arrangements unless a substantial voluime of commerce is foreclosed thereby." This "not-insubstantial commerce" requirement appears in both *International Salt* and *Northern Pacific*.

[8] Whinston, Michael D. 1990. "Tying, Foreclosure, and Exclusion." *American Economic Review* 80, no. 4, pp. 837–859 presents the market foreclosure theory, however, the explanations for the tie-in in that paper are not confined to the market foreclosure argument.

group of customers. He now has the opportunity to extract monopoly rents from B-only customers, an opportunity that he wouldn't have without the tie. Note also that the good-A monopolist, now also a good-B monopolist, derives a benefit from the tie-in event if his good-A customers use goods A and B in fixed proportions. (In fact, Whinston assumes fixed proportions.)

This model of tie-in sales is one more model of the "it-could-happen-that" variety. The model does describe a feasible case and it is internally consistent. The problem is that it has very limited applicability. We have elsewhere referred to this as a Goldilocks theory of tie-in sales.[9] Everything has to be just right for the model to provide a reason for tying. Users of good A must constitute a large enough share of the market for good B that other potential suppliers of B are crowded out by a tie-in. But if A's customers are too large a share of the B market, there won't be enough B-only customers to make the tie-in worthwhile. If the minimum efficient scale is not large enough, then the good-A monopolist will have difficulty crowding out rivals in the B market. Further, the average cost curve must be steep enough that entry at output levels below the minimum efficient scale is deterred even as prices for B increase. Also, if the increasing returns to scale are great enough in market B, it might have been monopolized to begin with so that consumers would not be harmed by the switch in monopoly that could result from the tie-in. So the problem with this theory isn't that the circumstance that it describes couldn't happen, but rather that it is unlikely to explain very many cases of actual tie-in sales.

Whinston's paper, along with several others that appeared in the early 1990s, are heralded as the beginning of a new "post-Chicago antitrust economics." This new school of thought was understood as providing formal models that rehabilitated theories of predation or coercion that had been dismissed by Chicago school critics. Among these discarded theories was the naïve leverage model of tie-ins presented in the first paragraph of this section. In the 1990 paper, Whinston quotes Posner as an example of this line of Chicago critics:[10]

[A fatal] weakness of the leverage theory is its inability to explain why a firm with a monopoly of one product would want to monopolize complementary products as well. It may seem obvious . . . , but since the products are by hypothesis used in conjunction with one another . . . , it is not obvious at all. If the price of the tied

---

[9] Jefferson Parrish Hospital District v. Hyde, 466 U.S. 16–17; Carlton, Denis W. and Michael Waldman. 2006. "Why Tie an Essential Good?" In Antitrust Policy and Vertical Restraint. Edited by Robert Hahn, pp. 10–37. Washington, DC: AEI–Brookings Joint Center for Regulatory Studies.

[10] Whinston, 1990, ibid.

product is higher than the purchaser would have to pay on the open market, the difference will represent an increase in the price of the final product or service to him, and he will demand less of it, and will therefore buy less of the tying product.

Following that, Whinston goes on to fault the analysis that Posner is recounting for its "[P]ervasive (and sometimes implicit) assumption that the tied good market has a competitive, constant-returns-to scale structure. With this assumption, the use of leverage to affect the market structure is actually impossible." Accordingly, he introduces a framework that assumes increasing returns to scale in the tied good market and then explains the possibility of foreclosure in this increasing returns world. Whinston presents an internally consistent theory and explores it quite fully. It has rightfully influenced a great deal of economic theory.

The problem, however, with this contribution to the post-Chicago renaissance is that the possibility of foreclosure was not overlooked in the Chicago analysis; rather, it was intentionally excluded because it appeared to lack much empirical relevance. Tie-in contracts were observed to allow the seller to charge a price for the tied good that was above the price *available elsewhere*. Competitors were not foreclosed from the market. That was the phenomenon that presented a puzzle, and the two-monopoly-margins explanation was unsatisfactory. In many cases the seller of the tying good purchased the tied good from producers already in that market and turned around and resold it at a higher price, as IBM did with the Hollerith cards. IBM was not interested in and had no chance to monopolize the paper or cardboard market.

In the paragraph immediately prior to the one Whinston quotes, which we just reproduced Posner writes,[11]

One striking deficiency in the traditional, "leverage" theory of tie-ins, as the courts have applied it, is the failure to require any proof that a monopoly of the tied product is even a remotely plausible consequence of the tie-in.[12]

He then cites the AB Dick case:

In the AB Dick Case, for example, the defendant had tied ink to its mimeograph machines. It is hardly credible that A.B. Dick was attempting to monopolize the ink industry; only a small fraction of the ink sold in this country is purchased for use in mimeograph machines.[13]

[11] Posner, Richard. 1976. *Antitrust Law: An Economic Perspective*. Chicago: University of Chicago Press.
[12] Posner, 1976, ibid.
[13] Posner, 1976, ibid.

This is not to say that Posner anticipated the particulars of Whinston's theory, but he clearly provides evidence that foreclosure was contemplated and dismissed as the explanation for observed tie-in sales.[14] Later, after defending the importance of the price discrimination argument against certain criticisms, Posner writes:[15]

Only in the rare case where the sale of the tied product for use with the tying product represents a substantial share of all sales of the tied product might preventthe independent producers of the tied product from selling it to the customers of the tying product substantially affect competition in the market for the tied product.[16]

In quoting Posner, Whinston amends Posner's statement, using appropriate markings, and subtly changes his meaning. Whinston's quote is "[A fatal] weakness ... " when what Posner actually writes is, "A second – and fatal – weakness ... "

The first weakness, as quoted above, is that in the available cases, foreclosure is not even a remote possibility. What is obscured is that Chicago antitrust law and economics had not failed to consider exclusion. Clearly they had considered exclusion, or at least one of them had, but found it lacking in empirical importance. Posner favors the price discrimination argument not because he was unable to imagine the possibility of exclusion, but rather because price discrimination had empirical relevance and exclusion did not.

This point requires one final note. As noted previously, sellers practicing tie-ins are often not the producer of the tied good. They often purchase a tied good to re-price it. In such circumstances, the exclusionary consequences that are the thrust of Whinston's model become even more remote, if not impossible. Such cases clearly should be distinguished from those in which the bundler produces the tied good. This is important because many of the new-technology examples of bundling are exactly this arrangement: Tying sellers are intermediaries that package, market, re-price, and deliver goods that are produced by others. Rhapsody offers all-you-can-eat bundles of other producers' music. Time Warner offers all-you-can-eat bundles of other producers' television programming.

D. Metering: Price Discrimination or Risk Shifting

Tie-in sales, by which we mean that the purchase of good A requires that any purchases of good B come from the same vendor, therefore allowing variable

[14] Whinston, 1990, ibid.
[15] Whinston, 1990, ibid.
[16] Posner, Richard. 1976. Ibid.

proportions, are usually explained as either price discrimination or, far less frequently, risk reduction. The explanations, although often repeated, are usually fragmentary and lacking in depth.

Almost every textbook discussion of tie-in sales mentions the basic price discrimination explanation, which goes something like this: The tied good is a metering device that measures the usage of the tying good. So the Hollerith cards measured the usage of the IBM calculation machine and the toner measured the use of the Xerox machine. By metering the usage of the tied good the seller can identify the intense users, and this information can be used to charge them higher prices since intense users are also likely to be the least elastic demanders of the calculating machines (or to have the highest reservation prices). By raising the price of the tied good and lowering the price of the tying good, the more intense user pays more for the machine than the less intense user. QED.

Why do we claim that this explanation is superficial and incomplete? For one thing, although we are told that price discrimination is occurring, the item whose price is being altered is not usually defined. By this we mean that the actual item being purchased is neither the tying good nor the tied good but the services jointly produced by the two. If a tie-in sale discriminates against intense users, then they are presumably paying more for these services than are less intense users. After all, isn't that how price discrimination works?

In fact, however, the intense user does not pay more for the joint services. If an intense user and a slack user each purchase a machine and the intense user generates three times as much service using three times as much of the tied good, the intense user will pay three times as much for the tied good but the same price for the tying good as the less intense user. Thus the intense user pays less than three times as much, in total, and yet receives three times as much service. No matter how much we raise the price of the cards or lower the price of the machine toward zero, the intense user always pays a lower price per unit of service. Is this really a case of price discrimination against the intense user?

Further, this story is simplistic in its assumption that the intense user pays the same amount for the tying good as the less intense user. Eventually the product will wear out, and it will likely do so more rapidly for the intense user. In fact, it is possible that, because the intense user has three times the usage, he will need to purchase three machines for each machine purchased by the slack user. If this is the case, then it is readily apparent that both parties pay the same price for the services jointly produced by the tied products no matter how much the prices of the tied and tying goods are altered. The intense user always pays three times as much for three times the service, giving identical prices for the service to the two users.

Left out of the traditional metering story, therefore, are the nature of the product (service) being purchased, the relative prices paid for the service, the form of depreciation of the tying good, and the nature of the contract, that is, whether the tying good is rented or sold. A fuller explanation of how these items interact can be found in Liebowitz.[17]

Neglected from most tie-in discussions is an alternative explanation of tie-in sales focusing on the possibility that the tie reduces customers' risks. If individual customers of the tied goods are uncertain about the value of the tied goods to them, the seller can help to offset this concern by lowering the price of the tying good and by doing so helping to reduce the number of customers who decide not to purchase the tying good even though it has a positive expected value. This is a particularly effective strategy if one element of the consumer uncertainty is a random shock in the business of the customer-firm that can be predicted and internalized by a seller of the tied goods catering to an entire customer base, just as an insurance company can internalize many of the predictable individual risks facing the population of users.

For example, take the case of a calculating machine (using Hollerith cards) that can be used by accounting firms who are nevertheless unsure that the purchase of the machine will be a wise decision. If the firm has a good year relative to other accounting firms, the machine will be worthwhile, but if it has a bad year, the purchase of the machine will not be a good investment. Assume that the typical firm has a positive expected value for the machine over both states of the world, but that the risk of a bad year deters many from making the purchase. The seller of the machine, by instituting a tie, can lower the price of the machine (while raising the price of cards) and decrease the financial harm to those firms who have a bad year. Since the risk involved is internal to the industry, a seller of machines can easily take on the risk of the individual firms. In this situation both the seller of the accounting equipment and the purchasers are better off due to the insurance component of the tie. Although the same result can be achieved by selling the services a-la-carte (through a rental based on use), the costs of doing so will often be prohibitive.

A key difference between these two explanations is that under the risk reduction hypothesis both the seller and the buyer are better off under the tie.

[17] Liebowitz, Stan. 1983. "Tie-in Sales, Risk Reduction and Price Discrimination," *Economic Inquiry*, pp. 387–399.

The tie-in provides a valuable form of insurance. There are no antitrust or welfare concerns to deal with. The price discrimination hypothesis benefits the seller, harms some and perhaps most buyers, and has unclear welfare effects.

E. Surplus Extraction (Stigler, Bakos, and Brynjolfsson)

The previous section considered explanations of tie-in sales that relied on variable proportions. Different customers used different amounts of the tied good with a unit of the tying good. Here we consider explanations of bundling that relies on the producer being able to extract additional surplus from consumers. Typically, these bundles involve one of each of several, sometimes very many, distinct goods.

The basic idea for this explanation goes back to Stigler, who sought to explain block booking of movies by movie distribution companies.[18] Under block booking, television stations were being "forced" to take movies that had little value as a condition for getting access to desirable movies. On the face of it, the idea makes little sense. If the distribution companies could extract large payments for desirable movies, they were free to do that directly; they didn't need to do it through forced sales of overpriced dogs. Stigler's explanation relies on differences between consumers regarding their evaluation of the movies. It works as follows. Suppose there are two types of customers, say red and blue. Suppose the blue customers value movie A at 10 and movie B at 4. And suppose the red customers value movie A at 8 and movie B at 6. With simple pricing of each movie, revenue would be maximized with movie A renting for 8 and movie B renting for 4. Total revenue from a representative pair would be 24. However, red customers would be willing to pay 14 for a bundle of the two movies, and blue customers would be willing to pay 14. The revenue maximizing price for the bundle would be 14, and the revenues from a representative pair would be 28.

In this example the bundling extracts more of the consumer surplus than individual-item pricing allows. The price for A alone leaves a blue customer with a consumer surplus of 2. The price of B alone leaves a red customer with a surplus of 2. But the bundle extracts all of the surplus from both customers. Intuitively, the variation in reservation prices is greater for individual movies than for the movie bundle. This means that pricing

---

[18] Stigler, George J. 1963. "*U.S. v. Lowes Inc.*: A Note on Block Booking." *Supreme Court Review*, pp. 152–157.

individual goods leaves some money on the table for each type of customer whereas bundle pricing leaves less surplus on the table. This sort of pricing is quite common, although the bundling is easily obscured by offering to sell each of the goods individually at the highest reservation price offered by either part, and offering the bundle as a discount. Using the values in the example, movie A is offered at 10, movie B is offered at 6, and the bundle is offered as a discount of 2.

Stigler's bundling story has been generalized and extended by several authors. Among those extensions, Bakos and Brynjolfsson's work, which specifically addresses the pricing of information goods, extends the argument in two useful ways.[19] They assume the marginal costs of the potential components of a bundle to be zero and they consider bundles with large numbers of components. Generally, Stigler-type bundling is more likely to be profitable where the marginal cost is low relative to the price. Otherwise, the discounts offered to lower value consumers are likely to generate marginal revenues less than cost. This issue was elided in the previous example by speaking specifically of maximizing only revenues, implicitly assuming that the seller would sell each item to each customer. But that wouldn't necessarily occur. It would not occur, for example, if the marginal cost of each of the movies was 6.

As in the previous example, Stigler's explanation of bundling requires that the buyer who would be the high bidder for one good will be the low bidder for the other. Other writers have generalized Stigler's explanation for bundling to consider cases where bundling merely reduces the dispersion of reservation values. Bakos and Brynjolfsson[20] consider the bundling of large numbers of information goods. Consumers demand one unit of a good or none, and the distributions of their reservation prices need only be bounded and independent. These distributions can have different means; one component can be worth more than another. But a consumer's departure from the mean of the distribution for any component does not predict that consumer's departure from the mean valuation on any other component. Bakos and Brynjolfsson[21] also allow for the possibility that the valuation of any component in a bundle depends on the number of goods in the bundle.

Under these assumptions, the law of large numbers assures that the variance of the average valuation of components in a bundle gets smaller as the number of components in the bundle gets larger. Equivalently, this implies

[19] Bakos, Yanis and Eric Brynjolfsson. 1999. "Bundling Information Goods: Pricing, Profits, and Efficiency." *Management Science* 45, no. 12, pp. 1613–1630.
[20] Bakos, 1999, ibid.
[21] Ibid.

that the variation of the total value of the bundle gets smaller in proportion to the total value, as the bundle gets large. In turn, for large bundles, the seller confronts demand that is very elastic around the median value of the bundle, and very inelastic away from the median values. For large bundles, sellers will find it profit-maximizing to charge a price for the bundle just below the price at which reservation prices are concentrated.

While the setting for Bakos and Brynjolfsson's model is quite different from Stigler's, something similar is going on.[22] In Bakos and Brynjolfsson's model, the consequence of large numbers of goods is that for an individual consumer, the money on the table that would be left for the goods they value relatively highly is offset by short money on the goods that they value less than the typical consumer.

It is fairly intuitive to see that this averaging out will break down if valuations are highly positively correlated, that is, the consumer who places a relatively low value on one good is likely to place a relatively low value on other goods. Such an assumption is reasonable, for example, for consumer goods where valuations of the entire set of goods might be correlated with income. But two considerations bear on this. First, consumers may well face a common set of substitutes for the goods in a bundle, therefore limiting the correlation between valuation and income. Second, where bundles are provided in competitive markets consumers may face alternative sources for the very same goods.

F. Public Goods Problems

Bakos and Brynjolfsson build their model around information goods.[23] Not only are information goods topical, but the zero marginal cost assumption highlights both a challenge for private supply and a potential contribution of bundling. For public goods, or more specifically nonrival goods, the cost of serving an additional user is zero. In that circumstance, confronting a user with a positive price for using a nonrival good is inefficient. The positive price will discourage some uses of the public good, which results in some potential surpluses going unrealized.

Bakos and Brynjolfsson's model offers an important result: If values of the individual elements of a bundle are uncorrelated, as the number of elements in a bundle gets large, the fraction of potential users that are priced into the market approaches one. So long as the individual's willingness to pay exceeds the necessary threshold, the marginal price of any element in the bundle is zero. If the information goods in the bundle are of the all-you-can-eat variety (i.e., consumers can reuse the particular information good to their hearts' content and are not limited to a single use so that the consumer never consumes more than one "unit"), then we have the analogy to the buffet.

As understood from the Bakos and Brynjolfsson model, bundling offers an imperfect and partial solution to the public goods problem. Pricing of a bundle allows the seller to cover the cost of creating the public goods that make up the bundle, while confronting the buyer with zero marginal cost for any element of the bundle. It is imperfect, of course, because consumers are confronted with a positive price for the bundle, and some consumers will elect to forgo the bundle event even though the marginal cost of providing it is less than the consumer's willingness to pay.

There are two margins of underconsumption of nonrivalrous goods that can be addressed by bundling. The first is whether people purchase the bundle at all. If the bundle reduces variance in values, this diminishes this dimension of the underproduction problem. The same is true if the bundle contains items that tend to be used together so that there would be few consumers wanting to purchase only a small portion of the bundle. The second margin concerns how much consumption of any given intellectual property occurs. If the products sold in the bundle are of the all-you-can-eat type, then the problem with underconsumption at this margin does not arise.

Another difficulty with bundling as a solution is that it does not solve the standard problem of determining which public goods to produce. A seller is not confronted with data on consumers' willingness to pay for individual items in the bundle, only the willingness to pay for the whole thing. This is the ordinary public goods problem, the free rider problem, seen in a different context. Of course, the seller of a bundle does at least confront consumers' willingness to pay for the entire bundle, which distinguishes a bundling seller from a government. And depending on the nature of the sales, the seller may be able to note which elements of the bundle are being consumed in greater quantities than others (cable operators might know which channels are being watched just as a buffet operator will note which dishes require more frequent replenishment), which should provide some feedback to the production loop.

The problem of identifying the value of individual components is not absent from the very common types of private goods bundles that we discussed previously. Restaurants will experiment with portion size and ingredient combinations. Customers will reveal the values they place on various bundles, and although their behavior will reveal something about the quantity of demand for different components of the bundle, it does not reveal the values that they place on individual items.

Finally, markets in which bundled public goods are sold are not necessarily monopolies. Many, like cable companies, telephone providers, and music subscription services, face one or more rivals offering competing bundles made up of many of the same components. Some of these are intermediaries, resellers of the public goods that are created by other entities. Consider iTunes, a partial a-la-carte model (partial in the sense that you do not pay each time you listen) where consumers purchase permanent rights to digital songs. iTunes, which sells songs and albums, competes against Napster-to-go, Rhapsody, and Yahoo, each of which provides rentals of a giant bundle of songs that expire when the membership expires. In these cases, sellers can compete on the appropriateness of the bundles they offer but also may appeal to different audiences. Either of these forms of competition provides a forum in which consumers can reveal their preferences.

Markets like these, where there is competition in bundles, are quite similar to the public goods markets in Tiebout models. Charles Tiebout argued that the competition among jurisdictions that offer differing bundles of public goods and differing tax policies constitute an approximation to a market that addresses the information problems inherent in public goods.[24] In regard to such competition, people were characterized as revealing their preferences for public goods by voting with their feet. In the type of competition in bundles we are talking about there are fewer rivals than there are jurisdictions, but at the same time consumers can more cleanly make decisions about individual items of consumption as opposed to blunt actions such as moving to another locality.

Of course, Tiebout's public goods are not pure nonrival public goods, but instead are local public goods, subject to crowding beyond some level of use. Were that not the case, the multiple jurisdiction schemes that Tiebout considered would trade one inefficiency for another – the local provision of a pure public good occurs on too small a scale.

Nevertheless, the Tiebout model might be a closer match to reality than models with a single monopolist foreclosing a market through a tie-in sale. City Hall may understand this one better than the Federal Communications Commission.

[24] Tiebout, Charles M. 1956. "A Pure Theory of Local Expenditures." *The Journal of Political Economy*, 64, No. 5: 416–424.

III. Seven Naughty Bundles?

If Department of Justice officials can talk about the nine no-nos of licensing, we can have a section head called Naughty Bundles. Sadly, we have only seven. Nine naughty bundles has a nice ring to it. But we are working on it. Here are the seven:

1. *Patent pooling*: Patent pools or patent sharing agreements have aroused patent abuse or antitrust concerns in the past. In some instances, particularly where the pools charge royalties, there has been an antitrust concern that the pool serves as a mechanism for cartelization. But elsewhere the common all-or-nothing bundling of patents by these pools has raised objections.

2. *Blanket licenses*: These licenses, issued by copyright cooperatives such as BMI and ASCAP, permit the use of the entire catalogs of these cooperatives. Users have objected that they wished to carve out pieces of the blanket and pay for them directly, outside the blanket. Is it efficient to allow this type of carve-out?

3. *Selling CDs, selling individual songs, or selling (renting) each second of music listening (micropayments)*: Digital rights management can in principle allow the latter to occur, much to the consternation of many legal scholars. Yet this form of selling is closest to a-la-carte. Although selling CDs is thought to be the typical bundling story in the current discussion, any selling of individual or group of songs, as opposed to renting songs, is also a form of bundling involving an all-you-can-eat approach.

4. *MP3 players and download services*: Apple's iTunes works only with Apple's own MP3 players, and Apple's MP3 players are directly compatible only with the iTunes service. The attempt by Apple to create a virtual tie-in has raised concerns categorized under the guise of "interoperability." The practice has not raised much concern on our side of the Atlantic, but the European Commission and the governments of several countries have objected. iTunes sells both albums and individual songs. Other models (Napster, Yahoo) also sell all-you-can-eat bundles of songs for a fixed price. Which model is more efficient? Which makes the most business sense?

5. *Cable television*: Cable television providers typically offer programming channels only in bundles, often called "tiers." These bundles are all-you-can-eat. Kevin Martin, the chair of the Federal Communications Commission, has publicly advocated pricing for individual channels. A true and complete a-la-carte system, however, would be

full pay-per-view for all programs, which no one seems to be advocating. The analysis here is similar to that for albums, songs, and DRM (digital rights management) micropayments.

6. *Telephone*: Among other things, the Telecommunications Act of 1996 was intended to unbundle the local telecommunications grid from switching services, allowing competitive local exchange carriers to compete with facilities based on former Bell operating companies.

7. *Software*: Much of the 1998 Microsoft antitrust case was concerned with the bundling of Internet Explorer with the Windows operating system. Related controversies continue, with the European Commission objecting to security and multimedia software being included in operating systems. In principle, similar objections could be raised whenever a software product incorporates new features that were not contemplated in the earliest versions of the product.

Certainly examples of bundling are not confined to this list. Many products incorporate components that could, in principle and sometimes in actual practice, be sold separately. Phones are becoming PDAs, MP3 players, and GPS devices. The list above, however, does illustrate that a number of current controversies regarding high technology do revolve around some common themes related to bundling. Further, the margin of innovation in many of these technology products is the addition of new functionality.

IV. Special Applications to Innovation and Information Markets

A. Patent Pools

An invention is a nonrival good. Trade secrets can make inventions private property, or a patent can secure an invention as private property for a limited time.

Either of these forms of protection provides an incentive for inventors and a means of recovering the costs of inventing. Patent law further provides an incentive and the context for disclosure of the invention. Under either form of protection, an inventor will capture a return to invention by charging a price for its use that is greater than the marginal cost of using the idea, which generally would be zero. That price may be explicit, in the form of a royalty, or implicit, in the form on an elevated price for a good that embodies the invention. Any price greater than zero creates a marginal welfare loss because some useful applications of the idea are not made. This trade-off between incentives to invent and efficiency in use is well known.

Patent pools are created for a variety of reasons. A common one is to settle patent disputes. Rather than litigate conflicting patents, patent owners may pool their properties and jointly manage the use or licensing of the patents. Another reason for entering patent pools is to alleviate holdup problems where several patents are required to produce a satisfactory product.

Patent pools vary in details but generally involve creating an entity that holds the patent rights for the members of the pool. Members may be required to contribute new patents for free or for fees that are determined by arbitration or some other means of assessment. Members may have the privilege of using patents in the pool without any royalty or with some established royalty or set of royalties.

George Bittlingmayer presents an extensive analysis of the Manufacturers Aircraft Association, a patent pool that grew out of the longstanding and bitter patent disputes between the Wright brothers and Glenn Curtis.[25] The association was formed in 1917 largely in response to wartime exigencies. It was dissolved in 1975 as a result of a consent decree after a long series of government investigations. The main criticism of the pool was that it constituted an agreement to reduce competitive innovation. This seems a strange perspective, given that the pool spans a time interval that brought the aerospace technology from the World War I–type biplanes through the 747.

While the pool was in place, members paid a flat fee per airframe built and were licensed, with a few exceptions, to use all of the patents owned by the organization. Payment schemes varied over the life of the organization, and payments declined sharply after the expiration of key Wright and Curtis patents, but generally involved members paying a flat fee per airplane they produced.

Bittlingmayer notes a number of concerns that may lead patent owners to participate in pools. Most of these are related to negotiating, contracting, and enforcement costs of various sorts. He also notes the issue of "coordination of access to a public good".[26] In the context of a broad argument that patent pools serve the purpose of reducing losses form forgone gains from trade, he notes, "[A] patent right is a public good. There are jointly realizable gains to the firms in an industry from allowing a particular patent to be used in all applications in which its marginal net contribution is greater than zero."

---

[25] Bittlingmayer, George. 1988. "Property Rights, Progress and the Aircraft Patent Agreement." *Journal of Law and Economics* 31, pp. 227–48.
[26] Bittlingmayer, 1988, ibid.

A patent pool offers a bundle to insiders and outsiders. Often licenses are granted, for a set fee, for the use of all of the patents owned by the pool. In this circumstance there is no marginal price for the licensees for the use of individual patents owned by the pool. Patent pools are examples of the kind of large-number bundles of nonrival goods that are modeled in Bakos and Bryndjolfsson.[27]

Hazeltine Research Inc. is another patent pool that faced repeated legal action for offering bundles of patent licenses. In 1950, in *Automatic Radio Mfg v. Hazeltine Research Inc.*, the Supreme Court found that Hazeltine's bundling practices were not per se a misuse of patents.[28] At the time, Hazeltine owned 570 patents that were used in radio receivers. For royalties that the Court deemed a "small percentage of the selling price of receivers," Hazeltine granted license to all of these patents. Automatic Radio had refused to pay royalties on the grounds that it had not used the patents in the goods it had produced. The lower court had granted summary judgment to Hazeltine and the Court of Appeals affirmed.

The Supreme Court held that it was not a per se abuse of patents to "require a licensee to pay royalties based on its sales, even though none of the patents are used." They further rejected an argument that "requiring payment on the basis of the licensee's sales constitutes patent abuse because it ties in a payment on unpatented goods." Later they add, "What [the plaintiff] acquired by the agreement into which it entered was the privilege to use any or all of the patents and developments as it desired to use them. If it chooses to use none of them, it has nevertheless contracted to pay for the privilege of using existing patents plus any developments resulting from respondents' continuing research."[29] The Court also took note that the lower courts had sustained the licensing agreement "on the theory that it was a convenient mode of operation designed by the parties to avoid the necessity of determining whether each type of petitioners' product embodies any of the numerous Hazeltine patents."[30] Here we see, in 1950, the Court anticipating transactions costs and option value arguments that would become familiar to economists over the decades to come.

Not twenty years later, in *Zenith Radio Corporation v. Hazeltine Research*, the Supreme Court is less friendly to percentage-of-sales agreements.[31] Although the Court affirmed that percentage-of-sales royalties do not

---

[27] Ibid.
[28] 339 U.S. 827 (1950).
[29] Ibid. at 834.
[30] Ibid. at 833, quoting the district court, 77 F. Supp at 496.
[31] *Zenith Radio Corp. v. Hazeltine Research et al.*, 395 U.S. 100 (1969).

constitute patent abuse if they are chosen for the convenience of the parties, citing *Automatic Radio*, it held that it was patent abuse to use the patent monopoly to "override protestations of the licensee that some of his products are unsuited to the patent or that for some lines of merchandise he has no need or desire to purchase the privileges of the patent."

What distinguishes *Zenith* from *Automatic Radio* is that in the latter there was no record established that Hazeltine had refused to license individual patents or exclude from royalty calculations the items that did not use any of the Hazeltine patents. In Zenith, the district court concluded that Hazeltine had refused to offer a license that covered only goods covered by Hazeltine's patents. (The case was remanded to examine whether the district court had decided that properly.) The Supreme Court found that such a refusal would constitute patent abuse. But transactions costs arguments as well as the public goods management argument provide support for a percent-of-total-sales royalty. A lower royalty rate on a larger base can collect the same royalty revenues but can reduce monitoring costs and avoid a positive marginal price on the use of the public good that a patent represents.

The series of Hazeltine cases parallel the increasingly hostile treatment of bundles from the 1920s through at least the 1970s. The Chicago influence reversed this trend, at least for time.

B. Blanket Licenses

Early in the twentieth century composers of music decided that they would like to be paid for the use of their music when played in public, such as in restaurants and bars, and the courts agreed they had the right to collect payments. Later, these rights were extended to radio and television. Composers formed an organization, the American Society of Composers, Authors, and Publishers (ASCAP), to sell the rights for the public performance of their music. Since then many other such organizations have arisen throughout the world.

These organizations generally sell what is known as a "blanket licenses," meaning that the purchaser of the license is allowed unlimited access to all the works represented by the license. Due to reciprocal arrangements between these organizations, the works covered by the blanket represent virtually all the commercial music in the world under copyright.

The bundle, however, is not the usual fixed proportions bundle found in economic models of bundles. It is, in fact, the equivalent of an all-you-can-eat bundle with virtually every dish in the world, musically speaking, included.

The bundle, in this case, has economic attributes that are superior to those we might expect from a-la-carte pricing, making it similar to the patent pools just discussed. Because the musical composition is an information good – a nonrivalrous good with zero marginal reproduction cost – there are no social benefits to excluding users from using particular songs or in having them economize on the usage of music. This means that the blanket license induces the efficient usage of music for all consumers who take the license. This is a case where we want all the customers to eat until they burst. An a-la-carte model, on the other hand, would reduce a customer's consumption of each product below the efficient level.

As far as the number of customers goes, this is somewhat trickier. It is conceivable that the blank license might be priced at a level that would deter some consumers unwilling to pay the admission fee. Fortunately, the pricing of these licenses is normally quite discriminatory, often a percentage of revenues, so that there do not appear to be many television or radio stations, say, that do not purchase the license. This may be due, in part, to the fact that radio and television stations are regulated and their markets do not "suffer" from free entry.

As we have seen for patent pools, the blanket license has come under antitrust scrutiny as well. In *Alden-Rochelle* (1948), ASCAP was told by the court that its "exclusive" license form of membership, whereby its members were not allowed to negotiate separately to sell the rights to their music outside of ASCAP, was an antitrust violation. That led to a consent decree whereby ASCAP agreed to change the nature of its membership agreements. In addition, it agreed to not exercise its performing rights over movie theaters (who had brought the case) and that the price for the blanket license would be put under the jurisdiction of a court in New York.

Part of the court's decision was based on ASCAP's treatment of its members, and whether some members were able to disadvantage other members (and potential members) through ASCAP's methods of calculating payments to members and its voting rules among members. A part of the consent decree concerned a "through-to-the-audience" clause, which meant that composers could negotiate directly with movie producers for their performance rights since they were already negotiating the synchronization right (involved with putting music into a audiovisual product) and one of the arguments in favor of a copyright collective, the savings on transactions costs, was thus invalid in this instance. Related to this through-to-the-audience clause was a portion of the consent decree requiring ASCAP to provide "per program" licenses whereby a radio or television station could clear the rights at the source and then have a reduction in its blanket license payment.

This latter issue is one that attempts to allow a form of a-la-carte pricing to arise when transaction costs allow it. The belief seems to be that a-la-carte pricing is conducive to competition whereas the regulation of a bundle in not. The logic was that a monopoly would be the rule if only the bundle is purchased, even though the price of the bundle is not controlled by the seller but by a regulatory agency. Such thinking presumes that the regulated rate is too high, although there is no evidence for this belief.

Allowing such "carve-outs" completely vitiates the benefits of the blanket vis-à-vis the nonrivalrous nature of the products in question. The extra "competition" does not necessarily mean that there is more competition, however. Evidence for this extra competition is often taken from the fact that carve-outs occur, but such behavior may have nothing to do with having a more competitive price on carve-outs.

When carve-outs occur it is necessary to determine how much the blanket license payment should be reduced for those songs that are negotiated outside the blanket license. There is no obvious answer. It cannot be by the amount that the music user pays to the composer for the upfront rights, since the music user would never have an incentive to negotiate upfront payments because it would not save on overall costs. Thus some system, based on the number of minutes of programming covered by per program licenses, say, relative to the total amount of programming, would need to be implemented. This then becomes an instance whereby the savings are calculated on some sort of crude per pound basis, as mentioned when we discussed the value of automobile parts. This also allows for cherry picking by users since the blanket license is determined for a large group of programs that have different music uses. The users can remove below-average music use programs (say news) from the blanket license calculation and save as if they had removed a typical music use program. This latter type of behavior is not efficiency inducing because it allows users to game the system to their advantage against the conditions that would lead to market efficiency and because it induces a use of music that is too low.

If the regulated price of the blanket license is thought to be competitive (admittedly a difficult decision but presumably one arrived at by the courts), then allowing carve-outs is likely to lead to inefficiency since it merely means that consumers have found ways to lower their payments by gaming the system. The inherent inconsistency of the logic involved with setting the price but then allowing carve-outs does not seem to have been understood by the courts.

V. Music, MP3s, CDs and DRM

Although file-sharing has dominated discussions of digital music files, there are several other current concerns about "bundling" and music files that have arisen in the last few years. The first has to do with business implications from the "bundling"of individual songs onto CDs and the ability of individual consumers to unbundle these songs and purchase individual songs, one at a time, online. The second has to do with the theoretical possibility that DRM might allow sellers of music to charge for each individual listening experience as opposed to selling the permanent rights to listen to a piece of music, a selling format that is akin to "renting" the music.

A music CD contains a bundle of songs (with a current average of fourteen). Although singles (usually pairs of songs sold together) have historically had a presence in the market, the importance of singles has diminished greatly in recent decades. Singles contributed about 10 percent of total sound recording revenues in 1972, 8 percent in 1982, 5 percent in 1992, and less than 1 percent in 2002. Digital downloads seem likely to increase the importance of singles back toward their prior level (they were at almost 7% in the first half of 2006) although claims that the singles floodgate has been broken are as yet premature.

Discussions on many music blogs during the last few years have rained down criticism on record companies for reducing the number of physical singles being sold during the last few decades. These are the inevitable criticisms from consumers who believe they will benefit from a-la-carte pricing, a la Jack Nicholson. As we have already seen, a-la-carte pricing always provides consumers with greater freedom than do bundles, although it might do so at a prohibitive cost. As we have also seen, a-la-cart pricing engenders its own set of inefficiencies, particularly in the case of nonrivalrous goods. The agitation for a-la-carte pricing seems to stem from an imaginary world in which individual components of a bundle of N items would be available for the bundle price divided by N.

Among the small number of people debating these topics, there is a group that decries the possibility of DRM (digital rights management) which, in principle, could allow individuals to be charged every time they listen to a particular piece of music. This is in addition to the group that decries attempts by the industry to "force" consumers to purchase CDs instead of individual songs. Both CDs and individual songs are bundles. Neither is a pure a-la-carte purchase. Pure a-la-carte would only occur if users paid by the minute, or for each listening event, for the songs they hear. One could argue that these two cases can be distinguished from one another and that

that there is a difference between the two bundles. In the case of CDs, some consumers may not value some of the songs on a CD at all, yet may be "forced" to purchase them if they want the other songs. Where songs are sold individually, all purchasers at least enjoy the song to some extent and no one is forced to purchase something that they do not want at all.

But this is a false distinction. Where songs are sold "permanently" (allowing unlimited use), some users who may only be interested in listening 20 times would be forced to pay the same price as others who listen 50 times or 500 times. Having to pay for unlimited "listens" when only a small number of listens are actually demanded is not different in any fundamental way from having to pay for a CD containing songs in which one is not interested. Why should this bundle of an unlimited number of listens be unobjectionable to critics who do not like the fact that purchasers of CDs may be forced to purchase individual songs that they do not like? The same "problem" – that consumers pay for something they do not want (non a-la-carte) – exists in both cases.

There actually is an answer based on economics, although we do not believe it plays any role in the seemingly contradictory positions mentioned previously. First, music, being a nonrivalrous good, requires that consumers not be given an incentive to economize on its use once it is created (and shipped). The purchase of a recorded piece of music, which is an all-you-can-eat affair, presents consumers with a zero marginal cost for listening to the song one more time. This should lead to more efficient consumption of the song than would a pay-per-listen scheme set up by a sophisticated digital rights management system. But it is only superior to "renting" songs once consumers purchase a song. Selling a song has a higher bundled price than would exist for a-la-carte pricing where payment occurred each time they listened to a song. Consumers who would only listen to the song a few times are priced out of the market by the "bundle" purchase price but might not be priced out by the pay per listen a-la-carte price.

We thus see the same two margins of consumption here that we find for other nonrivalrous goods: the number of consumers consuming the product versus the amount of consumption per consumer. A-la-carte is better on the first dimension and all-you-can-eat is better on the second dimension.

Let's start with the welfare implications of the sale of albums versus the sale of individual tracks. It is probable that most consumers who like a particular song tend to like other songs from the same artist(s). If so, the bundle created by the CD will appeal to many consumers and should not deter much consumption, although differences over which songs are most valuable should average out, allowing the bundle to deter fewer consumers than would the sale of individual songs.[32] Further, there are efficiencies inherent in the creation of a CD that do not go away just because of digital distribution. Studio time costs money, not just in terms of the usage of the facility but also the setup costs of having a producer on site, having any backup musicians on site, and in general just getting prepared for making a recording. Further, many fans want multiple songs by the same group. In the case of physical distribution it was perfectly reasonable that CDs would be preferred to the sale of singles. This would be for the same reason that individual short stories are not sold alone but rather in anthologies, that individual articles are not sold alone but instead are sold in magazines, and that French fries are sold in packages and not individually. It is likely that if the choice between songs and bundles required one or the other, bundles might be the welfare-maximizing solution.

This leaves us with the pay-per-listen option versus the all-you-can-eat bundle of a permanent song. We begin by assuming that music that is purchased lasts forever. The all-you-can-eat bundle is not combining different products in the same way that bundles of separate products do. There is most likely a strong positive correlation between the value of the early song consumption and later song consumption for a given song. Thus the permanent song "bundle" is unlikely to even out demand among users and therefore it will not enhance consumption. To the contrary, the bundle will tend to restrict consumption to those consumers with the highest value for the product whereas a-la-carte pay per listen will allow greater access to the song. Nevertheless, it is more efficient to allow users to listen as many times as they want, favoring the bundle. Since it is difficult to know which of these margins of consumption is more important in the generation of welfare, we do not have a likely answer without more information.

That additional information may come from examining the revenues that can be generated. When we produce the song we are likely to generate revenues that provide too little reward relative to what would be required to produce the ideal quantity of songs.[33] Perfect price discrimination is the

---

[32] Bakos, 1999, ibid.

[33] Efficient production of a nonrivalrous good, in other words a title, requires that all consumers' demands be summed together to make sure that all titles with value greater than costs get produced. Except for perfect price discrimination, this cannot be achieved. Thus too few titles will be provided compared to the ideal. This is Arrow's point in his information and efficiency paper. Demsetz points out that efficiency is not necessarily the ideal, but just the best that can be achieved. Arrow, Kenneth J. (1962) "Economic Welfare and the Allocation of Resources for Invention, in the Rate and Direction of Resources for Invention." Journal of Law and Economics; Demsetz, Harold. (1969) "Information and Efficiency: Another Viewpoint." Journal of Law and Economics. 12, no. 1: 1–22.

theoretical market structure that is required to overcome this limitation, and ordinary price discrimination should help us move at least partly in that direction. The producer seems more likely to be able to achieve revenues for the song closer to the ideal level if he can rent the song rather than if he sells it since this allows for the seller to charge more to customers who listen to the music more, which seems closer to correct pricing than to let such users get a lower price per use (which is what happens if the music is sold at a fixed price). This is an argument in favor of DRM and a-la-carte selling.

Fortunately, we do not have to choose among these stark trade-offs. Instead, record companies can (and do) engage in mixed bundling, which should increase their profits and allow somewhat greater flexibility for consumers, although the welfare consequences may be uncertain.

VI. Tying iPods to iTunes

Apple has created a virtual tie-in by using a proprietary music format that, to the extent it is not circumvented, requires owners of iPods to purchase downloaded music from its own iTunes site since the iPod cannot accept music purchased from any other download site.

Although not a contractual tie, Apple's proprietary music format has all the characteristics of a traditional tie-in sale. There is no requirement that consumers purchase any digital music at all (they could just use music ripped from CDs or downloaded from unauthorized sites), but if they do purchase authorized digital music it must come from Apple's web site.

What distinguishes this "tie" from more traditional tie-in sales is that Apple does not appear to lower the price of iPods or raise the price of iTunes songs as a result of the tie-in. For this reason the traditional price discrimination and risk reduction hypotheses would seem to not apply.

Under the largely discredited leveraging theory, the claim might have been made that Apple was using its near-monopoly in the MP3 player market to achieve a monopoly in the music download market. Under the more modern version of this theory Apple might achieve some monopoly if it prevents other firms from being able to compete in the digital download market because the remaining nontied market is too small to allow them to achieve scale efficiencies to survive, and if it then is able to sell iTunes to individuals who do not have iPods. Although this is possible, it requires circumventing the copy protection, so this version of leveraging seems not to apply.

Other facts are also inconsistent with these monopoly scenarios. First, and most importantly, digital downloads are close substitutes for music on physical CDs. CDs, which still make up 90 percent of the market, will constrain the prices of digital downloads. Second, the monopolizing argument hinges on competitors being driven from the market because they cannot reach a size sufficient to make economies of scale viable. There is no evidence of important economies of scale. In the CD business there are many small independent record labels and many small CD retailers, so, on the nondigital side of the market, economies of scale do not seem overwhelming. The digital retail market is quite new, but recently we have seen entry into this market, by Microsoft with its Zune player and digital download store and most recently by Yahoo, SanDisk, and Zing with complete ecosystems. In addition, there are numerous other websites selling digital music. Since, if anything, the costs of setting up retail distribution seem lower in the digital realm, it seems unlikely that economies of scale could be larger in the digital realm than in the bricks-and-mortar realm.

Apple's recent entreaties to the recording industry to stop protecting their content and switch to the unprotected MP3 format also are inconsistent with a monopoly story since any digital music retailer can sell MP3 files and they will work with any digital music player (except for an early generation Sony that did not play MP3 files).

On the other hand, Apple may feel that its major competitor to iTunes consists of the alternative business model of "rentals," currently dominated by Napster and Yahoo, which allow consumers access to a vast collection of songs for a monthly fee, but where access to those songs disappears if subscription payments end. By making digital downloads more valuable to consumers, the rental alternative loses some luster since rentals must be kept in a protected form to keep the consumer from paying his monthly fee and copying large collections of music. It is also the case that by dropping copy protection, Apple would nullify criticism from the European Union regarding interoperability problems with its copy protection scheme. Therefore, Apple's motivation for its move to MP3s may be more self-serving than it looks at first glance.

Still, the evidence leads to a conclusion that the main purpose of Apple choosing a proprietary technology for its iTunes stores and iPods would be the welfare-enhancing goal of giving consumers a simple and effective experience when purchasing music and transferring the music to the digital music player, an experience that is generally considered to be the best in the industry by various industry pundits. Its "tie," therefore, occurs for the same reason that the vast majority of ties or bundles occur: to provide a superior consumer experience that increases market share and profits for the firm.

VII. Cable Television

Consumers of cable or satellite television offerings are given choices that consist of large bundles of stations, usually labeled basic, extended basic, and then premium channels. Critics of these companies complain that these practices force consumers to pay for channels that they do not watch.

This criticism is akin to the claim that consumers in restaurants are forced to pay for food that they do not want if a meal contains food that they do not like and if substitutions are not allowed. More precisely, it is akin to a claim that consumers in an all-you-can-eat buffet may not partake in every dish but nonetheless must pay for every dish that is available. It is true that consumers would get more flexibility if restaurants were required to make substitutions on the menu (after all, who doesn't root for Jack Nicholson when he tells the waitress where to hold the chicken), but since no one denies that the restaurant market is competitive, it is generally understood that such a requirement would raise the cost of restaurants and in the end harm consumers. We know this because consumer sovereignty in this competitive market indicates many consumers prefer to patronize restaurants that have limits on such substitutions and government regulations on such bundles would go against those preferences.

What is it that might replace the current system? One possibility would be to force cable and satellite operators to go to a partially a-la-carte pricing system that we call pay-by-station, whereby consumers get to pick only the channels that they desire and bundles are eliminated.[34] Some critics of the current system claim that they only want to introduce mixed bundling into the system and not require full a-la-carte.[35] We discuss these choices in turn.

The choice between picking individual stations versus bundles of stations is discussed by Hazlett,[36] who correctly points out that the price of individual stations would be higher than the prorated share of the bundle price.[37] This can be easily illustrated by assuming that the current markets are competitive and that all the players earn normal returns on their investments (such an

---

[34] We refer to this as pay-by-station in spite of the fact that it has been referred to as a-la-carte because full a-la-carte would be full pay-per-view where viewers only pay for the content they watch on any given channel, by the hour or minute. Since no one is proposing full a-la-carte, we do not discuss it here.

[35] Cooper, Mark and Gene Kimmelman "Reply Comments of Consumers Union and The Consumer Federation Of America" August 13, 2004 Before the Federal Communications Commission.

[36] Hazlett, Thomas W. 2006. "Shedding Tiers for A-La-Carte? An Economic Analysis of Cable TV Pricing." George Mason University Law and Economics Research Paper Series.

[37] Hazlett, Thomas W. 2006. Ibid.

assumption should not alter the arguments made in favor of pay-by-station that tend to focus on consumers being forced to purchase products they do not want). Under such an assumption, the revenues generated are just able to pay for the costs of creating the programming. If we rearrange consumers so that they only pay for programs that they watch, we would need to generate the same revenues as previously in order to cover the costs of the same amount of programming. On average, it would be impossible for consumers to save anything if they watched the same stations as before. Cable operators and program creators would be indifferent if the same revenues were generated and their costs didn't change, but this will not be the case.

Consumers as a whole would be harmed in one particular and important manner. If consumers were to choose their sets of stations for the month, they might discover that there is some program that they wish to watch but for which they have not signed up. These are specific instances out of potentially many instances where consumers might value some small amount of programming that would fall below the critical value that would lead them to subscribe to that channel. This is the option value in having available channels you don't usually watch. In a pay-by-station world these consumers would not get to watch those programs. And for most products this would be fine since the value of the program would presumably be less than the cost. But the programs on cable are nonrivalrous goods and do not require any incremental cost to have an additional viewer. Thus it is inefficient to prevent the viewer from seeing these programs. The bundle allows them to indulge in this small level of consumption per network and to generate value from that while pay-by-station would not.

Admittedly, there may be consumers who would like to watch some programs but are unwilling to pay for the entire bundle, and in this case the bundle would cause harm to this other margin. But as Hazlett ably demonstrates, it is unlikely that such consumers would be willing to cover the fixed costs involved with being connected to cable in the first place, and those incremental costs are real, so that the former harm seems likely to be greater than the latter harm.[38]

One might argue that even if consumers do not benefit from pay-by-station, the market would benefit from the superior economic signals being revealed by consumer choices on networks actually purchased as opposed to relying on cable operators to make these choices. This is always, however, an advantage of a-la-carte, but, as we have seen, it is usually outweighed by

---

[38] Hazlett, 2006, ibid.

the cost savings in producing bundles. That is presumably the case here as well.

This last point is made more forcefully in the case of mixed bundling. It is always possible, if there are no transactions costs, for a seller to make greater profits with mixed bundling than with pure bundling. This can be achieved merely by making the price of individual items high enough that the profit on them is greater than the profit on the bundle, so that any defections away from the bundle to individual stations increase overall profits. (Because individual stations, even with a high markup, can be much less expensive than the entire bundle, certain viewers might prefer to pay for individual stations.) In this case, why would cable operators not embrace mixed bundling?

The answer must be that there are costs involved with going to a mixed bundling scheme, the same costs involved with going to a pay-by-station scheme. These costs include switching away from analog to digital converters since it is only the latter that allow for frequent and relatively low-cost switching of station availability. There are other costs as well, including the costs of changing the billing to the consumer and the payments to the cable networks every time a consumer changes his mind about what stations to order, requiring extra staff to answer questions about these options, and so forth. It seems likely that these costs are large, and that explains why there is no mixed bundling. But even if all consumers had digital converters, these other costs might still be larger than the benefits. It is likely that the costs of allowing pay-by-station choice are greater than the benefits, as we presume is true for buffet-only restaurants. If technology lowers these costs sufficiently, we would expect that cable operators will move to a mixed bundling system on their own since it is in their self-interest to do so.

Further, it is likely that cable operators oppose mixed bundling because they expect that imposed pay-by-station would be accompanied by price regulation. After all, absent some price regulation, cable operators could circumvent a mixed bundling pay-by-station requirement by charging very high prices for individual channels, so any meaningful unbundling requirement would have to include price controls.

Customers may naïvely believe that the single channel price will be their bundle price divided by the number of channels in the bundle. Regulators may cynically give them pay-by-stations options. But since customers will be unhappy with the likely result, some regulatory alternatives will be found, none of which are likely to enhance efficiency.

VIII. Unbundling as Market Foreclosure

Antitrust cynics sometimes observe that charging a relatively low price is illegal because it is predatory, charging a relatively high price is illegal because it proves you are a monopolist, and charging the same price as everyone else is illegal because it means you're colluding. Unbundling may offer its own version of the joke. It is rare, but unbundling can certainly expose a firm to public criticism and even legal action. Examples of the former concern intellectual property products that are sold with reduced functionality. The famous example is Intel's SX microprocessor that was sold with a coprocessor incapacitated. In that case, the functionality that was being removed from the processor was available at zero (arguably even negative) marginal cost. The criticism, not entirely ill founded, was that Intel could have made the fully capable processor available, but chose not to, instead preferring to "force" people who sought greater capacity to pay a higher price for the fully functional device.

Microsoft has been criticized for everything, of course, so going to that well for an example might be likened to using a gun for indoor fishing. Still, there is a lesson. In an amicus brief submitted by Wilson, Sonsini, Goodrich & Rosati, in opposition to the 1995 consent decree, an unbundling is deemed predatory:

With the introduction of Windows 3.1 in April, 1992, Microsoft removed the debug kernel from the operating system and bundled it with its own language application program. If a user wanted to run the competitive Borland program, it had to buy the debug kernel separately from Microsoft, at a price Microsoft set to make the Borland product less competitive. Microsoft even conspicuously advertised the fact that its own product was cheaper than the Borland product because the user had to buy the debug kernel separately from Microsoft. Byte, May 1992, at 159 (Ex. 6). Whatever pro-competitive benefits Microsoft might advance to justify its bundling of new functionality into the operating system, it is difficult to imagine any justification for unbundling operating system technology, other than harming competition.

It is, in fact, easy to imagine such a justification. With the change, Microsoft was able to sell more of its own products, presumably at profitable prices. Predation in antitrust typically is limited to the circumstance that an action is unprofitable, but for the expected departure of a competitor. In this case, their strategic action allowed them to increase revenues. The unbundling may well have made a rival's products less attractive. What we have here is a novel theory of both antitrust and bundling that the firm has an obligation to provide components of a bundle that make a rival's products more attractive. Note further the implicit logic of the amicus brief. Because the debug kernel is a public good, it costs Microsoft nothing to include it in the bundle, so Microsoft has an obligation to include it as part of the operating system.

There is a cockeyed symmetry between this instance of unbundling, for which Microsoft was criticized before the court, and the bundling of Internet Explorer, for which Microsoft was also criticized before the court. Both items, arguably, were middleware. In one case, excluding middleware was predatory because it hampered one rival's application. In the other case, including middleware was predatory because it competed with a different rival's middleware.

Unbundling is also considered bad behavior in consumer lending and medical billing. In consumer lending, lenders appear to run up the trans-actions fees by charging high prices for many individual items instead of presumably charging a lower price for an available bundle of services. In medical "coding" a similar practice charges for many individual procedures instead of charging for the comprehensive procedure that bundles a number of individual components at a much lower price. In both fields the practice is considered unethical and, in some instances, illegal, and probably should be. In both instances, some agent is making a selection of purchases on behalf of the customer that is not in the interest of the customer, and about which the customer is not fully informed. What is interesting in these cases is the regulatory presumption that bundling is in the consumers' interests, as it almost certainly is. This bundling has much in common with efficient bundles that we commonly see in competitive markets.

IX. Hope for Bundling Policy?

As evidenced previously, bundling is addressed in multiple areas of the law, including antitrust laws, patent abuse doctrines, and telecommunications regulation. Through the early 1970s, antitrust treatment of bundling, like antitrust treatment of most things, became progressively more interven-tionist. That trend was reversed somewhat in the 1980s, under the dual influences of the Reagan administration and the Chicago School. Some cases began to cite theories of tie-in sales that find the practice to be benign or even efficient. In the 1990s, in spite of the rise of a post-Chicago antitrust economics, there has been something of a trend toward a rule of reason regarding tie-in sales. Arguably it is now telecommunications law that is the arena that is most hostile to bundles and tie-in sales.

In telecommunications, the major thrust of the Telecommunications Act of 1996 was to compel owners of telecommunications networks to accommodate connection by competitive carriers, in effect unbundling switching services from a signal transport. Similarly, cable television operators were compelled to allow access to their networks by competitive Internet service providers, unbundling Internet services and cable connections. Both regimes imported price regulation schemes that required facilities owners to rent their facilities at "cost," somehow determined. The Federal Communications Commission, through its chair, has steadily attacked the practice of cable television providers of marketing their services as bundles of channels.[39] Legislation requiring net neutrality would, in effect, prohibit firms that provide broadband connections from offering bundling content.

While the FCC appears to be becoming ever more hostile to bundling, antitrust law may be moving the opposite direction. In *International Salt*,[40] tie-in sales are brought under section 1 of the Sherman Act, with the court finding that it is "unreasonable, per se to foreclose competitors from any substantial market."[41] This treatment is more fully articulated in *Northern Pacific*. After citing a litany of the wrongs done by tying agreements, the *Northern Pacific* court says of tie-in sales, "For these reasons, tying agreements fare harshly under the laws forbidding restraints of trade." And then, "They are unreasonable in and of themselves whenever a party has sufficient economic power with respect to the tying product to appreciably restrain free competition in the market for the tied product and a 'not insubstantial' account of interstate commerce is affected." *Jefferson Parrish*[42] draws on *Northern Pacific* and further develops the per se doctrine. *Jefferson Parrish* confronted the court with the issue of whether the tied good was distinct from the tying good. These rulings are commonly summarized by three conditions that, if satisfied, render at tie-in per se illegal: 1) the tying good and the tied good are distinct, 2) market power in the tying good, and 3) not insubstantial commerce in the tied good.[43]

There are well-known exceptions, such as *Jerold Electronics*,[44] where a company's interest in assuring and demonstrating the performance of a technology was held to be a justification of a tie, but only until the technology

---

[39] "FCC May Endorse Cable à la Carte In a Policy Shift," Amy Schatz in Washington and Joe Flint in New York, *The Wall Street Journal*, November 29, 2005.

[40] *International Salt v. U.S.*, 332 U.S. 392 (1947).

[41] Ibid. at 397.

[42] *Jefferson Parrish Hospital District no. 2 v. Hyde*, 466 U.S. 2 (1984).

[43] Sharer, F.M. and David Ross, 1990, Industrial Market Structure and Economic Performance, 3rd ed. Boston: Houghton Mifflin, pp. 567–68.

[44] *United States v. Jerold Electronics Corp.*, 187 F. Supp. 545 (E.D. Pa. 1960), aff'd per curiam, 365 U.S. 567 (1961).

became established. In both *International Business Machines* and *International Salt*, the courts noted that an interest in quality control could justify a tie but rejected the legitimacy of the quality claims in the cases before them. These exceptions have led some to offer a fourth requirement for per se unreasonableness, the absence of any efficiency defense.[45]

Jefferson Parrish is mostly noticed for its treatment of the two-goods question. On that issue, the court found that the tied good was distinct if there is sufficient demand for the tied good alone, in the absence of a tie, to sustain a separate market. Otherwise, the tie could not foreclose anything. That, in itself, is a limitation on the per se rule. But the court's decision on the case rested on its conclusion that a per se rule did not apply because the hospital didn't have sufficient market power to trigger the per se rule, and ultimately that the plaintiff had not presented a case that would allow a finding that the tying practice had, in fact, unreasonably restrained competition in the anesthesia market.

The *Jefferson Parrish* court also acknowledges the commonplace value of tie-ins: "Buyers often find package sales attractive; a seller's decision to offer such packages can merely be an attempt to compete effectively – conduct that is entirely consistent with the Sherman Act."[46] And later, "Thus the law draws a distinction between the exploitation of market power by merely enhancing the price of the tying product, on the one hand, and by attempting to impose restraints on competition in the market for a tied product, on the other. When the seller's power is just used to maximize its return in the tying product market, where presumably its product enjoys some justifiable advantage over its competitors, the competitive ideal of the Sherman Act is not necessarily compromised."[47]

This position significantly raises the bar in regard to the required showing of market power and the likelihood of competitive harm. In earlier cases,[48] the tie itself was treated as sufficient evidence of adequate market power in the tying good to trigger the per se rule. Ultimately, the *Jefferson Parrish* court does decide the case on this point, finding that East Jefferson Hospital does not have market power sufficient to affect the tied market. The court is fairly explicit in adopting a market foreclosure standard: "Of course, as a threshold matter, there must be a substantial

---

[45] Greer, Douglas F., 1992, *Industrial Organization and Public Policy, 3rd ed.* New York: Macmillan, p. 569.
[46] *Jefferson Parrish* at 12.
[47] Ibid. at 14.
[48] *Northern Pacific Railroad Co. v. U.S.*, 356 U.S. 1 (1958) at 7–8.

potential for impact on competition in order to justify per se condemnation."[49]

The opinion of the D.C. Circuit Court of Appeals in *U.S. v. Microsoft* (2001) is something of a treatise on tie-in sales. It goes further down a path of acknowledging both the potential value of bundling and its pervasiveness before rejecting a per se rule for computer software. In examining the *Jefferson Parrish*'s market-demand test for the existence of separate goods, the court goes on at some length on the subject of the efficiencies of tie-in sales in general, making arguments not too different from our comments about car parts:

Indeed, if there were not efficiencies from a tie (including economizing on consumer transaction costs such as the time and effort involved in choice), we would expect distinct consumer demand for each individual component of every good. In a competitive market with zero transactions costs, the computers on which this opinion was written would only be sold piecemeal – keyboard, monitor, mouse, central processing unit, disk drive, and memory all sold in separate transactions and likely by different manufacturers.[50]

The court then makes this general and useful observation:

In the abstract, of course, there is always direct separate demand for products: assuming choice is available at zero cost, consumers will prefer it to no choice.

Later the court adds,

The ubiquity of bundling in competitive platform software markets should give courts pause before condemning such behavior in less competitive markets.[51]

Finally, the court gets to the heart of the problem with the *Jefferson Parrish*'s test for the existence of separate products:

In fact, there is merit to Microsoft's broader argument that Jefferson Parrish's consumer demand test would "chill innovation to the detriment of consumers by preventing forms from integrating into their products new functionality previously provided by standalone products – and hence, by definition, subject to separate consumer demand."[52]

The court then struggles to distinguish software integration from other forms of bundling. Indeed, it does succeed in distinguishing software

[49] *Jefferson Parrish* at 16.
[50] *United States v. Microsoft Corporation*, 253 f. 3d 34 p 74 in original opinion,
[51] Ibid at 83.
[52] Ibid, p. 76.

integration from some particular instances in bundling, but then uses cases of nonsoftware integration to expose the problems with the per se doctrine:

Under per se analysis, the first firm to merge previously distinct functionalities (e.g., the inclusion of starter motors in automobiles) or to eliminate entirely the need for a second function (e.g., the invention of the stain-resistant carpet) risks being condemned as having tied two separate products because at the moment of integration there will appear to be a robust "distinct" market for the tied product.

With these arguments, the D.C. Circuit carves out an exception for the per se doctrine concerning tie-in sales that applies to software. But the court also observes that the characteristics that justify the carve-out for software are not limited to software. "We fear that these efficiencies are common in technologically dynamic markets where product development is especially likely to follow an easily foreseen linear pattern."

In short, markets for innovative goods of all sorts will involve products that combine new functionalities or enjoy economies of marketing bundles of goods. A per se standard will be a cudgel available wherever a product achieves a degree of market power, that is, wherever an innovation succeeds.

XI. Conclusion

We have argued, as others do, that bundling is pervasive in the economy. For many of the goods with which we have a great deal of experience, we do not even perceive bundles; the bundle of components has become a single good. Such bundles typically offer substantial economies in production, transportation, and marketing costs. New products will often be new bundles of characteristics.

Economists have offered many explanations of bundling and tying. Many of these show the practices to be efficient in one way or another. Some explanations show that bundling is a means to extract greater profit from a monopoly but that nevertheless has ambiguous welfare effects. The surviving explanation of tie-in sales that shows the practice to have antitrust implications is the market foreclosure argument. That explanation requires that conditions are just so. For foreclosure to occur, the tied market must be not too big but not too small. The same must hold for the tied share and the minimum efficient scale. Nevertheless, it could happen that a tie-in will foreclose a market, providing two monopolies where there was only one before. Foreclosure has long been recognized as a possibility; it just hasn't been thought to be common.

Contemporary markets in new products are probably not all that different from old markets in new products, combining attributes and capabilities that were once understood as being distinct goods. "Technologically dynamic markets" or, for that matter, institutionally dynamic markets, or socially dynamic markets, seem regularly to give rise to controversies around tying and bundling. Dynamisms of many sorts will be hindered by policies that condemn all such combinations, failing to distinguish the few instances that may be harmful from the great majority that are not.

4

Unlocking Technology

Antitrust and Innovation

Daniel F. Spulber

Introduction

"Technology lock-in" has joined the pantheon of highly honored justifications for government intervention in innovation that should be laid to rest. The concept of technology lock-in has begun to exert influence in antitrust policy, appearing in *Microsoft v. Commission*.[1] Advocates argue that technology lock-in occurs when markets adopt an inferior technology and that government action is required to remedy the situation. Yet, the notion that governments can make the best choice among innovations, while markets cannot, is the "fatal conceit" of technology lock-in.

In this chapter I demonstrate that the arguments supporting the idea of technology lock-in are fundamentally flawed, as is much of the evidence for

---

[1] The Commission of the European Communities (Commission) predicted that Microsoft's Media Player would dominate other forms of players. The arguments supporting the prediction were fundamentally flawed, and not surprisingly the prediction proved to be wildly inaccurate, with the rise of Adobe Flash Player, Apple iTunes, and other market alternatives. The Commission further maintained that Microsoft's server operating system would have an unfair advantage over other server operating systems. See *Microsoft Corporation against Commission of the European Communities*, Case T-201/04, Ruling on September 17, 2007 by the European Court of First Instance. See also Commission of the European Communities, Commission decision of March 24, 2004, relating to a proceeding under Article 82 of the EC Treaty (Case COMP/C-3/37.792 Microsoft), Brussels, April 21, 2004, C(2004)900 final.

Presented at the Searle Center on Law, Regulation and Economic Growth, Northwestern Law School, Research Roundtable on the Law & Economics of Innovation. For their helpful comments, I thank Henry Butler, F. Andrew Hansen, D. Bruce Johnsen, F. Scott Kieff, Lynne Kiesling, Peter Klein, Bruce Kobayashi, Stan Liebowitz, Geoffrey Manne, Stephen Margolis, Scott Masten, Francesco Parisi, Matthew Sag, Henry Smith, Jim Speta, Scott Stern, Christopher Yoo, and Martin Zelder for helpful comments. This is an edited version of the article by the same title originally published in the *Journal of Competition Law and Economics*, Advance Access published on May 8, 2008. doi:10.1093/joclec/nhn016.

the phenomenon. The desirability of government intervention is suspect as well, particularly as government remediation is built right into the definition of the problem. I show how markets effectively coordinate decisions to adopt innovations. Market participants have economic incentives to make efficient choices among innovations. The concept of technology lock-in thus is likely to misguide public policy. To avoid disrupting incentives for innovation, public policy-makers should exercise more forbearance than usual in markets for technology.

The concept of technology lock-in predicts market failure on a colossal scale. For Brian Arthur, the economy experiences "lock-in by history."[2] Since technological advances are ubiquitous in the modern economy, such a systematic market failure potentially would entail losses equal to a substantial share of the gross domestic product. In addition, since technological progress is an important contributor to increases in productivity, a systematic failure of technology markets would impact significantly the rate of economic growth. So large a danger to the economy begs the question, how likely is technology lock-in?

Technology lock-in is almost entirely based on one concept – "network externalities."[3] Network effects refer to the mutual benefits that consumers receive from consuming the same good, such as telecommunications.[4] If consumers cannot coordinate their purchases, they may miss out on some of these "social benefits," leading to a market failure from "positive externalities." The concept of "externalities" refers to those economic interactions that are inefficient because they take place outside of market transactions.

The technology lock-in assertion transfers the "network externalities" story from the decision to purchase a product to the decision to adopt an innovation. These decisions are one and the same when the innovation takes the form of a new product. Technology lock-in is said to occur when

---

[2] W. B. Arthur, 1989, "Competing Technologies, Increasing Returns, and Lock-In by Historical Events," *Economic Journal*, 97, March, pp. 116–131. Arthur claims that recognizing positive feedbacks creates an entirely new economics. See also Arthur, 1994, *Increasing Returns and Path Dependence in the Economy*, Ann Arbor: University of Michigan Press; P. David 1985, "Clio and the Economics of QWERTY," *American Economic Review*, 75, pp. 332–337, and P. David, 1992, "Heros, Herds and Hysteresis in Technological History: The Battle of the Systems Reconsidered," *Industrial and Corporate Change*, 1, pp. 129–180.

[3] There is some mention of switching costs, but the network externalities explanation is predominant in the literature. I address switching costs later in the discussion.

[4] For a critical discussion of the concept of network effects that is closely related to the arguments in the present chapter, see D. F. Spulber, 2008, "Consumer Coordination in the Small and in the Large; Implications for Antitrust in Markets with Network Effects," *Journal of Competition Law & Economics*, 4, June, pp. 1–56.

consumers choose between products, each of which has network effects. Technology lock-in thus recycles the idea of network effects.

Technology lock-in is an inevitable consequence of network externalities because of the presumption that the market has already failed. Yet, there should not be two social costs from one market failure. If the market failure were corrected, or indeed if the market failure did not happen, further inefficiencies in technology adoption would not occur either. Network effects are the underlying problem, not technology lock-in. Technology lock-in thus rises or falls depending on whether network externalities exist.

Network externalities lead to inefficient technology adoption decisions because of the assumed presence of network effects, and the assumed lack of consumer coordination. Consumers get stuck with an inferior technology because they are inefficiently chasing expectations about which technology will be popular and yield the desired benefits of network effects. Alternatively, consumers form incorrect expectations and split their technology choices among multiple technologies, thus missing out on the mutual benefits of network effects. Still further, consumers are reluctant to switch to a better technology because they enjoy the benefits of network effects, or they are too eager to adopt a new technology, ignoring the network benefits their adoption would confer on the existing base of users.

Although technology lock-in has captured the imaginations of some public policy-makers and academics, the phenomenon appears rare. There is some anecdotal evidence for lock-ins, but some of these studies have been challenged and shown to be flawed.[5] There is no support for a prediction of widespread inertia in technology adoption. Basic research advances are widespread in practically every field of science and mathematics. Technological change exists throughout the economy. Firms continue to make significant investments in research and development (R&D), indicating that they anticipate returns to innovation. New products, industrial processes, and transaction methods continue to be adopted in practically every industry.

Despite being rarely observed, technology lock-in remains influential in competition policy. This makes it necessary to understand whether technology lock-in has any economic consequences. I show in the present discussion that three crucial factors explain why technology lock-in is unlikely. These factors limit any potential economic damage from technology lock-in.

---

[5] See particularly S. J. Liebowitz and S. E. Margolis, 1990, "The Fable of the Keys," *Journal of Law and Economics*, 33, pp. 1–26, and S. J. Liebowitz and S. E. Margolis, 1999, *Winners, Losers, and Microsoft: Competition and Antitrust in High Technology*, Oakland, CA: Independent Institute.

First, consumer coordination mitigates or eliminates technology lock-in. Even if network effects do exist, consumer coordination is likely to take advantage of any potential benefits. When there are small numbers of consumers, they can engage in Coasian bargaining, what I call "coordination in the small." Consumers can coordinate their innovation adoption decisions in light of any mutual benefits from consumption. When there are large numbers of consumers, firms can apply various instruments to coordinate the choices of large numbers of consumers corresponding to Hayek's "spontaneous order," what I call "coordination in the large."[6] Coordination by consumers and firms internalizes the benefits of network effects, eliminating network externalities and avoiding technology lock-in.

Second, if technology lock-in exists, it is necessarily confined to particular network industries. Consumer interactions through networks are ubiquitous in the economy, encompassing social networks, transaction networks, and transport networks. However, network effects depend on particular features on goods and services. These product features require the use of physical and virtual networks in the transmission of information. The relevant network industries are the information and communications technology and selected electronics (ICTE) industries.[7] This helps to explain why examples and applications of the concept of technology lock-in are almost invariably being drawn from the ICTE industries. Technological change occurs in every part of the economy, but technology lock-in necessarily is limited to the ICTE industries.

Third, firms in network industries have strong incentives to provide interoperability when necessary. This guarantees that the potential benefits from network effects are realized without the need to choose a single technology. Interoperability is common in the network industries. In communications, almost all communications networks interoperate. Access to telecommunications is nearly universal and almost all networks are interconnected. An individual user that connects to any network can communicate with almost any user on any other network. In information systems, interoperability is the norm with significant exchange of information across computers, operating systems, and software applications. Interoperability is built into products in the ICTE industries. In addition, ICTE industry associations promote technology standards that bring benefits from technology adoption due to network effects. Also, firms have incentives to supply conversion

---

[6] See Spulber, 2007, *supra* note 3.
[7] For a comprehensive overview, see C. Forman and A. Goldfarb, 2006, "Diffusion of Information and Communication Technologies to Business," in T. Hendershott, ed., *Handbook in Information Systems*, v. 1, Amsterdam: Elsevier B.V., pp. 1–52.

technologies that bridge diverse product standards in the ICTE industries. Of course, not all products need to interoperate. The sheer diversity of products, even some that do not interoperate, indicates areas where the benefits of product diversity outweigh the benefits of standardization.

The concept of network effects has made its influence felt in antitrust. The combination of network effects and technology lock-in plays a prominent role in *Microsoft v. Commission*.[8] Network effects were said to lead to market dominance in *United States v. Microsoft*.[9] The concept of network effects plays a role in various other cases.[10] The Department of Justice's (DOJ's) complaints against Visa and Mastercard emphasize the card issuers' networks of banks, and the District Court found that "network services output is necessarily decreased and network price competition restrained by the exclusionary rules."[11] Technology lock-in and network effects are critical aspects in the policy debate of network neutrality.[12] In *Kodak*, the court applied lock-in arguments based on switching costs. The court in *Kodak* found tying to be a problem because the high cost of purchasing copiers resulted in switching costs, making customers subject to increases in the prices of service and replacement parts.[13]

George Priest argues that antitrust law and policy should take into account the economic theory of networks.[14] He suggests that network effects should guide a new interpretation of such antitrust cases as *Visa/Mastercard*,

---

[8] *Microsoft Corporation against Commission of the European Communities*, Case T-201/04, Ruling on September 17, 2007 by the European Court of First Instance.

[9] The appellate court in *Microsoft* stated that, "In markets characterized by network effects, one product or standard tends towards dominance, because the utility that a user derives from consumption of the good increases with the number of other agents consuming the good," *United States v. Microsoft Corp.*, 253 F.3d 34, 49 (D.C. Cir.), *cert. denied*, 534 U.S. 952 (2001). See also *Novell, Inc. v. Microsoft Corp.*, 505 F.3d 302 (4th Cir. 2007).

[10] *Alabama Power Co. v. F.C.C.*, 311 F.3d 1357 (11th Cir. 2002); *Flying J Inc. v. Comdata Network*, Inc., 405 F.3d 821 (10th Cir. 2005); *Covad Communications Co. v. Bellsouth Corp.*, 314 F.3d 1282 (11th Cir. 2002); *Poller v. Columbia Broad. Sys.*, Inc., 284 F.2d 599 (D.C. Cir. 1960) rev'd, 368 U.S. 464, 82 S. Ct. 486, 7 L. Ed. 2d 458 (1962); *LiveUniverse, Inc. v. MySpace*, Inc., 304 F. App'x. 554 (9th Cir. 2008); *New York Mercantile Exch., Inc. v. Intercontinental Exch.*, Inc., 323 F. Supp. 2d 559; (S.D.N.Y. 2004).

[11] Visa I, 163 F. Supp. 2d at 379.

[12] See Tim Wu and C. S. Yoo, 2007, "Keeping the Internet Neutral?: Tim Wu and Christopher Yoo Debate", 59 Federal Communications Law Journal 575; C. S. Yoo, 2008, "Network Neutrality, Consumers, and Innovation," University of Chicago Legal Forum, forthcoming, C. S. Yoo, 2005, "Beyond Network Neutrality," Harvard Journal on Law & Technology, 19, pp. 1–77.

[13] 112 S. Ct. 2072 (1992).

[14] G. L. Priest, 2007, "Rethinking Antitrust Law in an Age of Network Industries," Research Paper No. 352, John M. Olin Center for Studies in Law, Economics, and Public Policy, Yale Law School.

American Airlines, BMI/ASCAP, NCAA, Associated Press, and *Dr. Miles.*
Most closely related to technology lock-in, Priest contends that *Radiant
Burners* and modern telecommunications cases such as *Terminal Railroad*
and *Trinko* should be examined in terms of technological interoperability
within a network.

This chapter extends to technology lock-in the discussion of network
effects that I presented earlier.[15] For an additional discussion of the legal
and regulatory aspects of access to networks, see the work by Spulber and
Yoo.[16] Sidak and Spulber discuss legal and economic dimensions of deregulation in network industries.[17] The article builds on path-breaking work
by Stanley J. Liebowitz and Stephen E. Margolis.[18] They present critiques
of the discussions of network externalities and technology lock-in that are
related closely to the present analysis. The notion of technology lock-in is

---

[15] D. F. Spulber, 2008, "Consumer Coordination in the Small and in the Large: Implications
for Antitrust in Markets with Network Effects," *Journal of Competition Law and Economics*,
4, June, pp. 1–56.

[16] D. F. Spulber, and C. S. Yoo, 2003, "Access to Networks: Economic and Constitution
Connections," *Cornell Law Review*, 88, pp. 885–1024; D. F. Spulber and C. S. Yoo, 2005,
"Network Regulation: The Many Faces of Access," *Journal of Competition Law and Eco-
nomics*, 1 (4), December, pp. 635–678; D. F. Spulber and C. S. Yoo, 2005, "On the Regulation
of Networks as Complex Systems: A Graph Theory Approach," *Northwestern University
Law Review*, 99 (4), Summer, pp. 1687–1722; D. F. Spulber and C. S. Yoo, 2007, "Man-
dating Access to Telecom and the Internet: The Hidden Side of *Trinko*," *Columbia Law
Review*, forthcoming; D. F. Spulber and C. S. Yoo, 2007, *Networks in Telecommunications:
Economics and Law*, Cambridge: Cambridge University Press.

[17] J. G. Sidak and D. F. Spulber, 1997, "The Tragedy of the Telecommons: Government
Pricing of Unbundled Network Elements Under the Telecommunications Act of 1996,"
Columbia University Law Review, 97, pp. 1201–1281; J. G. Sidak and D. F. Spulber, 1997,
"Network Access Pricing and Deregulation," *Industrial and Corporate Change*, 6 (4), pp.
757–782; J. G. Sidak and D. F. Spulber, 1997, *Deregulatory Takings and the Regulatory
Contract: The Competitive Transformation of Network Industries in the United States*, Cambridge: Cambridge University Press; J. G. Sidak and D. F. Spulber, 1998, "Deregulation
and Managed Competition in Network Industries," *Yale Journal on Regulation*, 15, Winter, pp. 117–148; J. G. Sidak and D. F. Spulber, 1998, "Cyberjam: Internet Congestion
of the Telephone Network," *Harvard Journal on Law and Public Policy*, 21 (2), Spring,
pp. 327–394.

[18] S. J. Liebowitz and S. E. Margolis, 1994, "Network Externality: An Uncommon Tragedy,"
The Journal of Economic Perspectives, 8, pp. 133–150; S. J. Liebowitz and S. E. Margolis, 1995,
"Path Dependence, Lock-in and History," *Journal of Law, Economics and Organization*, 11,
pp. 205–226; S. J. Liebowitz and S. E. Margolis, 1995, "Are Network Externalities a New
Source of Market Failure?," *Research in Law and Economics*, 17, pp. 1–22; S. J. Liebowitz
and S. E. Margolis, 1996, "Market Processes and the Selection of Standards," *Harvard
Journal of Law and Technology*, 9, pp. 283–318; S. J. Liebowitz, and S. E. Margolis, 2002,
"Network Effects," in *Handbook of Telecommunications Economics*, Volume 1, M. E. Cave
et al., eds., Amsterdam: Elsevier Science B.V.

closely related to the broader concept of "path dependence" advanced by some economic historians.

Liebowitz and Margolis point out that economies may be "path dependent" in benign ways.[19] Dependence on initial conditions exists in many economic situations that are consistent with optimizing behavior. For example, investment by a firm can depend on its initial capital stock, particularly in the presence of adjustment costs. In addition, optimization decisions made under uncertainty depend on the information available at the time that the decision is made. These forms of path dependence are present in any type of dynamic decision making. As Liebowitz and Margolis demonstrate, the path dependence that corresponds to technology lock-in "supposes the feasibility, in principle, of improvements in the path." In other words, the market is on the wrong path, but it is assumed that the government is capable of both discerning the right path and taking appropriate policy actions to correct the market failure.[20]

The discussion is organized as follows. Section I shows that the concept of technology lock-in rests on the underlying assumption of network effects. Sections II, III, and IV examine the three major factors that limit technology lock-in. Consumer coordination captures the benefits of network effects, hence eliminating this potential cause of technology lock-in. Since network effects tend to be confined to the ICT and selected electronics industries, interactions between network effects and technology adoption also will be confined to these specific industries. Firms in network industries have incentives to pursue interconnection and interoperability when it is efficient to do so. Finally, Section V considers implications for antitrust policy that result from rejecting the concept of technology lock-in.

I. Network Effects and Technology Lock-In

The concept of technology lock-in is based on underlying network effects. It bears emphasis that the presence of network effects in economic models is an *assumption*, not a result of economic analysis.[21]

---

[19] S. J. Liebowitz and S. E. Margolis, 1995, "Path Dependence, Lock-In, and History," *Journal of Law, Economics & Organization*, 11, April, pp. 205–226.

[20] Liebowitz and Margolis refer to optimization based on initial conditions as "first-degree path dependence," and optimization under uncertainty based on available information as "second-degree path dependence," and the assumption that markets make incorrect choices in technology that governments can correct as "third-degree path dependence." Liebowitz and Margolis, 1995, id.

[21] M. L. Katz and C. Shapiro, 1994, "Systems Competition and Network Effects," *The Journal of Economic Perspectives*, 8 (2), Spring, pp. 93–115. See also M. L. Katz and C. Shapiro, 1985,

The network effects assumption is the foundation of economic models of technology lock-in. The discussion in this section is not meant as a criticism of these interesting and important economic analyses. Rather, the discussion is intended to distinguish assumptions from conclusions to assist public policy makers in understanding the technology lock-in debate.

Katz and Shapiro distinguish between direct and indirect network effects.[22] A *direct network effect* refers to the effect of one person's consumption of the network good on another person's benefit obtained from the network good. An *indirect network effect* refers to the effect of prices and features of complementary goods on a consumer's benefit from the network good. Both types of network effects appear in technology lock-in arguments and in antitrust policy. The theoretical literature in economics on technology lock-in employs both types of network effects.[23]

Technology lock-in also is known as "path dependence."[24] What Arthur refers to as "increasing returns to adoption" is when each consumer's payoff is increasing in the number of past adoptions. This definition thus corresponds to network effects from prior consumption of the network good.

Farrell and Klemperer point out that if consumer preferences are similar, strong network effects still are not a problem because the efficient outcome is an equilibrium.[25] Communication, side payments, and commitment to a technology will address the problem, as they point out. If consumer

---

"Network Externalities, Competition, and Compatibility," *American Economic Review*, 75, June, pp. 424–440, at 426; M. L. Katz and C. Shapiro, 1986, "Technology Adoption in the Presence of Network Externalities," *Journal of Political Economy*, 94, August, pp. 822–841, at 826; M. L. Katz and C. Shapiro, 1992, "Product Introduction with Network Externalities," *Journal of Industrial Economics*, 40, March, pp. 55–83, at 58; J. Farrell and G. Saloner, 1985, "Standardization, Compatibility, and Innovation," *Rand Journal of Economics*, 16, Spring, pp. 70–83, at 73; J. Farrell and G. Saloner, 1986, "Installed Base and Compatibility: Innovation, Product Preannouncements, and Predation," *American Economic Review*, 76, December, pp. 940–955, at 941; J. Farrell and G. Saloner, 1992, "Converters, Compatibility, and the Control of Interfaces," *Journal of Industrial Economics*, 40, March, pp. 9–35; J. P. Choi and M. Thum, 1998, "Market Structure and the Timing of Technology Adoption with Network Externalities," *European Economic Review*, 42, pp. 225–244.

[22] Katz and Shapiro, 1994, id.

[23] Liebowitz and Margolis (1994, 2002, supra note 6) demonstrate that direct and indirect network effects have substantially different economic implications.

[24] See B. Arthur 1989, "Competing Technologies, Increasing Returns, and Lock-In by Historical Events," *Economic Journal*, 97, pp. 116–131, at 117. See also B. Arthur, 1990, "Positive Feedbacks in the Economy," *Scientific American*, 262, February, pp, 92–99, and B. Arthur, 1994, supra note 2. See also R. Cowan, 1991, "Tortoises and Hares: Choice Among Technologies of Unknown Merit," *Economic Journal*, 101, July, pp. 801–814, at 801–802.

[25] J. Farrell and P. Klemperer, 2007, "Coordination and Lock-In: Competition with Switching Costs and Network Effects," in *Handbook of Industrial Organization*, v. 3, Berkeley: University of California.

preferences differ, then strong network effects can lead to inefficient technology adoption. In this way, the strong network effects assumption forces technology adoption by consumers to depend on their ability to coordinate their decisions.

If network effects were not sufficiently strong that they outweigh individual preferences, market outcomes would tend to be efficient. Consumer choices in the marketplace would reflect their relative preferences for goods. This would eliminate the technology lock-in problem.

Economists typically abstract from the basic model of interdependent demand in two ways. First, they assume that the volume of information does not matter, so that all subscriptions to the network represent the same amount of consumption of network services. For example, Rohlfs, Artle, and Averous assume that consumers derive benefits only from their own and others membership.[26] The second abstraction that is typical in the network effects literature is that the identity of subscribers to the network does not matter, only the number of subscribers.

Consider the technology lock-in problem when there are many consumers. Again, discussions of lock-in assume that network effects drive the economy. Consider Arthur's dynamic version of technology lock-in.[27] Arthur's argument assumes that one technology has an advantage if there is a small number of consumers while the other technology has an advantage if there is a large number of consumers. Arthur further assumes that consumers cannot communicate with each other to coordinate their adoption decisions. Also, consumers are fully myopic in that their technology adoption choices depend only on past adoptions, without any expectations of future adoption. Consumers behave in a myopic manner because the benefits they receive from network effects are only those from previous adopters. Thus, consumers initially adopt the technology that offers benefits with few

---

[26] See J. Rohlfs, 1974, "A Theory of Interdependent Demand for a Communications Service," *The Bell Journal of Economics and Management Science*, 5 (1), Spring, pp. 16–37. Artle and Averous examine interdependent demand in communications based on the number of subscribers; see R. Artle and C. Averous, 1973, "The Telephone System as a Public Good: Static and Dynamic Aspects," *Bell Journal of Economics and Management Science*, 4, Spring, pp. 89–100. On network effects, see also N. Economides, 1996, "The Economics of Networks," *International Journal of Industrial Organization*, 14 (2), March, pp. 673–699; N. Economides and C. Himmelberg, 1995, "Critical Mass and Network Evolution in Telecommunications," in *Toward a Competitive Telecommunications Industry: Selected Papers from the 1994 Telecommunications Policy Research Conference*, Gerard Brock, ed., Manwah, NJ: Lawrence Erlbaum.

[27] B. Arthur 1989, "Competing Technologies, Increasing Returns, and Lock-In by Historical Events," *Economic Journal*, 97, pp. 116–131.

consumers. Consumers who arrive later continue to adopt that technology as benefits grow further with additional subscribers. As a consequence, many consumers adopt the technology that offers greater benefits for only a few adopters. The outcome is inefficient because the consumers missed choosing the technology that offered greater benefits for a large number of consumers.

Path dependence in Arthur's model thus relies on consumer myopia and an absence of even tacit coordination. The first few consumers adopt technology B because benefits are greater with few consumers. The next adopters always prefer technology B because it has increasing benefits due to network effects, so that the benefits of B to the marginal consumer of B will always exceed the benefits of the first consumer adopting technology A, which equals zero. This is also true if a few consumers can coordinate their adoption decisions, because the benefits of technology B grow with each set of adopters and the benefits for the first few adopters of technology A remain at the same low level.

In Arthur's framework, consumers only derive network effects benefits from prior adopters – not future ones. Consumers act myopically by assumption. It should not be surprising that a technology that offers greater benefits for early adopters would be the one adopted by myopic consumers. The logic is purely circular; myopic adopters behave myopically. When consumers benefit from future adopters they will form expectations about the behavior of those adopters and make their decisions accordingly.

II. Consumer Coordination and Adoption of Innovations

This section considers how consumer coordination both in the small and in the large addresses the problem of technology lock-in. With consumer coordination of technology adoption choices, the network effects problem is addressed. Then, consumers can make efficient technology adoption decisions. When the number of consumers is small, consumers can coordinate their adoption decisions efficiently. When the number of consumers is large, firms offering the technology can help consumers to coordinate their technology adoption decisions.

A. Consumer Coordination in the Small and Adoption of Innovations

Technology lock-in depends on the underlying assumption that there are network effects that result from the social benefits of technology adoption. The consumers face a problem of social benefits because they do not take into account the benefits their technology adoption choices would confer on other potential adopters. Ronald Coase analyzed the closely related problem of negative externalities in his classic work on the problem of social cost.[28] He argued that with small numbers of consumers, low transaction costs, and well-defined property rights, bargaining would lead to an efficient outcome. Coasian bargaining has important implications for the problem of technology adoption.

This section refers to coordination with small numbers of consumers. I refer to bargaining with small numbers of consumers as "coordination in the small." The preconditions for efficiency discussed by Coase for negative externalities are more likely to exist in the case of network externalities; that is, transaction costs are low and property rights are well-defined.

With network effects and small numbers of consumers, transaction costs of bargaining are likely to be low. Consumers who will benefit from network effects are likely to be connected by family, friendship, business, or other social relationships. Consumers obtain benefits from network effects often because they wish to communicate with those with whom they already have relationships. Such relationships form a basis for agreeing to subscribe to the same communications network.

Consumers who benefit most from exchanging information in the small numbers case are those with close social ties. They obtain network benefits from subscribing to a telecommunications network to maintain those social ties. Consumers wish to exchange documents, photos, videos, and other information with those with whom they already are connected. Catherine Tucker finds that potential adopters of video-messaging systems within a firm only react to adoption by those people with whom they wish to communicate.[29]

Transaction costs should be lowered since the consumers seeking to coordinate are not in an adversarial relationship. Since potential adopters of virtual or physical network goods already have a cooperative relationship, transaction costs should be low. Also, since the negotiation deals with mutual benefits, the negotiation itself will not be adversarial, further lowering the potential costs of negotiation. In pollution abatement, enforcement may be needed to make sure that pollution is reduced and that transfer payments are made. Coordination does not require outside enforcement both sides have an incentive to adopt the technology they have agreed on. Adoption

---

[28] R. H. Coase, 1960, "The Problem of Social Cost," *Journal of Law and Economics* 3, October, pp. 1–44.

[29] C. Tucker, 2006, "Interactive, Option-Value and Domino Network Effects in Technology Adoption," Working Paper, MIT, Sloan, February.

of the technology is easily observed by both parties, so monitoring costs are minimal. Transfer payments may not be needed because the adoption is mutually beneficial.

Coase's condition that property rights should be well defined is meant to apply to pollution abatement, where either the polluter or the recipient of pollution has property rights. Such an issue does not arise in the case of network effects. Network effects are bilateral; both sides obtain benefits, so no assignment of property rights is necessary. Agreement to coordinate adoption yields benefits to both sides, which provides the motivation for coordination without any assignment of rights.

Farrell and Klemperer argue based on case studies that efficient equilibria need not be realized.[30] Consumers may be "confused" due to imperfect information about other players' strategies. Alternatively, "splintering" may occur if individuals cannot coordinate within groups. There may be many equilibria that involve splintering. These equilibria are not "coalition-proof" since individuals would benefit by forming coalitions to take advantage of network effects. Farrell and Klemperer further observe that consumers may coordinate on the wrong equilibrium. In the technology adoption game, technology B may be Pareto inferior to A, but the two groups may coordinate internally and interact with the other group to choose technology B due to expectations about which technology will be successful. Alternatively, the groups may choose the inferior technology due to imperfect rules of thumb used for coordination.

Consider again the technology adoption game in Table 4.1, where network effects are strong. With small numbers of consumers and low transaction costs, efficient bargaining will solve the coordination problem. Suppose that the two groups of consumers agree on what is the best technology. Then, the game of technology choice with strong network effects is a "ranked coordination game." If consumers can communicate, they will choose the best equilibrium, and they will reach the equilibrium without the need for monetary transfers. The consumers will agree to select the best technology, and only the most efficient technology will be adopted. Splitting and out-of-equilibrium outcomes will be avoided. Policy makers should treat the small numbers situation carefully since there should be a presumption that consumer coordination can address effectively the benefits of network effects.

Next, consider the technology adoption game in Table 4.1 where network effects are strong and differences in idiosyncratic preferences imply that

---

[30] J. Farrell and P. Klemperer, 2007, "Coordination and Lock-In: Competition with Switching Costs and Network Effects," in *Handbook of Industrial Organization*, v. 3, Berkeley: University of California.

Table 4.1. *The per-consumer payoffs for the technology adoption game with common network effects and idiosyncratic preferences with two groups of consumers*

	Group 2	
Group 1	Adopt technology A	Adopt technology B
Adopt technology A	$g^A(N_1 + N_2) - h^{1A}$, $g^A(N_1 + N_2) - h^{2A}$	$g^A(N_1) - h^{1A}$, $g^B(N_2) - h^{2B}$
Adopt technology B	$g^B(N_1) - h^{1B}$, $g^A(N_2) - h^{2A}$	$g^B(N_1 + N_2) - h^{1B}$, $g^B(N_1 + N_2) - h^{2B}$

the two equilibria cannot be Pareto ranked. The adoption game presents a quandary since communication alone is not sufficient to resolve the impasse. When monetary transfers are feasible, consumers will achieve the outcome that yields the greatest total surplus by making compensatory transfers to the group that would prefer the less desirable technology. If monetary transfers are not feasible, the two groups must find a way to choose between the two Nash equilibria.

Sequential adoption selects a single Nash equilibrium. Idiosyncratic preference effects change the nature of the sequential technology adoption game. In the game shown in Table 4.1, the first mover determines the outcome of the game. When consumers disagree on the best technology, group 1 as the first mover would adopt technology A and group 2 would then also adopt A since network effects override idiosyncratic preference effects. Group 2 as the first mover would adopt technology B, and group 1 would follow by adopting technology B. As a result, each group is made better off if it moves first. The sequential technology adoption game is a simplified version of the framework presented by Farrell and Saloner.[31] They consider a game in which one of the technologies is available and adopted before the other, and users decide whether to switch to the new technology. If the new technology is preferred by all when everyone adopts, the unique sequential equilibrium involves all users switching to the new technology.[32]

Whether or not the two Nash equilibria are Pareto ranked, sequential adoption addresses network effects and solves the technology lock-in problem. The assumption of strong network effects implies that either

[31] J. Farrell and G. Saloner, 1985, "Standardization, Compatibility, and Innovation," *Rand Journal of Economics*, 16, Spring, pp. 70–83.

[32] Farrell and Saloner (1985) find that with asymmetric information, the equilibrium of the adoption game fails to be Pareto efficient when users cannot communicate. Allowing some communication eliminates such excess inertia when preferences coincide but increases it when preferences differ.

group knows that by adopting one of the technologies, the other group will get on the bandwagon, thus achieving coordination without prior communication.[33] Then, if either group is a first mover, they will adopt technology A and the follower will choose to adopt technology A as the best response. In this way, sequential adoption results in the Pareto dominant outcome.

The efficiency criterion itself raises an issue for public policy. In the absence of monetary transfers between consumers, the Pareto criterion is appealing for evaluating the efficiency of technology markets. The two welfare theorems of neoclassical economies apply the Pareto criterion to the study of product markets. In considering the neoclassical general equilibrium setting, it is worthwhile to recognize the possibility of multiple market equilibria.

Total consumers' surplus is another effective criterion.[34] Maximizing total surplus implicitly involves the possibility of monetary transfers between consumers. The total surplus criterion for efficiency generally differs from the Pareto criterion. Applying a total surplus efficiency criterion distinguishes between the two equilibria depending on the relative levels of the total surplus.[35] Although the total benefits approach is highly useful in a variety of contexts, it has limited value in the present evaluation of technology adoption decisions. One of the technologies will most likely yield greater surplus.

To interpret the lower surplus outcome as representing inefficiency imposes a tough standard on technology adoption decisions. Consumers would not only need to coordinate their adoptions decisions; they would also need to make agreements involving compensating monetary transfers. This would certainly be of limited value as a guide to public policy. Government agencies would not have sufficient information to determine which technology generates the greatest consumers surplus. Doing so would require not only measuring idiosyncratic preference effects but also determining the benefits of network effects. Moreover, providing incentives for consumers to adopt the desired technology when private transfers are not feasible would require government mandates of technology choices or, worse

---

[33] See J. Farrell and G. Saloner, 1985, "Standardization, Compatibility, and Innovation," *Rand Journal of Economics*, 16, Spring, pp. 70–83.

[34] This means comparing $(N_1 + N_2)g^A(N_1 + N_2) - N_1 h^{1A} - N_2 h^{2A}$ with $(N_1 + N_2)g^B (N_1 + N_2) - N_1 h^1 B - N_2 h^{2B}$.

[35] Farrell and Saloner (1985, 1986) apply a total surplus criterion in defining "excess inertia." They add the benefits of new adopters and those of the installed base. They state that "the installed base may cause excess inertia" (1986, p. 942).

yet, public monetary transfers. When private transfers are not feasible and public transfers are not desirable, the Pareto criterion seems more useful for evaluating technology adoption decisions. The Pareto criterion is better suited for evaluating consumer decisions in a strategic setting with multiple equilibria.

B. Consumer Coordination in the Large and Adoption of Innovations

When there are a large number of consumers, it becomes more difficult for consumers to coordinate their technology adoption decisions. However, there are market mechanisms for coordination. Firms can act as intermediaries that provide instruments of coordination.

Friedrich Hayek referred to such coordination by firms as "spontaneous order."[36] Instruments of coordination not only include prices, but also mass marketing, mass media, and mass distribution. Through their marketing and sales efforts, firms help consumers to make choices and learn about the choices of others. This is instrumental in overcoming the potential lack of coordination that concerns advocates of network effects.

If a firm owns a particular technology, it has economic incentives to promote the technology. The firm will invest in assisting consumers in coordinating their adoption decisions. F. Scott Kieff points out that intellectual property rights can facilitate coordination.[37] Even if the technology is not owned by an individual firm, intermediaries will have incentives to enter the market to assist consumers with coordination. For example, firms can provide customer services that are complementary to open source software, thus promoting the adoption of a particular type of open source software. Thus, even in the absence of technology ownership, there are economic incentives for firms to help consumers coordinate their adoption decisions.

Instruments of coordination provided by firms increase the information available to consumers. As a result, consumers are no longer playing a simple Nash noncooperative game. Rather, consumers have additional

---

[36] See F. A. Hayek, 1991, "Spontaneous (Grown) Order and Organized ('Made') Order," in *Market, Hierarchies & Networks: The Coordination of Social Life*, G. Thompson, J. Francis, R. Levacic, and J. Mitchell, eds., London: Sage Publications, pp. 293–301; F. A. Hayek, 1976, *Law, Legislation and Liberty, Volume 2: The Mirage of Social Justice*, Chicago: The University of Chicago Press, and F. A. Hayek, 1977, "The Creative Powers of a Free Civilization," in Essays on Individuality, F. Morley, ed., Liberty Fund Inc.

[37] F. S. Kieff, 2006, "Coordination, Property, and Intellectual Property: An Unconventional Approach to Anticompetitive Effects and Downstream Access," *Emory Law Journal*, 56, pp. 327–438.

information about the choices of others. With sufficient information, consumers can coordinate in more sophisticated ways, such as choosing between noncooperative equilibria to select a Pareto dominant outcome.

If the number of consumers is small, they can enter into formal or informal agreements to join the network. If the number of consumers is large, coordination between consumers must take place through mechanisms of spontaneous order. Groups of consumers with common interests band together to join the network. Mass marketing, mass media, mass communications, and other types of coordination stimulate consumers to choose the outcome that offers the greatest benefits to subscribers. Consumer coordination without side payments selects the high-output Nash equilibrium outcome. This is the only outcome that does not involve foregoing benefits.[38]

III. Potential Technology Lock-In is Largely Confined to the ICTE Industries

In public policy discussions, "network goods" generally refer to information networks, which are confined to the ICTE industries. These industries have developed institutions that address interconnection and interoperability. These take advantage of network effects and thus limit the potential for technology lock-in that is attributed to network effects.

A. Physical and Virtual Networks

Although potential network effects are present throughout the economy, it is important to distinguish information networks from social, transaction, and transport networks. Although consumers experience mutual benefits of consumption in each of these types of networks, only information networks tend to raise policy concerns. What makes the ICTE industries the locus of potential network effects is the nature of the physical and virtual networks that connect the economic actors. Information networks require coordination of the consumption of network goods.

Information networks involve the communication of data in a form that allows for computation. Information networks are critical to the policy debate over technology adoption. The definition of an information network

[38] For a comprehensive examination of network effects, see D. F. Spulber, "Consumer Coordination in the Small and in the Large; Implications for Antitrust in Markets with Network Effects," *Journal of Competition Law & Economics*, 4, June, pp. 207–263.

derives from the general concept of an information system. *Information systems* comprise these two components: communication and computation.[39]

An information network connects economic actors by linking information systems. Accordingly, information networks require that the information that is exchanged is in a form that allows for communication and computation. A network in which information can be exchanged and processed is said to exhibit *interoperability*.[40] The technical standards that allow for the creation of physical and virtual information networks require the interoperability of software and hardware. Because of the key role played by interoperability, the discussion of network effects on technology adoption necessarily focuses on information networks.

The concept of interoperability is related to that of a *platform*, which refers to a collection of related technology standards. Platforms play an important role in information systems, both in communications and in computing. In computers, a platform is a "reconfigurable base of compatible components on which users build applications" and is identified with "engineering specifications for compatible hardware and software."[41] For example, IBM devised standards for the personal computer that were adapted by manufacturers of software designers; internal components, such as memory and microprocessors; and peripheral devices, such as printers and monitors.

In communications networks, platforms permit the compatible transmission of information in communications and the interconnection of transmission equipment.[42] Platforms in telecommunications include computer hardware and software standards for computer-based switching and

---

[39] Committee T1A1 [renamed Network Performance, Reliability and Quality of Service Committee (PRQC)], 2000, *ATIS Telecom Glossary 2000*, Washington, DC: Alliance for Telecommunications Industry Solutions.

[40] The definition of interoperability is based on that of the Institute of Electrical and Electronics Engineers, 1990, *IEEE Standard Computer Dictionary: A Compilation of IEEE Standard Computer Glossaries*, New York, NY.

[41] T. Bresnahan and S. M. Greenstein, 1997, "Technical Progress and Co-invention on Computing and in the Uses of Computers," *Brookings Papers on Economic Activity: Microeconomics*, Vol. 1996, (1996), pp. 1–83, pp. 1–78; T. Bresnahan and S. M. Greenstein, 1999, "Technological Competition and the Structure of the Computer Industry," *Journal of Industrial Economics*, 47, March, pp. 1–40; S. M. Greenstein, 1998, "Industrial Economics and Strategy: Computing Platforms," *IEEE Micro*, 18, May–June, pp. 43–53.

[42] D. F. Spulber and C. S. Yoo, 2005, "Network Regulation: The Many Faces of Access, *Journal of Competition Law and Economics*, 1 (4), December, pp. 635–678; D. F. Spulber, and C. S. Yoo, 2005a, "On the Regulation of Networks as Complex Systems: A Graph Theory Approach, *Northwestern University Law Review*, 99 (4), Summer, pp. 1687–1722; D. F. Spulber and C. S. Yoo, 2007a, "Mandating Access to Telecom and the Internet: The Hidden Side of *Trinko*," *Columbia Law Review*, 107, pp. 1822–1907, forthcoming.

transmission systems. Platforms in communications include computer software standards such as the Transmission Control Protocol/Internet Protocol (TCP/IP) used for Internet communications between computers. A network is said to be *modular* or to exhibit an *open architecture* if most suppliers of complementary services can gain access to the network.[43]

In the communications industries, firms establish physical transmission networks to provide communications services. Examples include traditional telecommunications, mobile telephony, and the Internet. Communication over transmission networks involves network effects because of the mutual benefits to subscribers of joining a network.[44] A consumer who joins the network can communicate with other subscribers. The consumer obtains benefits from communication with others, so that the consumer benefits from others' consumption of network services. If such benefits are not somehow accounted for, an externality is said to exist. There is a potential for market failure if a consumer does not recognize the benefits that his subscription to the phone network confers on others. If the consumer only recognizes his personal benefits from consumption, he may consume less of the network service than is socially optimal. Proponents of the network effects view may recommend that the activity be subsidized to overcome the problem of underconsumption resulting from the positive externality.

In the information technology industries and selected electronics industries there also exists the potential for network effects that are associated with interoperability. Economic actors obtain mutual benefits from exchanging information when connections between information systems facilitate communication and computation. Connected information systems form *virtual networks*. The exchange of information and the processing of information that is exchanged are an important feature of the services provided by physical communications networks. The general concept of interoperability extends these properties to virtual networks. These include software–hardware interactions, software–software interactions, and hardware–hardware interactions. In electronics, for example, devices such as media players share storage media, and computers and peripheral

---

[43] Graph theory provides an important tool for the study of networks. For an introduction to graph theory see J. M. Aldous and R. J. Wilson, 2000, *Graphs and Applications: An Introductory Approach*, New York: Springer-Verlag; B. Bollobás, 1998, *Modern Graph Theory*, New York: Springer-Verlag; R. Diestel, 2000, *Graph Theory*, 2nd ed., New York: Springer-Verlag; W. T. Tutte, 2001, *Graph Theory*, Cambridge: Cambridge University Press; J. Gross and J. Yellen, 1999, *Graph Theory and Its Applications*, Boca Raton, FL: CRC Press; J. Gross and J. Yellen, eds., 2004, *Handbook of Graph Theory*, Boca Raton, FL: CRC Press.

[44] See J. Rohlfs, 1974, "A Theory of Interdependent Demand for a Communications Service," *The Bell Journal of Economics and Management Science*, 5 (1), Spring, pp. 16–37.

equipment have plug-and-play compatibility. Interoperability is associated with network effects because users benefit from joining the same virtual network.

The benefits of joining the same virtual network are analogous to those obtained from joining physical networks. End users derive benefits from exchanging information. When joining the same virtual network is necessary for that communication to occur; an individual who joins the network benefits from another individual joining that network. The compatibility of computers, software, and electronic devices forms the *links* of the virtual network. Individual users access the virtual network at *nodes* that consist of compatible devices.

The benefits of communication on a virtual network derive from the value of the information that is received. The same information can be shared by two or more individuals. If there is nonrivalrous consumption of information, the shared information acts as a local public good. Multiple individuals benefit from consuming the same data, music, photographs, or videos. The information that is transmitted may be a product that is consumed by each individual, such as news, financial data, and entertainment. The interoperability of virtual networks also makes possible the operation of other types of networks, particularly transport networks and transaction networks.

B. Interconnection Is Standard in the ICTE Industries

In practice, the problem of network effects is likely to be eliminated since markets provide sufficient incentives for interconnection and interoperability. When the products and services of firms in network industries are interconnected and interoperable, consumers benefit from any potential industry-wide network effects. The technology lock-in argument becomes moot since underlying network effects do not pose a problem.

Firms have a strong incentive to adapt their products to market standards to obtain a share of the market. The global market for ICTE industries is huge, with one estimate suggesting that it exceeds 6 percent of the world economy with growth rates exceeding those of the world economy.[45] This trend suggests that the world ICTE industry is approaching $3 trillion. Markets within the ICTE industries that depend on very specific technical

---

[45] These estimates are for 1997; see H. Miller and J. Sanders, 1999, "Scoping the Global Market: Size is Just Part of the Story, *IT Pro*, March-April, pp. 49–54. See also *Digital Planet 2000: The Global Information Economy*, World Information Technology and Services Alliance, 1999.

standards are substantial. For example, the Internet employs particular pro-tocols and represents significant data traffic and electronic commerce trans-actions. Local networks are a multi-billion-dollar industry that depends on specific IEEE (Institute of Electrical and Electronics Engineers) standards.[46]

Forman and Goldfarb survey empirical evidence of network effects in the information and communications technology industries. They point out two identification problems. Statistical correlation between user adoption decisions can be the result of relationships between the users or common unobserved factors. This means that network effects may be difficult to distinguish from lower adoption costs. Second, even if network effects could be identified, their source might not be. As they point out: "Bandwagon effects may be the result of network externalities, social network effects, or even competitive effects."[47]

For example, network effects may be present within firms due to com-munication between employees regarding adoption decisions in the case of video conferencing. Adoption of the technology by managers and by workers has an important effect on other employees who wish to commu-nicate with them.[48] However, it would be incorrect to characterize decisions within the firm as "externalities." Such adoption decisions within the firm are likely to reflect coordination rather than market failure.

Cargill and Bolin refer to standardization as a "failing paradigm." They characterize standardization as a management technique that firms employ to reduce risk and suggest that in the information and communication technology industries, standardization "has moved from being viewed as a technical discipline to being viewed as a 'cool' marketing tool." They are concerned about the "excessive proliferation" of specifications and standard-setting organizations and suggest that public policy should *limit* standardization.[49]

As Anton and Yao point out,

Standards and standard-setting organizations have been an important feature of the economic landscape for many years, particularly in the information technology and communications industries.[50]

---

[46] See J. Hurd and J. Isaak, 2005, "IT Standardization: The Billion Dollar Strategy," *Journal of IT Standards & Standardization Research*, 3, January–June, pp. 68–74.

[47] Forman and Goldfarb, 2006, supra note 7.

[48] *See* Tucker, 2006, supra 29.

[49] C. Cargill and S. Bolin, 2007, "Standardization: A Failing Paradigm," in *Standards and Public Policy*, S. Greenstein and V. Stango, eds., Cambridge: Cambridge University Press, pp. 296–328.

[50] J. J. Anton and D. A. Yao, 1995, "Standard-Setting Consortia, Antitrust, and High-Technology Industries," *Antitrust Law Journal*, 64, Fall, pp. 247–265, at p. 247.

There are various explanations for the prevalence of interface standards in these industries. When firms adopt standards, the pace of adoption and overall market size are increased, according to Hurd and Isaak.[51] Given the size of the ICTE industries, the incentives for standardization are substantial. IT standardization drives increases in the size of the market while reducing transaction costs, reducing production costs, and increasing returns on investment.[52] According to an industry survey, those firms that migrated to new standards soonest received the highest returns on investment.[53] The survey of 340 computer server and storage sites around the world found that *all* of the respondent sites used standardized servers (Intel processors and Windows or Linux operating systems).[54]

Initially, most servers were proprietary, including the IBM 3090, Digital Vax, and the Hewlett-Packard 3000. In the early 1990s, less than one-third of all of the servers sold were a standardized Intel system. By 2001, 88 percent were Standard Intel Architecture Servers. Most standardized servers are in the "entry level server category, those costing under $100,000."[55] Standardization of servers makes possible specialization and division of labor among different types of servers. Splitting tasks among server appliances, data base servers, and general purpose servers yields increased benefits from scalability, reliability, manageability, and connectivity."[56] Gantz and Turner conclude that standardization of servers "is inexorable, paralleling similar standardization adoption experiences in IT over the past 40 years."[57]

Widespread interoperability and interconnection is apparent in the ICT and electronics industries. In communications, practically everyone already is connected with everyone else. A subscriber to any communications network anywhere in the world can reach every other subscriber anywhere in the world. Practically every telecommunications network is interconnected with practically every other telecommunications network. In addition to telecommunications, the Internet is a network of networks, with nearly complete global interconnection, limited only by some authoritarian governments but not by the private sector.

Network effects cannot drive technology lock-in in the design of communications networks because different types of networks are compatible.

---

[51] Hurd and Isaak, id.
[52] This is according to a study by J. Gantz and V. Turner, 2002, "Standardization: The Secret to IT Leverage," IDC White Paper, sponsored by Dell Computer Corp., Framingham, MA.
[53] Gantz and Turner, 2002, ibid.
[54] Gantz and Turner, 2002, ibid.
[55] Gantz and Turner, 2002, ibid.
[56] Gantz and Turner, 2002, ibid.
[57] The information in this paragraph is drawn from Gantz and Turner, 2002.

The incremental benefits of subscribing to the same network are reduced or eliminated if consumers can subscribe to different networks and still communicate with each other. All kinds of communications networks are interconnected, thus reducing or eliminating the potential benefits of having one type of network. For example, there are interconnections between traditional analog telecommunications networks, cable television–based networks, digital fiber optic networks, and wireless mobile networks. The benefits of network effects are achieved along with the benefits of a variety of network services and technologies. There is no need to have a single network or even a single type of network to capture network effects.

Also, network effects cannot drive technology lock-in for communications devices. Communicating networks can handle connections with very different end-user technologies. Thus, a telecommunications system can accommodate transmissions to and from traditional analog telephones, digital phones, mobile phones, fax machines, and computers. There is no possibility of technology lock-in deriving from the sacrifice of product variety to obtain network effects.

The joint benefits of subscribing to the same network are reduced further because consumers often subscribe to multiple networks, so that not all consumers need be on the same network for communications to take place. Consumers often belong to multiple communications networks including traditional telecommunications, mobile telephony, the Internet, and Wi-Fi systems. Consumers often have access to different communications networks at home and at work. The question of access to communications networks is essentially moot in developed economies, where access to telephony is practically universal and Internet access is nearly so.[58] In addition, the Telecommunications Act of 1996 expands the regulatory concept of universal service to one that expands with the development of new technologies.[59]

Network effects are unlikely to drive technology lock-in in software used for Internet communications. Multiple browsers are available at no cost and can be readily downloaded from the Internet. Consumers often have more than one browser. Providers of browsers have an incentive to allow users to reach as many web pages as possible. A similar situation exists with search engines. Consumers can access multiple search engines online and can switch easily between them. Providers of search engines seek to

---

[58] See D. F. Spulber and C. S. Yoo, 2008, for additional discussion of access.

[59] On regulation of broadband, see R. W. Crandall and J. G. Sidak, 1995, "Competition and Regulatory Policies for Interactive Broadband Networks," *Southern California Law Review*, 68, pp. 1203–1237.

maximize the benefits of users, which means that such engines will not exclude users who wish to search the web, nor will they exclude web pages that users wish to find.

Various market forces handle the network effects associated with multiple media player formats. Computer media player software exists in multiple formats including Microsoft Media Player, Adobe Flash Player, and RealPlayer. Network effects create the potential for a virtual network of players and media in different formats. However, the players are available for free, easily downloaded from the Internet, and not mutually exclusive since a computer user can have installed the software for multiple players on a single computer. Thus, any computer user can employ whatever media player is needed to read a particular file. In addition, the same information can be made available in multiple formats. As a consequence, most computer users can choose between formats for many types of information.

Even if a company offers a proprietary format for a media player, there are competing alternatives. For example, the Apple iTunes Store offered a vast library of songs and other content subject to a proprietary format. Apple iTunes could only be played on the Apple iPod portable device and are subject to "digital rights management" (DRM) copying restrictions. A competitor, eMusic, offered downloads of songs without restrictions for customers who pay subscription fees. Competitive alternatives expanded significantly when Internet retailer Amazon.com started to offer songs from many music companies that are free of DRM restrictions in the MP3 format that is used in practically any media player. Suppliers of recordings to Amazon include 20,000 independent recording labels and major labels such as EMI and Universal Music Group.[60] At least initially, Amazon's restriction-free songs were offered at a lower price than the restricted offerings of iTunes.

Platforms exist in electronic commerce, in the form of technical standards for the electronic exchange of data between companies. Innovations in communications and computation as applied to business documents avoid the need to translate computer files into paper documents, thereby increasing the speed and accuracy of transactions. There is a wide-ranging set of standards for electronic data interchange (EDI) on private networks that predate the Internet. Extensible markup language (XML) provides standards for documents and data transmission over the Internet developed by the World Wide Web Consortium. The advantage of document standardization is ease of communication and computation in retail, wholesale, and general interbusiness transactions.

---

[60] See Jonathan Richards, 2007, "Amazon Launches Music Download Service to Challenge iTunes," September 26, *Times Online*.

Collections of technical standards exist in many industries where independent producers supply substitute products that are interchangeable and complementary products that work together. Thus, cameras and film share technological standards that allow the products to be used together, and there are multiple providers of cameras and of film that follow the technical standards. These standards exist in many high-tech industries such as audio systems, video systems, and mobile phones. Platforms exist in many other types of industries in which compatible components are needed, including automobiles, aircraft, and industrial machinery.

There are more than 100 national and international standard-setting bodies in the ICTE industries. Among the major international standard-setting organizations are the International Organization for Standardization (ISO), the International Telecommunications Union (ITU), ECMA International, the Institute of Electrical and Electronics Engineers (IEEE), the Internet Engineering Task Force (IETF), the World Wide Web Consortium (W3C), the International Electrotechnical Commission (IEC), and the Internet Society (ISOC). International organizations also coordinate with each other through such mechanisms as the ISO/IEC/Joint Technical Committee 1 (JCT1) and through overlapping memberships. Standard-setting organizations develop and promulgate a wide range of technology specifications and product standards. For example, ECMA International deals with ICT and consumer electronics (CE) standards. These include standards for Scripting and Programming Languages; Communications Technologies: Product Safety, Environmental Design Considerations, Acoustics and Electromagnetic Compatibility (EMC), Optical Storage, Volume and File structure, Universal 3D open file format, Holographic Information Storage Systems (HISS), Office Open XML Formats, and XML Paper Specification (XPS).[61]

IV. Markets Provide Incentives for Coordination and Interoperability

Firms that provide innovations have economic incentives to coordinate product standards with each other. These standards should address potential network effects and thus eliminate the possibility of technology lock-in. Network effects, where they exist, increase the incentives for standardization and interoperability. This suggests that network effects should not be identified as causing technology lock-in but rather they may enhance the diffusion rates of new technologies.

Consumer coordination addresses the problem of social benefits potentially posed by network effects. Moreover, the possibility of network effects

---

[61] This list is from www.ecma-international.org.

largely is confined to the ICT and electronics industries. Even if network effects are present, market institutions capture many of the potential benefits, eliminating the possibility that network effects can cause technology lock-in.

A. Firms Have Incentives to Provide Interoperability

Potential externalities due to network effects that potentially underlie technology lock-in are eliminated if firms offer compatible products. Consumers obtain all of the mutual benefits of consumption when physical and virtual networks are interconnected. The question is whether firms have incentives to interconnect when it is efficient to do so. Katz and Shapiro show that firms need not engage in interconnection even when doing so is socially optimal.[62] Their result is predicated on quantity competition between firms. However, their results can be reversed when firms engage in price competition. Then, under some conditions, profit-maximizing firms choose to interconnect if it is socially efficient to do so. Firms may even choose to interconnect when it is socially inefficient. Forcing firms to interconnect through antitrust and government regulation may make consumers worse off than they would be otherwise.

Firms' decisions to engage in costly interconnection depend on the nature of competition. When firms employ quantity instruments such as capacity setting, they are said to compete using "strategic substitutes." When firms employ price instruments they are said to compete using "strategic complements."[63] The technology lock-in results obtained with strategic substitutes can be reversed when firms compete with strategic complements. Price competition tends to be a more accurate description of competition than quantity competition.[64] In practice, firms generally compete through price adjustment. Other competitive instruments, such as product features, innovation, marketing, sales, and service, accompany price competition.

Consider how competitive firms decide whether to make their technology compatible. Total welfare generally is composed of firms' profit and

---

[62] See also M. L. Katz and C. Shapiro, 1985, "Network Externalities, Competition, and Compatibility," *American Economic Review*, 75, June, pp. 424–440, at 426.

[63] See J. Bulow, J. Geanokoplos, and P. Klemperer, 1985, "Multiproduct Oligopoly: Strategic Substitutes and Complements," *Journal of Political Economy*, 93, pp. 488–511. The actions of two firms are strategic substitutes (complements) if an increase in one firm's action lowers (raises) the marginal effects on its profits of the other firm's action.

[64] This was the substance of Bertrand's 1883 critique of the 1838 Cournot model. This debate lies at the foundation of much of the economic field of industrial organization. See D. F. Spulber, 1989, *Regulation and Markets*, Cambridge, MA: MIT Press, ch. 17.

consumers' surplus. If firms decide to make their products compatible, the welfare effects are composed of the changes in profits (Π) and consumers' surplus (CS):

$$\Delta W = \Delta \Pi + \Delta CS.$$

Making products compatible is costly. Accordingly, it is efficient to make products compatible when the welfare benefits exceed the cost of compatibility. If the cost of compatibility is F, then compatibility is desirable if and only if

$$\Delta W \geq F.$$

Firms will choose to make their products compatible if and only if

$$\Delta \Pi \geq F.$$

If profits increase with compatibility, this will motivate firms to provide compatibility. The critical issue is whether compatibility increases consumers' surplus. If compatibility increases consumers' surplus, then compatibility increases social welfare more than firms' profits, so that firms are less motivated to choose compatibility than is socially optimal. Conversely, if compatibility decreases consumers' surplus, then firms are more motivated to choose compatibility than is socially optimal.

Katz and Shapiro show that when firms compete through quantities, compatibility always increases consumers' surplus.[65] This implies that firms do not supply enough compatibility since there are situations in which doing so is not profitable even though it is socially optimal. Their result depends on the fact that compatibility not only yields network effects but also increases the effects of competition, increasing total industry output and reducing the price paid by consumers. The public policy implications of this result, as emphasized by Katz and Shapiro, are for government to favor compatibility through industry coordination and other means.

Consider now the implications of price competition. To illustrate the effects of price competition, consider the classic model of differentiated products competition in a duopoly.[66] There is a continuum of N consumers represented by the interval of addresses from 0 to N. This also represents the space of possible products with firm A located at zero and firm B located at N. The number of consumers who buy technology A is n and the number of consumers who buy technology B is the remainder, $N - n$.

---

[65] Katz and Shapiro, 1985.
[66] This is the standard Hotelling model of a differentiated duopoly.

Suppose that there are common network effects as well as idiosyncratic preference effects. If the two products are not compatible, network benefits are $g(n)$ for technology A and $g(N-n)$ for technology B. If the two products are compatible, then network benefits are $g(N)$ for both technologies. The idiosyncratic benefit effect of the *marginal* consumer is $h(n)$ for technology A and $h(N-n)$ for technology B. The firms offer prices p^A and p^B, respectively, and choose prices to maximize profits.[67]

Network effects only play a demand-side role when products are not compatible. Thus, the price elasticity of demand only depends on network effects when products are not compatible.[68] This means that demand will be more elastic without compatible products and less elastic with compatibility. As a result, firms will choose higher prices at equilibrium with compatibility.[69]

Compatibility thus raises prices when firms engage in price competition. The price increase due to compatibility offsets the gain in consumers' surplus that is due to the network effects of compatibility. This means that compatibility can increase or decrease consumers' surplus depending or whether the network effects of compatibility are greater than or less than the price effects of compatibility.[70] When the price effects of compatibility outweigh the benefits, consumers' surplus falls. Then, the profitability of

---

[67] Profits are, respectively, $\Pi^A = p^A n$ and $\Pi^B = p^B(N-n)$. The marginal consumer is indifferent between the two technologies. Without compatibility, the marginal consumer is determined by $g(n) - h(n) - p^A = g(N-n) - h(N-n) - p^B$. With compatibility, the marginal consumer is determined by $g(N) - h(n) - p^A = g(N) - h(N-n) - p^B$.

[68] Demand elasticity for product A without compatibility equals

$$\eta^A = -\frac{\partial n}{\partial p^A}\frac{p^A}{n} = \frac{-1}{(g'(n) - h'(n)) + (g'(N-n) - h'(N-n))}\frac{p^A}{n}.$$

Demand elasticity for product A with compatibility equals

$$\eta^A = \frac{\partial n}{\partial p^A}\frac{p^A}{n} = \frac{-1}{-h'(n) - h'(N-n)}\frac{p^A}{n}.$$

[69] The equilibrium when marginal costs are zero equals a zero marginal revenue, so that $p(1 - 1/\eta) = 0$. The equilibrium prices are chosen so that, for each firm, elasticity of demand equals one. Without compatibility, firm A's price equals $p^A = Nh'(N/2) - Ng'(N/2)$. With compatibility, firm A's price equals $p^A = Nh'(N/2)$, so that the price effect is $\Delta p^A = Ng'(N/2)$. At equilibrium in either case, the two firms split the market at $N/2$. Compatibility increases prices and the firms' profits. The analysis generalizes to positive marginal costs.

[70] The formal representation of these two effects is

$$\Delta CS = g(N) - g(N/2) - Ng'(N/2).$$

If $g(n) = \sqrt{n}$, for example, $\Delta CS = \sqrt{N}(1 - \sqrt{2})$, which is less than zero.

making products compatible outweighs the social welfare effects. Firms will choose compatibility whenever it is socially efficient to do so. Firms also will choose compatibility in some situations when it is not socially efficient because they obtain greater private benefits from compatibility.

Farrell and Saloner, in their 1992 article on technological compatibility, present a Hotelling-type model with product variety. In their setting, the customers of the two firms decide whether to purchase converters. They observe that consumer decisions about purchasing converters illustrate the "irresponsibility of competition" because it may lead to less standardization and compatibility. They also find that both firms favor efficient converters due to the pricing game. Assuming that one technology is "dominant," they point out that a consumer that buys the dominant technology confers a greater network externality on others than a consumer who buys the minority technology and a converter. They conclude that "social welfare may be higher if converters are not available."[71]

In a setting without network externalities, Matutes and Regibeau find that firms will choose to make their products compatible to reduce the effects of price competition.[72] Economides shows, also in a model without network externalities, that firms in oligopolistic competition will choose compatibility.[73]

Antitrust policy makers should not assume that markets supply insufficient product compatibility. My analysis shows that when firms compete on price, as is almost always the case in practice, they benefit from compatibility, and these benefits can outweigh the costs of providing compatibility. Firms' net benefits of providing compatibility can be greater than the social benefits, so that firms provide compatibility at least when it is socially efficient to do so. Antitrust efforts to promote compatibility when firms do not choose to do so can be socially inefficient and can result in reductions in consumers' surplus. Antitrust efforts to promote compatibility need not be in consumers' best interests.

B. Benefits from Product Differentiation Can Overshadow Network Effects

The assumption that network effects are "strong" clearly is an even stronger assumption than simply assuming that network effects exist. The "strong"

---

[71] Farrell and Saloner, 1992, at 32, supra note 7.
[72] C. Matutes and P. Regibeau, 1988, "'Mix and Match': Product Compatibility Without Network Externalities," *Rand Journal of Economics*, 19, Summer, pp. 221–234.
[73] N. Economides, 1989, "Desirability of Compatibility in the Absence of Network Externalities," *American Economic Review*, 79, December, pp. 1165–1181.

network effects requirement means that it is better to have a single network than a variety of networks. However, this powerful assumption denies the benefits to consumers of product variety.

Consumers also benefit from consuming diverse products when there are different underlying technologies. Generally, different technological solutions offer trade-offs. Depending on the purpose a glass jar, or a plastic container, or a metal can may be the best container. Each container has advantages and disadvantages. Similarly, there are diverse technologies underlying product diversity in computer software, pharmaceuticals, medical devices, lasers, engines, textiles, and so on. Public policies that require standardization eliminate the benefits of multiple technologies.

Technological progress is by no means confined to the ICTE industries. Innovation occurs in practically every industry. Innovations involve new production processes, new products, and new transaction methods in almost any sector of the economy. Advances in materials sciences, mechanical engineering, biology, chemistry, physics, optics, electronics, and aerospace translate into a broad range of process and product innovations. The claim that technology standards and compatibility generate network effects does not apply to all goods. Examples of standardization occur almost everywhere, including nuts and bolts, hot dogs and buns, engines and sparkplugs, and anything covered by the National Bureau of Standards.[74] The problems attributed to network effects are likely to be confined to the ICTE industries. Therefore, discussions of technology lock-in should not continue to make general claims that extend across the economy.

The benefits of product differentiation can overcome potential benefits from joining the same virtual network. In this case, the network effects externality does not occur because it is efficient for consumers to choose a variety of products. As a result, technology lock-in cannot occur because it is efficient for there to be multiple technologies in the market place.

Technology lock-in is an issue only if the adoption of one technology somehow prevents the adoption of another, better technology. However, for most technologies there are substitutes that deliver different features. The technologies are embodied in consumer products that are horizontally differentiated. Consumers have heterogeneous preferences and may prefer different combinations of product features.

Thus, some consumers may prefer an IBM-compatible personal computer (PC) while others may prefer an Apple computer. There may be many types of software applications that solve the same problem. Substitute goods

---

[74] See, for example, Farrell and Saloner, 1985, supra 7.

may employ different technologies, so that, for example, a voice mail, an e-mail, a text message, or an instant message all provide substitute messages. Individual consumers may differ in their preference rankings of products based on these technologies. It can be efficient for there to be multiple substitute products. Correspondingly, it can be efficient for economies to adopt multiple substitute technologies.

Moreover, a mixture of technologies can be better than a single technology. For example, a consumer is often better off with a combination of communications technologies. Many consumers subscribe to multiple communications networks even if two technologies are vertically differentiated in terms of quality, but this does not imply that there should be only one technology adopted. Technologies can have different costs. Consumers have different preferences over price – quality combinations so that multiple technologies are desirable. When having multiple technologies is efficient, the technology lock-in story breaks down. It can be desirable to adopt more than one technology. The notion that being stuck on the wrong one prevents a switch to the best one no longer applies.

C. Economies of Scale and Increasing Returns to Innovation Do Not Create Technology Lock-In

Economies of scale and the related concept of increasing returns to innovation do not create technology lock-in. Benefits that firms derive from the standardization of inputs to production do not create network externalities because firms coordinate with their suppliers to address any potential network effects.

Some sources of network effects, and hence technology lock-in, are attributed to the demand side of input markets. Firms benefit from purchasing standardized inputs, including parts and components. The use of interchangeable parts facilitates mass production and generates economies of scale.[75] The argument is that firms that purchase interchangeable parts from suppliers experience network effects on the demand side of the market for parts. If more firms adopt a particular technological standard in their production processes, they will benefit from joining a broader demand for a particular type of part. The greater the demand by auto makers for a particular type of sparkplug, the better or the cheaper will be the sparkplug. Then auto makers can employ the standard sparkplug in assembling automobiles.

[75] See, for example, Farrell and Saloner, 1986.

The economies of scale argument is another form of an indirect network effect. As Liebowitz and Margolis observe, these indirect effects are mediated by markets.[76] Firms' transactions with suppliers internalize the benefits and costs of parts. These are nothing more than standard market transactions without external effects. If firms benefit from using standardized parts, suppliers will provide them with standardized parts. Firms also can choose to coordinate their adoption of technological standards as it affects their demand for parts by tacit coordination, by merger, by the formation of trade associations, or by participation in standard-setting organizations.

The same objection applies to a related argument based on "increasing returns" that occur over time. Arthur, for example, suggests that the adoption of a technology leads to experience and improvements in the technology.[77] Nate Rosenberg refers to this effect as "learning by using."[78] This effect is necessarily dynamic because it refers to a time-consuming process of technological improvements. The technology in question is not embodied in a specific product but rather in a series of different products developed and introduced over time.

The dynamic increasing returns type of network effect requires inventive activity by firms. Arthur illustrates the concept of increasing returns by noting the "constant modification" and significant improvements in the structure, wings, capacity, and engines of the Boeing 727. Clearly, these types of improvements result from the research and development (R&D) of Boeing and its suppliers. This should not be classified as a demand-side effect because it is clearly on the production side.

The fact that improvements in technology are made by a firm suggests that the firm owns that technology. Alternatively, there may be many firms that create improvements in a technology – but that possibility suggests that the next generation of products might be better characterized as multiple technologies offered by different firms. In this way, "learning by using" seems incompatible with the assumption that the technology is unsponsored. If the technology is not sponsored and is being improved by many firms, the technology must have some sort of "open source" arrangement with

---

[76] Liebowitz and Margolis, 1994, p. 139, conclude that indirect network externalities "describe nothing more than welfare-neutral interactions that occur in properly functioning markets."

[77] See Arthur, 1989. See also R. R. Nelson and S. G. Winter, 1982, *An Evolution Theory of Economic Change*, Cambridge, MA: Belknap-Harvard University Press. See also A. B. Atkinson and J. E. Stiglitz, 1969, "A New View of Technological Change," *The Economic Journal*, 79 (315), September, pp. 573–578, and K. J. Arrow, 1962, "The Economic Implications of Learning by Doing," *The Review of Economic Studies*, 29 (3), June, pp. 155–173.

[78] N. Rosenberg, 1982, *Inside the Black Box: Technology and Economics*, Cambridge: Cambridge University Press.

a consortium of firms making improvements on a commonly available product. Accordingly, the concept of increasing returns explicitly requires ownership of the technology by firms or cooperation by firms to improve the technology.

When the benefits of a common technology are due to economies of scale in manufacturing, such cost savings are the same as any other type of economies of scale. Well-known sources of economies of scale include specialization and division of labor, amortization of fixed costs, automation and mechanization of production, and volume–surface relationships. These types of scale effects exist in practically any industry and usually require standardization of the products. When economies of scale are significant, firms will expand production through growth or mergers and acquisitions. Competition between firms will drive industries toward larger scale production. All other things equal, such competition is sufficient to guarantee that products are standardized for efficient large-scale production.

D. Switching Costs Do Not Create Lock-In

Another view of technology lock-in is based on consumer switching costs.[79] David, for example, restates the network externality argument in the context of the typewriter keyboard but adds that "The occurrence of this 'lock-in' as early as the mid-1890s does appear to have owed something also to the high costs of software "conversion" and the resulting *quasi-irreversibility of investments* in specific touch typing skills."[80] The argument is that because it is costly for consumers to adopt a new technology, they may get stuck with an old and inferior technology, and hence lock-in occurs.

The antitrust policy implications of switching costs are based on an analysis of competition. The presence of switching costs mitigates the effects of price competition. Initially, firms compete aggressively to attract customers. Once they have an installed base, the firms can raise prices and extract monopoly rents since it is costly for customers to switch to competing products. The competitive frictions created by switching costs are similar to those due to product differentiation, which confers some market power. There is no basis for government intervention in the market based on brand identification or attractive product features. There should be no basis for government intervention based on competition with switching costs.[81]

---

[79] For an overview of the literature see J. Farrell and P. Klemperer, 2006, supra note 29.

[80] David, 1985, supra note 2, at 335–336.

[81] In fact, switching costs can reduce the profits of incumbents; see G. Biglaiser, J. Crémer, and G. Dobos, 2007, "The Value of Switching Costs," Working Paper, University of North Carolina.

The argument that technology lock-in is based on past adoption costs is fundamentally flawed. David's point about the "quasi-irreversibility of investments" in learning about the old technology is simply the fallacy of sunk costs. Because learning costs are sunk, the consumer's past investments are irrelevant to the adoption decision. The only costs that matter are those related to the future adoption of a competing technology. The consumer's decision depends on the relative benefits of the two technologies in comparison with the costs of adopting the new technology.

The consumer costs of adopting a new technology certainly offset the benefits of the new technology. However, it is incorrect to interpret this as market failure. Purchasing almost any product involves some transaction costs. Changing to a new product or technology generally involves some related learning and costs of adjustment. Consider the learning costs involved in visiting a new restaurant, traveling to a new city, or buying a new car. The transaction costs and switching costs are just part of the total purchase costs. It is efficient for the consumer to take these costs into account in evaluating the net benefit of a new product. If switching costs raise the hurdle, the decision is still efficient.

Switching costs based on transaction costs, adjustment costs, or learning costs are ubiquitous. They are not confined to innovative products. These costs are simply normal economic frictions. Market institutions exist to address these costs. Companies expend resources on marketing and sales efforts to mitigate such costs. They offer price discounts to new customers to offset the costs of switching. Intermediary firms such as retailers help to reduce transaction costs. There is no basis for public policy interventions to mitigate transaction costs.

It is important to distinguish the choice between two new technologies and the decision to switch from an old technology to a new technology. Switching costs certainly do not create bias in how consumers choose between two new technologies. Consumers choose between the net benefits of the new technologies. They should evaluate all the features of the new technologies. The costs of learning and adapting to a new technology are certainly among its features and should be taken into account. If it is easier to learn to use one of two otherwise similar technologies, it is efficient to choose the one with the lower learning costs.

The economic literature generally assumes that individual consumers have heterogeneous switching costs. For example, one consumer may have higher costs of learning about a new technology that another consumer. Accordingly, some consumers find it easier to switch to new technology. Some consumers enjoy trying new products and sometimes become "early adopters." Not all consumers will switch when a new product comes along. The result is beneficial product variety, not market failure. The continual adoption of new products and technologies throughout the economy strongly suggests that if there are frictions associated with switching costs, they are an integral part of technological change.

E. Evidence Suggests Technological Change Rather Than Technology Lock-In

The persistence and acceleration of technological change throughout the economy strongly suggest that technology lock-in is imaginary. The rapid pace of technological advances in the ICT and electronics industries in comparison with other industries should be sufficient to reject the notion that technology is locked in by network effects. The extremely fast adoption of new products in the ICT and electronics industries indicates the ease of consumer adoption and the ability of markets to coordinate decisions. Such new products include laptop computers, DVDs, the iPod, and the iPhone. Clearly, developed economies lack systematic network effects.

The evidence for technology lock-in is both anecdotal and highly questionable.[82] Liebowitz and Margolis present a critical evaluation of path dependence.[83] There is scant evidence that governments are better than consumers and firms at making decisions about technology adoption.

The process of adoption of an innovation over time is referred to as *diffusion*. The diffusion of innovation has been widely studied in many disciplines.[84] Entrepreneurs and established firms create innovations by

---

[82] The main example given to show that markets fail due to technology lock-in is that of the design of the typewriter keyboard. The story of the keyboard is inaccurate as shown by Liebowitz and Margolis, 1990. As other evidence that markets tend to choose the wrong technology and then get locked in, economists usually point to the success of VHS over Beta in the market for video cassette recorders. Supposedly, the market standard VHS was inferior to the failed Beta technology but VHS was more established. However, there is substantial evidence that this example of technology lock-in is also historically and technically inaccurate; see Liebowitz and Margolis, 1999. Another questionable example of path dependence concerns the inefficiency of small rail cars used to carry coal in Great Britain. Va Nee L. Van Vlecks shows that the coal cars were part of a larger system that included local delivery by horse cart and later by truck. Large rail cars would have been likely to raise the total costs of delivery and so were efficient as part of a transportation system. See V. N. L. Van Vleck, 1997, "Delivering Coal by Road and by Rail in Great Britain: The Efficiency of the 'Silly Little Bobtailed Wagons,'" *Journal of Economic History*, 57, pp. 139–160.

[83] See Liebowitz and Margolis, 1994, 1995.

[84] See B. H. Hall, 2005, "Innovation and Diffusion," Chapter 17 in *The Oxford Handbook of Innovation*, J. Fagerberg, D. C. Mowery, and R. R. Nelson, eds., Oxford: Oxford University

commercializing inventions. After the innovation is introduced to the market, the process of diffusion begins. Sequential adoption decisions by consumers lead to dynamic patterns of total sales.

The presence of lags in the diffusion of technological advances need not indicate problems in the process of adoption. Diffusion rates depend on the costs of adopting the new technology and the costs of learning about the benefits of the new technology. Thus, adoption lags can be efficient responses to adjustment costs, learning time, and the resolution of uncertainty.[85]

Saloner and Shepard argue that network effects affect diffusion rates for innovation. They find that banks with more branches adopted automated teller machines (ATMs) more rapidly than smaller banks, even when adjusting for the size of the firm.[86] However, such a result does not indicate market failure due to network externalities. Rather, the adoption of ATMs depends on business decision by a profit-maximizing firm. Banks with a greater emphasis on retail consumers will have more branches and are likely to emphasize additional services such as the provision of access to ATMS.

Perceived "lags" in diffusion can be a matter of interpretation of the data. Building sales requires time-consuming communication with consumers through media, marketing, and sales. It also takes time for consumers to learn about the innovation, to decide whether to adopt the innovation by purchasing the product, to search across suppliers for the product, and to negotiate the purchase of the product. The time involved in communication, learning, search, and purchasing generates lags in sales. In addition, consumers may not have an immediate need for the product but may develop needs over time as their personal circumstances change. Consumers may delay their purchase of the product until they need to replace an existing product. Consumers may delay their purchase until they observe the consumption of others as a means of gathering information. Thus, imperfect information and transaction costs can help to explain the rate of diffusion.

Changes in economic variables, such as incomes and the availability and prices of substitute goods, are likely to impact diffusion rates. Finally,

---

Press, pp. 459–484. For a sociological overview, see E. M. Rogers, 1995, *Diffusion of Innovations*, 4th ed., New York: Free Press.

[85] Hall, 2005, ibid.

[86] G. Saloner and A. Shepard, 1995, "Adoption of Technologies with Network Effects: An Empirical Examination of the Adoption of Automated Teller Machines," *Rand Journal of Economics*, 26, pp. 479–501.

demographic factors that can affect diffusion rates include the rate of population growth and the age distribution of the population. The standard diffusion model can be generalized to include price effects among other market data.[87] The presence of network effects need not change the basic model of diffusion.[88]

Innovation rates are affected by changes in marketing expenditures, sales efforts, and product prices.[89] Diffusion rates also are explained by improvements in product quality, which boosts sales of the innovation. If the quality of innovation improves over time, the rate of adoption will increase as well. Increased benefits yield greater adoption levels and thus do not imply problems of diffusion. As an innovation diffuses, the number of adoptions provides innovators with information that indicates the market value of the innovation. The success of an innovation can signal the demand for improvements in product quality.

The path-dependence view argues that increased sales stimulate innovation, which creates network effects between past and future adopters. However, the decisions about product improvements are internalized by the decisions of the innovating firms. This interpretation of diffusion requires treating a series of improved products as if they represent a single innovation, although technically they comprise a series of innovations.[90]

---

[87] See particularly F. Bass, 1980, "The Relationship Between Diffusion Rates, Experience Curves, and Demand Elasticities for Consumer Durable Technological Innovation," *Journal of Business*, 53, July, pp. 551–567. See also S. Kalish, 1983, "Monopolistic Pricing with Dynamic Demand and Production Costs," *Marketing Science*, 2, Spring, pp. 135–159.

[88] The network effects model can also be included in the diffusion equation. Let $n^*(p)$ be the equilibrium adoption level generated by the network effects model (see Figure 4.1) Let a and b be fixed parameters and let $n(t)$ be the cumulative sales at time t. Then, the diffusion rate can be written as

$$\frac{dn(t)}{dt} = (a + bn(t))(n^*(p) - n(t)).$$

Let $n(0) = n_0$ be given. The dependence of the rate of adjustment on cumulative sales reflects the effects of sales on information received by prospective consumers. The diffusion rate yields a logistic curve that relates cumulative sales to time.

[89] For an overview of diffusion models in marketing, see Chapter 10 in G. L. Lilien, P. Kotler, and K. S. Moorthy, 1992, *Marketing Models*, Englewood Cliffs, NJ: Prentice-Hall, especially the review of work on advertising, prices, and sales effort on p. 473. The standard model of the diffusion of an innovation is due to F. Bass, 1969, "A New Product Growth Model for Consumer Durables," *Management Science* 15, January, pp. 215–227.

[90] This might apply to the often-cited example of improvements in Boeing aircraft; see Hall, 2005, ibid, p. 470; N. Rosenberg, 1972, "Factors Affecting the Diffusion of Technology," *Explorations in Economic History*, 10, pp. 3–33, and N. Rosenberg, 1982, "Learning by Using," in *Inside the Black Box*, N. Rosenberg, ed., Cambridge: Cambridge University Press, pp. 120–140.

V. Antitrust Implications of Technology Lock-In

Advocates of technology lock-in suggest that it provides an instrument of monopolization because network effects attract consumers to one technology standard. For similar reasons, it is argued that technology lock-in is an instrument of exclusion because consumers will not switch to products offered by entrants due to excess inertia. In addition, technology lock-in is said to provide incentives for monopolization and exclusion since firms will seek to be the technology winner.

The technology lock-in and network effects concepts are highly influential in antitrust policy making. For example, the European Commission's Microsoft decision mentions lock-in six times and network effects thirty-four times. In servers, the Commission argued that Microsoft should supply software interoperability information to its competitors because "Technologies that will lead to a further lock-in into Microsoft's products at the work group server and client PC level are quickly gaining traction in the market."[91] With regard to media players, the Commission stated that "The network effects characterizing the media software market . . . translate into entry barriers for new entrants."[92]

A. Technology Lock-In and Monopolization

The technology lock-in literature suggests that network effects change the connection between competition and information disclosure. According to this view, since consumer expectations drive the outcome, firms will mislead consumers. If consumers cannot coordinate effectively, imperfect expectations will lead to inefficient technology adoption decisions. If the lower quality innovation is expected to win, it will – leading to an inefficient outcome.[93] The heart of the argument is that firms will seek to manage consumer expectations so as to obtain a monopoly.

Firms compete not only through prices, product quality, and innovation. They also compete in the supply of information. Firms normally engage in advertising and sales efforts to attract customers. Such competition tends to increase the amount of information that is made available to consumers. Competitors will point out inaccuracies in each others' marketing

---

[91] Commission Decision at p. 207, supra note 1.
[92] Commission Decision at p. 115, supra note 1.
[93] See S. M. Besen and J. Farrell, 1994, "Choosing How to Compete: Strategies and Tactics in Standardization," *Journal of Economic Perspectives*, 8, Spring, pp. 117–131, and the references therein.

campaigns. When competitors disclose different information about product features, consumers will seek additional disclosures to aid in comparison shopping. The intensity of competition is likely to lead to greater amounts of information for consumers.

How one interprets the management of expectations is critical. One interpretation of the management of expectations is positive. Firms will provide information to consumers that helps the consumers to coordinate their technology adoption decisions. The result is "spontaneous order." The market thus captures the benefits of network effects. Consumers, without being coerced, use the signals provided by firms to choose the best technology and the market functions efficiently. The result is the intermediation of network effects and well-informed technology adoption decisions.

The other interpretation of management of expectations is a negative one. Besen and Farrell conclude that

[B]ecause the prize is so tempting, sponsors may compete fiercely to have their technologies become the standard, and this competition will generally dissipate part – perhaps a large part – of the potential gains.[94]

The question is whether market incentives for intense competition enhance economic efficiency or somehow contribute to anticompetitive behavior.

The "tempting prize" argument is not sufficient to establish incentives for monopolization and exclusion. Monopoly profits could be earned in any industry, whether or not network effects are present. There is no evidence to suggest that potential profits in network industries are any greater than in any other industry. Network industries provide profits that are neither more nor less tempting than in other industries. Competition exists throughout the economy and should have the effect of equalizing rates of return across industries. There are many factors that affect profitability and opportunities for entry. It is highly unlikely that network industries are systematically more tempting than other industries.

The "tempting prize" argument suggests that exclusion yields greater returns in an industry in which technology standards matter. Technological change occurs throughout the economy; it is not confined to any specific industry. Scientific progress in computers, software, biotechnology, chemistry, physics, electronics, materials sciences, and other areas affect multiple industries. Technology standards play an important role wherever technological change occurs because there are often many ways to configure

[94] Besen and Farrell, 1994, ibid, at p. 119.

products and production processes. There is no reason to suppose a priori that standards matter more in particular sectors of the economy.

Besen and Farrell apply the "tempting prize" argument to characterize potential competitive strategies of firms that have consequences of monopolization and exclusion. They identify four strategies. Competing firms whose products have incompatible technologies may offer low "penetration" prices to build market share; they try to attract the suppliers of complements, they preannounce new products, and they offer guarantees of low prices in the future.[95]

These four strategies do not provide a useful guide for antitrust policy because they are difficult or impossible to distinguish from normal forms of vigorous competition in any industry. They certainly do not appear unique to network industries.

Firms generally offer discounts to introduce new products, helping consumers to learn about new product features or building new brands. Firms generally enjoy benefits from producers of complementary products. Firms often announce new products whether to attract the attention of potential customers, to raise money from investors, or to signal to competitors. Vaporware is not confined to computer hardware and software. Firms often enter into contracts with customers that involve guarantees of future prices. These activities are not directly related to technology standards.

Why do some firms, and the technology their products embody, succeed while others fail? There are many explanations. The most appealing possibility is that the market test is effective. Better products win because many consumers, firms, and market intermediaries evaluate the technology. The winning technology reflects the combination of information gathering and decisions by a large number of economic agents. As with the efficient market hypothesis in financial markets, the prices of technology products embody all of the information available to market participants. Refuting the efficient market hypothesis for technology products would require a demonstration that the information available to market participants can be concealed or distorted or that markets cannot make effective use of the information.

Additional factors affect market outcomes in markets for technology without necessarily suggesting inefficiency. Firms offering the technology may be highly innovative and well managed. The firm may be located in a country that has a comparative advantage in developing the technology or in producing the good that employs the technology. The efficiency of the outcome depends on the benefits received by the final consumer.

---

[95] Besen and Farrell, 1994, ibid, at pp. 122–124.

For example, the success of the Japanese consumer electronics industry in the decade 1975 to 1985 depended on technologies developed by the Sony Corporation.[96] Also, Japanese companies supplied Europe with computer systems and provided the United States with memory chips.[97] At the same time, Europe's computer and consumer electronics industries declined significantly, as did the U.S. consumer electronics industry.[98] However, Japanese firms were not competitive internationally in chemicals and pharmaceuticals.[99] Also, U.S. firms were highly successful in the production of microprocessors, particularly Intel, Motorola, and Texas Instruments.

These systematic geographic aspects of technological innovation and diffusion transcend notions of network effects and imperfect competition. First-movers were not successful in either consumer electronics or in computers. For example, U.S. companies such as RCA, Philco, CBS, and Zenith were displaced b Japanese companies, particularly Sony and Matsushita. Among the underlying geographic aspects of comparative advantage are differences in scientific invention, product development capabilities, and management skills. The specializations observed in different countries do not necessarily reflect absolute advantages in skills but instead depend on the returns to specialization in particular activities including invention, commercial development, and manufacturing. In addition, relative wages combined with relative technological efficiency determine specialization and the direction of international trade.

B. Technology Lock-In and Exclusion

Technology lock-in also can lead to misguided antitrust policy toward exclusion. The policy prescription begins with the assumption that a given firm holds a dominant market position due to technology lock-in. Since network effects underpin the technology lock-in model, this effectively assumes that the firm's dominant position is due to network effects. The next step is to characterize the dominant firm's exclusionary behavior based on the network effects model.

If the dominant firm does not license that technology or otherwise make its technology available to its competitors, then that firm is alleged to exclude others from the market. In this context, establishing exclusionary behavior

---

[96] See A.D. Chandler, 2001, *Inventing The Electronic Century*, New York: Free Press, at p. 2.
[97] Chandler, 2001, ibid.
[98] Chandler, 2001, ibid. Chandler highlights the importance of various firm capabilities in R&D, marketing, production, and management.
[99] Chandler, 2001, ibid, p. 238.

does not require either an intent to exclude or actions to exclude. There is no need for a smoking gun. Rather, antitrust authorities merely would have to show that a firm does not make its technology available to others for purposes of interconnection or interoperability.

Antitrust authorities first need to establish the preconditions for technology lock-in, namely, the potential presence of network effects. It is perhaps not surprising that antitrust authorities tend to confine their efforts to the ICTE industries. Next, antitrust authorities need to identify a leading firm in the industry. There is no need to determine how the leading firm obtained its dominant position. Having a dominant position in itself is not a violation of antitrust law. The leading firm may have been successful due to its offering better products, better service, and lower prices.

By assuming or perhaps identifying the presence of network effects, however, antitrust authorities can suggest that the dominant position is protected by technology lock-in. Finally, there is a need for competitors to request access to the leading firm's technology. Refusing such a request, or failing to comply, becomes the necessary monopolizing behavior that violates antitrust law. A dominant firm's refusal to supply access to technology to entrants and other competitors also can be identified as exclusionary behavior. Thus, technology lock-in justifies the classification of refusals to supply access to technology as anticompetitive behavior. The result is that innovation and protection of intellectual property constitute anticompetitive behavior in markets that may exhibit network effects. Thus, technology lock-in mistakenly interprets vigorous competition by innovative firms as anticompetitive behavior.

Recall that interconnectivity or interoperability eliminates the problem of network effects that underlies the technology lock-in problem. Here again, failure to interconnect or to interoperate provides evidence of exclusionary behavior based on the technology lock-in view. Antitrust authorities need only establish that network effects exist and that products do not interconnect or interoperate fully. This relieves antitrust authorities from the burden of either establishing an intent to exclude or identifying exclusionary behavior. However, interconnection or interoperability can be costly, so that it need not be socially efficient. Failure to provide full interoperability may simply be an efficient response to these costs by competitive firms as was demonstrated earlier.

By requiring the standardization necessary for full interconnection or interoperability, antitrust authorities may discourage firms from creating new products. Consumers may benefit from product variety even with the potential loss of some network effects. The result of antitrust guided by technology lock-in again is stifling of innovation and reduction of product variety. Antitrust enforcement based on lock-in creates a self-fulfilling prophecy. Requiring technologies to interconnect or interoperate can restrict new technologies to be those that fit with existing technologies. The result is that technology lock-in occurs as a result of antitrust enforcement.

The focus on innovative industries as a source of exclusionary behavior is likely to be misplaced. Anton and Yao argue that constant and dramatic innovation, and large benefits from standardization should reduce antitrust concerns about high-tech industries. They further suggest that "Anticompetitive effects of interface standards are likely to be a matter of degree (raising costs differentially) rather than of exclusion."[100]

Hovenkamp argues that in network markets, cartels will raise prices, restrain innovation, and exclude others because firms will be more reluctant to defect from a cartel.[101] His argument is that a cartel enforces collusion by making technology standards available to members of the cartel. Those who do not participate in the cartel are excluded from the technology standard and must adopt a competing standard. Even if such a strategy made sense economically, this type of exclusionary behavior would not be very difficult to detect.

However, there do not appear to be economic returns to using technology standards for collusion. Network effects are reciprocal. Firms in the cartel would be harmed by excluding competitors from a technology standard. The customers of the excluded firms would be offered a competing technology. This would reduce the number of consumers who purchase the technology with the cartel's standard. The threat of exclusion is diminished if the effect of the exclusion is to harm the members of the cartel. The benefits to the cartel from the exclusion would need to exceed the effects of reducing the number of consumers who purchase the technology. In addition, the excluded firms would embrace a competing technology standard, which would strengthen the competing standard.

If there are network effects from embracing a common standard, firms will cooperate either by negotiating a technology standard or by licensing their technology. Myriad industry standards committees exist for all types of technological standards.[102] With many firms involved, the transaction costs of negotiating a standard are likely to be substantial. However,

---

[100] Anton and Yao, 1995 at 263.

[101] Hovenkamp at 2005, p. 281.

[102] See www.consortiuminfo.org for a list of more than 460 consortia, accredited standards bodies, and open source projects.

when the benefits of standardization are sufficiently high, there may be returns to standardization through bargaining. Standard-setting organizations (SSOs) increase competition between firms within the standard. Mark Lemley argues that SSOs are an instrument of private ordering and suggests that antitrust policy may unduly restrict their activities.[103]

Standard-setting organizations involve coordination between the firms in the industry. Although this may involve smaller numbers of players in comparison with coordination between many consumers, the transaction costs of coordination within standard-setting bodies may be high. These costs are likely to increase if coordination is adversarial and if intellectual property rights are not well defined. Conflicts over intellectual property rights may lead to legal challenges to SSO patents.[104] There is evidence that SSOs are capable of selecting and promoting successful technologies.[105]

The alternative to cooperative standard setting is competition between standards. Standards competition provides a market test of alternative technologies. Even though a common technology standard provides benefits due to network effects, there may be greater benefits from competition. Firms offering competing technology standards have an incentive to improve the quality of the innovations. Competing standards are likely to represent substantially different technologies that offer consumers different trade-offs in terms of product features.

Determining the best technology requires knowledge of how consumers evaluate the trade-offs between product features. Individual consumers are the most qualified to determine their own preferences over product features. Accordingly, there is no effective substitute for a market test for differentiated technologies. Firms compete to promote a technology standard by employing mechanisms of spontaneous order, including prices, marketing, and sales. Hayek points out that "scientific discoveries have ample time to

---

[103] Mark A. Lemley, 2002, "Intellectual Property Rights and Standard-Setting Organizations," Boalt Hall Working Papers in Public Law, UC Berkeley.

[104] Simcoe et al. found that "SSO patents have a relatively high litigation rate, and that SSO patents assigned to small firms are litigated more often than those of large publicly-traded firms" (T. S. Simcoe, S. J. H. Graham, and M. Feldman, 2007, "Competing on Standards: Entrepreneurship, Intellectual Property and the Platform Standard," NBER Working Paper No. 13632, November).

[105] See M. Rysman and T. S. Simcoe, 2007, "Patents and the Performance of Voluntary Standard Setting Organizations," Boston University, Department of Economics Working Paper, June. However, Simcoe found that the Internet Engineering Task Force (IETF) experienced a slowdown in standards production between 1993 and 2003 due to "distributional conflicts created by the increasing commercialization of the Internet during that time period" (T. S. Simcoe, 2006, "Standard Setting Committees," Working Paper, Rotman School of Management, University of Toronto, December).

demonstrate their value." In contrast, economic competition "exhibits a method of discovering particular temporary circumstances." Market competition between technologies is necessary precisely because we cannot know the winner in advance. Hayek emphasizes that "competition is important primarily as a discovery procedure whereby entrepreneurs constantly search for unexploited opportunities."[106]

Technology alliances provide a middle ground between cooperative standard setting and competing standards. Firms within alliances share a common technology and reap the benefits of network effects. Alliances compete with each other to establish a successful standard, thereby generating consumer benefits from competing prices and product improvements. The existence of such technology alliances in a wide variety of industries suggests that markets provide an efficient mix of cooperation and competition. The sizes of the alliances reflect the trade-offs between the benefits of common technology standards and the benefits of market tests of alternative technologies.

VI. Conclusion

Markets can be expected to guide the adoption of technology efficiently. Consumers and firms will pursue their economic self-interests in technology adoption decisions. Small numbers of consumers can easily coordinate their technology adoption decisions to take advantage of network effects. When there are large numbers of consumers, firms and other innovation intermediaries help to coordinate innovation adoption. A contracting environment that would produce network externalities is unrealistic. Absent such assumed network externalities, there are no market failures in technology adoption. Consumers and firms make efficient choices among products and innovations. As a result, technology is "unlocked."

The potential impact of network effects on technology adoption decisions are confined to the ICTE industries. These industries have developed market institutions that address such potential external benefits. As a result, the technology adoption biases ascribed to network effects have limited impact and should not drive public policy toward innovation in other industries. Evidence for lock-in is deficient, while innovation is abundant and continual. Innovation is a critical driver of economic growth and prosperity.

---

[106] F. A. Hayek, 2002, "Competition as a Discovery Procedure," *Quarterly Journal of Austrian Economics*, 5, Fall, pp. 9–23.

Even if it could be demonstrated that the economy was on the wrong path of technology adoption, is public policy the solution? Market adoption of innovations is a complex process in which individual consumers choose what products to buy, firms choose what products to supply, and inventors choose directions for R&D. As Schumpeter observed, entrepreneurs choose to innovate by making "new combinations" and offering new products, production processes, and transaction methods.

Governments are notoriously inept at picking technology winners. Understanding technology requires extensive scientific and technical knowledge. Government agencies cannot expect to replicate or improve on private sector knowledge. Technological innovation is uncertain by its very nature because it is based on scientific discoveries. The benefits of new technologies and the returns to commercial development also are uncertain. Friedrich Hayek emphasized that individuals have better information about conditions that apply to them and will be better at decision making than centralized government planners. Public policy makers lack the necessary information about the preferences of consumers, the objectives of firms, the ideas of inventors, and the insights of entrepreneurs.

The notion that markets get locked in to inferior technologies would suggest that the government should replace clear winners in the market place with what government planners think would be superior technology. As a consequence, government planners may feel justified in pursuing industrial policies that subsidize specific technologies or protecting domestic industries against international competition from companies using distinct technologies. Government planners would be expected to solve the impossible problem of predicting technological change, as opposed to multiple competing technologies offered by markets. Government agencies are unlikely to reflect accurately the diversity of customer preferences about new products. The notion of lock-in has another dangerous implication. If markets are consistently locked into inefficient choices, then antitrust policy should target successful high-tech companies that presumably suppressed technologies offered by competitors.

The technology lock-in view is comparable to many other questionable justifications for government intervention in technology markets. Among these justifications is the recommendation that the government should support innovative infant industries through industrial policy to protect firms from international competition as they try to catch up. Others assert that the government should set standards for new technologies because firms cannot coordinate standards. Some advocates of government intervention assert that public policy makers are better able than markets at identifying new technologies by picking winners. One recommendation that is connected to debates over patents and copyrights suggests that governments should strongly limit intellectual property rights in innovation so as to capture the benefits of public goods. Closely related to the network effects assumption is the traditional argument that governments should subsidize those innovations that have positive externalities, since markets may not adjust for the benefits of spillovers. Technology lock-in suffers, as does each of these justifications, from the danger that such government intervention will reduce incentives for innovation. This is the opposite of the intended result.

Antitrust policy toward lock-in risks causing the very problem that it tries to solve. Private sector experimentation is particularly valuable in resolving uncertainties in discovering and developing new technologies. Antitrust policy that targets successful innovators threatens to reduce such experimentation. By enforcing standardization, antitrust discourages the type of innovation that generates product variety. By requiring successful firms to disclose intellectual property, antitrust damages incentives to innovate both for leading firms and for their competitors. By requiring compatibility, antitrust raises prices and costs while discouraging the development of unique proprietary systems. By limiting the ability of successful firms to add product features and to bundle products, antitrust reduces incentives to improve technologies. Avoiding such misguided antitrust policies allows competitive markets to continue unlocking technology.

5

Creative Construction

Assimilation, Specialization, and the Technology
Life Cycle

Marco Iansiti and Gregory L. Richards

I. Introduction and Overview

All too often, practitioners, pundits, and academics take a pessimistic view of the value and longevity of today's technologies. We all fall in love with new, apparently "disruptive" technologies, like Linux or on-line music distribution, and preach the death of established organizations and existing capabilities. However, the reality is often different and more subtle: The old mantra of "creative destruction" seldom applies in a holistic fashion.[1] Old technologies and capabilities rarely disappear – they instead evolve and become the building blocks of tomorrow's innovations. They provide crucial, enduring value to established firms, new entrepreneurs, and consumers alike. This simple realization has crucial implications for managers and policy makers.

This chapter takes a new look at the innovation life cycle and its implications for competition and public policy. It draws from existing literature, case studies, and product innovation data to illustrate the workings of technological "assimilation," namely, how technological innovations that were once marketed as individual products become integrated into broader platforms, which in turn provide the building blocks of further innovation. As we will illustrate through our examples, assimilation can take various forms and impact various levels of integration, such as the incorporation of capabilities into a new distribution platform, the licensing of complementary capabilities, and, in some cases, acquisitions of entire companies with complementary products or technology assets. Not only are the pervasive forces of technological assimilation essential to the viability of many innovative products and industries, they often provide the basis

---

[1] Schumpeter, J. 1939. *Business Cycles: A Theoretical, Historical and Statistical Analysis of the Capitalist Process.* Porcupine Press.

for the commercial feasibility of future innovations that build on prior innovations.

Relying on the findings of recent patent citation studies, our chapter also finds that certain "core" innovations serve as a broad foundation for the long-term feasibility of future generations of innovative products, by providing resources that enable and sustain a proliferation of specialized applications over time. Research has shown that a very small percentage of all patents filed in the United States generate a disproportionately large volume of all forward citations, suggesting that core technologies form an integral part of successive innovation cycles. Specific "keystone" strategies followed by firms can increase the dissemination of such core innovations in an industry, shaping the evolution of sometimes vast ecosystems of beneficiaries.[2]

The final section of the chapter summarizes public policy implications and some of the enduring public benefits of technology assimilation for both producers and end users. Examples of such multifaceted benefits include lower entry barriers, higher adoption rates, affordable access, and broader choice in the selection of goods and services. These long-term beneficial outcomes suggest that the assimilation dynamic provides new opportunities for many players, fuels competition, and provides a foundation for future specialization and "niche creation."

II. Technological Assimilation

A. The Concept of Technological Assimilation

We begin our discussion by situating our focus on technological assimilation within the vast literature on innovation. Formal innovation studies constitute an extensive and rapidly growing body of scholarship that addresses topics ranging from understanding the sources of innovation and determinants of industry change,[3] to the potentially disruptive impact of innovation on existing markets and incumbent firms,[4] to the role and impact

[2] Iansiti, M. and R. Levien. 2004. *The Keystone Advantage* (Harvard Business School Press).

[3] Schumpeter, J. 1939. *Business Cycles: A Theoretical, Historical and Statistical Analysis of the Capitalist Process.* Porcupine Press; Abernathy, W. and J. Utterback. 1978. Patterns of Industrial Innovation. *Technology Review.* 80: 40–47; Von Hippel, E. 1988. *The Sources of Innovation* (Oxford University Press); Anderson, P. and M. Tushman. 1990. Technological Discontinuities and Dominant Designs: A Cyclical Model of Technological Change. *Administrative Science Quarterly*, 35: 604–633; Christensen, C. 1997. *The Innovator's Dilemma: When New Technologies Cause Great Firms to Fail* (Harvard Business School Press).

[4] Foster, R. 1986. *Innovation: The Attackers' Advantage* Summit Books; Christensen, C. 1997. *The Innovator's Dilemma: When New Technologies Cause Great Firms to Fail* (Harvard

of user adoption in disseminating technological innovation[5,6,7]; Moore 1999).[8]

Studies have also addressed the economic incentives and regulatory policies that promote innovation[9] and the valuation metrics of innovative output.[10] In addition, management studies have addressed the organizational aspects of innovation, such as how to best implement and manage innovation,[11] and how firms can strategically profit from commercializing innovative ideas.[12]

Business School Press); Henderson, R. and K. B. Clark. 1990. Architectural Innovation: The Reconfiguration of Existing Product Technologies and the Failure of Established Firms. *Administrative Science Quarterly*, 35: 9–30.

5 Gandal, N. 1994. Hedonic Price Indexes for Spreadsheets and an Empirical Test for Network Externalities. *RAND Journal of Economics*, 25(1):160–170.

6 Katz, M. L. and C. Shapiro. 1986. Technology Adoption in the Presence of Network Externalities. *Journal of Political Economy*, 94: 822–841; Katz, M. L. and C. Shapiro. 1994. Systems Competition and Network Effects. *Journal of Economic Perspectives*, 8: 2.

7 Rogers, E. 1995, 2003. *Diffusion of Innovations* (The Free Press).

8 Von Hippel, E. 2005. *Democratizing Innovation* (MIT Press).

9 Teece, D. J. 1986. Profiting from Technological Innovation: Implications for Integration, Collaboration, Licensing and Public Policy. *Research Policy*. 15: 295–305; Gallini, N. and S. Scotchmer. 2002. Intellectual Property: When Is It the Best Incentive System? In Jaffe, A., J. Lerner, and S. Stern (eds.), *Innovation Policy and the Economy*, Vol. 2 (MIT Press); Hall, B. and R. Ziedonis. 2001. The Effects of Strengthening Patent Rights on Firms Engaged in Cumulative Innovation: Insights from the Semiconductor Industry [working draft]; Scotchmer, S. 2004. *Innovation and Incentives* (MIT Press); Murray, F. and S. O'Mahony. 2007. *Exploring the Foundations of Cumulative Innovation: Implications for Organization Science. Organization Science*, 18: 1006–1021.

10 Pavitt, K. 1988. Uses and Abuses of Patent Statistics. In van Raan, A. F. J. (ed.) *Handbook of Quantitative Studies of Science and Technology* (Elsevier Science Publishers); Scotchmer, S. 1991. Standing on the Shoulders of Giants: Cumulative Research and the Patent Law. *The Journal of Economic Perspectives*, 5: 1; OECD. 1995. The Measurement of Scientific and Technological Activities: Proposed Guidelines for Collecting and Interpreting Technological Innovation Data. Oslo Manual. 2nd edition, DSTI, OECD / European Commission Eurostat, Paris; Hall, B. and R. Ziedonis. 2001. The Effects of Strengthening Patent Rights on Firms Engaged in Cumulative Innovation: Insights from the Semiconductor Industry [working draft]; Godin, B. 2002. The Rise of Innovation Surveys: Measuring A Fuzzy Concept. Project on the History and Sociology of S&T Statistics, Working Paper No. 16, OST, INRS/CIRST, Montréal, Canada.

11 Chesbrough, H. and Teece, D. 1996. Organizing for Innovation: When Is Virtual Virtuous? *Harvard Business Review*. 8: 127–135; Iansiti, M. 1998. *Technology Integration* (Harvard Business School Press); Tushman, M. L. and C. A. O'Reilly. 2002. *Winning Through Innovation: A Practical Guide to Leading Organizational Change and Renewal* (Harvard Business School Press).

12 Teece, D. J. 2000. Strategies for Managing Knowledge Assets: The Role of Firm Structure and Industrial Context. *Long Range Planning* 33: 35–54; Chakravorti, B. 2003. *The Slow Pace of Fast Change: Bringing Innovations to Market in a Connected World* (Harvard Business School Press); Davila, T., M. J. Epstein, and R. Shelton. 2006. Making Innovation Work: How to Manage It, Measure It, and Profit from It* (Wharton School Publishing).

The dominant view in many existing studies of innovation has been to frame the innovation life cycle as a series of discontinuous waves. Starting from Schumpeter's seminal work, innovations have been viewed to promote "creative destruction," effectively replacing older solutions. This classic "Schumpeterian" view is often reinforced by practitioners and academics, ranging from Foster to Christensen.[13] In this context, innovations are viewed largely as a threat to the status quo, as new technology waves, S-curves, and disruptive forces move quickly to displace established products, technologies, and capabilities. These waves begin with product innovation, which replaces the old solution, culminate in the establishment of a new dominant design,[14] and evolve through saturation with an increased focus on process innovation in incremental steps. Under this view, new technologies,[15] architectures (Henderson and Clark 1990), and business models[16] threaten the established wave and often replace it with new ones.

The reality is more complex than just discontinuous waves of newer, better technologies. Studies have established that the innovation process also involves aggregating existing technology elements in new combinations.[17] As surveyed in Fleming and Sorensen's[18] recent work, several studies have conceived of the innovation process as the "combining of technological components in a novel manner" (Fleming and Sorensen's (2004)).[19] For

---

[13] Foster, R. 1986. *Innovation: The Attackers' Advantage* Summit Books; Christensen, C. 1997. *The Innovator's Dilemma: When New Technologies Cause Great Firms to Fail* (Harvard Business School Press).

[14] Abernathy, W. and J. Utterback. 1978. *Patterns of Industrial Innovation. Technology Review.* 80: 40–47.

[15] Anderson, P. and M. Tushman. 1990. Technological Discontinuities and Dominant Designs: A Cyclical Model of Technological Change. *Administrative Science Quarterly*, 35: 604–633; Christensen, C. 1997. *The Innovator's Dilemma: When New Technologies Cause Great Firms to Fail* (Harvard Business School Press); Christensen, C. 2004. *Seeing What's Next: Using Theories of Innovation to Predict Industry Change* (Harvard Business School Press).

[16] Chesbrough, H. 2006. *Open Innovation: Researching a New Paradigm* (Oxford University Press).

[17] Henderson, R. and K. B. Clark. 1990. Architectural Innovation: The Reconfiguration of Existing Product Technologies and the Failure of Established Firms. *Administrative Science Quarterly*, 35: 9–30; Iansiti, M. and T. Khanna. 1995. Technological Evolution, System Architecture and Obsolescence of Firm Capabilities. *Oxford Journals: Industrial and Corporate Change*, 4: 2; Fleming, L. and O. Sorensen. 2004. Science as a Map in Technological Search. *Strategic Management Journal* 25: 909–928.

[18] Fleming, L. and O. Sorensen. 2004. Science as a Map in Technological Search. *Strategic Management Journal* 25: 909–928.

[19] Nelson, R. and S. Winter. 1982. *An Evolutionary Theory of Economic Change* (Harvard University Press).

example, Pisano[20] explains how biotechnology's use of combinatorial methods, which involve assembling chemical "building blocks" in every possible combination, enhanced by automated search and testing tools, has vastly increased the scientific community's weekly yield of molecular compounds for screening purposes, from 100 compounds 20 years ago to one million compounds today. This technological advance, in turn, has greatly raised the probability of discovering new life-saving drugs through such experimental combinatory methods.

Within the organizational context of product development, innovation through combination or technology integration also involves an informed selection process, the goal of which is to achieve a "fit" between an array of technology options and a given application context.[21] In this view, a firm's ability to manage the integration of new and old technologies can lead it to adapt to a changing competitive landscape. Baldwin and Clark[22] greatly expand on these notions by showing how the recombination of technology components drives the evolution of "industry clusters," in which multiple firms and industry segments coexist and build on technologies introduced by key firms. Another line of research using patent studies has also addressed this sequential dimension of innovation, that is, how innovations consequently spur further generations of innovation that extend this cumulative prior knowledge.[23]

Building on these frameworks, we argue in this chapter that technology assimilation, not technology obsolescence and displacement, is at the heart of what has commonly been known as the innovation life cycle.[24] Subsequent waves of change are not discontinuous, but indeed closely interrelated. Under this new approach, the innovation life cycle involves a selective assimilation of novel technologies into broader capabilities, which consequently gives rise to conditions that enable further innovation to occur, typically in increasingly specialized applications.[25]

---

[20] Pisano, G. 2006. Science Business: The Promise, The Reality, and the Future of Biotech. (Harvard Business School Press).

[21] Iansiti, M. 1998. *Technology Integration* (Harvard Business School Press).

[22] Baldwin, C. Y. and K. B. Clark. 1997. Managing in the Age of Modularity. *Harvard Business Review* (June). 5: 84–93.

[23] Scotchmer, S. 1991. Standing on the Shoulders of Giants: Cumulative Research and the Patent Law. *The Journal of Economic Perspectives*, 5: 1.

[24] Abernathy, W. and J. Utterback. 1978. Patterns of Industrial Innovation. *Technology Review*. 80: 40–47.

[25] While the comprehensive research needed to conclusively establish this premise is beyond the scope of this chapter, the concept of innovation predicated on the integration of multiple existing capabilities has parallels in other knowledge domains. For instance, the philosophical term "synthesis" is understood to be an integration of two or more elements

B. Foundational Innovations

Not all innovations have the same impact over time. Some innovations endure and play a truly "foundational" role in spawning a multitude of new innovations. One example is the impact of UNIX on subsequent operating systems. This impact is felt most directly in the development of the Linux server operating system (Linux O/S). Linux is perceived by many in the business and developer communities as one of the greatest (and most "disruptive") software "innovations." However, Linux versions are predominantly characterized by components and capabilities that replicate or draw from key functionalities contained in UNIX.[26] The Linux kernel bears strong resemblances to its UNIX predecessor.[27] Industry sources have noted that Linux operates in a similar fashion as UNIX, and that it contains UNIX-like features and commands. At least one commentator has noted that Linux resembles a UNIX variant as much as any UNIX variant resembles any other. Another study notes that Linux is a "re-implementation of UNIX" and that "the conscious choices ... to 'clone' pieces of UNIX enabled Linux to bootstrap adoption" based on the availability of "complementary assets" that support both systems.[28]

It is interesting to note that the assimilation of UNIX capabilities into Linux UNIX has provided interesting opportunities for existing firms. In contrast, with a view implying the inevitable disruption of established competitors, we have seen firms with significant strength in UNIX development and in the UNIX market – such as IBM and Novell – become leaders in the Linux environment.

embodying a new creation. In the biology context, "some authors argue that the process of integration may be an important and underappreciated driver of biological evolution – at least as important as mutation" (Iansiti 2004, citing L. Margulis and D. Sagan, *Acquiring Genomes: A Theory of the Origins of Species* [New York: Basic Books 2002]).

26 These include, for example, the journal file system (JFS) that was initially developed for UNIX in 1991 and which subsequently appeared in the 2.4 Linux kernel in 2001. Similarly, the logical volume manager (LVM) developed for UNIX in 1992 was also included in the 2.4 Linux kernel.

27 This appears to be have been a conscious decision to develop the Linux kernel in the Minix environment based on UNIX principles. In his autobiography *Just for Fun*, 2001 (HarperCollins) Linux's founder, Linus Torvalds, describes his early development work on the Linux kernel: "I was reading the standards from either the Sun OS manual or various books, just picking off system calls one by one and trying to make something that worked ... " (Chapter 7).

28 Dedrick, J. and J. West. 2003. Why Firms Adopt Open Source Platforms: A Grounded Theory of Innovation and Standards Adoption. Standard Making: A Critical Research Frontier for Information Systems MISQ Special Issue Workshop, Seattle, December, pp. 236–257.

Another way in which companies such as IBM deploy their advantage in foundational innovations is through licensing them to other companies; IBM received $1.9 billion in royalty payments for its intellectual property in 2001.[29] Other firms – Sun may be an example – have fared much less well, which implies that performance may be a function of firm conduct, not of the structure of technological change.

Patent analysis provides a way to more systematically indentify foundational innovations. Patents have generally been recognized as a reliable measure of innovation by both academic researchers and policy makers.[30,31] Studies have also shown how patents directly enable the innovation process, by disclosing prior research findings and disseminating this information publicly.[32] Building on this research about the information-sharing role of patents, more recent studies have focused on forensically mapping the innovation process by examining linkages between patent citations.[33]

The consistent findings among these patent citation studies support the notion that there exist certain foundational innovations that become assimilated into a large variety of future innovations. Specifically, these studies demonstrate a strong correlation between highly cited patents[34] and their

---

[29] Chesbrough, H. 2006. *Open Innovation: Researching a New Paradigm* (Oxford University Press).

[30] For example, the European Trend Chart, which monitors inventive activity in Europe, incorporates two patent-based indicators. See European Commission 2006, European Innovation Progress Report/Trendchart.

[31] Basberg, B. 1987. Patents and the Measurement of Technological Change: A Survey of the Literature. *Research Policy,* 16: 131–141; Griliches, Z. 1990. Patent Statistics as Economic Indicators. *Journal of Economic Literature,* 28: 4; Stuart, T. E. and J. M. Podolny. 1996. Local Search and the Evolution of Technological Capabilities. *Strategic Management Journal,* 17: 21–38.

[32] Ernst, H. 1997. The Use of Patent Data for Technological Forecasting: The Diffusion of CNC-Technology in the Machine Tool Industry. *Small Business Economics* 9:4; Arundel, A. 1999. How Useful Are Patent Databases to SMEs as a Source of Technical Information? In Inzelt A. and J. Hilton (eds.), *Technology Transfer: From Invention to Innovation,* Nato ASI Series 4: Science and Technology Policy, Vol 19, pp. 195–206 (Kluwer Academic Publishers); Arundel, A. and I. Kabla. 2000. Patenting Strategies of European firms: An Analysis of Survey Data, in Allegrezza S. and H. Serbat (eds.), *The Econometrics of Patents,* Applied Econometrics Association series.

[33] Hall B. 2002. "The Financing of Research and Development," Oxford Review of Economic Policy 18, No. 1, pp. 35–51; Hall, B. 2004. Patent Citations as Knowledge Flow Indicators. NBER.

[34] The "citation" refers in this case only to so-called "forward citations," which are those citations generated by a particular patent after its filing and grant. By comparison, "backward" citations refer to those antecedent citations on which a particular patent relies, as part of its filing disclosures.

"technological importance" for future inventions.[35] Most notably, the U.S. Patent and Trademark Office concluded that "the number of times a patent is cited may be a measure of its technological significance."[36] Following this 1976 report, a number of patent citation studies have further established this link between high citation frequency and technological significance, through various data groupings. These include studies measuring the extremely high citation frequencies of patents listed in the National Inventor's Hall of Fame, patents of Historical Significance (as defined by the U.S. Department of Commerce), and "pioneering patents" identified by U.S. courts.[37] Typically, these studies show a skewed distribution pattern among the number of citations earned by patents. For example, one citation count study[38] shows that .01 percent of all U.S. patents granted through 1999 generated an annually averaged 100 citations each, while the majority of patents yielded five or less citations each.

The Pareto distribution outcomes of these patent citation studies strongly suggest that a few core innovations yield disproportionately high levels of influence on future generations of inventors. These studies further suggest that the systematic disclosures afforded by the patent grant system may play an important role in enabling disparate innovations to build cumulatively in a given field. A good example of this is the RSA patent (#4405829) filed in 1983 by three MIT faculty members, which relates to a cryptography algorithm for data encryption in electronic transmissions.

The RSA patent has generated more than 500 citations in the 23 years since it was filed. Interestingly, more than half of these citations were generated after the patent expired in 2000. These forward citations pertain to follow-on innovations in the domains of Internet security, electronic commerce, online banking, biometrics, on-line gaming, and digital rights management (DRM). Each of these technology domains has been enabled, to some extent, by the core innovation manifested in the RSA patent. Interestingly, a British mathematician named Clifford Cocks had invented a similar encryption technology a decade earlier while working for British intelligence; however, due to the covert nature of his work, Cocks' work was not publicly

---

[35] Trajtenberg, M. 1990. A Penny for Your Quotes: Patent Citations and the Value of Innovations. *RAND Journal of Economics*, 21:1; Hall B. 2002. "The Financing of Research and Development," Oxford Review of Economic Policy 18, No. 1, pp. 35–51.

[36] USPTO 1976. Sixth Technology Assessment and Forecast Report.

[37] Winkless, B. 2000. Invention Quality Measurement. Patent Valuation. *The Methods That TRIZ Forgot.*

[38] Hall, B. 2004. Patent Citations as Knowledge Flow Indicators. NBER.

disclosed until much later in the late 1990s, two decades after the RSA patent grant.

C. The Critical Impact of Licensing

The RSA example just described underscores the important public disclosure and knowledge-sharing functions that the patent system provides in enabling follow-on innovations to occur.[39] The grant and enforcement of patents and other intellectual property rights provide incentives for innovators, not only to create, but also to publicly disclose and broadly disseminate their innovative findings.[40] In addition to such disclosure advantages, the patent system affords a specific tool for the assimilation of prior innovations, that is, licensing. For example, one study found that between 1990 and 1999, 60 percent of new drugs approved by regulators were either new formulations or new combinations of drugs already on the market.[41] The same NIHCM (National Institute for Health Care Management) study concluded that one of the key enablers of this synthesis process was the grant and enforcement of intellectual property patents, which allowed pharmaceutical companies to license and assimilate patented "building blocks" in new drug-formulating combinations.

Licensing is often used to obtain access to complementary capabilities that are necessary to a follow-on invention.[42] A good example of the important role that licensing plays in enabling innovation is the development of humanized monoclonal antibodies (MAbs). This ground-breaking discovery was the result of Genentech's licensing of patented recombinant DNA methods owned by Protein Design Labs. By licensing this innovation from its competitor, Genentech was able to pioneer a technology that has become one of the most influential discoveries in modern medicine. While originally used for cancer treatments, MAbs have become foundational for the development of such far-ranging applications as the treatment of asthma and allergies, organ transplant rejection, and inflammatory bowel disease.

[39] Arundel, A. 1999. How Useful Are Patent Databases to SMEs as a Source of Technical Information? In Inzelt A. and J. Hilton (eds.), *Technology Transfer: From Invention to Innovation*, Nato ASI Series 4: Science and Technology Policy, Vol 19, pp. 195–206 (Kluwer Academic Publishers).

[40] Gallini, N. and S. Scotchmer. 2002. Intellectual Property: When Is It the Best Incentive System? In Jaffe, A., J. Lerner, and S. Stern (eds.), *Innovation Policy and the Economy*, Vol. 2 (MIT Press).

[41] National Institute for Health Care Management (2000), "Prescription Drugs and Intellectual Property Protection," *Issue Briefing (August)*.

[42] Teece, D. J. 1986. Profiting from Technological Innovation: Implications for Integration, Collaboration, Licensing and Public Policy. *Research Policy*. 15: 295–305.

Due to their targeting abilities, MAbs are readily combined with other drugs to maximize their effects. For example, Seattle Genetics' next-generation chemotherapy methods use the targeting ability of MAbs to deliver toxic payloads to discrete cells, by attaching them to MAbs through proprietary linkers. Global sales of MAbs surpassed $13 billion in 2005, and seventeen FDA-approved MAbs-based drugs were on the U.S. market. As of early 2006, forty new MAb-based therapies were in late-stage trials, comprising 25 percent of all biotech-related products in clinical development.[43] The rapid growth of MAbs-based drug therapies illustrates the important role that licensing plays in enabling assimilative innovation.

D. Platforms and Applications

Not all innovations are conceived for the same purpose. Some innovations provide specific end-use "applications," such as digital photos, music playback, fly fishing, and cooking. By comparison, others provide explicit "platforms," which we define as solution building blocks that are made available to other organizations, which in turn create specific applications. Examples of platforms are automobiles, television, microprocessors, computer operating systems, and the Visa payment processing system. Applications and platforms can be transient or foundational, and they often gradually morph (see Figure 5.1).

Platforms help to to sustain niche offerings by providing key building blocks with which to create or commercialize novel applications. A good example is provided by global satellite positioning (GPS) navigation devices, which were first introduced as in-vehicle navigation systems starting in the early 1990s. GPS navigation devices provide location-tracking based on the Navstar GPS System, which consists of twenty-four satellites operating in six orbits launched in 1973. GPS navigation technology existed for two decades before it was integrated into automobile dashboards, similar to the way that in-car stereo systems became integrated as standard features in the mid-1970s.

Consequently, the total penetration of in-car navigation systems reached 10 percent in Europe and Japan and approximately 7 percent in the United States by the end of 2005.[44] Most of these early sales were driven by pre-integrated OEM (original equipment manufacturer) units. According to

---

[43] Pisano, G. 2006. Science Business: The Promise, The Reality, and the Future of Biotech. (Harvard Business School Press).

[44] Tom-Tom Investor Relations 2006; Telematics Research Group 2007; Masterlink Securities Equity Research 2005.

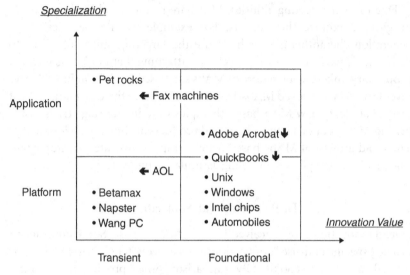

Figure 5.1.

one market research study, 90 percent of in-car navigation systems installed by the end of 2003 were factory or dealer installed, versus aftermarket products.[45] One cited reason for the overwhelming popularity of the pre-installed option was the technical ease and robustness of this approach. For instance, "navigation systems must be closely integrated with the vehicle's sensor speed, giving factory versions the edge."

As explained by a Mercedes-Benz spokesman: "Integrated systems can tell whether the wheels on one side of the car are moving faster than the other, and determine that you're going around a curve. That kind of invaluable data is always being processed even if you lose touch with a critical number of satellites." In 2006, GPS in-car unit shipments totaled two million units, up 66 percent from 2005 shipments, and 2007 shipments are projected at three million units.[46] As of 2007, approximately 69 percent of U.S. models will offer in-car navigation options up from 60 percent in 2006.[47]

This initial installation base of in-car navigation users led to lower production costs and growing demand for cheaper devices; consequently, in

---

[45] Frost & Sullivan 2003, quoted at www.bankrate.com (available here: http://www.bankrate .com/brm/news/auto/car-guide-2004/top-options-sider1.asp). Another study conducted by Telematics Research Group concluded that 85% were factory-installed as of 2004. However, this number has changed dramatically since the introduction of mobile navigation devices in 2005.

[46] Consumer Electronics Association 2007.

[47] Telematics Research Group 2007.

2005, other manufacturers introduced GPS navigation devices in two other formats: cell phones integrating GPS tracking capabilities, and the introduction of portable navigation devices (PNDs), which can be removed and transported from car to car. Notwithstanding the popularity of these second-generation mobile PNDs, their rapid take-up may stem from the public's introduction some fifteen years earlier to the prior generation of in-vehicle navigation systems. This example suggests that assimilation furthers the innovation process by initially providing a broadly familiar platform – that is, the automobile – with which to commercialize the new technologies.

Another example of this assimilation advantage is the history of plasma display technology, which was invented in the mid-1960s at the University of Illinois-Champagne and largely remained dormant until it was incorporated by Japanese manufacturers in production of high-definition television (HDTV) sets more than thirty years later. As its inventor Larry Weber is quoted as saying, "For most of its time, [plasma display] was a solution looking for a problem." Following numerous failed attempts at commercialization in the 1970s, it was not until the late 1990s and the widespread adoption of high-definition television (currently in use by over 30 million U.S. households[48]) that plasma's superior viewing resolution capabilities in the context of digital broadcast transmissions became commercially realized. Again, situating plasma's novel display properties within a broadly accessible and familiar platform – the ubiquitous television set – is the condition that allowed plasma technology to eventually find its true niche. The increasingly broad installation base of HDTV, in turn, has generated more specialized applications such as high-definition DVDs and Blu-ray disk formats.

The categories of platform and application do not remain static; instead, both evolve over time, in terms of their degree of specialization as well as their degree of innovativeness. For example, fax machines, which came to be regarded as an "all-in-one" communication platform with the integration of copy/print/scan functions, have since become largely outmoded by the advent of email communications and serve more as a niche device. Another example of a former communication platform that has been relegated to a niche offering is America OnLine (AOL), which at its peak boasted the largest installed base of Internet users (34 million worldwide subscribers in 2001). AOL's service platform consisted of a bundled offering of dial-up

---

[48] Jupiter Research 2005. Plasma display technology competes against LCD (liquid crystal display), another leading technology used in HDTV.

Internet access combined with e-mail and subscription-fee based content. However, the value proposition of AOL's "walled garden" approach largely disappeared with the widespread availability of broadband Internet and the massive proliferation of free content offerings that it enabled. By mid-2004, the number of U.S. broadband subscribers (26.9 million) surpassed the 25.8 million AOL dial-up users for the first time.[49]

On the other hand, some former niche applications such as QuickBooks instead gradually evolve into platforms. QuickBooks started out as a niche application providing financial accounting software for small- to midsize businesses (SMBs). Since then, it has broadened its features and capabilities through a series of acquisition-based product integrations. These acquisitions include online payroll service providers, merchant account services, and payment processing solutions, to create a complementary suite of full-service software offerings targeting SME (small and medium enterprise) users. Consequently, QuickBooks is now considered the "dominant small business software tool" with more than an 80 percent market share of accounting software in the SMB software segment. QuickBooks launched its own software development kit (SDK) in 2001 and presently hosts more than 600 supporting third-party applications.[50]

The QuickBooks example illustrates another point about the relationship between platforms and niche applications. While it is widely accepted that a given platform's value proposition may depend on the attractiveness of its hosted applications, that is, the "killer app principle,"[51] a topic that has been less examined in business management theory is, conversely, the role of certain technology platforms in sustaining the multitude of third-party applications that they engender.[52] Such "keystones" appear to play an important role in fostering innovation through the growth and proliferation of specialized application providers, in a given business ecosystem[53]

---

[49] CNET News.com, "Broadband Leaps Ahead of AOL," published on ZDNet News (May 13, 2004).

[50] Bolan, B., Jackson Securities. Equity research note dated September 15, 2006.

[51] The "killer app" notion became widely disseminated as a result of Larry Downes' and Chunka Mui's *Unleasing the Killer App: Digital Strategies for Market Dominance* (Harvard Business School Press, 1998), which sold more than 100,000 copies, was translated into a dozen languages, and appeared on the *BusinessWeek* and *New York Times'* best-seller lists soon after its publication.

[52] Iansiti, M. and R. Levien. 2004. Strategy as Ecology. *Harvard Business Review* 82(3): 68–78; Gawer, A. and M. A. Cusumano. 2004. *What Does it Take to be a Platform Leader: Some Recent from Palm and NTT DoCoMo*, Hitotsubashi Business Review, 52: 6–20.

[53] Iansiti, M. and R. Levien. 2004. Strategy as Ecology. *Harvard Business Review* 82(3): 68–78; Gawer, A. and M. A. Cusumano. 2004. *What Does it Take to be a Platform Leader: Some Recent from Palm and NTT DoCoMo*, Hitotsubashi Business Review, 52: 6–20.

QuickBooks has helped to transform the small business accounting software segment from a niche offering to a large industry. Its rapidly growing user base and release of its SDK has spurred the concurrent growth of its third-party developer community, who rely on QuickBooks' APIs (Application Programming Interfaces), totaling 28,000 developers at the end of 2006. This example shows how the presence of a keystone such as Intuit can promote the growth of a business ecosystem that allows more specialized applications to build on the foundational resources they provide.

III. Assimilation and Specialization

A. Assimilation of Innovations

Technological assimilation is an important driving force of technological progress. In software innovations, building blocks such as operating systems and developer tools are essential to the creation of specialized applications, just as in cooking new recipes leverage basic "platforms" such as gas stoves, barbecue grills, and even pots and pans. At the same time, new specialized software applications, just like new recipes, will push the envelope in platform capabilities and force platform providers themselves to innovate. Assimilation and specialization are thus both critical engines of the innovation life cycle, each important to the other's success.

Not all specialized innovations will endure. Many will be assimilated into broader applications or platforms over the long term. This trend is borne out, for example, by our survey of the top 100 software companies (ranked by revenues) listed in Softwaremag.com's database as of 1995. Ten years later, 51 percent of these software firms had been assimilated into larger firms (through acquisition), and only 17 percent remained in the top 100 rankings. The other one-third firms, while remaining independent, were unable to maintain a pace of performance and growth consistent with their prior 1995 rankings, despite significant overall industry growth (see Figure 5.2). The fifty-one acquisitions that took place within this group show a clear pattern of larger companies incorporating the complementary capabilities of smaller rivals into their broader technology portfolios. This appears to be consistent with larger industry trends during this timeframe, characterized by growing numbers of acquisitions targeting innovative capabilities.[54]

---

[54] Generally, "acquisitions for less than $50 million indicate that a smaller company has been purchased by a larger one seeking access to an innovative product or process. In 1995

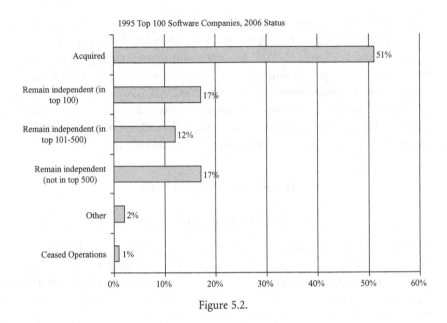

Figure 5.2.

B. Assimilation Encourages Specialization

Despite the many acquisitions, it is important to underline that during this same time period (1995–2005), the U.S. software industry was generally characterized by an *increase* in the overall level of specialization, as reflected in the relatively low Hirschfeld-Herfindahl Index (HHI) for the software industry as a whole.[55],[56] According to our internal analysis of this same

there were 322 such acquisitions, in 2004 there were more than 1400." Source: Mergerstat (mergerstat.com) 2006.

[55] Merges, R. 2006. Patents, Entry and Growth in the Software Industry. *Social Science Research Network Working Paper Series* [online database], No. 926204. Merges' recent study points out that the Hirschman-Herfindahl Index (HHI) for the software industry as a whole is 244, compared to "an average of 334 for U.S. manufacturing industries" (p. 7). However, no exact date is provided for these HHI readings. The results of our internal survey of the top 100 software firms, showing that over half the firms were acquired, is also consistent with Merges' conclusion that "there is evidence of significant turnover over time as well – a key indicator of a dynamic industry." Id.

[56] Kramer, R. 2004. Technology Neutrality in Software Procurement: The Soundest IT and Procurement Policy. UNCTAD: Expert Meeting on Free and Open Source Software Policy and Development Implications, Session 3: Government Usage and Policy Implications (September 23, 2004); Merges, R. 2006. Patents, Entry and Growth in the Software Industry. *Social Science Research Network Working Paper Series* [online database], No. 926204; Mann, R. 2006. Commercializing Open Source Software: Do Property Rights Still Matter? *Harvard Journal of Law & Technology*, 20: 1.

top100 software sample set,[57] the modified HHI for this market segment grouping declined from a reading of 737 in 1995 to a reading of 588 in 2006, which suggests an overall trend of decreasing market share concentration amoung the leading software companies. This increasing specialization in the software industry, despite high acquisition rates and strong revenue growth, suggests that assimilation and specialization can indeed go hand in hand. Interestingly, during this same period, total software revenues expanded greatly, at a compound annual growth rate of 27.6 percent, from $20 to $30 billion, in 1994 to more than $350 billion in 2005.[58] At a high level, the software innovation life cycle certainly appeared to increase the overall set of opportunities for firms.

One theory that has been advanced to explain this prolific increase in industry niche specialization is the overall trend toward encouraging stronger patent protections since the mid-1990s.[59] It has been observed, for example, that "a shift toward stronger patent rights could facilitate vertical specialization within the industry and lead to the emergence of 'technology specialists.'"[60] Similarly, other studies have concluded that U.S. policies of strengthening intellectual property protection starting in the mid-1990s encouraged the growth of smaller, more specialized firms, which may display a higher propensity for innovation than larger firms.[61]

A useful framework to explain how assimilative tendencies encourage the proliferation of specialized niche companies is the concept of the business

---

[57] The analysis was carried out based on data provided in *Software Magazine*'s "1995 Software 100" (available at http://www.findarticles.com/p/articles/mi_m0SMG/is_n7_v15) and "2006 Software 500" <http://www.softwaremag.com/S_FocusAreas.cfm?Doc=The500> lists, using the top 100 companies by revenue. Due to the lack of sufficient data for earlier periods, we have employed a modified HHI for purposes of this analysis.

[58] Keystone Strategy analysis 2007.

[59] Hall, B. and R. Ziedonis. 2001. The Effects of Strengthening Patent Rights on Firms Engaged in Cumulative Innovation: Insights from the Semiconductor Industry [working draft]; Merges, R. P. 1998. "Antitrust Review of Patent Acquisition: Property Rights, Firm Boundaries, and Originization," in *Competition Policy and Intellectual Property Rights in the Knowledge-Based Economy*. Robert D. Anderson and Nancy T. Gallini, eds. Calgary: University of Calgary Press, pp. 111–32.

[60] Hall, B. and R. Ziedonis. 2001. The Effects of Strengthening Patent Rights on Firms Engaged in Cumulative Innovation: Insights from the Semiconductor Industry [working draft].

[61] Arora, A. 1995. Licensing Tacit Knowledge: Intellectual Property Rights and Market for Know-How. *Economics of Innovation and New Technology*, 4: 41–59; Merges, R. P. 1998. "Antitrust Review of Patent Acquisition: Property Rights, Firm Boundaries, and Originization," in *Competition Policy and Intellectual Property Rights in the Knowledge-Based Economy*. Robert D. Anderson and Nancy T. Gallini, eds. Calgary: University of Calgary Press, pp. 111–32; Arora, A. and R. Merges. 2004. Specialized Supply Firms, Property Rights, and Firm Boundaries. *Industrial & Corporate Change* 13: 451–475.

"ecosystem".[62] Under this ecosystem view, keystones play a foundational role in giving rise to propensities for niche creation based on increasingly specialized capabilities. At the same time, keystones also serve to balance the creation of niches to avoid over-proliferation that could threaten system equilibrium.[63] In this regard, the high acquisition and turnover rates in this industry example can be seen as a means for consolidation (i.e., eliminating redundancies) to promote the flourishing of truly innovative applications that build sequentially on prior applications.

IV. Assimilation, Specialization, and the Life Cycle

A. The Technological Life Cycle

The processes of technological assimilation and specialization provide crucial building blocks of the technological life cycle. A variety of authors[64] have described the evolution of technology as a series of "cycles" between *different* generations of technology. In this work, we motivate a different view of the life cycle. Rather than competing technological "paradigms" fighting for dominance,[65] we argue that the engine behind the life cycle is provided by cycles of assimilation and specialization. In other words, technological capabilities are not always replaced – they are instead assimilated into broader innovations. As a classic example, the personal computer (PC) *accelerated* the diffusion of potentially disruptive internet technologies. In turn, the Internet *accelerated* the diffusion of PCs, rather than thwart their existence. Today's PCs are a fairly good assimilation of PC client and internet technologies. It is becoming more and more difficult for a user to understand where the PC ends and where the Internet begins.

---

[62] Moore, J. 1997. *The Death of Competition: Leadership and Strategy in the Age of Business Ecosystems* (Harper Business); Iansiti, M. and R. Levien. 2004. Strategy as Ecology. *Harvard Business Review* 82(3): 68–78.

[63] Moore, J. 1997. *The Death of Competition: Leadership and Strategy in the Age of Business Ecosystems* (Harper Business); Iansiti, M. and R. Levien. 2004. *The Keystone Advantage* (Harvard Business School Press).

[64] Abernathy, W. and J. Utterback. 1978. Patterns of Industrial Innovation. *Technology Review*. 80: 40–47; Anderson, P. and M. Tushman. 1990. Technological Discontinuities and Dominant Designs: A Cyclical Model of Technological Change. *Administrative Science Quarterly*, 35: 604–633; Christensen, C. 1997. *The Innovator's Dilemma: When New Technologies Cause Great Firms to Fail* (Harvard Business School Press).

[65] Dosi, G, O. Marsili, L. Orsenigo, and R. Salvatore. 1995. Learning, Market Selection and the Evolution of Industry Structures. *Small Business Economics*. 7: 411–436.

B. Digital Video Recording

The history of the digital video recorder (DVR) industry provides another illustration of how technology assimilation drives the technological life cycle. Analogous to the PC and the *Internet*, it shows how an existing technology platform (in this case cable television) can *accelerate* the commercialization of innovative products and services by allowing them to reach "critical mass" user adoption levels. The development of the U.S. DVR market in the late 1990s illustrates how assimilation into a broader capability platform plays a key role in sustaining the viability of innovative products, and also in determining the competitive outcome. From 1999 to 2002, several new entrants tried to capitalize on the growing consumer market for DVR capabilities. DVRs typically consist of programming and playback software combined with a nonremovable hard-disk storage hardware unit. DVR technology allows users to selectively pause, rewind, and record television programming content for optional viewing, at their choice of time and venue.

The best-recognized DVR brand among U.S. consumers is designed and licensed for OEM manufacturing by TiVo, a publicly traded company established in 1997. In addition to licensing designs for the DVR hardware, TiVo also provides a monthly subscription fee–based service, which provides the bulk of its revenues. Since 2002, TiVo has offered subscribers the choice of signing up for its monthly service either (1) directly by purchasing its hardware through retail channels such as BestBuy, or (2) through its revenue-sharing agreement with DirecTV, which acts as a reseller of TiVo's hardware/subscription service offerings. Under the latter arrangement, TiVo's software is integrated into the DirecTV satellite receiver. The resulting "DirecTiVo" recorder processes the incoming satellite MPEG-2 digital stream directly to a hard drive disk without digital conversion.

Significantly, of the numerous entrants in the DVR field, the suppliers that emerged as "winners" in this domain by 2006 – TiVo, OpenTV, and Scientific-Atlantic – had entered into licensing or revenue-sharing arrangements in the early 2000s with satellite and cable television operators to mass deploy and integrate their DVR capabilities into the latters' digital set-top boxes and broadband service platforms. In some cases, this involved upgrading digital subscribers' existing satellite receivers to incorporate the DVR software. This DVR capability integration proved to be the key winning strategy for companies such as TiVo and OpenTV, which entered into distribution arrangements with satellite television operators.

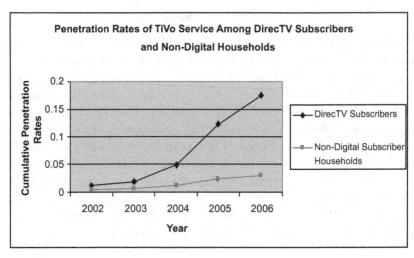

Figure 5.3.

In the case of TiVo, a comparison of the user adoption rates in its two distribution channels provides clear evidence of how integration into DirecTV's digital programming service platform played a key role in its marketing success. Figure 5.3 compares the cumulative penetration rates from 2002 through 2006 of TiVo's bundled service offering among DirecTV subscribers (18% combined total penetration in the integrated channels) versus those among nondigital households (3% total penetration in the nonintegrated channel). This large variance in outcome underscores the important role that platform integration played for TiVo's penetration success: While in 2001 subscribers accessing TiVo through DirecTV accounted for less than 15 percent of the total subscriber base, within three years DirecTV subscribers accounted for more than half of all TiVo users by 2004, and nearly two-thirds of all TiVo users by 2006.[66] TiVo reported in its 2004 third fiscal quarter, for instance, that 75 percent of new subscriber additions were sourced through the DirecTV channel.[67]

---

[66] In 2005, DirecTV announced it was discontinuing its revenue-sharing alliance with TiVo, resulting in a marked drop-off in new subscriber additions in the quarter. Starting in January 2007, TiVo entered into a new distribution alliance with the largest digital cable services provider, Comcast, which enabled a similar integration approach as with DirecTV. Under the new arrangement, Comcast's cable subscribers can integrate TiVo's DVR software into their existing set-top boxes. See link at http://www.dmwmedia.com/tags/ce/dvr; article also found at: http://www.foxnews.com/story/0,2933,242448,00.html.

[67] See article at http://www.usatoday.com/money/industries/technology/2004–11-29-dvr_x .htm.

Comparing the penetration results by industry segments confirms the same pattern: satellite television subscribers (18%), digital cable subscribers (16%), and nondigital households (7%). OpenTV employed a similar integration strategy for the distribution of its middleware, most notably through DirecTV's rival, EchoStar. Starting in 2003, OpenTV licensed its middleware to various manufacturers of digital set-top boxes, which were then sold through network operators' distribution channels. These distribution channels included EchoStar, DirecTv's satellite TV competitor that had integrated OpenTV's software into its DISH subscriber network set-top boxes.[68]

By end of 2006, OpenTV's DVR software had been integrated into 1.5 million set-top boxes offered by EchoStar and others, representing about 30 percent of the entire installation base in the satellite television segment. A similar dynamic played out in the digital cable subscriber segment, where Scientific-Atlanta was able to achieve high penetration for its Explorer 8000 DVR set-top box among digital cable subscribers through integration deals with Comcast, Cox, and Charter Communications. By early 2006, Scientific-Atlanta had shipped 4.5 million total DVR-equipped units,[69] approximately the same number as TiVo.

By contrast to these successful deployment strategies, early entrants such as ReplayTV and UltimateTV did not succeed with similar integration deals with broadband network operators. Consequently, neither remained commercially viable. Despite claims of technological superiority over rival TiVo, ReplayTV did not gain user traction and sold less than 10,000 hardware units before being acquired in 2001 by SonicBlue, which filed for bankruptcy less than two years later.[70] UltimateTV set out to compete against TiVo, and discontinued hardware manufacturing in 2002 after TiVo announced its distribution alliance with digital satellite provider DirecTV. WebTV also developed its own console with DVR capabilities designed to be compatible with satellite receivers, but it was unable to enter into distribution alliances with either EchoStar or DirecTV and gave up this effort.

These competitive outcomes among DVR contenders underscore the important role that assimilation into digital set-top boxes played in promoting the viability of DVR capabilities, and in accelerating their adoption rates among DVR users. As of June 2006, it was estimated that overall DVR penetration rates among U.S. households had reached 11 percent (up from

---

[68] See article at http://findarticles.com/p/articles/mi_m0DIZ/is_4_14/ai_83031517.

[69] Scientific Atlanta Second Fiscal Quarter 2006 10-Q public filing.

[70] SonicBlue's assets, which included the ReplayTV logo and technology, were in turn acquired out of bankruptcy by a Japanese electronics firm, D&M Holdings, which discontinued hardware sales in the United States in 2005.

4.5% in 2004), or 12.3 million households.[71] Another interesting aspect is that free DVR applications such as MythTV have not made significant inroads into the market share of commercial applications such as TiVo. The modest user bases of these free do-it-yourself kits for stand-alone boxes illustrate that ease of functional integration – not innovation alone – is the compelling value proposition among DVR users.

Furthermore, it is interesting to note that, separated by distribution channels, the user adoption rate in the integrated channel has surpassed that critical threshold defined as the "chasm," that is, above 15 percent. "Crossing the chasm" refers to a point of critical mass adoption, or the tipping point where it is expected that large-scale user adoption will follow.[72] What is interesting about the DVR example is that, as a direct consequence of the integrated approaches, user adoption rates for DVRs have crossed the threshold of the "early adopter" stage to the "early majority" stage, which ensures some degree of long-term viability.[73] Having reached this tipping point, it is anticipated that DVR penetration rates will begin to accelerate; by some forecast estimates, DVR penetration is expected to reach 50 percent of all U.S. households by 2011[74] Assuming these projections are accurate, one could directly attribute the DVR segment's ability to achieve critical mass and transition from a niche application to a mainstream offering to DVRs' capability assimilation into digital TV set-top boxes and subscriber platforms.

B. Payment Processing

The assimilation of technology is critical in driving the creation and evolution of broad-based platforms, as we saw in the example in the previous subsection. These, in turn, enable more economic specialization, which fuels a thriving ecosystem of niche competitors. eBay's acquisition of on-line payment services provider PayPal in 2002 is a prime example. It illustrates how the assimilation of technology into a broader platform can enhance the long-term sustainability of niche applications, which is beneficial to a large ecosystem of customers and organizations.

---

[71] ITFacts.com, found at www.itfacts.biz/index.php?id=P6688. According to this source, breakdowns by distribution channel are 40% by satellite, 30% by cable, and 30% are stand-alone users.

[72] Moore, G. 1999. *Crossing the Chasm* (Harper Business).

[73] Moore, G. 1999. *Crossing the Chasm* (Harper Business).

[74] Leichtman Research Group (2007), quoted at: http://www.afterdawn.com/news/article .cfm/2007/09/26/dvr_use_expected_to_reach_50_of_us_households_by_2011.

PayPal is one of the best-known "survivors" of the dotcom era, and succeeded in revolutionizing the electronic payments processing industry by creating a robust payment network through widespread user adoption. In contrast, numerous competitors[75] failed despite heavy financial backing. PayPal quickly became a leader in this emerging domain, mostly due to its ability to rapidly penetrate the eBay community user base. By the time of its initial public offering in late 2001, it had captured 65 percent of the market share of the on-line payments processing segment[76] and derived 60 percent of its revenues from eBay users. One unique aspect of PayPal's business model was that, unlike its competitors, its service tied the facilitation and tracking of payment transactions to a user's email address and relied on conventional currencies such as the U.S. dollar. Some business models such as Beenz.com and Flooz.com tried unsuccessfully to create new Internet currencies. Other competitors built their on-line payment models around traditional *off-line* capabilities such as checking accounts (Check-Free, ProPay, PayDirect) and money orders (BidPay, PayingFast, MoneyZap). By comparison, PayPal's integration of a broadly available *on-line* convention – e-mail – to identify, originate, and track electronic payments provided greater familiarity and convenience to on-line users.

Despite its early rapid growth and market dominance, PayPal's operations were beset by numerous difficulties that ranged from use of fraudulent accounts to money-laundering allegations and tens of thousands of complaints of freezing customer accounts. As a result, PayPal's transactional costs remained a high percentage of its operating revenues and total overhead. Just prior to its acquisition, PayPal's transactional costs (including both transactional processing expenses and loss provisions) were nearly half – 47 percent – of its total operating revenues, and its fraud losses peaked at 1.2 percent of total payment volume in late 2000. PayPal's high transactional losses were one of the main reasons for its inability to achieve profitability.

By comparison, eBay's acquisition and subsequent integration of PayPal into its on-line retail platform has greatly stabilized the latter's operations. It has also significantly increased PayPal's active user base, which grew 400

---

[75] These include BidPay, CheckFree, Citigroup Bank's C2It, PayingFast, ProPay Western Union's MoneyZap and Yahoo's PayDirect. Even eBay's own on-line payment division, Billpoint, was unable to compete against PayPal and later merged into the acquired company.

[76] See article at http://www.fundinguniverse.com/company-histories/PayPal-Inc-Company-History.html. While it's unclear how the article defined this segment as of 2002, it is interesting to note that eBay constituted less than 10% of the entire on-line commerce segment in 2003. This implies that the percentage of on-line payment users on eBay was much greater than for on-line commerce as a whole.

percent between 2002 and 2006. In addition to creating a more robust and seamlessly integrated on-line transactional experience for both users and sellers, the two companies' functional integration allowed PayPal to make even deeper inroads into eBay's user base. This convergence in their user bases is shown by the increasing percentage of eBay participants who rely on PayPal to close transactions. As of mid-2005, 78 percent of all eBay transactions were closed via PayPal,[77] up from 40 percent of all eBay transactions closed in 2002.[78] Currently, more than 90 percent of eBay listings accept PayPal as a payment method, according to its website.

As a consequence of PayPal's integration, eBay's ecosystem of buyers and sellers has benefited from faster closing times, as well as greater reliability in closing transactions, given that "buyers and sellers complete transactions days faster using electronic payments."[79] At the same time, PayPal users benefited post-integration from enhanced security against fraud, as evidenced by the sharp decline in its transactional loss[80] rates from .41 percent of total payment volume in 2002 to .27 percent in 2005. eBay also instituted several financial protection policies, user guarantees, and stricter operational guidelines to provide greater assurances to both buyers and sellers using PayPal. For example, eBay's management stepped up internal efforts to police against fraud, counterfeiting, and prohibited transactions (e.g., gambling), which had plagued PayPal's reputation earlier.[81] In sum, PayPal's assimilation into the eBay retailing platform afforded PayPal users the stabilizing advantages of eBay's stronger reputation for completing on-line transactions and its depth of operational experience in dealing with on-line fraud issues.

---

[77] L. Walker, "PayPal Looks To Evolve Beyond Its Auction Roots" (*Washington Post*, May 19, 2005). See article at http://www.washingtonpost.com/wp-dyn/content/article/2005/05/18/AR2005051802187_pf.html.

[78] Whitman, speaking on a conference call in 2002, stated that about 40% of eBay transactions are settled with electronic payments, a figure she hopes will "increase dramatically" with the PayPal acquisition (CNN article, July 2002).

[79] CNN article, July 8, 2002. While eBay does not disclose its average transaction closing times in its public filings, one of eBay's stated goals at the time of the acquisition was to "increase the number of electronic payments made via eBay" given that "the bulk of transactions on eBay [were] still conducted via check or money order." EBay CEO Meg Whitman noted at a 2002 press conference that "the PayPal acquisition will help both customers and the company's bottom line by speeding up the payment process."

[80] eBay's public filings define "transaction loss" as "failure to deal effectively with fraudulent activity and customer disputes."

[81] At one point, eBay's management tasked more than 1000 employees with investigating and controlling fraud and related problems in the PayPal division (Eisenmann and Barley 2006).

C. Assimilation, Specialization, and the Life Cycle

These examples are not isolated. Prior studies have recognized that "innovation is, more often than not, cumulative to the extent that it builds and incorporates prior knowledge from diverse sources".[82,83] The cumulative assimilation of innovation is evidenced in product development cycles in software, biotechnology, and creative industries.[84] It has also been recognized as a driving force in organizing knowledge production in the domains of patent applications,[85] academic scholarship,[86] and biomedical research.[87]

[82] Murray qualifies this by pointing out that "accumulation is not an inherent property of the innovation process itself" but requires certain institutional mechanisms such as patent enforcement that "enable knowledge accumulation" to occur (p. 6).

[83] Murray, F. and S. O'Mahony. 2007. Exploring the Foundations of Cumulative Innovation: Implications for Organization Science. *Organization Science,* 18: 1006–1021.

[84] Edwards, M., F. Murray, and R. Yu. 2003. Value-Creation and Sharing Among Universities, Biotechnology and Pharma. *Nature Biotechnology,* 21: 6.

[85] To date, cumulative innovation has mostly been studied in the context of legal doctrinal analysis (i.e., patents). Studies of cumulative innovation have focused on understanding its legal and economic implications, Scotchmer, S. 1991. Standing on the Shoulders of Giants: Cumulative Research and the Patent Law. *The Journal of Economic Perspectives,* 5: 1; Scotchmer, S. 1996. Patents as an Incentive System, Suzanne Scotchmer. Ch. 12, pp. 281–296, of Economics in a Changing World, Volume 2, Beth Allen, ed., McMillan Press (London) and St. Martin's Press (New York); Scotchmer, S. 2004. *Innovation and Incentives* (MIT Press); Dasgupta, P. and P. David. Toward a New Economics of Science, *Research Policy,* 1994, 23: 487–521; Romer, P. 2002. When Should We Use Intellectual Property Rights? *The American Economic Review.* 92: 213–216; Aghion, P., C. Harris, P. Howitt, and J. Vickers. Competition, Imitation and Growth with Step-by-Step Innovation. *Review of Economic Studies* (July 2001): 467–92 and in particular, "the importance of adequate economic incentives for investment in cumulative innovation" such as patents, and the "appropriate distribution of rewards across different generations of innovators". Murray, F. and S. O'Mahony. 2007. Exploring the Foundations of Cumulative Innovation: Implications for Organization Science. *Organization Science,* 18: 1006–1021. This analysis has implications, for instance, for the division of patent grants and royalties between upstream and downstream innovators. Murray, F. and S. O'Mahony. 2007. Exploring the Foundations of Cumulative Innovation: Implications for Organization Science. *Organization Science,* 18: 6. One limitation of this prior research focus on the allocation of legal and economic rights between patentholders and their downstream licensees is that it does not specifically address the societal benefits that may arise from cumulative innovation. Stern, S. 2004. Do Scientists Pay to be Scientists? *Management Science.* 50:6; Scotchmer, S. 1996. Patents as an Incentive System, Suzanne Scotchmer. Ch. 12, pp. 281–296, of Economics in a Changing World, Volume 2, Beth Allen, ed., McMillan Press (London) and St. Martin's Press (New York); Murray, F. and S. O'Mahony. 2007. Exploring the Foundations of Cumulative Innovation: Implications for Organization Science. *Organization Science,* 18: 1006–1021.

[86] Scotchmer, S. 1991. Standing on the Shoulders of Giants: Cumulative Research and the Patent Law. *The Journal of Economic Perspectives,* 5: 1.

[87] Long, C. 2000. Patents and Cumulative Innovation. *Re-Engineering Patent Law.* 2 *Wash. UJL & POL'Y* 229–46; Rai, A. K. 2001. Fostering Cumulative Innovation in the Biopharmaceutical Industry: The Role of Patents and Antitrust. *Berkeley Technology Law Journal,*

One particularly useful framework that examines how prior innovations enable a sustained pathway for future innovations is the work of Scotchmer,[88] who differentiates between innovations that reduce costs and those that enable or accelerate the sequential development of further innovations. "If the second generation could not be developed without the first, then the social value of the first innovation includes the incremental social surplus provided by second-generation products" (Scotchmer, p. 31).[89] Scotchmer explains that "if the first innovation accelerates development of the second, but at the same cost, then its social value includes the value of getting the second innovation sooner" (Scotchmer, p. 31).[90]

Building on Scotchmer's framework of conceiving of innovation as a sequential process, one could further distinguish between two pathways of cumulative innovation: (1) *assimilative* innovations, which assimilate technology capabilities into a broader platform; and (2) *derivative* innovations, which build sequentially on a subset of existing platform capabilities toward more specialized applications. Using the TiVo example, its DVR software application builds on the Linux kernel,[91] and in this regard it could be considered a derivative application of Linux. At the same time, its hardware mostly consists of a nonremovable hard drive, a generic storage component also found in digital cameras, and audio recording devices. Some recent models also incorporate DVD-R/RW drives that allow the transfer of recordings from the built-in hard drive to most modern DVD systems.

By recombining and integrating these existing software and hardware capabilities into a new DVR offering, TiVo could be regarded as an assimilative innovation. In turn, TiVo's software integration into the digital set-top boxes of satellite television providers provides a second instance of assimilation into a broader platform. In the next paragraph we describe how video-on-demand employs a subset of these assimilated DVR capabilities

16: 813; Murray, F. and S. O'Mahony. 2007. Exploring the Foundations of Cumulative Innovation: Implications for Organization Science. *Organization Science,* 18: 1006–1021.

[88] Scotchmer, S. 1991. Standing on the Shoulders of Giants: Cumulative Research and the Patent Law. *The Journal of Economic Perspectives,* 5: 1.

[89] Scotchmer, S. 1991. Standing on the Shoulders of Giants: Cumulative Research and the Patent Law. *The Journal of Economic Perspectives,* 5: 1.

[90] Scotchmer, S. 1991. Standing on the Shoulders of Giants: Cumulative Research and the Patent Law. *The Journal of Economic Perspectives,* 5: 1.

[91] TiVo's proprietary software incorporates and modifies the Linux kernel and open-source tools, by adding an unbuffered scatter/gather API for disk access, real-time disk scheduling capability, an advanced DMA management subsystem, and support for demand paging and real-time processing. TiVo also relied on the GNU toolset and TCL to develop its software.

to develop a specialized application (i.e., derivative innovation). Thus, the various innovation pathways related to TiVo illustrate how both assimilative and derivative innovations occur in tandem within the innovation cycle.

The aftermath of TiVo's assimilation into digital set-top boxes illustrates how the technology assimilation process furthers next-generation innovation. Consequently, the DVR market has provided the basis for another level of product innovation, namely, the emerging market for video-on-demand (VoD) services in the satellite television segment. The large-scale assimilation of DVR capabilities into the digital set-top boxes of satellite and cable platform providers has enabled the latter platform providers to move rapidly into the multi-billion dollar market for VoD services. Both satellite and cable providers are leveraging existing DVR subscriber bases to offer VoD services into this same segment. In the case of satellite television operators, the large downstream bandwidth requirements of streaming VoD made it impractical to offer such services in the past.

Recently, both DirecTV and EchoStar announced new VoD services that will rely on the hard-drive storage capabilities of existing digital DVR subscribers to download and store VoD movies for discretionary viewing. EchoStar announced in early 2005 that network subscribers would be able to have VoD movies downloaded to the storage drive of their DISH Player-DVR 625 receivers for future viewing. DirecTV is similarly offering its existing DVR subscribers VoD service upgrades. One reason that the prior integration of DVR into digital set-top boxes has consequently enabled the rapid deployment and adoption of VoD services is the transformation in consumer television watching behavior brought about by the advent of DVR. Consumers "love the control DVRs give them. The ability to record programs, pause live TV, and skip ads creates a powerful change in the way they view television."[92] One recent survey found that approximately 60 percent of existing digital cable subscribers with DVR access had also used VoD services.[93]

Other studies suggest that DVR users have a higher propensity for adopting VoD services, and are 50 percent more likely to use VoD services than non-DVR users.[94] DVR users' newfound ability to control the pace and content of television viewing has created new behavioral expectations among television viewers, which VoD accommodates by providing similar control

---

[92] Quote from Josh Bernoff, Vice President, Forrester Research (2004), found at www.ITFacts.biz/index.php?id=P1548.

[93] Leichtman Research Group 2006, "On-Demand TV 2006: A Nationwide Study on VOD and DVRs." See article at http://www.leichtmanresearch.com/press/022106release.html.

[94] Lyra 2004. See article at http://lyra.ecnext.com/coms2/summary_0290–129_ITM.

over viewing content. Thus, DVR's broad-based assimilation into digital subscriber television platforms has consequently furthered the commercial feasibility and rapid adoption of VoD, a technology that previously existed but was not widely deployed.[95]

PayPal's post-acquisition foray into new markets and development of innovative services provides a further illustration of this point. Assimilating PayPal's on-line payment processing capabilities into eBay's broader on-line retailing platform has given rise to significantly broader opportunities for participants of both user networks. One of the key post-integration effects has been both eBay's and PayPal's rapid expansion into cross-border transactions. eBay's international market segments, which comprised 25 percent of its total revenues in 2002, now account for nearly half of its $5 billion annual revenues and gross merchandising volume. eBay's total international market revenues and user numbers have grown by 330 percent since 2002. eBay's Europe division was the "fastest-growing" market for eBay as of the end of 2005, and generated 37 percent of its revenues and one-quarter of its user base.

At the same time, PayPal's metrics also show rapid international growth as a result of its integration. International revenues constituted 36 percent of PayPal's total revenues in 2005, up from 20 percent in 2002.[96] The international segment of eBay's gross merchandising volume addressable to PayPal stands to surpass its U.S. segment growth by 2007.[97] Similarly, PayPal's penetration rates in eBay's international transactions segment have increased from 23 percent to 31 percent in the past two years, while its U.S. payment transactions segment has remained flat. The acquisition of PayPal enabled eBay's rapid international expansion, through its own growth in facilitating cross-border transactions. In addition to creating new secondary markets for its resellers, and expanding its global reach among market participants, PayPal's assimilation into the eBay retailing platform has allowed PayPal to develop a more robust and expanded user network that has become the basis for a broad range of on-line merchant banking services aimed

---

[95] For example, a CNN article from 1999 refers to VoD trials at the 1999 Western Show; see article at http://news.com.com/Video+on+demand+may+trouble+digital+video+recording+upstarts/2100-1040_3-234765.html. Comcast started offering VoD in limited service areas as of 2003 (http://www.cable360.net/cableworld/operators/msos/15707.html).

[96] Eisenmann, T. and L. Barley. 2006. *PayPal Merchant Services.* Harvard Business School Case Study No. 9–806-188.

[97] Keung, P. "eBay, Inc.: Assessing the PayPal Opportunity," CIBC Equity Research Note, July 10, 2005, Ex. 1.

at SME online proprietors who would otherwise lack market liquidity and distribution access.

One year after PayPal's acquisition, PayPal launched a new "merchant banking services" initiative targeting off-eBay SME on-line proprietors. These on-line merchant banking services build on the liquidity-enabling capabilities of PayPal's original business model and include branded debit/ credit cards and advanced transaction management services, and mobile interfaces. Most notably, PayPal's merchant banking services division has expanded into the emerging domain of micropayments processing for low-cost digital content. This domain consists of several emerging business segments – ringtones, digital music downloads, on-line greeting cards, podcasting, patent searches, on-line text delivery – where vendors deliver content on-line. By some market estimates, this low-cost digital content market is projected to become a $15 billion industry by 2008.[98] PayPal's foray into this micropayments processing service will make it the only publicly traded company actively targeting the servicing of this sub-$5 category of on-line digital content. In the past, the prohibitively high transaction costs for processing payments in this sub-$5 digital content segment previously discouraged investment in this domain.

By lowering the processing fee structure through the scale economies afforded by its large user base, PayPal is enabling the growth of a new domain. In addition, start-up firms like Peppercoin and BitPass are building on PayPal's existing on-line transaction capabilities and broad-based user network by offering "pre-loaded card" services to support micropayments processing. Bitpass has attracted 1,100 sellers of low-cost digital content ranging from photos and comics to patent searches and independent musicians' file downloads. Such new supplier aggregation models may become the basis of future ecosystems, similar to eBay.

Assimilation has resulted in new innovations in the automotive industry as well. The growing installation base of in-car GPS navigation systems is enabling numerous telematic applications that build on the GPS frequency and location tracking capabilities to enhance public safety. These next-generation applications include real-time information services such as weather and traffic updates, which are already being implemented. For example, GM's XM NavTraffic is an optional upgrade that "can fully integrate with the vehicle's on-board navigation system to display current information about traffic, average traffic speed along specific roadways,

---

[98] Peppercoin website 2007, www.peppercoin.com.

and estimated travel times based on traffic conditions."[99] Other next-generation innovations in the emerging telematics field include vehicle-to-vehicle (V2V) wireless communications featuring road condition alerts; autonomous vehicle function enhancements such as collision warnings, lane-keeping mechanisms, and auto-pilot safety devices; and the development of comprehensive public transport radar networks to improve emergency location tracking and auto safety coordination. These telematics applications including navigation systems are projected to become a $38 billion global industry by 2011.[100]

Furthermore, the European Commission has confirmed a new proposal for regulation that requires all 15 million automobiles sold in Europe annually to be equipped with a telematics unit including a GPS satellite navigation device, starting in 2012.[101] Because many of the public safety applications require wholesale participation by auto manufacturers to be feasible, the ostensible goal of such mandates is to create scale economies that accelerate the broad adoption of these future innovation platforms and give rise to sweeping industry transformations. One General Motors senior research engineer predicts about the emerging V2V domain: "this would be the reinvention of the car."

V. Public Benefits of Technology Assimilation

There are substantial public benefits of technological assimilation. In contrast to other studies that have set out to measure innovative output through proprietary indicators such as market value, product development time, and shareholders' investment returns,[102] our focus is on the public benefits that collectively accrue to all participants in the value chain.[103] This includes the public benefits to both producers as well as consumer (end users) of a given innovation. As illustrated by our examples, the types of public benefits

---

[99] Frost & Sullivan, supra 9.

[100] ABI Research August 2006.

[101] Car Scoop 2008 found at http://carscoop.blogspot.com/2008/05/eu-electronic-stability-control-to-be.html.

[102] Hall, B., A. Jaffe, and M. Trajtenberg. 2005. Market Value and Patent Citations. *Rand Journal of Economics* 36 (Spring).16–38; Merges, R. 2006. Patents, Entry and Growth in the Software Industry. *Social Science Research Network Working Paper Series* [online database], No. 926204.

[103] Previous studies have noted that commercial "innovation" and technological "invention" are distinct phenomena that require different measures of valu. (Schumpeter 1939; Marquis 1969; Nelson and Winter 1982; Trajtenberg 1990). Our focus on measuring the public benefits is more related to the concept of "social innovation value," which Trajtenberg defines as the incremental change in producer and consumer surplus (Trajtenberg 1990).

that may arise from innovative assimilations include not only new products or downstream applications. In some instances, entire new domains arise through increasing specialization and niche creation, such as the emerging on-line retailing segment of low-cost digital content enabled by micropayments processing.

A. Producer Benefits

Many of the collective advantages that arise in connection with assimilative innovation benefit producers. One important way in which producers benefit is through accelerated adoption of their innovative products through assimilation into a familiar user context, such as the television or car. Our case study on DVRs illustrates the enhanced "survival advantage" that winning suppliers in the DVR segment were able to obtain by having their product capabilities assimilated into digital TV set-top boxes and digital subscriber platforms. As a whole, the DVR industry has benefited from this arrangement, through accelerated user adoption rates, allowing this product segment to reach sustainable, critical mass levels.

Another means of producer benefit is the lowering of entry barriers by the assimilation of on-line capabilities into traditional retailing formats. Numerous studies have shown that digital retailing formats have significantly lowered inventory, storage, and distribution costs for on-line retailers.[104] For example, the low-cost on-line distribution channels afforded by such business models as iTunes and Rhapsody have allowed more independent musicians to distribute their music files on-line, generating approximately $250 million in annual revenues and raising their per-track earnings.[105] In the case of our eBay example, on-line SMB merchants have benefited by lower integration costs resulting from PayPal's assimilation into eBay's on-line retailing platform. Leveraging eBay's experience in dealing with SMB retailers, PayPal has launched a series of initiatives addressing the needs of this growing segment both on and off the eBay site, including a turnkey storefront retailing platform that considerably lowers the start-up costs for an on-line merchant. PayPal's integrated ability to facilitate cross-border transactions has also enabled eBay's merchants to

---

[104] Brynjolfsson, E., J. Hu, and M. Smith. 2003. Consumer Surplus in the Digital Economy: Estimating the Value of Increased Product Variety at Online Booksellers. *Management Science.*16: 131–141; Brynjolfsson, Erik, and Michael Smith. 1999. "Frictionless Commerce? A Comparison of Internet and Conventional Retailers," 1999 Computing in Economics and Finance (CEF) Conference; Boston, Massachusetts; June 24–26.
[105] Recording Industry Association of America (RIAA) 2006.

access new markets and expand customer bases for their goods. In addition to lowering market entry costs, one EU-commissioned study found that on-line commerce lowers competitive entry barriers typical to traditional retailing formats by reducing incumbent advantages based on switching costs, lock-in effects, and brand recognition.[106]

B. Consumer Benefits

At the same time, consumers have benefited significantly from the innovative outcomes of technology assimilation. These end-user benefits include faster adoption, greater user choice, affordable access, enhanced performance and value, and broad-based participation in directing future innovation. Our DVR case study illustrates how faster adoption of DVR capabilities through bundled offerings has enabled new service innovations such as the introduction of VoD, which increasingly afford consumers greater control over the timing and venue of content viewing. In our GPS navigation system example, manufacturers are increasingly offering more integrated features such as built-in infotainment systems that "result in enhanced value-price ratio of navigation systems, thereby increasing their uptake."[107] Thus consumers get "more bang for the buck."

Studies have shown that web-based integration of traditional commerce models incorporating on-line search, listing, and other functions has enabled the mass adoption of on-line retailing formats, which, in turn, has greatly expanded the diversity of consumer choices, including the availability of more niche offerings.[108] The same applies to the mass proliferation of niche offerings in digitally downloaded videos.[109] To illustrate this increased efficiency of digital retailing, Walmart.com is able to offer six times more inventory to consumers than its own brick-and-mortar stores. On-line bookseller Amazon boasts the "world's largest selection" of books, and

---

[106] Buccirossi, P., C. Cambini, L. Bravo, and P. Siciliani. 2005. Competition Issues in the Provision of Content and E-Commerce Services. *Competition, Contents and Broadband for the Internet in Europe* (EU Framework Programme 6 Specific Support Action/Thematic Priority: Information Society Technologies).

[107] Frost & Sullivan, supra 9.

[108] Brynjolfsson, E., J. Hu, and M. Smith. 2003. Consumer Surplus in the Digital Economy: Estimating the Value of Increased Product Variety at Online Booksellers. *Management Science.* 16: 131–141; Brynjolfsson, Erik, Yu "Jeffrey" Hu, and Michael D. Smith. 2006. From Niches to Riches: The Anatomy of the Long Tail. *Sloan Management Review,* 47(4 Summer) 67–71.

[109] Elberse, A. and F. Oberholzer-Gee. 2006. Superstars and Underdogs: An Examination of the Long-Tail Phenomenon in Video Sales. Harvard Business School Working Paper [unpublished draft].

offers twenty-three times the number of shelf offerings of a typical off-line superstore bookseller. Brynjolfsson et al.'s[110] study on on-line booksellers estimates that the enhanced consumer welfare engendered by the dramatic increase in product variety allowed by digital distribution formats is "seven to ten times as large as the consumer welfare gain from increased competition and lower prices in this market."

In the realm of television broadcast content, the move to digital platforms has enabled a proliferation of specialized programming targeting specific niche audiences.[111] Similarly, the industry shift toward the on-line distribution of music files that now constitutes 8 percent of all music sales by revenues has increased consumers' access to more meaningful choices in music selection.[112] This increased access includes a 300 percent increase in the past three years in the number of on-line music offerings by independent musicians through iTunes and other similar on-line music venues. The result is a greater selection and proliferation of user choices in music files, including more diverse selections from indy musicians. The digital distribution format allows users to customize their music selections by downloading and combining individual song tracks, instead of purchasing entire albums.

In addition to increasing the diversity of consumer choices, the integration of web-based tools has also allowed end users to have more direct participation in the innovation process. For example, in the case of Quick-Books' growing ecosystem, the introduction of new feature sets has been driven in many instances by rapid user feedback cycles facilitated through its on-line forums, which help direct the next generation of specialized applications in future product releases. This increase in the diversity of offerings has also been accompanied in many instances by a significant reduction in consumer prices. For example, one study has shown that prices for books and CDs sold on the Internet are 15–16 percent lower than those sold through traditional brick-and-mortar stores.[113] Cost -savings for on-line shoppers have also been observed in on-line automobile portals such as Autobytel.[114]

---

[110] Brynjolfsson, E., J. Hu, and M. Smith. 2003. Consumer Surplus in the Digital Economy: Estimating the Value of Increased Product Variety at Online Booksellers. *Management Science*.16: 131–141.

[111] CoCombine 2005, citing Armstrong and Weeds 2004; OECD 2005.

[112] RIAA website, found at www.riaa.com. RIAA is the largest music-recording industry association in the United States, representing more than 85% of all music commerce by revenues.

[113] Brynjolfsson, E., J. Hu, and M. Smith. 2003. Consumer Surplus in the Digital Economy: Estimating the Value of Increased Product Variety at Online Booksellers. *Management Science*.16: 131–141.

[114] Morton Scott, Fiona, Florian Zettelmeyer, and Jorge Silva-Risso. Internet Car Retailing. *The Journal of Industrial Economics* 49, 4 (2001): 501–519.

Apart from increasing consumer access to greater choices and value in goods and services, perhaps the most profound example of collective benefits stemming from innovation is found in our car navigation example. The goal of enhancing collective road safety is undeniably a public good, and was enabled by the innovative assimilation of GPS receivers into that most familiar and basic technology: the car. Insofar as telematics promises to not only further the goals of collective public safety but also transform the user experience of the car, the (re)invention of the car has come full circle.

VI. Conclusion: The Diffusion of Intellectual Property

We have shown how the technological life cycle may be viewed as interacting cycles of assimilation and specialization. Rather than disrupting the existing status quo, "discontinuous" stand-alone innovations are often commercialized by becoming assimilated into an existing familiar technology. As the assimilation process continues, technologies coalesce into increasingly broad platforms. These platforms in turn provide significant value to large ecosystems of specialized application providers. This process can be observed in a broad variety of industries, from software to consumer electronics, and from automotive to telecommunication services.

We have emphasized the importance of assimilation in driving future innovation. Intellectual property (IP) incentive systems such as patent grants and licensing are crucial to the assimilation process – they afford the rewards necessary to stimulate follow-on innovation and encourage inventors to disclose their intellectual property and maximize its diffusion.[115] The breadth and duration of protection afforded by an IP system can be designed to minimize the social costs of excessive imitation as well as deadweight losses. IP protection has increased importance as a means of stimulating investment in new foundational technologies, given the latter's potential for spawning future derivative applications and other public benefits.

The process of assimilation creates additional considerations for determining how regulatory policy and competition-based incentive systems drive innovation. IP protection reflects one way in which competition furthers innovation[116] and has been shown to be an effective means of

---

[115] Arora, A. and M. Ceccagnoli. 2005. Patent Protection, Complementary Assets and Firms' Incentives for Technology Licensing. *Management Science*. 52: 293–308.

[116] Dasgupta, P. and J. Stiglitz. "Industrial Structure and the Nature of Innovative Activity," with P. Dasgupta, Economic Journal, 90(358), June 1980, pp. 266–293. Reprinted in The Economics of Technical Change, Elgar Reference Collection, International Library of Critical Writings in Economics, 31, Edwin Mansfield and Elizabeth Mansfield (eds.), Aldershot, UK: Elgar. pp. 133–160.

stimulating R&D investment that benefits the entire ecosystem. In a cumulative innovation process where "foundational" innovations are necessary for future innovation, well-designed IP incentive systems become even more essential. The novelty requirement for patents, for example, becomes important in determining what level of incremental improvement to a platform is afforded protection. In related work on open innovation incentives, we further explore licensing and the role of intellectual property – how "licensing in" and "licensing out" are necessary assimilation tools for innovative platforms to evolve, and for downstream innovations to flourish.

PART III

INNOVATION AND COMPETITION POLICY

6

Favoring Dynamic over Static Competition

Implications for Antitrust Analysis and Policy

David J. Teece

This chapter asks how competition policy should be shaped if it were to favor Schumpeterian competition over neoclassical static competition. Schumpeterian competition is the kind of competition that is engendered by product and process innovation. Such competition not only brings price competition – it tends to overturn the existing order. A framework that favors dynamic over static competition would put less weight on market share and concentration, and more weight on assessing potential competition and enterprise-level capabilities. Developments in evolutionary economics and the behavioral theory of the firm in recent decades indicate how the machinery of a new framework can be engineered and applied to antitrust.

I. Introduction

In 1988, in anticipation of the centennial of the Sherman Act, my Berkeley colleagues and I held a conference on campus that led to the 1992 volume titled *Antitrust, Innovation, and Competitiveness*, with contributions from many of the leading scholars in antitrust law and economics. The conference was designed to alert the law and economics communities to a set of emerging issues on antitrust and innovation. With hindsight, we believe it was a watershed event, and a slow and reluctant awakening to antitrust and innovation issues is now underway.

In the introduction to the *Proceedings* of the conference, Thomas M. Jorde and I as editors endeavored to reframe antitrust questions. The issue, we asserted, was that scholars and practitioners needed to take a more dynamic approach to competition declaring that "as Schumpeter[1] suggested half a

I would like to thank my UC Berkeley colleague Howard Shelanski for many helpful comments.
[1] Schumpeter, J. A. (1942): *Capitalism, Socialism, and Democracy*. New York: Harper & Row.

century ago, the kind of competition embedded in standard microeconomic analysis may not be the kind of competition that really matters if enhancing economic welfare is the goal of antitrust. Rather, it is dynamic competition propelled by the introduction of new products and new processes that really counts. If the antitrust laws were more concerned with promoting dynamic rather than static competition, which we believe they should, we expect that they would look somewhat different from the laws we have today."

We further proclaimed that our "antitrust laws may be at odds with technological progress and economic welfare. We do not by any means wish to assume that all the authors of the various chapters follow our point of view. Indeed, we are confident that several of them do not" (p. 3). In three subsequent papers, efforts were made to move the original agenda forward.[2]

Over the last decade, the intellectual winds have slowly begun to come around. Innovation and dynamic competition are on the radar screen. There is no doubt that the agencies are now taking innovation issues more seriously. The Federal Trade Commission (FTC) and Department of Justice (DOJ) staff and FTC commissioners understand that innovation is important to competition. My colleagues Michael Katz and Howard Shelanski at Berkeley in 2005 published a provocative piece titled "Schumpeterian Competition and Antitrust Policy in High-Tech Markets." The Intellectual Property Guidelines make the exercise of the intellectual property rights more confident, and the FTC-DOJ joint venture guidelines outline acceptable forms of cooperation amongst competitors. While these guidelines do not constitute law, the courts seem to have accepted the revised principles that the agencies have advanced.

II. Economic Theory and the Structuralist Tradition

We remain bereft of evidence that antitrust intervention has benefited the consumer. Indeed, Crandall and Winston[3] conclude that "we find little empirical evidence that past interventions have provided much direct benefit to consumers" (p. 4). Amongst the causes for this unfortunate state of affairs they cite "substantial and growing challenges of formulating and implementing effective antitrust policies in a new economy characterized

---

[2] Hartman, R. S., Mitchell, W., Jorde, T. M., and Teece, D. J. (1993): Assessing Market Power in Regimes of Rapid Technological Change. *Industrial and Corporate Change*, 2:3, 317–350; Teece, D. J. and Coleman, M. (1998): The Meaning of Monopoly: Antitrust Analysis in High-Technology Industries. *The Antitrust Bulletin*, 43:3/4, 801–857; Pleatsikas, C. and Teece, D. J. (2001): The Analysis of Market Definition and Market Power in the Context of Rapid Innovation. *International Journal of Industrial Organization*, 19:5, 665–693.

[3] Crandall, R. W. and Winston, C. (2005): Does Antitrust Policy Improve Consumer Welfare? Assessing the Evidence. *Journal of Economic Perspectives*, 17:4, 3–26.

by dynamic competition, rapid technological change, and important intellectual property" (p. 23).

The lack of compelling evidence indicating that antitrust is not aiding consumers is a matter of concern, and motivates inquiry here. The working hypothesis of this chapter is that the employment of static analysis to address antitrust issues in a dynamic economy is unlikely to improve consumer welfare, and that the chances of helping more than hurting go up if antitrust analysis can create and apply a more dynamic framework.

The problem may be that (a) much of economic theory is still permeated with static analysis; (b) the antitrust practitioner community seems unaware of what is now a substantial literature, much of it now quite robust, on evolutionary theory and the economic, organizational, and behavioral foundations of innovation; and (c) while this new literature has generated meaningful general descriptions of market and organizational behavior, it has only recently caught the attention of antitrust scholars. Because of this, (d) the enforcement agencies are not confident about discarding "conventional wisdom," despite the fact that many of them are aware that much of it is deeply discredited.

This chapter endeavors to help explain why static analysis appears to dominate, even though thoughtful policy makers are aware of dynamic competition. Unfortunately, policy makers are left wielding static analysis in part because of a wrong perception that scholars have not yet filled the intellectual void. Indeed, until this perception changes, not much is likely to happen. As Richard Posner has observed, "antitrust doctrine has changed more or less in tandem with changes in economic theory, albeit with a lag".[4] If scholars do not embrace the now robust behavioral/evolutionary approaches, economists are unlikely to analyze dynamic considerations properly.

Unfortunately, many economists seem to be stuck in a well-traveled and largely irrelevant debate, now half a century old, as to what form of market structure favors innovation, labeling this as the "Schumpeterian" debate. Regrettably, this is all that many have been absorbed from the rich work of Schumpeter, the Austrian School, and extensive development in behavioral and evolutionary economics. This so-called Schumpeterian debate casts Schumpeter too narrowly and is not of much interest anymore. However, it can still bog discussions about competition policy and innovation.

A more careful reading of Schumpeter will reveal at least three Schumpeterian propositions relevant to antitrust policy. (The first two are discussed in this section, the third in the next). The first proposition relates to

---

[4] Posner, R. A. (2001): Antitrust and the New Economy, *Antitrust Law Journal*, 68: 925–944.

the impact of market structure on innovation. On this topic, Schumpeter himself articulated conflicting and inconsistent perspectives. In *The Theory of Economic Development*[5] he spoke of the virtues of competition fueled by entrepreneurs and small enterprises. By the time he wrote *Capitalism, Socialism, and Democracy* (1942), Schumpeter's revised (second) proposition was that large firms with monopoly power are necessary to support innovation.[6] This transformation was no doubt in part a reflection of the transformation that had occurred with respect to the principal sources of innovation in the American economy.

So with respect to the impact of market structure on innovation, Schumpeter seems to have maintained two almost diametrically opposite positions. We will call his first position Schumpeter I and the second position Schumpeter II.

Schumpeter I is perhaps more appealing today than Schumpeter II. Indeed, I believe that the debate over whether to favor competition over monopoly (as the market structure most likely to advance innovation) was won long ago in favor of some form of rivalry/competition.

However, the line of causation that is most commonly discussed runs only from competition to innovation. Indeed, as noted by the FTC: "Competition can stimulate innovation. Competition amongst firms can spur the invention of new or better products or more efficient processes...."[7] While this is undoubtedly correct, it does not recognize that innovation may impact competition and market structure. Nor does it suggest what type of market structure is desirable – only that competition can drive innovation.

Unfortunately, we do not appear to have found a great deal of evidence that market concentration has a statistically significant impact on innovation, despite fifty years of research. The main takeaway is probably that this is not a useful framing of the problem, in that market concentration alone does not stack up even theoretically (let alone empirically) as a major determinant of innovation.

In short, framing competition issues in terms of monopoly vs. competition appears to have been unhelpful, at minimum inconclusive. Rivalry matters, but market concentration does not necessarily determine rivalry.

In briefly reviewing the theory, one can note that some industrial organization theories suggest that innovation is bound to decline with increasing

---

[5] Schumpeter, J. A. (1911): *The Theory of Economic Development: An Inquiry into Profits, Capital, Credit, Interest, and the Business Cycle.* Cambridge, MA: Harvard University Press.

[6] Schumpeter, J. A. (1942): *Capitalism, Socialism, and Democracy.* New York: Harper & Row.

[7] "To Promote Innovation: The Proper Balance of Competition and Patent Law and Policy," Report of the FTC, October 2003.

competition, since the monopoly rents for new entrants will decline with increasing competition.[8]

Other studies, following Arrow,[9] hypothesize a positive relationship between competition and innovation. But Arrow set aide the appropriability problem (i.e., how to capture value from innovation) and posited a perfect property right in the information underlying a specific production technique.

One can perhaps interpret Arrow's property right as a clearly specified and costlessly enforceable patent of infinite duration. The principal focus of Arrow is on how the (pre-invention) structure of the output market affects the gain from invention. Competition wins out because competitive output is larger than with monopoly. Hence, a given amount of unit costs reduction is more valuable if the market is initially competitive. Protected by a perfect patent, the inventor simply licenses the invention at a whisker below the cost saving that the invention makes possible. Put differently, competition will win out and advance innovation when the business environment is characterized by what I call elsewhere a strong appropriability regime.[10]

Absent strong appropriability, the presumption that (perfect) competition is superior to alternative arrangements cannot be built on Arrow.[11] In fact, it is important to note that despite how Arrow's paper is usually interpreted (to claim that competition spurs innovation), Arrow's general position in his writings is, much like Schumpeter, that competitive markets provided inadequate incentives to innovate.

As Sidney Winter points out, Arrow's analysis also sidesteps business model choices.[12] The producer and the inventor are one in the same.

Of course, one must also recognize that business (model) innovation is important to economic welfare, along with technological innovation. But the economics literature (theoretical and empirical) does not seem to address whether market structure is important to this type of innovation.

[8] Dasgupta, P. and Stiglitz, J. (1980): Industrial Structure and the Nature of Innovation Activity. *Economic Journal*, 90, 266–293; Kamien, M. J. and Schwarz, N. C. (1982): *Market Structure and Innovation.* Cambrodge" Cambridge University Press.

[9] Arrow, K. (1962): Economic Welfare and the Allocation of Resources for Invention, in R. R. Nelson (ed.), *The Rate and Direction of Inventive Activity.* Princeton, NJ: Princeton University Press.

[10] Teece, D. J. (1986): Profiting from Technological Innovation. *Research Policy*, 15:6, 285–305.

[11] Arrow, K. (1962): Economic Welfare and the Allocation of Resources for Invention, in R. R. Nelson (ed.), *The Rate and Direction of Inventive Activity.* Princeton, NJ: Princeton University Press.

[12] Winter, S. G. (2006): The Logic of Appropriability: From Schumpeter to Arrow to Teece. *Research Policy*, 35:1100–1106.

Empirical evidence is equally murky. Cohen and Levin[13] review the literature and conclude that there isn't a strong linkage between market concentration and innovation. The endogeneity of market structure is perhaps one reason why a robust statistical relationship between concentration and innovation is yet to be found. Nor is there any significant relationship between market concentration and profitability. As Joskow[14] notes, "we have spent too much time calculating too many kinds of concentration ratios and running too many regressions of these against profit figures of questionable validity" (p. 278).

III. Static and Dynamic Competition

As discussed earlier, there is a third (usually overlooked) but very important proposition embedded in Schumpeter: Dynamic competition should be favored over its poorer cousin, static competition. I will describe both static and dynamic competition in turn. In doing so, I recognize that these styles of competition sometimes do not have bright lines separating them. Certainly, Schumpeter did not provide crisp delineation.

In this chapter I try to give some substance to Schumpeter's intuition. Unfortunately, static competition is frequently favored unwittingly by antitrust economists. Dynamic competition is a style of competition that relies on innovation to bring forth new products, processes, and concomitant price reductions. It improves both productivity and consumer welfare. Promoting it may well mean recognizing that competitive conduct may involve holding short-run price competition in abeyance.[15]

Dynamic competition is not embraced as widely as it needs to be in part because the overwhelming focus in economic research is (implicitly) inside the paradigm of static competition. Indeed, a major contribution can come from simply revealing to judges, juries, the enforcement agencies, and legislators that most economic analysis is static, when it should be dynamic, and as a consequence innovation may well get harmed by superficial answers derived from implicitly held static notions about desirable forms of competition. This bias stems merely from the analytical tools used, as most every economist recognizes the importance of innovation, and then

---

[13] Cohen, W. M. and Levin, R. C. (1989): Empirical Studies of Innovation and Market Structures, in R. Schmalansee and R. Willig (eds.), *Handbook of Industrial Organization.* Amsterdam, The Netherlands: North-Holland.

[14] Joskow, P. (1975): Firm Decision-Making Processes and Oligopoly Theory. *American Economic Review,* 65:2, 270–279.

[15] The argument against generic drugs may be of this kind.

usually proceeds to apply analytical approaches that ignore it. Recognizing this state of affairs should deflate the hubris with which many antitrust scholars approach issues. To the extent they wield analytical tools of static competitive analysis, antitrust analysts are quite likely to make prescriptions that harm both innovation and competition, and sap productivity.

To come up with prescriptions that do more good than harm, it is necessary to inquire about the determinants of innovation, and the impact of antitrust activity on innovation. Dynamic competition is advanced by rapid technological change. And this is where the problem starts. The analytical framework most commonly used by economists stubbornly adheres to the view that market structure and little else determines the rate of technological change. This framework is grossly inadequate.

For instance, in merger analysis, as in many other forms of antitrust analysis, one is required to define a market and look at market shares. If a merger augments concentration above an accepted threshold, it may be blocked. Merger analysis usually proceeds this way, even though there are a growing number of economists who are beginning to think otherwise, particularly in differentiated product contexts.[16]

More often than not, however, avid antitrust economists (perhaps inadvertently) adopt the mantle of static competition. Because of its familiarity, they (unwittingly and inappropriately) use the apparatus of static microeconomics to analyze contexts where innovation is important. Innovation is at best an afterthought in static microtheory. The presence of innovation complicates the analysis, destroys equilibrium, and debases the value and utilities of the tool bags that most economists carry. This is unsettling, and tends to be resisted by the profession. Thus, dynamic analysis is shunned either because it isn't known or, if known, it is feared that recognizing it will be too hostile to well-accepted and well-practiced analytical frameworks. Competition policy advocates should not accept this state of affairs any longer.

To preview what is to follow, this chapter recognizes that dynamic competition is associated with the change in external circumstances and/or the generation of new products, new processes, and new business models. As Schumpeter said, competition fueled by the introduction of new products and processes is the more powerful form of competition: "Competition from the new commodity, the new technology, the new source of supply, the new type of organization – competition which commands a decisive

---

[16] In these contexts, that emerging consensus seems to be that what matters are the particular firms one is dealing with.

cost or quality advantage and which strikes not at the margins of the profits and the output of existing firms, but at their foundations and their very lives".[17]

In today's vernacular, dynamic competition is heavyweight competition; static competition is the "lite" version. Advocates of strong competition policy must surely favor the former. Static competition is anemic compared to dynamic competition. More on this in the following.

A. Static Competition

Static competition reflects an intellectual framework, generally not a state of the world. Absent innovation, (static) competition manifests itself in the form of existing products offered at low prices. No new products are introduced, and rapid price reductions driven by innovation simply do not exist. There is no hurly burly competition. Without innovation, all firms have the same technology and the same business models. Markets are in a comfortable equilibrium. Nobody makes any money, of course, but nor do they innovate. Price gets squeezed down to marginal cost.

Agents are nevertheless rational and well informed. Prices are drawn down to the floor of long–un marginal cost; but that floor becomes their resting place. Firms just make their cost of capital and cover long run marginal costs, and consumers are bereft of new products and true bargains. They never get overcharged, but there is nothing to charge them up.

While the framework has a simple theoretical simplicity and elegance, the industrial dynamics behind it are uninteresting. Absent innovation, there is unlikely to be much or any new entry – if incumbents can satisfy demand, new entrants are not needed. Absent scale economies, no firm is likely to become dominant, and the ecology of firms is unchanging.

The static economics paradigm is what infuses, at least the undergraduate economics textbooks. It is not a recognizable state of the world, except perhaps in a few local markets somehow insulated from competition. Unfortunately, it is what tends to spill over into antitrust economics as a normative paradigm. However, it is not and has never been a good abstraction of the economy. Nor has it ever been a state to which we should aspire.

B. Dynamic Competition

Dynamic competition is driven by innovation, but not exclusively. The term "dynamic" is a shorthand for a variety of rigorously competitive activities

---

[17] Schumpeter, J. A. (1942): *Capitalism, Socialism, and Democracy*. New York: Harper & Row.

such as significant product differentiation and rapid response to change, whether from innovation or simply new market opportunities ensuing from changes in "taste" or other forces of disequilibrium. Dynamic competition is in fact more intuitive and much closer to today's everyday language view of competition than is the (textbook) notion of static competition.

Dynamic competition is of course embedded in the Austrian economics framework of Carl Menger and his fellows (e.g., Kirzner). The Austrian treatment is quite different from neoclassical economics. The focus of the latter is on a static equilibrium in which there are a minimum number of known exogenous variables. Austrian economics does not purport to compute any equilibrium, because the essence of competition is taken to be the dynamic pattern by which it comes about, not the equilibrium itself. The truth is, Hayek argued, that "competition is by its nature a dynamic process whose essential characteristics are assumed away by the assumptions underlying static analysis".[18] The wishes and desires of consumers cannot be regarded as given information to producers but ought to be regarded as problems to be solved by the process of competition.

With dynamic competition, new entrants and incumbents alike engage in new product and process development and other adjustments to change. Frequent new product introductions followed by rapid price declines are commonplace. New innovations stem from investment in research and development (R&D), and/or the improvement and combination of older technologies. There are continuous introductions of product innovations, and from time to time dominant designs emerge. With innovation, there are explosions in the numbers of new entrants, but once dominant designs emerge implosions are likely and markets become more concentrated. As with dynamic competition, innovation and competition are tightly linked.

The model of dynamic competition recognizes that competition is a process, and that entrepreneurs and entrepreneurial managers are essential to it. Stagnation is defeated by perennial gales of competition. Maintaining innovation depends on the existence of entrepreneurs and institutional structures that support innovation.

Technological innovation comes in waves, based on different technologies. These waves cause what Schumpeter called "creative destruction".[19] A large fraction of new (radical) technologies are introduced by enterprises new to an industry; however, incumbents do sometimes pioneer, and if not

---

[18] Hayek, F.A. (1948): *The Meaning of Competition in Individualism and Economic Order.* Chicago: Chicago University Press.

[19] Hayek, F.A. (1948): *The Meaning of Competition in Individualism and Economic Order.* Chicago: Chicago University Press.

are often able to imitate or improve on the new entrants products. The benefits of creative destruction may not come immediately; changes take time. Innovation drives competition, and competition is in turn driven by innovation.

This paradigm of industrial change has been refined by Abernathy and Utterback[20] and given some theoretical motivation by Burton Klein.[21] There is now considerable evidence supporting it over a wide range of technologies.[22] It implicitly recognizes inflexion points in technological and market evolutions. The advent of new technological ensembles or paradigms is usually marked by a wave of new competitors entering an industry to sustain success. Incumbents must master discontinuities as well as incremental change and improvement.

There are many other complementary "models" of innovation. At their core, most can be related to an evolutionary theory of economic change and a behavioral theory of the firm. As Sydney Winter once said, the methodological imperative of evolutionary theories is "dynamics first"; the methodological imperative of behavioral theory is that internal firm structure (not market structure) and internal processes such as learning, diffusion, sensing, seizing, and reconfiguring impact firm behavior.

Evolutionary theory in economics is sometimes understood to be economic Darwinism, but the logical structure of an evolutionary theory is much broader than its biological versions. Evolutionary theory draws attention to what went before. As a general principle, novelty comes about by changing and combining existing artifacts and structure. "Descent with modification" crystallizes this key point.[23] Selection leaves behind variants that are unfit according to the selection criterion at work.

Selection processes include not only births and deaths of individual firms[24] but also the ability to adapt to the changing environment by changing

---

[20] Abernathy, W. J. and Utterback, J. M. (1978): Patterns of Industrial Innovation. *Technology Review*, 80:7, 40–47.

[21] Klein, B. H. (1977): *Dynamic Economics*. Cambridge, MA: Harvard University Press.

[22] Klepper, S. and Grady, E. (1990): The Evolution of New Industries and the Determinants of Market Structure. *Rand Journal of Economics*, 21:1, 27–42; Utterback, J. and Suarez, F. (1993): Innovation, Competition, and Industry Structure. *Research Policy*, 22:1, 1–21; Malerba, F. and Orsengio, L. (1996): Schumpeterian Patterns of Innovation are Technology-Specific. *Research Policy*, 25:3, 451–78.

[23] *See* Durham, W. (1991): Coevolution: Genes, Culture, and Human Diversity. Stanford, CA: Stanford University Press. Durham sets out five requirements for an economic theory of change: units of transmission (e.g., ideas, values); sources of variation (e.g., invention); mechanisms of transmission; processes of transformation; and sources of isolation.

[24] Hannan, M. T. and Freeman, J. H. (1989): *Organizational Ecology*. Cambridge, MA: Harvard University Press.

strategies and structures.[25] Scholars disagree on the amount of adaptation that is possible. Some evolutionary economists see firms as strongly constrained; strategic management scholars claim much greater capacity for change effectuated by managers. All recognize that the advance of change in the context of changing markets and technologies will lead to diminished prospects for the enterprise.

Another common thread to behavioral/evolutionary mechanisms is that they are probabilistic rather than determinative.[26] Rigorous evolutionary theories will make probabilistic statements like "there is a Z probability that individual Y will not replicate (die when the entity has a limited life span) under the selection environment X".[27]

Because business enterprises are guided by routines that interact in highly complex ways, managers more often than not find it difficult to figure out what makes the enterprise successful. This ambiguity around causation becomes a problem when the environment changes, as causal ambiguity makes it difficult to figure out what the enterprise should do differently. When Japanese auto manufacturers started to take a large share away from the U.S. manufacturers in the 1980s, a string of explanations were put up by the U.S. auto industry to explain the phenomenon, including a view that the cost of capital was lower in Japan, that unfair trade barriers in Japan prevented exports from the United States, to concerns that the U.S. firms were falling behind in the use of robotics, and so on. It took nearly two decades for the U.S. auto industry to figure out for itself that labor-management issues, and management itself, were key causal factors associated with decline.

Once causation was more accurately diagnosed, management and organizational changes were made that began to make a difference. As explained in Teece,[28] often it is necessary to create a breakout structure to unshackle the new from the old.

There are a number of assumptions and propositions that characterize dynamic competition. Many of them are rooted in an evolutionary theory of economic change. As Schumpeter said, "in dealing with capitalism, you

---

[25] Teece, D. J. (2007): Explicating Dynamic Capabilities: The Nature and Microfoundations of (Sustainable) Enterprise Performance, *Strategic Management Journal*, 28:13, 1319–1350; Augier, M. and Teece, D. J. (2008): Strategy as Evolution with Design: The Foundations of Dynamic Capabilities and the Role of Managers in the Economic System. *Organization Studies*. 29: 1187–1208.

[26] Aldrich, H. (1999): *Organizations Evolving*. London: Sage Publishing.

[27] Murmann, J. P. (2003): *Knowledge and Competition Advantage: The Coevolution of Firms, Technology, and National Institutions.* Cambridge: Cambridge University Press.

[28] Teece, D. J. (2007): Explicating Dynamic Capabilities: The Nature and Microfoundations of (Sustainable) Enterprise Performance, *Strategic Management Journal*, 28:13, 1319–1350;

are dealing with an evolutionary process." Features of evolutionary theory are outlined in the next section.

IV. Relevant Aspects of Evolutionary/Behavioral Economics

Evolutionary economics and the behavioral theory of the firm are separate but related frameworks. Both have been in existence for half a century or more. Both embrace firms and markets as we see them. Both recognize a capability to discover new technologies and business models in the economic system. Entrepreneurial activity by individuals and enterprises is critical to this capability.

Some endogenous generation of innovative opportunities is likely. Evolutionary theories recognize some process of imperfect (mistake-ridden) learning and discovery on the one hand, and selection on the other. Whereas neoclassical theory can recognize bad outcomes due to bad luck and uncertainty, evolutionary theory accepts the systematic mistakes associated with ignorance or wrong-headed understanding. Clearly, the canons of rational choice theory and equilibrium economics provide only a very limited basis for the study of innovation.

Neoclassical theory almost completely neglects the specificities of competencies and skills that each firm possesses. The relatively tacit and organizational capabilities that cannot be imputed to individuals are especially neglected. This neglect impedes any satisfactory analysis of the innovative capabilities of firms.

Bounded rationality is assumed as agents have an imperfect understanding of the environment they live in, and what the future will deliver. Because of limits to rationality, enterprise behavior is often rule guided/based. There are relatively invariant routines shaped by the learning history of the enterprise.

Adaptation and learning generate variety. Managerial action inside firms (at headquarters)[29] and market and factor market competition between firms act as selection mechanisms, leading to the disappearance of some firms and the rapid growth of others.

Knowledge of specific technologies determines how technology is going to advance. Technological paradigms shape the direction of future change. There is no innovation possibility frontier.

Technologies develop along relatively ordered paths (or trajectories) shaped by specific technical properties, search rules, technical "imperatives,"

---

[29] Managers act as the proximate agent of selection when they pull resources from underperforming units and reallocate them to growing units.

and cumulative expertise. As a consequence, diversity between firms is a fundamental and permanent characteristic of environments undergoing technical change.

Firms differ because of different technological capabilities with respect to innovation, differing degrees of success in adapting technologies developed externally, and different cost structures. They may also differ because of differing search/sensory procedures and capabilities, and differing strategies (behaviors).

One should expect path dependencies when there are increasing returns of some kind. This will be especially true for (a) information goods and (b) cumulative technological advances. How strong path dependencies are is mainly an empirical question.

Market concentration is a function of two opposing forces: (a) Selection mechanisms tend to increase the standing of innovating firms, while (b) learning and imitation mechanisms spread innovations/new knowledge throughout the potential adapters, thereby reinforcing existing disparities via cumulative mechanisms internal to the firm.

Abilities to innovate and imitate are firm specific and depend on a firm's past innovative record – learning is cumulative. Chance matters, but chance favors those firms that are prepared.

Although some of the economic benefits from innovation and the adaptation of new products and processes can be appropriated by the innovators themselves, there are learning externalities.[30] The ease of imitation depends on the intellectual property regime (strong or weak) with the nature of the relevant knowledge (codified or tacit). Skills and know-how almost always leak out from individual generators/first adapters to the whole industry.

Innovation in products and processes is nevertheless to a fair degree endogenous via in-house R&D, technological acquisition (e.g., in licensing), as well as by learning mechanisms.

There is considerable dispersion in costs, profitability, and growth rates inside an industry. Asymmetries in capabilities are a direct consequence of the cumulative, idiosyncratic, and appropriable nature of technological advances. The more cumulative the technological advances at the firm level, the higher the likelihood of success breeding success.

Moreover, the higher the opportunity for technological progress, the higher the possibility of differentials between innovators and laggards. High technological opportunity associated with a high degree of appropriability provides incentives to innovate for a firm on or near the frontier but possibly low incentives for firms with relatively lower technological capability.

---

[30] Teece, D. J. (1986): Profiting from Technological Innovation. *Research Policy*, 15:6, 285–305.

"Normal" technical progress proceeds along trajectories defined by an established paradigm and extraordinary technical advance associated with the emergence of new paradigms. As shown by others[31] market processes are generally weak in directing the emergence and selection of radical technological discontinuities. Put differently, when the process of innovation is highly exploratory, its direct response to economic signals is weaker and its linkage with scientific knowledge is greater. Institutional and scientific contexts are more important than the market.

Institutions and markets co-evolve. Industrial, technological, and institutional factors interact. In particular, research and training bodies and the intellectual property system help to shape industrial outcomes. The competitive strengths of individual enterprises as well as the industry depend on such factors. For instance, according to Murmann,[32] German firms achieved global superiority in dyestuffs by 1914 not because they had superior strategies and organization, but because there were a large number of new entrants, and a large number of exits, giving the German dye industry more room to experiment with different firm strategies and structures. By 1900 the leading dye firms had all developed in-house R&D capabilities and could match new product introductions by competitors in the UK and the United States, as well as in Germany. The German firms also patented heavily in the UK, and their innovative efforts at home were built on an extremely strong university system in chemistry. "Germany had it easier than Britain in bringing forth competitive firms."[33] The British government also imposed higher tariffs on industrial alcohol, an important input in dye making. Strong organizational capabilities in R&D, manufacturing, marketing, management, and strong patent portfolios allowed the German dye industry to capture 70–90 percent of the world market share.[34] Strength in both the supplier industry and in supporting institutions aids innovation. The German firms actively shaped their selection environment – particularly education and training, tariffs, and patents. German firms not only benefited from governmentally supported education and training; they helped upgrade them.

Indicators of dynamic competition include heterogeneous firms engaging in experimentation and innovation. New products and processes

[31] Dosi, G. (1984): *Technical Change and Industrial Transformation*. London: MacMillan.
[32] Murmann, J. P. (2003): *Knowledge and Competition Advantage: The Coevolution of Firms, Technology, and National Institutions*. Cambridge: Cambridge University Press.
[33] Murmann, J. P. (2003): *Knowledge and Competition Advantage: The Coevolution of Firms, Technology, and National Institutions*. Cambridge: Cambridge University Press.
[34] Murmann, J. P. (2003): *Knowledge and Competition Advantage: The Coevolution of Firms, Technology, and National Institutions*. Cambridge: Cambridge University Press.

are developed and introduced, and internal processes are reworked and adjusted. Firms constantly battle unanticipated events. Rivalrous behavior is the norm.

An evolutionary approach underscores the importance of maintaining variety in the economic system. Competition policy authorities as well as other agencies must be concerned with protecting economic diversity and meaningful variety in organizational forms. The focus need not be a particular market – it should be broader as what is outside the market tends to be among the best candidates for Schumpeterian entry and radical innovation.

These propositions, derived mainly from behavioral and evolutionary theories of firms and markets, promise to expand our understanding of firm behavior particularly in domains of rapid innovation. Following Joskow,[35] I would like to believe that the field of industrial organization, to which antitrust economics owes so much, can "play an important leadership role in the extension and revision of the conventional theory of the firm rather than be its prisoner."

V. Implications

A. General

Static and dynamic competition have elements in common. Current law embraces both,[36] although in my view, when it relies on economic theory to inform it, the law gets a larger injection of static analysis than dynamic analysis. But dynamic analysis has always been embraced to some degree by the law.

Traditional static analysis focuses on detecting market power in product markets. Dynamic analysis views competition through a broader lens and focuses less on outcomes and more on process. It favors maintaining rivalry, but it also protects property. The working assumption is that intellectual property rights are desirable institutional/legal arrangements providing necessary appropriability mechanisms to promote and reward innovation.

The framework also recognizes that the benefits of dynamic competition do not arrive immediately; some short-run static inefficiencies may have to

---

[35] Joskow, P. (1975): Firm Decision-Making Processes and Oligopoly Theory. *American Economic Review*, 65:2, 270–279.

[36] Katz M. and Shelanksi, H. (2007): Mergers and Innovation. Antitrust Law Journal, 74:1, 1–85. As noted by Kartz and Shelanksi, Judge Learned Hand wrote as early as 1916 that "the consumers interest in the long run is quite different from an immediate fall in prices" and spoke of competition as a proper stimulus to maintain "industrial advance."

be tolerated to support innovation. Wooden policies blind to innovation and fixated on short-run efficiencies are likely to hurt innovation, and thereby hurt competition.

If policy is to favor dynamic over static competition, a role for vigorous antitrust enforcement still remains, but it proceeds less self-confidently. Uncertainty and complexity are hallmarks of dynamic market environments. In particular, the tools of static analysis should be used sparingly, if at all. Simple rules based on static analysis may well stand in the way of competition. In particular, concentration analysis should be deemphasized, as Ordover and Willig indicate (perhaps for different reasons).[37] To prohibit mergers merely to manage concentration is unlikely to help consumers.

More generally, the presumption that more competitors is always better is overturned – once the goal is not just lowering price but also protecting innovation.

Barriers to entry may need to be examined over a longer time period and must be examined at the firm level.[38] The roles of supporting structures and government funding for research also affect entry conditions. They may purely reflect capabilities that incumbents have developed that newcomers should not expect to possess. Capabilities are likely to reflect the search for unique advantages. Their possession drives competition.

In stark contrast to the basic assumption of the structure–conduct–performance paradigm, in dynamic contexts, conduct in this framework is not a function of market structure. Market conduct is driven more by internal organizational factors: standard operating procedures, investment routines, and improvement routines. Performance depends on the (relative) organizational capabilities and behavioral traits of the enterprise. Enhanced industrial performance also stems from the improvement in individual technologies and the expansion in the use of more productive technologies.

As discussed previously, some typical evolutionary patterns to industry dynamics can be observed – perhaps one can call it an industry life cycle. In the early stages of the evolution of an industry, firms tend be small, and entry relatively easy, because of the diversity of technologies being employed. However, as the dominant design emerges, the costs of entry rise as an established scale for competition activity becomes apparent.

---

[37] Ordover, J. A. and Robert D. Willig (1983): The 1982 Department of Justice Merger Guidelines: An Economic Assessment, 71 Calif. L. Rev. 535.

[38] The firm-level analog is what is referred to in the strategy literature as "isolating mechanisms."

Learning becomes cumulative, and established firms are somewhat advantaged over the new entrants. After an industry shakeout, established firms settle into a more stable industry structure. This may sooner or later be overturned by a new technology that has the promise of being superior. Under normal circumstances, with entry and exit, the life of firms tends to be short.[39]

New technologies can be competency enhancing or competency destroying. The essence of the dynamic competition approach is that technological change itself shapes industry structure. Also, path dependencies and dynamic increasing returns are likely to be present in many circumstances.

Put differently, the rate and direction of innovation at the level of the firm do not depend on market structure but on the competences of the firm, the internal and external knowledge the firm can draw on, the IP regime, and its complementary assets. Entry conditions are a function of appropriability and cumulativeness. Learning and innovation will also shape the boundaries of the firm.

Market concentration is likely to be an outcome of market selection, which in turn depends on the uneven exploitation of learning opportunities; that is, concentration has little to do with market power.

Moreover, if the degrees of selection are interpreted as a proxy for how well markets work – in the sense that they quickly reward winners and weed out losers – then more efficient markets tend to yield, in evolutionary environments, more concentrated market structures, rather than more "'perfect" ones in the standard sense.[40]

The possibility of innovation rests on the permanent existence of unexploited technological opportunities. A growing body of evidence from the microeconomics of innovation supports the notion that unexploited opportunities permanently exist and that what firms actually explore is a small subset of what is available.[41] Accordingly, firms are not constrained by nature, but by their own capabilities – therefore there are almost always opportunities to be sensed and seized.

[39] Geroski, P. A. (1995): What Do We Know About Entry? *International Journal of Industrial Organization*, 13, 421–440; Geroski, P. A. and Schwalbach, J. (eds.) (1991): *Entry and Market Contestability: An International Comparison*. Oxford: Basil Blackwell.

[40] Dosi et al. (1995): "Learning, Market Selection and the Evolution of Industrial Structures," *Small Business Economics*, 411–436.

[41] Rosenberg, N. (1976): *Perspectives on Technology*. Cambridge University Press; Rosenberg, N. (1982): *Inside the Black Box*. Cambridge: Cambridge University Press; Freeman, C. (1982): *The Economics of Industrial Innovation*, 2nd Edition. London: Pinter; Dosi, G. (1988): Sources, Procedures and Microeconomic effects of Innovation. *Journal of Economic Literature*, 26, 1120–1170.

B. Market Definition

Market definition issues typically play a central role in antitrust analysis, especially as they relate to Sherman Section II and Clayton Act issues. Defining the boundaries of one or more markets is the first step under the Merger Guidelines.

Economists recognize that market definition is merely an analytical tool. As Ordover and Willig[42] put it, "Arguments for and against a merger that turn upon distinctions between broad and narrow markets definitions are, to an economic purist, an inadequate substitute for, and a diversion from, sound direct assessment of a merger's effect." While Ordover and Willig are undoubtedly correct, in practice the courts and agencies seem to require market definition.

An evolutionary/dynamic competition perspective would appear to support Ordover and Willig's position, as market share/concentration is unlikely to have much power in explaining conduct decisions, including those surrounding pricing. There is no general theorem establishing that higher concentration leads to higher prices or less output. There may be some theoretical support in static models to show that equilibrium output falls and equilibrium prices rise as the number of firms decline.

There is a modicum of empirical work in some markets like telecom and airlines to support the structure–conduct–performance paradigm. But the evidence supporting it is weak, and when innovation is significant, theoretical connections and empirical correlations become even weaker.

Fortunately, the Merger Guidelines are clear that at least in the merger context, market share is only a starting point – market definition is merely a tool. But it may not be even a good starting point or a good tool when the industry is characterized by rapid technological change. As discussed earlier, high market share may simply indicate that selection/competition processes are working well.

Also, as Katz and Shelanski[43] note, in practice the hypothetical monopolist test is hard to apply in the context of innovation. Hartman et al.[44] note that when innovation is present, products are likely differentiated in quality, and price is not the main or only competitive weapon. Furthermore, we note that innovation can make it difficult to define relevant product

[42] Ordover, J. A. and Robert D. Willig (1983): The 1982 Department of Justice Merger Guidelines: An Economic Assessment, 71 Calif. L. Rev. 535.
[43] Katz, M. and Shelanski, H. (2005b): Schumpeterian Competition and Antitrust Policy in High-Tech Markets. *Competition*, 14, 47.
[44] Hartman, R. S., Mitchell, W., Jorde, T. M., and Teece, D. J. (1993): Assessing Market Power in Regimes of Rapid Technological Change. *Industrial and Corporate Change*, 2:3, 317–350.

markets because business executives and government officials alike may not yet know what the future products will be.

The hypothetical monopolist test to establish relevant markets may be better suited for quasi commodity products than for high-tech companies. With innovation, value disparities are likely to exist among substitute products. In the context of the earlier discussion, before the emergence of the dominant design, competition takes place on features, not price. Hence, the hypothetical monopolist test might not be applicable before the emergence of a dominant design. In the case of autos, an application of the test circa 1910 may have put steam cars, electric cars, and internal combustion engine cars in separate markets, despite the fact that competition among these technologies was already fierce, and over the next few years it led to the obliteration of producers who were not able to transition to the design and production of internal combustion engine autos.

More importantly, if one is to adopt a future looking posture, then neither the agencies nor the courts are likely to know which products are likely to be good substitutes in the future. Since innovation produces new product and lowers the cost of existing products, it is necessary to include in the market such future products; but this is quite difficult to do in many instances.

C. Market Share and Actual vs. Potential Competitors

In traditional analysis, a market is first defined, and then actual competitors within it are identified and allocated a market share. In conventional analysis, actual but not potential competitors are included in the market. Potential competitors are recognized only when certain conditions of probability and immediacy of entry are met.

In dynamic contexts, potential competitors can be of very considerable importance. As discussed, what today may be thought of as a potential competitor can obliterate incumbents tomorrow in acts of Schumpeterian creative destruction. To exclude such competitors from the boundaries of the market would clearly be a mistake.

As discussed earlier, what is required is an assessment of capabilities. These are difficult to quantify, but a very large literature now exists in the field of strategic management.[45] This provides many clues about how to how to assess the capabilities of both actual and potential competitors.

---

[45] Teece, D. J., Pisano, G., and Shuen, A (1997): Dynamic Capabilities and Strategic Management. *Strategic Management Journal*, 18:7, 509–533; Teece, D. J. (2007): Explicating Dynamic Capabilities: The Nature and Microfoundations of (Sustainable) Enterprise Performance, *Strategic Management Journal*, 28:13, 1319–1350;

Furthermore, snapshots on market shares, whether present or forward looking, will not tell you much if markets are in turmoil, as they frequently are in dynamic contexts. Moreover, a high market share by no means suggests market power. Not only are today's market shares a poor indicator of the future but, as already noted, a high market share may indicate not just superior performance but strong selection (competition) at work in the industry.[46]

Accordingly, in both merger analysis and in the Section II cases, when dynamic competition is at work, one must look beyond market share data. Serious consideration of potential competitors is required. After all, studies show that new entrants almost always drive innovation in established industries.

A focus on potential competition will help to ensure that market analysis is forward thinking. Market share is likely to be irrelevant in regimes of rapid change, and competition for the market is likely to be as significant as the competition within it.[47]

Katz and Shelanski[48] likewise note that market share may be altogether irrelevant in some cases because there may be markets in which innovation is so characteristic and sustained that firms compete not just for market share but for markets as a whole. A firm's monopoly today may say little about the firm's prospects one, two, and five years down the road.

One should note that there have already been efforts to come up with new analytic approaches to market definition in recognition of the fact that defining the market at the level of the product is difficult when successful future products cannot be predicted with any degree of certainty. I refer to Gilbert and Sunshine's proposal for innovation markets.[49] They put

---

[46] Katz, M. and Shelanski, H. (2007): Mergers and Innovation. *Antitrust Law Journal*, 74:1, 1–85. "Even absent innovation, there are reasons to be cautious about the interpretation of market share data. In order to generate sensible predictions of the effects of a merger, the measurement and analysis of market shares should always be tied to a coherent theory of competitive effects that fits the facts of the industry under consideration. Put another way, the analysis of market shares can most confidently be used to predict adverse competitive effects of a merger when one has an empirically supported theory that market shares are informative of competitive conditions and that an increase in concentration will harm competition and consumers."

[47] Teece, D. J. and Coleman, M. (1998): The Meaning of Monopoly: Antitrust Analysis in High-Technology Industries. *The Antitrust Bulletin*, 43:3/4, 801–857; Pleatsikas, C. and Teece, D. J. (2001): The Analysis of Market Definition and Market Power in the Context of Rapid Innovation. *International Journal of Industrial Organization*, 19:5, 665–693.

[48] Katz, M. and Shelanski, H. (2005a): Merger Policy and Innovation: Must Enforcement Change to Account for Technological Change, in Lerner and Stein (eds.), *Innovation Policy and the Economy*, Volume 5 Boston: The MIT Press, pp. 109–165.

[49] Gilbert, R. and Sunshine, S. (1995): Incorporating Dynamic Efficiency Concerns in Merger Analysis: The Use of Innovation Markets. *Antitrust Law Journal*, 63, 569–601.

potential competition to one side and focused instead on what they call "innovation markets," by which they seem to mean R&D markets. Although this concept was used in U.S. vs. G.M., the concept seems to have been forgotten.

Despite its shortcomings, the innovation market approach did shift the attention away from product markets to activity upstream. This required antitrust authorities to determine what skills and assets are needed to innovate, and determine who possesses those skills. This can be a fundamentally different inquiry from examining demand-side substitution, which is now quite familiar to economists and many courts. The innovation market approach might have been pushed to its logical conclusion, which is the analysis of capabilities, which we now discuss.

D. Analyzing Capabilities to Assess Competitor Positions and Economic Power

As was noted by Edith Penrose, an enterprise should be defined not by its current products but by its (upstream) "resources," or what some prefer to call capabilities.[50]

Penrose defined the internal resources of the firm as "the productive services available to a firm from its own resources," particularly those from management experience. "A firm is more than an administrative unit; it is a collection of productive resources". She saw that "many of the productive services created through an increase in knowledge that occurs as a result of experienced gained in the operation of the firm as time passes will remain unused if the firm fails to expand". Penrose saw the capabilities of management – not exhaustion of technologically based economics of scale – as determining whether a firm could expand to take advantage of opportunities. In reality of course, the resources/capabilities of the firm are defined by other assets, too – like innovation capabilities – but it is important to note that Penrose laid out a model that implicitly eschewed market shares as a measure of how a firm is "positioned" to compete.

Subsequent research has established that firms exhibit more stability in their capabilities than in their products. In this sense, capabilities are easier to analyze than products. Capabilities are a proxy for those interrelated and interdependent aspects of the enterprise that govern its competitive significance. They are arguably a better proxy for competitive position than (downstream) market share.

---

[50] Penrose, E. (1959): *The Theory of the Growth of the Firm.* New York: John Wiley.

Strategy refers to the broad set of commitments made by the firm that define and rationalize its objectives and how it intends to pursue them. Some of this may be explicit, and some implicit in its culture and values. Strategy is often more a matter of faith and determination, not one of calculation. Structure refers to how a firm is organized and governed and how decisions are made and implemented. Strategy and structure shape capabilities, but what an organization can do well is likely to be partly a function of what it has done in the past. However, its R&D activities and success at acquiring external technologies can mold its going forward capabilities. Strategy helps to determine what capabilities one should own and protect.

The world is too complicated for a firm to have "an optimal strategy," and while its capabilities are always in a state of flux, existing capabilities are a good guide to what a company can do in the future.

The capabilities approach would be quite a break from standard analysis. It would calibrate a firm's competitive standing not by reference to products but by reference to more enduring traits.

In a dynamic context a firm will have a changing kaleidoscope of products – yet its underlying capabilities are likely to be more stable. For instance, rather than analyzing Honda's market share in outboard motors, lawnmowers, and small electric generators, perhaps a more meaningful approach for antitrust analysis would be to look at a capability "market." Here the relevant capability might be around small four-stroke internal combustion engines. A capabilities approach may lead to "markets" defined narrower or broader than product markets.

The tools for assessing capabilities may not be well developed yet, but they are developed enough to allow tentative application. Clearly, product market analysis can be unhelpful and misleading in dynamic contexts. Using the right concepts imperfectly is better than a precise application of the wrong ones.

The question arises as to whether simply doing a better job on analyzing potential competition would help. Clearly it might. In the end, however, one would be forced to look at the capabilities of potential competitors – so there is probably no escape from developing the analytics of a capabilities approach.

The innovation market approach introduced by Gilbert and Sunshine implicitly recognizes that focusing on product market analysis is inadequate.[51] But it too narrowly focuses on R&D as the arena for measuring

---

[51] Gilbert, R. and Sunshine, S. (1995): Incorporating Dynamic Efficiency Concerns in Merger Analysis: The Use of Innovation Markets. *Antitrust Law Journal*, 63, 569–601.

innovation competition. Even if it is defined quite broadly, R&D is usually just one element of the resources and problem solving that goes into innovation. The resources that must be committed – and the skills that must be employed – to succeed at innovation are usually much greater than those needed for just R&D. Furthermore, R&D concentration has little to do with innovation outcomes, except possibly in industries characterized by cumulative technological change – and even here, the linkage can be expected to be weak. The widespread adoption of elements of an open innovation[52] model – whereby elements of the innovation process are outsourced – makes this point even more compelling.

E. Merger Analysis

Despite the misgivings of an increasing number of economic scholars, in practice merger policy in the United States, the European Union, and most other jurisdictions where there are competition law focuses on how the merging party's combinations will effect concentration in one or more product markets. In effect, an increase in concentration is taken as a proxy for a decrease in competition that, if of sufficient size, will lead to an increase in the prices faced by consumers.

Focus on dynamic competition is likely to be especially relevant in high-technology industries. The evolutionary/behavioral economics approaches outlined here are not ones that lead to the abandonment of antitrust, or even necessarily to its restriction. But they do lead to a more careful approach that recognizes uncertainty and complexity and relentlessly asks, does this practice support/discourage innovation? Will this merger assist or burden dynamic competition?

The evolutionary/behavioral economics framework that we advance suggests a number of modifications in the way that some analysts may view a particular merger:

1. Market structure is not a meaningful concern, at least not until a dominant design has emerged, and the evolutionary paradigm is established and likely to remain for quite some time.
2. If the analysis is to be deflected away from products in the market, the natural place to look is at capabilities. These transcend products.
3. Only if the merger entities are the only ones with the necessary capabilities to innovate in a broad area should concerns arise. Katz and

---

[52] Chesbrough, H. W., Vanhaverbeke, W., and West, J. (2006): *Open Innovation: Researching a New Paradigm.* New York: Oxford University Press.

Shelanski[53] suggest that if new product development efforts are under-way to create or improve products and processes, and these products are not yet in the market, then harm arises from a merger because it may cripple future product market competition in a market that does not exist. A capabilities approach would soften such concerns – the question should be framed not in terms of whether product market competition will be impaired – as that is too much of an immedi-ate concern – but whether capabilities will be brought under uni-tary control, thereby possibly thwarting future variety in new product development.

F. Intellectual Property Issues

Favoring dynamic (over static) competition does double duty. It also softens the patent–antitrust debate. Static analysis looks on patents with consid-erable awkwardness – and fuels tension between the patent system and antitrust.

The DOJ-FTC intellectual property guidelines have endeavored to rec-oncile the tension between intellectual property and antitrust, by declaring intellectual property just another form of property, and by noting that patents only imply market or monopoly power if they enable control of a relevant market, which is rarely the case. Still, justifying the exclusivity pro-vided by the patent system is not easy for many competition policy advocates. In practice, neoclassical economists are often hostile to patents, believing that the appropriability problem is naturally solved by other mechanisms, which is often not the case.

Embracing dynamic competition causes the tension between intellectual property and antitrust to soften. The patent system provides some amount of exclusion; and some amount of exclusion is required to foster innovation, particularly in more competitive market environments.

Of course, once antitrust doctrine sees the promotion of innovation as its major goal, innovation and competition snap into greater harmony. But the harmony is not perfect, as questions remain with respect to the degree of intellectual property protection needed to foster innovation and competition. The cumulative/sequential nature of innovation means that intellectual property protection needs to be calibrated in a careful manner.

---

[53] Katz, M. and Shelanski, H. (2005a): Merger Policy and Innovation: Must Enforcement Change to Account for Technological Change, in Lerner and Stein (eds.), *Innovation Policy and the Economy*, Volume 5 Boston: The MIT Press, pp. 109–165.

There will almost always be more users of intellectual property than generators of it, so the danger particularly is that the users will try to crimp the scope of intellectual property rights provided to the generators.

V. Conclusion

Antitrust scholars must confront an inconvenient truth: Innovation drives competition as much as competition drives innovation. This requires that antitrust analysis recognize that advancing dynamic (nonstatic) competition will benefit consumers most, certainly in the long run if not in the short run. The law has already begun to move in this direction, as have the agencies. The pace is glacial, however, in part because antitrust economics has trouble grappling with dynamic concepts. The Chicago school in large measure inadvertently (by embracing static microtheory) ignored it; the post-Chicago economics have been almost as reluctant because their tools are inadequate too. Fortunately, a large body of research in evolutionary economics, the behavioral theory of the firm, and corporate strategy has emerged that can be exploited to hasten the transition toward an enlightened approach to antitrust that has a better chance of minimizing the unintended negative consequences of (static) antitrust analysis. If nothing else, the recognition of dynamic issues will temper the hubris that the uninformed sometimes bring to antitrust analysis.

7

Antitrust, Multidimensional Competition, and Innovation

Do We Have an Antitrust-Relevant Theory of Competition Now?

Joshua D. Wright

Harold Demsetz once claimed that "economics has no antitrust relevant theory of competition." Demsetz offered this provocative statement as an introduction to an economic concept with critical implications for the antitrust enterprise: the multidimensional nature of competition. Competition does not take place on a single margin, such as price competition, but several dimensions that are often inversely correlated such that a liability rule deterring one form of competition will result in more of another. This insight has important implications for the current policy debate concerning how to design antitrust liability standards for conduct involving both static product market competition and dynamic innovative activity. The primary purpose of this chapter is to revisit Demsetz's broader challenge to antitrust regulation in the context of the frequently discussed trade-offs between innovation and price competition. I summarize recent developments in our knowledge of the relationship between competition and innovation, highlighting the deficiencies that significantly constrain antitrust enforcers' abilities to confidently calculate inevitable welfare trade-offs. I conclude by discussing policy implications that follow from these limitations.

I. Introduction

Understanding the complex relationship between competition and innovation is essential to the execution of the antitrust enterprise in our modern

This chapter was prepared for the GMU/ Microsoft Conference on the Regulation of Innovation with financial support from the Microsoft Corporation, however, the views expressed in this paper are my own and not necessarily those of Microsoft Corporation. I thank Jeff Armstrong, Jon Baker, Geoff Manne, and Todd Zywicki for helpful comments and Jan Rybnicek and Brandy Wagstaff for research assistance.

economy. The relationship has posed a significant challenge to antitrust economists at least since Joseph Schumpeter's suggestion that dynamic competition would result in "creative destruction" leading to a competitive process where one monopolist would replace another sequentially as new entrants develop a superior product.[1] Schumpeter's argument is often relied on in support of the proposition that antitrust enforcers should be reluctant to intervene in product markets because short-run welfare gains are likely to be swamped by a reduction in dynamic efficiencies associated with less innovation.[2] Of course, the Schumpeter argument can be pushed too far. In theory, it need not be the case that all welfare trade-offs between static product market competition and dynamic efficiencies tilt in favor of the latter.

The well-known and oft-discussed tensions between monopoly, innovation, and product market competition have generated a substantial literature concerning the appropriate role of antitrust enforcement in innovation.[3] This debate has prompted numerous proposals from commentators concerning the best way to incorporate innovation into antitrust analysis, including the development of the "innovation market" concept[4] as well as other frameworks for addressing innovation concerns in merger analysis.[5] Federal agency officials have also demonstrated a concern for antitrust policy that overreaches by attempting to increase short-run product market competition at the expense of dynamic efficiencies created by innovation.[6]

---

[1] Joseph Schumpeter, CAPITALISM, SOCIALISM, AND DEMOCRACY (New York: Harper & Row, 1942).

[2] For an economic analysis of antitrust analysis in innovative industries focusing on single firm conduct, see David S. Evans and Richard Schmalensee, *Some Economic Aspects of Antitrust Analysis in Dynamically Competitive Industries*, in 2 INNOVATION POLICY AND THE EECONOMY 1–49 (Josh Lerner and Scott Sterns eds., Boston: MIT Press, 2002); Richard Schmalensee, *Antitrust Industries in Schumpeterian Industries*, 90 AM. ECON. REV. 192 (Papers and Proceedings, 2000).

[3] Jonathan Baker, *Beyond Schumpeter vs. Arrow: How Antitrust Fosters Innovation*, 74 ANTITRUST L.J. 575 (2007). For an excellent survey of the literature discussing the relationships between competition and innovation, see Richard Gilbert, *Looking for Mr. Schumpeter: Where Are We in the Competition-Innovation Debate?*, 6 INNOVATION POLICY AND THE ECONOMY 159 (Adam B. Jaffe, Josh Lerner, and Scott Stern eds., 2006).

[4] Richard Gilbert & Steven Sunshine, *Incorporating Dynamic Efficiency Concerns in Merger Analysis: The Use of Innovation Markets*, 63 ANTITRUST L.J. 569 (1995).

[5] Michael L. Katz and Howard A. Shelanski, *Mergers and Innovation*, 74 ANTITRUST L.J. 1 (2007).

[6] See, e.g., Thomas O. Barnett, Assistant Attorney General, Antitrust Division, The Gales of Creative Destruction: The Need for Clear and Objective Standards in Enforcing Section 2 of the Sherman Act (June 20, 2006), available at http://www.ftc.gov/os/sectiontwohearings/docs/Barnett-statement.pdf; Gerald F. Masoudi, Deputy Assistant Attorney General, Antitrust Division, Intellectual Property and Competition: Four Principles for Encouraging Innovation (April 11, 2006), available at http://www.usdoj.gov/atr/public/speeches/

There have also been discussions concerning whether reform of the antitrust laws is necessary in industries where innovation, intellectual property, and technological change are essential components of the competitive process. The emerging consensus appears to be that economic analysis and learning are a sufficient basis to conclude that antitrust *should* incorporate dynamic efficiencies into the current framework by accounting for the impact of competition to engage in research and development for new or improved goods, services, or processes. For example, the Antitrust Modernization Committee recommendations and findings conclude that:

[C]urrent antitrust analysis has a sufficient grounding in economics and is sufficiently flexible to reach appropriate conclusions in matters involving industries in which innovation, intellectual property, and technological change are central features.[7]

The debate thus appears to be moving beyond a discussion of "whether" antitrust should account for innovation and toward a fruitful discussion regarding the appropriate methodology for doing so. These developments have the potential to improve antitrust analysis and benefit consumers. An antitrust regime that ignores dynamic efficiencies and innovation and focuses solely on static product market competition is unlikely to improve consumer or total welfare. A regime paralyzed by the fear of deterring innovation such that it fails to intervene in product markets where consumers are threatened by anticompetitive conduct would not fare any better. Accounting for dynamic efficiencies in antitrust analysis is consistent with current antitrust law and policy objectives and would be a desirable goal if such an accounting could be carried out in a manner that the benefits outweigh the sum of administrative and error costs.

The condition in the last sentence is not trivial. Our economic knowledge regarding innovation itself, conduct affecting innovation, and how to assess competitive outcomes involving trade-offs between product market competition and innovation are far less impressive than our knowledge in a purely static setting. The costs of false positives leading to a chilling of pro-competitive innovation are significant. It is therefore critical to assess the state of our economic learning related to antitrust analysis of competitive effects in markets where innovation is an important component of the competitive process. Can economic theory and empirical knowledge

---

215645.htm; Todd J. Zywicki, Director, Office of Policy Planning, Federal Trade Commission, How Should Competition Policy Transform Itself (Nov. 20, 2003), available at http://www.ftc.gov/speeches/other031120zywickijapanspeech.pdf.

[7] Antitrust Modernization Committee Recommendations and Findings 38 (2007).

provide a sufficient basis for identifying those instances in which innovation or conduct impacting innovation will harm consumers?

While the emerging consensus appears to answer this question in the affirmative, this chapter argues that the incorporation of innovation considerations into antitrust analysis is a more difficult enterprise than has generally been appreciated if one is faithful to the theoretical and empirical underpinnings of antitrust analysis. The primary reason for this difficulty is that antitrust enforcers must predict competitive outcomes in the context of rivalry on multiple dimensions that are negatively correlated. The concept that rivalry between firms occurs on a multitude of margins, and not just on price or innovation, is generally well understood. Firms compete on price, output, reputation, quality, innovation, and cost. In many cases, though not all, these forms of rivalry are negatively correlated. This inverse correlation implies that regulators or judges must determine which bundle of competitive forms maximizes efficiency (or consumer welfare) in the face of welfare trade-offs between these activities. The motivation of this chapter is to reexamine the policy implications of the multidimensional nature of competition in light of the current focus on innovation in antitrust analysis.

This chapter is a *reexamination* of the implications of multidimensional competition for antitrust analysis because the problem was long ago recognized and discussed in greater detail by Harold Demsetz. Demsetz began an address in honor of the 100th anniversary of the Sherman Act with the provocative claim: "We do not yet possess an antitrust-relevant understanding of competition."[8] Demsetz argued that the ubiquity of multiple and negatively correlated forms of competitive rivalry, such as price and innovation, had important implications for the antitrust enterprise. Specifically, antitrust intervention would result in a substitution of a different mix of competitive forms. The ability of antitrust intervention to improve consumer welfare depends on our knowledge of these technical rates of

---

[8] Harold Demsetz, *100 Years of Antitrust: Should We Celebrate?*, Brent T. Upson Memorial Lecture, George Mason University School of Law, Law and Economics Center (1991) (including comments by Robert Pitofsky, Richard Schmalensee, Robert H. Bork, and Ernest S. Gellhorn) [hereinafter "*100 Years*"]. Demsetz closed the speech with the following assessment of the antitrust enterprise: "I see little cause to rejoice greatly or to be remorseful over the 100-year history of the Sherman Act," id. at 12. Former Federal Trade Commission Commissioner Thomas Leary described the reaction of the audience as "stunned when one of the vocal proponents of what came to be known as Chicago-School antitrust – a school of thought that was popularly supposed to believe in the supremacy of simple, straightforward theories – opened his lecture with [this] shocking statement." Thomas B. Leary, *Antitrust Economics: Three Cheers and Two Challenges* (paper based on earlier speeches), available at http://ftc.gov/speeches/leary/learythreecheers.htm. Commissioner Leary has noted that the antitrust community "did not pay enough attention to the arguments on which [Demsetz] based his ultimate conclusions." Id.

substitution between various competitive forms. Economic theory, Demsetz argued, provided no such basis.

Section II begins with a more detailed articulation of Demsetz's claim that economics offers no theory on which antitrust regulators and judges could confidently determine which business practices maximize "competition," efficiency, and consumer welfare. Section III summarizes some recent proposals for incorporating innovation effects into antitrust analysis in light of the Demsetz critique explored in Section II. Section IV discusses recent developments in economic theory and empirical learning concerning the relationship between competition and innovation. Section V explores the policy implications of the analysis.

II. The Multidimensional Nature of Competition

That competition takes place on many different margins is not or should not be controversial.[9] Firms devote resources to any number of activities in the pursuit of profit maximization. Firms might reduce prices, innovate by improving existing products or creating new ones, invest in their reputation, lower costs by increasing firm size and exploiting scale economies, or attempt to influence consumer tastes. Antitrust commentators would characterize these activities as "*competition on the merits.*"[10] But not all forms of competitive rivalry are or should be considered "meritorious" from an antitrust perspective. Consider, for example, the well-worn example of the firm that blows up a rival's factory. These forms of competition are beyond the scope of this analysis as it suffices to point out that consumer-welfare–enhancing forms of rivalry are numerous and go well beyond price competition.

A description of the multiplicity of competition is merely the jumping off point for Demsetz's critique of the antitrust enterprise. A proper understanding of the competitive process identifies the error in an antitrust policy that favors maximizing one dimension of competition, such as price competition, which merely encourages substitution toward some other form of competition. Whether this substitution represents an improvement in

---

[9] Acceptance of this proposition, however, illustrates the folly in reliance on the model of perfect competition for antitrust policy. Demsetz notes that the model of perfect competition is only "incidentally" related to price competition and explicitly ignores innovation in the form of technological change, competition by size of firm to exploit scale economies, and reputational competition. *100 Years*, supra note 8, at 3.

[10] The D.C. Circuit in *Microsoft* defined "competition on the merits" as conduct that results in "greater efficiency or enhanced consumer appeal." See *United States v. Microsoft Corp.*, 87 F. Supp. 2d 30 (D.D.C. 2000), rev'd in part, aff'd in part, 253 F.3d 34 (D.C. Cir. 2001), cert. denied, 534 U.S. 952 (2001).

antitrust policy cannot be determined without knowledge of the technical substitutabilities involved between these forms. Our lack of knowledge regarding these technical rates of substitution between forms of competition is the key premise of Demsetz's argument.

Demsetz claimed both that the appropriate policy goal for antitrust regulation cannot be to *increase* competition in the absolute but "*to select the 'best' mix of competitive forms,*"[11] and that economics had been incorrectly presumed capable of moving regulators toward that goal in large part because of a heavy and misplaced reliance on the model of perfect competition.[12] These claims rest on three economic propositions.

The first is that competition may, and usually does, take place on multiple dimensions. The multidimensional nature of competition has already been mentioned and is easily verified through casual empiricism with a walk through the supermarket. This proposition is the least controversial of the three and requires little elaboration.[13]

The second is that the degree of competition associated with one activity is often *negatively correlated* with the degree of competition associated with others and that this negative correlation means that a policy selecting the optimal mix of competitive forms *requires* knowledge of the technical rates of substitution between these forms.

The third proposition is that economic theory does not provide an analytically coherent method to equalize measures of intensity, efficiency, or consumer welfare. The third proposition entails both a theoretical and an empirical component. On one hand, economic theory does not tell us enough about these technical rates of substitution between competitive forms to contribute to policy analysis. On the other hand, empirical knowledge might substitute where theory falls short. Therefore, the claim also depends, at least to some degree, on a level of empirical knowledge regarding the rates of technical substitution between competitive forms insufficient to determine which competitive mix maximizes consumer welfare in a given setting.

The combination of these three propositions led Demsetz to the following *antitrust impossibility theorem*:

If we agree that many relevant forms of competition relate inversely to each other and that no plausible method exists for converting intensities of different forms of competition into a common unit of intensity, then, it would seem, we also must agree that the Sherman Antitrust Act is logically impossible to carry out if its goal

---

[11] *100 Years*, supra note 8, at 4.
[12] Harold Demsetz, *The Intensity and Dimensionality of Competition, in* THE ECONOMICS OF THE BUSINESS FIRM: SEVEN CRITICAL COMMENTARIES 137, 142 (1995) [hereinafter *"Intensity and Dimensionality"*].
[13] Id.

is interpreted as increasing the overall intensity of competition (or to reducing the overall intensity of monopoly).[14]

In Demsetz's view, ignorance regarding these policy-relevant technical rates of substitution across competitive activities would lead to the substitution of political whims and an antitrust policy that can only be described as an expression of tastes.[15] Demsetz concluded that the satisfaction of these subjective preferences rather than any objective measure of competitive intensity was the only "conceptually feasible" goal.[16]

Of course, modern antitrust commentators will probably agree with Demsetz on this claim, but point out that there is now consensus that antitrust analysis proceeds by asking whether the challenged business practice harms consumers or reduces total welfare.[17] At least one commentator responded to Demsetz's address by pointing out that these welfare standards were likely to provide a more fruitful avenue for antitrust policy:

> I would argue that antitrust, to the extent that it's driven by economics, is not about the process of competition, but about welfare-enhancing or consumer-welfare-enhancing outcomes. It does not follow from accepting these points that Professor Demsetz's conclusions are wrong, however. Indeed, the framework to which they lead supports his basic point: we don't have an antitrust-relevant understanding of competition; not necessarily the process of competition, but the consequences it produces.[18]

However, the improvement offered by objective standards is not that it resolves the need to understand the technical rates of substitution between competitive forms when multidimensional competition is at issue, but rather imposes a mode of analysis that would generate substantial agreement over a larger set of antitrust cases.[19] Demsetz had the foresight to anticipate

---

[14] Id. at 144.

[15] *100 Years*, supra note 8, at 4–5.

[16] Id.

[17] *See* Ken Heyer, *Welfare Standards and Merger Analysis: Why Not the Best*, 2 COMPETITION POLICY INT'L 29 (2006) (advocating the total welfare standard); Steven C. Salop, *Exclusionary Conduct, Effect on Consumers, and the Flawed Profit-Sacrifice Standard*, 73 ANTITRUST L.J. 311 (2006) (advocating the consumer welfare standard).

[18] *100 Years*, supra note 8, at 18–19. Schmalensee also noted that the modern industrial organization literature produced results "only slightly less nihilistic than the results that emerge from Professor Demsetz's framework." Id. at 19. Professor Muris has made a similar point in discussing the economic literature on bundling. Timothy J. Muris, Comments on Antitrust Law, Economics, and Bundled Discounts, submitted to the Antitrust Modernization Commission (July 15, 2005), available at http://www.amc.gov/commission_hearings/pdf/Muris.pdf.

[19] *100 Years*, supra note 8, at 19 ("Professor Demsetz and I – and indeed this whole panel – would undoubtedly agree about a large set of antitrust cases, that is, we would agree that

this objection and noted without much elaboration that the underlying logic of his critique applied equally to efficiency.[20]

Antitrust enforcement will generally result in a substitution from one bundle of competitive forms to another where post-intervention we observe more of some types of competition and less of others. This complicates consumer-welfare calculations because it requires some knowledge of the magnitude of this substitution effect and how to make welfare trade-offs in this setting. A primary theme of this chapter is that neither economic theory nor empirical evidence, at this stage, provides a sufficient basis for confident predictions regarding antitrust enforcement in this context.

III. Accounting for Innovation in Antitrust

There is general agreement that antitrust enforcement should account for innovation, that is, ensure that antitrust is neither an obstacle to techno-logical progress that results in desirable innovation nor permits the exercise of monopoly power to impede innovation. The interesting policy question is not whether, but how, antitrust analysis should incorporate innovation concerns into its framework.[21]

At least two approaches to incorporating dynamic efficiencies into antitrust analysis have been considered. The first approach involves expand-ing the existing standard framework for analyzing product markets to con-sider dynamic efficiencies. For example, the Antitrust Modernization Com-mittee appears to endorse this approach with its recommendation that the antitrust laws not be changed to apply different rules to industries where innovation is important and that antitrust enforcers "carefully consider market dynamics in assessing competitive effects."[22] A second approach, which has stimulated much debate in the antitrust literature, involves the "innovation market" concept,[23] which would shift the focus of antitrust

---

certain outcomes were or were not likely to enhance consumer welfare or overall economic efficiency").

[20] Id. at n.1 ("[V]ery little of the discussion to follow needs to be changed if the promotion of efficiency were to be substituted for [competitive intensity]. We also do not yet possess an antitrust-relevant understanding of efficiency").

[21] See Katz and Shelanski, supra note 5, at 4 (2007) ("there is little consensus among scholars, policy makers, or practitioners about . . . the appropriate degree of governmental interven-tion in markets with significant actual or potential innovation").

[22] Antitrust Modernization Commission Report 38–46 (2007). For the purposes of discussion here, the use of "technology markets" is a subset of conventional product market analysis.

[23] DOJ/ FTC Antitrust Guidelines for the Licensing of Intellectual Property § 3.2.3 ("an innovation market consists of the research and development directed to a

analysis from potential product market competition to innovative rivalry as
the unit of analysis.

The choice of framework is critically important to antitrust analysis, as are
the details regarding what evidence will be sufficient to shift plaintiffs' prima
facie burden and what presumptions will apply, if any, in the innovation
context. One important concern regarding how dynamic efficiencies and
innovation-related welfare gains and losses are incorporated into either
mode of antitrust analysis is that the presumptions of the conventional
analysis, such as those associated with industry concentration and firm size,
need not carry over to innovation as a theoretical or empirical matter. I
briefly summarize the two competing approaches.

A. Innovation Effects in Conventional Product Markets

The prevailing approach to dynamic efficiencies has been to incorporate
the potential consequences of innovative activity into conventional product
market analysis. While some have argued that this approach does not sufficiently account for the significance of innovative rivalry, there is no doubt
that antitrust analysis of both mergers and single firm conduct is generally
not limited to solely static concerns.

Conventional merger review, for example, is necessarily forward looking.
Pursuant to the analytical approach set forth by the Horizontal Merger
Guidelines,[24] agencies challenge mergers that they believe will result in
the post-merger firm gaining the power to control market output and
prices and thereby reduce consumer welfare. The presence of significant
innovative activity by merging firms introduces complications at both the
market definition and competitive effects stages of the analysis.

The market definition stage, where economists evaluate which goods and
services are sufficiently close substitutes to those produced by the merging
firms, is complicated by innovation considerations.[25] Innovation blurs the
boundaries at the heart of product market definition because the Merger
Guidelines' framework requires predicting future substitution possibilities

---

particular new or improved goods or processes, and the close substitutes for that research
and development"). See Gilbert and Sunshine, supra note 4.

[24] U.S. DEP'T OF JUSTICE & FEDERAL TRADE COMM'N, HORIZONTAL MERGER GUIDELINES
(1992, revised 1997), available at http://www.ftc.gov/bc/docs/hoizmer.htm [hereinafter
"*Merger Guidelines*"].

[25] For a discussion of these complications, see Katz and Shelanski, supra note 5, at 32–38
(describing these complications and advocating that merger analysis relax its requirement
that "bright-line boundaries" be drawn between products separately from competitive
effects analysis).

in the context of a rapidly changing competitive landscape. Such concerns have led some to argue that market definition will systematically lead to overly narrow markets in the context of rapid innovation.[26]

Innovation considerations also complicate the competitive effects analysis.[27] For example, a merger that may impact the incentive of the post-merger firm to innovate might have both static price effects as well as impact innovation in a manner that will be felt by consumers in terms of increasing competition in a product market. The central challenge for merger analysis in this setting is to determine how changes in post-merger incentives to innovate and increased control over research and development assets that might impact future product market competition will be addressed under the Merger Guidelines.[28]

Monopolization analysis also incorporates dynamic considerations at both the market power and competitive effects stages. For instance, Schumpeterian competition in dynamic industries makes it more difficult to ascertain whether a firm has antitrust market power.[29] Part of this difficulty stems from the relatively weaker inferences about antitrust market power that can be drawn from large market shares in dynamic settings. Conventional monopolization analysis also deals with dynamic considerations when assessing whether single firm conduct has or is likely to generate anticompetitive effects. For example, assessment of competitive effects in dynamic industries includes understanding whether emerging technologies will arise in the near future and understanding industry conditions at a detailed level to make sensible predictions about the dominant firm's incentives to innovate.

B. Innovation Markets

While conventional antitrust analysis incorporates dynamic considerations at some level, some commentators have encouraged an approach that would

---

[26] See, e.g., Christopher Pleatsikas and David J. Teece, *The Analysis of Market Definition and Market Power in the Context of Rapid Innovation*, 19 INT'L J. INDUS. ORG. 665, 671 (2001); David J. Teece & Mary Coleman, *The Meaning of Monopoly: Antitrust Analysis in High Technology Industries*, 43 ANTITRUST BULL. 801 (1998).

[27] See Katz and Shelanski, supra note 5, at 38–49.

[28] For a defense of conventional product market analysis in mergers implicating innovation concerns, see Richard T. Rapp, *The Misapplication of the Innovation Market Approach to Merger Analysis*, 64 ANTITRUST L.J. 19 (1995) (critiquing innovation markets and arguing that potential product market competition and conventional merger analysis is sufficient to address these concerns).

[29] This is a reference to market power in the sense that the term is used in antitrust law rather than the ability of nearly every firm in the modern economy to price above marginal cost.

focus on future product market competition by examining current research and development efforts as a proxy for the future competition itself. These commentators often point to arbitrary cutoffs in the Merger Guidelines, such as the two-year time horizon for consideration of entry,[30] arguing that the conventional approach places too much emphasis on the short run without justification.

Richard Gilbert and Steve Sunshine describe the innovation market procedure as follows: (1) Identify the overlapping research and development activities of the merging firms; (2) identify the alternative sources of research and development; (3) evaluate actual and potential competition from downstream products; (4) assess the increase in concentration in research and development and competitive effects on investment in research and development; and (5) assess research and development efficiencies.[31]

The innovation market concept has been subjected to a considerable amount of criticism on both economic and legal grounds,[32] although most favor the notion that innovation considerations should be incorporated into antitrust analysis.[33] Much of the criticism, and particularly the critique offered by Richard Rapp,[34] emphasizes that innovation markets were built on empirical foundations that were unreliable and too weak to provide the basis for the presumptions applied in conventional merger analysis and thus threaten to decrease the reliability of antitrust enforcement. In the next section I offer a related critique of antitrust analysis, not limited to innovation markets, favoring shortcuts for assessing whether some mixture of competitive conduct involving innovation would harm consumers on the grounds that insufficient theoretical or empirical basis exists in favor of such presumptions.

---

[30] *Merger Guidelines*, supra note 24, at § 3.
[31] See generally Gilbert and Sunshine, supra note 4.
[32] Katz and Shelanski, supra note 5, at 42–43 (summarizing the criticisms while endorsing the "underlying idea of the innovation markets approach").
[33] See, e.g., Ronald W. Davis, *Innovation Markets and Merger Enforcement: Current Practice in Perspective*, 71 ANTITRUST L.J. 677 (2003).
[34] Richard T. Rapp, *The Misapplication of the Innovation Market Approach to Merger Analysis*, 64 ANTITRUST L.J. 19 (1995); see also Dennis W. Carlton, Testimony Before the Federal Trade Commission Hearings on Global and Innovation-Based Competition: Antitrust Policy Towards Mergers When Firms Innovate: Should Antitrust Recognize the Doctrine of Innovation Markets (Oct. 25, 1995), *available at* http://www.ftc.gov/opp/global/carlton .htm (noting that adoption of the innovation market concept would decrease predictability and reliability in terms of improving welfare).

IV. Do We Have an Antitrust-Relevant Theory of Innovation?

Many scholars have recognized that our empirical knowledge of the relationship between market structure and innovation, as well as between market structure and consumer welfare, is limited relative to our understanding of static price effects in conventional product markets.[35] The limits of our empirical knowledge are just one important constraint on the ability of regulators to confidently prosecute "innovation" cases on behalf of consumers. While highlighting our empirical deficiencies in this arena, I also argue that there is an additional, and underappreciated, challenge to incorporating innovation effects into antitrust analysis.

Specifically, the multidimensional nature of competition implies that antitrust analysis seeking to maximize consumer or total welfare must inevitably calculate welfare trade-offs when innovation and price effects run in opposite directions. I argue that such welfare trade-offs are very likely to be debated in antitrust cases where innovation is at issue and contend that, at this point, neither economic theory nor our empirical knowledge of competition and innovation provides a reliable basis to confidently answer the relevant policy question: Which *mixture* of competitive activities will produce greater welfare?

A. Antitrust Analysis of Innovation Will Generally Require Welfare Trade-Offs between Inversely Correlated Forms of Competition

Competition involves a remarkably heterogeneous set of activities. The competitive process requires various forms of rivalry that occur on multiple dimensions: output, price, quality, and innovation. The key point for antitrust policy, highlighted by Demsetz, is that these forms of competition are frequently inversely correlated.[36] Consider the classic Schumpeterian trade-off between innovative and price competition. Innovative competition, which generally increases consumer welfare, is encouraged by limiting output and price competition on already invented goods.

The negative correlation between various forms of competition necessitates that, as a general matter, an antitrust policy that increases one form of

---

[35] See, e.g., David S. Evans and Keith N. Hylton, *The Lawful Acquisition and Exercise of Monopoly Power and the Implications for the Objectives of Antitrust*, 4 COMPETITION POL'Y INT'L 2 (2008) (arguing that economic literature guiding antitrust analysis is based on models of static competition and thus biased against dynamic competition).

[36] *Intensity and Dimensionality*, supra note 12, at 142–44.

rivalry relative to others must also decrease others. The question is whether we can identify the conditions under which a policy that encourages innovative rivalry by limiting output and price competition can be said to make consumers better off. Demsetz argued that the answer is no. He claimed that the multiplicity of competitive activities undermines the ability of "scholars, lawyers, judges, and politicians" to "agree that a policy has increased (or decreased) the general level of competitive intensity."[37] He further asserted that the proposition that consensus can be reached regarding which mixture of competitive activities increased competition was "plain wrong" and the product of "our heavy reliance on perfect competition, monopoly, and oligopoly models, all of which focus only on imitative output competition."[38]

These welfare trade-offs are also a substantial obstacle to creating an antitrust policy that can be said to unambiguously increase consumer welfare in the context of multiple forms of competition.[39] This is not to say that antitrust policy has no sensible basis from which to proceed. The trade-offs between innovative activity, competition, and efficiency have led to a substantial theoretical and empirical literature.[40] In the next section, I argue that neither economic theory nor the state of our empirical knowledge provides a sufficient basis for confidence that antitrust policy can be used to promote consumer welfare where multiple, inversely correlated forms of competition are involved.

B. What Do Economists Know about Dynamic Welfare Trade-Offs?

The central problem in applying an antitrust standard to innovative activity in terms of the inverse correlation between multiple forms of competition is that one must know something about the marginal rates of technical

---

[37] Id. at 142.

[38] Id.

[39] Demsetz himself argued that the combination of inversely correlated forms of competition and the absence of a "plausible method . . . for converting intensities of different forms of competition into a common unit of intensity" would render it impossible to justify "competitive intensity" as a logical guide to antitrust policy. Id. at 144. In *Intensity and Dimensionality*, Demsetz concedes that "efficiency is at least a conceptually feasible goal," though "not an easy one to pursue." Id. He further notes in *100 Years* that "we also do not yet possess an antitrust-relevant understanding of efficiency." *100 Years*, supra note 8.

[40] The literature has its roots in the seminal analyses of Schumpeter, supra note 1, and Kenneth J. Arrow, *Economic Welfare and the Allocation of Resources for Invention, in* THE RATE AND DIRECTION OF ECONOMIC ACTIVITIES: ECONOMIC AND SOCIAL FACTORS 609 (Richard Nelson ed., 1962). Jonathan Baker summarizes the economics literature linking industry structures to incentives to innovate in a recent paper. See Baker, supra note 3.

substitution between forms to answer the question sensibly. Take, for example, an antitrust liability rule that makes certain business conduct illegal on the theory that it will reduce consumer welfare by depressing future innovation. Will the policy increase consumer welfare? The answer turns on a comparison of how two different bundles of "competition" – combinations of price, innovation, quality, and cost competition – translate to consumer welfare. Where these forms of competitive rivalry are negatively correlated, evaluating the benefits of these alternative bundles in terms of consumer welfare requires knowing the marginal rates of technical substitution between competitive forms to convert different forms into common units of consumer welfare. I briefly survey in the following subsections our existing theoretical and empirical knowledge of the relationship between product market competition, consumer welfare, innovation, and market structure.

1. Economic Theory and Incentives to Innovate

While others have documented this extensive literature in greater detail than is required for our purposes,[41] I offer a brief survey. Recent surveys have usefully summarized four principles of competition and innovation that have emerged from this literature.[42] The first principle is that competition in innovation is a form of competition itself. In other words, competition encourages innovation by providing an incentive for each competitor to win the "prize" associated with appropriating the gains from the innovation.

The second principle is that product market competition encourages competitors to innovate to face less competition and earn greater profits. The converse can also hold: A firm that does not face substantial product market competition may have less incentive to innovate. This effect is at the heart of John Hicks's observation that the "best of all monopoly profits is a quiet life,"[43] and has been referred to as the "escape-the-competition" effect.[44] The third principle is related to the second and posits that firms that face greater product market competition post-innovation will have less incentive to engage in research and development.

---

[41] See, e.g., Gilbert, supra note 3, at 159; Katz and Shelanski, supra note 5, at 16–31 (discussing the relationship between concentration, research and development, and consumer welfare in the merger context).

[42] *See* Richard J. Gilbert, *Competition and Innovation*, 1 Issues in Competition Law and Policy 577 (W. Dale Collins ed., 2008); Baker, supra note 3.

[43] John R. Hicks, *Annual Survey of Economic Theory: The Theory of Monopoly*, 3 Econometrica 1, 8 (1955).

[44] See, e.g., Philippe Aghion et al., *Competition, Imitation and Growth with Step-by-Step Innovation*, 68 Rev. Econ. Stud. 467, 468 n.4 (2001).

The fourth principle is often referred to as the "preemption effect," which illustrates that a firm may have an additional marginal incentive to innovate if the innovation will discourage rivals and potential entrants from investing in research and development themselves.

By themselves, these economic principles do not tell us what role antitrust should play in innovative industries. The first principle, that innovation is a form of competition, offers little guidance for antitrust policy. All agree that innovative activity is an essential part of the competitive process. But the antitrust-relevant question is if we can confidently predict whether antitrust policy might increase or decrease innovative activity in a way that makes consumers better off. If firms are engaging in an endogenously determined mixture of competitive activities and an antitrust policy designed to encourage innovation is successfully introduced, we can expect the new mixture of competitive forms to involve more innovation and less of other forms of competition. But it is unclear that the first principle tells us anything more about the likely consumer-welfare effects of the policy.

The second and third principles do not offer better policy guidance on their own. Leaving aside the methodological issue of how one measures competition in these models, these principles teach that product market competition might increase or decrease the incentive to innovate under different conditions.

Finally, the fourth principle, the "preemption effect," teaches that dominant firms may have a greater incentive to innovate to reduce the innovation incentives of rivals and potential entrants. The preemption effect applies not only to "sham" innovations, but innovations that offer consumers immediate and tangible benefits such as offering a new product or increasing product quality.

The current state of the theoretical literature relating to competition and innovation is alone insufficient to instill any great confidence in our ability to determine what antitrust policies will encourage innovation and result in net consumer-welfare gains. Specifically, our ability to apply antitrust standards depends on our ability to predict how a rule will impact the *mixture* of competitive forms that will exist after the policy is implemented and to rank these mixtures on consumer welfare or efficiency criteria. At this point, economic theory does not appear to provide a reliable method of making such a determination.[45] First, as discussed previously, our theoretical knowledge

---

[45] *Accord* Gilbert, supra note 42, at 583 ("economic theory does not provide unambiguous support either for the view that market power generally threatens innovation by lowering the return to innovative efforts nor the Schumpeterian view that concentrated markets generally promote innovation"). Katz and Shelanski, supra note 5, at 19, conclude that

cannot yet confidently predict the direction of the impact of additional product market competition on innovation, much less the magnitude. A second reason is that the multidimensional nature of competition implies that the magnitudes will be important as innovation and other forms of competition will frequently be inversely correlated as they relate to consumer welfare. Thus, weighing the magnitudes of opposing effects will be essential to most antitrust policy decisions relating to innovation. Again, at this stage, economic theory does not provide a reliable basis for predicting the conditions under which consumer-welfare gains associated with greater product market competition resulting from some antitrust intervention will outweigh losses associated with reduced innovation.[46]

2. The Evidence: What Do We Know about Competition and Innovation?

Regulators, policy makers, and judges need not rely only on this developing branch of economic theory that has heretofore not produced results sufficient to guide policy on its own. Rather, one expects policy makers to turn to our empirical knowledge of the relationship between competition, innovation, and consumer welfare. There are at least two empirical relationships that are relevant to policy making in this area. The first is the relationship between product market competition and innovative activity, and the second is the link between firm size and research and development. I argue that the state of the empirical literature is also indeterminate at this stage and an insufficient basis on which to ground policy decisions.

Early studies of the link between product market competition and innovation supported the Schumpeterian hypothesis by finding an inverted-U relationship: Innovative activity is at its maximum at intermediate levels of market concentration and decreases as concentration approaches monopoly or more atomistic structures.[47] But the failure of these early studies to account for differences between industries, and the endogeneity

---

"although economic intuition suggests an overarching presumption that innovation will be greatest for firms facing competitive pressures and the prospects of supracompetitive returns to innovation, it is also clear that, depending on assumptions, the theoretical balance could swing toward either a greater number of competitors or toward monopoly in a given case." See also Wesley M. Cohen and Richard C. Levin, *Empirical Studies of Innovation and Market Structure, in* 2 HANDBOOK OF INDUSTRIAL ORGANIZATION 1074–79 (Richard Schmalensee and Robert D. Willig eds., 1989).

[46] This assertion echoes Demsetz's claim that economics does not yet have an "antitrust relevant understanding of efficiency." *100 Years*, supra note 8.

[47] There are several excellent discussions of the empirical literature linking product market competition and innovation. See, e.g., Baker, supra note 3, at 582–86; Katz and Shelanski, supra note 5, at 19–31; Gilbert, supra note 3.

in the relationship between market structure and innovation, undermine their value.[48] A recent study by Philippe Aghion et al. suggests that the link between market structure and markups of price over average costs may indeed have an inverted-U shape,[49] though commentators have noted that the study does not provide a basis for policy decisions regarding the role of innovation in antitrust analysis.[50] Other studies have examined the impact of changes in market structure within a single industry over time to analyze the relationship between product market competition and productivity or innovation with mixed results.[51] Others have examined whether competition policy enforcement is associated with greater competition or productivity, again, with mixed results.[52] Another strand of empirical literature examines the relationship between firm size and research and development. Richard Gilbert summarizes the findings in this literature as consistent with the theory that the effects of firm size and competition on innovation should be greater for process than product innovations.[53]

Gilbert's careful examination of the empirical record concludes that the existing body of theoretical and empirical literature on the relationship between competition and innovation "fails to provide general support for the Schumpeterian hypothesis that monopoly promotes either investment in research and development or the output of innovation" and that "the theoretical and empirical evidence also does not support a strong conclusion that competition is uniformly a stimulus to innovation."[54]

---

[48] Katz and Shelanski, supra note 5, at 22, conclude that "the literature addressing how market structure affects innovation (and vice versa) in the end reveals an ambiguous relationship in which factors unrelated to competition play an important role").

[49] Philippe Aghion et al., *Competition and Innovation: An Inverted U Relationship*, 120 Q.J. Econ. 701 (2005).

[50] This is largely because the Aghion et al. analysis control for industry effects at the two-digit SIC code level, which is not likely to meaningfully control for cross-industry differences and certainly does not correspond with antitrust markets. This point is addressed by both Baker, supra note 3, and Katz and Shelanski, supra note 5, at 23.

[51] Many of these studies are discussed by Baker, supra note 3, at 585–86 (and accompanying citations).

[52] See, e.g., Keith N. Hylton and Fei Deng, *Antitrust Around the World: An Empirical Analysis of the Scope of Competition Laws and Their Effects* 74 Antitrust L.J. 271 (2007) (finding no significant causal relationship between the scope of a nation's competition laws "on the books" and competitive intensity").

[53] Gilbert, supra note 42, at 597–98.

[54] Id. at 600. It should be noted that Gilbert concludes from this mixed evidence that a presumption that competition promotes innovation is warranted under certain conditions and justifies a fact-intensive, case-by-case approach (Id.).

C. Making Welfare Trade-Offs When Competition Is Multidimensional

The theoretical and empirical literature reveals an undeniably complex interaction between product market competition, innovation, and consumer welfare. While these complexities are well understood, this chapter emphasizes that recognition of the multidimensional nature of competition adds another degree of difficulty to this problem.

The critical implication of multidimensional competition is that such welfare trade-offs are ubiquitous. Acknowledgement that the optimal bundle of competitive forms is endogenous to antitrust policy implies that any enforcement policy or action will likely reduce one form of competition and increase another. Therefore, any analysis of whether such a policy will make consumers better off requires information concerning both the marginal rates of substitution between competitive forms and a method available for courts, judges, and regulators to calculate these welfare trade-offs.

The critical antitrust question is how policy makers will deal with the problem of welfare trade-offs in the antitrust analysis of innovation. A number of approaches have been suggested. For example, Jonathan Baker proposes that the theoretical and empirical literature is sufficient to allow regulators to use enforcement efforts to increase competition and consumer welfare by selecting the appropriate industries at which to target enforcement.[55] Baker's "prosecutorial selection" approach posits that antitrust enforcement can systematically benefit innovation by focusing on competition in "winner-take-all" markets and by "threading the needle" between the second and third principles discussed previously, because post-innovation competition will not be affected in such markets.[56] Baker also identifies a second type of industry where antitrust enforcement in product markets will systematically increase innovation: markets where future product market competition is unaffected by current product market

---

[55] Baker, supra note 3, at 589 ("through such selection, antitrust intervention can systematically promote innovation competition and pre-innovation product market competition, which will encourage innovation, without markedly increasing post-innovation product market competition, and, thus, without detracting from the pro-innovation benefits").

[56] Baker, supra note 3, at 593–95. Baker cites *United States v. Microsoft*, 253 F.3d 34 (D.C. Cir. 2004), as an example of intervention benefiting consumers (Id. at 593 n.54). Cf. Benjamin Klein, *The Microsoft Case: What Can A Dominant Firm Do to Defend Its Market Position*, 15 J. Econ. Persp. 45 (2001); David S. Evans, Albert L. Nichols, and Richard Schmalansee, *United States v. Microsoft: Did Consumers Win?*, 1 J. Competition L. & Econ. 497 (2005).

competition because of pending technological or regulatory developments or growing demand.[57]

A second approach avoids the welfare trade-off problem altogether by finding the rare case where competition is truly one dimensional. The "no trade-off" approach requires identifying cases where the benefits from enforcement on innovation are not offset by a reduction of some other competitive form now or in the future. This approach is consistent with Baker's suggestion that enforcement efforts be focused, at least in part, on industries where future product market competition is unlikely to be altered by enforcement actions in today's product market. Some applications of the "innovation market" concept might be viewed as consistent with this approach, such as an analysis of the consolidation of research and development assets by merger where no product market competition exists. A third potential set of "no trade-off" cases involve so-called "sham innovations."[58]

Michael Katz and Howard Shelanski's recent and insightful proposal advocating a more sophisticated method for incorporating innovation effects and uncertainty over future events into antitrust analysis may offer a third approach to these welfare trade-offs.[59] Recognizing the complexity of predicting the effects of a merger on innovation, Katz and Shelanski offer a number of concrete and practical suggestions to improve merger review in this regard. For example, they suggest developing a set of agency guidelines for incorporating analysis of innovation, moving away from formal market definition where feasible, and incorporating decision theory into policy-making decisions so that true expected welfare payoffs are the basis of policy decisions rather than the imposition of arbitrary cutoffs and probability thresholds.[60] Each of these recommendations is desirable in principle, though it is unclear whether such standards can be adopted without substantial administrative costs.

In their proposal to modify merger review where innovation concerns are implicated, Katz and Shelanski also recognize that the predicted competitive effects in product markets and from innovation might run in opposite directions and thus necessitate a welfare trade-off, noting that such a case

---

[57] Baker, supra note 3, at 597. Baker also notes that antitrust enforcement will increase innovation in cases such as naked price-fixing or "naked exclusion" without any plausible efficiency justification (Id. at 599).

[58] See, e.g., Richard Gilbert, *Holding Innovation to an Antitrust Standard*, 3 COMPETITION POL'Y INT'L 47 (2007) (discussing the problems associated with application of various antitrust standards innovation in the form of new products or design changes).

[59] Katz and Shelanski, supra note 5.

[60] Id. at 77–79.

calls for "a more careful analysis of the comparative benefits of price effects and innovation effects."[61] But how does one go about carrying out this trade-off in practice? For example, how does an agency or court assess what post-merger competition looks like when firms compete on both price, innovation, and other measures? The authors do not propose a specific answer to this problem, but in the spirit of their general approach to account for the "true" consumer-welfare impact of the merger over time, with uncertainty, and in both current and future product markets, they agree it is a significant issue and call for agency guidance on how they would make these trade-offs.[62]

Katz and Shelanski's suggestion that a more sophisticated, more realistic, and less arbitrary and subjective approach to uncertainty and welfare trade-offs would improve merger analysis is well taken and almost certainly correct in principle. This chapter highlights that accounting for the multidimensional nature of competition and substitution between competitive forms is consistent with an approach based on consumer-welfare measures and calls attention to the shortcomings in our current technology for applying this type of framework.

I am not suggesting that the multidimensional nature of competition renders sensible antitrust analysis impossible. To the contrary, economists are developing tools, though primarily in the merger context, to generate more precise and reliable predictions of post-merger outcomes when firms engage in multidimensional competition.[63] Moreover, the proposition that appropriate antitrust analysis should both account for innovation and deal with uncertainty more seriously, rather than imposing arbitrary time horizons, is quite sensible. For example, truncating merger analysis at a two-year time horizon invokes an arbitrary subjective preference in our consumer-welfare calculation for consumers who are purchasing today rather than those purchasing in the future.

This agreement comes with two important caveats. First, if imposing arbitrary preferences in our consumer-welfare calculations is antithetical to sound antitrust enforcement when it involves uncertainty of future events and market conditions, arbitrary preferences weighting one form of competition over another or not accounting for substitution between competitive forms resulting from intervention are no better. A policy that weights effects from innovation disproportionately relative to product market effects

---

[61] Id. at 49.
[62] Id. at 78.
[63] See, e.g., Luke Froeb et al., Mergers when Firms Compete on Price and Promotion (unpublished working paper, 2007).

without justification from economic theory or empirical evidence is likely to harm consumers. Alternatively, a standard applied to innovative activity that measures the competitive effects of innovation, including the exclusion of rivals, without understanding that the latter produced an incentive for the innovation itself is equally misguided and likely to harm consumers in the long run. The second caveat is that antitrust liability rules that attempt to engage in more sophisticated analyses of uncertainty and welfare trade-offs almost necessarily involve higher administrative costs. The selection of the appropriate approach to incorporating innovation concerns into antitrust analysis must be sensitive to the administrative and error costs associated with its implementation.

V. Antitrust Implications of Multidimensional Competition

This chapter has focused on two central points. The first is that the current state of economic theory and empirical knowledge regarding the relationship between innovation and competition does not yet provide a general and reliable basis for antitrust intervention. The second point is that the economic reality that competition takes place on multiple margins complicates antitrust analysis when innovation concerns are implicated in a particular way. Specifically, antitrust enforcement will generally result in a substitution from one bundle of competitive forms to another where post-intervention we observe more of some types of competition and less of others. This combination creates significant complications for consumer-welfare calculations because it requires some knowledge of the magnitude of this substitution effect and how to make welfare trade-offs in this setting. Economics and economists have improved the coherence of antitrust a great deal over the past fifty years, but at this stage, existing economic knowledge provides little basis for confidence that regulators and judges can carry out these calculations even with specialized skills and perfect knowledge of the literature.[64] But what do these difficulties tell us about optimal antitrust enforcement under these conditions?

Former Federal Trade Commission Chairman Timothy Muris articulates three useful normative propositions for integrating economic analysis into

---

[64] For a study indicating that some antitrust cases involve economic questions that are simply too complex for generalist judges, and that judicial economic training improves performance in relatively simple cases, see Michael R. Baye and Joshua D. Wright, Is Antitrust Too Complicated for Generalist Judges? The Impact of Economic Complexity & Judicial Training on Appeals, 51 J. L. & Econ. __ (Forthcoming, February 2011).

competition policy: (1) reassessment, (2) administrability, and (3) the centrality of empirical testing.[65] These normative propositions suggest at least two antitrust policy implications related to our analysis: (1) Competition policy research and development efforts, and in particular those focused on measuring the competitive effects of various business practices in innovative markets and dynamic competition more generally, are likely to improve the accuracy of antitrust enforcement efforts by reducing both false positives and negatives; and (2) plaintiffs should be allocated clear burdens of proof concerning competitive harm in markets involving multidimensional competition under conditions when theoretical and empirical uncertainty renders presumptions of actual competitive harm inappropriate and without sufficient scientific basis.

A. Competition Policy Research and Development

Economics is at its best when its insights are used to produce administrable rules and techniques for analyzing business conduct. Empirical knowledge of the relationship between competition and innovation is essential to creating the presumptions, grounded firmly in empiricism, required by efficient administration of the antitrust laws. Though the growing body of empirical knowledge linking competition, innovation, and efficiency is too underdeveloped to provide the basis for reliable presumptions, antitrust agencies would be well advised to continue to support this type of research.[66] The potential for antitrust to systematically promote innovation and improve efficiency depends largely on our ability to increase our understanding of this relationship to develop sound and workable antitrust rules.

B. The Burden of Proving Harm to Competition

Currently, neither economic theory nor empirical evidence suggests that antitrust agencies or courts have reliable knowledge concerning the types of conduct implicating innovation that are systematically likely to make consumers worse off. Under these conditions, where reliable presumptions concerning harm to consumers are not yet plausible for broad ranges of conduct, it is appropriate to allocate clear burdens of proof and persuasion

---

[65] Timothy J. Muris, *Improving the Economic Foundations of Competition Policy*, 12 Geo. Mason L. Rev. 1 (2003).

[66] For examples of such research initiatives at the Federal Trade Commission, see Muris, supra note 65, at 24–28.

to those claiming that some conduct reduces consumer welfare in violation of the antitrust laws.

There is a danger that our incomplete understanding of the competition and innovation might lead to a tendency to condemn conduct because it is difficult to understand or might appear to potentially harm innovation without also finding an anticompetitive effect. This dangerous tendency may be most severe when antitrust analysis focuses on how firm conduct might harm a rival's ability to innovate or compete. The competitive process generally disadvantages competitors and benefits consumers. It is critical that antitrust policy not adopt an analytical framework that presumes harm to competition when the pro-competitive rationale for the conduct is not facially obvious. The requirement that plaintiffs demonstrate an anticompetitive effect is a sensible safeguard against this danger and especially pertinent in cases involving complex innovative activity.[67]

Even where courts are willing to prematurely apply presumptions concerning harm to competition, our inability to consistently and reliably make the welfare trade-offs necessitated by antitrust analysis where innovation and product market competition are involved suggests that agencies should carefully select cases to prosecute to avoid chilling the normal competitive process that generates consumer benefits.

VI. Conclusion

Sound antitrust policy requires constantly updating our analytical framework to reflect improvements in economic theory and current empirical knowledge. While our understanding of the relationship between competition and innovation has increased markedly over the past several decades, we do not yet possess a sufficient knowledge of the complex interactions to provide a reliable basis for presumptions of harm to competition based on observables such as market structure, firm size, and conduct.

In addition to the conventionally understood difficulties in identifying the relationship between product market competition and dynamic efficiency, this chapter revisited an underappreciated source of difficulty for antitrust analysis. Harold Demsetz noted that antitrust analysis, assuming a goal of maximizing efficiency or consumer welfare, requires knowledge of the

---

[67] For a discussion of why the complex relationship between antitrust and innovation in the patent holdup context may favor the use of state common law remedies to prevent over-deterrence, see Bruce H. Kobayashi and Joshua D. Wright, *Substantive Preemption, Federalism, and Limits on Antitrust: An Application to Patent Holdup* 5 J. Comp. L. & Econ 469 (2009).

technical rates of substitution between various competitive forms and a reliable methodology for making welfare trade-offs between these negatively correlated forms.

The complexity of this problem does not imply that antitrust must never, as some contend, intervene on the grounds that some conduct will reduce innovation and ultimately harm consumers. Intervention in markets with significant innovative activity need not necessarily make consumers worse off by chilling innovation or product market competition. However, the nature of the problem does warrant caution and humility with respect to predictions of efficiency consequences of antitrust intervention in markets characterized by innovative activity. In particular, it is critical to note that the limits on predictive power are not only those that derive from the general challenges of making *ex ante* predictions about the innovative process but also, as discussed here, economics does not yet tell us a great deal about how to weigh trade-offs between various forms of competitive activity. It may be the case that future empirical research will justify presumptions of competitive harm in specific circumstances. But this relatively young literature does not yet justify such presumptions. The normal competitive process entails competition on many dimensions. And it is this process that generates a multitude of benefits for consumers. Where there is little evidence to suggest that antitrust enforcers and courts can systematically identify conditions when intervention will stimulate innovation and improve consumer outcomes net of reductions on other important margins of competitive activity, humility regarding the current state of knowledge implies that deference to the competitive process is an appropriate guiding principle in the absence of clear and convincing evidence of substantial consumer harm.

8

American and European Monopolization Law

A Doctrinal and Empirical Comparison

Keith N. Hylton and Haizhen Lin

This chapter focuses on the differences between Article 82 and Section 2, reflecting largely on the American experience. We start with a discussion of the American experience and use that as a background from which to examine the European law on monopolies. American law is more conservative (less interventionist), reflecting the error-cost analysis that is increasingly common in American courts. The second half of this chapter provides an empirical comparison of the American and European regimes. Although a preliminary empirical examination suggests that the scope of a country's monopolization law is inversely related to its degree of trade dependence, the actual relationship between trade dependence and the scope of monopolization law appears to be an inverted U.

I. Introduction

Although there are more than 100 competition law regimes around the world, the United States and the European Union are by far the most important. Both systems have laws constraining the conduct of monopoly firms. In the United States this part of competition law is called monopolization law, while in the EU it is called dominance law. We will use the terms interchangeably here. This chapter will survey the doctrinal differences and empirically examine the determinants of monopolization law in the United States and the EU.

This paper was originally prepared for the Conference on Economics of Competition and Innovation, George Mason University School of Law, May 4, 2007. A later draft of the paper was presented at the Triangle Antitrust Research Conference, University of North Carolina at Chapel Hill, May 3, 2008. We have benefited from comments by participants in these conferences. We also thank Roger Blair, Ron Cass, Luke Froeb for helpful suggestions. Nicola Leiter and Corinne McLaughlin provided excellent research assistance. The authors thank Boston University and Microsoft for research support.

In the United States, the law governing monopolies is provided by Section 2 of the Sherman Act and the judicial opinions interpreting it.[1] In the EU, monopolization law is provided by Article 82 of the European Community Treaty and related case law.[2] Sherman Act Section 2 says that "[e]very person who shall monopolize, or attempt to monopolize, or combine or conspire with any person or persons, to monopolize any part of trade or commerce among the several States, or with foreign nations, shall be deemed guilty of a felony."[3] Article 82 says that "[a]ny abuse by one or more undertakings of a dominant position within the common market or in a substantial part of it shall be prohibited as incompatible with the common market in so far as it may affect trade between member States."[4] It then provides several examples of types of abuse.[5]

Both of these provisions are invitations to their respective courts to develop a common law of competition governing dominant firms. In this respect, the American experience is illuminating because it began much earlier than the European effort. The Sherman Act was enacted in 1890, giving us more than 100 years of case law interpreting it. The case law interpreting Article 82 goes back to the early 1970s.[6]

This chapter focuses on the broad differences between Article 82 and Section 2, reflecting largely on the American experience.[7] We start with a discussion of the American experience and use that as a background from which to examine the European law on monopolies. In general, American law is more conservative (less interventionist) – reflecting the error-cost analysis that is increasingly common in American courts.

Although a preliminary empirical examination suggests that the scope of a country's monopolization law is inversely related to its degree of trade

---

[1] For an overview and discussion of statute and case law on monopolization, see Phillip Areeda et al., Antitrust Analysis 368–342 (6th ed. 2004).

[2] For an overview, see Faull and Nikpay, The EC Law of Competition (Jonathan Faull & Ali Nikpay eds., USA: Oxford University Press, 1999).

[3] The Sherman Antitrust Act, 15 U.S.C. §2 (2000).

[4] Treaty Establishing the European Community, Dec. 24, 2002, 2002 O.J. (C 325) 33, 65 [hereinafter EC Treaty].

[5] EC Treaty Article 82 provides, "Such abuse may, in particular, consist in: directly or indirectly imposing unfair purchase or selling prices or other unfair trading conditions; limiting production, markets or technical development to the prejudice of consumers; applying dissimilar conditions to equivalent transactions with other trading parties, thereby placing them at a competitive disadvantage; making the conclusion of contracts subject to acceptance by the other parties of supplementary obligations which, by their nature or according to commercial usage, have no connection with the subject of such contracts."

[6] Faull & Nikpay, supra note 2, at 117–203.

[7] For a recent comparison focusing on general enforcement issues, see Douglas H. Ginsburg, *Comparing Antitrust Enforcement in the United States and Europe*, 1 J. Comp. Law & Economics 427 (2005).

dependence,[8] the actual relationship between trade dependence and the scope of monopolization law appears to be an inverted U. As import penetration rises from an initial base level, dominance law increases in scope and then reaches a point where it declines. This is consistent with the theory that domestic firms seek legal protection from competition until a point is reached at which the benefits from additional protection no longer exceed the costs of obtaining it.

The empirical evidence also has implications for the comparison between the United States and the EU. Any such comparison should control for factors that determine the scope of monopolization law. In comparison to the European countries that were members of the EU before 2004, monopolization law in the United States does not appear to be narrower in scope when one controls for the economic and demographic factors that influence it. However, in comparison to the post-2004 enlarged EU, U.S. monopolization law is narrower in scope. Monopolization law is narrower in EU countries with a socialist background. The scope is broader in EU countries with a Scandinavian legal background.

The empirical analysis is for the most part a search for the contemporary determinants of monopolization law, and an inconclusive one at that. The factors that one would expect to be important – wealth, international trade, sectoral composition, size of government – all turn out to be so, but in complicated ways. Wealth, as measured by per capita gross domestic product (GDP), is by far the most important factor influencing the scope of monopolization law in the United States and the EU.

II. Monopolization Law in the United States and the EU

A. Section 2 Law

Almost every statute is an invitation to courts to develop a common law based on it.[9] That is because the text of a statute is hardly ever sufficient

---

[8] On the relationship between imports and monopolization law, see Table 1, infra. Andrew Guzman has offered one theory of the relationship between trade and competition law, see Andrew T. Guzman, *The Case for International Antitrust*, in COMPETITION LAWS IN CONFLICT, ANTITRUST JURISDICTION IN THE GLOBAL ECONOMY 99, 101 (Richard A. Epstein & Michael S. Greve eds., 2004). Guzman's thesis is that net importer states (trade-dependent states) will tend to have strict antitrust laws because those laws will apply to foreign firms operating in their markets. States that are net exporters will tend to have less strict antitrust laws because they will not want to hamper the competitive efforts of their dominant firms. He suggests that this is externalizing the costs of anticompetitive conduct to foreign consumers.

[9] This overview borrows heavily from earlier conference remarks by one of the authors; see Hylton, Keith N., "Section 2 and Article 82: A Comparison of American and European

to resolve all disputes concerning its meaning. Disputes over interpretation inevitably arise, and those disputes wind up in court. Judges are called on to fill in the interpretive gaps of the statute.

However, even if we start with an acceptance of the commonplace observation that statutes are invitations to develop common law, Section 2 of the Sherman Act is an unusually broad invitation. The American federal legislature invited courts in 1890 to develop a common law of monopolization. What existed before then as English common law on monopolization was scant and unlikely to be of much use to courts in interpreting the Sherman Act.[10]

The American judges took a conservative approach initially. With virtually no case law other than that based on Section 1 to draw on for guidance, they stayed close to the familiar shore, extending the reach of Section 2 only to conduct that seemed most clearly to violate it.[11] The most comprehensive early effort to interpret Section 2 appears in the *Standard Oil* decision of 1911.[12] Areeda described *Standard Oil* as "remarkable for its cloudy prolixity."[13]

In spite of its flaws, *Standard Oil* manages to deliver some important lessons about the early understanding of Section 2. It adopts the "abuse standard" of monopolization.[14] Under that standard, a firm can be found guilty of violating Section 2 if it engages in conduct that would violate Section 1 if engaged in by a combination of firms. Moreover, the abuse standard requires a finding of specific intent to monopolize.[15]

Specific intent to monopolize, in turn, is inferred by conduct that cannot be justified on the basis of legitimate competitive goals, conduct that can be understood only as an effort to destroy competition from rivals. The early

---

Approaches to Monopolization Law" (October 2005). Boston University School of Law Working Paper No. 06-11, available at SSRN: http://ssrn.com/abstract=902655.

[10] Some scholars have questioned the existence of a pre–Sherman Act common law of monopolization, see William Letwin, LAW AND ECONOMIC POLICY IN AMERICA: THE EVOLUTION OF THE SHERMAN ANTITRUST ACT 19 (1965).

[11] See, e.g., Keith N. Hylton, ANTITRUST LAW: ECONOMIC THEORY AND COMMON LAW EVOLUTION 186–188 (2003) (discussing early Section 2 case law).

[12] *Standard Oil Co. v. United States,* 221 U.S. 1 (1911).

[13] Phillip Areeda, ANTITRUST ANALYSIS: PROBLEMS, TEXT, AND CASES 148 (3rd ed. 1981).

[14] E.g., Hylton, supra note 10, 187.

[15] Id. This is also clear from perusing the early opinions. See, e.g., Areeda et al., *supra* note 1, 369–372 (providing excerpts from *Standard Oil,* 221 U.S. at 58, 61, 67, 75, and *United States v. American Tobacco Co.,* 221 U.S. 106, 181–183 (1911), stating that the defendant was found guilty of violating Section 2 because its conduct indicated an intent to monopolize by excluding or destroying rivals).

opinions, including *Standard Oil*, suggest that it is an objective inquiry based on facts.[16]

The early cases also made clear that monopoly status by itself is not unlawful.[17] The statute was interpreted to prohibit efforts to monopolize, say by destroying competitors. However, the statute was not interpreted to prohibit the setting of the monopoly price or the monopoly quantity. This part of the early understanding of Section 2 remains valid in American law today.

This conservative approach to Section 2 was not without controversy. Proponents of strong antitrust enforcement wanted a more aggressive interpretation and found their position vindicated, in their eyes, by the government's loss in the *United States Steel* case of 1920.[18] On the other hand, the conservative approach discouraged judges from attempting to conduct their own consumer-welfare tests of dominant firm conduct. The specific intent test originally adopted asked courts to determine whether there were plausible pro-efficiency or competitive bases for the defendant's conduct. If so, the specific intent test implied that the defendant should not be found guilty of violating Section 2.

The conservative approach came to an end in 1945 with Judge Learned Hand's decision in *Alcoa*.[19] The *Alcoa* opinion is a marvel in clarity in comparison to *Standard Oil*. However, its statement of the new monopolization standard leaves room for alternative interpretations.[20] One point appears to be absolutely clear: The specific intent test is no longer required under Section 2.[21] Beyond that unambiguous point, Judge Hand's decision suggests that, as a general rule, violations of Section 2 will be determined by a balancing of the pro-competitive and anticompetitive effects of the defendant's conduct. In other words, under Hand's test, the defendant may have substantial efficiency justifications for its conduct, yet it may still be found

---

[16] See, e.g., Areeda et al., supra note 1, 369–372 (excerpts from *Standard Oil*, 221 U.S. at 61, 62, 75 and *American Tobacco*, 221 U.S. at 181–183).

[17] See e.g., *Standard Oil*, 221 U.S. at 62 ("[T]he statute... *by the omission of any direct prohibition against monopoly* in the concrete... indicates a consciousness that the freedom of the individual right to contract... was the most efficient means for the prevention of monopoly") (emphasis added).

[18] *United States v. U.S. Steel Corp.*, 251 U.S. 417 (1920).

[19] *United States v. Alum. Co. of America*, 148 F.2d 416 (2d Cir. 1945) [hereinafter *Alcoa*].

[20] See, e.g., Steven C. Salop and R. Craig Romaine, *Preserving Monopoly: Economic Analysis, Legal Standards and Microsoft*, 7 GEO. MASON L. REV. 617 (1999) (interpreting *Alcoa* as a "no-fault" or strict liability standard), versus Ronald A. Cass and Keith N. Hylton, *Preserving Competition: Economic Analysis, Legal Standards, and Microsoft*, 8 GEO. MASON L. REV. 1 (1999) (interpreting *Alcoa* as a balancing test).

[21] *Alcoa*, 148 F.2d at 432 ("no monopolist monopolizes unconscious of what he is doing").

in violation of Section 2 because the anticompetitive effects were deemed too severe by the court.

As a summary of American monopoly law, Judge Hand's statement of it remains valid. Courts continue to refer to it as a starting point in discussions of the monopolization test.[22] But a more detailed look reveals that the standard for monopolization has been altered in practice substantially since *Alcoa*, and largely in a direction that favors dominant firm defendants. The date at which the change in Section 2 law began appears to be 1975, with the publication of the Areeda and Turner article on predatory pricing.[23] Areeda and Turner noted the uncertainty surrounding predation charges and the costs of error, and proposed a cost-based test to screen out predation claims with high error costs. Following their article, courts began to adopt their cost-based screen and to take seriously the costs of false convictions.

The changes in Section 2 case law have not occurred across the board, but in specific pockets. One pocket in which the law has changed is predatory pricing. The *Matsushita*[24] and *Brooke Group*[25] line of cases require, in order to hold a firm guilty of predatory pricing under Section 2, a price below some measure of cost (average variable cost usually) and objective evidence that the defendant would be able to recoup the losses incurred in the predatory (low-price) period.[26] The *Brooke Group* test is equivalent to a specific intent test.[27] The reason is that if the requirements of the *Brooke Group* test are satisfied, then one can say that the objective evidence implies that the defendant's intent was predatory.

As this example suggests, the type of monopolization test, or how it is framed, may not be important in the end. Whether the monopolization test is framed, as in the pre-1945 period, in terms of specific intent or, as in the post-1945 period, as a consumer-welfare balancing test, the underlying question is the evidentiary burden placed on plaintiffs in a monopolization case. In general, the specific intent test, as historically applied, puts the

---

[22] See, e.g., *F. Hoffman-La Roche Ltd. v. Empagram S.A.*, 542 U.S. 155, 165 (2004); *Eastman Kodak Co. v. Image Tech. Svces.*, 504 U.S. 451, 483 (1992); *Aspen Skiing Co. v. Aspen Highland Skiing Corp.*, 472 U.S. 585 (1985); *United States v. Microsoft Corp.*, 253 F.3d 34, 44 (D.C. Cir. 2001), cert. denied, 534 U.S. 952 (2001).

[23] Phillip Areeda and Donald Turner, *Predatory Pricing and Related Practices under Section 2 of the Sherman Act*, 88 Harv. L. Rev. 697 (1975).

[24] *Matsushita Elec. Indus. Co. v. Zenith Radio Corp.*, 475 U.S. 574 (1986).

[25] *Brooke Group, Ltd. v. Brown & Williamson Tobacco Corp.*, 509 U.S. 209, 226 (1993) (evidence of below-cost pricing is not alone sufficient to permit an inference of probable recoupment and injury to competition).

[26] Id. at 240–242; Matsushita, 475 U.S. at 595–598.

[27] Salop and Romaine, supra note 21, at 17, 24, 35; Cass and Hylton, supra note 21, at 639, 671.

greatest evidentiary burden on the plaintiff. The consumer-welfare test, by its terms, places a much lighter burden on the plaintiff. But if the consumer-welfare test were coupled with several additional evidentiary burdens – for example, standards requiring proof by clear and convincing evidence – it could present roughly the same obstacles to plaintiffs as the specific intent test. Conversely, if the specific intent test were applied in a way that put too little weight on defendant's evidence and too much weight on the plaintiff's anticompetitive theories, the results might be indistinguishable from a consumer-welfare balancing test applied with a pro-plaintiff bias. The issue at bottom is one of evidentiary burden.

Another pocket of Section 2 case law in which courts seem to have drifted back to the specific intent formulation is that involving "essential facilities."[28] The decision in *Aspen*,[29] which suggested that the defendant lost solely because it failed to provide a credible competitive justification for its conduct, carried the implication that the mere provision of such a justification would immunize a defendant from liability in an essential facilities case. That implication was apparently confirmed with Justice Scalia's opinion in *Trinko*.[30]

The most celebrated non–Supreme Court Section 2 case of recent history, *Microsoft*,[31] suggests a broader shift toward the specific intent formulation. The D.C. Circuit's opinion initially states the monopolization test as a consumer-welfare balancing test.[32] Then, when it gets around to actually

---

[28] See generally Philip E. Areeda, *Essential Facilities: An Epithet in Need of Limiting Principles*, 58 ANTITRUST L.J. 841 (1990); Keith N. Hylton, *Economic Rents and Essential Facilities*, 1991 BRIGHAM YOUNG UNIV. L. REV. 1243; Abbott B. Lipsky, Jr. and J. Gregory Sidak, *Essential Facilities*, 51 STAN. L. REV. 1187 (1999); Glen O. Robinson, *On Refusing to Deal with Rivals*, 87 CORNELL L. REV. 1177 (2002).

[29] *Aspen Skiing Co. v. Aspen Highlands Skiing Corp.*, 472 U.S. 585 (1985).

[30] *Verizon Communications Inc. v. Law Offices of V. Trinko, LLP*, 540 U.S. 398 (2004). Scalia's opinion, expressing skepticism toward the essential facilities doctrine, described *Aspen* as a case "at or near the outer boundary of Section 2 liability." *Trinko*, 540 U.S. at 409. Scalia described the defendant's conduct in *Aspen* as refusing, without a competitive justification, to supply a product at retail price to one's competitor, Id., at 408–409, which suggested an intent to harm. The defendant in *Trinko* failed to provide a pro-competitive justification for its actions. However, the Court refused to find an antitrust violation based solely on the defendant's failure to accept a statutory burden to support rivals. Thus, *Trinko* implicitly holds that a sufficient justification for denying access to an essential facility is the desire to avoid providing a benefit to a rival. If that is a sufficient justification for denying liability, then it follows that a plaintiff, in order to prevail in an essential facilities case, has to present evidence indicating that the defendant had an *intent to harm* its rival.

[31] *Microsoft*, 253 F.3d at 34.

[32] Id. at 58.

applying the test to Microsoft's conduct, it moves into a specific intent analysis. The court repeatedly condemns Microsoft's conduct because it appeared, to the court, to have no credible pro-efficiency or competitive rationale.[33] As an illustration of the inability of verbal formulations to tightly constrain the decision making of courts, the D.C. Circuit's application of the specific intent test put so little weight on Microsoft's justifications that it was arguably equivalent to a balancing test conducted with a pro-plaintiff bias. For example, in examining the complaints concerning Microsoft's integration of Internet Explorer with its Windows operating system, the court found that two of the three complaints (excluding Internet Explorer from the Add/Remove Programs function and commingling browser and operating system code) were violations of the Sherman Act, because Microsoft offered no credible pro-competitive justification, while one (overriding the choice of an alternative default browser in certain circumstances) was not a violation because Microsoft's justification was sufficient.[34] Yet it seems that the technical justifications offered by Microsoft, and accepted by the court, in response to the complaint that was rejected should apply just as well to the other two complaints.[35]

Summing up, American courts have been conservative in interpreting Section 2 of the Sherman Act, in the sense of showing reluctance to penalize a firm simply because of its monopoly status and of allowing wide scope, at least at the level of pure legal doctrine, for efficiency defenses to be asserted. Of the roughly 115 years that the Sherman Act has been in effect, courts applied a specific intent test under Section 2 for 55 of those years – from 1890 to 1945, the date of *Alcoa. Alcoa* introduced a balancing test in 1945 and scrapped the specific intent test. However, since roughly 1975 and beginning with the predatory pricing cases, we have seen the reemergence of versions of the specific intent approach.

B. Judging Article 82 in Light of the American Experience

Viewed in light of the American experience, Article 82 reflects a more interventionist approach toward antitrust law. The best illustration of this is the fact that Article 82 has been interpreted to make unlawful, as a form

---

[33] Id. at 72, 74, 76, 77.

[34] Id. at 66–67.

[35] If Internet Explorer should be allowed to override an alternative browser to allow the user to get to Microsoft's "HELP" site, then it would seem to follow that the company would want to prevent the user from removing Internet Explorer from the list of programs integrated into the operating system.

of monopoly abuse, the charging of a monopoly price. The first general application provided in the text of Article 82, referring to a type of abuse that violates the treaty provision, is "directly or indirectly imposing unfair purchase or selling prices or other unfair trading conditions."[36]

1. America versus Europe: Some Examples

American antitrust courts decided early on not to regulate pricing under Section 2 of the Sherman Act. In the first case interpreting the Sherman Act to reach the Supreme Court, *U.S. v. Trans-Missouri*,[37] the Court majority argued against adopting a reasonableness test on the ground that the Court would be required by such a test to determine the reasonableness of prices. The Court viewed this as beyond the capacity of judges.[38]

As an argument against using some notion of reasonableness in interpreting the Sherman Act, *Trans-Missouri* is unpersuasive. Pre–Sherman Act common-law decisions on contracts in restraint of trade employed the reasonableness test without being led into an examination of the reasonableness of prices or profits.[39] The reasonableness test applies to the defendant firm's allegedly anticompetitive conduct, not to the prices or profits that result from that conduct.

However, as an argument against using law to establish appropriate guidelines for price or profit levels, *Trans-Missouri*'s argument is no less valid today than it was 100 years ago. American courts have consistently rejected the notion that the Sherman Act calls on judges to take on the functions of regulatory commissions with power over pricing decisions.[40]

Predation is another good illustration of the sizeable differences between European and American courts in applying monopolization law. The *Matsushita* and *Brooke Group* cases in America require from the plaintiff, in order to survive a summary judgment motion, proof that the dominant firm priced below average variable cost and that the firm was likely to recoup its losses from pricing below cost. In contrast, the European Court of Justice, in cases such as *AKZO* and *Tetra Pak II*, has held that pricing below average variable cost violates the law against predation, and prices below average cost also violate the law although the defendant can rebut the

---

[36] EC Treaty Article 82.
[37] *United States v. Trans-Missouri Freight Assn.*, 166 U.S. 290 (1897).
[38] Id. at 331.
[39] Hylton, supra note 10, at 33–34.
[40] See, e.g., *Trinko*, 540 U.S. at 415 ("No court should impose a duty to deal that it cannot explain or adequately and reasonably supervise" (quoting Areeda, supra note 29, at 853)); *United States v. United Shoe Machinery Corp.*, 110 F. Supp. 295, 347 (D. Mass. 1953) (refusing to order the defendant's dissolution), *aff'd per curiam*, 347 U.S. 521 (1954).

presumption of a violation.[41] Moreover, there is no requirement on the part of the plaintiff to prove a high likelihood of recoupment.[42]

The "essential facilities" doctrine is a third illustration of the formal differences between European and American monopolization law. *Trinko* implies that the set of cases in which the essential facilities doctrine will be used by a court to force a dominant firm to share access to some input with a competitor is quite narrow. The Court's discussion in *Trinko* suggests that strong evidence of intent to monopolize is required. In contrast, the European Court of Justice has been considerably more receptive to the essential facilities doctrine and has not attempted to limit its application to a narrow set of circumstances.[43]

Microsoft v. Commission[44] provides an example of the difference between the United States and the EU on the essential facilities question. The European Court of First Instance found that Microsoft abused its dominant position by refusing to license, at a sufficiently low price, interoperability information to rivals in the market for server software. The Court of First Instance deferred to the European Commission's analysis of the effects of Microsoft's refusal but did not independently examine the record for evidence of a specific intent to monopolize.

2. Predation and Error Costs

It is commonplace by now to note that the differences between European and American law on predatory pricing reflect different views on the costs of error. The American approach puts a great deal of weight on the costs of false convictions. Erroneously holding firms liable for setting prices too low penalizes dominant firms for competing vigorously. This discourages competition, a result opposite to that intended by the Sherman Act. The European approach puts more emphasis on the costs of false acquittals. If false acquittal costs are constrained over time by competition, as Easterbrook argued,[45] the American approach would result in superior law.

---

[41] See, e.g., Case C-62/86, AKZO Chemie BV v. Commission, 1991 E.C.R. I-3359; Case T-83/91, *Tetra Pak Int'l SA v. Commission*, 1994 E.C.R. II-755, 4 C.M.L.R. 726 (1997), *aff'd* C-333/94, 1996 E.C.R. I-5951, 4 C.M.L.R. 662 (1997).

[42] See, e.g., Vickers, supra note 38, at F248.

[43] See Damien Geradin, Limiting the Scope of Article 82 of the EC Treaty: What can the EU Learn from the US Supreme Court's Judgment in *Trinko* in the Wake of Microsoft, IMS, and Deutsche Telekom, at 5–6, Common Market Law Review, December 2005, available at http://ssrn.com/abstract=617263.

[44] Case T-201/04, available at http://curia.europa.eu/jurisp/cgi-bin/gettext.pl?lang=en&num=79929082T19040201&doc=T&ouvert=T&seance=ARRET.

[45] Frank H. Easterbrook, *The Limits of Antitrust*, 63 Texas L. Rev. 1 (1984).

One could stop at the observation that the wisdom of the American approach depends on the balance of error costs. This would be a convenient and diplomatic statement because no one has carried out an empirical study of the balance of error costs in predatory pricing cases. Hence, noting that the relative wisdom of the two approaches depends on the balance of error costs leaves us with an invitation to do empirical research and perhaps not much more. Moreover, the prospect of answering the welfare question on the basis of empirical research seems slim, because it is hard to isolate the effects of different predation laws on consumer welfare.

An alternative and less diplomatic perspective is the decision-theoretic approach set out in the Hylton and Salinger article, and in the Evans and Padilla article.[46] Let the fraction of competitive price cuts be given by $P(C)$. Let the fraction of anticompetitive (i.e., predatory) price cuts be given by $P(A)$. Let the likelihood that a competitive price cut is ruled anticompetitive be given by $P(A' \mid C)$, and let $P(A' \mid A)$ be the rate of correct decisions given anticompetitive conduct. Bayes' rule tells us that the fraction of competitive instances within the sample of decisions in which the competition authority has deemed the price cutter's conduct anticompetitive is

$$P(C \mid A') = \frac{P(A' \mid C)P(C)}{P(A' \mid C)P(C) + P(A' \mid A)P(A)}.$$

Let us suppose that the vast majority of price cuts are pro-competitive, say 95 percent. Suppose that the competition authority makes mistakes in only 5 percent of all cases. It follows that the likelihood that a case that has been deemed anticompetitive by the competition authority is really competitive is $1/2$. In other words, half of the cases in which the court finds the conduct anticompetitive were instances in which the conduct really was competitive.

The decision-theoretic approach focuses on the background rate of competitive instances within a certain class of conduct and on the rate at which competition authorities are likely to err in evaluating the conduct. If we take price cuts as a class of conduct, we are likely to find that the vast majority of them are pro-competitive. Moreover, a competition authority is likely to have difficulty, *ex post*, in distinguishing competitive and anticompetitive price cuts. Suppose, for example, that instead of the 5 percent error rate assumed in the previous example, competition authorities make mistakes

---

[46] See generally Keith N. Hylton and Michael A. Salinger, *Tying Law and Policy: A Decision-Theoretic Approach*, 69 ANTITRUST L.J. 469 (2001); David S. Evans and A. Jorge Padilla, *Antitrust: Designing Antitrust Rules for Assessing Unilateral Practices: A Neo-Chicago Approach*, 72 U. CHI. L. REV. 73 (2005). For more recent decision-theory arguments, see also James C. Cooper, Luke M. Froeb, Dan O'Brien, Michael G. Vita, *Vertical Antitrust Policy as a Problem of Inference*, 23 INT'L J. INDUSTRIAL ORGANIZATION 639 (2005).

in 20 percent of predatory pricing cases. Using the Bayes' rule approach just described, the rate of false positives jumps from 50 percent to 83 percent. Moreover, holding error rates fixed and letting the proportion of competitive price cuts rise toward 100 percent causes the rate of false convictions to approach 100 percent.

One might argue that this discussion merely shows that when the law is working, in the sense of inducing actors to comply with it, there will be a high rate of false convictions.[47] However, the message here is different. It is quite plausible in the pricing context to presume that the vast majority of price cuts would be pro-competitive even in the absence of antitrust law. Competition already provides a substantial if not sufficient spur for firms to engage in price cutting. Given this, it is not the law that gives us the 95 percent background rate of competitive price cuts; it is competition. If competition gives us a high rate of competitive price cuts, then we need to worry about the effects of a high rate of false convictions on the incentives already put into place by competition.

In other words, the competitive price cut example in antitrust should be distinguished from that of compliance with tort law rules. In the tort law setting, there are not, as a general rule, substantial private-interest motivations that would lead one to take costly precautions to avoid harming others. A person who drives does not, in the typical case, have strong private-interest motivations to take care to avoid harming strangers. When we see a high rate of compliance with the law in the torts context, it is quite likely due to the threat of liability. A high rate of false convictions may simply be a reflection that the law is working as intended. In the antitrust setting, in contrast, competition already provides a substantial private-interest motivation for firms to make price cuts. A high rate of false convictions, then, is not necessarily a sign that the law is compelling firms to comply with its provisions. Given this, there is a much greater likelihood in the antitrust than in the torts setting that the law distorts unilateral conduct away from the socially preferable.

This argument is clearly capable of being generalized from the predatory pricing example. In general, when the law imposes penalties on conduct that is typically pro-competitive, there is a high risk of false convictions that both discourage pro-competitive conduct and encourage wasteful litigation. Legal and evidentiary standards should be adjusted to take these costs into

---

[47] See, e.g., Keith N. Hylton, *An Asymmetric Information Model of Litigation*, 22 INTL REV. LAW ECON. 153–75 (2003).

account. The evolution of American predatory pricing law toward the *Brooke Group* standard reflects precisely this sort of adjustment.

III. An Empirical Approach

A. Measuring Dominance Law

Aside from the decision-theoretic critique briefly recounted here, the only other basis for telling whether the American or European approach to monopolization law is superior is an empirical examination. Since the European approach is more interventionist, the proper question is whether it leads to superior economic results. This would be a difficult project.[48] Economic outcomes are determined by many factors in addition to monopolization law.

An alternative empirical question to ask is what factors seem to explain the variation in monopolization laws within the EC countries and between the United States and the EC. Table 8.1) shows a *Dominance Law Score* (for the year 2003) for the United States and countries that were members of the European Community before 2004. The *Dominance Law Score* reflects the number of different practices explicitly mentioned in the nation's laws governing the conduct of dominant firms.

The *Dominance Law Score* was tabulated as follows. Each country is given a score of 1 if the part of its competition statute covering dominance (monopolization) prohibits one of the following practices: (1) limiting access (restricting supply), (2) abusive acts, (3) price setting, (4) discriminatory pricing, (5) resale price maintenance, (6) blocking entry, or (7) predatory pricing. Thus, 7 is the maximum Dominance Law Score possible, and 0 is the minimum.[49] In Table 8.1, Luxembourg has the sparsest law of

---

[48]   Keith N. Hylton and Fei Deng, *Antitrust Around the World: An Empirical Analysis of the Scope of Competition Laws and Their Effects*, 74 ANTITRUST L.J. 2 (2007)

[49]   The scores were compiled by reading the competition law statutes for each country and, where necessary, supplementing the information from case law or other legal reports. For the underlying data, see Keith N. Hylton et al., Antitrust World Reports, available at http://antitrustworldwiki.com. The Dominance Law Score is the sums of the totals for the dominance portion of each country's template, and then the score for predatory pricing is added; see id., *Predatory Pricing Report*, Antitrust World Reports, *available at* http://antitrustworldwiki.com/antitrustwiki/index.php/Predatory_Pricing_Report. An earlier version of the data used in this chapter is examined in Keith N. Hylton and Fei Deng, *Antitrust Around the World: An Empirical Analysis of the Scope of Competition Laws and Their Effects*, 74 ANTITRUST L.J. 2 (2007). The scoring approach used is based on the approach in Michael Nicholson, "Quantifying Antitrust Regimes" (February 5, 2004). FTC Bureau of Economics Working Papers No. 267. Available at SSRN: http://ssrn.com/abstract=531124

Table 8.1. *Dominance score and trade dependency*

Country	Dominance score 2003	Imports/GDP
Austria	5	44.81
Belgium	4	76.60
Germany	6	31.67
Denmark	6	38.97
Spain	6	28.60
Finland	6	30.71
France	5	24.55
Greece	6	29.19
Ireland	4	67.64
Italy	6	24.00
Luxembourg	2	113.31
Netherlands	5	56.32
Portugal	6	34.82
Sweden	5	36.91
United Kingdom	7	28.32
United States	5	14.16

them all, with a dominance score of 2. It is followed by Belgium and Ireland with Dominance Law Scores of 4.

There appears to be a correlation between the dominance score and the share of imports in the gross domestic product (GDP). The country with the lowest dominance score, Luxembourg, also has the highest share of imports in its GDP (113 percent). The country with the next lowest dominance score, Belgium, also has a relatively high import share (73 percent). Countries with relatively low import shares have relatively high dominance scores. The strength of a country's laws on monopolization seems to increase as the share of trade in the GDP declines. Put another way, as a country becomes more dependent on trade, it tends to relax its laws governing dominant firms. What might explain this pattern?

Before offering any hypotheses to explain the correlation in Table 8.1, we should note that the laws of the individual EU member countries are to some extent preempted by Article 82 of the EC treaty. The relationship

or DOI:10.2139/ssrn.531124. The Dominance Score reported in Table 8.1 is a broad measure of monopolization law on the books. It makes no attempt to capture enforcement zeal. Of course, enforcement zeal may be positively correlated with the amount of law on the books. It would clearly be desirable to develop a more finely grained measure of the scope of the law. That is a problem to address in the future.

between national laws and EC law is as follows. For those matters that do not involve commerce among the several EC member states (i.e., intrastate, small business matters) the laws of the individual states govern.[50] For those matters that involve commerce among the EC member states, Article 82 governs.[51] However, Article 82 provides a floor and not a ceiling on monopolization laws. Individual member states are permitted to go beyond Article 82 in prohibiting conduct not prohibited by Article 82 (e.g., price cuts when price is above average cost) and in specifying penalties.[52] But even in this instance, the individual nation laws may be of interest as a signal of the individual nation's own priorities with respect to enforcement. For these reasons it is worthwhile to examine the variation in the dominance laws of various nations.[53]

B. Demand- versus Supply-Side Theories of Dominance Law

The roughly inverse correlation between the strength of dominance law, as reflected in national statutes, and the share of trade in the GDP could reflect pressures from the supply side or from the demand side of the legislative process. Consider the demand side. The demand-side victims of monopolization are domestic consumers and domestic producers operating downstream from a monopolist. In a trade-dependent economy, the potential victims of monopolization may not find a need for a statute constraining the conduct of dominant domestic firms, because those firms are already disciplined by the traded goods sector. If the dominant domestic firms were to attempt to raise their prices to monopoly levels, they would invite importing firms to invade their customer bases. Given this type of limit-pricing equilibrium, domestic pressure groups consisting of potential demand-side victims of monopolization would see little need in pressuring the legislature to enact a statute constraining dominant firms.

Supply-side pressure, or the lack of it, provides an alternative explanation for the inverse correlation between trade and the strength of dominant firm

---

[50] See, e.g., Eleanor M. Fox, *The Central European Nations and the EU Waiting Room – Why Must the Central European Nations Adopt the Competition Law of the European Union?*, 23 BROOKLYN J. INT'L L. 351, 354 (1997).

[51] See, e.g., Wouter P.J. Wils, *The Modernization of the Enforcement of Articles 81 and 82 EC: A Legal and Economic Analysis of the Commission's Proposal for a New Council Regulation Replacing Regulation No. 17*, 24 FORDHAM INT'L L.J. 1655, 1656 (2001).

[52] See, e.g., William M. Hannay, *Transnational Competition Law Aspects of Mergers and Acquisitions*, 20 NW. J. INT'L L. & BUS. 287, 291 (2000).

[53] If we examined Article 82 rather than the national competition laws, there would be no variation in the dominance laws of the EU. The national laws offer a sample with some variation that still reflects harmonization pressures created by membership in the EU.

law. The supply-side victims of firms that monopolize are direct competitors who are frozen out of markets as a result of the conduct of dominant firms. These potential victims always have an interest in some level of protection from competition. Put another way, whether the national economy is trade dependent or not, every domestic firm that perceives itself to be the potential victim of exclusionary conduct by a dominant firm has an interest in legislation that offers protection from such conduct.[54]

However, even if a firm has an interest in legislation that protects it from aggressive competitive conduct, the costs of securing such legislation may exceed the benefits to the firm. The pressure group formed of these firms may be unable to overcome opposition or indifference from other legislative coalitions. This is a plausible scenario in a trade-dependent state. As a result, the inverse correlation between trade dependency and monopolization law may reflect a lack of effort on the supply side – that is, on the part of domestic firms – in securing protective legislation.

Indeed, the (supply-side) relationship between the scope of dominance law and the level of trade may be nonlinear. Starting from a base level of trade (measured by imports as a percentage of the domestic economy), domestic firms may first push for more dominance law to protect them from competition as trade increases. Suppose, as seems plausible, that competitive pressure from importers comes initially from dominant foreign firms. That pressure is likely to cause domestic dominant firms to compete more aggressively. During this period of intensifying competition from dominant foreign firms, domestic firms will have a strong incentive to seek protection through the enactment of a dominance law. Over time, trade may reach a level at which the costs of seeking more protection from dominance law exceed the benefits. The reason for this turnaround is that as the market becomes less concentrated and more intensively competitive as a result of trade, seeking a more expansive dominance law would do little to protect a domestic firm from competition. As the market becomes less concentrated, fewer firms operating in the market would be constrained by dominance law.

Under this theory, as Figure 8.1 illustrates, the relationship between trade and the net benefit to domestic firms from dominance law would have an inverted-U shape. Assuming the relationship between trade and the net benefit to domestic firms also applies to dominance law itself, we should observe an inverted-U relationship across a sample of firms with different import levels.

---

[54] One exception to this might be observed when the domestic firms are roughly equal in ability to inflict competitive harm on one another and view such harms as live-and-let-live nuisances. However, this is unlikely to be observed.

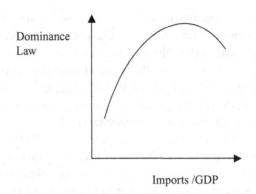

Figure 8.1. Inverted-U relationship between dominance law and trade.

Determining whether the demand-side or the supply-side explanation of monopoly legislation is valid is an empirical project. However, legislation is understood today as the product of concentrated rather than diffuse interest groups. The demand-side theory – that the inverse correlation between the strength of monopoly law and trade dependency is due to a lack of demand from consumers – posits the existence of pressure from diffuse interest groups. The supply theory, on the other hand, explains observed legislation as a function of the strength or weakness of concentrated interest groups. The supply-side theory has the advantage of being consistent with modern explanations of legislation.

C. Regression Evidence

In this section we use a regression model to explore the importance of supply- and demand-side explanations of the determination of dominance law. Treating the Dominance Law Score as the dependent variable, we estimated an equation of the following form:

$$Dominance\ Law = \alpha + \beta_1 GDP + \beta_2 GDPcap + \beta_5 Education$$
$$+ \beta_6 Elder + \beta_7 GovSpend + \beta_8 LegalOrigin. \quad (8.1)$$

1. Variables and Hypotheses

GDP is the gross domestic product, and *GDPcap* is the gross domestic product per capita. The variable *Imports* is a measure of imports as a percent of the GDP. *Agriculture* is the percentage of the workforce in the agricultural sector. *Education* is measured as the ratio of secondary school enrollment to the secondary school–aged population. *Elder* is the percentage of the population aged sixty-five and over.[55] *Govspend* is a measure of government spending as a percentage of the GDP. *LegalOrigin* is a dummy variable identifying the legal origin of the country.

The key variable in this analysis is the measure of imports relative to the GDP (*Imports/GDP*). As the previous discussion implies, a negative coefficient estimate is consistent with both demand- and supply-side theories of the production of dominance law. In other words, a negative coefficient is consistent with a regime in which consumers are the major interest group pushing for dominance law (demand side) and also consistent with a regime in which producers are pushing for such laws (supply side) but are unable to enact them because of indifference from other factions.

A positive estimate for the imports variable coefficient would be inconsistent with the demand-side theory. As imports increase relative to the GDP, consumers should perceive less need to seek legislation protecting them from monopoly abuses. However, a positive estimate for the imports variable would not be inconsistent with the supply-side theory. Even if imports are high relative to the GDP, some producers will still desire protection from aggressively competitive conduct by dominant firms. Indeed, the desire for such protection may be stronger when import penetration is high, because competition from both foreign and domestic firms would be more intense.

Although *Imports/GDP* is the key variable of concern, some of the other variables could mimic its effect, by having both supply- and demand-side influences on the production of dominance law. This complicates any effort to predict the signs of the coefficients in the regression equation. On the other hand, each estimated coefficient sheds light on the competing theories of the transmission effect of that variable. Rather than attempt to predict the coefficient signs, we will discuss transmission-effect theories here.

We controlled for gross domestic product (*GDP*) on the theory that larger economies will differ in significant respects from smaller ones. There are potentially conflicting effects of economy size on the dominance score. Larger economies will be less dependent on imports to dampen the market power of domestic firms. This suggests that *GDP* will have the same

---

[55] All of the explanatory variables used in this chapter are from the World Bank database except for two. First, Imports/GDP is missing for the United States in 2004 in the World Bank's data. The number we used is based on the data from the Economic Report of the President, 2005, available at http://www.gpoaccess.gov/eop/tables05.html. Second, for the United States, the data on Education were taken from the 2007 statistical abstract from the census bureau, available at http://www.census.gov/compendia/statab/labor_force_employment_earnings/labor_force_status/.

impact as the imports variable, though weaker. On the other hand, sectoral composition affects the scope of monopolization law: Antitrust laws were first enacted in industrialized economies.[56] The sectoral composition effect implies the scope of monopolization law will be greater in larger economies.

The per capita GDP (*GDPcap*) is included as an explanatory variable for the obvious reason that wealthier countries should be willing to spend more, other things being equal, on their regulatory preferences. Specifically, if monopolization law is a response to public preferences for protection from monopolistic pricing, then wealthier economies should be willing to spend more on such protection. On the other hand, wealthier economies are associated with larger markets for goods and services, and this suggests that wealth could mimic the effect of the imports variable.

We controlled for the workforce in agriculture (*Agriculture*) on the theory that dominance law is less likely to be observed as that share increases. Historically, the first antitrust laws in the world were enacted in the United Statesand Canada (relatively advanced economies) as a consequence of the power of the railroads and trusts.[57] Agricultural economies are not typically associated with the concerns that led to the first antitrust statutes.

However, our sample consists of the United States and European countries, and there are no primarily agricultural economies in this group. The percentage of the workforce in agriculture may capture something other than sectoral composition within our sample. For example, within a sample of wealthy countries, the percentage of the workforce in agriculture could capture the strength of farm lobbies rather than the effect of sectoral structure.

We controlled for education (*Education*) because it should be easier for legislators to persuade a more educated population of the dangers of monopolization. The first antitrust laws in the world were enacted in the United States and Canada following widespread press reports critical of the conduct of the railroads and the trusts.[58] This implies that dominance law's scope should be greater in more educated countries.

The variable measuring the percentage of elderly (*Elder*) is an attempt to get at the degree of risk aversion in the population. Older workers and business owners probably would perceive a stronger need to be protected from business losses that might result from aggressive competition. This would lead to a greater scope of dominance law as the percentage of elderly increases.

[56] See, e.g., Hylton, supra note 12, at 37–39.
[57] Hylton, supra note 12, at 37–39.
[58] Id.

The amount of government spending relative to the GDP (*Govspend*) is relevant to the production of dominance law because an economy dominated by the government will probably generate fewer demands for protection from dominant firms. Such firms are likely to be under considerable government regulation already. In addition, the government itself may be less willing to effectively surrender some of its power to consumers directly (as in the case of the Clayton Act, which permits private lawsuits) or to special government agencies.[59] This scope of dominance law will decline as the share of government spending in the economy increases.

The final set of regressors control for the legal origin of the country.[60] Legal origin is treated as an indicator of the inclination toward market regulation, on the assumption that countries with similar legal origins are more likely to take similar approaches to competition law. We control for English, Scandinavian, Socialist, French, and German legal origins.

2. Regression Approaches

In theory, equation (1) would describe the relationship between a continuous dominance law variable and several explanatory variables. In fact, we have a discrete dependent variable that measures categories in which a country's dominance law falls. Technically, ordered probit is the preferred regression method given our data.

The dominance score ranges from 1 to 7. As the difference between the scores of 2 and 3 may not be the same as that between 3 an 4 (and so on) due to the coding of the statute, it is important to examine the determinants of dominance law using an ordered probit model. Suppose that the latent variable depends on a vector of observable characteristics as we used in the previous OLS (ordinary least square) regressions,

$$y_{it}^* = X_{it}'\beta + \varepsilon_{it},$$

where ε_{it} follows a standard normal distribution. We observe only the dominance score y but not the latent variable y^*, where

$$y = 1 \quad \text{if } y^* \le \mu_1$$
$$y = j \quad \text{if } \mu_{j-1} < y^* \le \mu_j$$
$$y = J \quad \text{if } y^* > \mu_{J-1}$$

---

[59] See Franz Kronthaler and Johannes Stephan, *Factors Accounting for the Enactment of a Competition Law – An Empirical Analysis*, 52 ANTITRUST BULLETIN 137, 147 (2007).

[60] La Porta et al., *The Quality of Government*, 15 J. LAW, ECON. & ORG. 222 (1999).

We set J equal to 5 in our analysis. Given in our sample, the frequency of having dominance no bigger than 3 is small, we combine and set up $y = 1$ for dominance scores equal to 1 or 2 and $y = 2$ for dominance scores equal to 3 or 4. As a result, we have five individual categories with four thresholds. The model is estimated using the maximum likelihood estimation procedure. Again because observations of each individual country may be correlated to each other, the estimation is clustered at the country level.

Given the estimation of the parameters and the thresholds, the probability of having a dominance score equal to j could be calculated as

$$\Pr(y = 1 \mid X) = \Pr(y^* \leq \mu_1 \mid X) = \Phi(\mu_1 - X\beta)$$
$$\Pr(y = j \mid X) = \Pr(\mu_{j-1} < y^* \leq \mu_j \mid X) = \Phi(\mu_j - X\beta) - \Phi(\mu_{j-1} - X\beta)$$
$$\Pr(y = J \mid X) = \Pr(y^* > \mu_{J-1} \mid X) = 1 - \Phi(\mu_{J-1} - X\beta)$$

The interpretation of the parameters is not as straightforward because those parameters are of limited interest. To calculate the marginal effect of each variable, we have

$$\frac{\partial \Pr(y = 1 \mid X)}{\partial X_k} = -\beta_k \phi(\mu_1 - X\beta)$$
$$\frac{\partial \Pr(y = j \mid X)}{\partial X_k} = -\beta_k \left[\phi(\mu_j - X\beta) - \phi(\mu_{j-1} - X\beta) \right]$$
$$\frac{\partial \Pr(y = J \mid X)}{\partial X_k} = \beta_k \phi(\mu_{J-1} - X\beta)$$

where $\phi(\cdot)$ is the probability density function for normal. Note here that the marginal effect will change as the underlying values of X changes.

An alternative model to consider is the fixed effects framework

$$y_{it}^* = X_{it}'\beta + \theta_i + \varepsilon_{it},$$

where θ_i is a time-invariant effect on the scope of dominance law in each country. Although we have attempted to control for time-invariant effects (e.g., *LegalOrigin*), if the variables incorporated in X do not effectively control for such effects, the fixed effects estimator would be preferable to the ordinary least squares approach.

The greatest drawback with the fixed effects estimator is that our data are not well suited for it. Estimation in the fixed effects model requires temporal variation in y and X, but our dominance law measure y is relatively stable. The dominance score changes in very few countries over the time period of our sample. Still, we present the fixed effects results later because they are helpful in interpreting the least squares and ordered probit results.

3. Ordered Probit and Least Squares Results

Tables 8.2 and 8.3 present the results of ordered probit and ordinary least squares regression of equation (1) for the European Union member countries and the United States. We have decided to present both ordinary least squares and ordered probit results because of the greater ease of interpreting the least squares results.

For the period of the sample (2000 to 2004 inclusive) the EU consisted of fifteen members: Austria, Belgium, Denmark, Finland, France, Germany, Greece, Ireland, Italy, Luxembourg, Netherlands, Portugal, Spain, Sweden, and the United Kingdom. During this period, ten countries were waiting to join the EU: Cyprus, Czech Republic, Estonia, Hungary, Latvia, Lithuania, Malta, Poland, Slovakia, and Slovenia. Because of missing observations, Cyprus had to be dropped from the sample.

The first two columns of Tables 8.2 and 8.3 present results for the EU15 and the United States. The last three columns present results for the EU25 (excluding Cyprus) and the United States. Both the GDP and the GDP per capita are logged in the regressions.

D. Imports

The imports (relative to the GDP) measure is statistically significant in most of the columns in both Tables 8.2 and 8.3. In general, the imports estimate suggests that trade dependency is negatively related to the scope of dominance law – put simply, more trade-dependent states have less dominance law. But this general impression weakens as more variables controlling for heterogeneity are included in the regression. The imports variable loses statistical significance in the EU15 regression that includes the legal origin variables. It also loses significance in the last regression and changes slope when interacted with a dummy variable representing non-EU countries (i.e., the ten countries waiting to join the EU during the sample period).

The first and third columns, which drop the legal origin variables, permit one to see how much the estimated import effect changes as additional variables controlling for heterogeneity are added. In general, the imports measure doubles in impact when the legal origin variables are excluded.

These results suggest that the apparent negative relationship between imports and the scope of dominance law is not as strong as suggested by Table 8.1. As more variables controlling for heterogeneity among the

Table 8.2. *OLS regression, with year dummies; standard errors are clustered at country level*

Dependent Variable: Dominance Score	Reg. 1 (EU15)	Reg. 2 (EU15)	Reg. 3 (EU25)	Reg. 4 (EU25)	Reg.5 (EU25)
Independent Variables:	Coefficient (|t-stat|)				
GDP	−0.204	0.069	−0.112	0.137	0.529**
	(0.63)	(0.39)	(0.66)	(0.91)	(2.98)
GDP per capita	−1.73	−2.893**	−0.528**	−1.867**	−0.943*
	(1.45)	(2.58)	(2.30)	(5.61)	(1.97)
Imports/GDP	−0.043**	−0.016	−0.043**	−0.019**	−0.006
	(4.92)	(1.41)	(5.38)	(2.36)	(0.74)
Agriculture	−0.15	−0.139	−0.113**	−0.085**	0.048
	(1.01)	(1.50)	(2.81)	(2.86)	(0.95)
Education	−0.008	−0.019	0.000	−0.006	−0.003
	(1.06)	(1.99)	(0.00)	(1.19)	(0.67)
Elder	−0.149**	−0.051	−0.069	−0.015	0.06
	(2.73)	(0.69)	(0.88)	(0.13)	(0.57)
Government Spending	−0.013	0.017	−0.068**	−0.06*	−0.051*
	(0.29)	(0.40)	(2.52)	(1.96)	(1.89)
US	−1.399	−1.219*	−1.984**	−1.741**	−2.367**
	(1.65)	(1.76)	(2.97)	(2.54)	(3.43)
Legal Origin_England		0.713*		0.647	0.76
		(1.85)		(1.27)	(1.55)
Legal Origin_French		−0.303		−0.065	−0.096
		(1.45)		(0.31)	(0.42)
Legal Origin_Scan		0.954*		1.093**	1.469**
		(1.95)		(2.56)	(3.17)
Legal Origin_Socialist				−1.888**	−2.517**
				(4.59)	(6.65)
Imports/GDP* NEU					0.038**
					(2.89)
Constant	34.393	36.399**	18.594**	23.547**	0.825
	(1.53)	(2.43)	(3.89)	(6.06)	(0.09)
Rsquared Adjusted	0.712	0.764	0.468	0.602	0.664
N	80	80	125	125	125

Note: ** $p < 0.05$ and * $p < 0.1$.

countries are included in the regression, the relationship between dominance law and imports weakens substantially.

The last column of Table 8.2 further undermines the implied negative relationship of Table 8.1 (comparing dominance law scores and import percentages). Here we include an interaction between imports and non-EU

Table 8.3. *Ordered probit regression, with year dummies; standard errors are clustered at country level*

Dependent Variable: Dominance Score	Reg. 1 (EU15)	Reg. 2 (EU15)	Reg. 3 (EU25)	Reg. 4 (EU25)	Reg. 5 (EU25)
Independent Variables:	Coefficient (|t-stat|)				
GDP	−1.032*	−0.491	−0.118	0.392	1.141**
	(1.73)	(0.87)	(0.43)	(1.32)	(2.93)
GDP per capita	−4.75**	−7.204**	−0.595*	−3.266**	−1.842*
	(2.35)	(2.56)	(1.77)	(3.83)	(1.72)
Imports/GDP	−0.099**	−0.048	−0.058**	−0.024	−0.001
	(3.78)	(1.45)	(3.87)	(1.42)	(0.05)
Agriculture	−0.538**	−0.556**	−0.171**	−0.154**	0.079
	(2.09)	(2.46)	(2.90)	(2.44)	(0.79)
Education	−0.052**	−0.076**	−0.009	−0.03**	−0.029**
	(3.10)	(2.93)	(0.90)	(3.03)	(2.98)
Elder	−0.221	0.009	−0.081	0.035	0.174
	(1.54)	(0.05)	(0.62)	(0.17)	(0.89)
Government Spending	−0.022	−0.022	−0.122**	−0.152**	−0.14**
	(0.22)	(0.22)	(2.44)	(2.41)	(2.18)
US	−1.982	−2.182	−3.488**	−4.02**	−5.396**
	(1.16)	(1.28)	(3.06)	(2.73)	(3.15)
Legal Origin_England		2.246*		1.712	1.914
		(1.77)		(1.36)	(1.52)
Legal Origin_French		0.134		0.432	0.321
		(0.21)		(0.86)	(0.57)
Legal Origin_Scan		2.797*		3.023**	3.853**
		(1.77)		(3.67)	(4.08)
Legal Origin_Socialist				−3.015**	−4.577**
				(2.53)	(3.89)
Imports/GDP* NEU					0.07**
					(2.87)
Log Likelihood	−54.544	−45.871	−117.487	−95.502	−87.897
N	80	80	125	125	125

Note: ** $p < 0.05$ and * $p < 0.1$.

status. The slope of the imports variable is positive in this column for the non-EU countries.

E. Other Variables

The U.S dummy variable is negative and statistically significant in the EU25 sample and not in the EU15 sample. This suggests that the United States is not more conservative than the core EU members, if judged on the basis of the scope of statutory law. However, the United States is more conservative than the enlarged EU. Thus, even after controlling for variables affecting the scope of the law, dominance law in the United States appears to be more conservative (or less interventionist) than that in Europe. In light of our earlier discussion of monopolization doctrine, these results probably understate the degree to which U.S. monopolization law is more conservative than the laws of the EU members. First, the laws of the individual nations, which were used in the regression analysis, are not more expansive and some are less expansive than EU law. It follows that if the United States appears to be conservative in comparison to the laws of the individual EU member states, it is even more conservative in comparison to EU law. Second, our coding of monopolization laws fails to incorporate some important details, such as the approach of a given regime toward essential facilities cases.[61] In this special area of dominance law, the United States is more conservative than the other nations with competition laws.

Legal origin affects dominance law. The European countries with a socialist legal background have a narrower dominance law than the rest of Europe. Those with a Scandinavian legal background have broader monopolization laws.

There are varying levels of statistical significance observed in the remaining variables. The per capita GDP appears to have the greatest effect overall and has a consistently negative impact. This is inconsistent with a view of monopolization law as responsive to public preferences. It is consistent with the prediction that the GDP per capita would mimic the effect of the imports measure – in the sense that wealthier economies are associated with larger and more competitively intense economies.

Percent elderly, which we predicted would have a positive impact as a more risk-averse population would demand more protection from competition law, has an insignificant impact for the most part and a negative and significant impact in one regression. This goes against the view that dominance law responds to the risk preferences of the population.

1. Marginal Effects from Ordered Probit Regressions

The ordered probit model permits us to examine marginal effects for each of the explanatory variables and for each category of dominance law. Recall that the ordered probit model assumes five categories: Category 1 consists of

---

[61] However, we have incorporate information on predatory pricing laws in the dominance measure used for the regressions. This should limit the degree to which the dominance measure understates the gap between U.S. law and that of EU member states.

Table 8.4. *Marginal effects of the explanatory variables on dominance score*

United States				
Dominance score	GDP	GDP per capita	Imports/GDP	Government spending
1,2	0.386%	1.945%	0.191%	0.399%
3,4	3.745%	18.892%	1.851%	3.879%
5	−0.655%	−3.307%	−0.324%	−0.679%
6	−3.448%	−17.393%	−1.704%	−3.571%
7	−0.027%	−0.137%	−0.013%	−0.028%
Europe				
Dominance score	GDP	GDP per capita	Imports/GDP	Government spending
1,2	0.065%	0.329%	0.032%	0.067%
3,4	2.225%	11.226%	1.100%	2.305%
5	2.399%	12.101%	1.185%	2.484%
6	−4.494%	−22.671%	−2.221%	−4.655%
7	−0.195%	−0.985%	−0.096%	−0.202%

dominance law scores 1 and 2; category 2 consists of dominance law scores 3 and 4; and categories 3, 4, and 5 consist of dominance scores 5, 6, and 7, respectively.

Table 8.4 presents marginal effects from the ordered probit regressions. We used the third regression of Table 8.3 to calculate marginal effects.

The marginal effects for the United States show that an increase in *Imports/GDP* increases the likelihood of being in the low dominance score ranges of 1 through 4. Increasing imports reduces the likelihood of being in dominance score range of 5, 6, and 7. For the EU, an increase in imports increases the likelihood of being in the dominance score range of 1 through 5 and reduces the likelihood of being at the highest levels of 6 and 7.

The marginal effects for the both the United States and the EU are consistent with the inverted-U hypothesis. They suggest that the point at which the benefits provided to domestic firms from monopolization law declines earlier in the United States than in Europe.

2. OLS Again

The relationship between imports and dominance law is more complicated than the negative correlation observed in Table 8.1. Table 8.2 shows that when controlling for heterogeneity both in the sample (column 2 of

Table 8.2) and in the slope of the imports variable (column 5 of Table 8.2), the negative relationship fails to hold. One explanation for this failure is provided by the marginal effects from the ordered probit model. The marginal effects suggest that the imports variable has an inverted-U relationship with the dominance law measure.

In this section, we use ordinary least squares for an alternative test of the inverted-U hypothesis. Specifically, Table 8.5 presents results in which the imports and the square of imports are included as regressors. Moreover, we have divided the variable into two categories depending on the scale of imports. The slope for the imports variable is allowed to differ for countries with imports less than 50 percent of the GDP (*Imports/GDP* Small*), and for countries with imports greater than 50 percent of the GDP (*Imports/GDP* Big*).

The reason for suspecting a nonlinear relationship is that domestic firms may initially seek additional protection from competition as imports enter the domestic market. However, at some point the marginal benefits of protection fall below the marginal cost, after which imports no longer generate a greater push by domestic firms for legal protection.

We have divided the countries according to the level of imports on the theory that the baseline relationship between imports and dominance law should differ between large economies and small dependent economies. In a small dependent economy, the baseline level of imports (measured when dominance law is at a minimal level) will be large as a percentage of the GDP. For a large economy, the baseline level of imports will be relatively small. If, as we have hypothesized, an inverted-U shape explains the relationship between imports and dominance law within both sets of countries, a regression that failed to separate the two groups would confuse the nonlinear relationships observed in both sets of countries.

The results of Table 8.5 are consistent with the nonlinear relationship theory. For both small import and trade-dependent economies, one observes a statistically significant, inverted-U–shaped relationship between imports and dominance law. The cross-over points for the large (small import) economies occur at 36.5 percent and 31.2 percent in the first and second columns, respectively. For trade-dependent (big import) economies, the cross-over points occur at 53.5 and 51 percent.

3. Fixed Effects Regressions

Because of the small number of changes in the dominance law variable, our sample is not well suited for the fixed effects framework. We ran the fixed effects model anyway to examine its implications. Table 8.6 presents

Table 8.5. *OLS based on the size of imports/GDP*

Dependent variable: Dominance score	Reg. 1	Reg. 2
Independent Variables:	Coefficient (|t-stat|)	
Imports/GDP* Big	0.107*	0.102*
	(1.98)	(1.95)
Imports/GDP* Big^2	−0.001*	−0.001**
	(1.96)	(2.03)
Imports/GDP* Small	0.292**	0.312**
	(2.45)	(2.71)
Imports/GDP* Small^2	−0.004**	−0.005**
	(2.41)	(2.86)
GDP	0.186	−0.012
	(1.47)	(0.14)
GDP per capita	−0.963**	−1.168**
	(3.19)	(4.08)
Agriculture	−0.044	−0.079**
	(1.60)	(4.25)
Education	−0.009	−0.006
	(1.31)	(1.02)
Elder	0.055	−0.006
	(0.83)	(0.11)
Government Spending	−0.05**	−0.047**
	(2.94)	(2.66)
US	−0.091	0.163
	(0.12)	(0.22)
NEU	1.332**	
	(2.19)	
Legal Origin_England	0.835**	0.618**
	(2.51)	(1.99)
Legal Origin_French	0.210	0.100
	(0.78)	(0.39)
Legal Origin_Scan	0.994**	0.55*
	(2.25)	(1.66)
Legal Origin_Socialist	−1.54**	−0.872**
	(3.19)	(2.03)
Constant	6.312	14.711**
	(0.99)	(3.40)
Rsquared Adjusted	0.659	0.644
N	125	125

Note: ** $p < 0.05$ and * $p < 0.1$.

Table 8.6. *Fixed effects*

Dependent variable: Dominance score	Reg. 1 (EU15)	Reg. 2 (EU15)	Reg. 3 (EU25)	Reg. 4 (EU25)
Independent Variables:	Coefficient ($|$t-stat$|$)			
GDP	7.235	2.952	3.82	6.03
	(0.82)	(0.41)	(0.63)	(1.15)
GDP per capita	1.057	3.727	−2.19	−3.921
	(0.13)	(0.48)	(0.43)	(0.87)
Imports/GDP	0.069**	0.067**	0.044**	0.045**
	(2.74)	(2.67)	(3.35)	(3.38)
Agriculture	0.279	0.24	0.083	0.088
	(1.58)	(1.41)	(0.82)	(0.87)
Education	0.008	0.01	0.007	0.005
	(0.99)	(1.20)	(1.02)	(0.87)
Elder	0.274		−0.159	
	(0.84)		(0.72)	
Government Spending	0.245*	0.182	0.137	0.166*
	(1.70)	(1.48)	(1.45)	(1.97)
R-squared:				
Within	0.224	0.214	0.182	0.178
Between	0.159	0.001	0.094	0.124
Overall	0.144	0.000	0.085	0.111
N	80	80	125	125

Note: ** $p < 0.05$ and * $p < 0.1$.

fixed effects regressions, both with the EU15 sample and the EU25 sample. The most noticeable difference is that the imports variable has a statistically significant and positive coefficient in the fixed effects regressions.

However, the relatively small number of changes in the dominance law variable over the period of the sample provides a strong reason to discount the fixed effects results. The countries that experienced changes in the dominance law scope are the Czech Republic, Ireland, Luxembourg (two changes over the sample period), and the Slovak Republic. Each of these countries is a relatively small, trade-dependent economy (imports as a percent of the GDP exceed 50 percent in each country). These results provide additional support to the inverted-U hypothesis.

Moreover, since two of the four countries in the group with changes are in the non-EU subsample, the positive estimate in the fixed effects regression confirms the finding of the last regression of Tables 8.2 and 8.3, where the imports variable has a positive slope for the non-EU countries.

7. Discussion

We have distinguished supply- and demand-side theories of dominance law and attempted to find evidence for these theories in the regression results. Under a demand-side theory, dominance law is produced in response to demands for protection from monopolistic pricing. Under a supply-side theory, dominance law is produced in response to demands by domestic firms for protection from the aggressive competitive conduct of dominant firms.

Both demand- and supply-side theories are consistent with the observed negative correlation between the scope of dominance law and the level of import penetration. However, we argue that only the supply-side theory is consistent with a positive relationship between import penetration and the scope of dominance law.

The regression evidence supports neither theory as a general account of the process by which dominance law is generated in the wealthiest economies. The regression evidence is consistent with a third theory advanced here, that of an inverted-U relationship between import penetration and the scope of dominance law. Under the nonlinear relationship theory, dominance law and import penetration are positively related initially, as import penetration rises above a baseline initial level. As import penetration increases, a point is reached at which the benefits of legal protection to domestic firms are no longer greater than the costs of seeking protection.

Under the nonlinear relationship theory, the slope of the imports variable in the dominance law regression will depend on the type of country and the level of import penetration. Regressions that fail to disaggregate the countries will generate unreliable results. The negative coefficient in the OLS regressions and the positive coefficient in the fixed effects regressions are both incorrect as general descriptions of the relationship between import penetration and dominance law. Indeed, the positive result for the fixed effects regressions probably reflects the disproportionate share of small dependent countries among the countries that experienced changes in the scope of dominance law in the period of the sample.

IV. Conclusion

This chapter is both a survey and an empirical assessment of U.S. and EU monopolization law. The empirical results raise questions about the forces that generate monopolization law.

American monopolization law has evolved to be more conservative than European law in its present stage. Roughly since the publication of Areeda and Turner's article on predation, American courts and commentators have shown a concern for potential false conviction costs under monopolization law. This concern has been especially evident in predation law (*Brooke Group*) and the law governing unilateral refusals to deal (*Trinko*).

Our empirical analysis has focused on the factors that explain broad variations in the scope of monopolization law in the United States and the EU. One factor of special interest is international trade. Monopolization law appears to have an inverted-U relationship with import penetration, rising first with import penetration and then falling. This finding is inconsistent with the theory that monopolization law in the most important competition law regimes develops in response to consumer demands for protection from monopoly pricing.

APPENDIX

I. Variable Definitions and Sources

Agriculture: Employment in agriculture (% of total employment).

Education: The ratio of secondary school enrollment to the secondary school–aged population.

Elder: Percentage of total population aged 65 and above.

Government spending: The ratio of general government final consumption expended to the GDP.

Legal origin:

Legal origin	Country
England	Cyprus, Ireland, United Kingdom, United States
French	Belgium, Spain, France, Greece, Italy, Luxembourg, Malta, Netherlands, Portugal
Germany	Austria, Germany
Scan	Denmark, Finland, Sweden
Socialist	Czech Republic, Estonia, Hungary, Lithuania, Latvia, Poland, Slovak Republic, Slovenia

Sources: All of the explanatory variables used in this chapter are from the World Bank – World Development Indicators except for the following cases:

1. *Imports/GDP* is missing for the United States at 2004. This number was calculated based on the data from an economic report of the president, 2005. http://www.gpoaccess.gov/eop/tables05.html.

2. Employment in Agriculture for France is obtained from the *CIA World Factbook*. https://www.cia.gov/library/publications/the-world-factbook/geos/fr.html. (CIA provides data for the year of 1999.)

II. Descriptive Statistics

Variable	Mean	Std. Dev.	Min	Max
Dominance Score	5.29	1.16	1	7
GDP (log)	26.60	1.47	23.70	30.01
GDP per capita (log)	10.05	0.37	9.26	10.83
Imports/GDP	45.05	26.98	13.73	129.01
Agriculture	4.91	3.90	1.30	17.40
Government spending	20.24	3.69	13.96	28.32
Education	110.99	16.86	89.48	160.15
Elder	15.66	2.04	10.93	19.67
$N = 80$				
Dominance Score	5.21	1.07	1	7
GDP (log)	25.57	1.93	22.06	30.01
GDP per capita (log)	9.53	0.79	8.09	10.83
Imports/GDP	52.20	25.50	13.73	129.01
Agriculture	6.55	5.12	1.30	19.30
Government spending	19.89	3.58	10.19	28.32
Education	105.99	15.45	86.58	160.15
Elder	15.09	2.00	10.93	19.67
$N = 125$				

PART IV

THE PATENT SYSTEM

9

Rewarding Innovation Efficiently

The Case for Exclusive Rights

Vincenzo Denicolò and Luigi Alberto Franzoni

I. Introduction

The law provides various forms of legal protection for innovations, depending on the subject matter (manufactured items, artistic works, design, etc.) and degree of novelty. Patents are usually regarded as a strong form of protection, since they provide an exclusive right on the innovative technological knowledge. Copyrights and trade secrets, by contrast, are regarded as weak forms of protection, since they prohibit direct copying but not independent duplication.

The recent literature on the optimal breadth of IP rights has underscored the positive role of such independent duplicators in increasing the degree of product market competition, and hence in reducing the social costs of IP protection.[1] This literature, while recognizing the risks of permitting outright copying of innovations, argues that parallel development and independent discovery should not be discouraged, since the benefits they induce on the competition side may outweigh their adverse effects on innovation. In this perspective, the optimal form of IP protection appears to be that provided by copyrights and trade secrecy, which do not prevent independent developers from practicing the innovation.

---

[1] See, among others, La Manna M., R. MacLeod, and D. de Meza, 1989, The Case for Permissive Patents, *European Economic Review*, 33, 1427–1443; Farrell, J, 1995, Arguments for Weaker Intellectual Property Protection in Network Industries, *Standard View*, Vol. 3/2, 46–49; Leibovitz, J., 2002, Inventing a Nonexclusive Patent System, *The Yale Law Journal*, Vol. 111/8, 2251–2287; Kultti, K. J. Toikka, and T. Takalo, 2006, Simultaneous Model of Innovation, Secrecy, and Patent Policy. *American Economic Review*, vol. 96, 82–86; Shapiro, C., 2006, Prior User Rights, *American Economic Review*, 96, 92–96; Shapiro, C., 2007, Patent Reform: Aligning Reward and Contribution, *NBER Working Paper No. 13141*; Bessen, J. and E. Maskin, 2009, Sequential Innovation, Patents, and Imitation, *RAND Journal of Economics*, 40/4, 611–35; Henry, E. 2009. Disclosure of Research Results: The Cost of Proving Your Honesty," *Economic Journal*, 119 (539), 1036–1064.

Building on the original insight of La Manna, Maurer and Scotchmer, Shapiro, Kultti and Takalo, and Henry, among others, have argued that patent protection should be weakened so as to allow second independent inventors to practice the innovations they obtain by parallel development.[2] More specifically, they argue that independent inventors should be granted a defense to patent infringement (independent inventor defense). This proposal has spurred an interesting debate, which has mostly focused on the practical problems posed by its implementation.[3]

Even if the focus of this stream of literature centers on the rights of the patent holders against second inventors, its insights have a more general bearing. They suggest that exclusive rights are an inefficient system of rewarding innovation when multiple parties are likely to discover the same innovation more or less at the same time. If this is so, then the analysis also can be applied to the case where duplication *is forced* by the policy maker, for example, by compulsory licensing or by mandatory disclosure of secret technological knowledge and know-how. And there are many other instances in which IPRs (intellectual property rights) and competition law may collide, and courts have to decide whether to favor *ex ante* innovation or *ex post* competition.[4]

The stance taken by antitrust authorities and the courts on these issues varies over time and across countries. In the United States, there seems to be a general consensus – reinforced by *Trinko* (540 U.S. 398, 2004) – that competition rules should not trump IP law.[5] In Europe, antitrust authorities and the courts follow a different approach, which tends to set a closer boundary to IPRs. According to the European approach, a refusal to license

---

[2] La Manna M., R. MacLeod, and D. de Meza, 1989, The Case for Permissive Patents, *European Economic Review*, 33, 1427–1443; Maurer, S. M., Scotchmer, S., 2002. The Independent Invention Defence in Intellectual Property. *Economica*, 69, 535–547; Shapiro, C., 2006, Prior User Rights, *American Economic Review*, 96, 92–96; Kultti, K. and T. Takalo, T., 2008, Optimal Fragmentation of Intellectual Property rights. *International Journal of Industrial Organization*, 26/1, 137–149; Henry, E. 2009. Disclosure of Research Results: The Cost of Proving Your Honesty," *Economic Journal*, 119 (539), 1036–1064.

[3] Blair R. and T. Cotter, 2001, Rethinking Patent Damages, *Texas Intellectual Property Law Journal* 10/1, 1–93; Vermont, S., 2006, Independent Invention as a Defense to Patent Infringement, *Michigan Law Review*, vol. 105, December; Vermont, S., 2007, The Angel is in the Big Picture: A Response to Lemley, *Michigan Law Review*, Vol. 105/7, 1537–1544; Lemley, M, 2007, Should Patent Infringement Require Proof of Copying? *Michigan Law Review*, Vol. 105, 1525–1536.

[4] Vickers, J., 2009, Competition Policy and Property Rights, University of Oxford: Department of Economics Discussion Paper Series 436; Hovenkamp, H, 2008, Parents, Property and Competition Policy. 34 *Journal of Corporation Law* 1243.

[5] See, for instance, U.S. Dept. of Justice and Fed. Trade Commission, 2007, Antitrust Enforcement and Intellectual Property Rights: Promoting Innovation and Competition.

an IPR by a dominant undertaking constitutes an abuse if certain "exceptional" conditions hold, outlined by the European Court of Justice in the *Magill* case. Encouraged by its success in the *Microsoft* case, the European Commission seems to support a "balancing of interests" approach, where the positive effect of more intense competition should be weighted on a case-by-case basis against the adverse impacts on innovation.[6]

From a law and economics viewpoint, when an innovator is forced to license its innovative technological knowledge, the protection afforded to him or her degrades from a property rule to a liability rule in the sense of Calabresi and Melamed.[7] That is to say, the owner of the innovative knowledge is not entitled to enjoin other parties from it, but has to content himself with compensation (a license fee) decided by the court. However, in this context the traditional comparison between property rule and liability rule needs to be extended to account for their effects on the incentives to innovate.[8]

In what follows, we will develop an analytical framework that is simple and tractable and yet helps bring to the fore some effects omitted in the previous literature. Building on our previous work (Denicolò and Franzoni, 2010, we will compare strong and weak IP rights using Kaplow-like ratio tests, which relate the social costs (in terms of deadweight losses) and benefits (in terms of incentives to innovate) of alternative forms of protection. We investigate firms' incentives in an innovation race where two or more firms that target the same innovation race to discover first, and show how the standard Kaplow test should be corrected so as to account for the adverse effect on the incentives to innovate of the "consolation prize" netted under nonexclusive rights by the loser. We conclude that the policy prescriptions obtained by the previous literature need to be qualified.

II. The Ratio Test

The optimal design of IP rights inevitably rests on the resolution to the fundamental trade-off between the need to reward the innovator and the need to diffuse the innovation. This trade-off involves many dimensions, the

---

[6] DG Competition, 2008, Discussion paper on the Commission's Enforcement Priorities Applying Article 82 Ec Treaty to Abusive Exclusionary Conduct by Dominant Undertakings, Brussels.

[7] Calabresi, G. and A. D. Melamed, 1972, Property Rules, Liability Rules, and Inalienability: One View of the Cathedral, *Harvard Law Review*, Vol. 85/6, 1089–1128.

[8] See, for instance, Lemley, M. and P. Weiser, 2007, Should Property or Liability Rules Govern Information? 85 *Texas Law Review* 783–841.

best explored of which is the duration of the exclusive right.[9] More recent contributions also have explored the issue of the optimal breadth of the exclusive right with respect to producers of similar products,[10] follow-on innovators,[11] and prior (secret) users.[12]

Another important issue, which is the focus of this chapter, concerns the right of the IP holder to exclude imitators and duplicators. Here, the law follows two basic models, associated with patent and trade secrets protection, respectively. Patent protection provides a fully exclusive right to the patent holder, who can enjoin all others from the use and commercialization of the innovation, independently of how they have obtained it.[13] Under trade secrets protection, by contrast, the inventor is protected against copying, but not against independent discovery or duplication through reverse engineering.[14] Other forms of IP protection lie somewhere in between these two extremes and borrow elements from each of them. Copyright law, for instance, allows for parallel development but tends to put restrictions on reverse engineering ("circumvention of digital locks").

For simplicity, we focus on the comparison between patents and trade secrets protection in a very simple setting. We start in this section by presenting a basic ratio test. In the subsequent sections, we introduce several extensions and analyze how the appropriate ratio test changes accordingly.

Let us consider the case where one firm (firm 1) discovers an innovation and another firm (firm 2) duplicates it. Duplication by firm 2, either through independent discovery or reverse engineering – which are taken to be equivalent for the time being – introduces some degree of competition in the market: Prices go down, and a larger share of consumers is served.

---

[9] See, also, Nordhaus, W. 1969. *Invention, Growth, and Welfare*, Boston: MIT Press.

[10] Gilbert, R. and C. Shapiro, 1990. Optimal Patent Length and Breadth, *Rand Journal of Economics*, 21, 106–112; Klemperer, P., 1990 How Broad Should the Scope of Patent Protection Be? Rand Journal of Economics 21, 113–130; Denicolo, V, 1996. Patent Races and Optimal Patent Breadth and Length, 44 *The Journal of Industrial Economics* 3, 249–265.

[11] Scotchmer, S., 2004, *Innovation and Incentives*, Boston: MIT Press; Bessen, J. and E. Maskin, 2009, Sequential Innovation, Patents, and Imitation, *RAND Journal of Economics*, 40/4, 611–35.

[12] Denicolo V. and L. Franzoni, 2004, Patents, Secrets, and the First Inventor Defense, *Journal of Economics and Management Strategy*, 13/3, 517–538; Shapiro, C., 2006, Prior User Rights, *American Economic Review*, 96, 92–96.

[13] In this sense, patent infringement resembles a strict liability offense. However, the analogy is not perfect, since the determination of damages depends on whether the violator was put on notice (Blair R. and T. Cotter, 2001, Rethinking Patent Damages, *Texas Intellectual Property Law Journal* 10/1, 1–93.)

[14] The law and economics of reverse engineering are discussed in Samuelson, P. and S. Scotchmer, 2002, The Law and Economics of Reverse Engineering, *Yale. Law Journal*, 111, 1575–1663.

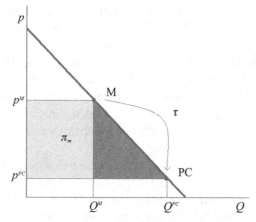

Figure 9.1. Patent protection.

Thus, let us assume that the price of the "new" product decreases from its monopoly price p_M to a duopoly price p_D, with $p_D < p_M$ (see Figures 9.1 and 9.2).

Under patent protection (Figure 9.1), discovery spans a temporary monopoly followed by perfect competition at the end of the patent term. During the patent life, of expected duration τ, the innovator earns monopoly profits π_m while society bears the deadweight loss Δ_m (the shaded area in the figure).

To make some progress, the literature has concentrated on the problem of the efficient provision of the incentives to innovate. In other words, it has proceeded by taking the desired level of remuneration of the innovator as

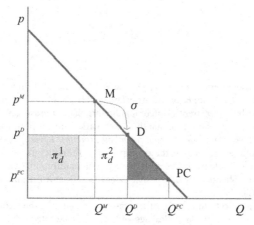

Figure 9.2. Trade secrets protection.

given, and asking which form of protection yields the target remuneration at the least social cost.[15,16] Thus, the comparison focuses on the social loss entailed by the target level of the innovator's profit in the different regimes.

Initially, under both regimes there is a temporary monopoly, which entails the same costs and benefits. The comparison between the two regimes therefore hinges on the second period. In the strong regime there is a monopoly until the patent expires. In the weak regime, by contrast, there is a duopoly until the secret leaks out. For simplicity, we rule out leakage, so in our model secrecy lasts forever.[17]

Let us focus on the comparison between the two regimes from the time when the innovation is duplicated. Let h be the present discounted value of a perpetual constant annuity, and let e be the present discounted value of a constant annuity over the patent lifetime E; obviously $e \leq h$. Then, in order for the innovator's expected discounted profit to be the same under the two regimes, we must have $e\pi_m = h\pi_d$, that is,

$$e = h\pi_d/\pi_m.$$

The social cost of patents is measured by the deadweight loss Δ_m. Under trade secrecy, social costs comprise both duopoly deadweight loss Δ_m and duplication costs d_u, which are sunk to reproduce an innovation already available. Hence, trade secrets protection entails a lower social cost than patents if

$$h\Delta_d + d_u < e\Delta_m,$$

Using the definition of e, trade secrets protection is preferable if

$$h\Delta_d + d_u < \Delta_m \frac{h\pi_d}{\pi_m},$$

---

[15] In Denicolo V. and L. Franzoni, 2010, On the Winner-take-all Principle in Innovation races, *Journal of the European Economic Association*, Vol. 8/5, 1133–1158 we show that this method tallies with two apparently different policy problems: the assessment of a marginal policy variation on the assumption that the benchmark regime is optimally calibrated (as in Shapiro, C., 2006, Prior User Rights, *American Economic Review*, 96, 92–96), and the comparison of different regimes on the assumption that the policy maker is able to calibrate the incentives to innovate by different means (e.g., patent duration, ease of duplication).

[16] Gilbert, R. and C. Shapiro, 1990. Optimal Patent Length and Breadth, *Rand Journal of Economics*, 21, 106–112.

[17] Trade secrecy may also terminate for other reasons, e.g., because the technology becomes obsolete. However, accounting for leakage and other similar effects does not modify the qualitative results of the analysis.

that is,

$$\frac{\Delta_d}{\pi_d} + \frac{d_u}{h\pi_d} < \frac{\Delta_m}{\pi_m},$$

Note that the ratio $\Sigma = \frac{d_u}{h\pi_d}$ ($=$) represents the share of discounted duopoly profits that firm 2 invested in the duplication process, and hence are wasted from the social viewpoint. Then, trade secrets are preferable if the following ratio test is met:[18]

$$\text{Basic Ratio Test } \frac{\Delta_d}{\pi_d} + \Sigma < \frac{\Delta_m}{\pi_m}.$$

The deadweight loss to the individual profit ratio under duopoly depends on the intensity of competition. Generally speaking, the tougher the competition, the lower the prices, and hence the lower is the deadweight loss to profit ratio (see Figure 9.2).[19] In the case of homogenous goods and linear demand, for instance, the deadweight loss to profits ratio under a duopoly is the same as that under a monopoly if firms compete à la Cournot (where each firm behaves like a monopolist on the residual demand). The duopoly ratio is lower than the monopoly ratio if competition results in lower prices than under Cournot competition.[20] The share Σ of duopoly profits that are dissipated, instead, depends on the ease of duplication and on the nature of duplication costs.[21] Hard to duplicate innovations entail larger costs.[22]

---

[18] Although the basic ratio test follows the same logic as the original test developed by Kaplow (1984, The Patent-Antitrust Intersection: A Reappraisal, 97 Harvard Law Review) there are important differences between our basic test and Kaplow's, which are discussed in details in Denicolo V. and L. Franzoni, 2010, On the Winner-take-all Principle in Innovation races, *Journal of the European Economic Association*, Vol. 8/5, 1133–1158. On the use of Kaplow tests in IP, see Scotchmer, S., 2004, Innovation and Incentives, Boston: MIT Press.

[19] The implications for optimal taxation of deadweight loss increasing exponentially with prices were first explored by Ramsey (1927). See Ramsey, F.P., 1927. A Contribution to the Theory of Taxation. 37 *The Economic Journal* 145, 47–61.

[20] Product differentiation tends to tilt the balance in favor of weak IP rights. Here, however, several factors come into play, since differentiation affects both the social cost of monopoly (depriving consumers of product variety) and the social cost of duopoly (since differentiation attenuates competition). See Denicolo V. and L. Franzoni, 2010, On the Winner-take-all Principle in Innovation Races, *Journal of the European Economic Association*, Vol. 8/5, 1133–1158. If duopoly is asymmetric, because of a cost advantage of the innovator, then duopoly also entails production inefficiency, and the balance is tilted against weak IP rights.

[21] More generally, this share would also depend on the number of firms able to duplicate the innovation. See Gallini, N., 1992, Patent Policy and Costly Imitation. *RAND Journal of Economics*, Vol. 23/1, 52–63; Denicolo V. and L. Franzoni, 2008, Rewarding Innovation Efficiently: The Case for Exclusive Rights, GMU/Microsoft Conference on Innovation.

[22] Clearly, the expenditure of the first inventor to fence off his technological knowledge would also count as social waste.

The main insight that we get from this analysis is that weak protection (trade secrets) is likely to be preferable if the competition brought about by duplication is intense and duplication costs are low (as a share of the expected duopoly profits). By contrast, strong protection is likely to be preferable when competition ensuing from duplication is weak and the duplicative process is costly.

III. IP Law and Antitrust

Under certain circumstances, the right to exclude provided by patents and other IP rights may run against antitrust law. Take, for example, the case of a firm holding a monopolistic power that refuses to license its proprietary know-how to a rival. In Europe, such a practice may fall under the scrutiny of antitrust agencies, which will try and ascertain if the firm is engaging in an anticompetitive exclusionary conduct. In certain circumstances – as when the proprietary knowledge is regarded as an "essential facility" – the refusal to license may be deemed illegal, and the owner of the innovative technology may be forced to share it with its rivals. In this case, the protection afforded to the innovator is degraded to a liability rule, where the compensation for the "taking" is decided by the court.

The basic ratio test developed in the previous section can be used to provide a first-cut analysis of this issue. Consider the case of a patent holder who is subject to mandatory licensing. The patent holder loses her right to exclusive use, and rivals are allowed to compete with the first inventor. While under trade secrecy rivals can access an innovator's original knowledge by sinking duplication costs, under mandatory licensing they can do it by paying the compensation decided by the court. In the latter case, no resources are devoted to the wasteful duplication of an existing technology. However, the innovator's profit goes down, with a negative effect on the incentives to innovate. Again the policy maker has to trade off lower incentives to innovate with more intense competition in the product market.

Let us consider, as before, the case where the policy maker intends to provide a pre-specified reward to the innovator and decides which type of protection to grant.[23] The case of weak patent protection now is taken to mean that the innovator is forced to disclose the innovation to the rival on payment of a compensation, the amount of which is decided by the

---

[23] This problem might be directly relevant, for instance, in those cases where the policy maker intends to reduce the reward to the innovator and has to decide whether to do it by either shortening the patent term or by reducing the scope of protection.

court and can range from nil to full duplication profits.[24] Since mandatory disclosure reduces the innovator's profit, the pre-specified reward can only be achieved if the weak patent has a longer duration than the standard one. In other words, we make the analytically convenient but rather unrealistic assumption that when a patent holder is forced to license its patent, the duration of the patent is suitably extended.

Let w be the present discounted value of a constant annuity over the extended patent lifetime, W, and let e be the present discounted value of a constant annuity over the normal patent lifetime, as before. Now we have $e \leq w$.

The upper bound on the licensing fee to be paid by the duplicator is its expected profit $e \, \pi_d$. It is convenient to express the mandatory licensing fee as a fraction α of the duplicator's expected profits, with $0 \leq \alpha \leq 1$. Then, under a weak patent regime, the innovator's expected reward is $w\pi_d$ (her own profits after duplication) plus $\alpha w\pi_d$ (the licensing fee paid by the duplicator), that is, $w\pi_d (1 + \alpha)$.

For the innovator's profit to be the same amount in both regimes, we must have $e\pi_m = w\pi_d (1 + \alpha)$, that is, $e = w\pi_d (1 + \alpha)/\pi_m$.

Assuming, to fix ideas, that the patent holder is obliged to license his innovation as soon as he discovers it, the total social waste under the weak patent system amounts to a duopoly deadweight loss Δ_d for the duration of the patent term. Now there are no duplication costs, since competitors obtained the right to utilize the innovation by legal means, not by duplication. Hence, weak patents entail a lower social cost than strong patents if

$$w\Delta_d < e\Delta_m.$$

If e is set so as to provide the required reward to the innovator, we find that weak patents are preferable if

$$w\Delta_d < \Delta_m \frac{w\pi_d(1 + \alpha)}{\pi_m},$$

that is,

$$\frac{\Delta_d}{\pi_d(1 + \alpha)} < \frac{m}{\pi_m}.$$

---

[24] The timing of the disclosure is immaterial for our purposes. In the time period between invention and duplication, monopoly prevails and the innovator's profit and the deadweight loss are the same as under a standard patent.

Under Cournot competition, $\Delta_d/\pi_d = \Delta_m/\pi_m$. It follows immediately that the new ratio test is surely passed if product market competition is more intense than under Cournot.

More generally, the ratio test is more likely to be passed (and hence the weak patent system is more likely to be preferable) if the royalty rate α is high, and if product market competition (after disclosure) is intense. If α is equal to one, that is, if the innovator is able to appropriate the full industry profits – as in Maurer Scotchmer – then weak patents are preferable for any given linear demand function.[25] If, instead, α is equal to nil, that is, if the innovation is forcibly disclosed to rivals without compensation, then the ratio test becomes harder to pass (if competition is more intense than under Cournot).

Overall, the simple application of the ratio test seems to suggest that a weakening of IP rights is generally socially desirable. The virtues of *ex post* competition seem to have a greater weight than the adverse effects on the incentives to innovate. If, for some reasons, the policy maker wants to reduce the incentive to innovate – perhaps because innovators are over-rewarded – then a good way of doing so would be to enhance *ex post* competition, for instance by favoring competitors against the original inventors. We contend, however, that the analysis developed in this section abstracts from a crucial factor, namely, the fact that innovative activity is often rivalrous in nature. Accounting for this effect may change radically the policy conclusions, as we shall see in the next section.

IV. Rivalrous Innovation

The ratio test developed in the previous section is based on the special case where one firm serves the role of innovator and the other that of duplicator. In real life, the "roles" to be played in the innovation game are open for competition, and firms race to gain technological leadership. We now argue that the assumption of the previous section underestimates the adverse effects of weak IP rights.

Look again at Figure 9.2. Here the profits netted by firm 2 serve the purpose of stimulating duplication and thus, ultimately, a price reduction. They are not directly included in the ratio test, since the latter balances profits and deadweight loss from the perspective of the innovator only. Yet, a closer analysis shows that the profits of the duplicator affect the

[25] Maurer, S. M., Scotchmer, S., 2002. The Independent Invention Defence in Intellectual Property. *Economica*, 69, 535–547.

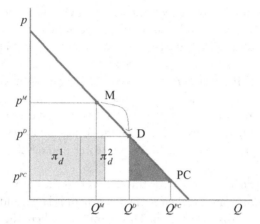

Figure 9.3. Mandatory disclosure ($\alpha = 1/2$).

incentives to innovate in a deeper way. First, as already recognized, they stimulate duplication. Second, and perhaps more important, they represent the reward to the loser of the race. As such, they provide an incentive **not to invest** in the race. This effect has been neglected so far, and it is the focus of this section.

When the innovation is the outcome of a race, firms will care about both the first prize and the second prize. The second prize is in fact a "consolation prize" for the firm that fails to invent first. As such, it affects incentives to innovate in a negative way: The larger the second prize, the less urgent it is to discover the new technology. Put differently, while strong IP rights make the race a winner-take-all contest, weak IP rights provide a reward to all firms. All contestants win, although the first obtains more than the second.

To see how the division of the total prize affects the incentives to innovate, consider Figures 9.2 and 9.3. The total expected profits to the firms are represented by industry profits $\pi_d^1 + \pi_d^2$ for the duration of the weak IP right. Incentives to innovate, however, are not proportional to the sum of the prizes, $\pi_d^1 + \pi_d^2$. They crucially depend on the *difference* between the first and second prizes, which is much higher under exclusive IP rights. The *structure* of the reward scheme matters.

If the presence of a consolation prize reduces the incentives to innovate, the ratio test developed in the previous section has to be modified, and the policy implications suitably qualified. Under what circumstances does the second prize matter? And how can the ratio test be adjusted so as to account for the consolation prize effect?

In Denicolò and Franzoni,[26] we reformulate the ratio test for the patent/ trade secrecy choice. A similar solution can be applied to the mandatory licenses case. From the point of view of a contestant, it is apparent that the importance of the second prize depends on whether the rival is about to discover soon. If the rival is perceived as "far away" from discovery, the contestant does not care about the presence of the second prize. It will instead concentrate on the first prize and invest to get it earlier. Conversely, if the rival is about to make the discovery, the contestant may very well settle for the second price and reduce his own research and development (R&D) investment.

In a symmetric innovation race, this means that the adverse effect of the consolation prize is largest when R&D investment is large, and each firm is likely to make the discovery soon. This is the case where the race is most "rivalrous," in the sense that the main aim of greater R&D investment is to preempt the other contestant. By preempting its rival, a firm is able to switch from the second to the first prize. Hence, only the difference between the first and second prizes matters, not the aggregate value of the prizes.[27] For the sake of the ratio test, in this case incentives to innovate are well proxied by the difference between the profits of the winner and the loser of the race. Thus, the denominator of the ratio test becomes $\pi_d^1(1 + \alpha) - \pi_d^2(1 - \alpha)$, that is, assuming symmetry, $\pi_d[(1 + \alpha) - (1 - \alpha)] = \alpha 2\pi_d$ Hence, the amended ratio test reads as follows: Mandatory disclosure is efficient if

$$\text{Ratio test with extreme rivalry}: \; \frac{\Delta_d}{\alpha 2\pi_d} < \frac{\Delta_m}{\pi_m}.$$

When the innovation race is extremely rivalrous, as in the case considered here, the ratio test is likely not to be passed if α is small, as it is likely to be in reality. For example, with homogenous goods, linear demand, and Cournot competition, the test is not passed if $\alpha < \frac{1}{2}$, that is, if the royalty paid to the innovator disgorges less than half of the duplicator's profits.

If the innovation race is "moderately" rivalrous, in the sense that firms invest both for bringing the date of discovery forward and to preempt the rival – who is likely to discover soon, but not too early – the adjusted ratio test depends on a parameter ρ (0,1) that captures the degree by which the profits

[26] Denicolo V. and L. Franzoni, 2010, On the Winner-take-all Principle in Innovation races, *Journal of the European Economic Association*, Vol. 8/5, 1133–1158.

[27] This effect has been labeled a "competitive threat" by the industrial organization literature. Beath J., Katsoulacos Y. and D. Ulph, 1989. Strategic R&D Policy, *Economic Journal* 97, 32–43.

to the duplicator delay innovation.[28] In this general setup, the denominator of the ratio test becomes $\pi_d^1(1+\alpha) - \rho\pi_d^2(1-\alpha)$ that is, under symmetry, $\pi_d[(1+\alpha) - \rho(1-\alpha)] = \pi_d[1 - \rho + \alpha(1+\rho)]$.

Mandatory disclosure becomes efficient only if

Ratio test with moderate rivalry: $\dfrac{\Delta_d}{[1 - \rho + \alpha(1+\rho)]\,\pi_d} < \dfrac{\Delta_m}{\pi_m}$.

If α is close to zero, the ratio test is passed only if

$$\frac{\Delta_d}{\pi_d(1-p)} < \frac{\Delta_m}{\pi_m}.$$

This is also a hard-to-pass condition, especially if ρ is large (that is, if the innovation race is tight and firms care about preempting the rival).

Overall, since the degree of rivalry of the innovation race depends on the amount of resources invested by the firms, we can conclude that **weak IP rights are not suitable for highly innovative sectors**, where firms make large R&D investments and technological leadership is subject to intense competition.

V. Final Remarks

Our analysis underscores the importance of *timing* for the optimal structure of of rewarding innovative effort. One desirable feature of the current patent system is that it rewards only the first inventor: The winner takes all. Laggard contestants, late independent inventors, imitators, and excluded competitors in principle get nothing.[29] This feature of the patent system makes the innovation race extremely sharp, yielding very strong incentives to innovate with the least amount of aggregate reward. Since monopolistic and duopolistic profits come at a cost, they should be handed out in a parsimonious way, so as to get the highest incentives with the least social cost. For this reason, weak IP rights – which provide a consolation reward to latecomers – may not represent an attractive alternative to the current system in industries where R&D competition is intense. In these industries, using nonexclusive rights as a means to decrease the reward to the innovator may be dominated by a policy of simply reducing the patent length.

---

[28] Denicolo V. and L. Franzoni, 2010, On the Winner-take-all Principle in Innovation races, *Journal of the European Economic Association*, Vol. 8/5, 1133–1158.

[29] In practice, things are different since patents can to some extent be circumvented.

10

Presume Nothing

Rethinking Patent Law's Presumption of Validity

Douglas G. Lichtman and Mark A. Lemley

Abstract

The United States Patent and Trademark Office is tasked with the job of reading patent applications and determining which ones qualify for patent protection. It is a herculean task, and the Patent Office pursues it subject to enormous informational and budgetary constraints. Nonetheless, under current law, courts are bound to defer to the Patent Office's decisions regarding patent validity. That is a mistake. Deference to previous decisions is appropriate in instances where those previous decisions have a high likelihood of being accurate. But to grant significant deference to the initial process of patent review is to defer to an unavoidably and significantly inaccurate signal. Put bluntly, early patent review is not reliable and is unlikely to become so. In this chapter, we explain why and propose the creation of a two-tier system of patent validity, with a strong presumption being given to patents after they have been subject to any of a number of intensive review procedures, but only a weak presumption being awarded as a matter of course on patent issuance.

Sincere thanks to the many readers who offered comments on earlier drafts, including Bob Armitage, Jason Bordoff, Chris Cotropia, Dennis Crouch, Michael Deich, John Duffy, Rob Gordon, Rose Hagan, Scott Hemphill, Tim Holbrook, Stephen Merrill, Joe Miller, Adam Mossoff, Peter Orszag, Andrew Pincus, Eric Posner, Meeghan Prunty, Arti Rai, Tim Taylor, Shashank Upadhye, Sam Vermont, and participants in workshops at George Mason and Microsoft Corp. This piece develops an idea that we first wrote about for a nonlegal audience over four years ago in a piece coauthored with Bhaven Sampat. *See* Mark Lemley, Doug Lichtman & Bhaven Sampat, *What to Do About Bad Patents*, REGULATION, Winter 2005–2006, at 10. This follow-on work was funded in part by the Hamilton Foundation.

Introduction: The "Bad Patent" Problem

The United States Patent and Trademark Office (PTO) is tasked with the job of reading patent applications and determining which ones qualify for patent protection. It is a herculean task. One problem is resources. About 450,000 patent applicantions are processed annually.[1] As of Fall 2009, there are 1.2 million unexamined applications in the PTO's backlog.[2] To accurately evaluate the merits of all of those purported inventions would cost billions. Add to that the administrative costs of both interacting with all of the relevant lawyers and documenting the entire process, and the required budget would make patent application fees prohibitively expensive.[3]

Information is a second significant impediment to PTO review. Patent applications are evaluated early in the life of a claimed technology, and thus at the time of patent review there is typically no publicly available information about matters such as how well the technology has been received by experts in the field or whether consumers have deemed the technology to represent in some way an advance over existing alternatives. Worse, patent examiners cannot solicit these sorts of credible outsider opinions, not only because for many technologies it is unclear at the early stages who the relevant experts and customers might be, but also because patent evaluation is at least in part a confidential conversation between applicant and examiner,[4] designed to keep an applicant's work secret in case the patent application is ultimately denied.[5]

---

[1] Invention Statistics, *found at* http://www.inventionstatistics.com/Patent_Backlog_Patent_Office_Backlog.html.

[2] Invention Statistics, *found at* http://www.inventionstatistics.com/Patent_Backlog_Patent_Office_Backlog.html.

[3] See Mark A. Lemley, *Rational Ignorance at the Patent Office*, 95 Nw. U. L. Rev. 1495 (2001).

[4] Until 1999, patent applications were kept secret in the United States. Most – but not all – applications are now published eighteen months after they are filed. 35 U.S.C. § 122(b) (2000). But they are kept confidential until then.

[5] For an interesting proposal to change this by instituting outside peer review of patents, see Beth Simone Noveck, *"Peer to Patent": Collective Intelligence, Open Review, and Patent Reform*, 20 Harv. J.L. & Tech. 123 (2006). The PTO is experimenting with such a procedure as a pilot project, but because of the confidentiality restriction they are doing so only for patent applicants who voluntarily agree to such review. That means that the pilot program requires volunteers on both sides of the transaction: The patent applicant must volunteer to participate in the review, and then reviewers must volunteer their time to actually do the evaluations. That latter condition strikes us as a significant hurdle. We know a lot of people who could be great "volunteer" patent examiners in their fields, but none of those individuals are likely to work for free, let alone do so on a project so intellectually unrewarding as poking holes in dud patent applications. Put differently,

Given all this, it is hardly a surprise that the PTO makes mistakes during the initial process of patent review, granting patents that, on the merits, should never have been issued.[6] The real surprise is that the law makes issuance mistakes hard to reverse.

The culprit is a legal doctrine known as *the presumption of validity*. Under that doctrine, courts are obligated to defer to the PTO's initial determination that an invention qualifies for patent protection unless the defendant can show by "clear and convincing" evidence that the PTO erred. Thus, if the PTO issues a patent covering a technology that the purported inventor did not in fact pioneer, the defendants face an uphill battle persuading the courts to overrule that errant determination. The theoretical justification is that patent examiners have expertise when it comes to questions of patent validity, and, thus, if patent examiners have decided that a given invention qualifies for protection, judges and juries should not second-guess the experts.[7] But the reality is that PTO expertise is brought to bear under such poor conditions that any advantages associated with expertise are overwhelmed by the disadvantages associated with insufficient funding and inadequate outsider information. Contrast that to court review, where information is a natural product of the adversarial process, and where financial constraints are reduced because only a tiny fraction of all issued patents end up sufficiently valuable and contentious to warrant litigation.

---

open source models work well when the underlying work is fun and rewarding – hence the success of Linux, the various Wiki projects, and the like – but reading undeserving patent applications is like grading F term papers and may not draw qualified volunteer reviewers in sufficient numbers to make peer review more than a pilot project.

[6] Calls for patent reform have echoed loudly over the past several years, with industry organizations, patent scholars, and government agencies all publicly announcing that the patent system is broken and that the PTO in particular is letting a large number of undeserving patents be issued. See, e.g., Fed. Trade Comm'n, To Promote Innovation: The Proper Balance of Competition and Patent Law and Policy (2003), available at http://www.ftc.gov/os/2003/10/innovationrpt.pdf; Adam B. Jaffe & Josh Lerner, Innovation and Its Discontents (2004); A Patent System for the 21st Century (Stephen A. Merrill, Richard C. Levin & Mark B. Myers eds., 2004). Even the mass media has picked up on the theme, frequently poking fun at PTO mistakes that are so obvious that a lay audience can appreciate the errors. See Editorial, *Patently Ridiculous*, N.Y. Times, Mar. 22, 2006, at A24; Editorial, *U.S. Patent System Has Run Aground*, Boston Herald, July 24, 2005, at 26; Sara Schaefer Munoz, *Patent No. 6,004,596: Peanut Butter and Jelly Sandwich*, Wall St. J., Apr. 5, 2005, at B1.

[7] For an argument that the presumption can be justified as a matter of history based on an analogy to land title, see Adam Mossoff, *Who Cares What Thomas Jefferson Thought About Patents? Reevaluating the Patent "Privilege" in Historical Context*, 92 Cornell L. Rev. 953 (2007). Whether Mossoff is right as an historical matter, there seems to be no policy justification for a presumption of validity unearned by examiner expertise.

Thus, the presumption of validity backfires. Rather than protecting accurate initial decisions from inefficient later meddling, the presumption precludes what would often be a worthwhile second look. As a result, courts today regularly enforce overbroad and undeserved patents, and strategic applicants continue to apply for undeserved patents knowing that there is a good chance the PTO will err.

This is a substantial, real-world problem. Under normal circumstances, a patent holder earns a living first by patenting a genuine invention, and then by telling potential customers about the technology. The patent in this instance protects the inventor from having his idea stolen, but the patent is worth nothing unless and until the associated inventor can find customers for his idea. The system thus encourages both the creation of new ideas and their dissemination. Patents that are issued wrongly, however, do not follow this pattern. A patent holder whose patent covers a technology that was already obvious to those skilled in the art has a strong incentive to sit quietly after the patent is issued, knowing full well that other parties will stumble onto that same obvious technology in time. When that happens, the patent holder can step forward, threaten litigation, and in the end extract royalties from infringers who neither knew of nor benefited from the patent holder's work.[8] Sadly, a large and growing number of "patent trolls" today play this exact strategy, using patents on obvious inventions quite literally to tax legitimate business activity.

What to do? One tempting idea is to increase PTO funding, making possible more rigorous up-front screening of patent applications. That would obviously help weed out bad patents, but the drawback is that most of the money would be wasted. As one of us pointed out years ago, most patents lie dormant after issuance.[9] They claim technologies that ultimately fail in the marketplace. They protect firms from competitors who, for other reasons, never materialize. They are lottery tickets filed on the speculation that a given industry or invention will take off. Patents in these categories will never be read, never be licensed, and never be asserted in negotiation or

---

[8] For an economic analysis of such holdup strategies, see Joseph Farrell & Robert P. Merges, *Incentives to Challenge and Defend Patents: Why Litigation Won't Reliably Fix Patent Office Errors and Why Administrative Patent Review Might Help*, 19 BERKELEY TECH. L.J. 943, 952–60 (2004); Mark A. Lemley & Carl Shapiro, *Patent Holdup and Royalty Stacking*, 85 TEX. L. REV. 1991 (2007); Joseph Farrell & Carl Shapiro, *How Strong Are Weak Patents?* (Competition Pol'y Ctr., Univ. of Cal. at Berkeley, Paper No. CPC05-54, 2007), available at http://faculty.haas.berkeley.edu/shapiro/weak.pdf; Carl Shapiro, *Injunctions, Hold-Up, and Patent Royalties* (Competition Pol'y Ctr., Univ. of Cal. at Berkeley, Paper No. CPC06-062, 2006), available at http://faculty.haas.berkeley.edu/shapiro/royalties.pdf.

[9] See Lemley, supra note 3.

litigation. Money spent perfecting these documents, then, is money thrown away.[10] That obviously is unfortunate to the extent that those dollars are tax dollars. It is also unfortunate, however, if those dollars belong to patent applicants, because every dollar an applicant invests in the patent process is a dollar the applicant cannot spend in other ways promoting and developing the patented invention.

Our proposal, therefore, aims not to improve the overall quality of PTO review but instead to change the presumption of patent validity to more accurately reflect the realities of current patent practice. The goal is to discourage the filing of bad but not good patents,[11] and at the same time to empower the PTO to better distinguish between the two. Our overall point is not that patents should never be accorded a strong favorable presumption. It is instead that presumptions must be earned.

Specifically, we propose three related reforms: First, the strong "clear and convincing evidence" presumption of patent validity that today is accorded to every patent by default should be removed and replaced with a much weaker presumption that accused infringers could rebut under a "preponderance of the evidence" standard. With this weaker presumption in place, patent examiners would still play their customary role in terms of evaluating claim language and ensuring that applicants comply with the patent system's many rules about the form and content of patent disclosures. Patent examiners would also continue to weed out the most egregious applications and to force inventors to commit up front to details about their claimed

---

[10] This would not be true if competitors were nonetheless scared off by the mere existence of these patents. See Christopher R. Leslie, *The Anticompetitive Effects of Unenforced Invalid Patents*, 91 MINN. L. REV. 101 (2006). But we are skeptical that competitors are frequently deterred by patents that simply sit on a shelf. In many industries, particularly information technology, large companies tend to ignore patents unless they are brought to their attention by the patent owner (and sometimes the companies ignore them even then). Not only do patent attorneys in these industries advise their clients not to read patents (see Mark A. Lemley & Ragesh K. Tangri, *Ending Patent Law's Willfulness Game*, 18 BERKELEY TECH. L.J. 1085 (2003)), and perhaps not to conduct a prior art search, (cf. Bhaven N. Sampat, Determinants of Patent Quality: An Empirical Analysis 5 (Sept. 2005) (unpublished manuscript), available at http://siepr.stanford.edu/programs/ SST_Seminars/patentquality_new.pdf_1.pdf), but they even ignore letters that threaten suit, reasoning that if the patentee is serious, he or she will either file suit or at least send a follow-up letter. See Mark A. Lemley, Ignoring Patents 4 (2007) (unpublished manuscript, on file with authors). But cf. Josh Lerner, *Patenting in the Shadow of Competitors*, 38 J.L. & ECON. 463 (1995) (reporting an empirical study of small biotech firms suggesting that they were deterred by patents held by competitors).

[11] See also Matthew Sag & Kurt Rohde, *Patent Reform and Differential Impact*, 8 MINN. J. L. SCI. & TECH. 1 (2007) (suggesting this as a goal for patent reform).

accomplishments, thereby limiting the risk that a patent holder will be able to strategically alter details during litigation. Patent examiners, however, would no longer themselves make a definitive ruling with respect to validity. Examiners instead would document their reasons for allowance, and those reasons should certainly be considered by later decision makers,[12] but there would be only a modest presumption that the examiner's validity analysis was, in fact, correct. Courts would be free to deem that presumption fully rebutted in cases where the evidence, on balance, ultimately suggests that patent protection is inappropriate.

Second, and in essence to fill the hole created by the first reform, either Congress or PTO officials should create a new opportunity for patent applicants to "gold-plate" their patents – funding and submitting to a vigorous review process in the PTO, and in return earning a significant presumption in favor of patent validity. The procedure would be entirely optional. Applicants who forgo it would still be able to defend their patents in court should that need arise. Applicants who opt for this approach, however, would enjoy surer protection. Courts would be allowed to consider evidence that was not considered by the examiner at the time of this intense review, but courts would need to overcome a significant threshold before being allowed to second-guess the PTO's evaluation of evidence that was in fact considered. To provide funding sufficient to actually run an intense evaluation, the fees associated with this supplemental review would have to be significantly higher than the current fees.[13] Those higher fees would discourage patent holders from too readily invoking the process, allowing applicants to sort their inventions into those that need early additional review and those that do not.[14]

Finally, in addition to this proposed new form of PTO review, there are other procedures that result in reliable patent evaluation; either the courts or Congress should make available a presumption of validity in those settings as well. For instance, when a court or the United States

---

[12] Under current Federal Circuit case law, courts are required to all but ignore an examiner's statement of reasons for allowance. *Salazar v. Procter & Gamble Co.*, 414 F.3d 1342 (Fed. Cir. 2005). That rule makes no sense, and we think it should be reversed.

[13] As is already the case with respect to most other PTO procedures, reduced fees would be available to smaller entities.

[14] Indeed, the PTO is already considering something similar, though the carrot it offers is not a stronger presumption of validity but accelerated examination. See Changes to Practice for Petitions in Patent Applications to Make Special and for Accelerated Examination, 71 Fed. Reg. 36,323 (June 26, 2006), available at http://www.uspto.gov/web/offices/com/sol/notices/71fr36323.htm.

International Trade Commission (ITC) evaluates a patent in the context of litigation, that evaluation should be accorded substantial deference in any later litigation involving the same patent. Similarly, when under current law a challenger requests that the PTO reexamine an issued patent, the results of that intense look should be given heavy presumptive weight in later judicial proceedings. If Congress adopts one of the many proposals that would create a post-grant opposition process, there again decisions made as part of that more intense review should be accorded deference by later decision makers.[15] Deference in each of these instances should be calibrated to match the strengths and weaknesses of the relevant first-round decision. For instance, the more adversarial the process, the greater the appropriate deference, because adversarial interactions are particularly good at bringing forward evidence and arguments. Similarly, the more time that passes between issuance and evaluation, the greater the deference, this time because delay means that there was more opportunity for reliable outsider evaluations to come to light.

In summary, the presumption of validity is today recognized too readily, built into a one-size-fits-all patent system where every application is given the same – necessarily sparse – review. The result is a counterproductive system where patents are wrongly issued and then vigorously enforced. Our proposal would recalibrate the presumption of validity to better account for the realities of patent review. The courts or the PTO itself must take the first and most important step: voluntarily ratcheting down the presumption that, by default, is accorded every patent on issuance. Then Congress, the PTO, and the courts could combine to implement the second and third prongs, with Congress and/or the PTO creating new procedures through which presumptions could be earned, and the courts in turn recognizing tailored presumptions in any context where there is reason to believe that a prior decision maker made a reliable decision. The net effect would be to reduce applicants' incentive to file undeserved applications in the first

---

[15] Scholars have been debating the details of a possible post-grant opposition proceeding for years, and legislative proposals have been put forward several times, thus far to no avail. For a sense of the academic debate as well as links to some of the legislative proposals, see Mark D. Janis, *Rethinking Reexamination: Toward a Viable Administrative Revocation System for U.S. Patent Law*, 11 Harv. J.L. & Tech. 1 (1997); Robert P. Merges, *As Many as Six Impossible Patents Before Breakfast: Property Rights for Business Concepts and Patent System Reform*, 14 Berkeley Tech. L.J. 577 (1999); Craig Allen Nard, *Certainty, Fence Building, and the Useful Arts*, 74 Ind. L.J. 759 (1999); J. H. Reichman, *From Free Riders to Fair Followers: Global Competition Under the TRIPS Agreement*, 29 N.Y.U. J. Int'l L. & Pol. 11 (1997); John R. Thomas, *Collusion and Collective Action in the Patent System: A Proposal for Patent Bounties*, 2001 U. Ill. L. Rev. 305.

place, to reduce the disruption caused by any undeserved applications that might accidentally slip through, and at the same time to provide a greater degree of certainty to patentees who deserve it.

I. The Presumption Today

Patent law's presumption of validity derives from the language of the U.S. Patent Act itself. Specifically, in Section 282, the Act provides that "[t]he burden of establishing invalidity of a patent or any claim thereof shall rest on the party asserting such invalidity."[16] This language on its face sets an unobjectionable baseline: After issuance, the default outcome in litigation is a finding of validity, and a challenger must amass evidence before a patent can be declared invalid. The modern presumption of validity, however, goes troublingly farther. As courts apply the doctrine today, the only way to render invalid an issued patent is to present "clear and convincing" evidence that the patent was improvidently granted. This is a high evidentiary bar, and one that, in practice, often proves difficult for accused infringers to overcome.[17]

The court opinions that establish this rule do not explain the policies behind it.[18] However, two such policies are readily apparent. First, the presumption of validity forces courts to defer to the expertise of the PTO, thereby avoiding redundant and possibly inferior second looks by the courts. Presumptions are used throughout the law for precisely this reason. If

---

[16] 35 U.S.C. § 282 (2000).

[17] The statutory language was not always read this way. Indeed, prior to the formation of the Federal Circuit, courts varied considerably in terms of the degree of deference they would show, both by circuit and on the basis of how closely the patent examiner had considered the validity argument now being raised. See, e.g., *Mfg. Res. Corp. v. Graybar Elec. Co.*, 679 F.2d 1355 (11th Cir. 1982) (adopting the rule that only "considered art" was subject to the clear and convincing evidence presumption); *NDM Corp. v. Hayes Prods., Inc.*, 641 F.2d 1274 (9th Cir. 1981) (same); *Lee Blacksmith, Inc. v. Lindsay Bros., Inc.*, 605 F.2d 341 (7th Cir. 1979) (same). The Federal Circuit, however, has consistently applied the high bar (see *Connell v. Sears, Roebuck & Co.*, 772 F.2d 1542 (Fed. Cir. 1983)), and it continues to do so today (see, e.g., *Ultra-Tex Surfaces, Inc. v. Hill Bros. Chem. Co.*, 204 F.3d 1360, 1367 (Fed. Cir. 2000)); *Kahn v. Gen. Motors Corp.*, 135 F.3d 1472, 1480 (Fed. Cir. 1998) ("The presentation of evidence that was not before the examiner does not change the presumption of validity. . . . "). For a discussion of how the Federal Circuit changed the rules, see Don Martens & Guy Perry, *Re-Examining the Clear and Convincing Standard of Proof,* IPL NEWSL., Summer 1999, at 16.

[18] For a detailed discussion of the early opinions establishing this uniform deference and their problems, see Lee Hollaar & John Knight, Unclear and Unconvincing: How a Misunderstanding Led to the Heightened Evidentiary Requirement in Patent Litigation (May 20, 2007) (unpublished manuscript), available at http://digital-law-online.info/papers/jk/unclear.pdf.

some initial decision maker has made a decision about an issue, and if there is reason to believe that the decision is probably right, a presumption works to avoid wasteful reconsideration. This might in the aggregate reduce accuracy, but the point is that the first decision is sufficiently good that the odds of improving it are small and thus the costs of a second look are unwarranted.[19]

Second, to bring a patented technology to market, patent holders often must invest substantial resources in development and commercialization. The presumption of validity reduces the risk associated with those investments. A patent holder whose patent benefits from a presumption knows that, if his development and commercialization efforts turn out successful, he likely will have a valid patent that will empower him to exploit that success. The presumption thus encourages the patent holder to spend the necessary resources. Patent holders in the pharmaceutical industry, in particular, emphasize this benefit. In that industry, enormous expenditures are required after patent issuance, including expenditures related to testing and regulatory approval.

We do not quarrel with either of these rationales. The presumption of validity surely does at times reduce wasteful duplication of investigative efforts, and the presumption of validity also surely does encourage, under certain circumstances, patent holders to invest in development and commercialization. As discussed further later, however, the extent of these effects seems small. PTO review is so terse and imperfect that a later, second look is unlikely to be significantly redundant, and even less likely to increase the error rate. And while uncertainty regarding patent rights might discourage some types of investment, it would seem odd to focus too heavily on this effect, both because the presumption is not conclusive, which means that the validity and scope of a patent remain unclear even under current rules,[20] and because patent uncertainty is only one of a million uncertainties facing a firm that is actually endeavoring to bring a patented invention to market. Thus, these rationales do not seem sufficient to justify the presumption as it exists today.

---

[19] The presumption of validity in theory reduces court costs by reducing the incentive to litigate. An accused infringer has little reason to litigate if the presumption all but guarantees a win to the patent holder. In cases where litigation does occur, however, the presumption does not likely reduce costs; patent litigants today spend a fortune fighting over whether the presumption has been rebutted in each specific case.

[20] As one of us has emphasized elsewhere, patents are probabilistic rights – not rights to exclude with certainty, but rights to try to exclude. See Mark A. Lemley & Carl Shapiro, *Probabilistic Patents*, 19 J. ECON. PERSP. 75 (2005).

A. Deference to the PTO

We start with the first of these policy defenses: that deference to the PTO avoids redundant and likely inferior second looks. This argument is strong only if it is plausible to think that the PTO can, at the time of patent application, run a substantial and relatively reliable evaluative process. For reasons beyond the PTO's control, that seems unlikely.

We have already mentioned one problem: the budget. Several hundred thousand patent applications are filed every year,[21] and those applications cover the full range of technologies – from breakthroughs that involve the human genome to innovative new designs for consumer electronics. Patent examiners who are assigned to evaluate those applications are chosen, in part, because they have backgrounds roughly related to the technology at hand, but examiners are rarely experts on the precise details of the relevant invention. Thus, to evaluate an application, an examiner not only has to read the frequently voluminous documentation submitted by the applicant, but he or she also must use computerized databases and other available sources to learn about the state of the art. The examiner obviously also has to interact with the applicant's lawyers and document any decisions ultimately made. Strikingly, examiners are asked to do all of this in what turns out to be an average of between sixteen and seventeen hours;[22] and those hours are spread over what is often a three- to four-year period.[23] Given these numbers, it is hardly a surprise that bad patents routinely slip through.

To do more, however, would be enormously costly. Suppose, for example, that the PTO were to hire actual industry experts to participate in patent reviews, for instance hiring an expert on digital camera lens technology when a patent on such a lens was filed. Assume that these experts could evaluate the invention, identify relevant prior art, and communicate their conclusions to the patent examiner in forty hours total, and that these experts would be willing to do all that while being paid a very modest expert wage of $200 per hour. Ignoring both overhead and the salary owed to the

---

[21] In fiscal 2005, for example, the PTO reported receiving the following: 384,228 conventional patent applications; 46,926 applications that were filed pursuant to special rules that apply to foreign filings; and 111,753 provisional applications that are, in essence, place holders that can later mature into conventional applications. See U.S. PAT. & TRADEMARK OFFICE, PERFORMANCE AND ACCOUNTABILITY REPORT FOR FISCAL YEAR 2005, at 18 (2005), available at http://www.uspto.gov/web/offices/com/annual/2005/2005annualreport.pdf.

[22] See Thomas, supra note 15, at 314.

[23] See Kristen Osenga, *Entrance Ramps, Tolls, and Express Lanes – Proposals for Decreasing Traffic Congestion in the Patent Office*, 33 FLA. ST. U. L. REV. 119, 130 (2005).

patent examiners themselves, the aggregate costs of evaluating one year's worth of patent applications in this manner would top out at well over $3 billion.[24]

Now, admittedly, if patents were reviewed this aggressively, it is likely that fewer patent applications would be filed. It takes time and money to prepare an application, and applicants would be less likely to do that if the likelihood of patent issuance were low. Some applicants would similarly be dissuaded from applying if application fees were raised to cover fully the actual costs of rigorous patent reviews. Nevertheless, even a nontrivial reduction in the application rate would leave the basic numbers problem intact. Patent evaluation is scientific review at an extraordinary scale, and it will necessarily be flawed unless and until applicants, the government, or both are willing to pay a hefty price. (And remember, we do not advocate paying this price, for the simple reason that most patents will still never be read, never be litigated, and never be licensed, and so money spent here really is money wasted.)[25]

Another limitation on the extent and quality of PTO review is the fact that early patent review is not – and as a practical matter cannot be – adversarial. Adversarial processes tend to produce good evaluative information. The court system, for instance, is thought to work in large part because in every case there are opposing parties arguing for different outcomes, and thus all the judge and jury need do is evaluate the alternatives rather than identify arguments and weaknesses themselves.[26] Patent review does not benefit from this sort of competitive dynamic, however. Instead, the only parties that participate in the initial process of patent review are the applicant, the applicant's attorneys, and the examiner. This unavoidably yields an information-poor process. Bluntly, no matter how good the examiner, no examiner will ever know as much or be as motivated as a true market rival.

---

[24] Cf. Lemley, supra note 3, at 1508–09 (estimating additional costs to double the amount of time each examiner – who makes significantly less than $200 per hour – spends on an application at $1.52 billion).

[25] See id. at 1510–11.

[26] Among the abundant literature on the adversary system and its benefits and costs, see Geoffrey C. Hazard, ETHICS IN THE PRACTICE OF LAW 121 (1978); David Luban, *The Adversary System Excuse*, in THE GOOD LAWYER: LAWYERS' ROLES AND LAWYERS' ETHICS 83, 94 (David Luban ed., 1984); Stephen A. Saltzburg, *Lawyers, Clients, and the Adversary System*, 37 MERCER L. REV. 647, 656 (1986); cf. Lon Fuller, *The Adversary System*, in TALKS ON AMERICAN LAW 30, 31 (Harold J. Berman ed., 1961) (discussing the importance of "partisan zeal" in achieving a fair outcome). But cf. Stephen McG. Bundy & Einer Richard Elhauge, *Do Lawyers Improve the Adversary System? A General Theory of Litigation Advice and Its Regulation*, 79 CAL. L. REV. 315 (1991) (asking the distinct question whether legal advice benefits or harms the adversary system).

Adversaries are not welcome in the process today in part because the patent system tries to protect applicants from having their ideas leak out too early. This is important to applicants whose applications are ultimately rejected, because after rejection these applicants will want to rely on secrecy to protect their unpatented work. Even if society were to abandon the goal of protecting unsuccessful applicants,[27] however, it would still be difficult to implement a genuinely adversarial application process. After all, it would be an enormous burden on industry if every firm had to monitor filings at the PTO and then participate in any relevant application process. This is especially true in the information technology industries, where perhaps 100,000 patents are issued every year and where a given commercial product can implicate hundreds and perhaps even thousands of those patents. Worse, participation can be a double-edged sword. A participating firm would be identifying itself as a target for later litigation in the event the patent is issued, and such a firm would at the same time be acknowledging awareness of the patent and hence exposing itself to later charges of willful and/or contributory infringement.[28] Moreover, adversarial participation would be implausible in instances where, at the time of patent evaluation, the relevant market was still in its infancy. In such cases, firms that might ultimately be key competitors would not even exist at the time of patent review, let alone realize the need to fight the application or have the resources to do so. Finally, were adversarial interactions possible, they would raise the costs of patent review, and even that is unattractive given that both the government and the dueling parties likely can do better things with their cash than invest in grueling combat every time a patent application is filed.

The absence of third-party information is yet another constraint that calls into doubt the quality of early patent reviews. One of the central questions raised in patent reviews is whether the purported invention was obvious to those skilled in the art at the time it was supposedly invented.[29] Obviousness is difficult to judge at the time of patent application. Over time, however,

---

[27] To some extent Congress did this several years ago when it required publication of most patent applications eighteen months after they are filed. The bill actually passed merely required those who file counterpart applications abroad to publish their applications here, however. 35 U.S.C.A. § 122(b) (West 2007). Because the rest of the world already required publication at eighteen months, the practical effect of this new statute was negligible – it merely required publication in the United States of applications that were already being published abroad.

[28] On the current definition of willful infringement and its problems, see, for example, Lemley & Tangri, supra note 10; Matthew D. Powers & Steven C. Carlson, *The Evolution and Impact of the Doctrine of Willful Patent Infringement*, 51 SYRACUSE L. REV. 53, 102–04 (2001).

[29] See, e.g., *KSR Int'l Co. v. Teleflex Inc.*, 127 S. Ct. 1727 (2007).

objective evidence bearing on obviousness comes to light. Was the invention a significant market success? Did competitors copy the technology after it was unveiled? Did other inventors independently accomplish the same thing at approximately the same time? Was the invention greeted with praise or skepticism by industry experts?[30] This and comparable information are not available at the time a patent application is first filed, and hence cannot contribute to the accuracy of early patent review. By the time of a second look, however, secondary evidence along these lines can be introduced. Indeed, courts today are obligated to consider this sort of information, albeit subject to the presumption of validity.[31]

In short, to the extent that the presumption of validity is justified on an intuition about the quality or extent of initial patent review, that justification falls flat. The PTO simply cannot engage in particularly rigorous or accurate initial patent review,[32] and thus, although the PTO process is certainly helpful and revealing, it does not on any measure warrant the heavy deference that it is accorded today.

[30] For discussion of these "secondary considerations" of nonobviousness, see, for example, *Greenwood v. Hattori Seiko Co.*, 900 F.2d 238, 241 (Fed. Cir. 1990); *Hybritech Inc. v. Monoclonal Antibodies, Inc.*, 802 F.2d 1367 (Fed. Cir. 1986); Rochelle Cooper Dreyfuss, *The Federal Circuit: A Case Study in Specialized Courts*, 64 N.Y.U. L. Rev. 1 (1989); Edmund W. Kitch, Graham v. John Deere Co.: *New Standards for Patents*, 1966 Sup. Ct. Rev. 293; and Robert P. Merges, *Commercial Success and Patent Standards: Economic Perspectives on Innovation*, 76 Cal. L. Rev. 803 (1988). With the exception of Dreyfuss, the commentators cited are critical of the commercial success factor as evidence of nonobviousness, though they agree that other factors are important.

[31] Objective information such as this is also important because it helps to combat hindsight bias. There is always in the patent system the concern that a decision maker will see the purported invention and immediately think that it was obvious, even if no one had thought of it before. This problem is particularly troublesome in litigation because, by the time litigation begins, the patented invention will typically have been out in the world for many years and thus seem familiar. Objective evidence helps decision makers to combat this natural but troubling tendency.

[32] We focus in the text on reasons why, as a matter of first principles, PTO review cannot work. Our point is that even a benevolent dictator would have trouble making PTO review effective because early stage evaluations of every application that comes in the door are too costly, insufficiently adversarial, and come too early in time for there to be adequate, reliable third-party information about invention quality. If these obstacles were somehow removed, there would then be an additional layer of practical and bureaucratic problems to address – structural problems about how examiners are hired, how examiner work is evaluated, and the degree to which an examiner can ultimately and decisively reject a patent application. See, e.g., Mark A. Lemley & Kimberly A. Moore, *Ending Abuse of Patent Continuations*, 84 B.U. L. Rev. 63 (2004) (discussing the rules that today allow an applicant to persevere indefinitely even in the face of repeated rejections by his examiner). These problems are important, but we do not focus on them here because they are not unavoidable difficulties associated with PTO review. That is, these problems could be solved by the appropriate reforms; the financial and informational problems, by contrast, cannot be.

B. Patent Certainty

The second policy rationale in favor of the presumption of validity is that the presumption reduces uncertainty and thereby increases a patent holder's incentive to invest in the development and commercialization of his patented technology. We are sympathetic to the desire for certainty, but we doubt that it alone can justify the presumption.

For starters, note how odd it would be to emphasize stability in the context of the presumption of validity, given how little weight stability is accorded almost everywhere else in patent practice. Consider, for example, the rules that govern when a court determination regarding patent validity binds later litigants. A patent holder who successfully defends patent validity in the context of a first infringement suit must start afresh when he sues a second infringer. Again, the patent holder must rebuff arguments that the patent was improvidently granted. Again, the patent holder must establish his desired claim constructions.[33] A patent holder whose patent is found invalid in some first case, by contrast, is barred from ever again enforcing that patent.[34] If there is some randomness in litigation, the result here is to shift significant uncertainty onto patent holders. A lucky draw has implications only for the specific litigation at hand. An unlucky one has implications for every future interaction.

The interpretive rules under which patent claims are analyzed similarly undermine patent certainty, not because of their substance but because they are constantly in flux. One minute the PTO (United States Patent and Trademark Office) is approving claim language where some new apparatus is described in part by articulating how the apparatus should be used; the next, the Federal Circuit retroactively declares all such claims to be so unclear as to be invalid.[35] Similarly, one minute the practice of altering claim language during patent prosecution is seen as a natural part of the give-and-take between applicant and examiner; the next, the Federal Circuit and the Supreme Court combine to retroactively change the rules, this time announcing that almost every such language alteration will be construed as a concession that limits patent scope.[36]

---

[33] There is some question of whether a prior court's claim construction, as a legal ruling, is binding in subsequent cases involving the patent. See, e.g., *Hilgraeve Corp. v. Symantec Corp.*, 265 F.3d 1336, 1341–42 (Fed. Cir. 2001) (raising but not deciding this issue).

[34] *Blonder-Tongue Labs., Inc. v. Univ. of Ill. Found.*, 402 U.S. 313 (1971).

[35] See *IPXL Holdings, L.L.C. v. Amazon.com, Inc.*, 430 F.3d 1377 (Fed. Cir. 2005) (holding mixed system-method claims invalid).

[36] See *Festo Corp. v. Shoketsu Kinzoku Kogyo Kabushiki Co.*, 234 F.3d 558 (Fed. Cir. 2000) (holding that a narrowing amendment precludes reliance on the doctrine of equivalents altogether), vacated, 535 U.S. 722 (2002) (holding that a narrowing amendment precludes

And this is just the tip of the iceberg. The Federal Circuit regularly reverses lower court claim construction decisions.[37] The Supreme Court recently threw into disarray the previously established rule that patent holders were entitled to injunctive relief if they could prove infringement of a valid patent.[38] A patent can be held invalid because someone uncovers "secret" prior art – art that was not public at the time of invention but that is nevertheless admissible in court under one of several special exceptions.[39] We provide these examples not to question whether stability has value (of course it does), nor even to criticize these specific rules and decisions, but instead to point out how disingenuous it would be to put stability on a high pedestal in just this one context. The lesson from patent law more generally seems to be that stability is desirable, but the patent system is willing to pay only a remarkably modest price to achieve it.

One reason that patent law is so willing to sacrifice stability is that, in practice, legal uncertainty is only one among many types of uncertainty in play. Pharmaceutical companies, for instance, admittedly worry about the strength of their patent portfolios. But a little less certainty there is unlikely to radically alter firm behavior given that success in the pharmaceutical industry critically depends on other unavoidable uncertainties such as the uncertainty associated with FDA review and the very real risk that, because of some unexpected side effect, a blockbuster drug will suddenly lose all of its value and even become a source of devastating legal liability. Similarly, small firms and start-ups face enormous risks above and beyond the risks associated with patent validity. Indeed, every venture capitalist in the country can list dozens of innovative start-ups that today hold presumptively valid patents but have yet to generate a penny of revenue. Again, patent uncertainty is important, but its importance ought not be overstated.

Yet another reason to question whether a desire for certainty is enough to justify the presumption of patent validity is the simple fact that the presumption disproportionately helps patents for which validity would otherwise be in doubt. A patent that is clearly valid does not benefit much

---

reliance on the doctrine of equivalents except in very narrow, specified circumstances). For discussion of this particular patent issue, see Douglas Lichtman, *Rethinking Prosecution History Estoppel*, 71 U. CHI. L. REV. 151 (2004).

[37] See Kimberly A. Moore, *Are District Court Judges Equipped to Resolve Patent Cases?*, 15 HARV. J.L. & TECH. 1 (2001); Kimberly A. Moore, Markman *Eight Years Later: Is Claim Construction More Predictable?*, 9 LEWIS & CLARK L. REV. 231, 239 (2005) (stating that the Federal Circuit rejects at least one claim construction in 37.5% of cases, and reverses or vacates 29.7% of these cases).

[38] See *eBay Inc. v. MercExchange, L.L.C.*, 126 S. Ct. 1837 (2006).

[39] See, e.g., 35 U.S.C.A. § 102(e), (g) (West 2007).

from a presumption of validity. Even without a presumption, the relevant patent holder can be reasonably confident that the patent will survive court challenge.[40] A patent holder relying on a suspect patent, by contrast, gains significant ground by virtue of a strong presumption. Thus, to the extent a presumption encourages investment, it seems to encourage investment in the wrong inventions. The patent system is designed to encourage investment in technologies that are genuinely new, not technologies that are likely redundant to things society knew before.

There are still more problems with the view that the presumption of validity is justified on the ground that patent holders need legal certainty. For instance, there is an academic literature that suggests that the last marginal increase in patent certainty comes at an enormously high cost to society, in essence because a confident patent holder can be particularly aggressive when it comes to negotiating licensing deals or settling litigation.[41] There is also a literature suggesting that firms have other means by which to increase certainty, such as acquiring large numbers of overlapping patents and in that way creating a somewhat diversified patent portfolio.[42] Thus, a justification that explains the presumption of validity on the ground that it beneficially increases certainty is precarious at best. Certainty is important, but certainty is not a good reason to endorse the current presumption, especially given the obvious costs the presumption today imposes.

II. Layered Presumptions

To this point, we have argued that PTO review as it currently stands is not sufficiently intense or accurate to warrant deference, and that, while deference does somewhat reduce uncertainty, the case for reducing uncertainty in this manner is weak. Moreover, as we pointed out in the Introduction, the presumption of validity is affirmatively unattractive to the extent that it locks in mistakes that would otherwise be corrected by presumption-free litigation, and further unattractive to the extent that it encourages applicants

---

[40] It is always possible that a wayward judge and a wayward jury will combine to wrongly invalidate a patent that should have been held valid. But that possibility exists even with the presumption of validity. The only way to eliminate legal error entirely would be to eliminate judicial review of validity altogether, and that would increase the harm from PTO error.

[41] See, e.g., Ian Ayres & Paul Klemperer, *Limiting Patentees' Market Power Without Reducing Innovation Incentives: The Perverse Benefits of Uncertainty and Non-Injunctive Remedies*, 97 MICH. L. REV. 985 (1999).

[42] See, e.g., Gideon Parchomovsky & R. Polk Wagner, *Patent Portfolios*, 154 U. PA. L. REV. 1 (2005).

to submit questionable applications in the hope that those applications might slip through and then benefit from the presumption.

With that background in place, we offer three proposed reforms.

A. Eliminate the Clear and Convincing Evidence Presumption

First, the PTO should disclaim the strong presumption currently recognized in favor of its work. The presumption is for the most part a judicially created rule of deference under which courts acknowledge what they understand to be the PTO's desire to have its earlier evaluation respected. The PTO should speak up and disavow that desire. Specifically, the PTO should instruct patent examiners to do exactly what they do today but also to include, on patent issuance, boilerplate language welcoming the courts to revisit the question of patent validity in the event an issued patent ends up in litigation. The PTO obviously cannot, and in any event should not, reject the statutory baseline; that is, challengers should still have the burden of bringing forward evidence that the patent was wrongly issued.[43] However, the PTO should politely decline the heavier presumption that courts today recognize as a matter of course. To the extent that the PTO has valuable arguments and insights to contribute, it can do that by influencing how the issued patent reads and what documents are in the file. The PTO need not wield its influence through the use of a heavy presumption.[44]

It is admittedly hard to know whether a change of this sort would be enough to bind the courts. Patent examiners sometimes write notes to the file wherein they explain why they let a particular patent issue, and yet patent courts today knowingly – and in our view indefensibly – ignore those communications.[45] It is possible the same would hold true for a PTO policy such as the one we advocate. That said, it would seem untenable as a matter of administrative law for the courts to strongly "defer" to an agency decision in a case where the agency itself explicitly requests a lighter touch.[46]

---

[43] 35 U.S.C. § 282 (2000).

[44] Indeed, it is worth noting that when the PTO itself considers the validity of the patents it has already issued, in both reissue and reexamination proceedings, it ignores the presumption of validity and reconsiders the patent without any deference to the first determination. See 35 U.S.C. §§ 251 (reissue applications treated the same as original applications for patent), 305 (*ex parte* reexamination), 314(a) (*inter partes* reexamination) (2000).

[45] See, e.g., *Salazar v. Procter & Gamble Co.*, 414 F.3d 1342 (Fed. Cir. 2005). Under *Salazar*, examiner statements of reasons for allowance – as opposed to applicant statements clearly disavowing claim breadth – are given no weight.

[46] The Supreme Court held in 1999 that the Administrative Procedure Act (APA) applies to the PTO. *Dickinson v. Zurko*, 527 U.S. 150 (1999). For discussions of deference to the PTO

All this is admittedly contentious ground, and our proposal might ultimately need to be implemented either via statutory amendment[47] or by judicial reinterpretation of the existing statute and its associated case law.[48] The latter approach is more feasible than it might seem; not only is the clear and convincing evidence standard a judicial creation, but the uniform standard is of recent vintage. Before the 1980s, courts generally did not give substantial deference to PTO validity decisions in cases where the arguments made in court differed from the ones the examiner had expressly considered.[49] And while the Federal Circuit has long been the last word on patent issues, the Supreme Court has recently taken a more active role in reviewing substantive patent rules,[50] and indeed a few months ago explicitly expressed some discomfort with the very presumption at issue here.[51] The illogic of the clear and convincing evidence presumption, the fact that it departs from the prior rule in many other circuits, and the Supreme Court's skepticism might make this issue ripe for Supreme Court review should the Federal Circuit fail to act. Judicial reform may also be desirable because,

under the APA, see, for example, Stuart Minor Benjamin & Arti K. Rai, *Who's Afraid of the APA? What the Patent System Can Learn from Administrative Law*, 95 GEO. L.J. 269 (2007); Orin S. Kerr, *Rethinking Patent Law in the Administrative State*, 42 WM. & MARY L. REV. 127 (2000); Craig Allen Nard, *Deference, Defiance, and the Useful Arts*, 56 OHIO ST. L.J. 1415 (1995). The PTO does not have substantive rulemaking authority, however, so if PTO statements to this effect are to have force, they must be in the context of particular determinations of patent validity, not a general rule interpreting section 282 of the Patent Act.

47 Section 282 of the Patent Act currently states that "[t]he burden of establishing invalidity of a patent or any claim thereof shall rest on the party asserting such invalidity." 35 U.S.C. § 282 (2000). Congress could add a second sentence here that would clarify the extent of that burden; for example, "That burden is met whenever a party brings forward new evidence sufficient to show that, more likely than not, the patent would not have been granted had the patent examiner been aware of the new evidence at the time of initial patent review."

48 For an argument in favor of judicial reinterpretation, see Benjamin & Rai, supra note 46, at 319; Lemley, supra note 3, at 1531.

49 See, e.g., *Mfg. Research Corp. v. Graybar Elec. Co.*, 679 F.2d 1355, 1360–61 (11th Cir. 1982) (adopting the rule that the clear and convincing evidence presumption applies only to prior art considered by the examiner); *NDM Corp. v. Hayes Prods., Inc.*, 641 F.2d 1274, 1277 (9th Cir. 1981) (same); *Lee Blacksmith, Inc. v. Lindsay Bros., Inc.*, 605 F.2d 341, 342–43 (7th Cir. 1979) (same).

50 See John F. Duffy, *The* Festo *Decision and the Return of the Supreme Court to the Bar of Patents*, 2002 SUP. CT. REV. 273. Since Duffy's article was written, the Court has gotten more involved and, indeed, had more patent cases on its docket in 2006 than in any year since 1965.

51 See *KSR Int'l Co. v. Teleflex, Inc.*, 127 S. Ct. 1727, 1745 (2007) ("We nevertheless think it appropriate to note that the rationale underlying the presumption – that the PTO, in its expertise, has approved the claim – seems much diminished" where the examiners had not considered the art in question.).

unlike PTO reform, it would apply not only to new patents but also to existing patents.

If the current strong presumption of validity is in any of these ways successfully removed, the PTO would still play a central role in the patent process. Examiners would still weed out obviously flawed requests, they would continue to wield significant influence over claim language, and they would still generate a paper trail that might later limit an applicant's ability to make self-serving arguments about what was claimed, what was invented, and when. The only difference is that, with respect to patent validity, issued patents would not benefit from the heavy thumb courts today put on the scale in favor of the PTO's original validity decision. As we have argued here, that original decision will often be inaccurate, not due to any failing on the part of patent examiners, but instead due to the extraordinary budgetary and informational constraints under which initial patent review is by necessity accomplished.

B. Gold-Plated Patents

Second, Congress should create a new, much more rigorous patent review process that would be run by patent examiners and that would be entirely voluntary.[52] This supplemental review would be available only during prosecution – more on that later – and the fees associated with it would be sufficiently high that examiners would have the funding necessary not only to spend at least one full month researching each purported invention, but also to hire relevant outside experts to assist in that process.[53] In addition, applicants who trigger this process would themselves be obligated to conduct a thorough search for prior art and submit the results of that search to the patent examiner, thus giving the examiner and the outside experts a good starting point for their work. Applicants would also be obligated to submit with each piece of prior art an explanation as to why that prior art does not

---

[52] If Congress does not act, the PTO could implement a similar procedure. Indeed, it is already talking about something of this sort. See Changes to Practice for Petitions in Patent Applications to Make Special and for Accelerated Examination, 71 Fed. Reg. 36,323 (June 26, 2006), available at http://www.uspto.gov/web/offices/com/sol/notices/71fr36323.htm. If the PTO implemented such a procedure, it would be up to the courts to give a correspondingly stronger presumption of validity to the more thoroughly vetted patents.

[53] The goal of using outside experts is to make sure the PTO has the technical knowledge in the specific field necessary to understand how a person having ordinary skill in the art would view the application. Outside experts are not experts in patent law, and it would be unwise to delegate to them authority over the ultimate issues, like whether the invention is or is not "obvious" under Section 103.

preclude patentability, in that way reducing the likelihood that an applicant can simply bury a damaging reference in a large pile of disclosures.[54]

Patents that survive the supplemental review process would earn and therefore be accorded a strong presumption of validity. Specifically, courts would not be allowed to second-guess decisions based on any prior art that the patent examiner actually considered during this more intense review, and even new art would be considered only if it could first be shown not to be redundant to materials already reviewed. Structuring the presumption this way creates an incentive for applicants to look for and show the examiner the most relevant prior art. Only art seen by the examiner could trigger a conclusive presumption, and so applicants would want the examiner to see as much prior art as possible.[55] The only constraint from the applicant's perspective would be the obvious one: The applicant would not want to share so much prior art that the examiner would think the purported invention is not actually innovative.

As is the custom already today with respect to most PTO fees, fees for this procedure would be set such that individual inventors and smaller entities would be given a break on price. The fee would remain intentionally high, however, because a high fee would discourage applicants from invoking the procedure lightly, and that would drive most of the work of patent review to other – and hopefully even more reliable – processes. Put differently, the high fee here would be a selection mechanism that would force applicants to credibly distinguish patents that for one reason or another ought to be evaluated early from those that can instead wait for later (ideally adversarial) procedures such as patent litigation, *inter partes* reexamination, and post-grant opposition.

This supplemental review would be available only during patent prosecution. Like the high fee discussed previously, the idea here is to channel most patent review to other, and likely more reliable, procedures. That is, this window is intentionally tight, designed to make the process available only in those comparatively rare instances where a patent applicant knows early on that certainty would for some reason be particularly helpful. Patents

---

[54] Cf. Changes to Information Disclosure Statement Requirements and Other Related Matters, 71 Fed. Reg. 38,808, 38,810 (proposed July 10, 2006) (to be codified at 37 C.F.R. pt. 1), available at http://www.uspto.gov/web/offices/com/sol/notices/71fr38808.pdf (proposing to require applicants submitting more than twenty pieces of prior art to explain the relevance of each piece).

[55] The rule extending the conclusive presumption to duplicative art would both prevent applicants from having to submit duplicative art to the examiner and prevent accused infringers from avoiding the presumption by finding a reference that says the same thing in a slightly different way.

that do not fit into that category – including what some have called lottery ticket patents[56] – would, if ultimately determined to be valuable, thus end up being evaluated by patent litigation, *inter partes* reexamination at the PTO, or post-grant opposition. This again is by design. These other procedures are adversarial and hence likely to be more accurate than even a well-funded process that involves only the applicant, his lawyers, and the patent examiner.

Creating a second tier of patent applications might serve another purpose as well – allowing patent applicants to signal to the marketplace which of their inventions they consider the important ones. Our mechanism relies on the fact that many applicants have a pretty good idea up front about which applications are likely to be most valuable to them.[57] Gold-plating will not only let the PTO harness this private information, but it may enable the market to benefit from it as well.[58]

C. Deference to Adversarial Determinations .

Third, and relatedly, there are already today a number of moments in the existing patent process during which a decision maker takes a hard look at the merits of an issued patent. If patents are accorded only a featherweight presumption as a matter of course, and if very few patents earn a greater presumption by participating in gold-plated reviews, then additional weight could be recognized in support of patents that survive these other types of evaluation. For example, some issued patents are returned to the PTO after issuance and are reevaluated through an adversarial process known as *inter partes* reexamination. This is an evaluation to which some deference is appropriate.[59] It involves the applicant and a rival, it typically takes place several years after the application was first filed, and the only patents subject to this procedure are patents specifically targeted by a complainant and accepted for review by the PTO. Similarly, decisions made in litigation or in the context of a hearing at the International Trade Commission (ITC) should be accorded a substantial degree of deference. Under current law,

---

[56] See F.M. Scherer, *The Innovation Lottery*, in Expanding the Boundaries of Intellectual Property: Innovation Policy for the Knowledge Society 3 (Rochelle Cooper Dreyfuss et al., eds., 2001).

[57] See John R. Allison et al., *Valuable Patents*, 92 Geo. L.J. 435, 461 (2004).

[58] On patent signaling, see, for example, Clarisa Long, *Patent Signals*, 69 U. Chi. L. Rev. 625 (2002). Note that the private market could provide other ways to credibly signal this information. Indeed, private solutions might be better, for instance, if a private alternative could be even more rigorous or reliable than a PTO-run gold-plating process.

[59] Some deference is appropriate, but not the complete *res judicata* effect the law currently recognizes. See 35 U.S.C. § 315(c) (2000).

if a court or the ITC finds a patent valid and infringed, that finding does not officially increase the presumption of validity accorded the relevant patent;[60] but that is because a strong presumption of validity is already in place even prior to the case. With that prior presumption gone, it would be appropriate to introduce a new presumption that would require courts to defer to any reliable decision made as part of these earlier adversarial processes.[61]

Proposals are afoot to add still more opportunities for merit-based patent reevaluation. Decisions made in these contexts too should be entitled to deference. For example, many commentators (and members of Congress in both parties) have called for the introduction of a post-grant opposition proceeding that would allow potential infringers to bring a patent back to the PTO for a second look.[62] If those proposals are adopted, post-grant opposition would be the type of rigorous review that would warrant an eventual presumption in its favor.[63] (Inside the PTO, there would be no deference to the PTO's own initial decision to issue the patent, just as there is no deference today in a reissue or reexamination proceeding. If a patent survives post-grant opposition, however, the courts should presume the correctness of any factual findings specifically made as part of this adversarial process, just as we suggest they should for gold-plated patents.)

---

[60] There might be some effect in practice, however, as fact-finders might find themselves inclined to defer to the decisions of other fact-finders.

[61] Our overall theme here is that the presumption of validity should be tailored to the reality of patent review, and that obviously applies to decisions made in court and at the ITC just as to decisions made at the PTO. Thus, presumptions would not be appropriate to the extent a later court believes that the earlier litigation was a sham, or to the extent that important information was for some reason not available during the prior evaluative process. Put another way, one design issue here is to make sure that patent holders do not have too strong an incentive to sue weak defendants first in the hope of being awarded a presumption.

[62] See, e.g., H.R. 2795, 109th Cong. (2005); see also sources cited supra note 6 (collecting academic commentary). It is important to design a post-grant opposition system carefully, with an eye toward strategic behavior by both patentees and accused infringers. For instance, as the procedure is described in some of the literature, a strategic infringer could abuse the process by triggering post-grant opposition merely as a tactic to drain a small patent holder's resources. To avoid this, there should be limits on both the number of post-grant oppositions and the novelty of the issues raised, and perhaps a provision for fee shifting. At the same time, other proposals would allow post-grant opposition only within the first nine months after a patent issues. That would render the procedure largely useless, because in many situations the firms that would challenge a given patent are not even going to be in business at the nine-month mark, let alone know that the relevant patent is important enough to warrant the expense and investment associated with post-grant opposition.

[63] See Arti K. Rai, *Allocating Power over Fact-Finding in the Patent System*, 19 BERKELEY TECH. L.J. 907, 918–19 (2004) (arguing for deference to the results of a post-grant opposition, if implemented).

The touchstones – met here and in our previous examples – are, again, some combination of an adversarial inquiry, an inquiry that applies to a small enough number of patents that it can be sufficiently well-funded, and an inquiry that occurs late enough in a patent's life that some external information about the technology is available.

The theme that unifies our proposals is the need to better harness information that currently rests in private hands. The PTO needs help in assessing validity, but to make that assessment efficiently it also needs help in deciding which applications are worth the effort. Patentees have some of this information, both about importance and about validity, and allowing them to opt into special scrutiny will draw it out. Competitors have some of this information as well, and both post-grant opposition and litigation will elicit it. Further, post-grant opposition and litigation will elicit that information through the adversarial process, which we think far superior to even the best-intentioned government bureaucracy as a mechanism for finding truth. Finally, neutral experts have some of this information, and we support proposals to give examiners (through some sort of outside search or peer review process) and the courts (through the mechanisms of expert testimony and consideration of objective evidence of nonobviousness) greater ability to seek this information as well.

II. Objections

We expect five primary objections to our proposal: (1) It might harm cash-strapped inventors; (2) it might make litigation more costly; (3) it might shift the burden of determining patent validity to courts, which lack the necessary expertise; (4) it might be too easy to get a gold-plated patent; and (5) the whole project might be for naught, because presumptions are just words and as such they might not affect outcomes anyway. We consider each in turn.

A. Layered Presumptions Favor Patent Applicants Who Have Adequate Resources over Individual Inventors and Start-Ups

One part of our proposal involves a new, intensive PTO procedure through which an applicant could ultimately earn a presumption of validity. This procedure would be expensive by design, both because the PTO would need money to run that intensive review and because a high fee would discourage applicants from lightly requesting this procedure. A natural concern is that individual inventors and small entities will not be able to afford the fee, and that, as a result, these parties will in essence be relegated to a second-class patent system where patents must be defended from scratch in court.[64] In response, we have already suggested that the fee schedule ought to offer a price break for smaller entities, in much the same way that the PTO currently offers a small-entity discount on the fees associated with filing a patent application. Still, this is a serious objection that warrants further discussion.

The truth of the matter is that almost any change designed to improve the quality of patent review will hurt cash-constrained applicants, because almost any change will end up costing more money. If patent examiners commit to spending twice as much time on each application during the normal review process, for example, patent fees will go up. If patent law changes to require that applicants conduct their own prior art searches before applying for patent protection, that extra cost will again sting. If post-grant opposition procedures are created by statute, patent holders who are dragged into those proceedings will need to hire lawyers to defend their patents, again resulting in new costs. Against this backdrop, our proposal is comparatively attractive, not simply because we can dampen any harm by reducing the fee for smaller entities, but also because a cash-starved firm can choose not to participate in the new procedure. Yes, that would make any ultimate dispute over patent validity more precarious, but validity disputes are rare in the patent system. Remember, most patents are never read, never licensed, and never litigated. Besides, even a firm that expects litigation might prefer to put off investing in that litigation and instead focus in its early days on marketing, commercialization, and other investments that are likely more important determinants of long-run success.

Finally, we note that under the current system, a patentee who wants to enforce its patent will pay legal fees that run into the millions of dollars. Patentees who opt to pay more for a stronger presumption of validity are likely to be those who will ultimately enforce their patents in court; asking a patentee who plans to pay millions to lawyers to pay perhaps 1 percent of that to strengthen its patent from the get-go does not seem unreasonable.

B. Reducing the Presumption of Validity Will Encourage Frivolous Validity Challenges and Wasteful Searches for Obscure Prior Art

Accused infringers spend exorbitant amounts of money searching for prior art that might disprove the originality of the asserted patent. The necessary prior art might be a doctoral thesis, written in Greek, archived in a

---

[64] For a detailed expression of this concern, see Michael Meehan, An Economic Approach for Increasing Certainty in the Patent System 48–52 (Jan. 12, 2007) (unpublished manuscript, on file with authors).

government library, and completely unnoticed by the literature or industry. Nevertheless, if the liability associated with a finding of infringement is large enough, an accused infringer will gamely join the hunt. The trade-off for the infringer, after all, is a comparison between the costs of the search and the costs associated with losing the case. That balance will often fund a significant, indeed an excessive, search budget.

Any legal change that weakens the presumption of patent validity might amplify this incentive to search. The reason is that, the lesser the presumption, the greater the likelihood that the infringer will be able to find a piece of prior art sufficient to invalidate the patent. Whether that is a social benefit or a social harm depends on the circumstances. Invalidating patents that should not have been granted is clearly worthwhile. The relevant patent is stopped from further disrupting the industry, and, anticipating this, future patent applicants are dissuaded from filing overbroad patent applications in the first place. Allowing ridiculously obscure prior art to invalidate a patent, by contrast, seems a mistake. If society knew of an invention only in the very formal sense of there being a doctoral thesis, written in Greek, buried in a remote library, then the relevant patent probably ought not be invalidated even if a particularly resourceful litigant ultimately finds that document. The patent holder, after all, really did bring new and worthwhile information into public use.

In short, then, we are sympathetic to the idea that novelty and obviousness in patent law should be relative, not absolute.[65] Specifically, a patent should not be deemed invalid just because some ridiculously obscure piece of prior art can be found during litigation. If the prior art is that obscure, the patent holder should be treated like any other inventor, because, but for the patent holder, the invention would not have been available to society anyway. But the presumption of validity is not the instrument with which to address this problem. Prior art rules should ensure, and to some extent already do ensure, that too obscure a reference is treated as if it never existed.[66] The presumption of validity, by contrast, weighs against all prior art references, even prior art that was known to experts in the field but for some reason failed to catch the attention of the patent examiner. Thus, the presumption is a poor solution to the problem of obscure art, and courts should instead continue to develop practical rules about how public a prior art reference

---

[65] See Daralyn J. Durie & Mark A. Lemley, A Realist Approach to the Obviousness of Inventions (unpublished manuscript, on file with authors).

[66] See, e.g., *Atmel Corp. v. Info. Storage Devices, Inc.*, 198 F.3d 1374, 1385–86 (Fed. Cir. 1999) (requiring that, to be prior art, a reference must be reasonably accessible to the public). H.R. 2795, 109th Cong. (2005), would have enshrined this standard in the statute.

must be before it will be deemed admissible as evidence against patent validity.

C. Trained Patent Examiners Are Better at Determining Validity than Generalist Judges and Lay Juries

Patent litigation is, without doubt, a deeply flawed process. District court judges are poorly equipped to read patent documents and construe technical patent claims. Lay juries have no skill when it comes to evaluating competing testimony about the originality of a technical accomplishment. Even the specialized judges of the Federal Circuit are widely criticized for their inability to resolve intracircuit patent law splits.[67] All this leaves us with little confidence that court decisions in the patent arena will necessarily map well to the public policy motivations that justify the existence of a patent system in the first place.

Our proposal, however, is not designed to shift decision-making power away from patent examiners and toward judges or juries. Quite the opposite. The second prong of our proposal explicitly advocates a new pay-more/get-more examination process that would be based in the PTO, and the third prong endorses PTO procedures such as *inter partes* reexamination and post-grant opposition. Our argument here is therefore not that courts are necessarily better than the PTO in all contexts. Rather, our argument is that the PTO's initial review is so constrained by budgetary and informational limitations that decisions made in that context should be reevaluated by some other decision maker – be it courts, the PTO acting later in time, or even a third entity like the International Trade Commission.

Nevertheless, our proposal will admittedly shift some decision-making authority to the courts, because at least some patent holders will skip all of the PTO's second-look measures and thus will end up defending their patents in litigation. We worry about whether the courts will be able to handle those cases reliably, and we support wholeheartedly experiments and conversations about ways to improve the quality of litigation outcomes. To the extent that the choice is between initial patent review at the PTO and later patent review in court, however, courts have the clear advantage. After all, patent litigation is adversarial, it takes place later in time, and it applies to a small enough fraction of patents that the parties can devote

---

[67] See, e.g., William C. Rooklidge & Matthew F. Weil, *En Banc Review*, Horror Pleni, *and the Resolution of Patent Law Conflicts*, 40 SANTA CLARA L. REV. 787 (2000). To be fair to the Federal Circuit, we believe the conflict problem was much worse in the 1990s than it is today, in part because the court has taken several issues en banc to resolve conflicts.

significant resources to hiring experts, searching for prior art, and in other ways rigorously analyzing the merits of the case.

D. The PTO Will Have Incentives to Grant Bad Gold-Plated Patents

So far, we have been discussing primarily objections likely to be raised by patent owners. Those who fear being accused of infringement might have a different worry: that the PTO will simply grant gold-plated patents as a matter of course, just as it approves the overwhelming majority of applications under the current system.[68] This is likely to be a particular worry if the PTO becomes dependent on the higher fees associated with gold-plated applications, so that it has a bureaucratic incentive to encourage applicants to use the system, or if examiners of these gold-plated patents find it easier or more rewarding to grant than to deny patents, as some argue is the case today under the normal patent system. A gold-plated patent is only as good as the examination process that creates it, and, admittedly, if they are too easy to obtain, the point of the system will be lost.

We think these are serious design issues that need to be addressed, and they are a reason to prefer adversarial decisions where feasible, but the need for care in designing the system is not a reason to reject the system altogether. The resource problem can be mitigated by having a separate examiner unit evaluate gold-plated patents, as the PTO has recently done for reexaminations, and making that unit revenue-neutral. If the unit pays for itself, but is neither a drain on PTO resources nor a source of funding, there will be little incentive for the PTO to try to push applicants toward or away from the gold-plated option. A separate examining corps may also help to insulate the new examiners from the pro-patent mindset that has arguably infected the rest of the examining corps. Promotion and pay rules should similarly ensure some degree of neutrality. For instance, examiners in the new unit should not be paid based on the number of patents reviewed or (worse) approved, nor should their tenure turn on "customer" satisfaction, given that patent applicants all clearly want just one thing.

E. Presumptions Do Not Matter Anyway

Eliminating the clear and convincing evidence presumption of validity will not radically remake patent litigation. Accused infringers would still have

---

[68] See Mark A. Lemley & Bhaven Sampat, Is the Patent Office a Rubber Stamp? (2007) (unpublished manuscript, on file with authors) (reporting a PTO grant rate around 75% and that the PTO only actually rejects 15–20% of applications).

to persuade a jury to second-guess what the PTO had done. And some will argue that fact-finders do what they want, and that presumptions do not matter at all. But we think that goes too far. Admittedly, this is an area of uncertainty. We know far less than we should about how presumptions affect litigation decisions. The lack of empirical evidence on this point may be endemic: As Priest and Klein have suggested, changes in substantive legal rules also change the behavior of parties in deciding which cases to litigate,[69] so it is far from a simple matter to predict how changes in a legal presumption would change actual case outcomes.

While we cannot prove that presumptions matter, we believe that they likely do, at least at the margins. When the Federal Circuit strengthened the presumption of validity in the early 1980s, the rate at which patents were held valid increased significantly.[70] While there may be many causes for this increase, the stronger presumption of validity is one of the most plausible. And even if juries do not fully understand what the presumption means, courts do, and most validity determinations are made pretrial.[71] We do not know exactly how often the presumption makes a difference to a case outcome. But we are confident that it does in at least some cases,[72] and that a change in the presumption really can alter patent holder behavior.

Finally, it's worth noting that even if we are wrong – if the presumption of validity turns out to be just words that do not much change a decision maker's analysis – that is not a reason to reject our proposal. It means, at most, that our approach will not do any good, but for the same reason it also will not do much harm. Put differently, if we are wrong, then it does not matter how strong or weak the words of a presumption are, and thus our new rules will not matter; they will just be new words, equally powerless

---

[69] George L. Priest & Benjamin Klein, *The Selection of Disputes for Litigation*, 13 J. LEGAL STUD. 1, 16 (1984).

[70] See John R. Allison & Mark A. Lemley, *Empirical Evidence on the Validity of Litigated Patents*, 26 AIPLA Q.J. 185, 205–06 (1998) (noting increase in validity from 35% to 54% from the 1970s to the 1990s).

[71] See Jay P. Kesan & Gwendolyn G. Ball, *How Are Patent Cases Resolved? An Empirical Examination of the Adjudication and Settlement of Patent Disputes*, 84 WASH. U. L. REV. 237, 271 (2006) (reporting that more patent cases are resolved on summary judgment than at trial).

[72] For an example, see *Aventis Pharma Deutschland GmbH v. Lupin Ltd.*, 2006 WL 2008962, at *47 (E.D. Va. July 17, 2006) ("If the preponderance of the evidence standard was the standard to judge this case, the Court might agree with Lupin, but, as the Court has said many times, that is not the standard to be applied here since the '722 patent was granted. A patent is presumed valid and invalidity must be shown by clear and convincing evidence."). The court further noted, "It is quite possible that the '722 patent should have never been granted, but once it was granted, attacking its validity is a very difficult task indeed. Unfortunately, the law is the law." Id. at *49.

as the old. We therefore think that trying to design the right incentives is worth the attempt, even if it turns out that the cynics are right and legal niceties like presumptions in the end do not actually matter.

IV. Effects on Current Stakeholders

Our proposal will have implications for a large number of stakeholders who are in one way or another involved with the patent system. In this section, we consider which stakeholders might be helped by these reforms and which might be disadvantaged.

The primary beneficiaries of patent reform are not necessarily patent holders. Instead, the primary beneficiaries are the countless firms that, in the course of putting out some product or service, might inadvertently infringe a patent. These firms need the patent system to exercise due care to ensure that only genuine inventions are awarded patent protection, because these firms are the ones who will end up paying royalties, have to redesign their products, or in other ways have their businesses disrupted if some obvious idea is patented. For patent reform, this dynamic poses a problem. Reform efforts work best when the beneficiaries are a concentrated group that can be rallied to the cause. Here, the beneficiaries constitute an enormously diverse group, with members ranging from Internet start-ups to large manufacturing entities and financial institutions. Reforms of the sort we advocate here will, as a result, be difficult to accomplish, though the growing recognition of the patent troll problem by information technology companies is a start.

One important group that might be disadvantaged by these reforms is the group of firms that exploit today's rules by suing on patents that never should have been issued in the first place. A cottage industry has emerged to do exactly this, with certain firms widely accused of using the presumption of validity to turn dud patents into disruptive moneymakers. These "patent trolls" do not in any way contribute to innovation. They do not directly bring new ideas into public use, for instance, by producing products, nor do they bring new ideas into public use through indirect means, for instance, by introducing potential licensees to the patented technology. Instead, these firms wait for their victims to independently develop the obvious "inventions" their patents cover, and then sue or threaten to sue to extract their unearned reward. Patent reform will be difficult because these firms have substantial resources and they will use those resources to defend the status quo. But patent reform is at the same time essential because of the disruptions for which these firms are increasingly responsible.

At least two additional categories of patent holders might also oppose the reforms we suggest here: patent holders in the pharmaceutical industry and individual inventors. Patent holders in the pharmaceutical industry are cautious about any reform that might weaken patent strength, primarily because of the slippery slope concern that someday their patents might be targeted by well-meaning lawmakers who mistakenly think that weaker patents would mean lower drug prices and better drug availability. Individual inventors are similarly cautious when it comes to patent reform. The deck is already stacked so heavily against individual inventors in terms of their ability to detect infringement and to litigate high-stakes cases to completion that any reduction in their ability to enforce their rights is understandably viewed with enormous skepticism. We have tried to make our proposal as palatable to these inventors as possible without undermining the goal of weeding out bad patents.

Other patent holders will admittedly be nervous to see the presumption of patent validity weakened, but they ought to support these reforms nonetheless. The reason is that the underbrush of undeserving patents undermines the value of well-earned patent rights. This plays out in a number of ways. For instance, many patent holders produce products or offer services consistent with their patent grants. These firms should favor patent reform for the same reason that firms in general should: Bad patents are a tax on legitimate business activity, including the legitimate use of patents that were fairly earned. Other patent holders, meanwhile, do not produce products or offer services directly, but instead license their patents to other firms that in turn do those things. These patent holders should support reform for two reasons. First, their businesses are built on licensing revenue, and there will be more licensing revenue for them if their licensees do not have to pay for dud patents. Second, these firms in particular rely heavily on the existence of a strong patent system; the more the patent system is abused, the more likely it is that Congress and the courts will weaken patent rights in response. The recent Supreme Court case of *eBay, Inc. v. MercExchange, L.L.C.* is in this regard a clarion call.[73] The Court in that case significantly restricted what had been the standard remedy for patent infringement, and did so largely because particular patent holders have in recent years very publicly abused the stronger rights that had previously been the norm. Fortunately, that opinion gave courts the flexibility needed to weaken patent rights for patent trolls without interfering with more legitimate patent use. But the broader lesson should be clear: Legitimate patent holders need to drive their less

[73] 126 S. Ct. 1837 (2006).

honorable counterparts out of the tent, or the weakening of patent rights might become a dangerous trend.

V. Conclusion

Evaluating patent applications is a difficult task, and it is not a criticism of the PTO to point out that the current process results in the issuance of an uncomfortably large number of undeserving applications. Those errors can be corrected, but only if some second evaluative body is given an opportunity to revisit the initial decision to issue. The presumption of validity today makes that difficult. Thus, the patent system wastes the many advantages that a second decision maker might have: the opportunity for adversarial review, sufficient resources to devote to a smaller number of important patents, and reliable outsider information about (for example) how well the product was received and whether other inventors achieved roughly the same breakthrough at roughly the same time. The result is a patent system that needlessly and significantly disrupts legitimate business activity.

The patent system can be fixed. By tailoring the presumption of patent validity to the realities of patent review, the patent system could ensure that there is deference to decisions that are likely reliable, but it also provides a chance to revisit decisions that are hampered by budgetary and informational constraints. Reasonable minds might disagree over the details of how best to implement that reform. For instance, there are colorable arguments for giving slightly more or less of a presumption in various situations, and colorable arguments for tweaking the timing of the various patent procedures we describe. Importantly, however, there is no colorable defense for the status quo. The initial patent review done by the PTO is an important step in the patent process, but it cannot bear the substantial weight it is given under current patent doctrine and practice.

11

Patent Notice and Cumulative Innovation

Michael Meurer

Cumulative innovation, the process of one innovator building on the efforts of an earlier innovator, is common and important. Because of the work of Suzanne Scotchmer and others, economists recognize that cumulative innovation poses a serious challenge to those who try to design an optimal patent system. When one innovation builds on another, the patent system can be used to divide profits between two distinct innovators. But under normal conditions it cannot be designed to make both innovators full claimants on the flow of value created by their respective innovations.

Several articles have taken up the challenge of uncovering policy concerns that should help to determine the division of profit beyond early and late innovators. Green and Scotchmer[1] note that when different firms contribute innovations to a sequence, total patent-based profits will need to be higher than the profits required to induce a single firm to invest in the same sequence of innovations. Scotchmer and Green[2] observe that a weak nonobviousness standard encourages disclosure that has social value because it speeds further development and reduces redundant innovation. O'Donoghue et al.[3] argue for broad and short patents in a quality ladder model because broad patents reduce duplicative investment. In contrast, Denicolò[4] observes that a weak nonobviousness standard and narrow breadth reduce possibly wasteful racing to achieve a first-generation innovation.

[1] Green, J. and Scotchmer, S. 1995. "On the Division of Profit in Sequential Innovation." *RAND Journal of Economics* 26, 20–33.
[2] Scotchmer, S. and Green, J. 1990. "Novelty and Disclosure in Patent Law." *RAND Journal of Economics* 21, 131–146.
[3] O'Donoghue, T., Scotchmer, S., and Thisse, J.-F. 1998, "Patent Breadth, Patent Life and the Pace of Technological Progress." *Journal of Economics and Management Strategy* 7, 1–32.
[4] Denicolò, V. 2000. "Two Stage Patent Races and Patent Policy." *RAND Journal of Economics* 31, 488–501.

Curiously, the lessons from these articles best apply to what are usually classified as discrete rather than cumulative technology. Drug discovery is a discrete technology in the sense that there are few inventions and few patents per product. The standard models of cumulative innovation apply well to problems like how to divide patent profits between the inventor of a new drug and follow-on innovators who find a new use or new formulation of the drug.

The models do not work very well for cumulative technologies like the information and communications technologies (ICT). Three simplifying assumptions in these models are more problematic for richly cumulative technologies than they are for discrete technologies. First, the division of patent profits is often crucial in the pharmaceutical industry, but often not very important in ICT, because the patent-derived profits account for a relatively small portion of the return to innovation.[5,6] Second, the models assume that there is value in the disclosure contained in the early patent, and that the early invention is essential to later innovation. In ICT, independent invention and inadvertent patent infringement are common (Bessen and Meurer).[7] Third, the models emphasize *ex ante* licensing as an option for coordinating early- and late-stage innovations. But such coordination is impossible if the potential contracting parties cannot find each other. Cockburn and Henderson[8] surveyed large, research-intensive firms and found that they do not always do patent searches before they introduce a new product. Lemley[9] argues that ICT firms typically "simply ignore patents." Pharmaceutical firms, however, are religious about doing patent searches at several different decision points in the innovation process.[10]

My goal in this chapter is to modify a standard model of cumulative innovation to better account for some of the factors that cause patents (especially outside pharmaceutical technology) to perform badly as property. Bessen and Meurer show that patents fail as property in the sense that they deliver small net rewards to innovators (even negative rewards), because they fail to communicate information about patent-based property

---

[5] Cohen, W., Nelson, R. R., and Walsh, J. P 2000. "Protecting Their Intellectual Assets: Appropriability Conditions and Why U.S. Manufacturing Firms Patent (or Not)." NBER Working Paper No. 7752.

[6] Bessen, J. and Meurer, M. J. 2008. *Patent Failure: How Judges, Bureaucrats, and Lawyers Put Innovators at Risk*, Princeton University Press.

[7] *Id.*

[8] Cockburn, I. and Henderson, R. 2003. "The IPO Survey on Strategic Management of Intellectual Property." *Intellectual Property Owners Association*, Washington DC, November.

[9] Lemely, M. A. 2008. "Ignoring Patents." *Michigan State Law Review* 20, 19–34.

[10] Roin, B. N. 2009. "Unpatentable Drugs and the Standards of Patentability." *Texas Law Review* 87, 503–570.

boundaries to strangers. To lawyers this is known as failure of the notice function of property.[11]

I. Cumulative Innovation, Holdup, and *Ex Ante* Patent Licensing

In this chapter I combine a model of cumulative innovation and patent licensing that follows Green and Scotchmer[12] with a search model. The model has two players, a patent owner and an innovator. Initially, they are unaware of each other. If the innovator searches for and finds the patent and its owner thereafter, the patent owner and the innovator hold symmetric information about the patent and the innovation. In the first stage, the innovator conducts a search for a patented technology to incorporate into its innovation. The goal of the search is to find and license a patent that might be asserted against the innovator, and to reduce development costs by building on the patented technology held by the patent owner. Searching is costly because the patent system does not provide perfect notice.

If the search is fruitful and reveals a relevant patent (I assume there is at most one), then the innovator has a chance to negotiate a license before sinking its development cost. The parties simultaneously decide whether to implement an *ex ante* license that splits the surplus from the bargain equally. If either party objects, then there is no *ex ante* license. Regardless of whether an *ex ante* license is negotiated, the innovator then decides whether to develop the innovation. Lacking an *ex ante* license, the innovator is vulnerable to a patent lawsuit, and it may be forced to negotiate an *ex post* license following development.

If the search does not reveal a relevant patent, then the innovator can do nothing, or develop the innovation. Development exposes the innovator to a possible patent lawsuit, and it might negotiate an *ex post* license with the patent owner. I assume the development cost is (weakly) greater after a failed search.

In this section, I will analyze the subgame that follows a search that uncovers a relevant patent. The next section analyzes the subgame that follows a fruitless search, and the entire game including searching. Let V measure the value of the innovation. The cost of development is c, where $c \leq V$. Thus, the social planner always prefers development. If the firms go to trial, they each bear the litigation cost L. The probability of victory by the innovator is α; thus, the patent owner is sure to win at trial if $\alpha = 0$. If the patent owner wins at trial, the remedy is an injunction; the innovator cannot

---

[11] Bessen, *supra*, note 6.
[12] Green, *supra*, note 1.

profit from the innovation, which includes the patented technology, unless it gets permission from the patent owner. I will assume that the innovator can design around the patent and deploy an alternative innovation with value X, where $X \in [\ 0,\ V]$. I assume that the "design around" alternative is not available to the innovator until after the patent claims are interpreted at trial, and the innovator can determine the boundaries of the patent claims. The value X is net of additional development costs.

Licensing does not occur if the patent owner lacks a credible threat of going to trial. The patent owner's expected profit is

$$\frac{1-\alpha}{2}(V - X) - L. \tag{11.1}$$

This profit expression arises because the patent owner bears its own litigation cost L regardless of the trial outcome; the patent owner wins with probability $1 - \alpha$; and, following a win, the patent owner negotiates a post-trial license and equally splits the surplus achieved when the innovator deploys the original technology instead of inventing around the patent. If expression (11.1) is less than zero, then there is no license, the patent owner earns zero, and the innovator earns $V - c$. I will call this outcome *acquiescence*.

If expression (11.1) is greater than or equal to zero, then the parties simultaneously decide whether to implement an *ex post* license that splits the surplus from the bargain equally. My assumption of symmetric information means that a trial will not occur in equilibrium. Instead, it provides the threat point for *ex post* licensing (that is, a license after development but before trial). The threat point for the patent owner is given by expression (11.1), and the threat point for the innovator is $\frac{1-\alpha}{2}(V + X) + \alpha V - c - L$. The firms will negotiate a license to avoid the litigation costs. An equal split of the surplus implies the *ex post* license outcome gives the patent owner an expected profit of $\frac{1-\alpha}{2}(V - X)$, and the innovator gets an expected profit of

$$\frac{1-\alpha}{2}(V + X) + \alpha V - c, \text{ or } \Delta - c, \text{ where } \Delta \equiv \frac{1-\alpha}{2}(V + X) + \alpha V. \tag{11.2}$$

I have rewritten expression (11.2) to include Δ, the developer's share of the surplus from settlement gross of development cost. This term will be useful in subsequent analyses.

Green and Scotchmer[13] observe that because the innovator shares the rents from successful innovation with the patent owner, the innovator may find that *efficient* development $(0 \leq V - c)$ is not profitable without an

---

[13] Green, *supra*, note 1.

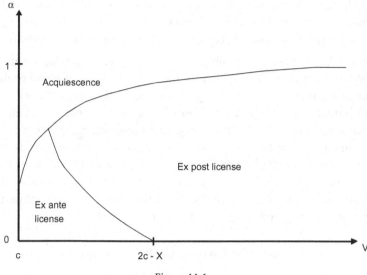

Figure 11.1.

ex ante license. In particular, if expression (11.2) is less than zero, then the innovator will not develop the technology unless the patent owner agrees to bear some of the development cost.

The equilibrium outcome is *ex ante* licensing when the patent owner has a credible threat to sue and the innovator has a credible threat to forego development. In other words, *ex ante* licensing requires expression (11.1) to be nonnegative and expression (11.2) to be negative. The threat points for the negotiation of an *ex ante* license are zero for both firms. The surplus is $V - c$, which is divided equally so that each firm gets $(V - c)/2$ from an *ex ante* license.

Figure 11.1 displays the set of (V, α) parameter values that correspond to different outcomes of the licensing subgame that occurs after a relevant patent is identified by the innovator's search. The figure is drawn on the assumption that $2L + X \leq c$. A relatively high development cost makes the region of *ex ante* licensing larger. If $2c \leq 2L + X$, then *ex ante* licensing is not an equilibrium outcome. The intermediate case, $1/2[2L + X] \leq c \leq 2L + X$, is similar to the case displayed in Figure 11.1, except that, for values of V sufficiently close to c, the patent owner does not have a credible threat to sue even if victory is certain, in other words, even if $\alpha = 0$.

Remark 1. As noted by Green and Scotchmer (1995), *ex ante* licensing has social value because it assures development of the innovation when its value exceeds development cost. Social value is realized only in the region of Figure 11.1 labeled *ex ante licensing*. There is no social (or private) value to *ex ante* licensing for sufficiently large values of α, L, V, and X, because either the patent owner lacks a credible threat of a lawsuit to induce licensing or because the innovator lacks a credible threat of foregoing development.

Remark 2. The innovator's possibly credible threat not to develop the innovation has a surprising implication for the division of patent-based profits. For certain parameter values, the patent owner makes more money if its patent is made weaker. This counterintuitive result arises because when the innovator has a credible threat to forego development, it shifts part of the development cost to the patent owner through the terms of the *ex ante* license. A small increase in α or X that changes expression (11.2) from negative to positive can shift the equilibrium outcome from *ex ante* licensing to *ex post* licensing, and raise the profit of the patent owner, because the innovator loses its credible threat to forego development.

II. Search, Development, and Patent Licensing

If the innovator conducts a fruitless search and decides to develop the innovation anyway, then it faces a potential dispute with the patent owner. I assume that the patent owner is sure to observe the innovation. I also assume that the innovator knows the strength of the patent, that is, the values of α and X, before investing in development. Then the parties will negotiate an *ex post* license unless the patent owner lacks a credible threat of going to trial. If expression (11.1) is negative, then the patent owner acquiesces. If expression (11.1) is nonnegative, then the parties agree to an *ex post* license yielding the same profits as those given in Section I.

Before I can analyze the development decision I need to specify the remaining features of the model. Rather than assuming the patent owner's technology is essential to the innovation, I assume that it reduces the development cost. Let $C \geq c$ be the development cost when the innovator has not located the relevant patented technology. In Section I, I assumed that when an innovator reads a patent, it gains the knowledge necessary to reduce the development cost from C to c, *regardless of whether there is an* ex ante *license.* In contrast, after a fruitless search, the innovator cannot learn from the patent, and thus it incurs the higher development cost. Later, I will comment on another scenario in which the development cost reduction comes from know-how that is transferred only with an *ex ante* license.

The innovator chooses whether to invest the lump sum S in search. It knows that there is at most one patented technology available that is relevant to the innovation it is contemplating. The probability that the relevant patented technology exists is given by p. Conditional on the existence of a relevant patent, a search finds it with probability f. Thus, pf is the probability of finding a patent, $p[1 - f]$ is the probability of finding nothing even though a relevant patent exists, and $1 - p$ is the probability that there is no relevant patent.

Given this search technology I can now evaluate the profitability of a decision to develop the innovation after a fruitless search. Recall that the innovator believes that there is at most one patent, and if that patent exists, it is characterized by parameters α and X. If there is no relevant patent, then the innovator will capture $V - C$ from development. If there is a relevant patent that the innovator did not find and the patent owner has a credible threat to sue, then the profit from an *ex post* license is $\frac{1-\alpha}{2}(V + X) + \alpha V - C$, or $\Delta - C$. Weighting these profits by the updated probabilities gives an expected profit of

$$\frac{1 - p}{1 - pf} V + \frac{p(1 - f)}{1 - pf} \Delta - C. \tag{11.3}$$

If this expression is nonnegative, then the innovator will develop the technology despite not finding a relevant patent. If the expression is negative, then the innovator will not develop the technology after a fruitless search. If the innovator does not search, then expression (11.3) applies with f set equal to zero.

If the relevant patent is weak and the patent owner does not have a credible threat, then the profit after a fruitless search or no search is simply

$$V - C. \tag{11.4}$$

The equilibrium investment in search is driven by three considerations. First, a successful search reduces the development cost by $C - c$, and thus searching increases with development cost savings. Second, searching grows more attractive as the probability that there is a relevant patent grows. The relationship between equilibrium searching and the profit-sharing problem is more complex. As noted in Section I, an *ex ante* license can overcome a profit shortfall to the innovator and assure development. This problem arises when $V \geq c$, but expression (11.2) is negative. Of course, an *ex ante* license is only possible if the innovator finds the relevant patent and its owner. Furthermore, a thorough, but failed search can give an innovator confidence to develop a technology when $V \geq C$. An intensive search that does not turn up a relevant patent reduces the *ex post* probability that there is a relevant patent and that profit-sharing will occur. In other words, expression (11.3) grows with search effectiveness (increasing f) and can change the value of expression (11.3) from negative to positive.

Proposition 1. Equilibrium searching occurs if and only if $pfG \geq S$, where G is the private gain to the innovator from a successful search. The private gain from a successful search depends on the outcome of the settlement subgame, and whether development is profitable following a fruitless search.

Proof. When the innovator chooses whether to search it knows which of the three licensing outcomes from Section I prevails. Let's consider the *acquiescence* outcome first. If $V \geq C$, then the innovator will develop regardless of the search outcome and the expected profit from the search is $V - pfc - (1 - p)fC - S$. The private gain from a successful search is simply the development cost savings $G = C - c$. The condition in Proposition 1 follows from a simple comparison of the profit with and without searching. If $V < C$, so that condition (11.4) is negative, then the innovator will only develop after a successful search and the expected profit from search is $pfV - pfc - S$. The private gain from a successful search is the development surplus, $G = V - c$, and the condition in Proposition 1 follows.

Next, suppose that the parameter values are such that the *ex post* licensing outcome prevails after the innovator has identified the relevant patent owner. The expected profit from a successful search when expression (11.3) is negative is $pf[\Delta - c] - S$. Thus, the private gain from search when expression (11.3) is negative is $G = \Delta - c$. The expected profit from searching when expression (11.3) is nonnegative is $p\Delta - pfc - p[1 - f]C + (1 - p)(V - C) - S$. Thus, the private gain from a successful search when expression (11.3) is positive is $G = C - c$.

Finally, suppose the parameter values are such that the *ex ante* licensing outcome prevails after the innovator has identified the relevant patent owner. The expected profit from search when expression (11.3) is negative is $pf \frac{V-c}{2} - S$. In this case the private gain from a successful search is $G = \frac{V-c}{2}$. The expected profit from a search when expression (11.3) is non-negative is $pf \frac{V-c}{2} + p[1 - f][\Delta - C] + (1 - p)(V - C) - S$. In this case the private gain from a successful search is $G = \frac{V-c}{2} - [\Delta - C]$.

To gain a better understanding of the equilibrium let's consider a special case. If the patented technology is unnecessary to the innovator, so that $C = c$, then there is no search given an acquiescence outcome. The patent owner does not have a credible threat to sue, and thus the only reason to search for the patent is to gain a development cost benefit. Next, notice that expression (11.3) is greater than or equal to expression (11.2) when the development costs are equal. Hence, if the *ex post* licensing outcome prevails given a fruitful search, development will occur following a fruitless search. This in turn means that the private gain from search $G = C - c = 0$, and there will be no search.

In contrast, an equilibrium search may occur given the *ex ante* licensing outcome, even when $C = c$. If the innovator foregoes development following a fruitless search (expression [11.3] is negative given a frutiless search), then searching is profitable because *ex ante* licensing overcomes the holdup problem. If the innovator develops despite a fruitless search, searching is still profitable because when a search is successful, the patent owner will share some of its rents with the innovator in the *ex ante* license.

III. Comparison of Private and Social Incentives to Search

The U.S. government has a variety of policy instruments that it could use to reduce patent search costs. It could require prompt publication of all U.S. patent applications. It could prohibit or limit claim language changes in continuing applications. It could limit the number of patents in force, by raising fees or standards of patentability. It could reward innovators that conduct product clearance searches, or at least it could reduce the penalties imposed on searchers through the operation of the willfulness doctrine (and possibly the inequitable conduct doctrine[14]).

Before we attempt to formulate policy reforms that encourage searching, we should ask whether the current search levels are too low. Or perhaps the easier question is, how do private incentives to search compare to social incentives? If the social planner were in charge of the search choice, but not the litigation, licensing, or development decisions, then the objective function given to searching when development always occurs would be

$$pf(V - c) + p[1 - f](V - C) + (1 - p)(V - C) - S. \qquad (11.5)$$

The objective function given no development after a fruitless search is

$$pf(V - c) - S. \qquad (11.6)$$

The same objective functions with f and S set equal to zero apply when there is no search.

Proposition 2. If a fruitful search yields an acquiescence outcome or an *ex post* licensing outcome in which expression (11.3) is nonnegative, then

[14] Lemely, M. A. and Tangri, R. K. 2003. "Ending Patent Law's Willfullness Game." *Berkeley Journal of Law and Technology* 18, 1086–1125.

the private and social incentives to search are the same. If the expression (11.3) is negative and a fruitful search yields an *ex ante* or *ex post* licensing outcome, then the innovator does too little searching compared to the socially preferred amount. If a fruitful search yields an *ex ante* licensing outcome in which expression (11.3) is nonnegative, then the innovator does too much searching compared to the socially preferred amount.

Proof. Looking back to the proof of Proposition 1 we see that the private gains to search are $G = C - c$ when innovation occurs regardless of the search outcome and when the acquiescence or *ex post* licensing outcome prevails. This matches the social gain that can be derived from expression (11.5). In other words, the social planner derives a benefit from searching when it reduces development cost. Because the entire benefit of a reduced development cost is captured by the innovator, the social and private incentives are aligned.

In the acquiescence outcome in which the innovator does not invest in development given a fruitless search, the private gain $G = V - c$. This matches the social gain that can be derived from expression (11.6).

In the cases in which a fruitless search leads to no development, and either *ex ante* or *ex post* licensing prevails, then there is too little searching (in the sense that there are conditions in which the social planner would invest S, but the innovator would not). Once again the social gain is $V - c$, but the private gain in the *ex ante* licensing case is only $G = \frac{V-c}{2}$, and in the *ex post* licensing case the private gain is $G = \Delta - c$. The private gains are smaller in both cases (recall that $X \leq V$). Private searching is too low because the innovator does not appropriate the full value of the innovation.

In the remaining case there is too much searching. The innovator develops the innovation regardless of the search outcome. The innovator seeks both the benefit of a reduced development cost and also the enhanced bargaining power associated with an *ex ante* license. The social planner cares about the former but not the latter. The social gain from searching is $C - c$, and the private gain is $G = \frac{V-c}{2} - [\Delta - C]$. The fact that expression (11.2) is negative is sufficient to prove that the private gain is larger.

IV. Discussion and Conclusion

Patents provide effective notice and perform well as property only if patent owners and potential infringers are aware of each other. In this chapter I have modeled searching by a potential infringer to create a match between the two parties. In the model, the gains from the cost savings created by technology transfer $(C - c)$ are captured entirely by the searching party, and thus the private and social incentives are the same. This feature of the model arises because I treat technology transfer as a spillover – the potential infringer gains the benefit of the inventor's technology simply by reading the patent. In other models, the private incentive to search associated with the benefits from technology transfer could be smaller than the social incentive if the gains are shared between the innovator and the patent owner.

A second factor influencing searching is the threat of a patent lawsuit. If the potential innovator conducts a fruitless search, and is discouraged from developing a technology because of the fear of a patent lawsuit, then there is a private and social loss from the missed development opportunity. Because the innovator generally does not capture the full value from development, the private incentive to search to avoid lawsuits is smaller than the social incentive.

Finally, successful searching may improve the bargaining position of the innovator and cause a wealth transfer from the patent owner to the innovator. In the model, the social planner does not care about this wealth transfer in cases in which the development decision is unaffected (NB: I have assumed that the invention and patent already exist). Thus, it is possible that there will be too much searching. This outcome seems unlikely except perhaps in the case of certain "patent trolls" – when the patents have little or no valuable technology, and the patents have significantly more value when asserted after the innovator has sunk its development costs.[15]

This model provides a modest starting point for a policy analysis of why innovators search for patents and why patent disputes occur. Much work remains to be done. A few of the most important extensions of the model should account for (1) the two sides of the search process – patent owners search for prospective licensees and infringers, (2) different licensing models associated with different stories about how an early match influences bargaining power (for example, patent owners who plan to innovate and exclude other innovators as in Meurer[16]), and (3) search for public domain technology as an alternative to invention).[17]

---

[15] Lemely, M. A. and Shapiro, C. 2007. "Patent Hold-up and Royalty Stacking." *Texas Law Review* 85, 1991–2050.

[16] Meurer, M. J. 1989. "Patent Litigation and Licensing." *RAND Journal of Economics* 20, 77–91.

[17] Merges, R. P. and Duffy, J. F. 2007. Patent Law and Policy: Cases and Materials, LexisNexis.

PART V

PROPERTY RIGHTS AND THE THEORY
OF PATENT LAW

12

Commercializing Property Rights in Inventions

Lessons for Modern Patent Theory from Classic Patent Doctrine

Adam Mossoff

In 1859, Abraham Lincoln famously observed that the "patent system . . . secured to the inventor, for a limited time, the exclusive use of his invention; and thereby added the fuel of interest to the fire of genius, in the discovery and production of new and useful things."[1] Lincoln understood this point all too well, as he remains the only U.S. president to have obtained a patent (which was still in force at the time he gave this speech).[2] Today, scholars and lawyers often quote this passage from Lincoln's 1859 speech as a poetic exemplar of the long-standing policy justification for the patent system – it promotes inventive activity and progress of the useful arts by "add[ing] the fuel of interest to the fire of genius."[3]

Yet this invocation of President Lincoln's justification for the patent system also reflects a deep ambivalence within modern patent theory about the function of the patent system. While repeatedly quoting the latter portion of Lincoln's statement about the patent system spurring on inventive activity, modern scholars always redact the all-important first clause in which Lincoln observed that patents "secured to the inventor . . . the exclusive use of his

---

[1] Abraham Lincoln, *Second Lecture on Discoveries and Inventions* (Feb. 11, 1859), in 3 THE COLLECTED WORKS OF ABRAHAM LINCOLN 356, 363 (Roy P. Basler ed., 1953).

[2] See Patent No. 6,469 ("Buoying Vessels over Shoals") (issued May 22, 1849).

[3] See, e.g., Jessica Silby, *The Mythical Beginnings of Intellectual Property*, 15 GEO. MASON L. REV. 319, 330 n.69 (2008); Christopher A. Harkins, *Fending Off Paper Patents and Patent Trolls: A Novel "Cold Fusion" Defense Because Changing Times Demand It*, 17 ALB. L.J. SCI. & TECH. 407, 407 (2007); Christopher Sprigman, *Reform(aliz)ing Copyright*, 57 STAN. L. REV. 485, 533 (2004); Margo A. Bagley, *Patent First, Ask Questions Later: Morality and Biotechnology in Patent Law*, 45 WM. & MARY L. REV. 469, 536 (2003); Gerald J. Mossinghoff, *Post-Grant Review of Patents: Enhancing the Quality of the Fuel of Interest*, 85 J. PAT. & TRADEMARK OFF. SOC'Y 231, 231 (2003); Lisa A. Dolak, *Declaratory Judgment Jurisdiction in Patent Cases: Restoring the Balance Between the Patentee and the Accused Infringer*, 38 B.C. L. REV. 903, 904 n.13 (1997); Justin Hughes, *The Philosophy of Intellectual Property*, 77 Georgetown L.J. 287, 304 (1988).

invention."[4] In fact, given Lincoln's syntax, it is clear that he believed that it is the legal guaranty of "exclusive use" that adds "thereby" the "fuel of interest to the fire of genius."[5] In other words, Lincoln believed it was commercialization – the "exclusive use" of a patented product in the marketplace – that spurs inventive activity and not merely the grant of the patent right itself. Modern scholars turn Lincoln's inspired justification for the patent system on its head, transforming his advocacy for the commercialization theory of patents into an early statement of the now-dominant theory of patent law: the reward theory.[6]

The translation of historical texts into modern policy parlance is nothing new within patent law scholarship,[7] and one might be inclined to conclude that this is simply another instance of "law office history" – the selective use of historical sources to support the reward theory of patent policy.[8] Yet there is nothing that indicates that this is an intentional misrepresentation of Lincoln's speech on the value of the modern patent system. Instead, the conversion of Lincoln's words – with, or more often without, the revealing ellipses[9] – seems to reflect merely an innocuous correction to anachronistic patent doctrine. That is, Lincoln believed that patents secured the "exclusive use" of a patent, whereas it is basic patent theory today that patents secure only the right to exclude.[10]

---

[4]   See supra note 3 (citing sources that commit this omission).
[5]   Lincoln, supra note 1 (the "fuel of interest" follows as a conclusion from his observation about the security in "exclusive use").
[6]   See F. Scott Kieff, *IP Transactions: On the Theory & Practice of Commercializing Innovation*, 42 Hous. L. Rev. 727, 732 (2005) (recognizing that "[t]he bulk of law and economics literature on U.S. IP regimes focuses on a reward theory of patents"); Mark A. Lemley, *Ex Ante Versus Ex Post Justifications for Intellectual Property*, 71 U. Chi. L. Rev. 129, 30 (2004) (characterizing the reward theory as the "standard economic explanation for intellectual property in the United States").
[7]   See generally Adam Mossoff, *Who Cares What Thomas Jefferson Thought About Patents? Reevaluating the Patent "Privilege" in Historical Context*, 92 Cornell L. Rev. 953 (2007).
[8]   Larry D. Kramer, *When Lawyers Do History*, 72 Geo. Wash. L. Rev. 387, 389–94 (2003) (complaining about the bad historiography of lawyers, who produce "law office history" intended only "to generate data and interpretations that are of use in resolving modern legal controversies") (citations omitted).
[9]   See supra note 3 (citing sources that convert the above statement without use of ellipses). See also Joseph Scott Miller, Fire of Genius Blog, at http://www.thefireofgenius.com (redacting "exclusive use" and using ellipses in quoting Lincoln's famous statement from his 1859 speech) (last visited April 29, 2008).
[10] See, e.g., 35 U.S.C. § 154(a) (defining the legal entitlement in a patent as comprising only "the right to exclude others from making, using, offering for sale, or selling the invention"); *Dawson Chem. Co. v. Rohm & Haas Co.*, 448 U.S. 176, 215 (1980) (recognizing "the long-settled view that the essence of a patent grant is the right to exclude others from profiting by the patented invention"); 5–16 Chisum on Patents § 16.02[1] (2006) ("Basically, a

As revealed in this subtle but important change to Lincoln's speech on patents, modern patent scholars have altered the positive definition of patent rights, fostering a formalism within patent law that has sown indeterminacy within the commercialization doctrines securing this "exclusive use" of patents in the marketplace. To be clear, my thesis here is not that modern patent theory is incorrect in its positive definition of patent rights; such a claim would require substantial conceptual and normative exegesis that goes far beyond the scope of this relatively short chapter.[11] My thesis here is far more limited in its scope: The positive account of patents as securing only the right to exclude does not necessarily provide positive guidance to courts in adjudicating a patentee's commercialization of his property rights.

In proving this thesis, this chapter will frame its analysis around three positive models that describe the methods by which a property owner commercializes his property interests and thus enjoys "the fruits of his honest labour and industry."[12] This positive framework is important because it elucidates the fundamental conceptual features of classic patent doctrine, to which the Supreme Court in recent years has repeatedly professed fealty.[13] As Chief Justice Roberts explained in *eBay v. MercExchange*, "historical practice[s]" set the positive baseline when "it comes to discerning and applying" any hoary patent doctrines today.[14] Accordingly, these three models explicate how nineteenth-century courts developed the legal doctrines that ensured effective commercialization of property rights in inventions – securing the "exclusive use" of inventions in the marketplace and thus "add[ing] the fuel of interest to the fire of genius."[15]

---

patent grants to the patentee and his assigns the right to *exclude* others from making, using, and selling the invention. It does not grant the affirmative right to make, use or sell.").

[11] See generally Adam Mossoff, *Exclusion and Exclusive Use*, 22 HARV. J.L. & TECH. 321 (2009).

[12] *Vanhorne's Lessee v. Dorrance*, 2 U.S. (2 Dall.) 304, 310 (1795) (Patterson, J.) ("[T]he right of acquiring and possessing property, and having it protected, is one of the natural, inherent, and unalienable rights of man. . . . No man would become a member of a community, in which he could not enjoy the fruits of his honest labour and industry.").

[13] See, e.g., KSR Intern. Co. v. Teleflex Inc., 127 S. Ct. 1727, 1734 (2007) (recognizing that modern nonobviousness doctrine follows "the logic of the earlier decision in *Hotchkiss v. Greenwood*, 11 How. 248 (1851), and its progeny"); *Festo Corp. v. Shoketsu Kinzoku Kogyo Kabushiki Co.*, 535 U.S. 722, 738 (2002) (affirming the doctrine of prosecution history estoppel in patent law given, in part, how courts construed this equitable defense in the nineteenth century); *Warner-Jenkinson Co. v. Hilton Davis Chemical Co.*, 520 U.S. 17, 26 n.3 (1997) (maintaining that nineteenth-century court decisions creating the doctrine of equivalents are controlling today despite the litigant's argument that Congress's enactment of the 1952 Patent Act impliedly repealed these decisions).

[14] *eBay v. MercExchange*, 547 U.S. 388, 394–95 (2006) (Roberts, C. J., concurring).

[15] Lincoln, supra note 1, at 363.

More important, these three commercialization models also illustrate how the Federal Circuit has created indeterminacy within these important commercialization doctrines today. Given the limited scope of this chapter's thesis, it will similarly limit its analysis to an important case within modern patent jurisprudence that reveals this indeterminacy: the Federal Circuit's 2001 opinion in *Jazz Photo Corp. v. International Trade Commission*.[16] The principal issue in *Jazz Photo* was the distinction between repair versus reconstruction by an end user given the exhaustion of patent rights after the unrestricted sale of a patented product in the marketplace. In discussing this distinction between an end user's acceptable repair and the impermissible reconstruction, the Federal Circuit followed basic, black-letter patent doctrine. In fact, patent law casebooks discuss this case or cite it for precisely this issue.[17]

Jazz Photo also handed down another holding that has far more reaching consequences: Unrestricted sales of a patented product in foreign jurisdictions do not exhaust patent rights.[18] This secondary holding was not only novel, it was reached with virtually no discussion or analysis whatsoever, taking up only a single paragraph in an opinion that spanned many pages.[19] Moreover, this holding on international patent exhaustion was not dicta, as it had an immediate impact in the case. Although the assignee lost the decision in *Jazz Photo*, it was able to pursue its infringement claims on the basis of this secondary holding of nonexhaustion and ultimately obtained a favorable decision several years later.[20] Yet when the Federal Circuit later confirmed in this follow-on decision that the *Jazz Photo* court "expressly limited first sales under the exhaustion doctrine to those occurring within the United States,"[21] it provided no additional explanation as to why this novel holding is justified.[22]

---

[16] 264 F.3d 1094 (Fed. Cir. 2001).

[17] See, e.g., Robert P. Merges & John F. Duffy, PATENT LAW AND POLICY 914 (4th ed. 2007).

[18] *Jazz Photo*, 264 F.3d at 1105.

[19] Id.

[20] See *Fuji Photo Film Co. v. Jazz Photo Corp.*, 394 F.3d 1368 (Fed. Cir. 2005).

[21] *Id.* at 1376 (reaffirming *Jazz Photo* with no further discussion).

[22] See, e.g., Rebecca S. Eisenberg, *The Role of the FDA in Innovation Policy*, 13 MICH. TELECOMM. & TECH L. REV. 345, 362–63 (2007) ("The U.S. Court of Appeals for the Federal Circuit once observed in passing, with no acknowledgment of controversy, that under U.S. patent law the first sale doctrine only applies if there has been a sale in the United States."); Daniel R. Cahoy, *Patent Fences and Constitutional Fence Posts: Property Barriers to Pharmaceutical Importation*, 15 FORDHAM INTELL. PROP. MEDIA & ENT. L. J. 623, 663 (2005) ("An intriguing aspect of Judge Newman's opinion in *Jazz Photo* is that she articulated the national exhaustion rule with such brevity."); Michelle Vockrodt, *Patent Exhaustion and Foreign Sales: An Analysis and Application of the Jazz Photo Decision*, 33 AIPLA Q. J. 189, 193–94 (2005) ("The *Jazz Photo* decision was the first time the Federal Circuit had addressed the issue of international patent exhaustion. In announcing its rule,

For this reason, *Jazz Photo* deserves attention because it provides insight into the degree to which modern patent theory is potentially indeterminate as a conceptual matter in defining the scope of a patentee's commercialization rights. It is not an accident that *Jazz Photo* was a case of first impression, as conceptual errors are typically revealed in such cases. Here, the Federal Circuit essentially defaulted to first principles in deciding a case on which it had no substantive guidance from preexisting case law, such as the venerable repair versus reconstruction doctrine similarly discussed in the same opinion.[23] In returning to first principles, modern patent theory informed the Federal Circuit that a patent comprises only the right to exclude, and the court therefore adopted a highly formalistic approach to enforcing this right to exclude. Again, the point here is not that *Jazz Photo* is right or wrong in its holding on international patent exhaustion – there are perhaps legitimate policy reasons for this secondary holding[24] – but rather that modern patent theory makes possible such pedantic decisions about commercialization rights as a result of how it defines the positive content of patent rights.

In three sections, this chapter will explain how *Jazz Photo* reveals a potentially fundamental indeterminacy concerning commercialization rights within modern patent theory. First, it will discuss three commercialization models that explain how courts have long secured the rights of use and disposition of property in inventions. These models further reveal how nineteenth-century courts drew on the conceptual framework of commercialization of real estate to craft similar legal doctrines governing the commercialization of patents. Second, it will discuss *Jazz Photo*, explaining the two holdings in this case, and how the court's secondary holding that there is no patent exhaustion for unrestricted international sales was both unprecedented and unexplained. This section will also show how *Jazz Photo* rejected the three commercialization models and created a fourth model for how a patentee may alienate and control its property interests in the marketplace. Third, this chapter will conclude with some observations about the role of commercialization within patent doctrine, and what historical doctrines, like patent exhaustion, may teach modern patent theory about how commercialization concerns may be built into patent doctrine. In this

---

however, the panel did not elaborate on its reasoning except to cite *Boesch v. Graff*, a Supreme Court case from 1890.").

[23] *Jazz Photo*, 264 F.3d at 1102–04.

[24] See Cahoy, supra note 22, at 663–664 (discussing several policy reasons supporting the *Jazz Photo* decision). But see Daniel Erlikhman, Note, *Jazz Photo and the Doctrine of Patent Exhaustion: Implications to TRIPS and International Harmonization of Patent Protection*, 25 Hastings Comm. & Ent. L.J. 307, 337 (2003) (criticizing *Jazz Photo* as "ill-advised, given the international efforts to harmonize patent protection and open borders to free movement of commercial goods").

way, classic patent doctrine can provide substantive guidance to courts in securing the legitimate expectations of inventors in the exclusive use of their property.

II. Three Models of Commercializing Property Rights

To understand the indeterminacy produced by modern patent theory with respect to commercialization rights, one must situate it within a positive account of how patent jurisprudence has defined commercialization rights generally. As a purely conceptual matter, one can model three different doctrinal approaches that explain how property owners, whether of land or inventions, might deploy their legal rights in the marketplace. Significantly, these three models are not just theory: They reflect historic real property doctrine, and nineteenth-century courts incorporated these real property doctrines into patent law on the basis of the classification of patents as property.[25]

In the first commercialization scenario, patentees may keep their fee interests in their property, choosing to manufacture and sell outright the patented products resulting from what nineteenth-century courts repeatedly called their "title deeds."[26] This is perhaps the easiest case of commercialization, as a patentee does not convey any property interest in the patent to others; rather, the patentee alienates in fee unconditionally the products resulting from the patent, thereby profiting from the use of its property interest in much the same way that a farmer sells apples from his orchard or the wheat sown from his field.[27] As a court observed in 1862, the patent statutes ensure that "inventors shall exclusively enjoy, for a limited season, the fruits of their inventions" by "authorizing them alone to manufacture, sell, or practice what they have invented."[28]

---

[25] See Adam Mossoff, *Patents as Constitutional Private Property: The Historical Protection of Patents under the Takings Clause*, 87 B.U. L. Rev. 689, 718–19 (2008); Mossoff, supra note 7, at 992–98.

[26] *Birdsall v. McDonald*, 3 F. Cas. 441, 444 (C.C.N.D. Ohio 1874) (No. 1,434) (observing that "[i]nventors are a meritorious class of men" and that "[t]heir patents are their title deeds"); see also *Earth Closet Co. v. Fenner*, 8 F. Cas. 261, 263 (C.C.D.R.I. 1871) (No. 4,249) (explaining that a "patent is prima facie proof of title"); *Evans v. Kremer*, 8 F. Cas. 874, 875 (C.C.D. Pa. 1816) (No. 4,565) (explaining that a plaintiff-patentee must "be prepared to maintain his title, in relation to the question of original discovery").

[27] See *Hovey v. Henry*, 12 F. Cas. 603, 604 (C.C.D. Mass. 1846) (No. 6,742) (observing that "[a]n inventor holds a property in his invention by as good a title as the farmer holds his farm and flock").

[28] *Clark Patent Steam & Fire Regulator Co. v. Copeland*, 5 F. Cas. 987, 988 (C.C.S.D.N.Y. 1862) (No. 2,866).

A corollary of the first commercialization case is when a property owner conveys its entire fee interest to a third party, and thus a patentee may sell its property outright. In such a case, the third party now owns the title in the patent and can do whatever it wants with its property, such as use the patent in the manufacture of products or engage in further conveyances of the property interests (see the second and third cases that follow).[29] Following common-law doctrine governing estates in land,[30] nineteenth-century courts identified an outright conveyance of title in a patent to a third party as an "assignment,"[31] and this usage continues to this day.[32] Ultimately, for purposes of commercialization of property interests, the difference between a patentee and an assignee is a distinction without a difference, as in both situations the owner of title in the patent is the person profiting from the unconditional sale of products in the marketplace.

In the second commercialization case, a property owner may convey to a third party a lesser estate interest carved out of the original title, such as creating the equivalency of a tenancy in terms of years and retaining a reversionary interest.[33] Thus, a patentee may convey a limited right either to use the patented invention[34] or to sell the invention in a particular city or state.[35] As one federal court observed in 1874, "[i]t is clear that the patentee may grant the right to use within any specified place, town, city

---

[29] See, e.g., *Lowell v. Lewis*, 15 F. Cas. 1018 (C.C.D. Mass. 1817) (No. 8,568) (both plaintiff and defendant were manufacturing patented pumps as assignees of separate patents).

[30] See Blackstone, 2 Commentaries 326–327 ("An *assignment* is properly a transfer, or making over to another, of the right one has in *any* estate, but it is usually applied to an estate for life or years. . . . [I]n assignments he parts with the whole property, and the assignee stands to all intents and purposes in the place of the assignor").

[31] See, e.g., *Moore v. Marsh*, 74 U.S. (7 Wall.) 515, 520 (1868) ("An assignee is one who holds, by a valid assignment in writing, the whole interest of a patent, or any undivided part of such whole interest, throughout the United States").

[32] See, e.g., *Rite-Hite Corp. v. Kelley Co.*, 56 F.3d 1538, 1551 (Fed. Cir. 1995) ("A conveyance of legal title by the patentee . . . is an assignment and vests the assignee with title in the patent, and a right to sue infringers").

[33] For instance, O may convey Blackacre "to A for 20 years." This conveyance creates a term of years leasehold estate in A, and O has a reversion. Conveyances like this constitute the bread-and-butter of real estate transactional practice, and are the primary reason why so many 1Ls each year consider their Property course to be an extremely painful experience.

[34] See, e.g., *McClurg v. Kingsland*, 42 U.S. (1 How.) 202, 206 (1843) (referring to a patent conveyance as "an express license or grant . . . giving the defendants a right to the continued use of the invention"); *Heaton-Peninsular Button-Fastener Co. v. Eureka Specialty Co.*, 77 F. 288, 290 (6th Cir. 1896) ("All alienations of a mere right to use the invention operate only as licenses"); *Gamewell Fire-Alarm Telegraph Co. v. City of Brooklyn*, 14 F. 255, 256 (C.C.N.Y. 1882) (dismissing a licensee's lawsuit as going beyond the scope of the limited rights of use and sale granted to it by the patentee).

[35] See *Farrington v. Gregory*, 8 F. Cas. 1088, 1089 (C.C.E.D. Mich. 1870) (No. 4,688) (noting that the license in this case contained a geographic restriction that limited the licensee's

or district, and he may make such right of use exclusive; and I deem it no less clear that he may limit the right to manufacture for such use."[36] Within nineteenth-century patent jurisprudence, courts held that patentees had the right to carve out such lesser interests through conveyances to third parties precisely because patents were defined as "property."[37] Although courts conceptualized patents as property rights and drew on legal doctrines in real property to define similar doctrines in patent law,[38] they recognized that they could not classify lesser interests in patents as lesser estates, such as a fee simple defeasible, because this taxonomy applied only to property interests in land.[39] As such, early courts identified a patentee's conveyance of a limited interest in its property as a "license,"[40] importing this concept from real estate doctrine and then using it as a catch-all category for conveyances of any lesser interests in a patent.[41]

In this second commercialization case, therefore, a patentee conveys only a portion of his use or alienation interests, retaining a reversionary interest that gives the patentee the right to sue the licensee to enforce the property rights retained by him. As one court stated in 1857: "If the licensee uses the

---

"right to use and sell machines in Calhoun and Kalamazoo counties, in the state of Michigan").

[36] *Dorsey Revolving Harvester Rake Co. v. Bradley Mfg. Co.*, 7 F. Cas. 946, 947 (C.C.N.D.N.Y. 1874) (No. 4,015).

[37] An anonymous essay published in the *Federal Cases* reporter at 3 F. Cas. 85, following *Belding v. Turner*, 3 F. Cas. 84 (C.C.D. Conn. 1871) (No. 1,243), explicitly drew the connection between the classification of patents as an "incorporeal chattel" or "personal estate" and the right to alienate this legal interest. This essay distinguished American patents from English patents on precisely these terms, as English patents were a mere "grant by the crown" and thus "inalienable unless power to that effect is given by the crown." 3 F. Cas. at 85.

[38] See Mossoff, supra note 7, at 992–1009 (applying liberal interpretative canons to patents on the basis of conceptualizing patents as similar to real estate); Adam Mossoff, *Patents as Constitutional Private Property: The Historical Protection of Patents under the Takings Clause*, 87 B.U. L. Rev. 689, 700–11 (2008) (securing patents as private property under the Takings Clause given their similarities as property rights to real estate).

[39] Cf. Dukeminier et al., Property 182 (6th ed. 2006) ("For historical reasons there is a fee simple only in land, not in personal property").

[40] See, e.g., *Suydam v. Day*, 23 F. Cas. 473, 473 (C.C.N.Y. 1845) (No. 13,654) (distinguishing between "an assignee of a patent [who] must be regarded as acquiring his title to it, with a right of action in his own name," and "an interest in only a part of each patent, to wit, a license to use"); *Whittemore v. Cutter*, 29 F. Cas. 1120, 1120–1121 (C.C.D. Mass. 1813) (No. 17,600) (Story, Circuit Justice) (recognizing in this case that there was "no assignment of the patent right" and thus "[t]he instrument could only operate as a covenant or license for the exclusive use of the patent right in certain local districts").

[41] See 2 James Kent, Commentaries on American Law 452–453 (George Comstock ed., 11th ed. 1866) (explaining that "a license is an authority to do a particular act, or series of acts, upon another's land, without possessing any estate therein")

patented invention beyond the limits of the license or grant, or in a way not authorized by the license or grant, then there has been a violation of a right secured to the patentee under a law of the United States giving to him the exclusive right to use the thing patented."[42] Accordingly, if a licensee uses a patented invention beyond the terms of the interest conveyed to it by the patentee, it is liable for infringement for the same reason that an owner of a life estate is liable for devaluing land under waste doctrine[43] or the owner of an easement who expands the right of way is liable for trespassing on the larger estate.[44] As a positive doctrinal matter, the patentee retains an interest in the property, what courts would identify as a reversionary interest in real property cases and even in some patent cases,[45] and it is this retained property interest that permits the patentee to sue its licensee for infringement.

Lastly, in the third commercialization case, a property owner may convey an estate interest, either a lesser estate or the entire "exclusive title,"[46] but create in the conveyance instrument express words of limitation that impose the equivalent of either a restrictive covenant or a defeasible condition restricting the use of the property interest purchased by the third party. When a property owner creates a restrictive covenant, and the covenant meets the legal requirements for enforcement either at law or in equity,[47] the covenant shall "run with the land" and the original property owner may thus sue any "heirs, successors and assigns" for breach of the use restriction.[48] Similarly, a defeasible condition created through words of limitation permits a property owner to sue to retake property on breach of the use restriction.[49]

---

[42] *Goodyear v. Union India Rubber Co.*, 10 F. Cas. 726, 727 (C.C.S.D.N.Y. 1857) (No. 5,586).

[43] See generally POWELL ON REAL PROPERTY §§56.01–56.12 (Michael A. Wolf gen. ed. 2005).

[44] See *Brown v. Voss*, 715 P.2d 514, 518 (Wash. 1986) (Dore, J., dissenting) (noting that "any extension of the use of an easement to benefit a nondominant estate constitutes misuse of the easement," and thereby "is a trespass").

[45] See, e.g., *Heaton-Peninsular Button-Fastener Co. v. Eureka Specialty Co.*, 77 F. 288, 290 (6th Cir. 1896) (recognizing that "[a]ll alienations of a mere right to use the invention operate only as licenses," and that in such cases, the interest conveyed to a licensee was "subject to a reverter in case of violation of the conditions of the sale").

[46] *Johnson v. M'Intosh*, 21 U.S. (8 Wheat.) 543, 574 (1823).

[47] See generally William B. Stoebuck, *Running Covenants: An Analytical Primer*, 52 WASH. L. REV. 861 (1977).

[48] *Neponsit Property Owners' Ass'n, Inc. v. Emigrant Industrial Savings Bank*, 15 N.E.2d 793, 795 (N.Y. 1938) (quoting a restrictive covenant that the court ultimately enforces against successors-in-interest).

[49] For instance, O may convey Blackacre "to A and her heirs as long as alcohol is never sold or consumed on Blackacre." This conveyance creates a fee simple determinable in A, and O has a possibility of reverter in the estate. O's future interest means that the estate will

In the nineteenth century, courts incorporated into patent law the right to impose use restrictions that had been secured to landowners through the enforcement of restrictive covenants and defeasible estates.[50] Accordingly, patentees were able to impose a whole litany of restrictions on the use of the property interest they conveyed to a licensee. For instance, a patentee could restrict a licensee in terms of the total quantity of patented products manufactured or sold,[51] the manner in which the patented product may be used,[52] the territorial scope in which the patented product may be used or sold,[53] and even the price that the licensee could charge in the marketplace.[54] Notably, the interest retained by the patentee in this third commercialization case was even greater than in the second commercialization case, because the patentee could sue for infringement not only for a breach of the estate interest but also for breach of any additional use restrictions imposed on the activities of the licensee, such as selling outside of the sales territory set forth in the license agreement.

Congress and courts in the nineteenth century secured to patentees their right to impose additional restrictive conditions on the interests they were creating in the conveyances of their patented property. In so doing, they continued to import from real property law the conceptual framework

---

automatically revert back to him if the use restriction is breached by A or any of her heirs, successors or assigns. See Joseph W. Singer, Introduction to Property 295 (2001).

50 See, e.g., *Heaton-Peninsular Button-Fastener Co.*, 77 F. at 290 (recognizing under the terms of the license that "[t]he buyer of the machine undoubtedly obtains the title to the materials embodying the invention, subject to a reverter in case of violation of the conditions of the sale"); *American Cotton Tie Supply Co. v. Bullard*, 1 F. Cas. 625, 629 (C.C.N.Y. 1879) (No. 294) (recognizing that patented products may be sold in which "a restriction may easily be attached, or where a license to use only may be sold, unaccompanied with any title or accompanied with a restricted title").

51 See, e.g., Charles Slack, Noble Obsession: Charles Goodyear, Thomas Hancock, and the Race to Unlock the Greatest Industrial Secret of the Nineteenth Century (2003) (describing quantity, territorial and field-of-use restrictions that Goodyear imposed on licensees of his patent for vulcanized rubber).

52 See, e.g., *American Cotton-Tie Co. v. Simmons*, 106 U.S. 89 (1882) (enforcing license restriction prohibiting re-use of a patented cotton-bale tie, on which the patented products were stamped "License to use once only"); *Providence Rubber Co. v. Goodyear*, 76 U.S. (9 Wall.) 788, 799–800 (1869) (enforcing against the defendants the express sale and use restrictions imposed in a license); *Chaffee v. Boston Belting Co.*, 63 U.S. (22 How.) 217, 220 (1859) (recognizing by "the terms of the instrument" created by Goodyear in this case that "it was understood that the right and license so conveyed was to apply to any and all articles substituted for leather, metal, and other substances, in the use or manufacture of machines or machinery").

53 See, e.g., *Farrington v. Gregory*, 8 F. Cas. 1088, 1089 (C.C.E.D. Mich. 1870) (No. 4,688) (noting that license contained a geographic restriction that limited the licensee's "right to use and sell machines in Calhoun and Kalamazoo counties, in the state of Michigan").

54 See, e.g., *E. Bement & Sons v. Nat'l Harrow Co.*, 186 U.S. 70 (1902).

for designing the doctrinal requirements for such use restrictions, such as requiring recordation and requiring reasonable notice for end users when patentees attempted to extend restrictions to downstream market activities.[55] By the end of the nineteenth century, it was well-settled patent doctrine that patentees could retain both a reversionary interest as well as an additional property interest secured through a restrictive covenant imposed on a licensee in commercializing their property interests in their inventions.[56]

In sum, the substantial weight of nineteenth-century patent jurisprudence evidenced the work of courts in importing from real property three conceptual frameworks that produced sound doctrine securing commercialization rights in patent law. Of course, the nineteenth-century case law on patentee's commercialization rights is not entirely consistent, as some courts were not cognizant of the positive doctrinal framework that was being adopted in patent law in common-law fashion from real property law.[57] Moreover, a few prominent judges, such as Chief Justice Roger Taney, viewed

---

[55] On the recordation requirement, see Patent Act of 1836, ch. 357, § 11, 5 Stat. at 121 (requiring an assignment to be "recorded in the Patent Office within three months from the execution thereof"); Patent Act of 1793, § 4, ch. 11, 1 Stat. at 322 (requiring an assignee to "record said assignment, in the office of the Secretary of State"). On the notice requirement, see *Heaton-Peninsular Button-Fastener Co.*, 77 F. at 291 (recognizing that a licensee and its wholesaler are both liable to a license restriction because the "jobber buys and sells subject to the restriction, and both have notice of the conditional character of the sale, and of the restriction on the use"); *American Cotton Tie Supply Co.*, 1 F. Cas. at 629 ("[W]here pins, nails, screws, or buckles are sold, if some of them are sold with a restricted and some with an unrestricted title, there are no means of identification which enable the purchaser, after they have passed into the market and common use, to distinguish the articles licensed or restricted in their use from those absolutely sold. In the case of articles of that description, the patentee may fairly be presumed to have received his royalty when he parted with the possession of the articles and allowed them to go into common and general use."); cf. *Adams v. Burke*, 84 U.S. 453 (1873) ("Whatever, therefore, may be the rule when patentees subdivide territorially their patents, as to the exclusive right *to make* or *to sell* within a limited territory, . . . when they are once lawfully made and sold, there is no restriction on their *use* to be implied for the benefit of the patentee or his assignees or licensees").

[56] See *Mitchell v. Hawley*, 83 U.S. 544, 548 (1872) (noting proposition in patent law that "[p]urchasers of the exclusive privilege of making or vending the patented machine hold the whole or a portion of the franchise which the patent secures, depending upon the nature of the conveyance").

[57] This is particularly true in *Bloomer v. McQuewan*, 55 U.S. (14 How.) 539 (1852), which is the Supreme Court case that formally gave birth to the patent exhaustion doctrine. Here, Chief Justice Taney engaged in dicta that was tantamount to his judicially rewriting the patent statutes to better reflects his anti-patent political prejudices. See Mossoff, *supra* note 11, at 341–342 (discussing how the *Bloomer* dicta reflects Taney's judicial activism and his minority-status anti-patent views).

patents with hostility, given their belief that patents were monopoly franchises that violated common-law property rights.[58] Yet these were minority viewpoints.[59] The property-based commercialization framework was sufficiently dominant in nineteenth-century patent case law that the Supreme Court could summarize it in 1902 as follows: "An owner of a patent has the right to sell it or to keep it; to manufacture the article himself or to license others to manufacture it; to sell such article himself or to authorize others to sell it."[60]

The Federal Circuit ostensibly follows this classic commercialization doctrine, declaring that "express conditions accompanying the sale or license of a patented product are generally upheld."[61] Yet, apart from such abstract declarations of fidelity to long-standing commercialization doctrine, the Federal Circuit's commercialization jurisprudence does not in practice reliably conform to the three classic commercialization models. In fact, the Federal Circuit has created a new, fourth model of commercialization. Before we can assess why this happened and what it portends, we must first understand what happened in the doctrine, and to grasp this, we must now turn to the cases in which the Federal Circuit has departed from classic commercialization doctrine.

III. The Federal Circuit's Fourth Model of Commercialization: *Jazz Photo v. ITC*

The Federal Circuit's commercialization jurisprudence reflects a conceptual indeterminacy within patent law, which is illustrated dramatically in its 2001 decision in *Jazz Photo Corp. v. International Trade Commission.*[62] Before we can assess what *Jazz Photo* might teach us about the function of commercialization doctrines within modern patent theory, we must first establish what happened in this case. This is necessary because, as noted in the Introduction, the primary holding dealt with the legal distinction between repair

---

[58] See Mossoff, *supra* note 7, at 966, 100 (discussing Taney's commitment to Jacksonian Democracy and his resulting inherent suspicion of any government grants of exclusive rights, such as corporate charters, franchises, and patents).

[59] See Mossoff, *supra* note 11, at 341–342.

[60] *E. Bement & Sons*, 186 U.S. at 88–89.

[61] *B. Braun Med., Inc. v. Abbott Lab.*, 124 F.3d 1419, 1426 (Fed. Cir. 1997). See also *Hewlett-Packard Co. v. Repeat-O-Type Stencil Mfg. Corp., Inc.*, 123 F.3d 1445, 1455 (1997) ("When a patentee sells a device without condition, it parts with the right to enforce any patent that the parties might reasonably have contemplated would interfere with the use of the purchased device").

[62] 264 F.3d 1094 (Fed. Cir. 2001).

versus reconstruction following a patentee's exhaustion of its rights in a patented product sold in the marketplace. Judge Newman's opinion in *Jazz Photo* dealt only peripherally with international exhaustion, which was when she departed from the three commercialization models. Even more frustrating Judge Newman discussed the international exhaustion issue and came to her conclusion within a single paragraph. Yet, despite this perfunctory discussion, commentators recognize that the "court's holding on national exhaustion is unmistakable" – there is no international patent exhaustion.[63] Here, I will discuss how the *Jazz Photo* court reached this decision, and how this decision creates a novel, fourth model of commercialization of property rights in a patented invention.

A. The Who, What, and Why of *Jazz Photo v. ITC*

The provenance of the Federal Circuit's decision in *Jazz Photo* was a bit unlike most patent infringement lawsuits. The case began normally for most patent lawsuits: Fuji Photo Film Co. sued twenty-seven defendants, including Jazz Photo Corp., for infringing fifteen patents on "lens-fitted film packages" (LFFP), or "single-use cameras" in the vernacular. Fuji chose, however, to file its action with the International Trade Commission (ITC), as the gravamen of its complaint against the defendants was that they were acquiring previously used LFFP cameras, reconstructing them overseas, and then importing the LFFP cameras for resale in the United States.[64] The ITC ruled in favor of Fuji and issued an injunction prohibiting the importation of any refurbished LFFP cameras that violated Fuji's patents. Jazz Photo and two other defendants (collectively, "Jazz Photo") appealed the ITC's order to the Federal Circuit, contesting the ITC's underlying judgment that they were infringing Fuji's patents.

Judge Newman's opinion, reversing the ITC's order in favor of Jazz Photo, is a bit difficult to untangle, as it assesses Jazz Photo's appeal along two different axes of analysis with respect to multiple patents on LFFP cameras: first, whether Jazz Photo's actions constituted repair or reconstruction of a patented product previously sold in the marketplace, and, second, whether

---

[63] Cameron Hutchison & Moin A. Yahya, *Infringement and the International Reach of U.S. Patent Law*, 17 Fed. Cir. B.J. 241, 268 (2008).

[64] Jazz Photo and the other defendants acquired previously used and discarded LFFP cameras, broke open the internal plastic camera, installed new film, reset the film counter, replaced the flash battery, resealed the plastic camera, and then put on a new cardboard cover so that it appeared as new. *Jazz Photo*, 264 F.3d at 1101.

Fuji exhausted its rights with the first sale of its patented products.[65] For our purposes here, I will only briefly summarize the first issue to lay the groundwork for understanding why the Federal Circuit ultimately reached the second issue on international patent exhaustion.

With respect to Fuji's product patents covering the LFFP cameras, Judge Newman concluded that only one of Fuji's product patents, Patent No. 4,884,087 ('087 patent), contained a claim directed to "a film roll of unexposed film," which covered Jazz Photo's activities of replacing the film in the used LFFP camera.[66] Jazz Photo's replacing the film roll, however, constituted only replacing parts "having a shorter life than is available from the combination as a whole,"[67] which was an activity that was similar to the "repair" of patented products deemed permissible under long-standing case law.[68] Thus, with respect to the '087 patent, Judge Newman concluded that Jazz Photo's replacement of the film was "characteristic of repair, not reconstruction,"[69] and therefore a permissible re-use of the LFFP camera.

With respect to Fuji's other product patents on the LFFP cameras, Judge Newman concluded that there was no replacement of parts covered by the patent claims, as these patents were directed to particular structural components of the cameras, such as the pushbutton for taking pictures.[70] Since these components were unaffected by Jazz Photo's replacement of the film rolls and similar reuse activities,[71] Judge Newman concluded: "If the claimed component is not replaced, but simply reused, this component is neither repaired nor reconstructed."[72] From the perspective of these other product patents, she characterized Jazz Photo's activities as "refurbishment,"[73] a legally neutral reuse of a patented product by a purchaser that falls within neither of the domains of repair or reconstruction.

Jazz Photo was not out of the infringement woods just yet, because Judge Newman's conclusions that its activities constituted permissible repair or refurbishment raised the further issue of whether Fuji imposed a license restriction prohibiting any reuse of the LFFP cameras. Such a restrictive

---

[65] Fuji also claimed that the defendants infringed its process patents, to which Judge Newman applied her exhaustion/repair and nonexhaustion conclusions, id. at 1108–09, but for ease of reference here, this chapter will refer to only the product patents.

[66] Id. at 1106–07.

[67] Id. at 1107.

[68] See id. at 1102–04 (discussing case law on permissible "repair" versus impermissible "reconstruction").

[69] Id. at 1107.

[70] Id. (discussing claim 1 of Patent No. 5,361,111).

[71] See supra note 64 (describing Jazz Photo's refurbishment activities on the LFFP cameras).

[72] Id.

[73] Id. at 1098 n.1.

covenant, if imposed on the first purchasers of the LFFP cameras, would legally prohibit what might otherwise be permissible activity, such as repair or refurbishment. In other words, Fuji may have retained some property interest in the initial conveyance, and thereby reserved the right to control post-sale uses of the cameras in downstream markets. If Fuji did not impose such restrictions, then it "exhausted" its right to control the reuse of the LFFP cameras.[74] If it did, then it could still prohibit Jazz Photo from engaging in its otherwise lawful activities of repair and refurbishment in reusing the LFFP cameras.[75]

Fuji argued, unsurprisingly, that it did impose such restrictions against reuse of the LFFP cameras in language that it printed on the covers of the LFFP cameras sold to consumers.[76] Judge Newman rejected these contentions, observing that the package "statements are instructions and warnings of risk, not mutual promises or a condition placed upon the sale."[77] Although Fuji intended the LFFP cameras to be only single-use cameras, it did not impose any license restrictions on the reuse or resale of the patented products that signaled this intent to purchasers of the LFFP cameras.[78]

It thus seemed that the Federal Circuit was going to conclude that Fuji exhausted its rights to control the reuse and resale of the LFFP cameras, regardless of whether such activities constituted repair or refurbishment. But Judge Newman then proceeded to distinguish between domestic and international sales of Fuji's patented products. By itself, this was not necessarily a problematic step in judicial decision making: Fuji raised the issue of exhaustion (or, more precisely, the lack thereof), and the underlying facts of the case indicated that some unrestricted sales occurred within the United States and some did not. Accordingly, the Federal Circuit could have used this case as an opportunity to address the nettling policy issues implicated in whether there should be an international patent exhaustion doctrine,

---

[74] Id. at 1105 ("The unrestricted sale of a patented article, by or with the authority of the patentee, 'exhausts' the patentee's right to control further sale and use of that article by enforcing the patent under which it was first sold").

[75] See, e.g., *Anton/Bauer, Inc. v. PAG, Ltd.*, 329 F.3d 1343, 1349 (Fed. Cir. 2003) (noting that the exhaustion doctrine is predicated solely on the "unrestricted sale of a patented article"); *Monsanto Co. v. Scruggs*, 342 F. Supp. 2d 584, 598–99 (N.D. Miss. 2004) (finding the exhaustion doctrine inapposite where the patentee "never made an unrestricted sale of its seed technology"); *Pioneer Hi-Bred Int'l, Inc. v. Ottawa Plant Food, Inc.*, 283 F. Supp. 2d 1018, 1032–34 (N.D. Iowa 2003) (finding the exhaustion doctrine inapposite due to express sale restrictions on the re-use of patented seeds).

[76] *Jazz Photo*, 264 F.3d at 1107.

[77] Id. at 1108.

[78] Id. at 1108.

such as arbitrage in international trade, the enforcement of TRIPS (trade-related aspects of intellectual property rights) and other international trade agreements, and the domestic enforcement of patent rights.

Unfortunately, it did not. In a single paragraph consisting of its first and only analysis of the issue of international patent exhaustion, Judge Newman concluded that patent exhaustion is limited to only domestic unrestricted sales of patented products. Although a bit long for recitation in this chapter, this paragraph bears quoting in full given its importance:

Fuji states that some of the imported LFFP cameras originated and were sold only overseas, but are included in the refurbished importations by some of the respondents. The record supports this statement, which does not appear to be disputed. United States patent rights are not exhausted by products of foreign provenance. To invoke the protection of the first sale doctrine, the authorized first sale must have occurred under the United States patent. See Boesch v. Graff, 133 U.S. 697, 701–03 (1890) (a lawful foreign purchase does not obviate the need for license from the United States patentee before importation into and sale in the United States). Our decision applies only to LFFPs for which the United States patent right has been exhausted by first sale in the United States. Imported LFFPs of solely foreign provenance are not immunized from infringement of United States patents by the nature of their refurbishment.

If there were any doubts as to the significance of this single paragraph, they were erased in 2005 when the Federal Circuit decided *Fuji Photo Film Co. v. Jazz Photo Corp.*,[79] affirming a district court's infringement decision against Jazz Photo on the basis of the imported LFFP cameras that originated from these unrestricted, albeit unexhausted, international sales.[80] Adding nothing additional, the *Fuji Photo* court simply reiterated and applied the holding of *Jazz Photo*: "The patentee's authorization of an international first sale does not affect exhaustion of that patentee's rights in the United States."[81] Significantly, one also learns in *Fuji Photo* that Judge Newman *sua sponte* addressed the issue of international patent exhaustion, as the issue "was not even raised by Fuji in the ITC or [before] the Federal Circuit" in the earlier *Jazz Photo* case.[82]

---

[79] 394 F.3d 1368 (Fed. Cir. 2005).

[80] Id. at 1376–77.

[81] Id. at 1376. Notably, Jazz Photo did raise the issue that "this court's explanation of the application of exhaustion to foreign sales decided a matter of first impression not clearly foreshadowed," which it used to argue that the holding should at least be given only prospective effect. Id. at 1077. The Federal Circuit refused to address Jazz Photo's argument on this issue, claiming that "Jazz in effect waived this argument by failing to raise it in a form that requested or required a decision from the district court." Id.

[82] Id. (quoting argument by Jazz Photo).

But what of the Supreme Court's 1890 decision in *Boesch v. Graff*, on which both *Jazz Photo* and *Fuji Film* were cited as supporting their conclusions that there is no international patent exhaustion? The *Boesch* case is not squarely on point with the patent exhaustion issue raised in *Jazz Photo*, and thus it is not a controlling precedent. The *Boesch* Court addressed the issue of whether a product purchased lawfully in Germany under a German patent permitted the purchaser to import and sell the product within the United States without permission of the U.S. patentee.[83] Unlike in *Jazz Photo*, the *Boesch* defendants argued that they were immune from liability because they had lawfully purchased the patented product in a foreign jurisdiction under the authority of a foreign patent.[84] The *Boesch* Court rejected this defense, concluding that "[t]he sale of articles in the United States under a United States patent cannot be controlled by foreign [patent] laws."[85]

In *Jazz Photo*, there was no question whether a foreign patent immunized Jazz Photo's activities. The only question in *Jazz Photo* was whether the unrestricted sale in a foreign jurisdiction by a U.S. patent owner exhausted its rights to enforce its U.S. patent rights. In fact, following *Boesch*, it was unclear whether there was an international patent exhaustion rule, and early-twentieth-century federal courts split over the issue with no definitive resolution.[86] Thus, *Boesch* was not determinative in *Jazz Photo*, as there were dispositive differences in the nature of the "lawful foreign purchase" at issue in the two cases.[87] Moreover, it was a long-standing controversy within American patent law whether there was a doctrine of international patent exhaustion.[88] Lastly, other U.S. intellectual property regimes, such

---

[83] *Boesch v. Graff*, 133 U.S. 697, 702 (1890).

[84] Id. at 701.

[85] Id. at 703.

[86] Compare *Curtiss Aeroplane & Motor Corp. v. United Aircraft Eng'g Corp.*, 266 F. 71 (2d Cir. 1920) (unrestricted foreign sale exhausted patentee's rights) with *Daimler Mfg. Co. v. Conklin*, 170 F. 70 (2d Cir. 1909) (unrestricted foreign sale did not exhaust patentee's rights).

[87] *Jazz Photo*, 264 F.3d at 1105 (quoting Judge Newman's inapt characterization of the *Boesch* holding).

[88] At about the same time that *Boesch* was decided, a federal appeals court noted that restrictions imposed by U.S. patentees on foreign wholesalers against importing patented articles into the U.S. "were customary." *Dickerson v. Matheson*, 57 F. 524, 526 (2d Cir. 1893). Such express restraints likely were customary because the law was long unsettled whether unrestricted conveyances abroad exhausted a patentee's right to enforce the exclusive right secured under the Patent Act within the United States. In the nineteenth century, the Supreme Court had ruled only that an unrestricted *domestic* sale exhausted a patentee's rights. See *Bloomer v. McQuewan*, 55 U.S. (14 How.) 539 (1852) (upholding domestic patent exhaustion rule).

as copyright, had already adopted an international exhaustion rule.[89] Given the lack of controlling precedent from the Supreme Court, the conflicting decisions in the federal appellate courts, and a definitive decision in favor of international exhaustion in copyright law, judicial decision-making norms would seem to have militated in favor of a court providing at least some analysis or explanation as to why it reached its decision on this novel issue in patent law. With two separate opportunities to do so over the span of four years – in *Jazz Photo* and in its follow-on decision in *Fuji Film* – the Federal Circuit chose otherwise.

In sum, the *Jazz Photo* Court *sua sponte* handed down a novel, substantive rule concerning the unrestricted sale of patented products by a patent owner in foreign jurisdictions – unrestricted sales in foreign jurisdictions did not exhaust a patent owner's rights under the U.S. patent. To emphasize again, the issue here is not whether *Jazz Photo* was correct or not in its decision; unfortunately, the Federal Circuit did not give any insight as to why it thought it ill-advised to adopt an international exhaustion rule in patent law, and thus we lack any basis within the four corners of the opinion in *Jazz Photo*, as well as within the subsequent opinion in *Fuji Film*, to assess the Federal Circuit's reasons for adopting this rule. It is for this reason that *Jazz Photo* serves as en exemplar of my thesis. It was the court's *methodological* approach to resolving a novel issue concerning the commercialization of patent rights for which it deserves special attention. It is in this respect that *Jazz Photo* provides insight into the potential indeterminacy of modern patent theory when it comes to the adjudication of patentees' commercialization rights.

B. *Jazz Photo* and a Fourth Model of Commercializing Patent Rights

As is clear from the prior section, *Jazz Photo* has added a fourth model for conceptualizing how a patentee may commercialize its property interests in the marketplace: A patentee may retain a reversionary interest following an outright unrestricted sale of patented product in the marketplace. Fuji Film, as the assignee for the patents on the LFFP cameras, manufactured and sold these patented products through outright, unrestricted commercial transactions. As such, in selling its patented property, Fuji chose the first commercialization model: It retained its title in the assigned patent and manufactured and sold its patented products (the LFFP cameras) in the

---

[89] See William W. Fisher III, *When Should We Permit Differential Pricing of Information?*, 55 UCLA L. Rev. 1, 16–17 (2007) (discussing international exhaustion of copyrights and the unsettled doctrine in patent law both before and after *Jazz Photo*).

marketplace. As the *Jazz Photo* Court recognized, Fuji imposed no words of limitation or express restrictions on purchasers of the LFFP cameras that signaled to the purchasers that they were acquiring anything less than the equivalent of a full-fee interest in their cameras.[90]

According to long-standing commercialization doctrine in patent law, Fuji conveyed its property interests outright, profiting from its patent only through each one-time sale of the products it lawfully produced and sold under its property right. As the Supreme Court recognized in the early twentieth century: "It is well settled . . . that where a patentee makes the patented article, and sells it, he can exercise no future control over what the purchaser may wish to do with the article after his purchase. It has passed beyond the scope of the patentee's rights."[91] Yet the Federal Circuit did not hold Fuji or its market participants to the terms of the commercialization doctrine under which Fuji profited by the sale of its property. Recognizing that Fuji did exhaust its rights in the LFFP cameras conveyed in domestic sales – applying the first commercialization model to Fuji's domestic sales – the Federal Circuit concluded that Fuji retained an exclusive property interest following the exact same unrestricted sales of the same cameras in foreign jurisdictions.

In sum, Fuji sold its fee interest outright in each patented LFFP camera, and the Federal Circuit permitted Fuji to revoke this fee interest, and thereby created *ex post* in Fuji a retained property interest in the form of a defeasible condition or a restrictive covenant. In other words, the Federal Circuit permitted an assignee that chose *ex ante* to profit from its property under the first commercialization model to then switch *ex post* to the third commercialization model. In so doing, the Federal Circuit created in *Jazz Photo* a fourth commercialization model – an amalgam of the first and third models in which a patentee initially sells its patented products outright and then later claims a retained property interest in the form of a defeasible condition or a restrictive covenant that permits it to sue a downstream owner for infringement.

It bears emphasizing again that this chapter's thesis is positive, not normative. Scholars might identify legitimate policy reasons for creating a fourth model of commercialization for intellectual property rights given the inherent differences between inventions and land. For instance, the differences in the legal provenance between these two types of property – land has long been secured in common-law decisions and inventions under federal

---

[90] *Jazz Photo*, 264 F.3d at 1108.
[91] *United States v. General Electric*, 272 U.S. 476, 489 (1927) (citing substantial nineteenth-century case law supporting this proposition).

statutes – suggest that there should be differences in their commercialization doctrines.[92] But such commentary misses the point, because judicial decision-making norms dictate that appellate courts should provide such analyses in explaining why they are crafting their legal rules. This is a particularly salient concern in the context of the commercialization models themselves, which have never been defined in the federal patent statutes, but rather are the result of common law decisions.[93] Yet, in *Jazz Photo* and again in *Fuji Film*, the Federal Circuit created a fourth commercialization model without any explanation as to why it was doing this. What accounts for this? An answer to this question is the purpose of the next section.

IV. Commercialization Doctrine in Patent Law:
Lessons for Modern Patent Theory

It is tempting to dismiss the adjudicatory approach in *Jazz Photo* as merely an outlier within a substantial sea of modern case law that hews closely to the three models for commercializing one's property interests. This is an understandable reaction to *Jazz Photo* because the commercialization of patented property remains firmly grounded in both the modern patent statutes and case law. The 1952 Patent Act re-codified the provisions in the earlier patent statutes that secured a patentee's right to convey its rights to third parties.[94] Moreover, the Federal Circuit and other federal courts ostensibly follow the historical case law that created the three commercialization models.

In 1992, the Federal Circuit announced its commitment to the commercialization patent doctrines reaching back two centuries in its famous decision in *Mallinckrodt, Inc. v. Medipart, Inc.*[95] There, the Federal Circuit declared "[t]hat a restrictive license is legal seems clear,"[96] quoting the Supreme Court's 1939 decision in *General Talking Pictures Corporation. v. Western Electric Company.*[97] For its part, the *General Talking Pictures* Court was simply restating the basic thrust of classic nineteenth-century commercialization jurisprudence.[98] In fact, a federal appeals court in 1939 succinctly

[92] Cf. *AT&T v. Microsoft Corp. v. AT&T Corp.*, 550 U.S. 437, 441 (2007) ("It is the general rule under United States patent law that no infringement occurs when a patented product is made and sold in another country").

[93] See supra Part II.

[94] See 35 U.S.C. § 261(b) ("the applicant, patentee, or his assigns or legal representatives may . . . grant and convey an exclusive right under his application for patent, or patents, to the whole or any specified part of the United States").

[95] 976 F.2d 700 (1992).

[96] Id. at 704 (quoting *General Talking Pictures Corp. v. Western Elect. Co.*, 305 U.S. 124, 127 (1939)).

[97] 305 U.S. 124, 127 (1939).

[98] Id. at 127 (citing *Mitchell v. Hawley*, 83 U.S. 544 (1872)).

summarized the status of commercialization doctrine in patent law: "In general, a patentee may grant licenses to whom he wants, and restrict the license as to time, territory, and purpose."[99] Fifty years later, another federal court again nicely captured the essence of the three models for commercializing property rights in inventions, noting that the "unilateral right to license, exclusively or otherwise, or to refuse to license at all, reflects the essence of the statutory patent monopoly."[100]

In this context, *Jazz Photo* seems uncontroversial. At worst, it is simply wrong. At best, the Federal Circuit simply made a mistake in failing to enunciate in this one case the policy reasons for its decision and thereby made it appear as if it is incorrectly creating a novel, fourth commercialization model.

As a preliminary matter, such a dismissal of *Jazz Photo* is too hasty, as the Federal Circuit has made it clear that it does not believe that *Jazz Photo* is an outlier. Judge Newman's opinion was joined by the other two judges on the panel, Judges Michel and Gajarsa. Moreover, *Fuji Film* reaffirmed *Jazz Photo*'s holding concerning international patent exhaustion with another unanimous panel (Judges Rader, Clevenger, and Linn). Thus, at least six judges on the Federal Circuit, representing 50 percent of the total sitting judges on the court, support *Jazz Photo*'s secondary holding that there is no patent exhaustion following the unrestricted international sale of patented products.

Beyond such institutional analysis, there are better reasons for highlighting *Jazz Photo* as an exemplar of a formalist methodology within patent law that is creating indeterminacy in the commercialization of patents in the marketplace. As noted earlier, the Federal Circuit *sua sponte* addressed the issue of international patent exhaustion in *Jazz Photo* as a matter of first impression.[101] In such a case, the court returns to first principles to properly frame the novel issue and to situate it within the relevant positive and normative framework. It is with respect to this methodological approach that *Jazz Photo* is important for what it potentially reveals about modern patent theory.

As a result of Judge Newman's decision in *Jazz Photo*, "the Federal Circuit adopted a *clear rule* of territorial exhaustion."[102] Given that this was a matter of first impression, despite *Jazz Photo*'s inaccurate allusion

---

[99] *American Lecithin Co. v. Warfield Co.*, 105 F.2d 207, 212 (7th Cir. 1939) (citations omitted).

[100] *United States v. Telectronics Proprietary, Ltd.*, 607 F. Supp. 753 (D. Colo. 1983).

[101] See supra notes 82–88 and accompanying text.

[102] Daniel Erlikhman, Note, *Jazz Photo and the Doctrine of Patent Exhaustion: Implications to TRIPS and International Harmonization of Patent Protection*, 25 Hastings Comm. & Ent L.J. 307, 313 (2003) (emphasis added).

to *Boesch* as controlling precedent, why was the Federal Circuit so interested in adopting a clear rule on international patent exhaustion? Notably, this was not the first time the Federal Circuit chose to adopt a "clear rule" in patent jurisprudence that lacked either support in prior precedent or, worse, effectively overruled long-standing case law.[103] Nor was it the last.[104] As one commentator recently remarked: "The Federal Circuit increasingly has articulated rules of law to promote certainty, at the expense of fairness."[105] Why is the Federal Circuit doing this?

Lawyers and commentators proffer several reasons for the Federal Circuit's positive commitment to clear rules (and its attendant normative commitment to certainty). One explanation is that the Federal Circuit has experienced a patent-specific version of agency capture, although in this case it is a specialized patent court that has been captured by the special interests of the patent bar favoring strong patent rights.[106] Another suggestion is that the Federal Circuit is aggrandizing its power as the sole appeals court hearing patent law appeals.[107] Such explanations, however, unnecessarily

---

[103] See *Festo Corp. v. Shoketsu Kinzoku Kogyo Kabushiki Co.*, 535 U.S. 722, 738 (2002) (rejecting the Federal Circuit's "absolute bar" rule for prosecution history estoppel as incompatible with the equitable nature of the doctrine); *Warner-Jenkinson Co. v. Hilton Davis Chemical Co.*, 520 U.S. 17, 26 n.3 (1997) (rejecting de facto repudiation of the doctrine of equivalents by the Federal Circuit given concerns about certainty in claim construction and infringement actions).

[104] See *IpVenture, Inc. v. Prostar Computer Inc.*, 503 F.3d 1324 (Fed. Cir. 2007) (refusing to apply California contract law in construing an employee-assignment agreement, and instead applying its own judicially created rule of requiring "hereby . . . grant/assign" as a formal legal requirement for contractually assigning patent rights). The Federal Circuit's formalism in contract cases is nothing new. See Christopher M. Kaiser, Note, *Take It or Leave It:* Monsanto v. McFarling, Bowers v. Baystate Technologies, *and the Federal Circuit's Formalistic Approach to Contracts of Adhesion*, 80 Chi.-Kent L. Rev. 487 (2005) (surveying and critiquing the Federal Circuit's formalistic approach in contract cases, which is justified as providing greater predictability and certainty).

[105] Timothy R. Holbrook, *The Supreme Court's Complicity in Federal Circuit Formalism*, 20 Santa Clara Computer & High Tech. L.J. 1, 1 (2003); see also Arti K. Rai, *Engaging Facts and Policy: A Multi-Institutional Approach to Patent System Reform*, 103 Colum. L. Rev. 1035, 1040 (2003) ("[T]he Federal Circuit has substituted formalist decisionmaking for the fact-specific, policy-oriented analysis that is required by the open-ended language of the patent statute").

[106] See John R. Thomas, *Formalism at the Federal Circuit*, 52 Am. U. L. Rev. 771, 792–94 (2003) (discussing how the Federal Circuit's "jurisprudence increasingly reflects a trend towards adjudicative rule formalism," which is explained in part as a response to the "lawyers [who] draft the exclusionary rules that are patent claims").

[107] See Holbrook, supra note 105, at 5 ("The Federal Circuit has promoted an agenda favoring the creation of bright-line legal rules which arguably aggrandize power at the appellate level and which create unfairness to various parties for the sake of certainty in the law."); Rai, supra note 105, at 1057–164 (claiming that the Federal Circuit has engaged in "arrogation" in creating bright-line legal rules requiring de novo review of all aspects of lower court

impugn the motives of federal judges, interposing into doctrinal and policy analysis the difficult task of inferring bad subjective states of mind.

An additional explanation may provide a less personal assessment of what is happening in *Jazz Photo* and in other cases in which the Federal Circuit has shown a proclivity for "clear rules" (and for the policy of certainty). One contributing factor that no one has assessed is the role that modern patent theory may be playing in the formalistic jurisprudence of the Federal Circuit. More specifically, the positive account of patents as securing only a right to exclude may be a basic underlying factor in the formalistic decision making represented by *Jazz Photo*, as the conceptual framework adopted by a court constrains what it sees as the appropriate doctrinal inputs in deciding a particular case.

At first blush, this may sound strange, because the Federal Circuit ostensibly follows the long-standing judicial protection of patentees' commercialization rights.[108] However, the Federal Circuit's foundational commercialization decision in 1992 in *Mallinckrodt* reflects an important conceptual shift between the historical and modern case law. In place of the nineteenth-century courts' reliance on real property doctrines and the protection of the rights of use and disposition, the Federal Circuit has reconceptualized the commercialization models solely in terms of the right to exclude: "The enforceability of restrictions on the use of patented goods derives from the patent grant, which is in classical terms of property: the right to exclude. This right to exclude may be waived in whole or in part."[109] This reconceptualization of the commercialization doctrines went unnoticed among patent lawyers and scholars, as it conforms to the accepted definition of patents today as securing only a negative right to exclude.[110] However, *Mallinckrodt*'s change in the positive definition of the legal right secured by the commercialization doctrines, while seemingly insignificant, was in fact of great import.

The Federal Circuit's positive redefinition of the legal rights secured by the three commercialization models shifted the doctrinal focus to a singular focus on the right to exclude. This is important insofar as the right to exclude is a purely formal, negative right that admits no conditional doctrinal applications in a case-by-case basis. Thus, for instance, trespass is the doctrine

decisions); see also *Phillips v. AWH Corp.*, 415 F.3d 1303, 1330 (Fed. Cir. 2005) (en banc) (Mayer, J., dissenting) (accusing the Federal Circuit of having "focused inappropriate power in this court" resulting from a "quest to elevate our own importance").

[108] See supra notes 61, 96–97, and accompanying text.
[109] *Mallinckrodt, Inc.*, 976 F.2d at 703 (citation omitted).
[110] See supra note 21–23.

enforcing the right to exclude in land, and trespass is a highly formalistic legal doctrine that provides absolute certainty in all cases as to whether one's property interest in a parcel of land has been breached.[111] Today, patents are defined as securing only a right to exclude, and, unsurprisingly, patent infringement is often analogized to trespass.[112] Patent claims are similarly analogized to the metes and bounds of real property – the bright-line physical boundary whose breach triggers absolute liability for trespass.[113] Thus, it is little surprise that the Federal Circuit talks often of the need for legal rules in patent law that provide certainty to patentees and the public,[114] as do patent scholars as well.[115]

This then provides a possible insight into how *Jazz Photo* came to its novel result in creating a fourth commercialization model never before seen

---

[111] Cf. *Loretto v. Teleprompter Manhattan CATV Corp.*, 458 U.S. 419, 436 (1982) (justifying a categorical rule that a breach of the right to exclude by a "permanent physical occupation of property" is a compensable taking on the ground that it "avoids otherwise difficult line-drawing problems").

[112] See *King Instruments Corp. v. Pergo*, 65 F.3d 941, 947 (Fed. Cir. 1995) ("An act of infringement . . . trespasses on [a patentee's] right to exclude"); *Markman v. Westview Instruments, Inc.*, 52 F.3d 967, 997 (Fed. Cir. 1995) (Mayer, J., concurring) (noting that "a patent may be thought of as a form of deed which sets out the metes and bounds of the property the inventor owns for the term and puts the world on notice to avoid trespass"); Frank H. Easterbrook, *Intellectual Property is Still Property*, 13 Harv. J. L. & Pub. Pol'y 108, 109 (1990) ("Patents give a right to exclude, just as the law of trespass does with real property").

[113] See Robert P. Merges & John F. Duffy, Patent Law and Policy 25 (3d ed. 2002) (noting that "innumerable cases analogize claims to the 'metes and bounds' of a real property deed").

[114] See, e.g., *Phillips v. AWH Corp.*, 415 F.3d 1303, 1323 (Fed. Cir. 2005) (en banc) (recognizing the need for "reasonable certainty and predictability" in claim construction rules); *Festo Corp. v. Shoketsu Kinzoku Kogyo Kabushiki Co.*, 234 F.3d 558, 578 (Fed. Cir. 2000) (en banc) (justifying adoption of absolute rule in prosecution history estoppel given the "certainty and predictability such a bar produces"), vacated 535 U.S. 722 (2002); *Cyber Corp. v. FAS Tech., Inc.*, 138 F.3d 1448, 1475 (1998) (justifying treating claim construction as a matter of law given the "early certainty about the meaning of a patent claim"); *Litton Sys., Inv. v. Honeywell, Inc.*, 87 F.3d 1559, 1580 (Fed. Cir 1996) (Bryson, J., concurring in part and dissenting in part) ("Patent counselors should be able to advise their clients. . . . The consequences of advice that turns out to be incorrect can be devastating, and the costs of uncertainty – unjustified caution or the devotion of vast resources to the sterile enterprise of litigation – can be similarly destructive").

[115] See, e.g., Michael J. Meurer & James E. Bessen, Patent Failure: How Judges, Bureaucrats, and Lawyers Put Innovators at Risk 46–72 (2008) (discussing fundamental function of certainty in property regimes, including the patent system); Michael J. Meurer & Craig A. Nard, *Patent Policy Adrift in a Sea of Anecdote: A Reply to Lichtman*, 93 Geo. L.J. 2033, 2035 (2005) (noting "the standard view in law and economics that fuzzy property rights frustrate investment decisions and impede transactions"); Joseph Scott Miller, *Enhancing Patent Disclosure for Faithful Claim Construction*, 9 Lewis & Clark L. Rev. 177, 195 (2005) ("Both due process norms and the economic analysis of property law support the view that claim scope should be predictable").

in more than 200 years of patent doctrine securing patent owner's rights in the marketplace. When the Federal Circuit returns to its first principles to address a novel issue in patent law, the positive framework within which it considers the issue is one that orients the court toward the necessity for bright-line, formalistic, absolute doctrinal rules to secure the singular right secured in a patent – the right to exclude. *Mallinckrodt* reveals that the court considers even commercialization issues through the prism of the right to exclude.[116] Accordingly, *Jazz Photo* employed a formalistic approach to crafting a new legal rule for a novel situation dealing with an assignee's unrestricted sales of its patented products in foreign jurisdiction. The result was a single paragraph creating a new bright-line rule – no exhaustion – and similarly perfunctory consideration of the issue when the court returned back to the same issue four years later in *Fuji Film.*

Of course, we do not know with absolute certainty why Judge Newman *sua sponte* crafted the secondary holding in *Jazz Photo* on international patent exhaustion, because she did not explain her reasons. She did not even cite any of the Federal Circuit's own case law on patent exhaustion, such as *Mallinckrodt.* And that is exactly the point of this chapter: Modern patent theory makes such formalistic decision making seem appropriate, because the positive theory defines patents in terms of the purely formal right to exclude. If trespass of real property is the well-accepted analogy for framing patent infringement, and trespass is understood today to be a property-rule regime par excellence,[117] then the Federal Circuit will frame its decision-making processes in novel cases in which it is unconstrained by controlling precedent in terms of formal legal rules securing the similarly formal right to exclude. Thus, any conclusion that secures this right to exclude with absolute formal certainty is in conformity with the basic positive structure of the patent system, at least according to the patent theory guiding the Federal Circuit today.

For this reason, the substantive policy analyses of *Jazz Photo* – defending or criticizing its decision on international patent exhaustion[118] – miss a more fundamental conceptual point. (Of course, they miss it because they share the basic positive premise with the Federal Circuit that patents secure only a right to exclude.[119]) These scholarly exegeses elide the all-important methodological question: Why would Judge Newman and five other judges

---

[116] See supra note 101 and accompanying text.
[117] Singer, supra note 45, at 27–28 (describing the objective rule-like features of a trespass action and its remedies).
[118] See supra notes 21–23 and accompanying text.
[119] See supra note 10 and accompanying text.

on the Federal Circuit consider a one-paragraph discussion of a novel and contested issue to be a valid exercise of judicial decision making?

This chapter maintains that Judge Newman's opinion in *Jazz Photo* is an exemplar of fundamental formalism in modern patent theory, which has infected commercialization doctrine with indeterminacy. To be clear, the point is not that *Jazz Photo* is substantively right or wrong, but rather that the methodology of modern patent theory, derived from defining patents as securing only a right to exclude, orients judges toward handing down bright-line rules whose sole justification is absolute certainty in the enforcement of this exclusive right. Moreover, the point is not that every commercialization case is going to be infected with the same excessively formalistic methodology adopted in *Jazz Photo*. In cases in which prior case law is squarely on point, such as with single-use restrictions, courts are constrained by black-letter doctrine and will reach the same result as dictated by one of the earlier three commercialization models.[120] In this respect, the nature of international patent exhaustion as an issue of first impression in *Jazz Photo* was important, as novel cases are the most illustrative examples of how the positive conceptual content of a legal entitlement can impose subtle blinders on judges, leading them to results they see as absolutely necessary, but only because they have created for themselves a myopic doctrinal perspective.

Lastly, it bears emphasizing that there is nothing intrinsic in modern patent theory that requires it to be indeterminate in commercialization cases. There are at least two possible ways that modern patent theory could resolve this indeterminacy on its own terms. First, since the right to exclude does not contain its own positive limits defining how it might be deployed in particular cases – beyond tilting judges toward adopting absolute, bright-line, formalistic rules – the indeterminacy may be resolved by developing an exogenous normative theory to guide the enforcement and limitation of the right to exclude in particular commercialization cases. (This is no less true for enforcing the right to exclude in land than it is for patents.)[121]

Unlike most areas of law, patent law seems uniquely situated to adopt this particular solution, as there is broad normative agreement within modern

---

[120] See, e.g., *Monsanto Co. v. Parr*, 545 F. Supp. 2d 836 (N.D. Ind. 2008) (finding the defendant liable for inducing infringement in cleaning patented seeds for reuse, which violated a single-use restriction imposed on the farmer in the first-sale of the patented seeds).

[121] Compare *State v. Shack*, 277 A.2d 369, 372 (N.J. 1971) (refusing to enforce the right to exclude given the complex web of social relations defining the "human values" by which the right to exclude is "limited") with *Jacque v. Steenberg Homes, Inc.*, 563 N.W.2d 154, 160 (Wis. 1997) (enforcing "a strong interest in excluding trespassers" even if damage is nominal given the need to protect the "integrity of the legal system" and to preclude "resort to 'self-help' remedies").

patent theory: Patents are justified according to economic theory.[122] Modern patent theory thus presents lawyers and judges today with a unified descriptive and policy framework for the American patent system: A patent comprises only the right to exclude, and economic analysis is the means by which courts and scholars evaluate how this right to exclude should function to "promote the Progress of. . . useful Arts."[123] Of course, the devil is in the details, and patent scholars strongly diverge over the appropriate metrics for assessing the economic goals of the patent system.[124]

Commercialization is one of the many examples of this policy divergence in patent law. As observed in the Introduction, it is unsurprising that most patent scholars today translate Lincoln's commercialization justification for patents into the reward policy, because the commercialization of patent rights is a highly controversial subject within the economic analysis of patents.[125] In fact, the role of commercialization within patent law proper is one of the principal points of divergence among scholars today.[126] Unfortunately, commercialization theory lacks widespread support within patent scholarship, and the dominant reward theory simply discounts commercialization as the necessary evil by which the patent system incentivizes inventive activity: It is the dangling carrot by which self-interested inventors are forced to disclose their inventions and thereby expand the public domain.[127] Moreover, even amongst those scholars who believe that

---

[122] See, e.g., Dan L. Burk & Mark A. Lemley, *Patent Policy Levers*, 89 Va. L. Rev. 1575, 1597 (2003) (recognizing that "courts and commentators widely agree that the basic purpose of patent law is utilitarian"); F. Scott Kieff, *Property Rights and Property Rules for Commercializing Inventions*, 85 Minn. L. Rev. 697, 697 (2001) ("The foundation for the American patent system is purely economic").

[123] U.S. Const. art. I, § 8.

[124] See Burk & Lemley, supra note 122, at 1597–1599 (observing that "[a]greement on basic utilitarian goals has not, however, translated into agreement on how to implement them").

[125] Compare Mark A. Lemley, *Ex Ante Versus Ex Post Justifications for Intellectual Property*, 71 U. Chi. L. Rev. 129 (2004) (criticizing commercialization theory in favor of reward theory) with F. Scott Kieff, *Property Rights and Property Rules for Commercializing Inventions*, 85 Minn. L. Rev. 697 (2001) (advocating commercialization theory).

[126] See, e.g., Mark F. Grady & Jay I. Alexander, *Patent Law and Rent Dissipation*, 78 Va. L. Rev. 305, 310 (1992) ("Two economic theories dominate the study of patent law: the more traditional reward theory, and the newer prospect theory as developed by Edmund Kitch").

[127] See *J.E.M. Ag. Supply, Inc. v. Pioneer Hi-Bred Int'l*, 534 U.S. 124, 142 (2001) ("The disclosure required by the Patent Act is the quid pro quo of the right to exclude"); Rebecca S. Eisenberg, *Patents and the Progress of Science: Exclusive Rights and Experimental Use*, 56 U. Chi. L. Rev. 1017, 1037 (1989) (explaining that the reward theory "assume[s] that the patent monopoly has already served its social function of promoting invention and disclosure as soon as the patent issues, and that enforcement of the patent thereafter is simply the regrettable price that society must pay in order to live up to its end of the bargain"); Paul J. Heald, *A Transaction Costs Theory of Patent Law*, 66 Ohio

commercialization is central to the incentive structure of the patent system, many shunt commercialization issues to legal doctrines external to patent law,[128] and disagreement remains as to the relevant metrics to be used in particular cases.[129]

Interestingly, the Federal Circuit ignores the current scholarly debates over economic policy.[130] Perhaps the court does not wish to wade into disputed theoretical territory, but this is largely irrelevant when it comes to its decisions, because it still embraces the positive definition of patents as securing only a right to exclude. Accordingly, the court repeatedly defaults in its decision making to the core positive right – the right to exclude – and the basic policy inherent in the enforcement of this formal right – certainty. The result is indeterminacy in the commercialization cases in which the right to exclude does not necessarily fit conceptually within the three classic commercialization models that inform the pre-existing doctrine, such as when the *Jazz Photo* court apparently decided that a clear rule providing certainty was preferable in the enforcement of the right to exclude in a novel exhaustion case. Nonetheless, if courts and scholars could coalesce around a single normative framework to guide the adjudication of the right to exclude when used positively in the commercialization of a patented invention, this would provide greater determinacy in the legal protection of patented innovation today.

A second way to resolve this indeterminacy is to develop commercialization doctrine within a conceptual framework that builds into the doctrine its own positive default presumption (as well as its own normative justification). But this would only be reinventing the wheel, because this is

---

Sᴛ. L. J. 473, 506 (2005) ("The traditional normative defense of patent law asserts that the public benefits of increased inventiveness, innovation, and disclosure of information offset the monopoly costs imposed by holders of exclusive rights."); cf. Mark A. Lemley, *Should Patent Infringement Requirement Proof of Copying*, 105 Mɪᴄʜ. L. Rᴇᴠ. 1525, 1530 (2007) (noting that from the perspective of the reward theory, "IP is a necessary evil").

[128] See, e.g., F. Scott Kieff & Troy A. Paredes, *The Basics Matter: At The Periphery of Intellectual Property Law*, 73 Gᴇᴏ. Wᴀsʜ. L. Rᴇᴠ. 174, 198 (2004) ("[I]t is inappropriate to suggest that some uses of a patent are not within its scope, since patents only give a right to exclude. The right to use is derived from sources external to IP law.").

[129] Compare Kieff, supra note 122 (transaction costs) with Henry E. Smith, *Intellectual Property as Property: Delineating Entitlements in Information*, 116 Yᴀʟᴇ L.J. 1742 (2007) (information costs).

[130] See Craig Allen Nard, *Toward a Cautious Approach to Obeisance: The Role of Scholarship in Federal Circuit Patent Law Jurisprudence*, 39 Hᴏᴜs. L. Rᴇᴠ. 667, 673–74 (2002) (observing that modern "empirical and economic scholarship . . . with a few notable exceptions, has largely been absent from the patent opinions of the Federal Circuit").

exactly what was achieved with the three commercialization models.[131] In developing these three models, historical patent case law incorporated from real property the same legal security in the "exclusive use" of one's property interests in the marketplace. In this way, historical patent doctrines can teach modern patent theory about how sound doctrine can be fashioned in a way that effectively secures patent owners' rights, especially their all-important right to secure the fruits of their inventive labors by profiting from the use or disposition of their property in the marketplace.

The commercialization doctrines in patent law – which are now collectively referred to as "patent exhaustion" doctrine – functioned so well for so long because they secured to patentees their property rights based on a broader conception of property as securing the exclusive rights to use and dispose of one's possessions.[132] Thus, both Lincoln's emphasis on "exclusive use" as the primary right that incentivized inventors to become patentees[133] and the hoary statutes and court decisions' emphasis on the "substantive rights" gave to patentees the "right to manufacture, the right to sell, and the right to use."[134] In nineteenth-century commercialization cases, patentees exercised the classic property rights of use and disposition, or what all pre-1952 patent statutes referred to as "the exclusive right to make, use, and vend the said invention or discovery."[135] It was on the basis of this

---

[131] The existence and validity of a normative principle internalized within doctrine to guide its adjudication is beyond the scope of this chapter, which addresses only the existence of the positive doctrine and its background conceptual framework (i.e., the four models of commercialization). Nonetheless, it bears noting that the original three commercialization models did build into the resulting commercialization doctrine a normative presumption that guided the courts in justifying their creation of the licensing rules: The courts employed a normative default presumption of maximum liberty in the use of one's property, which disaggregated decision making concerning the uses of property to the entitlement-owners, as owners are in the best position to know how to dispose of new inventions as commercial innovation. See *E. Bement & Sons v. Nat'l Harrow Co.*, 186 U.S. 70, 91 (1902) (observing that "the general rule is absolute freedom in the use or sale of rights under the patent laws of the United States"). For a further discussion of this normative principle and the need to create a private-ordering default rule for commercialization of unpredictable innovation, see Adam Mossoff, *A Simple Conveyance Rule for Complex Innovation*, 44 Tulsa L. Rev. 707).

[132] See, e.g., *McKeon v. Bisbee*, 9 Cal. 137, 143 (1858) ("Property is the exclusive right of possessing, enjoying, and disposing of a thing"); *Wynehamer v. People*, 13 N.Y. 378, 433 (1856) ("Property is the right of any person to possess, use, enjoy, and dispose of a thing."); William Blackstone, 1 Commentaries 138 ("The third absolute right . . . is that of property: which consists in the free use, enjoyment, and disposal of all his acquisitions. . . . ").

[133] Lincoln, supra note 1, at 363.

[134] *Adams v. Burke*, 84 U.S. 453, 456 (1873).

[135] Patent Act of 1870, ch. 230, § 22, 16 Stat. 198, 201 (repealed 1952); see also Patent Act of 1836, ch. 357, § 11, 5 Stat. 117, 121 (repealed 1870) (providing that "every patent shall

conceptual similarity between the legal interests secured in both land and patents that nineteenth-century courts were able to incorporate into patent law the commercialization doctrines already securing to landowners the free use and alienation of their property interests.[136]

The resulting commercialization case law in patent jurisprudence reflected an internal positive limit that courts took from real property doctrine and expressly designed into the patent system: "[T]he general rule is absolute freedom in the use or sale of rights under the patent laws of the United States,"[137] but this freedom must be exercised in the form of express restrictions provided in recorded instruments that gave notice to purchasers and their heirs, successors, or assigns.[138] If a landowner wishes to grant a license, an easement, a fee simple defeasible, or a fee simple with restrictive covenants, the grantor has to do so explicitly. Otherwise, the grantee may reasonably conclude that it is acquiring the unfettered exclusive rights to use and dispose of its newly acquired possession, and courts enforced such conveyances as creating a fee simple interest in the grantee.

On the basis of the same definition of patents as property, nineteenth-century courts designed into the patent system the exact same doctrinal requirements they used in defining the same rights in land:

[T]he general rule is that if a patentee made a structure embodying his invention, and unconditionally make a sale of it, the buyer acquires the right to use the machine without restrictions, and, when such machine is lawfully made and unconditionally sold, no restriction upon its use will be implied in favor of the patentee.[139]

Patentees knew that if they wished to convey anything less than "complete title" in a patented product – if they wished to adopt anything other than the first model of commercialization – then they had to impose express

---

be assignable in law" and that this "conveyance of the exclusive right under any patent, to make and use, and to grant to others to make and use, the thing patented" must be recorded in the Patent Office); Patent Act of 1793, ch. 11, § 1, 1 Stat. 318, 321 (repealed 1836) (providing that a patent secures "the full and exclusive right and liberty of making, constructing, using, and vending to others to be used, the said invention or discovery"); Patent Act of 1790, ch. 7, § 1, 1 Stat. 109, 110 (repealed 1793) (providing that a patent secures "the sole and exclusive right and liberty of making, constructing, using and vending to others to be used, the said invention or discovery")

[136] See generally Mossoff, supra note 11, at 347–360.

[137] E. Bement & Sons v. Nat'l Harrow Co., 186 U.S. 70, 91 (1902).

[138] See supra notes 55–56 and accompanying text.

[139] Heaton-Peninsular Button-Fastener Co. v. Eureka Specialty Co., 77 F. 288, 290 (6th Cir. 1896) (emphases added). See also Mitchell v. Hawley, 83 U.S. 544, 548 (1872) ("Complete title to the implement or machine purchased becomes vested in the vendee by the sale and purchase, . . . [and] when it rightfully passes from the patentee to the purchaser, [it] ceases to be within the limits of the monopoly).

restrictions in the license or sale.[140] In other words, as a positive matter, they had to impose defeasible conditions or restrictive covenants that reflected the second and third of our commercialization models. More important, the market participants who engaged in commercial transactions with patentees knew that an "unrestricted purchase and sale" of a "patented article" meant that they owned the product as "an ordinary article of commerce."[141]

In this respect, modern patent theory can learn important lessons from sound doctrine that was crafted by courts in a time when commercialization was viewed as central to the proper functioning of a patent system, but on very different positive grounds than today. This does not mean that the modern definition of patents as securing only the right to exclude is invalid, although this positive account of patents is rooted in a widespread misunderstanding of the nature of use rights in property.[142] This definition is nonetheless firmly set in the modern statutes and patent practice, and thus this topic is far beyond the limited scope of this chapter. For purposes of our analysis here, it is enough to realize that the American patent system once fostered a fundamental commercialization policy that was given life through judicially created doctrines that secured to patentees and their assignees their rights of use and disposition in the marketplace.

V. Conclusion

In seeking to rediscover commercialization as a fundamental policy of the American patent system, scholars and judges might learn how such a policy first animated patent doctrines under the first four iterations of the patent statutes in 1790, 1793, 1836, and 1870. In this earlier era, Congress and the courts deemed the commercialization of patents to be fundamental to the functioning of the patent system. The reason was that, in Lincoln's words, the "exclusive use" of patents in the marketplace was what "added the fuel of interest to the fire of genius."[143]

Within the theoretical constraints set by modern patent theory, scholars and judges miss this important insight, because this is viewed today as a historically anachronistic definition of patents. Patents do not secure

---

[140] *Mitchell v. Hawley*, 83 U.S. 544, 548 (1872) ("Complete title to the implement or machine purchased becomes vested in the vendee by the sale and purchase, ... [and] when it rightfully passes from the patentee to the purchaser, [it] ceases to be within the limits of the monopoly.").

[141] *American Cotton Tie Supply Co. v. Bullard*, 1 F. Cas. 625, 628 (C.C.N.Y. 1879) (No. 294).

[142] See Adam Mossoff, Patents as Property: Rethinking the Exclusive Right(s) in Patent Law (unpublished manuscript 2008)

[143] Lincoln, supra note 1, at 363.

exclusive rights of use and disposition; patents secure only the right to exclude. Regardless of whether this positive definition of patents is correct, it subtly tilts Federal Circuit jurisprudence toward a rarefied formalism within patent law that has produced a proclivity for bright-line rules justified by a policy concern of certainty. Of course, rule-based regimes and the concerns about certainty have their place – most notably within trespass and infringement doctrines – but they lack conceptual fit when it comes to commercialization doctrines, which are conditional and case-sensitive. The result, as typified by decisions like *Jazz Photo*, is indeterminacy in commercialization doctrines, in which the Federal Circuit adopts absolute bright-line rules enforcing the right to exclude.

Of course, modern patent theory, such as the reward and commercialization theories, is capable of incorporating the normative consequences of commercialization rights. The important point here is that the right to exclude has conceptually blinded the first forays into the economic analysis of patents by excluding as a positive matter the core commercialization rights – the rights of use and disposition – from the evaluation of the functioning policies in the patent system. Unsurprisingly, this is not a problem that is unique to patent law, as Professors Thomas Merrill and Henry Smith have similarly critiqued the modern economic analysis of property as having "blinded itself to certain features of property regimes – features that are important and cannot be accounted for on any other terms."[144] Historical patent doctrine points the way to rediscovering the fundamental commercialization policy within patent law, and in rethinking whether modern patent theory provides the best positive theoretical account for this policy today.

---

[144] Thomas W. Merrill & Henry E. Smith, *What Happened to Property in Law and Economics?*, 111 Yale L.J. 357, 398 (2001).

13

The Modularity of Patent Law

Henry E. Smith

Introduction

At the core of controversies over the correct scope of intellectual property lie grave doubts about whether intellectual property *is* property. Property covers a broad range of resources, from solid objects like land and cars, to fugitive resources like water, to intangibles like debts. But, as a resource, information is different from all of these. From the consumer point of view, information is nonrival; one person's enjoyment of the plot of *Hamlet* does not diminish another's (if anything, the opposite), and preventing people from using information – excluding them – is difficult.[1] Although information itself is a public good and, once known, would be consumed at zero marginal cost, discovering and making information useful requires inputs that *are* rival and are susceptible to efforts to exclude. Edison's labor in testing filaments for the light bulb (not to mention his lab equipment and working space) were as rival and excludible as shrimp salads or Blackacre

---

[1] If access to information has snob appeal on the consumer side, or affords some advantage on the producer side, it is rival in that sense. In this chapter I will be assuming the rivalness of information to show that exclusive rights can make sense even with a strong form of nonrivalness of information.

A longer version of parts of this chapter was published as Henry E. Smith, *Intellectual Property as Property: Delineating Entitlements in Information*, 116 YALE L.J. 1742 (2007). I would like to thank Barry Adler, Oren Bar-Gill, Bob Ellickson, Lee Fennell, James Grimmelmann, Bruce Johnsen, Scott Kieff, Tom Merrill, Eric Rasmusen, Carol Rose, Joe Sommer, Lior Strahilevitz, Katrina Wyman, Todd Zywicki, and the participants in workshops at Boston University, Fordham University, George Mason University, Harvard University, New York University, and the University of Virginia law schools, at the Korean Intellectual Property Association, the 2003 American Law and Economics Annual Meeting, and at the Conference on Commercializing Innovation at Washington University in St. Louis School of Law for helpful comments. I would also like to thank the Microsoft Corporation for its generous financial support. All errors are attributable to my inputs.

(the classic examples).[2] On various theories, patent rights are said to give incentives to invent, develop, and commercialize information such as the light bulb.[3] Other intellectual property rights regimes, such as copyright, focus more on creation, and yet others, like trademark, are concerned more with commercialization rather than creation. Yet all of these regimes reflect a concern that in their absence people will have too little incentive to engage in one or more activities with respect to information – from discovering it, to commercializing it, to using it to lower consumer search costs.

Intellectual property rights are conventionally said to solve an incentive problem – to create, to commercialize – but not an allocation problem. Regular property may serve to allocate resources to avoid use conflicts, but information can be used by more than one person – it is nonrival – and so need not be allocated to one person to the exclusion of another. Instead, intellectual property is supposed to encourage people to engage in the production or development of information. And if it is various activities we want to encourage, it would seem to follow that we should regulate or subsidize those activities. If there is an allocation problem connected with activities like invention and commercialization, it involves not the information itself but the inputs used to discover and enhance the value of the information.[4] But why we would provide for rights in information to solve this allocation problem when it would seem that we could simply give rights to appropriate the returns from these (rival) inputs like labor and lab space?

Although such questions are particularly pressing in intellectual property because of the special nature of information as a subject of property rights, these questions do arise in more familiar settings involving tangible property. In this chapter I will argue that the information cost problems solved by property rights do carry over into intellectual property. Because exclusive rights have underappreciated benefits, the main questions in intellectual property are ultimately even more empirical than most commentators recognize. Furthermore, attending to both the benefits and costs of exclusive

---

[2] See The Incandescent Lamp Patent, 159 U.S. 465 (1895). On the involvement of shrimp salads in legal relations, see Wesley Newcomb Hohfeld, *Fundamental Legal Conceptions as Applied in Judicial Reasoning*, 26 YALE L.J. 710 (1917), reprinted in FUNDAMENTAL LEGAL CONCEPTIONS AS APPLIED IN JUDICIAL REASONING AND OTHER LEGAL ESSAYS 65–114 (Walter Wheeler Cook, ed. 1923).

[3] See, e.g., A. Samuel Oddi, *Un-Unified Economic Theories of Patents – The Not-Quite-Holy Grail*, 71 NOTRE DAME L. REV. 267 (1996) (discussing theories of patent law).

[4] Edmund W. Kitch, *The Nature and Function of the Patent System*, 20 J.L. & ECON. 265, 275–76 (1977) ("There is, however, a scarcity of resources that may be employed to use information, and it is that scarcity which generates the need for a system of property rights in information.").

rights as a second (or third) best solution to problems inherent in delineating entitlements will point to new sources of data for resolving these
empirical questions.

This chapter proposes that intellectual property's close relationship to
property stems from the role that information costs play in the delineation
and enforcement of rights. Property differs from other areas like torts and
contracts in its heavier reliance on what I have elsewhere called the *exclusion*
strategy.[5] The exclusion strategy protects rights holders' interests in the
use of resources indirectly, by using a simple signal for violations. The
prototypical example is trespass to land where unauthorized crossing of a
boundary serves as a (very) rough proxy for harmful use; any voluntary
entry into the column of space defined by the *ad coelum* rule counts as a
trespass.[6] By contrast, some rights are defined more directly in terms of
proper use, under what I call a *governance* strategy: A person has a right to
perform a certain action, and the action, rather than some defined thing,
is the focus of delineation effort. Much of nuisance law is a classic example
of this approach: Certain activities, like emitting odors, are the focus of
attention, and contextual factors about the neighborhood and the relative
benefits to society of the conflicting uses are directly relevant. Indeed the
trespass–nuisance divide or the shift within nuisance from the exclusion-
like trespass doctrine to a use-based balancing-style governance approach
can be taken as paradigmatic of the relation between the core of property
and adjacent areas such as torts.[7] Governance rules can refine and extend
the basic rough exclusion strategy but at ever greater cost, as we move along
the spectrum from exclusion to governance. Building on this framework
that identifies exclusion and governance as complementary strategies for
defining property rights, I will show that exclusion rights in information

---

[5] See, e.g., Henry E. Smith, Exclusion and Property Rules in the Law of Nuisance, 90 Va. L.
Rev. 965 (2004).

[6] The full statement of the maxim is *cujus est solum, ejus est usque ad coelum et ad inferos* (he
who owns the soil owns also to the sky and to the depths). The maxim is routinely followed
in resolving issues about ownership of air rights, building encroachments, overhanging
tree limbs, mineral rights, and so forth, and is subject to certain limited exceptions for
airplane overflights, for example. See *Brown v. United States*, 73 F.3d 110, 1103 (Fed. Cir.
1996); Thomas W. Merrill, *Trespass, Nuisance, and the Costs of Determining Property Rights*,
14 J. LEGAL STUD. 13, 26–35 (1985); Henry E. Smith, *Exclusion and Property Rules in the
Law of Nuisance*, 90 VA. L. REV. 965, 992–96 (2004).

[7] See, e.g., Merrill, Trespass, supra note 6; Smith, supra note 6; see also *Victoria Park Racing
and Recreation Grounds Co. v. Taylor*, (1937) 58 C.L.R. 479 (Australia) (Evatt, J., dissenting)
(describing the law of nuisance as "an extension of the idea of trespass into the field that
fringes property"), citing 1 Thomas Atkins Sweet, FOUNDATIONS OF LEGAL LIABILITY
(Theory and Principles of Tort) 211 (1906).

outputs may serve as a low-cost way to establish property rights in the rival *inputs* to invention and commercialization.

Paradoxically, the main advantage of exclusive rights is their indirectness, or the lack of direct fit between exclusion as a mechanism and the purposes that it serves. As some legal philosophers have argued, if the right to exclude is the basic feature of property, it nonetheless serves our interests in the use of things.[8] Property rests on a foundation of simple rules like trespass, which tell duty holders to keep off. No direct reference need be made to information about either the duty holder or the owner: If I am walking through a parking lot, I know not to drive off with others' cars, and I need not know who the owners are, how virtuous (or not) they are, or whether they are actual people or corporations.[9] Likewise, the owners of the autos need not know much about me or the vast crowd of other duty holders – the "rest of the world" against whom *in rem* rights avail. Our interactions can be relatively anonymous precisely because they are mediated by a thing – in this instance the cars. The right to exclude from a designated thing protects our interests in the use of things like cars or Blackacre; if no use could be made of a given thing, there would be no reason to exclude. Further, the focus on exclusion – for reasons of simplicity and cheapness – only makes sense because of positive transaction costs – here broadly taken to include the nonzero cost of delineating property rights.[10] In a world of zero transaction costs we might accept for all purposes the economists' definition of a property right as a right to take one of a list of actions with respect to a thing, the thing being merely a backdrop to the direct specification of what actions are permissible as between any pair of members of society.[11]

---

[8] See, e.g., J.W. Harris, PROPERTY AND JUSTICE 63 (1996); J.E. Penner, THE IDEA OF PROPERTY IN LAW 68–74 (1997).

[9] Penner, supra note 8, at 75–76.

[10] See, e.g., Douglas W. Allen, *What Are Transaction Costs?*, 14 RES. L. & ECON. 1 (1991) (arguing that transaction costs are better defined as the costs of establishing property rights, in the economist's sense of a de facto ability to derive utility from an action, rather than narrowly as the costs of exchange); Steven N.S. Cheung, *The Transaction Costs Paradigm*, 36 ECON. INQUIRY 514, 515 (1998) ("'Transaction costs' must be defined to be all the costs which do not exist in a Robinson Crusoe economy.").

[11] See, e.g., Armen A. Alchian, *Some Economics of Property Rights*, in ECONOMIC FORCES AT WORK 127, 130 (1977) (reprinting 30 IL POLITICO 816 (1965)) ("By a system of property rights I mean a method of assigning to particular individuals the 'authority' to select, for specific goods, any use from a nonprohibited class of uses."); see also Thráinn Eggertsson, ECONOMIC BEHAVIOR AND INSTITUTIONS 33 (1990) (stating that "[w]e refer to the rights of individuals to use resources as *property rights*" and quoting Alchian's definition); Steven N. S. Cheung, *The Structure of a Contract and the Theory of a Non-Exclusive Resource*, 13 J.L. & ECON. 49, 67 (1970) ("An exclusive property rights grants its owner a *limited* authority to make decision on resource use so as to derive income therefrom.").

Of course we do not live in a zero-transaction-costs world, but it is easy to overlook that the role identified by philosophers for the right to exclude – its indirect protection of various privileges to use – is one of the features of our legal world that result from positive delineation and information-processing costs.

The basic presumption in property law is the right to exclude, which serves to economize on information costs. In effect, the exclusion strategy allows the system of uses of resources to manage complexity with modularity.[12] For our present purposes, a system is complex when the interactions are many and multiplex such that is it difficult to infer the properties of the whole from the properties of its parts.[13] Modularity is the key to managing complexity when a system is what Herbert Simon termed "nearly decomposable": A nearly decomposable system is one with clusters of elements that interact intensively among themselves but which are not intensely connected to the rest of the system. This allows chunks or components of the system to be partially walled off into modules in which the interconnection between these chunks and the rest of the system are deliberately limited (sometimes even at the expense of interdependencies that might have some value).[14] Interactions and interdependencies can be intense within such modules but are defined and relatively sparse across the interface with other modules. This allows actions within a module not to have hard-to-predict ripple effects through the entire system. The key is that the interface allows only certain information though; the rest is "hidden" in the module. Modularity is a key design principle in many areas and is important in evolutionary theory cognitive science, computer hardware and software, as well as all sorts of engineering and architecture.

In Section I, I argue that property law features modularity at its core and that modularity serves a similar function in intellectual property. On the information cost theory, the combination of exclusion and governance in property furnishes modules and interfaces for actors taking potentially

---

[12] See, e.g., Carliss Y. Baldwin & Kim B. Clark, DESIGN RULES: THE POWER OF MODULARITY (2000); MANAGING IN THE MODULAR AGE: ARCHITECTURES, NETWORKS AND ORGANIZA- TIONS (Raghu Garud, Arun Kumaraswamy, & Richard N. Langlois, eds. 2003); Richard N. Langlois, *Modularity in Technology and Organization*, 49 J. ECON. BEHAV. & ORGANIZ. 19 (2002); Ron Sanchez & Joseph T. Mahoney, *Modularity, Flexibility, and Knowledge Man- agement in Product Organization Design*, 17 STRATEGIC MANAGEMENT J. 63 (Special Issue, Winter 1996); see also Erich Schanze, *Legalism, Economism, and Professional Attitudes Toward Institutional Design*, 149 J. INSTITUTIONAL & THEORETICAL ECON. 122, 127–38 (1993).

[13] Herbert A. Simon, THE SCIENCES OF THE ARTIFICIAL 195 (2d ed. 1981) (1969).

[14] See Baldwin & Clark, supra note 12; Simon, supra note 13.

conflicting actions with respect to resources. Section II shows that patent law relies relatively more than copyright on modular exclusion. By contrast, separate delineation of uses in a more articulated governance regime is more feasible in copyright. This basic difference between the two areas is reflected in the greater reliance on lumpy exclusion rights in patent law, the greater scope of independent creation defense in copyright, greater reliance on compulsory licenses in copyright, and the greater number of exceptions in copyright. I then turn to how the greater range of normative theories of patent reflects a greater role of modular property rights than in copyright. Like regular property, intellectual property mixes exclusion and governance, but the appropriate mixture depends on the special nature of information as a resource and the problems in attributing the value of nonrival informational outputs to rival inputs. Section III draws out some dynamic implications of the information cost theory. The increasing value of information makes both the benefits and costs of exclusion rise. Overall, the degree of modularity of intellectual property law is an empirical question that cannot be answered by appeals to the nonrivalness of information on the one hand or the need for incentives on the other.

I. Modularity and the Problem of Rights in Information

The information cost theory allows us to draw out the fundamental similarity between property and intellectual property. The combination of exclusion and governance strategies in the delineation of property rights results in a modular structure in which limited information permeates the boundaries between the spheres defined by the exclusion rights. Intellectual property also manages complexity through modularity, and the devices that lend modularity to firms and information production often come from the property element of the law of intellectual property.

A. Modularity in Property

Much of property law can be thought of as specifying the interface conditions between property modules. Thus, the exclusionary strategy sets up basic modules and hides a great deal of information about uses and features of the owner. But we do make exceptions for overflights, and nuisance law does balance some high-stakes use conflicts. These refinements add to the interface and solve problems at the price of less modularity.

Property is the area of law concerned with those rights most based on exclusion. In our terms, this means that property law tends to define rights based on informational variables that that *bunch attributes and uses together* and treats them as a modular component of the legal system. Previously, I have argued that there are two strategies for delineating rights, which I term "exclusion" and "governance," and that these strategies fall on the poles of a spectrum of methods of informational variables (or, to use the term from neoinstitutional economics, proxy measurement).[15] For example, in the case of land, do we use simple on/off signals like boundary crossings (trespass, some nuisance) or more tailored variables involving the evaluation of conflicting uses (other nuisance law)? By distinguishing exclusion and governance based on their different cost structures at different levels of precision, we can explain a wide range of features of property law and its relations to adjacent areas.

The *exclusion* strategy delegates decisions about resource use to an owner who, as gatekeeper, is responsible for deciding on and monitoring how the resource will be used. To set up such rights, informational variables (or proxies) like boundaries and the *ad coelum* rule are used. Crossing the boundary does somewhat correlate with whether a person is imposing costs through use, but only in a very rough sense. Being on the land is necessary to engage in a wide range of such uses as picking fruit or parking cars. But those present on the land might or might not be causing harm (and could be causing more or less harm), but a rule based on a boundary does not distinguish these cases. In the case of land, the main informational variable relevant to the action of trespass (and much of the law of nuisance) is locational: Has a party invaded the column of space around the land?[16] By having the right to exclude, the owner is protected in a wide range of potential and actual uses, without the law ever having to delineate these use privileges separately. Indeed, many uses such as using air to blow away chimney smoke are not really rights at all; they are privileges in the owner that are implicitly and indirectly protected by the basic gatekeeper right, the right to exclude.[17]

In the case of intellectual property, as we will see shortly, the patent law relies heavily on the right to exclude. For example, in a chemical invention, the applicant can claim a substance by stating its structure. Any use of the substance, whether foreseen by the applicant at the time of the application or not, is protected by this right to exclude. The right to exclude others from using the substance bunches together a wide range of uses that the law

---

[15] Henry E. Smith, *Exclusion versus Governance: Two Strategies for Delineating Property Rights*, 31 J. Legal Stud. S453 (2002).

[16] See Smith supra note 6.

[17] Henry E. Smith, *Self-Help and the Nature of Property*, 1 J.L. Econ. & Pol'y 69 (2005).

need never specify individually. The law delegates to the patentee the choice among these uses. As a result, there is a wide range of activities that the patentee can take to promote the invention, including further development not resulting in improvement patents, advertising, marketing, and so on, the returns of which the patentee will be able to capture. Under certain circumstances, the patentee can also use the functionally broad right to exclude in its efforts to coordinate further innovation.[18]

For low levels of precision, rough informational variables (proxies) like the boundary in the *ad coelum* rule or the chemical structure of a substance are the cheapest method of delineating rights, but they would be very expensive if employed to pick out individual levels of use. As Robert Ellickson has noted, dogs can be taught to police boundaries but not to detect stealing by those with the privilege of access.[19] Similarly, enforcing the right to exclude from a substance or an apparatus is much easier than a right to specific types of uses of these "things." Generally, exclusion proxies are over- and underinclusive of the harms caused by individual uses.

The exclusion strategy also has implications for the correlative duty holders. Exclusion rights are used when the audience (of duty holders) is large and indefinite (*in rem*), and their simplicity reduces the processing costs, which would be high for such extensive audiences.[20] Recall the examples of the anonymously parked cars. When large numbers can contribute to the value of the resource by keeping off, rough informational variables of exclusion will be used to send this simple message.

If exclusion bunches uses together, the *governance* strategy, by contrast, picks out uses and users in more detail, imposing a more intense

---

[18] Perhaps because of the emphasis in the reward theory on innovation rather than (nonpatentable) commercialization, critics of Kitch's prospect theory, see Kitch *supra* note 4, have focused on the difficulties that patentees will have in coordinating further innovation where others can get improvement patents, leading to a situation of blocking patents. See, e.g., Mark A. Lemley, *The Economics of Improvement in Intellectual Property* Law, 75 TEXAS L. REV. 989, 1047 (1997) (patentee does not have exclusive control over further improvements); Robert P. Merges & Richard R. Nelson, *On the Complex Economics of Patent Scope*, 90 COLUM. L. REV. 839, 875–77 (1990) (based on empirical study, expressing skepticism about the ability of a holder of a broad patent to coordinate further research and development through "tailored licensing"). John Duffy shows that where others have a small enough incentive to engage in follow-on work or where the patentee can save on transaction costs, the prospect patent holder can coordinate (but not slow down) further innovation, usually through integration rather than licensing, and so avoid duplication. John F. Duffy, *Rethinking the Prospect Theory of Patents*, 71 U. CHI. L. REV. 439, 483–91 (2004). As Duffy points out, development activities that do not (or might not) result in improvement patents are even more firmly under the original patentee's control. Id.

[19] Robert C. Ellickson, *Property in Land*, 102 YALE L.J. 1315, 1327–28 (1993).

[20] See Smith, supra note 15, at S468–69; Henry E. Smith, *The Language of Property: Form, Context, and Audience*, 55 STAN. L. REV. 1105, 1151–53 (2003).

informational burden on a smaller audience of duty holders.[21] For example, a group of herdsmen have rights to graze animals, but the rights among themselves may be limited to a certain number of animals, time of grazing, and so on. In the case of land, if governance rules are those that pick out more specific activities for measurement, then a wide range of rules – from contractual provisions, to norms of proper use, to nuisance law and public environmental regulation – can be seen as reflecting the governance strategy.

Sometimes, use on multiple scales becomes important enough to allow for overlapping modules in which some attribute is subject to multiple property modules. A *semicommons* exists where private and common property regimes overlap physically and the two regimes interact: A semicommons must tolerate or address the strategic behavior made possible by the enhanced access from the overlap.[22] In the medieval open fields, throwing land owned in plots for graingrowing open as an area for common grazing in fallow periods and rights after harvests invited the strategic behavior of favoring one's own parcel with manure and trashing others with excessive trampling of sheep. I have argued that the scattering of strips was designed to prevent such behavior on the part of those with access.[23] Because access to information is more difficult to prevent and presumptively undesirable from its nonrival character, this type of overlap is even more likely in intellectual property.[24] Doctrines like fair use in copyright can be regarded as overlap between private rights and the public domain, and as a very complicated interface between the two.

B. Intellectual Property

Like other property, intellectual property rights provide simple ground rules and a platform for further contracting and forming organizations.[25] Officials and duty holders need not know as much as they do when they

---

[21] See Smith, supra note 15, at S455, S468, S471–74.

[22] Henry E. Smith, *Semicommon Property Rights and Scattering in the Open Fields*, 29 J. LEGAL STUD. 131, 131–32, 138–42 (2000).

[23] Id. at 134–38, 144–54.

[24] Like tangible property rights, IP rights are not absolute. Michael A. Carrier, *Cabining Intellectual Property through a Property Paradigm*, 54 DUKE L.J. 1 (2004). Multiple overlapping regimes can sometimes fill in the edges. See, e.g., Robert A. Heverly, *The Information Semicommons*, 18 BERKELEY TECH. L.J. 1127 (2003); Peter K. Yu, *Intellectual Property and the Information Ecosystem*, 2005 MICH. ST. L. REV. 1, 11–12; see also, e.g., Ellen P. Goodman, *Spectrum Rights in the Telecosm to Come*, 41 SAN DIEGO L. REV. 269, 379–403 (2004); Henry E. Smith, *Governing the Tele-Semicommons*, 22 YALE J. ON REG. 289 (2005).

[25] One of the roles of property rights is to serve as a platform for further contracting. For an exploration of this in connection with precontractual liability and enforcement flexibility,

choose to contract with the holder of the rights. Consider how much information is hidden behind the boundaries of an intellectual property right. As with other assets, someone must decide which combination of uses of the rival inputs to developing the information is best. The number of combinations is $n!/((n - r)!r!)$ for a set of n uses taken r at a time, but we may not know *ex ante* which uses are compatible with which. If some uses are compatible only in certain sequences (in the case of land this might be graingrowing and then hunting, but not vice versa), then the number of permutations (ordered combinations) is even greater, that is, $n!/(n - r)!$. With intellectual property rights that delegate to owners the development of information about uses and the choice among them, outsiders (officials and duty holders) need not know the exact makeup of the set; all officials and duty holders need to know are the "interface" conditions of when a violation of the right has occurred (as by crossing a boundary or practicing a patented invention).[26] Through use or subsequent transfer, the owner enjoys the fruits or the loss that flows from these complex choices.

The indirectness of the relation between the right to exclude and the interests in uses that it protects is also characteristic of intellectual property. With a right to exclude from a wide and indefinite range of uses, the intellectual property owner can take a correspondingly wide range of actions and appropriate the returns (positive or negative) from these efforts without outsiders – potential violators, officials, and, to some extent, contractual partners – needing to know much about these uses. Those who in a world of zero transaction costs might contract with commercializing "input" providers can do so while focusing their attention on low-cost, narrow, and indirect proxies instead.[27] In the case of patent law, this is whether someone not licensed by the patentee is making, using, or selling the invention.[28] If the uses delegated in this way were all *nonrival* with the

---

see Robert P. Merges, *A Transactional View of Property Rights*, 20 Berkeley Tech. L.J. 1477 (2005).

[26] For the role of delegation to owners in an information cost theory of property, see, e.g., Smith, supra note 6, at 1021–45.

[27] Paul Heald develops the similarity between patent law and the asset partitioning function of organizational law. See Paul J. Heald, *A Transaction Costs Theory of Patent Law*, 66 Ohio St. L.J. 473 (2005).

[28] Patent Act, 35 U.S.C. § 271; *Bloomer v. McQuewan*, 55 U.S. (14 How.) 539 (1852) (noting that "[t]he franchise which the patent grants, consists altogether in the right to exclude every one from making, using, or vending the thing patented, without the permission of the patentee. This is all he obtains by the patent;" and noting that right to use a machine is not within the scope and is governed by state property law"). See also Craig Allen Nard, *Certainty, Fence Building, and the Useful Arts*, 74 Ind. L.J. 759, 759 (1999) ("Patent law is about building fences."), citing *Centennial Proceedings of the United States Patent*

uses that might be prevented under the right to exclude, the case *against* intellectual property could not be clearer. However, the inputs to these uses – the labor, equipment, and so on – needed to develop the information *are* rival. The use of these and the return from them is swept along indirectly in the right to exclude.

Whether it would be better to separately value each input (and trace through its contribution to the overall return on the informational asset) is an empirical question. On the benefit side, unlimited tracing of this sort would allow unimpeded use of the informational asset, in accordance with its nonrival nature for consumers. On the cost side, the tracing would be far costlier than lumping these "uses" in within the functional scope of the exclusion right: By exercising the right to exclude, the interest in using these more causally "remote" rival inputs and appropriating their return comes along automatically – without a separate need for any third party to delineate or even identify these uses and inputs. In regular property, the right to exclude indirectly protects use privileges, but in the presence of positive transaction costs does prevent some beneficial, nonharmful – and in that sense nonrival – uses. The analogous rights in intellectual property likewise benefit from their indirectness, but at the price of foregone use. The right to exclude is both the greatest strength and weakness of intellectual property rights – as it is in regular property. In a way, the difference between property and intellectual property looks like a matter of degree rather than of kind.

Nevertheless, in intellectual property the nonrival nature of use makes rights more difficult to delineate and enforce. In the case of tangible property use, conflict itself can be the trigger of a right violation or at least bring the violation to the attention of the right holder. Where uses do not conflict in this way, mere use by another does not announce itself in the same way. If so, this is a reason to think that signals tailored to use – governance-type signals – tend to be more costly in the case of intellectual property than in tangible property. All else equal, this can push us toward no property rights (open access) or more reliance on exclusion. Thus, in a sense, it is nonrivalness that has some *tendency to polarize the choices of delineation* for intellectual property rights. This can go some way toward explaining the sharp disagreements over the proper strength and scope of intellectual property.

System 1891, at 43, 51 (Executive Comm. of the Patent Centennial Celebration ed., 1990) (Commissioner of Patents writing in the late 19th century that claims are important as "set[ting] definite walls and fences about the rights of the patentee").

Uses do not always conflict, and more than one ownership regime can govern an asset. Multiple overlapping regimes that can accommodate multiple uses are particularly likely in intellectual property (and are less modular than having a single level).[29] Intellectual property rights are likely to be semicommons around their edges.

As in property law, in intellectual property law, the governance strategy fine tunes the basic exclusionary regime by further specifying the interface between property modules. For example, with the patented chemical invention, the law provides a very narrow use-based exception for experimental use;[30] the exception focuses on the type of use and requires detailed evaluation of the experimental user's motivations. (For example, these days commercial motivation will usually disqualify a use as experimental.[31]) As another example, the law of patent misuse – as its name suggests – singles out particular uses that are thought to extend the patent beyond its lawful scope and withdraws enforceability from the patent.[32] As we will see, copyright makes even greater use of governance rules than does patent law, through its stick-by-stick definition of rights, compulsory licenses, and exceptions.

When we focus on property law as opposed to property rights in general, issues of institutional competence are central. The pattern of property law will depend in part on the relative cost of delineation of rights by courts as opposed to participants. Thus, the question is not just the Demsetzian one of whether additional definition and enforcement activity is worth the cost but whether informal or formal contracting, with or without *ex post* judicial enforcement, is cheaper than *ex ante* specification of rights by property law.

Property law serves two purposes, both of which are consistent with seeing property as generally more based on rough signals of exclusion and access than is contract. Property can either assign an entitlement in contexts in which further bargaining to modify or transfer the entitlement is not likely to take place, or property can furnish the starting point for private bargains.

[29] See, e.g., Heverly, supra note 24; Smith, supra note 24, at 131–132, 138–142. Robert Merges describes a regime under which scientists share with each other for research purposes but enforce rights against commercial entities, in a semicommons-like arrangement. See Robert P. Merges, *Property Rights Theory and the Commons: The Case of Scientific Research*, Soc. Phil. & Pol'y, Summer 1996, at 145.

[30] See Donald S. Chisum, Chisum on Patents §§ 17.02[4], 17.05, 19.04 (1997).

[31] The Federal Circuit has recently taken an expansive approach to what counts as commercial. See *Madey v. Duke University*, 301 F.3d 1351 (Fed. Cir. 2002).

[32] The trend in patent misuse is to rely less on per se rules and more on rule of reason analysis, which increases the governance-like aspect of patent misuse. See *Virginia Panel Corp. v. MAC Panel Co.*, 133 F.3d 860, 869 (Fed. Cir. 1997) (finding misuse where the patentee extended the term of the patent by requiring royalties after expiration).

In the latter case, it is likely that contracting will add to the precision of the rights; in addition to simple transfers, parties can contract to subdivide, to modify rights, or to allow access under limited conditions. Parties can also contract over specific uses to which resources can be put. Anything beyond a contract for simple transfer is likely to add to the precision of the collection of rights to the resource and hence increase reliance on the governance strategy. If, on the other hand, no further bargaining takes place, property law has the last word. This can happen because the gains from further precision are outweighed by the costs of further delineation by contract.

What is the problem to be solved in intellectual property? On the commercialization theory, it is not so much the creation of information as the actions taken with respect to it that make the invention useful commercially. In the commercialization process, rival inputs are used and the return from such inputs is not easy to measure.

On one version of commercialization theory, it is important that one actor coordinate others in the commercialization process. This is prospect theory, which points to broad rights to allow the owner the authority to coordinate the commercialization and development of the invention even after it has been invented.[33] This modular structure here crucially has a coordinating or command module.

But prospect theory is not the only version of commercialization theory. Others have highlighted the role of patent rights as platforms for contracting.[34] Property as opposed to contract allows for precontractual liability and enforcement flexibility.[35] The patent right announces to others who has complementary inputs.[36]

The patent allows actors to undertake commercialization efforts with some assurance of a return from their rival inputs. It is true that in principal these contributions could be more finely measured in a grand contractual process, without the need for exclusive rights. That is, providers of inputs could bargain for a payment for providing them if they had rights to withhold these inputs. In the face of team production problems this is not a trivial exercise.

---

[33] See Kitch, supra note 4.
[34] See, e.g., Heald, supra note 27; F. Scott Kieff, *Coordination, Property, and Intellectual Property: An Unconventional Approach to Anticompetitive Effects and Downstream Access*, 56 EMORY L.J. 327 (2006); Merges note 58.
[35] See Merges, supra note 25.
[36] Kieff, *supra* note 34.

Modular rights serve three purposes. They are a rough proxy for the right to enjoy the return from these rival inputs. Modular rights are also the platform for modification of the flows of returns to rival inputs. And modular rights allow certain actors to modify the modular structure itself. This last purpose is reminiscent of the prospect function, and it is only important where the gatekeeping function has a meta aspect: We are so unsure about the process that its solution is best handled by one specialist, and so it makes sense to delegate the entire architecture of the commercialization process to one party. That will only be true in some cases, and will be more true the broader the rights that are given. But it should be emphasized that modularization can be important even where prospects in the classical sense are not necessary.

Modularization allows patents to be treated as property for general purposes. Patent holders can use them as security for loans. Again, in a zero-transaction-cost world, the intellectual property holder might use the rights to the inputs to commercialization as security for loans – if security interests were even necessary in a zero-transaction-cost world, in which a contract over all states of the world could be costlessly written. In a positive-transaction-cost world, giving a security interest in the inputs to commercialization or to the (difficult-to-measure) financial flows from those inputs is likely to be less cost effective in many cases than simply to have a property right in the invention itself, which can then be subject to the security interest in favor of creditors.

In other words, patents and other intellectual property rights are like organizations and other property in general in that the short cut over the contracts that do not – and could not – be used instead is a general purpose one. Officials need not even know the purposes to which the modularity of the property rights need to be put in order for them to be effective.

II. Information Costs in Patent and Copyright Law

Intellectual property is a natural area to test the information cost theory of property, for two reasons. First, we are accustomed to thinking in terms of physical boundaries, but any account of exclusion and governance should be expected to accord with our intuitions about access to and use of nonphysical resources. Second, and more tentatively, we may be able to begin to explain some differences among areas of intellectual property law as a response to different costs of measuring the use of information and the role of modularity in managing complexity.

A. Patent versus Copyright Law

Exclusion and governance can be contrasted with respect to nonphysical attributes and assets as well as to the more familiar tangible "things." In the case of a nonphysical and nonrival resource such as information, the modular right to exclude is the right to deny access to a large collection of uses (and hence attributes), as in the case of a physical resource. But, unlike with a physical resource, the lowest cost boundary is not a spatial one. In the case of a nonphysical asset, governance still refers to norms of use defined over activities involving the asset.[37]

One problem in comparing patent and copyright is that the nature of the resource is sufficiently different between and within the two areas that commentators have disagreed as to whether the costs of delineating property rights in patent are higher or lower than in copyright. For example, Clarisa Long has argued that because the resource in copyright is more ethereal than in patent, the delineation costs are higher.[38] But this view fails to consider that inventions come in many different varieties, some of which are easier to define (e.g., chemicals) and others much less so (e.g., processes). The same can be said of copyright: Policing at the level of word-for-word expression is easy, but defining a protected literary character or style is difficult.[39] And, as we will see, the literatures on intellectual property valuation and invention economics suggest high delineation costs in the case of patent.[40]

It is useful to distinguish two kinds of information costs associated with the exclusion and governance strategies, respectively. *Exclusion* relies on

---

[37] Unlike with a spatial asset, it may be the case that attributes are easier to separate out; separating them may not involve the physical obstacles of intermingling. At the same time, there may be significant measurement costs to separating out the attributes and uses, and, as we will see, when these costs are high we expect the bundling of attributes characteristic of exclusion here, too.

[38] See Clarisa Long, *Information Costs in Patent and Copyright*, 90 Va. L. Rev. 465 (2004).

[39] See, e.g., *Nichols v. Universal Pictures Corp.*, 45 F.2d 119, 121 (2d Cir. 1930) (Hand, J.) ("Upon any work, and especially upon a play, a great number of patterns of increasing generality will fit equally well, as more and more of the incident is left out.... [T]here is a point in this series of abstractions where they are no longer protected, since otherwise the playwright could prevent the use of his 'ideas,' to which, apart from their expression, his property is never extended. Nobody has ever been able to fix that boundary, and nobody ever can."); *Steinberg v. Columbia Pictures Indus.*, 663 F. Supp. 706, 712 (S.D.N.Y. 1987). "No rigid principle has been developed, however, to ascertain when one has gone beyond the idea to the expression, and '[d]ecisions must therefore inevitably be ad hoc.'" (quoting *Peter Pan Fabrics, Inc. v. Martin Weiner Corp.*, 274 F.2d 487, 489 (2d Cir.1960) (L. Hand, J.)).

[40] See infra note 59 and accompanying text.

finding signals that correspond roughly with use but more tightly with some "thing," whether pre-carved by our conventions or delineated especially for legal purposes. *Governance* relies on signals tightly tied to use but not keyed to things or their attributes. In this section, I claim first and foremost that it is the relative costs that are different in the cases of patent and copyright. Indeed, patent law involves high stakes, high delineation cost, and much residual uncertainty about boundaries.[41]

Nevertheless, we can ask how cost effective exclusion is (and can be) as well as the different relative cost effectiveness of exclusion versus governance in the case of patent and copyright. If we hypothesize, consistent with the literature on valuation, that use is costly to separate out and measure in the case of inventions, relative to exclusion-like delineation based on other attributes of inventions (e.g., their basic features, such as chemical composition or the steps involved in a process), this helps to explain patent law's reliance on exclusion despite the high stakes involved. Conversely, in copyright, uses appear to be relatively less costly to delineate. Whether or not, as some have claimed, thing-attributes are more costly to delineate in copyright than in patent, the relative ease of delineating uses can explain the ways in which copyright is more regulatory and less property-like than patent – that is, is more of a governance regime.

Rules of physical access involve rough signals that are cost effective when a large number of uses are to be prevented or protected. Exclusion in intellectual property likewise prevents and protects a large class of uses. As with physical resources, if enough uses are bunched together in this way in the module, most all of those uses are protected, and it becomes economical to speak of rules as regulating access to attributes; that is, the rules become exclusion rules implementing the layperson's right to a "thing." The more uses are bunched together, the more exclusion-based the right appears and the more property-like the right becomes. A right to a thing could be regarded as a collection of use rights, but this misses something: A rule that employs cheap and rough signals like boundaries can leave implicit a large and indefinite class of uses as against a large and indefinite class of users.[42] As William Markby has analogized, ownership "is no more conceived as an aggregate of distinct rights than a bucket of water is conceived as an aggregate of separate drops."[43] This idea is an old one, going back at least

---

[41] See, e.g., James Bessen & Micahel J. Meurer, PATENT FAILURE: HOW JUDGES, BUREAUCRATS, AND LAWYERS PUT INNOVATORS AT RISK 29–72 (2008).

[42] See Smith, supra note 15, at S468–71.

[43] William Markby, ELEMENTS OF LAW 158 (6th ed. 1905).

to the Austinian notion that "indefiniteness" is the essence of property.[44] In terms of modularity, for many purposes, the individuation of drops (or molecules or even further) is not relevant; the fluid can be treated as an aggregate. A reservoir of unspecified uses under the control of an owner is the result of the use of rough signals of exclusion, and such signals are relatively cheap precisely because they sweep in these uses without needing to spell them out.

The question is whether it is less costly to measure use by signals very directly related to use or by signals that bundle so many uses together that we speak of exclusion. Patent and copyright differ in many ways, but especially in the costliness of delineating and evaluating use. And the two areas of law differ in the ways one would expect on the information cost model.

Patent and copyright differ along many dimensions and for many reasons, but delineation cost is a crucial difference, making patents more modular than copyrigths. Traditional criteria for distinguishing the realms of patent and copyright, such as utilitarian versus artistic values, correspond closely, I argue, to how difficult the uses of the information are to separate and evaluate. Utilitarian use often involves problems of attributing the value of interacting inputs and choosing among indefinite, novel, and therefore hard-to-assess uses. This distinction is reflected in the respective scopes of the two great nineteenth-century conventions on intellectual property, the 1883 Convention of Paris for the Protection of Industrial Property[45] and 1886 Berne Convention for the Protection of Literary and Artistic Works.[46] These two conventions helped to define the function/expression divide.[47]

Patents on average give rise to greater information costs, and greater complexity, than do copyrights – that is, the costs of devising and monitoring informational signals of the use of information as a resource. First, and most

---

[44] 2 John Austin, Lectures on Jurisprudence 827 (Robert Campbell ed., 4th ed. London, John Murray 1873) ("[I]ndefiniteness is of the very essence of the right; and implies that the right . . . cannot be determined by exact and positive circumscription."); see also Restatement of Property §§ 5 cmt. e, 10 cmt. c (1936) (defining "complete" ownership in terms of the maximum set of allowable interests, and noting that one can be an "owner" despite some decrease in interests); Bernard E. Jacob, *The Law of Definite Elements: Land in Exceptional Packages*, 55 S. Cal. L. Rev. 1369, 1388 (1982) (discussing how the *Restatement* definition of complete ownership requires "not only reasonably exclusive present control but also an indefinite reservoir of potential uses").

[45] Paris Convention for the Protection of Industrial Property, Mar. 20, 1883, as last revised July 14, 1967, 21 U.S.T. 1583, 828 U.N.T.S. 305.

[46] Berne Convention for the Protection of Literary and Artistic Works, Sept. 9, 1886, as last revised July 24, 1971, 25 U.S.T. 1341, 1161 U.N.T.S. 3.

[47] On the Paris and Berne Conventions as representing two approaches of intellectual property, see J. H. Reichman, *Legal Hybrids Between the Patent and Copyright Paradigms*, 94 Colum. L. Rev. 2432, 2434–36 (1994).

familiarly, patents involve a great deal of uncertainty.[48] Inventions protected by patent law are often subject to multiple uses, many of which are not foreseeable. Second, and relatedly, the range of actions taken to increase the value of the patent seem to be far greater in the case of patents than in the case of copyrights. Correspondingly, there is a rationale to employ signals of access to define the entrepreneur's residual claim.

Third, it is a well-known problem that the contribution of a patent to an overall product is very difficult to measure; this has not historically been as large a problem with copyrights.[49] One product may embody a large number of inventions and innovations. Furthermore, tracing the many further contributions of an invention like the light bulb to other products and activities would be very costly, even for the length of the patent term.[50] Relatedly, there is a large economics literature on spillovers, external benefits from one research and development project to another, again suggesting a major measurement problem in isolating the value of various activities with respect to inventions.[51] Again, the problem is like team production in that various contributors affect each other's productivity and are hard to disentangle.[52] Furthermore, the productive uses of an invention typically require a great deal of expertise, making it even more difficult for judges to evaluate those uses.

Fourth, combining these last two points, patents interact with each other, making officials' evaluations all the more difficult in patent than in copyright. Even for private parties who likely have an advantage in delineating fine-grained use rights, measuring the individual contribution of a

---

[48] See, e.g., Kitch, supra note 4, at 267–271; Robert P. Merges, *Uncertainty and the Standard of Patentability*, 7 HIGH TECH. L.J. 1 (1992).

[49] See, e.g., Russell Hardin, *Valuing Intellectual Property*, 68 CHI.-KENT L. REV. 659, 660 (1993); Kitch, supra note 4, at 271 (noting that "[e]ach significant innovation affects related aspects of the technology with which it interacts," and discussing how one innovation can alter the possibility set for the development of other related inventions, such that "the realization of the possibilities may have a significance that dwarfs [that of] the original invention considered alone"); Robert P. Merges, *The Law and Economics of Employee Inventions*, 13 HARV. J.L. & TECH. 1, 21 & n.69 (1999) (discussing measurement problems in R&D team production, and citing literature on managing complementary components of R&D projects); see also Giles S. Rich, *The Principles of Patentability*, 42 J. PAT. OFF. SOC'Y 75, 84–85 (1960) (noting that patent law need not determine the size of the reward because the popularity of the invention will be measured by the market).

[50] See, e.g., John P. Dawson, *The Self-Serving Intermeddler*, 87 HARV. L. REV. 1409, 1412 (1974); Wendy J. Gordon & Sam Postbrief, *On Commodifying Intangibles*, 10 YALE J.L. & HUMAN. 135, 157–58 (1998) (book review).

[51] See, e.g., Morton I. Kamien et al., *Research Joint Ventures and R&D Cartels*, 82 AM. ECON. REV. 1293 (1992); Kotaro Suzumura, *Cooperative and Noncooperative R&D in an Oligopoly with Spillovers*, 82 AM. ECON. REV. 1307 (1992).

[52] *See supra* notes – and accompanying text.

single patent to a product is evidently so difficult that licenses between sophisticated parties are rarely tailored to individual licensees.[53] The problem is not just undervaluation but the multidimensional nature of the activities that are the concern of patent law.[54] In our terms, it is difficult in patent to move beyond access-based rules to use-based rules.

Copyright, by contrast, raises these problems in lesser degree. In copyright, the set of such interlocking uses has historically been smaller, and often it is easier to attribute value to a copyrighted work, either because it corresponds more closely to a product demanded and sold on the market or because the copyright use does not involve expertise. Before turning to the statutory schemes for evaluating types of uses of protected works, it is worth remembering that judicial apportionment of profits from the use of a copyrighted work in a further work is more readily undertaken in copyright law, even though, as Judge Learned Hand put it, "[s]trictly and literally, it is true that the problem is insoluable."[55] Also, in part because copyright relies on use-based rather than access-based signals to define the right, copyright comes even less close than patent to protecting ideas themselves. But if copyright *did* protect ideas, many patent-like valuation problems would arise because new works typically incorporate many old ideas.[56] In sum, "industrial" exploitation of information involves different and more costly measurement than does cultural exploitation – at least before new forms of electronic communication arrived on the scene.[57]

---

[53] See Merges & Nelson, supra note 18, at 874 & n.148; see also Carl Shapiro, *Navigating the Patent Thicket: Cross Licenses, Patent Pools, and Standard Setting*, in 1 INNOVATION POLICY AND THE ECONOMY 119 (Adam B. Jaffe et al. eds., 2001) (discussing how overlapping patents lead to difficulties in licensing).

[54] Other countries do make some use of compulsory licenses in their patent laws, in situations such as blocking patents, see Robert Merges, *Intellectual Property Rights and Bargaining Breakdown: The Case of Blocking Patents*, 62 TENN. L. REV. 75, 104–05 (1994) (noting that the law provides for compulsory licenses for blocking patents in Australia, China, France, Japan, the Netherlands, New Zealand, and Switzerland), cases of public interest, and essential intellectual property rights, see Consolidated Version of the Treaty Establishing the European Community arts. 81(3), 82, Dec. 24, 2002, 2002 O.J. (C 325) 33, 64–65 (providing for compulsory licensing of essential intellectual property rights). The argument here is just that copyrights are comparatively more amenable to this approach than are patents.

[55] *Sheldon v. Metro-Goldwyn Pictures*, 106 F.2d 45, 48 (2d Cir. 1939) (apportioning only 20% of the profits from a movie to the holder of the copyright on a play, of which only a small part was used in the movie, and when the movie's success was mainly attributable to its stars rather than its script), aff'd, 309 U.S. 390 (1940).

[56] Creating a new work involves new expression and old ideas. See William M. Landes & Richard A. Posner, *An Economic Analysis of Copyright Law*, 18 J. LEGAL STUD. 325, 332 (1989).

[57] See infra notes 81–85 and accompanying text.

Furthermore, the differences between patent and copyright law do not stem mainly from differences in the benefits of precision in a richer interface between modules. On the benefit side, one would expect more precision when the stakes are higher, and there is reason to believe that the stakes are, if anything, higher in patent law. This is reflected in, for example, the expensiveness of obtaining and defending a patent. Private parties themselves often do delineate separate uses very finely in their licenses, suggesting benefits from doing so. Much delineation effort goes into each patent and into numerous licenses, such that a governance regime might emerge privately through licensing: Another party might be given the right to use the substance for some purposes (or in some markets but not in others), with royalties to be paid for different amounts of use.[58] And the literature on valuing intellectual property has an overwhelming focus on patents rather than copyrights.[59] Furthermore, questions of anticommons and the possibility of bargaining breakdown in the presence of multiple, tightly interrelated patent rights have been a focus in recent commentary on patent law, in a different way and to a greater extent than in copyright.[60] In patent, the fear is that the holders of narrow patents that need to be used together for further research or to develop a project will each engage in holdup behavior and that assembling the permission will be costly and time consuming.[61] This was a major concern with patents over gene fragments before the Patent and Trademark Office promulgated guidelines. The evidence on the significance

---

[58] See, e.g., Robert P. Merges, *Of Property Rules, Coase, and Intellectual Property*, 94 COLUM. L. REV. 2655 (1994).

[59] See, e.g., Gordon V. Smith & Russell L. Parr, VALUATION OF INTELLECTUAL PROPERTY AND INTANGIBLE ASSETS (3d ed. 2000); Robert S. Bramson, *Valuing Patents, Technologies and Portfolios: Rules of Thumb*, 635 PLI/Pat 465 (2001); Scott D. Phillips, *Patent & High Technology Licensing: Evaluation of Patent Portfolios*, 652 PLI/Pat 57 (2001); Lauren Johnston Stiroh & Richard T. Rapp, *Modern Methods for the Valuation of Intellectual Property*, 532 PLI/Pat 817 (1998).

[60] See Michael A. Heller & Rebecca S. Eisenberg, *Can Patents Deter Innovation? The Anticommons in Biomedical Research*, 280 SCIENCE 698 (1998); Michael S. Mireles, *An Examination of Patents, Licensing, Research Tools, and the Tragedy of the Anticommons in Biotechnology Innovation*, 38 U. MICH. J.L. REFORM 141, 230–34 (2004).

[61] *Compare* Mark A. Lemley & Carl Shapiro, *Patent Holdup and Royalty Stacking*, 85 TEX. L. REV. 1991, 2037–38 (2007) (arguing for systematic overcompensation from injunctive remedy); Gerard N. Magliocca, *Blackberries and Barnyards: Patent Trolls and The Perils of Innovation*, 82 NOTRE DAME L. REV. 1809 (2007) (analogizing the troll problem to nineteenth-century "patent sharks"); *with* Vincenzo Denicolò, *Do Patents Over-compensate Innovators?*, 22 ECON. POL'Y 679 (2007) (finding little evidence of overcompensation); John M. Golden, *"Patent Trolls" and Patent Remedies*, 85 TEX. L. REV. 2111 (2007) (critiquing case for overcompensation); Henry E. Smith, *Institutions and Indirectness in Intellectual Property*, 157 U. PA. L. REV. 2083, 2126–30 (2009).

of the anticommons effect comes primarily from surveys; it is mixed and provides little guidance as to how costly the problem is or how much to attribute it to the patent system.[62]

Even commentators who are optimistic about the ability of private transactions to lead to efficient exploitation recognize that patents are often highly complementary[63] in a way that copyrights seldom are.[64] Nor is it only the breadth of patent rights that is the sole problem here: Multiple narrow rights are thought to be problematic precisely because of their high

---

[62] See, e.g., Eric G. Campbell et al., *Data Withholding in Academic Genetics: Evidence from a National Survey*, 287 J. AM. MED. ASS'N 473, 477 (2002) (reporting that 47% of academic geneticists said that another academic had refused at least one of their requests for data or materials associated with a published article at least once in the preceding three years); Stephen Hilgartner & Sherry I. Brandt-Rauf, *Data Access, Ownership, and Control: Toward Empirical Studies of Access Practices*, 15 KNOWLEDGE 355, 359, 363–66 (1994) (discussing strategic issues involved in decisions to grant access to data); Fiona Murray & Scott Stern, *Do Formal Intellectual Property Rights Hinder the Free Flow of Scientific Knowledge? An Empirical Test of the Anti-Commons Hypothesis*, 63 J. ECON. BEHAV. & ORG. 648 (2007) (finding modest effect of property rights on flow of inforation); Shapiro, supra note 53, at 119; John P. Walsh et al., *Effects of Research Tool Patents and Licensing on Biomedical Innovation*, in PATENTS IN THE KNOWLEDGE-BASED ECONOMY 285 (Wesley M. Cohen & Stephen A. Merrill eds., 2003) (noting that a survey of industry participants found that patents on research tools generally have not caused much breakdown or even restricted access as anticommons theory would suggest, and documenting various solutions to the fragmentation problem, including licensing, inventing around, infringing, public disclosure, and litigation); John P. Walsh et al., Patents, Material Transfers and Access to Research Inputs in Biomedical Research 2 (Sept. 20, 2005), http://tigger.uic.edu/~jwalsh/WalshChoCohenFinal050922.pdf. Problems seem to be greater in the case of materials transfer than sharing of data. John P. Walsh et al., *View from the Bench: Patents and Materials Transfers*, 309 SCIENCE 2002, 2002 (2005); see also Rebecca S. Eisenberg & Arti K. Rai, *Harnessing and Sharing the Benefits of State-Sponsored Research: Intellectual Property Rights and Data Sharing in California's Stem Cell Initiative*, 21 BERKELEY TECH. L.J. 1187, 1200 n.47 (2006) (discussing studies surveying geneticists on sharing of data and materials).

[63] See, e.g., John J. Doll, *The Patenting of DNA*, 280 SCIENCE 689 (1998) (drawing an an analogy of the proliferation of patents on expressed sequence tags in genetics to earlier polymer chemistry in which initial patents were widely licensed); Shapiro, supra note 53, at 122–23; see also Richard A. Epstein, *Steady the Course: Property Rights in Genetic Material* (Chi. Working Paper Series, Paper No. 152, 2002), available at http://www.law.uchicago.edu/faculty/epstein/resources/rae.genome.new.pdf (noting the existence of a "patent thicket" and interdependency, and arguing against compulsory licensing but also against patents for expressed sequence tags).

[64] Someone making a movie will rarely have to use a particular piece of music, but someone wishing to parody a given work will need access to that particular work. Notice that here copyright avoids the apportionment problem as between the original author and the parodist by allowing a certain amount of free access to the parodist. See *Campbell v. Acuff-Rose Music, Inc.*, 510 U.S. 569 (1994) (holding that a commercial parody can fall within Section 107 fair use).

degree of interrelatedness.[65] Given all this evidence of the potential benefits of delineating uses, one would expect that patent law would focus more on specific uses – that it would present a more nuisance-like and less trespass-like regime. So the puzzle is why patent takes a more sweeping and indefinite strategy in this respect than does copyright law. I argue that high measurement cost leads to a more exclusionary, more strongly property-like regime in patent than the more governance-style regime in copyright.

Moreover, commentary that does compare patent and copyright law tends to see them as more similar than they are.[66] In particular, copyright serves as a model for those commentators who would like to see officials intervene more to solve patent transacting problems. The tendency is to see copyright as a model for patent law, precisely because it separates out various uses for special treatment. Once information costs are taken into account, however, we can explain some of the sharp differences between patent and copyright, differences that are otherwise somewhat mysterious.

Consider first the legal rules, which may or may not lead to further contracting. Patents and copyrights both give rights relating to information, and both areas can involve situations of high transaction costs. For a variety of reasons, the scope of the right in patent is broader than that in copyright. The different information cost strategies in patent and copyright are reflected in the contours of the law.

1. *Definition of Rights.* Most basically, the rights in patent and copyright are defined differently. Patent law grants the exclusive right to "make[], use[], or . . . sell[]" an invention,[67] which means that many uses are bundled together, so much so that commentators often adopt the metaphors of fencing, boundaries, and access.[68] Although it is sometimes overlooked, patent law is explicitly based on exclusion rather than on rights to use

---

[65] Interconnectedness would strengthen the anticommons argument against many fragmented rights. See Heller & Eisenberg, supra note 60; see also David E. Adelman, *A Fallacy of the Commons in Biotech Patent Policy*, 20 BERKELEY TECH. L.J. 985 (2005) (discussing the anticommons argument, and arguing that research opportunities in biotech are not currently a scarce resource).

[66] See, e.g., Maureen A. O'Rourke, *Toward a Doctrine of Fair Use in Patent Law*, 100 COLUM. L. REV. 1177 (2000); John Shepard Wiley Jr., *Copyright at the School of Patent*, 58 U. CHI. L. REV. 119 (1991).

[67] 35 U.S.C. § 271 (2000). To these traditional rights have been added the right to offer to sell and to import the patented invention into the United States. Id.

[68] See, e.g., Nard, supra note 28, at 759 ("Patent law is about building fences." (citing Mitchell, supra note 28)); see also, e.g., Patrick Croskery, *Institutional Utilitarianism and Intellectual Property*, 68 CHI.-KENT L. REV. 631, 648–56 (1993) (discussing "fencing" in intellectual property); Kitch, supra note 4, at 273–74 (comparing the limits of claims in patents to the physical boundaries of mineral claims); Merges & Nelson, supra note 18, at 845 (analogizing patent claims to metes and bounds); *Patent Rights and Licensing*, 6 B.U. J. SCI. & TECH. L. 3, ¶ 31 (2000) (remarks of Thomas Meyers).

(governance, in our terms).[69] Thus, patents give a right that relies heavily on the access-type proxies in a more modular exclusion strategy.[70]

Some of the differences between patent and copyright stem from patent law's effort to internalize the benefits and costs of the wider range of uses discussed earlier and the special information costs to which this extra effort gives rise. The greater costs of delineating and policing use in patent are a factor pushing in the direction of the exclusion strategy for delineating rights.[71]

Consistent with the exclusion strategy is today's "peripheral" approach to patent claims: The definition of claims focuses on the outer bounds of what is claimed as an invention, without the need to specify the interior. The earlier central claiming method, in which the central case of the invention was specified and the boundaries were worked out *ex post*, is more of a governance regime (in our terms), as is its pale reflection in the doctrine of equivalents, under which the scope of a claim can be extended beyond the literal reading.[72] Also, a primary focus on the patent specification rather than outside sources such as dictionaries tends to decrease the use of context and to increase the relative reliance on the exclusion strategy.[73]

By contrast, copyright law enumerates various use rights, making it more of a governance regime from the outset. Copyright law traditionally gives certain specific exclusive rights to reproduce; to prepare derivative works;

---

[69] See *Bloomer v. McQuewan*, 55 U.S. (14 How.) 539, 549–50 (1852) (emphasizing that a patent simply furnishes "the right to exclude every one from making, using, or vending the thing patented, without the permission of the patentee"); but cf. Adam Mossoff, *The Use and Abuse of IP at the Birth of the Administrative State*, 157 U. Pa. L. Rev. 2001 (2009) (discussing exclusion conceptions of property and the importance of use to definitions of patents in the nineteenth century).

[70] See, e.g., Kenneth W. Dam, *Some Economic Considerations in the Intellectual Property Protection of Software*, 24 J. Legal Stud. 321, 336 (1995) (noting that patents rarely confer monopoly power in any market, and that "[i]f this is true of patents, it seems even clearer in the case of copyrights *where no power to exclude is granted, where only the power to preclude copying is granted*, and where independent creation by competitors is a complete defense" (emphasis added)); see also id. at 337 (discussing the absence of the power to exclude independently created works in copyright, as well as the copyright doctrine of merger of expression and idea as a limit on the scope of the right).

[71] Notice that the marginal benefit of specifying rights in patent is unlikely to be lower than in copyright, and that, if so, a greater degree of legal definition in terms of use in copyright cannot be explained by different levels of the marginal benefit of precision.

[72] See *Warner-Jenkinson Co. v. Hilton Davis Chem. Co.*, 520 U.S. 17, 26, 27 & n.4 (1997); Henry E. Smith, Differential Formalism in Claiming Intellectual Property: A Response to Fromer (2010The Legal Workshop); see also Jeanne C. Fromer, *Claiming Intellectual Property*, 76 U. Chi. L. Rev. 719 (2009).

[73] For an argument that relying on the specification over outside sources reduces third-party information costs, see Christopher A. Cotropia, *Patent Claim Interpretation and Information Costs*, 9 Lewis & Clark L. Rev. 57 (2005).

and to distribute, perform, and display the work.[74] Copyright law does not simply define a work or an idea and then give rights to exclusive access to such a resource. Copyrightable works must be fixed in a tangible medium of expression, and the statute explicitly denies protection for any "idea, procedure, process, system, method of operation, concept, principle, or discovery."[75]

For this reason, copyright is sometimes even argued not to be property in the full sense. Historically in English law, a statutory limited-term exclusive right over publishing and selling competed with a more robust common law right that gave property in the work itself.[76] In our terms, common-law copyright is more based on the exclusion strategy. One argument against recent trends toward a broader and stronger copyright law is based on the theory that the Founders were aware of the two approaches to copyright and chose the more limited approach based on delineating certain uses of a work.[77] The notion that federal copyright "exclusion" sweeps less broadly than it did at common law continues to influence the courts.[78]

Nevertheless, some recent trends in copyright law have indeed had the effect of broadening the right. On the theory here, this could be because the benefits of doing so are higher – or at least because the benefits inure to those with an organized interest capable of lobbying Congress. Or it could be because the cost of "fencing" has become lower.[79] Evaluating these costs

---

[74] 17 U.S.C. §§ 106–106A (2000).

[75] Id. § 102. Under the useful article doctrine, something with aesthetic elements that are not conceptually severable from its utilitarian aspects is not copyrightable. See Robert C. Denicola, *Applied Art and Industrial Design: A Suggested Approach to Copyright in Useful Articles*, 67 MINN. L. REV. 707, 741–48 (1983) (proposing a test of conceptual separability); see also *Brandir Int'l, Inc. v. Cascade Pac. Lumber Co.*, 834 F.2d 1142 (2d Cir. 1987) (applying a modified form of Robert Denicola's test, and holding that a bicycle rack was not copyrightable because the designer modified a sculpture to serve as a bicycle rack). But see *Brandir*, 834 F.2d at 1151 (Winter, J., dissenting in part) (proposing as a test whether a reasonable observer would "perceive an aesthetic concept not related to the article's use").

[76] See, e.g., L. Ray Patterson, *Copyright Overextended: A Preliminary Inquiry into the Need for a Federal Statute of Unfair Competition*, 17 U. DAYTON L. REV. 385, 396–403 (1992).

[77] See id. at 401–03.

[78] See *Suntrust Bank v. Houghton Mifflin Co.*, 268 F.3d 1257, 1260–63 (11th Cir. 2001) (discussing the history and types of copyright).

[79] See, e.g., Trotter Hardy, *Property (and Copyright) in Cyberspace*, 1996 U. CHI. LEGAL F. 217, 238 (noting that the lower cost of monitoring or "fencing" using computer technology pushes in the direction of more "parcelization" of information, as in the case of barbed wire and land). Many authors have decried this tendency. See, e.g., James Boyle, SHAMANS, SOFTWARE, AND SPLEENS: LAW AND THE CONSTRUCTION OF THE INFORMATION SOCIETY 38 (1996); Yochai Benkler, *Free as the Air to Common Use: First Amendment Constraints on Enclosure of the Public Domain*, 74 N.Y.U. L. REV. 354, 420–21 (1999) (using the fence

and benefits is beyond the scope of this chapter, but one feature of this phenomenon deserves mention. As more uses are swept into the right, the fencing metaphor is more likely to be used. Copyright may be moving some way toward the exclusion pole of the spectrum of strategies for delineating rights. Often any tendency to employ copyright to deny access to published material is criticized as inconsistent with copyright law or policy, or with the First Amendment.[80] Even such criticisms of excessively strengthening copyright, or calls for patent rights to be attenuated along the lines of copyright, all implicitly take for granted that patents fall further toward the full property end of the spectrum.

For copyright, the fencing metaphor tends to be used when commentators argue that authors can in effect protect ideas – making copyright into an exclusion-like rule of access – especially in the electronic domain.[81] But, unlike in patent law, this exclusion may take the form of legal protection against the activities of others. For example, the Digital Millennium Copyright Act (DMCA) of 1998 prohibits an activity – that is, circumventing "a technological measure that effectively controls access to a [copyrighted] work."[82]

---

analogy, and arguing against information enclosure); Julie E. Cohen, *Lochner in Cyberspace: The New Economic Orthodoxy of "Rights Management,"* 97 Mich. L. Rev. 462 (1998).

[80] See, e.g., Shyamkrishna Balganesh, *Copyright and Free Expression: Analyzing the Convergence of Conflicting Normative Frameworks,* 4 Chi.-Kent J. Intell. Prop. 45 (2004); Benkler, supra note 79; Paul Goldstein, *Copyright and the First Amendment,* 70 Colum. L. Rev. 983 (1970); Lawrence Lessig, *Copyright's First Amendment,* 48 UCLA L. Rev. 1057 (2001); L. Ray Patterson, *Free Speech, Copyright, and Fair Use,* 40 Vand. L. Rev. 1, 5–7 (1987). But see, e.g., Christopher L. Eisgruber, *Censorship, Copyright, and Free Speech: Some Tentative Skepticism About the Campaign To Impose First Amendment Restrictions on Copyright Law,* 2 J. on Telecomm. & High Tech. L. 17 (2003); David McGowan, *Why the First Amendment Cannot Dictate Copyright Policy,* 65 U. Pitt. L. Rev. 281 (2004).

[81] See, e.g., Dan L. Burk, *Muddy Rules for Cyberspace,* 21 Cardozo L. Rev. 121, 168 (1999) (discussing new "technological fences"); Ejan Mackaay, *The Economics of Emergent Property Rights on the Internet,* in The Future of Copyright in a Digital Environment 13, 21 (P. Bernt Hugenholtz ed., 1996); Neil Weinstock Netanel, *Copyright and a Democratic Civil Society,* 106 Yale L.J. 283, 285 (1996) ("[S]uch technological fences would raise the specter of all-consuming copyright owner control."); Maureen A. O'Rourke, *Fencing Cyberspace: Drawing Borders in a Virtual World,* 82 Minn. L. Rev. 609 (1998); see also, e.g., Julie E. Cohen, *A Right To Read Anonymously: A Closer Look at "Copyright Management" in Cyberspace,* 28 Conn. L. Rev. 981, 983–89 (1996) (discussing technologies for monitoring and controlling access to information); cf. Wendy J. Gordon, *Asymmetric Market Failure and Prisoner's Dilemma in Intellectual Property,* 17 U. Dayton L. Rev. 853, 855 (1992) (analogizing any right to exclude to fences in real property).

[82] 17 U.S.C. § 1201(a)(1)(A) (2000) (emphasis added); see id. § 1201(a)(3)(B) ("[A] technological measure 'effectively controls access to a work' if the measure, in the ordinary course of its operation, requires the application of information, or a process or a treatment, with the authority of the copyright owner, to gain access to the work."). The DMCA includes

This set-up is reminiscent of trade secret, in which the law focuses on activities that circumvent the efforts of the trade secret holder to keep the secret. Trade secret itself is perched between a property-like regime of exclusion and a more tort-like, activity-based governance regime rooted in notions of fair competition. Like torts, trade secret sometimes focuses on activities and applies an evaluative standard to them, but it sometimes applies more modular bright-line rules to create an exclusive zone within which secrets may be kept.[83] Nonetheless, trade secret only provides protection for information that the owner can feasibly keep secret (typically processes and customer lists).[84]

Copyright is also less exclusionary and more governance-like than patent when it comes to refinement of the basic rights. This emerges in some of the main differences between patent and copyright law with respect to independent invention or creation and compulsory licensing.

2. Independent Invention or Creation. Patent law, but not copyright law, gives a right against independent inventors that can be crucial in areas such as software, in which both forms of protection are in principle available, at least for different program elements (e.g., function, structure, various interfaces, code).[85] Denying a defense of independent invention causes the right to rely on a more exclusion-like signal and allows more information hiding within the property module. The signal is bright-line and rough

provisions concerning manufacturing, importing, offering to the public, providing, or otherwise trafficking in technology that is "primarily designed or produced for the purpose of circumventing," has "only limited commercially significant purpose or use other than to circumvent," or "is marketed . . . for use in circumventing a technological measure that effectively controls access to a work protected under this title." Id. § 1201(a)(2).

[83] The leading case of making a trade secret an _in rem_ right is _E.I. duPont deNemours & Co. v. Christopher_, 431 F.2d 1012 (5th Cir. 1970), in which the court held that DuPont could sue photographers who had been hired by a competitor and had aerially photographed a plant under construction without committing any independent crime or tort. For a discussion of the two traditional approaches to trade secret, sounding in tort and property, see _Rockwell Graphic Sys., Inc. v. DEV Indus., Inc._, 925 F.2d 174 (7th Cir. 1991) (Posner, J.).

[84] The primary difficulty is defining what degree of secrecy suffices; absolute secrecy would prevent any dealings with outside contractors. See, e.g., _Metallurgical Indus., Inc. v. Fourtek, Inc._, 790 F.2d 1195, 1200 (5th Cir. 1986) (noting that "[a]lthough the law requires secrecy, it need not be absolute," and upholding a finding that the plaintiff's particular modification of a well-known process was secret); RESTATEMENT OF TORT § 757 cmt. b (1939) (stating that the holder of a secret may communicate it to employees and others pledged to secrecy without losing protection, but that "a substantial element of secrecy must exist, so that, except by the use of improper means, there would be difficulty in acquiring the information").

[85] See, e.g., Dam, supra note 70; Pamela Samuelson et al., _A Manifesto Concerning the Legal Protection of Computer Programs_, 94 COLUM. L. REV. 2308 (1994); cf. Reichman, supra note 47 (proposing a hybrid regime).

and does not require a detailed evaluation of activities with respect to the invention. Also, as Norman Siebrasse has pointed out, a defense of independent creation makes protection of the original more costly; the holder of a right in the original faces a claim that the defendant copied an independent creation.[86] Ruling out a defense of independent invention causes property rights to be clearer and the interface simpler, which can be seen as a by-product of employing the exclusion strategy. Various possible versions of an independent invention defense would be refinements characteristic of a governance regime. While they would address the problem of inadvertent infringement with its attendant surprises and would reduce an arguably excessive reward for some inventions, they would make rights more difficult to define and transfer.[87] Also, the more commercialization (as opposed to initial invention) is important to the patent system, the more moving from exclusion toward governance through an independent inventor defense will decrease the modularity of the rights involved.[88] As usual, whether the benefits of this tailoring outweigh the costs – especially if it involves any variation according to context, such as industry or features of the invention itself – is an empirical question.

3. *Compulsory Licenses.* Even more strikingly, patent and copyright differ in their degree of reliance on compulsory licenses. Patent law in the United States has never made much use of compulsory licenses.[89] Copyright is another story: The right to exclude in copyright is subject to a number of exceptions in which the statute provides for compulsory licenses.[90] These

[86] See Norman Siebrasse, *A Property Rights Theory of the Limits of Copyright*, 51 U. TORONTO L.J. 1, 22–42 (2001).

[87] See Samson Vermont, *Independent Invention as a Defense to Patent Infringement*, 105 MICH. L. REV. 475 (2006) (arguing for an independent invention defense); see also Mark A. Lemley, *Should Patent Infringement Require Proof of Copying?*, 106 MICH. L. REV. 1525, 1531–32 (2007) (pointing out that an independent invention defense would lessen the marketability of patent rights).

[88] Samson Vermont's proposal presumes that the reward to invent is the key to the patent system, Vermont, supra note 87, at 479, and to the extent that commercialization is important, this would counsel caution, see Lemley, supra note 87, at 1530–1531 (arguing that commercialization concerns are a reason for caution, but that commercialization is important only in some industries, like pharmaceuticals).

[89] See *Dawson Chem. Co. v. Rohm & Haas Co.*, 448 U.S. 176, 215 & n.21 (1980) (noting that "[c]ompulsory licensing is a rarity in our patent system," and that compulsory licensing of patents has often been proposed but never enacted); W.R. Cornish, INTELLECTUAL PROPERTY: PATENTS, COPYRIGHT, TRADE MARKS AND ALLIED RIGHTS 254 (3d ed. 1996) (remarking on "[t]he hostility of the United States to the very idea of compulsory patent licensing").

[90] On the four compulsory license provisions of the 1976 Copyright Act, see Paul Goldstein, *Preempted State Doctrines, Involuntary Transfers and Compulsory Licenses: Testing the Limits of Copyright*, 24 UCLA L. REV. 1107, 1127–39 (1977). The jukebox compulsory license of

exceptions for compulsory licenses cover secondary transmission by cable television, production and distribution of phonorecords of musical works, use by noncommercial broadcasters, satellite retransmission, and manufacturing and importing of digital audiotape devices.[91] Commentators have been divided over whether compulsory licenses really do provide significant benefits in terms of reducing transaction costs.[92] At least on the cost side, however, we can say that copyright is more susceptible to enrichment of modular rights through a more elaborate interface of compulsory licenses than is patent law because the measurement problems are not as great. Patent law is far less tailored to particular technologies,[93] and the use-based exceptions that do exist in patent law, such as for experimental use, are few and not favored.[94]

4. *Further Exceptions.* Other exceptions to copyright are likewise framed in terms of use and do not have counterparts in patent law. Most prominently, the doctrine of fair use is another limitation on copyright, and, as its name implies, it involves the measurement or evaluation of uses.[95] Gordon has

an earlier section 116 of the 1976 Copyright Act was considered incompatible with the International Union for the Protection of Literary and Artistic Works (Berne Convention) and was repealed and replaced with a voluntarily negotiated system. See 17 U.S.C. § 116 (2000).

[91] 17 U.S.C. § 111(c)-(e) (cable licenses); id. § 115 (phonorecords); id. § 118 (public broadcasting); id. § 119 (satellite retransmission); Audio Home Recording Act of 1992, Pub. L. No. 102–563, 106 Stat. 4237 (codified at 17 U.S.C. §§ 1001–1010) (digital audio tape devices).

[92] See, e.g., 2 Paul Goldstein, COPYRIGHT: PRINCIPLES, LAW AND PRACTICE 19 (1989) (describing and partially endorsing the conventional wisdom).

[93] The Trade-Related Aspects of Intellectual Property Rights (TRIPS) agreement contains a requirement that countries offer patents for inventions regardless of the field of technology, subject to a few exceptions. Agreement on Trade-Related Aspects of Intellectual Property Rights (TRIPS) art. 27(1), Apr. 15, 1994, Marrakesh Agreement Establishing the World Trade Organization, Annex 1C, pmbl., Legal Instruments – Results of the Uruguay Round, 33 I.L.M. 1197, 1208.

[94] See Kenneth W. Dam, *Intellectual Property and the Academic Enterprise* 7–8 (Chi. Working Paper Series, Paper No. 68, 2d ser., (1999); Rebecca S. Eisenberg, *Patents and the Progress of Science: Exclusive Rights and Experimental Use,* 56 U. CHI. L. REV. 1017, 1074–78 (1989) (arguing for a broad experimental use exception). As these authors have noted, courts are likely to reject the defense whenever the researcher might profit from the experimental use – a situation that is increasingly at issue.

[95] See 17 U.S.C. § 107. The statute defines fair use in terms of purposes "such as criticism, comment, news reporting, teaching (including multiple copies for classroom use), scholarship, or research." Id. It also calls for evaluation of the use mainly on the basis of use-based factors, which include: (1) the purpose and character of the use, including whether such use is of a commercial nature or is for nonprofit educational purposes; (2) the nature of the copyrighted work; (3) the amount and substantiality of the portion used in relation to the copyrighted work as a whole; and (4) the effect of the use on the potential market for or value of the copyrighted work. Id.

argued that fair use is a response to "market failure" in the sense that, given the copyright holder's rights, the copyright holder and other interested parties (including the public at large) may be unable to serve certain interests.[96] One might ask, as Maureen O'Rourke has, whether such an exception should be exported to patent law.[97] On the benefit side, as O'Rourke has shown, such an approach might well serve some interests, including those of a public good character such as basic research, that receive inadequate protection from the narrow and uncertain experimental use defense in patent law.[98] But on the cost side, the separation and evaluation of individual uses is likely to be costlier in patent than in copyright; in patent law, the scope of the right is broader and more exclusion-like – more modular – in the presence of multiple, indefinite uses that are difficult to evaluate.

Other exceptions in copyright are provided for performances at agricultural fairs, horticultural fairs, or exhibitions;[99] educational copying;[100] first sale;[101] and public performances for educational, religious, or charitable purposes.[102] Fair use and these other exceptions can be thought of as a compulsory license with a zero royalty rate.[103] Most recently, the DMCA provides a procedure whereby the Librarian of Congress can make exceptions, for certain classes of users, to the Act's prohibition on any circumvention of a "technological measure that effectively controls access";[104] in other words, even in its strongest, most exclusion-like (and most controversial) form, copyright features a detailed governance regime of fine-tuned balancing between access and use.

---

[96] *See* Wendy J. Gordon, *Fair Use as Market Failure: A Structural and Economic Analysis of the Betamax Case and Its Predecessors*, 82 Colum. L. Rev. 1600, 1601 (1982) ("[T]he courts and Congress have employed fair use to permit uncompensated transfers that are socially desirable but not capable of effectuation through the market.").

[97] See O'Rourke, supra note 66.

[98] See id. at 1198–1211. This is all the more so after the Federal Circuit's decision in *Madey v. Duke University*, 307 F.3d 1351, 1361–62 (Fed. Cir. 2002) (holding that the "very narrow and strictly limited experimental use defense" does not apply when allegedly infringing conduct is in furtherance of "the institution's legitimate business objectives, including educating and enlightening students and faculty participating in these projects," and that the nonprofit status of the defendant university was not determinative).

[99] 17 U.S.C. § 110(6).

[100] This is an outgrowth of fair use. See id. § 107.

[101] Id. § 109.

[102] Id. § 110(4).

[103] Hardy, supra note 79, at 253 n.96; see also, e.g., Robert P. Merges et al., Intellectual Property in the New Technological Age 268–273 (4th ed. 2006) (discussing compulsory licenses and excuses as exceptions to intellectual property rights); Burk, supra note 733, at 140 (analyzing fair use as a muddy entitlement).

[104] 17 U.S.C. § 1201.

Although these exceptions can be viewed as the product of interest group activity,[105] the argument here is that interest groups succeeded in copyright as opposed to patent law in part because the costs of separating out and policing uses in copyright are lower in the first place. Notice that if the range of uses is lower or the measurement of types of uses is easier in copyright, this is likely to facilitate legislative bargaining. Many have argued that the legislative process in copyright is characterized by interest groups responding to technological change with proposals for an ad hoc addition to the law, sometimes a new compulsory license. This legislation is complicated, and industry groups are so involved that some have argued that Congress delegates the fashioning of copyright law to representatives of these industries.[106] On the information cost theory, if the range of uses is narrow, then fewer, more concentrated interests will be involved and their heterogeneity will be lower. These are among the factors that promote deals concerning institutional change.[107] Likewise, if there is a range of relevant uses but they are easy to separate, narrow deals can be made without the expansion to additional groups of heterogeneous (and hence especially transaction-cost-increasing) interests. Interestingly, on notable occasions when potential deals did have such wider implications, copyright negotiations have broken down.[108]

B. Rewards and Prospects

These differences between patent and copyright are also reflected in the range of theories in each area. Both patent and copyright have been justified on a wide variety of partially overlapping grounds.[109] In this section, I use information costs to explain why "rewards" for invention or "encouragement" for creation have been invoked in both areas, but "prospects" for development and commercialization-based theories are largely limited to patent law.[110] These patent-specific theories of commercialization or

---

[105] See, e.g., Jessica D. Litman, *Copyright, Compromise, and Legislative History*, 72 CORNELL L. REV. 857, 870–79 (1987) (detailing the role of interest groups in the legislative history of the 1976 Copyright Act).

[106] See Jessica Litman, *Copyright Legislation and Technological Change*, 68 OR. L. REV. 275 (1989).

[107] See Gary D. Libecap, CONTRACTING FOR PROPERTY RIGHTS 19–89 (1989).

[108] Litman, supra note 106, at 279.

[109] See, e.g., Wendy J. Gordon, *An Inquiry into the Merits of Copyright: The Challenges of Consistency, Consent, and Encouragement Theory*, 41 STAN. L. REV. 1343 (1989); Oddi, supra note 3.

[110] The incentive to disseminate is sometimes offered as an additional rationale for copyright. 1 Paul Goldstein, GOLDSTEIN ON COPYRIGHT § 1.0 (3d ed. 2006) (explaining that copyright law seeks to "encourag[e] the production of the widest possible array of literary, musical

prospects are heavily based on the high cost of measuring uses – making the governance strategy relatively more costly than the exclusion strategy.[111]

Patents have been justified as rewards for invention. But others have argued that they are also "prospects" that promote a variety of actions to increase the value of the invention and, in particular, to commercialize it. Copyright is more straightforwardly a reward for creation; investment in improvement and commercialization do not seem to be as important in copyright – at least as compared to patent – as reasons for granting property rights and free speech concerns are raised by a very broad copyright.[112] The entitlement in copyright is correspondingly narrower and less modular; it includes the right to copy and related rights.

Commentators in the reward tradition focus on tailoring the reward to the value of the inventor's or creator's contribution, and this concern has led to calls for use of liability rules, buy-outs, and cash rewards.[113] Other, more "property-oriented" commentators have stressed the role of the patent as a prospect, allowing the patent holder (who need not be the inventor) to take actions to raise the value of the patent prospect – for example, through further research or through marketing efforts.[114] Just how much of a reward for invention is required, or how strong property rights for

and artistic works"); Robert A. Kreiss, *Accessibility and Commercialization in Copyright Theory*, 43 UCLA L. Rev. 1 (1995).

[111] Another theory of patent is based on rent-seeking, see, e.g., Yoram Barzel, *Optimal Timing of Innovations*, 50 Rev. Econ. & Stat. 348 (1968); Mark F. Grady & Jay I. Alexander, *Patent Law and Rent Dissipation*, 78 Va. L. Rev. 305 (1992); Jack Hirshleifer, *The Private and Social Value of Information and the Reward to Inventive Activity*, 61 Am. Econ. Rev. 561 (1971), although one of the functions of the patent prospect on Kitch's theory is to communicate claims and reduce duplicative effort, see Kitch, supra note 4, at 278.

[112] This is not to say that commercialization is of no concern in copyright. Copyright is sometimes justified on the grounds of dissemination as well as creation. See, e.g., *Eldred v. Ashcroft*, 537 U.S. 186, 188, 207, 228 (2003) (noting that Congress had a rational purpose in extending the term of the copyright to promote the restoration and dissemination of old works); id. at 239 (Stevens, J., dissenting) (arguing that restoration and dissemination cannot justify the extension); id. at 260 (arguing that overall dissemination is best promoted by the end of a copyright term). And, as copyright law is amended to cover more acts, critics cite its property-like and trespass-like features and the enclosure of the information commons. See supra notes 79, 733 and accompanying text.

[113] *See* sources cited supra note __.

[114] See, e.g., F. Scott Kieff, *Property Rights and Property Rules for Commercializing Inventions*, 85 Minn. L. Rev. 697 (2001) (arguing that the commercialization function requires property rule protection for patents); Giles S. Rich, *The Relation Between Patent Practices and the Anti-Monopoly Laws*, 24 J. Pat. Off. Soc'y 159, 177–81 (1942) (arguing that promoting the commercialization of inventions is the most important function of patent law); see also Kitch, supra note 4, at 276–277, 284 (discussing, inter alia, the role of patent prospect in giving "the patent owner . . . an incentive to make investments to maximize the value of the patent," including investments in manufacture, distribution, and market development).

commercialization should be, is beyond the scope of this chapter. But the information cost theory suggests an important role for exclusion, especially in patent law.

In terms of the model developed here, the decision to include a wide and indeterminate range of multidimensional, difficult-to-measure uses in patent favors access-based rather than use-based rules. However one resolves issues such as the size of rewards, market power (if any), and facilitating bargaining,[115] the wide range of interlocking and indefinite uses covered by patents leads to information cost problems that push the system toward exclusion and a more modular, property-like right. At any rate, it is striking that a prospect theory – under which broad rights facilitate coordination of development through control by the owner – has been proposed and debated extensively for patents but not for copyrights.[116] Moreover, the prospect theory responds to the information problems inherent when an "asset" requires costly measurement along many margins at once – a situation that has generally received less attention than it deserves.[117]

The information cost theory also sheds some light on the tension between the reward and prospect theories of patent law. Patents may both reward the inventor and provide property rights to secure a prospect. But information cost concerns mean that this prospect (or reward) cannot be too finely tailored to the nature and value of the activity; part of the point of granting prospects is that it is difficult for officials to value the contributions that someone commercializing an invention makes to the value of a product. Finely tailored rewards for inventors require exactly this kind of valuation when it comes to the inventor's contribution to the product. Both types of measurement – of the value of inventive and commercializing activities – will be very difficult, and for many of the same reasons;

---

[115] See, e.g., Ian Ayres & Eric Talley, *Distinguishing Between Consensual and Nonconsensual Advantages of Liability Rules*, 105 YALE L.J. 235 (1995); Ian Ayres & Eric Talley, *Solomonic Bargaining: Dividing a Legal Entitlement To Facilitate Coasean Trade*, 104 YALE L.J. 1027 (1995) (arguing that liability rules facilitate bargaining); Rachel Croson & Jason Scott Johnston, *Experimental Results on Bargaining Under Alternative Property Rights Regimes*, 16 J.L. ECON. & ORG. 50 (2000); Louis Kaplow & Steven Shavell, *Do Liability Rules Facilitate Bargaining? A Reply to Ayres and Talley*, 105 YALE L.J. 221 (1995); *see also* Carol M. Rose, *The Shadow of* The Cathedral, 106 YALE L.J. 2175 (1997) (noting the preference for property rules to protect certain classes of entitlements).

[116] See Mark A. Lemley, *Ex Ante Versus Ex Post Justifications for Intellectual Property*, 71 U. CHI. L. REV. 129 (2004); *see also, e.g.,* Wendy J. Gordon, *Authors, Publishers, and Public Goods: Trading Gold for Dross*, 36 LOY. L.A. L. REV. 159, 170 n.38 (2002) ("Moreover, the centralization argument [of the prospect theory] has little force when applied to copyright, a field whose merit is diversity rather than centralization.").

[117] See Henry E. Smith, *Ambiguous Quality Changes from Taxes and Legal Rules*, 67 U. CHI. L. REV. 647, 649–53 (2000).

separating out the contributions of inputs to novel products will consume resources. Thus, when inventive, and especially commercializing, activity presents these information problems, rewards for inventive activity will be correspondingly costly. And, to the extent that prospect theory is strong, the reward theory will tend to be weak. There is a trade-off between the benefits of accurate measurement for rewards and the costs of measurement that are reduced by prospect-like property rights.

The information cost theory also suggests that certain advantages to the patent owner are more important than others. Reward theory does not, without more, tell us much about whether rights that are substantively broader, or longer, or greater in other dimensions are the way to achieve the optimal reward. The information cost theory highlights the benefits of functionally broad rights, encapsulating information about uses within the modular right, particularly when uses are interlocking and indefinite, as they typically are in patent law.[118] The exclusion strategy's delegation of the gatekeeping function to owners is particularly important when the uses behind the gate are costly to delineate or even to foresee. Thus, among the various "levers" at the disposal of those designing an intellectual property system,[119] functionally broad rights to exclude are likely to be comparatively cost effective.

Finally, the model here is consistent with the observation by many commentators that electronic communication and other technological advances can decrease transaction costs and lead to contractual provisions that effectively extend intellectual property protection. Whether this is a problem has been very controversial,[120] but the fact that it might occur follows from the model. As bargaining costs decrease, the marginal cost curve for use-based contractual devices could lower, leading to a likely substitution away from more property-like devices and to an overall more precise level of

---

[118] Criticism of the prospect theory often assumes that it calls for substantively broad rights. See, e.g., Grady & Alexander, supra note 111, at 317; Merges & Nelson, supra note 18, at 875. This is less than clear, see Kitch, supra note 4, at 273 ("The mineral claim system restricts the area that can be claimed through rules that specify maximum boundaries in relation to the location of the mineralization. In the patent system, the applicant must limit his claims to his invention." (footnote omitted)), but both the mineral claim system and the patent system use a basic exclusionary approach to allow the holder of the claim or patent to choose between a wide variety of actions in developing the asset. Functional breadth is characteristic of rights under both systems, making Kitch's mineral analogy apt in this respect.

[119] See, e.g., Dan L. Burk & Mark A. Lemley, *Policy Levers in Patent Law*, 89 Va. L. Rev. 1575 (2003).

[120] See, e.g., sources cited supra note 733. For example, much controversy surrounds the DMCA.

delineation and enforcement of rights. With new technology, a bundle of *in personam* rights could tend to be substituted for off-the-rack *in rem* rights.

C. Intellectual Property and the Mix of Exclusion and Governance

Because the model offered here makes the mixture of exclusion and governance a matter of degree, it is not surprising that neither patent nor copyright – nor real property for that matter – instantiates an absolute or ideal right to exclude. Nonetheless, the model here, in conjunction with the massive information cost problems presented by sorting out issues involving returns, positive and negative, from assets and related inputs, sees exclusion as playing an otherwise unexpectedly large role in both the worlds of tangible and intangible assets. As in the case of real property, exclusion, because of its advantages in dealing in a rough way with many uncertain uses by delegating decisions to owners, is predictably used as a first cut in handling problems of appropriation (both intellectual property and property) and use conflict (mainly property). The central empirical question in both regular property and intellectual property is when – and how easily – to overcome the basic presumption for exclusion.[121]

What separates the information cost theory from those of the legal realists and their successors is the basic presumption for exclusion. Intellectual property commentators are quite correct in observing that the exceptions to property show that analogies to property furnish grounds for thinking about cabining intellectual property rights and that injunctions should not be automatically available in all cases.[122] Consider building encroachments.[123] Courts have long struggled with the problem of good faith improvers, those who build over the line in a good faith belief that they are building on their own property. Courts and statutes have moved to a regime of damages in cases of good faith building encroachment – but not in cases of deliberate encroachment – in part because we do not want people to expend excessive resources (multiple surveys, large buffer zones) in order

---

[121] See Smith, supra note 6, at 1021–1045 (setting out a framework of presumptive exclusion and refinement through governance in the context of nuisance law).

[122] See, e.g., Carrier, supra note 24 (surveying property doctrines that limit the right to exclude and drawing on them proposals to cabin intellectual property law); Mark A. Lemley & Philip J. Weiser, *Should Property or Liability Rules Govern Information?*, 85 Texas L. Rev. 783 (2007) (arguing for liability rules in case-by-case analysis using traditional tests for equitable relief).

[123] Smith, supra note 61, at 2128.

to avoid trivial encroachments.[124] Likewise, commentators are understandably worried about inadvertent infringement in patent law, in which the edges of the claim are not always well-defined *ex ante*.[125] If in certain contexts the problem of good faith "encroachment" becomes serious enough in patent law, a limited good faith user defense with damages rather than an injunction would be appropriate.[126] Another candidate might be cases in which the literal bright-line "boundary" of the claim acquires an uncertain penumbra under the doctrine of equivalents; one could lower the protection from injunction to damages where there is no literal infringement but only a violation of rights under the doctrine of equivalents. In intellectual property as in regular property law, moving from property rules to liability rules is but one method of softening the basic presumptive exclusion regime, but the information cost advantage of basic exclusion points toward the greater strength of the presumption for exclusion and property rules than would otherwise be expected.

Normatively, a shift from exclusion to off-the-rack governance is desirable in a context of both high stakes and comparative advantage for a court's *ex post* solutions. Again, where the switch should occur is an empirical question.[127] Moreover, if exclusion has the information cost advantages I am arguing for as a basic platform and the solution is not a reconfiguration of boundaries, then the switch is likely to be from exclusion to governance. This set-up – of basic regime of exclusion to refinement, extension, and partial override through governance – follows from the model offered here and some basic factual assumptions about information costs. Descriptively, such

---

[124] See, e.g., Merrill & Smith, supra note at 50–56, 62–67; Carrier, supra note 24, at 74–75 (discussing building encroachments).

[125] Bessen & Meurer, supra note 41; Lemley & Weiser, supra note 122, at 793–96 (arguing that uncertainty of definition of entitlements in intellectual property is a factor favoring liability rules); Smith, supra note 61, at 2127.

[126] Id. at 2129–32.

[127] My present purpose is not to make broad empirical claims but to develop a theoretical framework and to point to property aspects of intellectual property that have been overlooked. By contrast, the usual paradigm in intellectual property scholarship is to make normative claims based on empirical priors. In his recent response to an earlier article of mine, Michael Carrier claims to see the type of quasi-empirical claim I am trying to avoid, see Michael A. Carrier, *Why Modularity Does Not (And Should Not) Explain Intellectual Property*, 117 YALE L.J. POCKET PART 95 (2007) (mistaking information cost theory for a pro-exclusion prescription for intellectual property), as I have emphasized before, Henry E. Smith, *Intellectual Property as Property: Delineating Entitlements in Information*, 116 YALE L.J. 1742, 1745, 1750–51, 1761, 1764, 1779–81, 1811, 1818–19, 1821–22 (2007); see also Henry E. Smith, *Intellectual Property as Property: Delineating Entitlements in Information*, 117 YALE L.J. POCKET PART 87 (2007).

a structure seems roughly to fit both property and intellectual property –
and on a more micro scale, patent and copyright – and is hard to capture
from a pure legal realist point of view.

III. Dynamic Implications

The conventional skeptical view of intellectual property rights implies
an anti-Demsetzian view of their evolution. According to Demsetz's
famous thesis, rising resource values should result in the emergence and
development of property rights.[128] I have argued elsewhere that the rights
that emerge need not be exclusion rights; under some circumstances an
increase in value can lead to more elaborate rules governing use.[129] For
example, increased congestion on a commons can lead to stints and other
norms or formal rules of proper use.[130] Increases in pollution externalities
led to the development of nuisance law and later pollution controls.[131] If,
as seems to be the case, information is becoming more important in the
economy and the subject of more commercial activity, what new types of
rights, if any, should we expect to emerge?

The conventional view offers a clear answer: We should expect more
attenuation of exclusive rights and expect that any increase in exclusive
rights is the result of rent-seeking by producers. On this view, because
information is nonrival, the more important it is, the more the nonrival
aspect should dominate in the design of a legal regime for information. (In
a sense, this view adopts the anti-Demsetzian or pessimistic Demsetzian
story for the evolution of property rights in information.) More specifically,
many who are skeptical of intellectual property make affirmative arguments
for the increasing importance of the public domain. Exclusive intellectual
property rights derogate from the public domain and thus suffer from
presumptive illegitimacy.

At the other end of the spectrum, others point to the increasing importance of information as a reason to increase incentives though stronger
intellectual property rights. This approach is optimistically Demsetzian
in that increasing resource values call for "more" property rights. It also
assumes that more property means more exclusion.

---

[128] See Harold Demsetz, *Toward a Theory of Property Rights*, 57 AM. ECON. REV. (PAPERS &
PROC.) 350 (1967).

[129] See Smith, supra note 15.

[130] See Rose Carol M. Rose, *Rethinking Environmental Controls: Management Strategies for
Common Resources*, 1991 DUKE L.J. 1, 8–12.

[131] See, e.g., id. at 9–36; see also Smith, supra note 15, at S482–83.

Regarding intellectual property as like regular property in solving coordination problems in a modular fashion makes both positions look too hasty. Taking IP (intellectual property) optimistism first, the importance of incentives does not by itself answer the question of whether more reliance on the exclusion strategy makes sense. The importance of the attribution of returns to rival inputs could call for greater precision in the delineation of rights to the use of those inputs – a more articulated governance regime. As for the IP pessimists, if information is more valuable, tracing its value is likely to be more complex than ever; particularly in the area of commercializing patentable information, the interaction of inventions is likely to be more intense than ever. Each product will incorporate increasingly specialized innovations. Furthermore, the very nonrivalness of uses of information makes the problem of attributing returns for appropriation more difficult, because a nonrival use does not announce itself in the same way that a rival use does through its interference with other uses (think of classic crops and cattle). Coordinating all this activity and solving the appropriation problem may well call for more modularity through exclusive rights, not less. Only by ignoring the benefits of the modularity of the intellectual property system can its inferiority in a static or a dynamic sense be argued on theoretical grounds alone. The nonrival aspect of information does not preclude a need for a modular exclusion-based system to solve the coordination of commercialization when not all the inputs to the process are nonrival.

Thus, for more reliance on exclusion to make sense on the model presented here, we would have to be sure of two conditions. First, the benefits of exclusive rights must have risen faster than the costs of establishing them. Second, the relative costs of exclusion and governance must favor exclusion at the higher level of the property rights delineation effort. Again, how far the benefits carry us along the supply curve of property rights and how components of that curve for exclusion and governance may have shifted relative to each other are the essential empirical questions, not simply the rising importance of incentives.

If it is modularity that makes intellectual property rights most like property, this opens up avenues for empirical guesswork. As organizational theorists apply modularity theory to the production of artifacts, we might look for analogs of the intellectual property system on smaller scales where the designers of the system have incentives to get things right.[132] One theme that emerges from the organization literature on modularity is that

---

[132] The management and economics literature applying Simon's theory of modular systems to organizations is a start. See supra note 12 and accompanying text.

modularity of the production process can be implemented by providing for modular design of the product itself: By specifying only how components must combine (the interface), the within-module decisions can be made independently. This keeps many options open because there is less need to commit to a decision for the sake of other decisions relevant to other components.[133] There is a tendency for organizations to reflect the artifacts they design and produce. Furthermore, the question of whether firms should choose to bring a transaction within the firm or pursue it in a market – and, if within the firm, within a more articulated divisional structure or team – is parallel to the question of modularity in property. As noted earlier, the boundaries of a firm render the nexus of contracts more thing-like and partake of some of the information cost advantages of the exclusion strategy. Intellectual property may serve a similar coordinating function in a similarly modular way. Once we better understand these areas and their similarities and differences, developments in one area – such as private contracting in the setting of business organizations – can provide some clue as to the benefits and costs of exclusion and forms of governance in other areas – such as intellectual property. We have to make do with the best information available. But looking for such analogies as suggested by a theory of wide applicability throughout human activity and cognition is likely to be an improvement over the current state of empirical knowledge.

IV. Conclusion

Intellectual property is most like property when not viewed in isolation. Although it is true that the nature of the "resource" is very different – because it is nonrival – from the typical resource in the law of property, this is not the end of the story. Intellectual property, like property in general, can be seen as the solution of a complex coordination problem of attributing outputs to inputs. In the intellectual property area, different actors combine inputs with something that can be said to belong to the public. As long as the innovator's or commercializer's rival input is valuable enough and the overall coordination problem of investment, appropriation, and consumption is complex enough, the theory of systems and our experience with human artifacts should lead us to expect a major role for modular solutions. Property, with its boundaries and rights of exclusion indirectly protecting an

---

[133] See Baldwin & Clark, supra note 12; Kim B. Clark & Carliss Y. Baldwin, The Option Value of Modularity in Design: An Example from Design Rules, Volume 1: The Power of Modularity (Harvard NOM Working Paper No. 02-13; Harvard Business School Working Paper No. 02-078, Jan. 2009).

indefinite range of internally interacting uses, makes the system of commercializing innovation more modular. In both intellectual property and property more generally, exclusion rights – as modified by governance rules – furnish, at some positive cost, modularity to the system of providing inputs and appropriating benefits from assets. Ultimately, the desirability of intellectual property rights is an empirical question. The answer must take into account the crucial role of modularity in organizing the production of modular artifacts, which commercialized inventions themselves have increasingly become.

14

Removing Property from Intellectual Property and (Intended?) Pernicious Impacts on Innovation and Competition

F. Scott Kieff

Commentators have poured forth a loud and sustained outcry over the past few years that sees property rule treatment of intellectual property (IP) causing excessive transaction costs, thickets, anticommons, holdups, holdouts, and trolls unduly taxing and retarding innovation, competition, and economic growth. The popular response has been to seek a legislative shift toward some limited use of weaker, liability rule treatment, usually portrayed as "just enough" to facilitate transactions in those special cases where the bargaining problems are at their worst and where escape hatches are most needed. This chapter is designed to make two contributions. First, it shows how, through a set of changes in case law over just the past few years, the patent system has been hugely re-shaped from a system having several major, and helpful, liability-rule-pressure-release-valves into a system that is fast becoming almost devoid of significant property rule characteristics, at least for those small entities that would most need property rule protection.

The author gratefully acknowledges financial support for this work from the Northwestern University School of Law Searle Center Project on Innovation, Entrepreneurship, and Economic Growth. The author also gratefully acknowledges intellectual contributions from participants at the 2007 and 2008 Annual Conferences on the Law and Economics of Innovation presented by George Mason University and Microsoft, at the Research Roundtable on the Law & Economics of Innovation and the Research Symposium on Property Rights Economics and Innovation, both hosted by Northwestern University School of Law's Searle Center, as well as the Annual Meeting of the International Society of New Institutional Economics, and from workshop participants at George Washington University Law School, Washington University School of Law, the Max Planck Institute for the Study of Intellectual Property, and the Munich Intellectual Property Law Center, and appreciates more detailed comments provided by Harold Demsetz, Steve Haber, Troy Paredes, Matt Sag, and Henry Smith. This work is part of the Hoover Task Force on Property Rights, Freedom, and Prosperity, which studies the philosophical, historical, legal, and economic foundations of property rights, as well as the Hoover Project on Commercializing Innovation, which studies the law, economics, and politics of innovation and which is available online at www.innovation.hoover .org. Correspondence may be sent to fskieff.91@alum.mit.edu.

The chapter then explores some harmful effects of this shift, focusing on the ways liability rule treatment can seriously impede the beneficial deal-making mechanisms that facilitate innovation and competition. The basic intuition behind this bad effect of liability rules is that they seriously frustrate the ability for a market-challenging patentee to attract and hold the constructive attention of a potential contracting party (especially one that is a larger, more established party) while preserving the option to terminate the negotiations in favor of striking a deal with a different party. At the same time, liability rules can have an additional bad effect of helping existing competitors to coordinate with each other over ways to keep out new entrants. The chapter is designed to contribute to the literature on IP in particular, as well as the broader literatures on property and coordination, by first showing how a seemingly disconnected set of changes to the legal rules impacting a particular legal regime like the patent system can have unintended and sweeping harmful consequences, and then by exploring why, within the more middle range of the spectrum between the two poles of property rules and liability rules, a general shift toward the property side may be preferred by those seeking an increase in access and competition.

I. Introduction

Getting resources put to use by market actors requires them to interact with each other and with various government actors in various ways, depending on the set of applicable laws, rules, and norms (collectively, "institutions"), and their enforcement characteristics. This chapter uses the set of analytical tools from the field generally called new institutional economics (NIE)[1] to offer a comparative analysis of the various interaction mechanisms that result when the applicable institutions governing private sector entitlements take on the essential features of one of the two paradigmatic types that are generally labeled by the law, economics, and NIE literatures as either "property rules" or "liability rules." Property rules are seen as designed to generally keep an entitlement in the hands of its owner unless the owner consents to use or transfer; and emblematic property rules include injunctions designed to prevent such use or transfer, and enhanced damages designed to deter them. Conversely, liability rules are seen as designed to allow infringement when the owner refuses consent, or when the owner is not even asked, and

---

[1] See, e.g., Oliver E. Williamson, MARKETS AND HIERARCHIES: ANALYSIS AND ANTITRUST IMPLICATIONS: A STUDY IN THE ECONOMICS OF INTERNAL ORGANIZATION 1 (1975) (representative early work using the term NIE); Ronald Coase, *The New Institutional Economics*, 88 AM. ECON. REV. 72 (1998).

generally require the nonowner merely to pay, after a lawsuit the property owner elected to bring and maintain, whatever amount of money the property owner proves in court to be attributable to the objectively measured damages caused by the infringement.[2] While most debates about property and IP focus on questions of how many property rights would be best, generally with owners demanding more property rights and users demanding fewer, this chapter focuses attention instead on the different question of how these entitlements are structured, with an eye toward facilitating mechanisms for diverse sets of complementary users of an asset to coordinate with each other over ways to get the asset put to ever higher and better uses while frustrating mechanisms for existing competitors to coordinate with each other over ways to keep out new entrants.

In the vast majority of the intellectual property (IP) literature, property rule treatment of IP is said to cause excessive transaction costs, thickets, anticommons, holdups, holdouts, and trolls unduly taxing and retarding innovation, competition, and economic growth. The popular view of IP for the past several years has been that property rule treatment is stopping deals from getting done, leaving desired users of IP subject matter unable to engage in sufficient productive activities. For example, the injunction infamously sought against the provider of the BlackBerry service was said to threaten ongoing operations at the upper echelons of the American business, nonprofit, and government sectors, which were staffed by VIP's who had come to so depend on the devices that the nickname "Crackberry" was spawned.[3] To hear some tell it, one might have thought the American way of life was at stake and executive levels of our society would shut down if the injunction had been granted.[4]

---

[2] See, e.g., Guido Calabresi & A. Douglas Melamed, *Property Rules, Liability Rules, and Inalienability: One View of the Cathedral*, 85 HARV. L. REV. 1089, 1092 (1972). Of course, even property rules allow for compelled transfer by a host of mechanisms such as takings accompanied by just compensation, and even liability rules discourage taking to the extent of the risk of judgment enforcement and collection. The difference is both a matter of degree as well as the mechanisms by which such transfers are modulated; yet while the labels are thereby hugely imperfect, they are so well accepted in the law and economics literatures that their use easily conveys sufficient meaning to those in these fields.

[3] Blackberry maker Research in Motion is reputed to have strategically targeted such VIP's for free devices as a marketing ploy, recognizing that if the leadership of an organization liked the devices, it would both increase the willingness of the organization to invest in the infrastructure needed to support them and, at the same time, lend a level of prestige to having the devices.

[4] See, e.g., Ian Austen, *Bye Bye Blackberry?; A Patent Dispute Threatens To Cut Executives Off*, N.Y. TIMES Dec. 3, 2005, at C1; Jane Spencer & Jessica E. Vascellaro, *Imagining a Day Without BlackBerrys – Possibility of Shutdown Has Some Users Panicking, Others Dreaming of Freedom*, WALL ST. J. Jan. 25, 2006, at D1.

In response, many commentators suggested trying to solve these important problems of property by only slightly shifting toward some limited use of liability rule treatment. The idea was to facilitate transactions in those targeted cases where the bargaining problems are at their worst and where escape hatches are most needed.

One well-known problem with such a targeted response is that the number of targets is actually not small. Property can face serious pitfalls when the negotiations it would require involve one or both sides being made up of a large number of parties, thereby triggering problems of coordination, free-riding, holdouts, etc., such as when a large number of users would each require permissions from a large number of IP owners. Property's pitfalls also can be serious when the two sides of the negotiation are each individuals, who would still face problems of bilateral monopoly, strategic behavior, and cognitive biases. And mixed sized models raise a mix of both sets of problems.[5] But focusing on efforts to determine which of these situations should be targeted first would be a tragic mistake because a more troubling problem has crept up.

This chapter argues that just as Jonathan Swift's *A Modest Proposal* was a less than forthright title for its suggestion that the eighteenth-century Irish poor sell their children as food for the rich, the calls for targeted reforms in the patent system over the past few years by innovation's discontents[6] have not sufficiently acknowledged the important role played by liability rules long present in the patent system or the ways in which the reforms they were pushing would almost remove property rule treatment from this area of IP. Section II of this chapter begins the discussion by elucidating the several major, and largely helpful, liability-rule-pressure-release-valves that were already built into the patent system and the recent changes that have all but stripped away those few significant property rule characteristics that were remaining. Section III then explores some pernicious effects of this shift by focusing on the ways liability rule treatment can seriously impede the beneficial deal-making mechanisms that facilitate innovation and competition. The basic intuition behind this bad effect of liability rules is that they seriously frustrate the ability for a market-challenging patentee to attract and hold the constructive attention of a potential contracting party (especially one that is a larger, more established party) while preserving

---

[5] See, e.g., James E. Krier & Stewart J. Schwab, *Property Rules and Liability Rules: The Cathedral in Another Light*, 70 N.Y.U. L. Rev. 440, 450–51 (1995).

[6] Many of the reform proponents rely on the book by economists Adam Jaffee and Josh Lerner called Innovation and Its Discontents: How Our Broken Patent System is Endangering Innovation and Progress, and What to Do About It (2004).

the option to terminate the negotiations in favor of striking a deal with a different party. The discussion also elucidates the way other related and recent shifts in the law governing contracts over patents further frustrate the ability to strike such pro-competitive, pro-innovation helpful deals. Section IV concludes.

II. The Patent System's Liability Rules

Liability rules are no stranger to the patent system. Liability rule treatment is expressly provided in a number of areas within patent law, and a number of other areas of patent law have liability rule effect. In addition, patents are enforced only against a backdrop of general civil law, which itself contains a number of tools that effectively keep enforcement of an entitlement like an IP right limited to liability rule treatment in many contexts.

A. Liability Rules Long in Use

Most property rights systems recognize that an absolute right to exclude backed up by inexpensive, immediate, certain, and powerful enforcement could lead to serious risk that socially productive uses might be prevented or deterred, or that other collateral costs might be realized. For this reason, even most systems of real or personal property have a host of mechanisms for allowing trespass to occur without imposing an immediate death sentence. The patent system also has long recognized that it can be helpful to allow some extent of liability rule treatment, as a tool for facilitating some transactions. While there are a number of these liability rule provisions, they are not redundant or identical. Rather, each operates on its own terms and is the product of diverse debate and careful evolution.

1. Corporate Law, Bankruptcy Law, Litigation

One of the most important, but also most overlooked, sources of liability rule impact on the patent system are the generally applicable bodies of law relating to the corporate form, bankruptcy, and litigation. Indeed, it has been those often seen as being on the so-called pro-property side of the debates about IP who have pointed out this effect, and even urged its importance to certain types of deal structures.[7] Because these areas of general commercial

---

[7] See, e.g., F. Scott Kieff, *Property Rights and Property Rules for Commercializing Inventions*, 85 Minn. L. Rev. 697 (2001) (general importance); F. Scott Kieff & Troy A. Paredes, *Engineering a Deal: Toward a Private Ordering Solution to the Anticommons Problem*, 47 Boston College L. Rev. 111 (2006) (particular deal structure).

law exist largely independent of any one area of entitlement-creating law such as IP, it would be a stretch to say that these areas of law are part of IP in the narrow sense; but they do operate to burnish down the sharp edges one might otherwise imagine would be associated with IP. They also were very much on the mind of the leading champions of the long-operating version of our patent system – the 1952 Patent Act – since those champions – such as Judges Learned Hand and Jerome Frank – were at the same time leading voices in debates about commercial law generally.

While relatively new to the IP literature, the general finance and liability literatures have long focused on the ways the limited liability offered to shareholders under the corporate form[8] can be combined with the ability to seek protection from the bankruptcy laws to allow for a number of so-called judgment-proofing strategies such as sale-leasebacks, doing business through subsidiaries, franchising, off-shore asset sequestration, secured debt, and traditional asset securitization, each of which may have the effect of eliminating legal liability.[9] These techniques are equally

---

[8] For more on limited liability, see, e.g., Frank H. Easterbrook & Daniel R. Fischel, *Limited Liability and the Corporation*, 52 U. Chi. L. Rev. 89, 105–06 (1985); Timothy P. Glynn, *Beyond "Unlimiting" Shareholder Liability: Vicarious Tort Liability for Corporate Officers*, 57 Vand. L. Rev. 329 (2004); Joseph A. Grundfest, *The Limited Future of Unlimited Liability: A Capital Markets Perspective*, 102 Yale L.J. 387 (1992); Paul Halpern et al., *An Economic Analysis of Limited Liability in Corporation Law*, 30 U. Toronto L.J. 117 (1980); Henry Hansmann & Reinier Kraakman, *Toward Unlimited Shareholder Liability for Corporate Torts*, 100 Yale L.J. 1879 (1991); David W. Leebron, *Limited Liability, Tort Victims, and Creditors*, 91 Colum. L. Rev. 1565 (1991); Henry G. Manne, *Our Two Corporation Systems: Law and Economics*, 53 Va. L. Rev. 259, 261–65 (1967); Robert B. Thompson, *Unpacking Limited Liability: Direct and Vicarious Liability of Corporate Participants for Torts of the Enterprise*, 47 Vand. L. Rev. 1 (1994). While the focus here is on corporations, limited partners in a limited partnership and members in a limited liability company also enjoy the benefits of limited liability.

[9] For a sampling of the literature on judgment proofing, on which this chapter's discussion of the subject builds, see, e.g., Lynn M. LoPucki, *The Death of Liability*, 106 Yale L.J. 1 (1996) [hereinafter LoPucki, *Death of Liability*]; Lynn M. LoPucki, *The Essential Structure of Judgment Proofing*, 51 Stan. L. Rev. 147 (1998) [hereinafter LoPucki, *Essential Structure*]; Lynn M. LoPucki, *The Irrefutable Logic of Judgment Proofing: A Reply to Professor Schwarcz*, 52 Stan. L. Rev. 55 (1999) [hereinafter LoPucki, *Irrefutable Logic*]; Lynn M. LoPucki, *Virtual Judgment Proofing: A Rejoinder*, 107 Yale L.J. 1413 (1998) [hereinafter LoPucki, *Virtual Judgment Proofing*]; Charles W. Mooney, Jr., *Judgment Proofing, Bankruptcy Policy, and the Dark Side of Tort Liability*, 52 Stan. L. Rev. 73 (1999); Steven L. Schwarcz, *Judgment Proofing: A Rejoinder*, 52 Stan. L. Rev. 77 (1999) [hereinafter Schwarcz, *Rejoinder*]; Steven L. Schwarcz, *The Inherent Irrationality of Judgment Proofing*, 52 Stan. L. Rev. 1 (1999) [hereinafter Schwarcz, *Inherent Irrationality*]; Steven Shavell, *The Judgment Proof Problem*, 6 Int'l Rev. of L. & Econ. 45 (1986) [hereinafter Shavell, *Judgment Proof Problem*]; James J. White, *Corporate Judgment Proofing: A Response to Lynn LoPucki's The Death of Liability*, 107 Yale L.J. 1363 (1998); Steven Shavell, *Minimum Asset Requirements and Compulsory Liability Insurance as Solutions to the Judgment-Proof Problem* (Harvard, John M. Olin

available against patent infringement judgments, and indeed many are used by parties anticipating or engaged in patent litigation.

In addition, judgment proofing against tort creditors like patentees can be particularly easy – essentially all that need be done is operate within an outrage constraint.[10] For example, as long as those running the infringing business respect the corporate form and pay themselves nonfraudulent wages and dividends, and so on, they will be able to derive a vast amount of money and other benefits from an infringing business before an infringement lawsuit is brought and won and its judgment collected, and then they will be able to keep those gains from getting hauled back into the infringement estate.

An interesting question for further research might be to study why these techniques are not used even more widely. While some have suggested that such fears over the death of formal legal liability are overstated, because, for example, a parent corporation would rationally elect to pay for the debts of its subsidiary out of an interest in preserving goodwill and reputation, some recent decisions to not pay in the cases involving sex abuse charges against the Catholic Church and alleged human rights violations in Nigeria by a subsidiary of Chevron suggest the reputational constraints may not bind.[11] The bottom line for infringers is that as a practical matter they may not be on the hook, at least not for the full amount, even if they are found to have infringed.

Even when the careful corporate structuring and planning needed to reduce liability have not been taken, the award of liability can be significantly deterred or delayed by the ordinary process of civil litigation. Patents are wasting assets in that they only remain in force for up to about seventeen years, and for most patents it is not until several years into the patent term that the patented technology even becomes commercially significant. Meanwhile, trying a patent case typically takes at least three to five years, and the appeal typically adds another two to three years. If the patent suit is not likely to end before the patent expiration, any threat of injunction will significantly decrease if not become a nullity.

Cost also is a significant deterrent. Patent litigation typically costs each side 3 to 5 million dollars, although it is not rare for cases to take more than

---

Discussion Paper No. 456, 2004), available at http://www.law.harvard.edu/programs/olin_center/papers/pdf/456.pdf [hereinafter Shavell, *Minimum Asset Requirements*].

[10] That is, avoid behavior that is so totally outrageous that it would generate some type of social backlash.

[11] I thank Lynn LoPucki for pointing this out. See also Lynn M. LoPucki, *Toward a Trademark-Based Liability System*, 49 UCLA L. Rev. 1099, 1131–34, n. 153 (2002).

five years and cost each side 20 to 30 million dollars. Much hay is made by commentators about the threat of damages awards in patent cases frequently reaching into the hundreds of millions and sometimes billions of dollars. But regardless of its size, no judgment is likely to be worth more than the amount that can actually be collected and the judgment proofing strategies can keep collections to a minimum. Decisions to pursue litigation have to weigh the certainty of the several million dollars in litigation expenses against the possibility of collecting on a judgment as well as the possibility of the judgment being awarded.

2. Uncertain Enforcement Mechanisms

As Ayres and Klemperer point out, uncertainty and delay in the patent system have the same effect as liability rule treatment.[12] While Ayres and Klemperer complain about the large degree of certainty in the system, Lemley and Shapiro explore the many ways in which the system is properly seen as a probabilistic game of great uncertainty.[13]

3. Experimental Use and the Hatch-Waxman Act

Some commentators have long suggested that patent law should permit noncommercial, experimental use of a patented invention as an exception to infringement under a so-called experimental use exemption or research use exemption. To the extent this doctrine exists, it was severely limited in the case of *Roche v. Bolar*,[14] in which the court held that limited experimental use by a generic drug company to obtain Food and Drug Administration (FDA) approval for use after the patent expired was an infringing use.

Congress responded to *Roche* with the enactment of the Hatch-Waxman Act in 1984, which added Section 271(e) to the Patent Act, and which essentially deems activities reasonably related to FDA approval to be non-infringing, so as to streamline FDA approval of so-called Abbreviated New Drug Applications (ANDAs). At the same time, the Act requires the sponsor of the ANDA to make a certification that the drug will not infringe any valid claim and deems the filing of such a certification to be a jurisdictionally creating act of infringement so that a patentee can bring suit on the patent

---

[12] Ian Ayres & Paul Klemperer, *Limiting Patentees' Market Power without Reducing Innovation Incentives: The Perverse Benefits of Uncertainty and Non-Injunctive Remedies*, 97 Mich. L. Rev. 985, 92 (1999) (criticizing the crispness of the present patent system).

[13] Mark A. Lemley and Carl Shapiro, *Probabilistic Patents*, 19 J. Econ. Persp. 75 (2005).

[14] 733 F.2d 858 (Fed. Cir. 1984).

during the FDA approval process and, if victorious, keep the competition from coming to market until after the patent expires. At the same time, the competition is allowed to make progress on obtaining FDA approval before the expiration of the patent so that he is ready to come to market soon after expiration. Thus, in the field of biotechnology, the experimental use exception has been viewed as rather liberal but restrained by the mechanisms of the Hatch-Waxman Act; and in other fields of technology the exception is very limited by the holding of *Roche*, if the exception exists at all.

It makes sense for the research use exemption to be limited because it turns out that most research uses are in effect permitted via a different mechanism than some formal legal rule of excuse or exception. The transaction costs of dealing with a patentee's right to exclude are not carried entirely by those wanting to obtain permission for use. Unlike the copyright system, the patent system does not have criminal liability or statutory damages, and so the costs of enforcement for patents are born by the property owner. The presence of these significant enforcement costs and the lack of significant enforcement benefits in many cases, especially those against low-value users for whom damages are likely to be low and even high-value users who are judgment proof or judgment remote, combine to make it rational for patentees to greatly underenforce. Importantly, the theory just reviewed is borne out by the facts. Empirical studies of the impact patents have had on basic scientists, for example, have shown that very large numbers of low-value infringements are routinely allowed for free.[15]

4. Acts of Infringement by or for the Government

As demonstrated in the infamous post-9/11 anthrax scare during which the federal government wanted the owner of the patent on Cipro to provide large quantities of the drug at a low price, the federal and state governments have some protection from infringement by the doctrine of sovereign immunity. The federal government is subject to suit in the United States Court of Claims by a patentee for "his reasonable and entire compensation"[16] but not for an injunction. In the case of Cipro in the post-9/11 anthrax scare, the government's threat to either make the drug or have it made was enough

---

[15] Timothy Caulfield, Robert M. Cook-Deegan, F. Scott Kieff, & John P. Walsh, *Evidence and Anecdotes: An Analysis Of Human Gene Patenting Controversies*, 24 NATURE BIOTECH. 1091 (2006).

[16] 28 USC § 1498. This may either be seen as a limited waiver of sovereign immunity or as a statute that assigns jurisdiction for a cause of action that exists as of the right to seek just compensation for a taking under the 5th Amendment. Compare Zoltek.

to get Bayer, the patentee, to drop its price and increase its output. To be sure, decisions to do this are cabined by the political process as well as the constitutional and statutory requirements that the government pay just compensation, but, as seen in cases like *Kelo*, that outrage constraint does not always bind, and parties in need of use are welcome to simply ask the government to make the decision to infringe or to arrange for the infringement.

State governments also are immune. The Supreme Court decided that state governments were immune from suit for patent infringement and that Congressional efforts to abrogate that immunity were unconstitutional under the 11th Amendment.[17] While state officials likely may be enjoined,[18] they may not be personally sued for those patent infringements that are properly part of their official acts.

B. Liability Rules Recently Added

While the patent system had long contained the mix of property and liability rules described previously, the mix was radically shifted over the past few years with a slew of high-profile cases that have almost decimated the property rules remaining in the system. These many new, and overlapping, liability rules are each discussed in the following subsections.

1. Injunctions Eliminated by the *eBay* Case

For a long time, a central part of the value in a patent was the credible threat of an injunction. But the recent Supreme Court decision in *eBay* may weaken this long-standing practice.[19] Some see this case as having raised the bar for patentees seeking an injunction after there has been a full adjudication of patent validity and infringement by injecting more discretion in the determination of essentially whether an injunction is in the broadly defined public interest. Others see the case as merely restating the established practice that an injunction should issue once validity and infringement have been decided in court. In the final analysis, the full impact of the *eBay* case remains an open question for debate.[20]

---

[17] See *Florida Prepaid Postsecondary Education Expense Board v. College Savings Bank*, 527 U.S. 627 (1999).
[18] Ex Part Young.
[19] See *eBay Inc. v. MercExchange, LLC*, 126 S.Ct. 1837 (2006).
[20] For more on why and how the *eBay* decision's four-factor test for injunctions should not be read to be such an open-ended analysis, see F. Scott Kieff, & Henry E. Smith, *How Not*

But in the short term it looks as if even the Federal Circuit is treating the case as making it very hard to get an injunction except if the patentee is a large manufacturing entity. In October of 2007 the court issued an opinion in *Paice v. Toyota* affirming the power of a district court to impose a post-verdict "ongoing royalty" on future sales of a product adjudicated to infringe a patent adjudicated to be not invalid after a full trial by sophisticated and well-financed defendants.[21] The court took pains to write that this was merely an "ongoing royalty" and "not a compulsory license" because it did not apply to nonparties to the lawsuit. What the court seems to have overlooked is that the defendant elected to be a party by electing to infringe and the patentee was compelled to be a party and compelled to accept the royalty, leaving open the suggestion to future parties interested in this and other patents that the season for infringement is open.

2. Enhanced Damages Eliminated by the *Seagate* Case

The victorious patentee in an infringement suit is supposed to be awarded at least actual, objective, damages "adequate to compensate for the infringement, but in no event less than a reasonable royalty."[22] In the past, the patentee also was generally able to receive enhanced damages for willfulness, which is a question of fact to be proven by clear and convincing evidence, and which, if found by fact-finder, would then leave within the judge's discretion a decision about whether to treble damages and award attorney fees.[23]

However, the ability for patentees to obtain enhanced damages for willfulness may have been significantly curtailed by the Federal Circuit's August 2007 decision in *Seagate*.[24] In that case, the Federal Circuit seemed to have established a new requirement for proving willful infringement, a showing of "objective recklessness" on the part of the infringer, based on a two-step test: (1) The infringer acted despite an objectively high likelihood that its actions infringed a valid patent, treating the infringer's subjective state of mind as irrelevant; and then (2) that the objectively high risk was

---

to Invent a Patent Crisis, in REACTING TO THE SPENDING SPREE: POLICY CHANGES WE CAN AFFORD, Terry L. Anderson and Richard Sousa, eds., Hoover Institution Press, 2009; Stanford Law and Economics Olin Working Paper No. 384; Harvard Public Law Working Paper No. 10-02. Available at SSRN: http://ssrn.com/abstract=1496990, at 68–69.
21 *Paice LLC v. Toyota Motor Corp.* 504 F.3d 1293 (Fed. Cir. Oct. 18, 2007).
22 35 USC § 284.
23 35 USC §§ 284–85.
24 See In re Seagate Technology, LLC, 497 F.3d 1360 (Fed. Cir. 2007) (en banc).

either known or should have been known to the infringer.[25] The court took pains to emphasize that "[b]ecause we abandon the affirmative duty of due care, we also reemphasize that there is no affirmative obligation to obtain opinion of counsel."[26] The court also strongly suggested that a substantial question regarding infringement or validity that is sufficient to avoid a preliminary injunction also is likely sufficient to avoid a willful infringement finding. But because permanent injunctions are likely to be significantly harder to obtain after *eBay*, the preliminary injunctions contemplated by *Seagate* are even more unlikely. In addition, because the general substantive uncertainty discussed above, especially when enhanced by the added uncertainty discussed below, is likely to leave most patent infringement cases in a bad position for a preliminary injunction, the new *Seagate* test probably means that all those cases now are also in a correspondingly bad position for enhanced damages. Put differently, after *Seagate*, it is hard to imagine a patentee who can win enhanced damages regardless of the notice he gives the defendant.

3. Expanded Hatch-Waxman Immunity by the *Merck* Case

The common-law research use exemption discussed previously seems to have been reaffirmed recently to be extremely narrow in exempting only those uses that are "for amusement, to satisfy idle curiosity, or for strictly philosophical inquiry."[27] For academic researchers, who do much if not all of their work in furtherance of philosophical inquiry, the legal test in essence allows only for a very limited amount of research to be conducted on patented technologies to confirm whether they work as described in the patent. It does not allow for the user of a patented technology to be legally exempt from infringing simply because their use has to do with research or is for research purposes. The distinction here is between researching with and researching on, which basically distinguishes between a business purpose that would not be exempt and a purely philosophical interest that could be. The bottom line is that only a limited number of uses to genuinely test whether a patented technology works will be good candidates for the common-law exemption.

Nevertheless, and despite the clear legislative intent to limit the Hatch-Waxman Act's exemption for infringement, the Supreme Court in the recent *Merck* case treated the statutory exemption so broadly that the Court gave

---

[25] Seagate, 497 F.3d at 1371.

[26] Id.

[27] *Madey v. Duke University*, 307 F.3d 1351 (Fed. Cir. 2002).

a free pass from infringement for work relating to preclinical studies of a new drug seeking FDA approval.[28] A careful reading of the *Merck* decision would of course not extend its impact beyond the narrow facts of the case. Any other view would not only be an overly strained reading of the opinion; it also would undercut the important policies of the patent system. But the language of the *Merck* opinion seems to suggest that the statutory exemption now is not limited only to the development of information for submission to the FDA and that instead Congress "exempted from infringement all uses of patented compounds 'reasonably related' to the process of developing information for submission under any federal law regulating the manufacture, use, or distribution of drugs."[29] This language seems to cover almost any use by any company that is in some way regulated by the government, and which therefore may reasonably be anticipating submitting data to a regulatory body.

4. Increased Uncertainty by *KSR*, *Bilski*, and Other Cases

Two key areas of the law allocating or awarding the initial patent entitlement have undergone a dramatic increase in uncertainty in the past year. The first relates to the patent law requirement of nonobviousness and the second relates to the requirement of statutory subject matter.

The April 2007 U.S. Supreme Court decision in *KSR* is seen by many as having raised the bar for the nonobviousness standard by injecting more discretion into the determination of this central issue for most patent cases.[30] The central issue presented in *KSR* is whether expert opinion testimony in court when adopted at the discretion of a federal judge is enough to prove what would have been obvious to a person having ordinary skill in the art of the patentee at the time in history when the patentee made an invention. Patent critics see the *KSR* case as standing for the proposition that government decision makers, like judges, now have increased discretion to pronounce what the prior art teaches; and they applaud that result, hoping to see it applied in court and during initial Patent Office examination. For example, examiners would be able to block patents on the basis of their own assertions about what the state of the art was at a particular time in history, without having to rely on the factual proof, such as documents and sample products, which has long been required. Others think the case was narrowly decided on its facts and that the relevant inquiry remains

---

[28] *Merck KGaA v. Integra Lifesciences I, Ltd.*, 545 U.S. 193 (2005).

[29] *Merck*, 545 U.S. at 206.

[30] See *KSR International Co. v. Teleflex Inc.*, 127 S. Ct. 1727 (2007).

an objective determination of precisely what was taught by the particular combination of relevant pieces of prior art. If the case is ready broadly, then it injects a great degree of flexibility into the nonobviousness analysis.

Similarly, the Federal Circuit has just recently issued three opinions that inject a great degree of flexibility and uncertainty into the law of statutory subject matter. The Supreme Court and the Federal Circuit formerly treated as patentable subject matter "anything under the sun made by man."[31] In a case that effectively opened up the field of computer programs to patent protection, the Federal Circuit in banc upheld as directed to statutory subject matter a patent claim on a computer program for printing a smooth curve on a compute screen.[32] Then, in a case that effectively opened up the field of financial services to patent protection, the court did the same for a patent on a hub-and-spoke mutual fund accounting system, disposing of the so-called algorithm and business method exceptions to patentable subject matter.[33] Thus, until recently, the touchstone for patentable subject matter had been merely that the claimed invention must cause some concrete and tangible result, and, as a result, patentable subject matter itself presents a very low hurdle to patentability.

This all changed in September 2007, when the court issued its decision in *In re Comisky*.[34] This decision seems to limit the scope of the *State Street Bank* decision by requiring a pure mental process be connected to a machine (e.g., a computer) in order for a claim to recite subject matter that can be patentable. As a result of this decision, patent drafters and inventors of mental processes will be required to combine a particular technology such as a computer with such mental processes for the subject matter to meet the statutory requirement of patentable subject matter. While this seems like an easy decision to draft around, it is strikingly similar to the slippery slope we previously occupied in the 1970s and 1980s, during which we effectively made every software patent subject to discretionary review for being too close to a mental step and therefore invalid. Indeed, in a case handed down the same day as *Comisky*, *In re Nuijten*,[35] the Federal Circuit examined the patentability of claims to a digital watermark for a computer data file and simply declared it to be not within any patentable subject matter. While

---

[31] *Diamond v. Chakrabarty*, 447 U.S. 303 (1980). See also Diamond v. Diehr, 450 U.S. 175 (1981).

[32] See In re Alappat, 33 F.3d 1526 (Fed. Cir. 1994)(in banc).

[33] *State Street Bank & Trust Co. v. Signature Financial Group, Inc.*, 149 F.3d 1368 (Fed. Cir. 1999).

[34] 499 F.3d 1365 (Fed. Cir., 2007).

[35] 500 F.3d 1346 (Fed. Cir., 2007).

some may have thought that *Comisky* and *Nuitjen* were outliers, the Federal Circuit's October 30, 2008 in banc decision in *Bilski* seems to all but fully jettison the approach of cases like *State Street Bank* in deciding that to be eligible for patent protection the claimed subject matter must either (1) be tied to a particular machine or (2) transform a particular article.[36] It is difficult to imagine judges or anyone else viewing the precipitous drop in their own stock accounts caused by the fall 2008 economic collapse as not being a meaningful transformation; and yet the claim at issue in *Bilski* was directed to a process of managing financial risk of exactly that type. As a result, it looks like the definitional line drawing that will have to be done after *Bilski* to determine how much of a transformation in risk[37] or financial value is sufficiently transformative is at least as unpredictable as it was during the period of greatest recent uncertainty in this area – between the Supreme Court's 1972 *Benson*[38] and 1981 *Diehr* decisions. This type of "know it when you see it" decision making by a court re-injects massive uncertainty into the law of patentable subject matter.

While flexibility sounds attractive whether used in these areas or others, it has a serious Achilles Heel. By increasing the discretion of government bureaucrats, flexibility increases uncertainty, not decreases it, and it gives a built-in advantage to large companies with hefty lobbying and litigation budgets. That is a big reason why some big firms want it. And even if certain, it is now certainly much harder to get patents in this area.

III. How Liability Rules Frustrate Deals

A central and underexplored problem with liability rules is that they seriously frustrate the ability for the patentee to attract and hold the constructive attention of a potential contracting party while preserving the option to terminate the negotiations in favor of striking a deal with a different party. This comparative effectiveness of property rules in achieving these goals is the mechanism by which property rules facilitate both innovation and competition. That is, property rules help get done the deals needed to build the small- and medium-sized businesses that create new lines of business to compete against existing ones.

---

[36] In re Bilski, 545 F.3d 943 (Fed. Cir. 2008)(en banc), *petition for cert. granted, sub nom,* Bilski v. Doll, 129 S.Ct. 2735 (Jun 01, 2009). Given the oral argument in the case before the Supreme Court, it is likely that the predictable approach of cases like *Diehr, Alappat,* and *State Street Bank* is not likely to be embraced by the Court at this time.

[37] Would you feel you had been meaningfully transformed if you were warned sufficiently in advance to step aside from the freight train fast approaching you from behind?

[38] *Gottschalk v. Benson,* 409 U.S. 63 (1972).

A. Direct Impact of Recent Changes from Property to Liability Rules

Many scholars have focused on the relative overall information costs and transaction costs of liability rules compared with property rules, and the way liability rules tend to overall provide lower compensation than property rules.[39] In addition, Haddock, McChesney, and Speigel have explored the threat posed by a large number of potential takers in the liability rule setting and its net impact in decreasing *ex ante* incentives to invest in the underlying entitlement.[40]

Yet, the literature has not devoted much focus to the mechanism by which an actual breakdown in bargaining occurs (the "bargain effect" of property rules), let alone to the way the credible threat of exclusion associated with a published patent acts like a beacon in the dark, drawing to itself all those interested in the patented subject matter (a "beacon effect"). Knowing there is a good chance that a court employing a liability rule approach will set a lower price than the IP owner would accept, some potential infringers may first try for a low damage award from the court, rather than consummate a deal up front with the IP owner, and then later make a deal if the court award is too high. The prospect that infringement may be an attractive option to some can decrease the incentives for all others to attempt or consummate a deal up front, thereby weakening both the beacon effect and the bargain effect that are associated with property rules.[41]

The decrease in incentives in part occurs because each potential taker must worry about other potential takers following suit. That is, liability rules for one mean nonexclusive licenses for all.

---

[39] See, e.g., Richard A. Epstein, *A Clear View of The Cathedral: The Dominance of Property Rules*, 106 YALE L.J. 2091 (1997) (information costs and transaction costs); Robert P. Merges, *Of Property Rules, Coase, and Intellectual Property*, 94 COLUM. L. REV. 2655 (1994) (same); Henry E. Smith, *The Language of Property: Form, Context, and Audience*, 55 STAN. L. REV. 1005 (2003) (same); Richard R.W. Brooks, *The Relative Burden of Determining Property Rules and Liability Rules: Broken Elevators in the Cathedral*, 97 Nw. U. L. REV. 267, 268 n.8 (2002) (elucidating analytical framework for assessing "the relative burden (or costs, or difficulty) faced by judges when attempting to determine property rules and liability rules"); Louis Kaplow & Steven Shavell, *Property Rules Versus Liability Rules: An Economic Analysis*, 109 HARV. L. REV. 713 (1996) (undercompensation); see also Louis Kaplow & Steven Shavell, *Property Rules Versus Liability Rules: An Economic Analysis*, 109 HARV. L. REV. 713, 732–33 n.61 (1996) (same).

[40] David D. Haddock et al., *An Ordinary Economic Rationale for Extraordinary Legal Sanctions*, 78 CAL. L. REV. 1, 16–17 (1990); F. Scott Kieff, *Property Rights and Property Rules for Commercializing Inventions*, 85 MINN. L. REV. 697, 733 (2001).

[41] See F. Scott Kieff, *On Coordinating Transactions in Information: A Response to Smith's Delineating Entitlements in Information*, 117 YALE L.J. POCKET PART 101 (2007); F. Scott Kieff, *Coordination, Property, and Intellectual Property: An Unconventional Approach to Anticompetitive Effects and Downstream Access*, 56 EMORY L.J. 327 (2006).

The problem also is due to the way in which the incentive to consummate a deal is decreased by the availability of the option to get a court to force the deal. A central argument in favor of liability rule treatment is that it is most needed as a pressure release for those cases in which one side to a negotiation is acting irrationally or strategically and simply not getting along with the other. But, if the ability to avoid the property rule treatment hinged on the failure of a deal getting done, then there would be a markedly increased incentive for those wanting to obtain use through court-ordered terms to resist striking licensing deals. A legal test that rewards a failure to cooperate would lead to a decrease, rather than an increase, in cooperation.[42] Simply put, instead of the problem being a fear that the patentee is engaging in a holdout or a holdup game against the one desiring use, the problem will instead become that the patentee will be unable to hold its potentially bargaining partner in the negotiation, since that partner will instead want to engage in tactics designed to make the patentee act irrationally, such as by engaging in a proverbial Three Stooges poke in the eye, and then run off to simply wait for the court to issue what the Federal Circuit in *Paice v. Toyota* refused to call a compulsory license.[43]

What is more, not only is the patentee unable to hold this party in a negotiation, the patentee is unable to hold on to the option to end the negotiation and deal with some other user over an exclusive license or assignment. That is, not all deals should get done, and liability rule treatment forces them to get done.

What is worse, it appears that in the post-*eBay* world the only party that can count on an injunction will be a large manufacturing entity. Ironically, these are the parties that need the protection of the injunction the least. First off, large players will usually be better able to finance the litigation and so bring a more credible threat to bear against infringers. Second, large players are more likely than small players to be able to keep their potential contract counterparts engaged in a contract relationship without the credible threat of the injunction, relying instead on broader relationships, reputation effects, and bargaining power.

B. Other Deal-Breaking Changes in Rules about Patent Contracts

In addition to the recent shift toward overall liability rule treatment generally frustrating the ability of a patentee get done appropriate deals, another set

---

[42] Id.
[43] See supra note 22, and accompanying text.

of recent changes further frustrate that ability for the patentee to even settle or avoid cases. These involve the law governing two areas of contracting over patents, as discussed in the following subsections.

1. Inability to Settle or Avoid Litigation after the *Medimmune* Case

Invoking some kind of general and nonstatutory public policy against those patents that enjoy a statutory presumption of validity,[44] but that are likely to be held invalid by a court if adjudicated, the Supreme Court decided in the 1969 *Lear* case to allow a party to a patent license to contest the validity of the licensed patent even if there is an express promise in the contract license to not raise such a challenge.[45] The general rule of *Lear* had been interpreted to require a challenger to do more than simply stop paying the royalties or performing the other obligations under the contract – he must also go so far as to formally challenge the patent's validity.[46]

The balance these cases created essentially gave the licensee the benefit of not being bound to his promise to not challenge, but at the same time saddled the licensee with the obligation to actually walk away from the entire license agreement when challenging the patent. The basic point was that the challenger could renegotiate the entire deal by electing to challenge, but could not selectively hold the patentee to all terms binding the patentee while allowing the licensee to have a shot at renegotiating some decrease in payment or other obligation once the patent had been adjudicated invalid.

Concerned that this balance of interests was out of alignment, the January 2007 Supreme Court decision in *Medimmune* makes it particularly easy for the licensee to bring such a challenge by no longer requiring the licensee to have to go all the way to break the entire license contract itself, instead allowing the licensee to challenge while keeping the patentee bound by the remaining contract terms.[47] The court in that case held that the patent licensee in that case was "not required, insofar as Article III is concerned, to break or terminate its 1997 license agreement before seeking a declaratory judgment in federal court that the underlying patent is invalid, unenforceable, or not infringed."

---

[44] 35 U.S.C. § 282.
[45] *Lear v. Adkins*, 395 U.S. 653 (1969); see also *Beckman Instruments, Inc. v. Technical Dev. Corp.*, 433 F.2d 55 (7th Cir. 1970) (*Lear* applies to exclusive licensees); *Bull v. LogEtronics, Inc.*, 323 F. Supp. 115 (E.D. Va. 1971) (*Lear* applies to assignees).
[46] See, e.g., *Rite-Nail Packaging Corp. v. Berryfast, Inc.*, 706 F.2d 933 (9th Cir. 1983).
[47] See *MedImmune, Inc. v. Genentech, Inc.*, 549 U.S. 118 (2007).

Some might think that a contractual workaround to this case is the use of an express provision in the contract promising not to challenge the validity of the patent. But the broad public policy articulated in cases like *Lear* does not on its own terms have a constraint against being read so broadly as to make such a contractual provision against that public policy, and thereby unenforceable as against public policy or unenforceable as pre-empted by a federal policy. In addition, it is not clear what the remedy would be for such a breach. *Lear* itself prevents an injunction against challenging since *Lear* allows for a challenge in the face of a nonchallenge promise. It also is not clear what the damages would be. Even if the expectation damages were viewed as including the cost of litigation, in most of these cases the central goal of the patentee will be to either keep the licensee bound to all terms or to leave both parties unbound to any terms. It is not at all clear that some damages award could achieve either of these goals even if a court were included to try to award it. For example, some scholars, like Sean O'Connor, have suggested that parties enter into structured deals with stock and stock options in the licensee, to provide the patentee with a functional equivalent to a patent royalty stream.[48] A central shortcoming of approaches like these is the shortcoming that plagues any damages award. Damages do not cover for the many nonprice terms that are in patent license agreements – after all, if patent license agreements were only about price, they would be a single sentence listing price instead of being many pages in length. But patent license agreements are often very textured contracts having many terms, including price and a host of seemingly esoteric and unique provisions – such as technical support, field-of-use or territory limitations, grant-backs, cross-licenses, payment schedules, and most-favored-nation provisions.

As a result, it is likely that parties will pursue other contractual work-arounds. If maintaining the enforceability of these nonfinancial clauses is important to contracting parties, then one approach they might adopt is to split their patent licenses deals into two bundles, with one set of deals each being labeled as a simple patent license for a stated price, with the recognition that this one may be avoided through a one-sided challenge as in *Medimmune* and the second set being a single deal arranging through a complex relational contract the many other important terms. At least two problems arise with this strategy: It increases the overall social costs of contracting with little social benefit, and the complexity of such sets of deals

---

[48] Sean O'Connor, *Using Stock and Stock Options to Minimize Patent Royalty Payment Risks after* MedImmune v. Genentech, 3 N.Y.U. J. Law & Bus. 381 (2007).

will be pierced as courts treat them as essentially a single deal subject to the same treatment as in *Medimmune*.

The bottom line is that the medium and strong readings of *Lear* and *Medimmune* suggest that patentees will always have to recognize that when they give "peace" from litigation by executing a license agreement they will not be able to at the same time gain "peace" from litigation. This substantially reduces incentives to license by removing the central element – mutual and symmetrical "peace" – from the economics of a licensing transaction. A license is a promise not to sue, and those promises are now only enforceable one-way, which means they are of significantly less value to both sides of the deal.

2. Disincentive to Settle or Avoid Litigation after the *Quanta* Case

In June 2008 the Supreme Court issued its most recent patent decision in *Quanta v. LG*,[49] which involves a patentee's decision to settle out a dispute with one party, Intel, but giving that party a limited license for that party's own use. The contract in that case expressly provided that Intel's customers would not be licensed under the patent and expressly required Intel to give notice to those customers of this lack of license. Those customers were large computer manufacturers on actual notice of this lack of license and yet brought their case to the Supreme Court, arguing that the patentee in effect created an improper restrictive covenant running with the computer chips.

It made sense for Intel and the patentee to enter into this limited license because, essentially, the patentee and Intel were entering into a blanket settlement of IP cases that bought Intel freedom, but only bought freedom for Intel. Intel needed the freedom because, for example, Intel might otherwise have been guilty of inducing third parties to infringe when it sold its products, computer chips. This settlement made clear that it let Intel free but not Intel's customers, and the price reflected this limited ambition.

The petitioner in the case successfully argued that the so-called first sale doctrine makes the broad unrestricted license required. Under the long-established view of this doctrine, a patentee's unrestricted voluntary introduction of a patented article into commerce, such as through a sale, may prevent the patentee from exercising his right to exclude others from the particular article so introduced. For example, a patentee who makes an unrestricted sale of a patented widget may not be able to sue the buyer, or any other downstream user of that particular widget, for infringement. After all,

---

[49] *Quanta Computer v. LG Electronics*, 128 S.Ct. 2109 (2008).

the buyer presumably paid the patentee not only for title to the good in the sales sense, but also for permission to use it for its intended purpose. Thus, the first sale doctrine was long viewed safely as a contract-based doctrine that implied into contracts for unrestricted sales of patented articles a term that conveyed some authority to use the article free from a suit for infringement. But this long-established view of the doctrine treated it as merely a default rule, because courts had long recognized that restrictive terms in a sale – such as a sale accompanied by a promise to make only a single use of the patented article – would be enforceable as long as they do not violate some other rule of positive law, is not adhesionary, unconscionable, and so on.[50]

Importantly, in general, when you buy something you are not entitled to think that it is free of a patent – especially if you are a large commercial player. Under the long-established view of the first sale doctrine, it only got triggered if you bought the patented thing from the patentee, because it made sense in that case for you to have thought that you were buying a thing and also a license to use the thing under the patent – that is presumably why you bought it from the patentee rather than from someone else or made it yourself. The key was your reasonable impression as a buyer that you were getting a license. In *Quanta*, the "buyers" only came to know of Intel's license by reading it, and its text made explicit that only Intel was licensed and not Intel's customers. So, there was on the facts no chance of confusion or mistake or duress, and so on. Quite the opposite, the buyer had to argue that it was seduced into thinking it was licensed by reading only half the document that seduced it. But that seems to be what the Supreme Court decided.

The Court's decision in the case creates a very strong disincentive to settle a case with any one of the many possible infringers in a market. In view of *Quanta*, any such settlement is now likely to create some kind of license that could be used to launder all other members of the market. As a result, now settlements may have to be with all at a very high price or with none at all.

A range of structured workarounds may be attempted after *Quanta*. Each is discussed in the following, and each may be used alone or in combination with the others. But it is not clear whether any of these will be viewed by courts as being consistent with the broad policy statements made in the *Quanta* opinion. As a result, and as with attempted workarounds for *Medimmune*, the costs of transacting may increase with little benefit, or the attempted fixes may not even work.

---

[50] See *Mallinkrodt v. Medipart*, 976 F.2d 700 (Fed. Cir. 1992).

The first attempted fix for *Quanta* is to make clear that the contract being struck is not, in fact, a patent license. Under this approach, the contract should be labeled as a "restricted and limited agreement to release and not sue." All operative clauses should avoid using the word "license" and its variants and instead use variants of the phrase "restricted and limited agreement to release and not sue." To the extent that the court in *Quanta* is making broad statements about federal patent policy that impact patent licenses, structuring the deal in this suggested fashion places the deal more outside of the reach of that potential policy of federal patent law. Indeed, this approach also places the deal more within the zone of more favored policy of resolving and avoiding federal court litigation, a policy that is federal itself and so is not merely a matter of state contract law of the type that might be preempted by a potentially conflicting federal patent policy.

The second attempted fix, which assumes the parties strongly prefer labeling their contract a patent license, is to make clear in all references to the license in that contract, especially in the grant clause, that the license is, itself, on its own terms, restricted. The *Quanta* case and many patent first sale cases focus a great deal on there being an "unrestricted sale." To increase the chance that the parties take their license out of the reach of those cases, the parties should be sure to explicitly restrict all licenses and all sales of patented subject matter. That is, the license should be restricted to whatever limits they want to place on it, and in addition it should be restricted to reaching only those sales that are themselves made in a way that is expressly restricted.

The third strategy uses two guidelines that come from the *Quanta* decision itself. The Court in Quanta stated that so-called "patent exhaustion" occurs when: (1) the only "reasonable and intended use" of the component product sold was to practice the combination or method patent; and (2) the component product sold "embodies essential features" of the combination or method patent. As a result, the more the parties take a range of steps in the contract to make clear that the parties do not intend to have certain uses meet both of these tests, the more a court may determine those uses are not covered by the reach of "patent exhaustion." For example, if the contract can make clear what uses are "intended" and what uses are not, the more likely a later court will determine that "patent exhaustion" is not triggered. The central concern with this approach is that some courts may make their own determination of what use is reasonable and extend patent exhaustion to reach all of those uses regardless of the language in the contract to the contrary.

The fourth strategy is to make sure that any restrictions or limits or obligations that are associated with any grant are expressly structured as *conditions* rather than as contractual *obligations*. This is because if a contracting party does not meet all of its contractual obligations, then the only recourse is a suit for breach for which the remedy will be at most expectation damages. Moreover, only those breaches that are material will give rise to a cause of action, since substantial performance is all that many courts require. In contrast, if a material condition is not met, then the benefit the party seeks from the patentee is not itself triggered. The recourse for the patentee is more automatic and complete – the permission, or the license, or the promise not to sue, would not be given.

Only further empirical research will let us know which, if any, of these several contractual workarounds to *Medimmune* and *Quanta* are tried, whether they work, and so on. But one effect that is likely to evolve is that the most stable patent licenses after these cases will be those cross-licensing large portfolios, because only those types of licenses avoid the need for both precise evaluation and firm commitment for each patent – what holds together deals of that type is fear of mutually assured destruction, or a symmetrical threat of large numbers of litigations. If this prediction is correct, then the outcome will be a web of contractual arrangements between large players to the exclusion of market entrants, which is decidedly anticompetitive.

IV. Conclusion

The patent system presently seems to be devoid of property rules, especially for small market entrants trying to sue or license larger, more established market participants, and except perhaps for large established participants when suing market entrants. The stated purpose of stripping away this protection was to facilitate bargaining and avoid holdout and holdup effects. But while the property literature has long recognized and endeavored to mitigate the problems of property rules, we now face the problems of liability rules without the aid of a developed set of tools for mitigating them.

There are several basic intuitions underlying the problem caused by using liability rules only. First, while liability rules force deals, some deals just should not get done. Second, a rule that allows for liability rule intervention in those cases where the parties disagree on deal terms encourages disagreement and frustrates transactions. Third, and most importantly, liability rules make it significantly more difficult for owners of IP rights like patents to attract and hold the constructive attention of a potential contracting party (cannot hold in the counterparty), and eliminate the patentee's option to terminate the negotiations in favor of striking a deal with a different party (cannot hold on to option). This problem hits small firms worse than large firms because large firms have an easier time keeping their contracting parties tethered to deals through various devices such as bargaining power, access to resources needed to finance litigation and its threat, and reputation effects. Fourth, liability rules actually help large established firms to coordinate with each other in an anticompetitive fashion to keep out market entrants.

Worse yet, the problems that have recently been introduced into the patent system through the removal of property rule treatment are only compounded by shifts in other rules governing patent contracts. Even when patent deals are struck, they no longer seem to be enforced post-*Medimmune*. Alternatively, the licenses that a patentee does grant one party may be granted to all third-party buyers after *Quanta*, thereby creating a strong disincentive to even attempt to strike deals through patent settlements and other licenses. And the only firms well positioned to mitigate the transaction-inhibiting effects of these new contract law rules are those large firms that can use a strategy of swapping large portfolios of patent licenses, thereby further enhancing their ability to coordinate with each other to keep out market challengers.

The bottom line is that under the patent system newly created by the courts, it is very hard to see how patents can have significant positive effect in facilitating the coordination and contracting that can lead to increased competition and access. Instead, the prevalence of liability rules may actually be causing a substantial negative impact, the *keiretsu* effect of facilitating collusive anticompetitive coordination among large established market participants.[51] These problems explored here, which are seriously underexplored, if not totally ignored, by most of the contemporary literature combine to make the present system a strong candidate for change in the opposite direction called for by most other commentators.

Nevertheless, it is essential to keep in mind that even the present system, with its increased access to liability rules, is still a far cry from a full compulsory licensing system that some might advocate. The essential distinction

---

[51]   See, F. Scott Kieff, *On Coordinating Transactions in Information: A Response to Smith's Delineating Entitlements in Information*, 117 Yale L.J. Pocket Part 101 (2007); F. Scott Kieff, *Coordination, Property, and Intellectual Property: An Unconventional Approach to Anticompetitive Effects and Downstream Access*, 56 Emory L.J. 327 (2006).

here is between the compulsory licensing that involves a plea to the government for an exemption accompanied by some very modest payment, often from the government itself, and each of the detailed mechanisms that a party seeking to use a patented invention must employ to even take advantage of the various liability rules discussed in this chapter. At a minimum, this distinction should be preserved to prevent the United States from becoming a compulsory licensing regime.

PART VI

INTELLECTUAL PROPRETY AND ANTITRUST:
THE REGULATION OF STANDARD-SETTING
ORGANIZATIONS

15

Increments and Incentives

The Dynamic Innovation Implications of
Licensing Patents under an Incremental Value Rule

Anne Layne-Farrar, Gerard Llobet, and Jorge Padilla

A number of recent policy papers have called for patents to be priced according to a so-called incremental value rule, where licensing fees would be restricted to the value the patent adds as compared to licensees' next best alternative. Incremental value pricing is a common approach for physical goods and services, but intellectual property is different in a number of important ways. We evaluate the proposal to cap licensing fees at the incremental value of the patent. We find that while the incremental value rule has intuitive appeal, it is based on *ex post* reasoning in that it relies on the presumption that all needed innovations have already been developed. We consider the dynamic implications of the innovation process, assessing how the imposition of an incremental value licensing cap would impact a firm's decisions to invest in R&D and, when relevant, to participate in cooperative standard-setting efforts. Shifting the analysis to fully *ex ante*, before either licensors or licensees have made any irreversible investments, we find imposing an incremental value cap on licensing fees would lower R&D investments among innovators, it would lower SSO participation rates among patent holders, and it would even lower aggregate earnings for SSO members as a whole.

I. Introduction

A fundamental result in economics is that a firm facing competition for a particular product will be able to charge at most the incremental value

The authors thank Dhiren Patki for research assistance. Financial support from Qualcomm is gratefully acknowledged. The ideas and opinions in this chapter, as well as any errors, are exclusively the authors'. Comments should be sent to alayne@lecg.com, llobet@cemfi.es, and jpadilla@lecg.com.

that the product offers to customers over the next best alternative.[1] The intuition behind this result is straightforward: If product A offers customers on average $20 more value, say, than does the next closest product (call it B), then customers will be willing to pay a price up to $20 more for A as compared to B. At these pricing levels, the average customer's cost-benefit comparison of the two goods is equivalent. If the firm offering good A attempts to charge more than a $20 differential, customers will simply purchase product B instead, which is now relatively more attractive given its price advantage. Only in the rare instance where products are identical due to competition will all firms set prices equal to marginal cost.[2]

This incremental value pricing rule is well established for traditional goods, but recently it has been suggested that the rule should apply equally to intangible goods as well and, in particular, for patent licensing. For example, in the pharmaceutical industry, where intellectual property is particularly important, the incremental value cap logic is based on notions of "fair" remuneration for innovation, but which at the same time hold consumer drug prices at "reasonable" levels. For instance, a former Canadian Competition Bureau Economist argues that "[t]he key to unblocking the impasse of high drug prices is to reward drug innovators based on the therapeutic value their products create through national government-funded Pharmaceutical Innovation Funds."[3] Moreover, many organizations responsible for managing healthcare budgets "increasingly require evidence on value for money. To be good value drugs have to provide health gain at a price that is deemed affordable."[4]

---

[1] See Joseph E. Stiglitz, PRINCIPLES OF MICROECONOMICS 92 (Norton 1997) (discussing how price is related to marginal value); Sherwin Rosen, *Hedonic Prices and Implicit Markets: Product Differentiation in Pure Competition*, 82 J. POL. ECON. 34 (1974) (discussing market equilibrium in a competitive market with goods differentiated by quality).

[2] Of course, this discussion is based on the idea that all consumers agree regarding which product has the higher quality. Whenever this is not the case and products have attributes that make them preferred by some consumers but not by others, firms might choose prices higher than marginal cost.

[3] Aidan Hollis, *An Efficient Reward System for Pharmaceutical Innovation* 1 (June 2004), available at https://www.who.int/intellectualproperty/news/en/Submission-Hollis6-Oct.pdf. Specifically, Hollis argues that "government would not be involved in the market at all, but would retrospectively determine the therapeutic benefit of an innovation in order to make a payment to the patentee." Id. at 2.

[4] Christopher McCabe, Karl Claxton, and Anthony O'Hagan, *Why Licensing Authorities Need to Consider the Net Value of New Drugs in Assigning Review Priorities – Addressing the Tension Between Licensing and Reimbursement*, 24 INT'L J. TECH ASSESSMENT IN HEALTH CARE 140, 140 (2008).

The argument in favor of the incremental value rule also has been put forth (and generated controversy) in the context of organizations that cooperatively develop standards. These organizations gather a large number of firms that contribute technologies for the creation of new products (for example, smart phones). Firms willing to produce goods in these markets must purchase a license from each of the essential patent holders participating in the development of the standard. In this context, it has been argued that, for these licenses to be provided on "reasonable and non-discriminatory" (RAND)[5] terms (as patent holders typically promise to standard-setting organizations, or SSOs), the licensing rates should be set according to the *ex ante* value they contribute to the standard – in other words, the incremental value rule should be used within SSOs. Thus, if two technologies are competing with one another for inclusion in a particular standard and, for example, one would reduce the cost of producing a good embodying the standard by $20 per unit as compared to the other technology, then the better technology could charge up to $20 per unit more in licensing fees, which is its incremental value.

The previous two examples show that, just as with traditional goods, at first sight the application of the incremental value rule to intellectual property is intuitively appealing and easy to understand. In this chapter we argue, however, that there are a number of crucial distinctions between tangible and intangible goods, many of which have the potential to render the incremental value rule inapplicable to intellectual property licensing. While the applications of our analysis are far broader, as the pharmaceutical example suggests, we focus primarily on a distinction that is particularly important for firms that participate in standard-setting organizations. For those firms there is a significant span of decisions required to commercialize a product or promulgate a standard, including research and development (R&D) investment decisions necessary to generate innovative technologies, decisions to participate in an SSO's efforts, and, finally, decisions regarding the licensing of patents reading on the developed standard.[6] In particular, we consider the dynamic implications of the innovation process, assessing how the imposition of an incremental value licensing cap would impact a firm's

[5] Standards organizations in Europe often request FRAND licensing, with "Fair" preceding RAND. While it is possible that "fair" adds something different to the commitment, most commentators view RAND and FRAND as equivalent.

[6] Note that we assume all innovations that can be patented are patented. In practice, this is clearly not the case, as firms may decide not to pursue a patent for every patentable innovation. For example, firms may choose to maintain certain patented innovations as trade secrets instead.

decisions to invest in R&D and, if relevant, to participate in cooperative standard-setting efforts.

We find that while the incremental value rule has intuitive appeal, it is based on *ex post* reasoning in that it relies on the presumption that all needed innovations have already been developed. The cap therefore ignores the risky nature of R&D investment and the inevitable unsuccessful endeavors that must nonetheless be paid for out of the rewards earned from the successful ones.[7] Furthermore, for licensing within standard setting, the incremental value rule adds the presumption that all innovators are already participating in the SSO. Neither of these assumptions matches the real-world process of innovation and standard setting, however, where continuing investments in innovation are frequently quite important to the development of a product or commercialization of a standard and where firms can and do decide not to participate in standard-setting efforts, even when the standard at issue is relevant for the firm's business.[8] In other words, the model on which the incremental value licensing rule rests is static and does not account for the decisions that firms make over time. This is a serious flaw in a pricing rule applied to products dependent on an innovation process that entails significant uncertainty.

Intellectual property typically has very low marginal costs of production (licensing does not tend to involve significant recurring costs) but commonly involves substantial upfront fixed costs (e.g., R&D). When innovation investments and participation decisions are accounted for, we find that imposing an incremental value rule for licensing patents would lead to a number of undesirable effects. It would lower R&D investments among innovators, it would lower SSO participation rates among patent holders, and it would even lower aggregate earnings for SSO members as a whole. In fact, we find that in the SSO context, members have incentives to pay more in licensing than what the incremental value rule dictates to ensure patent holder participation and thereby eliminate the risk of outside firms charging even higher royalty rates.

Our results stem from a general observation: Innovation is risky. This risk is relevant not only for the success of any R&D efforts but also for the

---

[7] This is a fundamental concept in finance economics, but for some reason risk-adjusted rewards are often overlooked in other areas. For a discussion of risk and reward in a financial context, see Stephen A. Ross, Randolph W. Westerfield & Jeffrey Jaffe, CORPORATE FINANCE 255–337 (McGraw-Hill Irwin 2005).

[8] Anne Layne-Farrar & Josh Lerner, *To Join or not to Join: Examining Patent Pool Participation and Rent Sharing Rules* 7 (Working paper, Jan. 7, 2008), available at http://papers.ssrn .com/sol3/papers.cfm?abstract id=945189.

commercial value that the new product will have. Absent such uncertainty, an incremental value rule that rewards a firm *ex post* (when the technology exists) with its contribution to the value of the product or standard (before investments have been made to commercialize that product or standard) might deliver the optimal outcome. However, our research indicates that once we account for uncertainty, the results are likely to change. For example, in our model innovators that face other competing technologies during the development phase of a standard and that are rewarded according to the incremental value rule might decide not to participate in the SSO, hoping that *ex post* their technology offers a substantially better option than the one obtained by the competitors, and thus enabling them to charge a higher *ex post* price outside of the constraints (like RAND) imposed by the SSO.

The point we make here in the case of standard-setting technologies might be extended to other areas that rely on intellectual property. For example, in the case of the pharmaceutical industry, recent papers have shown that the payment that firms should receive for a drug (through a regulated price or the reimbursement by insurers) should not, in general, be determined solely by its incremental contribution over the next best alternative. Once firms account for this payment cap, they tend to bias their investment decisions toward small innovations for which this rule tends to provide higher net profits.[9] The long-term result could well be fewer pioneering drugs and lower overall social value from drug research. Uncertainty might also make the incremental value rule suboptimal in other contexts. If innovators are risk adverse, for example, payments made according to the fully *ex ante* (before R&D investments) expected contribution as opposed to the partially *ex ante* contribution (before implementation investments) might lead to different outcomes.

Finally, the incremental value rule might also fail to promote an optimal level of innovation in the context of intellectual property in the same instances where this rule fails for physical goods. The existence of externalities is an obvious example of this failure. When goods generate an externality – such as when manufacturing creates pollution, for instance – the valuation that buyers associate with them does not coincide with their social valuation. If this externality is positive (negative), there will be underprovision (overprovision) of the good if firms charge the incremental "private" value of their product.

---

[9] See Juan José Ganuza, Gerard Llobet, & Beatriz Domínguez, *R&D in the Pharmaceutical Industry: A World of Small Innovations*, 55 MGMT. SCI. 539 (2009).

In the case of intellectual property positive externalities seem to abound, particularly for what it is denoted as basic research. It often has been argued that to the extent that patent licensing can only capture the private contribution that licensees assign to the technology (akin to the incremental value), public funding might be complementary to private investments. This insight was one of the primary motivations behind government funding for basic research at universities and the creation of national research labs.[10] But, as society eventually discerned, while universities and labs were generally good at conducting basic research, they did little to ensure that its fruits ever emerged from the ivory tower, to the broader benefit of society. This in turn led to the passage of the Bayh-Dole Act, whose impetus is to provide incentives for university and government lab research to be disseminated more widely, eventually benefiting consumers in the form of new products and services.[11]

As this brief historical tour of innovation policy amply illustrates, obtaining the optimal level of innovation is a thorny problem, with different insights emerging over time. The complexities of the issue suggest a slow and careful approach to implementing new policies affecting innovation that could upset the balance, as the imposition of an incremental value licensing rule surely could do.

The remainder of this chapter is organized as follows. Section II provides a brief review of the literature proposing that patent holders within SSOs charge no more than the incremental value that their patents provide to the standard under development over the next closest alternative. This section discusses the potential competitive problems that can arise in standard-setting efforts and that have provided the motivation for the incremental value licensing proposals. In Section III, we turn to a nontechnical presentation of an economic model we developed in a companion publication hat evaluates the application of the incremental value rule to patents within standards.[12] This model acknowledges the time dimension and uncertainty associated with innovation and standard setting and thus incorporates both

---

[10] Richard. R. Nelson, *The Simple Economics of Basic Scientific Research*, 67 J. POL. ECON. 297 (1959); Kenneth J. Arrow, ECONOMIC WELFARE AND THE ALLOCATION OF RESOURCES FOR INVENTION 1–2 (Economics Division, The RAND Corporation 1959) available at http://wwwcgi.rand.org/pubs/papers/2006/P1856.pdf.

[11] Richard Jensen & Marie Thursby, *Proofs and Prototypes for Sales: The Licensing of University Inventions*, 91 AM. ECON. REV. 240 (2001); Nancy T. Gallini, *The Economics of Patents: Lessons from Recent U.S. Patent Reform*, 16 J. ECON. PERSPECTIVES 131 (2002).

[12] Anne Layne-Farrar, Gerard Llobet, & Jorge Padilla, *Payments and Participation: The Incentives to Join Cooperative Standard Setting Efforts* (Working Paper, February 2010), available at http://www.cemfi.es/~llobet/joinSSO.pdf.

the decision to invest in innovation in the first instance (R&D) and also the decision to participate or not in voluntary standard setting efforts. Section IV concludes.

II. The Literature on IP Licensing within Standards

As more and more firms are filing for more and more patents, standard setting in high-technology fields has become a more complex process. Whereas simple cross-licensing deals among a relatively small group of large, vertically integrated firms used to suffice for handling all intellectual property issues for a particular standard, today specialist entities – both upstream (research firms, universities, patent aggregators) and downstream (manufacturing outsourcing firms) – participate in voluntary industry standard-setting efforts.[13] Upstream specialists earn their revenues solely through out-licensing and rarely need cross-licenses; thus they require an explicit royalty rate or upfront payment in exchange for the use of their intellectual property rights. Downstream specialists have no patents of their own to offer in exchange, and thus even vertically integrated firms will tend to want higher royalty/fee payments from these manufacturing firms. Taken together, these trends have led to a variety of licensing schemes that are now seen within SSOs.[14]

Not surprisingly, as the heterogeneity of participants has increased within SSOs, so too has the number of disputes emerging from cooperative standard setting. The licensing issues generating the most concern today are patent holdup, royalty stacking, and non-RAND ("excessive") royalty rates. Patent holdup occurs when a firm holding patents for specific technologies included in a standard charges a licensing price that exploits other SSO members' costs of switching to a different technological solution after a standard is defined.[15] Under holdup, any irreversible investments in implementation made by potential licensees are held hostage by the patent holder, who raises

---

[13] See Rudi Bekkers & Isabelle Liotard, *European Standards for Mobile Communications: The Tense Relationship Between Standards and Intellectual Property Rights*, 21 EURO. INTELLECTUAL PROP. REV. 110, 111–12 (1999).

[14] See Damien Geradin, Anne Layne-Farrar, & A. Jorge Padilla, *Elves or Trolls? The Role of Non-Practicing Patent Owners in the Innovation Economy* (TILEC Discussion Paper No. 2008–018, May 2008), available at http://papers.ssrn.com/sol3/papers.cfm?abstract_id=1136086.

[15] See Mark A. Lemley & Carl Shapiro, *Patent Holdup and Royalty Stacking*, 85 TEX. L. REV. 1991 (2006–07); Joseph Farrell et al., *Standard Setting, Patents, and Hold-Up*, 74 Antitrust L. J. 603 (2007). See also, Anne Layne-Farrar, Gerard Llobet, & A. Jorge Padilla, *Are Joint Negotiations in Standard Setting "Reasonably Necessary"* (CEMFI Working Paper No. 0808, May 2008), available at ftp://ftp.cemfi.es/wp/08/0808.pdf.

the license fee to just under the cost of switching to the next best alternative, thereby capturing more than the value contributed by its patented technologies. Royalty stacking occurs when the number of patent licenses required to implement a standard is so high and the coordination among patent holders is so low that the cumulative royalties form a stack that impedes or eliminates the profitable commercialization of the standard.[16] Lastly, non-RAND royalty rates are those deemed to exceed the economic value of the underlying patents.[17] Whereas patent holdup involves surprise (since firms implementing a standard would not make irreversible investments in the full knowledge of relevant patents without first securing a license), non-RAND rates occur when the patent holder reneges *ex post* on its *ex ante* promise to license its relevant patents on a RAND basis.[18]

Ex ante licensing – or at least binding *ex ante* announcements of licensing terms – has been suggested as a solution to all three of these opportunistic licensing problems within SSOs. During the development of a standard, before any vote over the technologies to include in the standard has occurred, technologies vying for inclusion may face competition that can be leveraged to help maintain RAND rates. If a patent holder attempts an "excessive" rate *ex ante*, SSO members can simply shift to the next best option for the standard, so that the would-be hold-up firm faces a choice of reasonable rates or no royalty earnings at all. Starting from this base of competition, a number of different variations on the *ex ante* theme have been proposed, including *ex ante* auctions, where auctions would be held within an SSO among the technologies to be included in a standard with the royalty rates (and other licensing terms) forming the "bids,"[19] and incremental value licensing caps, which is the focus of this chapter.

Several policy-oriented papers have suggested that the incremental value rule is the best licensing approach for patents within standard setting. For

---

[16] See Lemley & Shapiro, supra note 15. See also Damien Geradin, Anne Layne-Farrar, & A. Jorge Padilla, *The Complements Problem Within Standard Setting: Assessing the Evidence on Royalty Stacking*, 14 B. U. J. SCI. & TECH. L. 144 (2008); and Anne Layne-Farrar & Jorge Padilla, *Royalty Stacking in Mobile Telecommunications: A Closer Look at the Evidence* (Oct. 19, 2009) (unpublished manuscript, on file with authors).

[17] See Farrell et al., supra note 15, at 636–637; see also, FED. TRADE COMM'N, COMPLAINT IN THE MATTER OF NEGOTIATED DATA SOLUTIONS, Docket No. C-4234 (2008) at ¶¶ 26–35.

[18] Carl Shapiro, *Patent Reform: Aligning Reward and Contribution* 11–14 (NBER Working Paper No. W13141, May 2007), available at http://papers.ssrn.com/sol3/papers .cfm?abstract id=989952. Some competition agency cases have involved allegations of this sort. See, e.g., E.U. COMMISSION, D.G. COMPETITION, Case COMP/39.247 – Qualcomm, which was officially dismissed on November 24, 2009.

[19] See Daniel G. Swanson & William J. Baumol, *Reasonable and Nondiscriminatory (RAND) Royalties, Standards Selection, and Control of Market Power*, 73 ANTITRUST L. J. (2005–06).

instance, Dolmans, O'Donoghue, and Loewenthal put forth the following argument:

> But assuming that some innovative value is conveyed, and that price squeezing is avoided, what should the [patent licensing] price be? The economic theory seems relatively clear. In competitive conditions, if the technology to be licensed is equivalent to alternative available technology, there is no reason to believe that the IPR owner, absent its monopoly, would find a buyer or be able to charge a positive price for it. Indeed, in a competitive and non-collusive environment, royalties for equivalent and competitive technical solutions would tend towards marginal costs, which is often close to zero in the case of IT. Where technologies are not equivalent, the fee for the lesser solution would tend to approach zero, with the owner of the better solution being able to charge no more than the incremental value that the licensee expects from the use of the better solution (for instance, because it saves costs, leads to expansion of demand, or allows the licensee to charge higher prices to end users). The fee for the better solution is no higher than the opportunity cost that the licensee would incur if it used the next best alternative.[20]

In a similar vein, in considering patent reform Shapiro argues that, "In principle, the courts could correct for [a patent holder overcompensation] problem by making it clear that royalties should be based on the underlying value of the patented feature, in comparison with the best non-infringing ex ante alternative, and not based on the entire value of the infringing product."[21] Likewise, Farrell, Hayes, Shapiro, and Sullivan maintain that one "can align rewards fairly well when there is a good market test of the invention's . . . superiority to the alternatives. . . . If the patent holder demands more than its inherent advantage, . . . the producer will use the alternative, unpatented technology."[22] And, finally, Lemley and Shapiro set their benchmark for a RAND royalty rate at *less* than the incremental value contributed by the patent.[23] In their model, they begin with the incremental

---

[20] Maurits Dolmans, Robert O'Donoghue, & Paul-John Loewenthal, *Article 82 EC and Intellectual Property: The State of the Law Pending the Judgment in Microsoft v. Commission*, 3 Competition Pol'y Int'l 107, 139 (2007). Observe that the implicit assumption in this proposal is that the next best alternative is priced at zero, meaning the incremental value rule sets price at exactly the incremental value. For any alternative whose price is not zero, the incremental value rule sets price at the alternative good price *plus* the incremental value.

[21] Carl Shapiro, supra note 18, at 35.

[22] Joseph Farrell et al., supra note 15, at 11–12. Under their version of the incremental value rule, the assumption is that an unpatented alternative exists – an assumption that may or may not pan out in reality however.

[23] See Lemley & Shapiro, supra note 15. As with Dolmans et al.'s argument above, supra note 20, the model developed by Lemley and Shapiro assumes that the next best alternative is priced at zero. If it had a positive price, that price would be added to the incremental value to obtain the price of the superior technology.

value but then weight that amount by the probability that the patent is valid (a factor that is less than one) and by the bargaining power of the patent holder (another factor that is also less than one).

It is these proposals, and others like them outside of standard setting, that have spurred the inquiry presented in this chapter. In the following section, we consider the implicit assumptions behind the arguments presented in the above quotes as well as the implications that imposing such a licensing rule could be expected to have on innovative firms.

III. The Implications of Incremental Value Licensing

In a companion technical publication, we develop an economic model that explores an innovative firm's R&D investment and SSO participation decisions.[24] Our model makes clear how innovative firms can be expected to respond to an incremental value licensing rule imposed, say, by an SSO or by a government agency (mandating SSO policy). In this chapter, we present a simplified version of the model and focus on its policy implications.

Consider an SSO that aims to promulgate a standard comprised of several components, for which new inventions are required. Denote these inventions as 1, 2, 3, up to N. Assume that innovation is a risky, uncertain process that unfolds over time, such that R&D is successful with a probability less than one. The standard is valuable, however, only if all inventions are successfully achieved. In other words, the product involves full complementarity between the innovators. Denote the commercial value of a successfully developed standard as $v > 0$. The members of the SSO obtain a share of profits corresponding to the value generated by the standard, net of the development costs involved.

Although in our technical companion publication we discuss the general case meeting these criteria, for illustration purposes here we focus on the case where all innovations except the first have already been obtained.[25] Thus, the success of the standard depends on the success of the first invention (or component). For invention 1, there is a potential patent holder that can devote resources to research in an effort to obtain the innovation, at which point it would be patented. The probability of successful innovation,

---

[24] Anne Layne-Farrar, Gerard Llobet, & Jorge Padilla, *Payments and Participation: The Incentives to Join Cooperative Standard Setting Efforts* (Working Paper, February 2010), available at http://www.cemfi.es/~llobet/joinSSO.pdf.

[25] In the next section we discuss the subtle differences that the general case contributes to our discussion. The main mechanism at work, however, can be explained in this simpler setup.

denoted by ρ, depends on the individual investment expended by the firm, such that higher R&D expenditures (greater effort) lead to greater odds of a successful invention.[26]

Alternatively, the invention can be replaced with what we call *default* technology. By this we mean that the standard can be implemented by SSO member firms uncovering existing technology and adapting it to the standard under development, analogous to the Farrell et al. assumption that a nonproprietary technology option exists. This discovery-adaption procedure requires a positive fixed cost, $F > 0$, and is successful with constant probability s.[27] We assume that a newly invented technology is superior to its default counterpart, even accounting for the R&D expenditure. So, while the standard can go forward with the default technologies, the SSO members would all prefer to base the standard on the newly invented technology for component 1 because it generates a higher value for the standard.[28] We therefore focus on the case in which it is efficient that only the component 1 technology created by the patent holder is researched and developed and the default is not attempted.

Finally, we assume that a patent holder's invention may be used for other purposes, independently of whether it is accepted as part of the standard or not. These additional uses lead to positive profits for the patent holder (denoted by π), even if its technology is not chosen for the standard. The availability of an outside option emphasizes the voluntary nature of SSO participation (and out-licensing in general, outside of an SSO context).[29]

As proposed by the papers discussed in the previous paragraph, we assume that the SSO establishes a payment rule that members must follow for licensing any proprietary invention to be included in the standard. Alternatively, a competition agency could urge that a particular licensing rule be followed,[30] especially for those SSOs with governmental ties. Regardless of

---

[26] Specifically, we assume that the cost of achieving a probability of success of ρ is $C(\rho) = 1/2\rho^2$.

[27] We assume $0 < s < 1/2$. Thus, if the SSO relies on the default technology, the probability of success for the standard is simply s.

[28] As pointed out previously, our technical companion publication also considers the case where all components can be supplied by newly invented or default technologies.

[29] Observe that the results of our model are not affected by π. In particular, we could set $\pi = 0$ and all of our findings would remain unchanged. We include the variable here as it helps to clarify the choices that patent holders make and, as stated in the text, underscores that patent holders may not need to join an SSO to earn a return on their innovation investments.

[30] In fact, in a speech made in the fall of 2009, the former Competition Commissioner Neelie Kroes made such a suggestion. She stated, "Ex ante disclosure helps those involved make a properly informed decision, and competition law should not stand in the way...

its origin, in the context of our model, an incremental value licensing rule mandates license fees to be set according to the rule $L^{IV} = v\,(\rho - s)$. The expression in parentheses represents the incremental improvement in the odds of achieving a standard of value v that is obtained by investing in R&D for technology 1.[31]

A patent holder decides whether to participate in the standard-setting efforts after the SSO has set the licensing rule. If the innovative firm decides to participate, it then selects an R&D investment amount to obtain a new invention for the standard, for which, if successful, other SSO members will pay licensing fees.

We assume that if a patent holder does not participate in the standard-setting efforts, the firms in the SSO will automatically attempt to implement the default alternative technology for the missing component. If the default technology works out (with probability s), then the nonparticipating patent holder will obtain no revenue from the SSO members (although, as long as its own R&D is successful, the patent holder will still have its outside profit opportunities). If the default technology fails, however, while the patent holder is successful, the patent holder can negotiate with the SSO members an *ex post* license, unconstrained by the payment rule or any other norms or contracts established by the SSO. We assume that in this case the inventor can extract the entire surplus created by the standard: Because technology 1 is essential for the standard to exist at all, the patent holder can extract with a licensing fee more than the *ex ante* incremental value.[32]

The setup assumed here provides the worst case scenario for firms implementing a standard and thus presents the best framework for testing the efficacy of an incremental value licensing rule. It is precisely when patent holders face no other constraints but the SSO's rules that they can be

unilateral ex ante disclosure of maximum royalty rates and the most restrictive licensing terms that would apply should a company's technology be made the standard." Neelie Kroes, European Commissioner for Competition Policy, Address at Harvard Club of Belgium, "De Warande" (Oct. 10, 2009), available at http://europa.eu/rapid/press ReleasesAction.do?reference=SPEECH/09/475&format=HTML&aged=0&language=EN &guiLanguage=en.

[31] Alternatively, the model can be rewritten as a setup where the quality of the innovation is uncertain but the patented technology (with the appropriate level of investment) is more likely to lead to a high-quality product. In that context, we can interpret L^{IV} as the difference in *expected* quality. It is easy to show that such a setup leads to identical results.

[32] Here we focus on the case where the patent holder has, *ex post*, all the bargaining power. This is consistent with the fact that the incremental value rule will have an impact precisely in those cases where the patent holder would have, otherwise, a large bargaining power. Nevertheless, in the companion publication we show that similar results may arise even if both parties have similar bargaining positions in the negotiation.

expected to exploit any market power that might be gained through their inclusion in a standard. It is therefore under these circumstances that potential licensees will be most interested in instituting licensing restrictions, such as an incremental value rule.

For simplicity, we assume that the cost (F) of adapting default technology 1 is sufficiently large that it is never optimal to develop both the default technology and the one sponsored by the innovator.

If some benevolent social planner were dictating all of the firms' behaviors, we would have that the patent holder always joins the SSO and puts in just enough effort to maximize the sum of its profits together with those of the (other) members of the SSO while minimizing its costs of doing so.[33] Under this "first best" solution (from a social, but not necessarily a private perspective), R&D investment increases with the value of both the standard (v) and the private profits that the patent holder can accrue outside of the standard (π); the greater the potential reward, the more effort the patent holder will put in. Mathematically, the social first best R&D effort is described by $\rho^{fb} = v + \pi$. This first best effort rule forms the benchmark for our analysis in the next section. We have normalized cost parameters and profits so that the probability of success does not exceed one in the first best.[34]

A. The Implications of Incremental Value Licensing for R&D Investment

Of course, social planners do not make decisions for firms. Instead, firms make choices that are privately profitable and which may or may not coincide with the social optimal. To find a solution that describes firm 1's behavior in the face of an incremental value licensing scheme, we work backward from the participation decision, considering what R&D investment decisions a patent holder will make when it participates in the SSO as compared to when it does not participate. After exploring the R&D decision, we turn to the participation decision.

Start with the case in which the patent holder does not join the SSO. The patent holder will obtain licensing profits only if its R&D has been successful, but an additional condition is necessary as well. Namely, to earn licensing revenues from the SSO members, the default technology

---

[33] For the mathematical exposition of the arguments presented in this section, along with the proofs of our conclusions, see the companion publication, supra note 24.

[34] In particular, given the cost function proposed in footnote 26, it is enough to impose the restriction that $v + \pi \leq 1$.

1 must *not* have been successful so that the (outside) patented technology contribution is essential to the standard. In this latter case, the patent holder can extract all the surplus from the SSO through *ex post* licensing because the patent offers the only option for completing and commercializing the standard but the patent holder is unconstrained by any SSO rules. That is, the profit-maximizing *ex post* license that the patent holder will demand equals the entire value of the standard, $\hat{L} = v$, not just the incremental value, $L^{IV} = v(\rho - s)$. As a result, in comparison to the benchmark, in this case the patent holder sets "excessive" licensing fees.

To reach this "excessive" licensing outcome, in the previous time period the patent holder chooses the level of effort (which in our model is synonymous with the patent holder choosing the probability of R&D success ρ) to maximize the chances of obtaining a profitable and successful technology 1. Consider again the two conditions that must hold for the patent holder to earn both the outside option revenue plus revenue from the SSO members. Earning this larger pool of revenue depends not just on the patent holder's efforts to obtain a successful technology 1, but also on the SSO members' failure to successfully develop the default technology 1. As a result, even if the potential earnings are large, the uncertainty surrounding their achievement lowers their importance in driving firm behavior. In particular, *ex ante* the potential earnings are weighted by both the probability that the patent holder is successful with technology 1, $\rho < 1$, as well as the probability that the SSO members are unsuccessful with the default technology 1, $(1 - s)$.

From an *ex ante* perspective, as it decides how much to invest in R&D, the patent holder weighs the relatively limited odds that it will be able to charge "excessive" royalties *ex post*, which leads the patent holder to underinvest in R&D as compared to the social optimum. Mathematically, in the case where the patent holder chooses not to join the SSO, its effort level will be set at $\hat{\rho} = (1 - s)v + \pi$. Compared to the first best effort level given above, the new term is $(1 - s)$. Since this term is less than 1, it follows that $\hat{\rho} < \rho^{fb}$, meaning R&D efforts will fall below the socially first best benchmark.

Turn next to the case in which firm 1 chooses to participate in the SSO. Since the SSO has adopted the incremental value licensing rule, the patent holder will be rewarded for a successful technology 1 according to that technology's incremental value for the standard (i.e., $v(\rho - s)$). Note that, unlike the above scenario, where the patent holder remains outside of the SSO, in this case the licensing earnings will not be weighted by the additional probability that the search for default technology 1 fails since the default technology 1 will not even be attempted given that the patent holder chose to join the SSO.

The patent holder will again select the effort level that maximizes its expected profits, which now leads to $\rho^{IV} = v + \pi$. Compared to the case where the patent holder does not join the SSO, the incremental value rule leads to an efficient investment choice, identical to the effort expended under the social optimum, ρ^{fb}. This is one of the properties that make the incremental value licensing scheme appealing: Conditional on innovators participating in the standard-setting process, an incremental value rule will induce them to exert the optimal R&D effort.[35] This outcome occurs in spite of the lower licensing proceeds that the firm obtains when joining the SSO as compared to those possible outside of the SSO. This result follows from the higher probability of being rewarded in the first instance. In other words, although the potential earnings are lower (there is no "excessive" licensing fee), the chances of getting a positive reward are higher, which leads to more R&D investment as compared to not participating in the standard-setting efforts.

To summarize, we find that, conditional on the patent holder joining the SSO with an incremental value rule in place, R&D investment for technology 1 is higher than when the patent holder abstains from the SSO, and actually equals the first best investment amount. The question, however, is whether the innovative firm will in fact join the SSO when that SSO adopts an incremental value licensing rule. We turn to that question next.

B. The Implications of Incremental Value Licensing for SSO Participation

Optimal investment levels and a higher surplus for the SSO members as a whole are well and good, but unless the patent holder sees a private benefit, it will not choose to join the SSO. The response to this question therefore amounts to comparing patent holder profits under both of the scenarios just described, joining and not joining.

We return to the first case, in which the patent holder chooses not to join the SSO. Conditional on achieving a successful invention, the patent holder will earn at least the outside profits, π. If the other two conditions listed hold as well, the patent holder will also earn "excessive" licensing fees from the SSO members. Putting these elements together and weighting them by the odds of success (since uncertainty implies that the patent holder is considering expected profits, before joining the SSO and before

---

[35] Analogously for patent holders outside of standard setting contexts, such as those referenced in the introduction, the condition would be that the innovative firm commits *ex ante* to compulsory RAND licensing *ex post*.

Table 15.1.

	Participation	No participation
Patent Holder	$\Pi^{IV} = \frac{1}{2}(v + \pi)^2 - sv$	$\hat{\Pi} = \frac{1}{2}((1-s)v + \pi)^2$
SSO members	$V^{IV} = sv$	$\hat{V} = sv - F$

investing in any R&D), we have that when the patent holder's R&D effort is given by $\hat{p}$, then the patent holder's expected profits are given by $\hat{\Pi} = \frac{1}{2}((1-s)v + \pi)^2$. The first term inside the brackets represents the SSO earnings – the value of the entire standard v (the "excessive" licensing fee) weighted by the probability that default technology 1 is not successful $(1-s)$, which makes the patented technology 1 essential for the standard. The second term inside the brackets (π) is the profit from the outside option.

When the patent holder stays outside, however, the SSO will have to incur the cost F of developing the default technology, which is successful with probability s. Thus, the SSO profits become $\hat{V} = sv - F$.

In the second case, where the patent holder joins the SSO, it s expected profits are given by $\Pi^{IV} = \frac{1}{2}(v + \pi)^2 - sv$. The second term (sv) is subtracted as that is the value the default technology brings to the standard, leaving the patent holder with its incremental contribution. Notice that the probability that the default technology 1 fails $(1-s)$ does not enter this expression. The SSO will incur no development costs, since the default is not attempted when the patent holder joins the SSO, so the SSO obtains profits $V^{IV} = sv$. Table 15.1 summarizes the different payoffs.

Comparing the payoffs of the different parties, notice the following results. First, SSO members are better off under the incremental value rule when the patent holder commits to participate. The reason is that they get the value the default technology would have provided to the standard, and yet they do not need to incur the costs necessary to develop it. In other words, by participating in the SSO, the patent holder reduces the other SSO members' expenses.

Second, the expressions for profits of the patent holder illustrate the trade-off that the patent holder faces when joining the SSO. By joining, the firm loses the term sv, which is the value the default technology provides to the standard. However, by staying out, the patented invention is less likely to be accepted by the SSO, which will invest in the default technology to replace the patent holder. This is reflected in the term $1 - s$, which leads to lower profits and thus lower incentives to innovate for the patent holder.

The mathematical manipulation of these expressions shows that the patent holder will obtain higher profits by staying out of the SSO as long as $2(v + \pi) < 2 + vs$. This will always hold when $\pi + v < 1$.[36] In words, the patent holder expects to earn lower profits when joining an SSO with an incremental value licensing rule as compared to the profits it expects to accrue by remaining outside of the SSO, taking account of the chance that its invention will become essential for the standard. This abstention strategy is, of course, detrimental to the members of the SSO, who will face "excessive" royalties if they fail in their efforts to develop default technology 1.

Because SSO members expect lower profits when the patent holder decides to stay out than when the patent holder participates (as explained previously), there is room for the SSO to allow the patent holder to charge a royalty above what the incremental value rule would prescribe to entice the patent holder to join. In particular, a royalty above the incremental value by up to F units will still be preferred by SSO members to the alternative in which the patent holder does not participate. This follows because the cost of developing the default technology is equal to F; any inducement less than that cost makes the SSO better off as long as it ensures the patent holder's participation. It is easy to show that, because the default technology is inferior to the patented one and the redundancy in the development costs that occur when the patent holder does not participate destroys the overall value (i.e., there is duplicative investment), increasing the royalty enough (but by less than F) will lure the patent holder into joining the SSO and thus lead to the optimal level of investment.

To summarize, when the patented technology is expected to be superior to the default technology, then the SSO members can make an additional payment to the patent holder (one that is unconditional on the patent holder's effort level ρ) that ensures the patent holder's participation, achieves the first best R&D investment, and improves the SSO members earnings compared to the alternative of relying solely on default technologies, even after accounting for the supplemental payment.

IV. Conclusions and Extensions

The main idea that this chapter has attempted to convey is that although the incremental value rule has interesting properties, such as promoting the optimal amount of investment conditional on SSO participation, it does

---

[36] As with all of the model findings, please see the companion technical publication for proofs.

not take into account the uncertainty inherent in the innovation process. In particular, firms that must make risky upfront investments in innovation will be willing to participate in an SSO (or otherwise commit to *ex post* licensing) only if they get an appropriate risk-adjusted reward. The previous section shows that the participation problem can be easily solved if the payments that the firm obtains are increased somewhat above the incremental value amount, taking into account the opportunities that the firm would face outside of the SSO.

As with all models, the one we discussed in this chapter is based on some important simplifications. Some of them are considered in our companion publication In the next paragraphs we discuss the main ones and their implications.

In this chapter we have assumed that the patent holder has all the bargaining power. This feature is consistent with the fact that, precisely, the incremental value rule is meant to limit the bargaining power that this firm would otherwise have. Still, one may wonder whether the results hinge on this idea as powerful licensees will have countervailing bargaining power. Our results go through even if the bargaining power is split more evenly among the parties, provided that the profits derived from the innovation (either π or v) are sufficiently high.

Another important feature that this model assumes away is the existence of several innovations that might be developed simultaneously, as when all components of the standard may be researched *de novo*. Our companion publication undertakes this case and shows that the main mechanism still operates in the more general setup with multiple potential patent holders. Interestingly, though, an opposing force may appear when the number of patent holders is greater than one but remains small. For simplicity, suppose that there are two such patent holders. In that case, an interesting complementarity may arise between them. A patent holder sees the odds of the standard being successful increase when the other one participates, since, as we have seen, the patented invention is superior to the default one. But, of course, the more likely the standard is to succeed, the more incentives the patent holder has to innovate, creating a virtuous circle. This force may lead under very specific circumstances to situations where the incremental value rule might offer enough compensation for innovative firms to participate. This case holds only for small numbers of patent holders, though. In the technical companion publication we show that this virtuous circle becomes less important as we increase the number of patent holders so that eventually firms are not interested in participating under the incremental value rule when a modest threshold of patent holders is reached. As most SSOs involve numerous patent holders, the force described in this chapter is likely to prevail.

An additional condition of the finding presented here is that the cost of the default technology for component 1 is relatively high. For those components of a standard for which readily available nonproprietary technologies exist, SSOs need not worry about incenting the participation of innovative firms. The analysis we present is aimed at those situations in which standards development is complex and difficult and requires a measure of innovation. We believe that many, if not most, standard-setting efforts fit that description.

Finally, consider that if the supplemental payment that patent holders require to participate in the SSO is too high, then the SSO members will prefer the default technology be developed, even when it is costly to do and thus the first best would not be optimal. This can happen when the patent holder's outside option, π, is sufficiently large. In that case, the patent holder has relatively less to gain from joining the SSO. Because some surplus above the incremental value needs to be granted to the patent holder to guarantee its participation, a higher π leads to a larger additional payment needed, making the contract more costly for the SSO members compared to relying on the default technology.

We conclude that the incremental value rule is a double-edged sword. For those SSOs that feel confident in attracting (and maintaining) the participation of key innovators, imposing an incremental value licensing cap can induce those innovators to invest the optimal amount in R&D. That is, however, a considerable gamble as our analysis indicates that in most instances (all situations except for those uncomplicated standards involving a small number of innovators) imposing an incremental value cap on licensing fees will lead innovative firms to abstain from participating in cooperative SSO efforts.

16

What's Wrong with Royalties in
High-Technology Industries?

Damien Geradin

I. Introduction

Over the past few years, there has been an unprecedented degree of interest among competition authorities, scholars, legal practitioners, industry analysts, and trade associations with respect to the level of royalties that are charged by holders of intellectual property rights (IPRs), especially when their patents are essential to an industry standard.

In particular, the last couple of years saw a lot of action on the antitrust front in the United States and Europe. The U.S. Federal Trade Commission (FTC) adopted a decision in which it found that by concealing its ownership of certain patents, Rambus persuaded the members of JEDEC, a standard-setting organization (SSO), to adopt two standards for computer memory (SDRAM and DDR SDRAM) incorporating those patents that, in turn, significantly contributed to Rambus's unlawful acquisition of monopoly power.[1] The remedy imposed by the FTC consisted in imposing a cap on the level of royalty rates that could be charged by Rambus to the firms needing access to its technology to implement the standards in question. This decision was, however, reversed in April 2008 by the U.S. Court of Appeals for the District of Columbia Circuit.[2] In the two years preceding, the U.S. Department of Justice (DoJ) granted business letter clearances to two SSOs – VITA and IEEE – to implement new IPR policies essentially designed to control the IPR costs for the standards they promulgate.[3] Further, in

---

[1] See In the Matter of Rambus, Inc., Docket No. 9302, available at http://www.ftc.gov/os/adjpro/d9302/060802commissionopinion.pdf.

[2] See Reuters, "Appeal court overturns FTC order against Rambus", 22 April 2008, available at http://www.reuters.com/article/technologyNews/idUSN2230474020080422.

[3] See Thomas O. Barnett, Response to VMEbus International Trade Association (VITA)'s Request for Business Review Letter, Dep't Just. Antitrust Division (2006), available at http://www.usdoj.gov/atr/public/busreview/219380.htm; Thomas O. Barnett, Response

April 2007, the DoJ and the FTC jointly released a report on "Antitrust Enforcement and Intellectual Property Rights," in which the level of royalties charged by essential patent holders is analyzed at length.[4]

The interest is not, however, limited to the United States. For instance, the European Commission is currently investigating the compatibility of licensing regimes and conduct within SSOs against EC competition law in the context of its investigations of several essential patent holders, such as Rambus,[5] Qualcomm,[6] and IPCOM.[7] Although the practices of (and the allegations made against) these firms tend to be quite different, the investigations in question relate to the level of royalties provided for in these firms' licensing agreements.

Reflecting the debate at the policy level, scholars have produced a large body of legal and economic literature on IPR and standardization issues, including patent holdup (where the patent holder exploits ill-gotten market power in "excessive" licensing fees) and royalty stacking (where multiple patents must be licensed and thus the royalty rates stack up to "excessive" amounts).[8] There is no consensus in this literature. While some scholars

to Institute of Electrical and Electronics Engineers, Inc.'s Request for Business Review Letter, Dep't Just. Antitrust Division (2007), available at http://www.usdoj.gov/atr/public/busreview/222978.htm.

[4] See FTC, "Antitrust Enforcement and Intellectual Property Rights: Promoting Innovation and Competition," available at http://www.ftc.gov/reports/innovation/P040101 PromotingInnovationandCompetitionrpt0704.pdf.

[5] The European Commission sent a Statement of Objections to Rambus in August 2007 on the ground that it infringed EC Treaty rules on abuse of a dominant position (Article 82) by claiming unreasonable royalties for the use of certain patents for dynamic random access memory' chips (DRAMs) subsequent to a so-called patent ambush. See Memo/07/330, "Commission confirms sending a Statement of Objections to Rambus," Brussels, 23 August 2007. In June 2009, Rambus reached a tentative settlement with the European Commission. See "Rambus Reaches Tentative Settlement with the European Commission," Press Release, 6 June 2009, available at http://www.rambus.com/us/news/press_releases/2009/090611 .html.

[6] In October 2007, the European Commission also decided to open formal antitrust proceedings against Qualcomm following complaints lodged with the Commission by Ericsson, Nokia, Texas Instruments, Broadcom, NEC, and Panasonic, alleging that Qualcomm's licensing terms and conditions are not fair, reasonable, and nondiscriminatory (FRAND) and, therefore, may breach EC competition rules. See MEMO/07/389, "Commission Initiates Formal Proceedings against Qualcomm," 1 October 2007.

[7] See Bill Ray, "Nokia Calls Foul Over Patent Spat," *The Register*, 7 January 2009, available at http://www.theregister.co.uk/2009/01/07/nokia_ipcom/.

[8] See, for instance, Daniel Swanson & William Baumol, "Reasonable and Nondiscriminatory (RAND) Royalties, Standards Selection, and Control of Market Power," 73 Antitrust Law Journal 1; Douglas G. Lichtman, "Patent Holdouts and the Standard-Setting Process," University Chicago Law and Economics, Olin Working Paper No. 292, May 2006, available at SSRN: http://ssrn.com/abstract=902646; Mark Lemley and Carl Shapiro, "Patent Hold

argue that the above issues are both serious and widespread, and thus require reforms of the IPR policies of SSOs (or of patent law in general),[9] others – including this author – consider that these issues have been grossly exaggerated and that most of the proposed reforms are not only unnecessary, but would be generally harmful for social welfare.[10]

Against this background, this chapter addresses the issue of whether something has gone wrong with royalties in high-technology industries. This chapter seeks to answer this question by looking at a number of simple, concrete scenarios where firms holding essential IPRs seek to obtain a return on their patent portfolios through licensing or cross-licensing. As will be seen, the licensing strategy of these firms essentially depends on whether they are vertically integrated or nonvertically integrated. Vertically integrated firms engage in research and development activities, patenting at least some of their inventions, and also manufacture products based on their own innovations and the innovations produced by others. Nonverticallyintegrated firms, in contrast, specialize in one or the other layers of production. Pure upstream firms conduct research and development activities and patent their innovations, but they do not engage in manufacturing. Pure downstream firms specialize in manufacturing, but do not engage in R&D.[11]

In order to narrow the scope of the discussion, this chapter focuses on royalties paid by firms seeking to implement an industry standard.[12] Standard-setting activities aim to achieve device interoperability and product compatibility.[13] Many SSOs – ike ETSI – have a prominent role in

---

Up and Royalty Stacking" (2007), 85 *Texas Law Review*, 1989; John Golden, "'Patent Trolls' and Patent Remedies, " 85 (2007), *Texas Law Review*, 2111; Greg Sidak, "Holdup, Royalty Stacking, and the Presumption of Injunctive Relief for Patent Infringement: A Reply to Lemley and Shapiro" (2008), 92 *Minnesota Law Review* 713.

[9] See, e.g., Gil Ohana, Marc Hansen, & Omar Shah, "Disclosure and Negotiation of Licensing Terms Prior to Adoption of Industry Standards: Preventing Another Patent Ambush" (2003), 24 *European Competition Law Review*, 644; Robert Skitol, "Concerted Buying Power: Its Potential for Addressing the Patent Holdup Problem in Standard-Setting" (2005), *Antitrust Law Journal*, 727.

[10] See Damien Geradin & Miguel Rato, "Can Standard-Setting Lead to Exploitative Abuse? A Dissonant View on Patent Hold-up, Royalty-Stacking and the Meaning of FRAND" (2007) 3 *European Competition Law Journal*, 101.

[11] For a good discussion of the conflicting incentives of these firms, see David Teece & Ed Sherry, "Standards Setting and Antitrust" (2003), 87 *Minnesota Law Review*, 1913, at 1929.

[12] Note that royalties are but one element of the consideration agreed on between the parties. Other elements susceptible of pecuniary valuation, such as a cross-licence to the licensees' IPR or an upfront fee, are taken into account and their value is often significantly higher than that of the royalty itself.

[13] See D. Geradin, "Standardization and Technological Innovation: Some Reflections on Ex-ante Licensing, FRAND, and the Proper Means to Reward Innovators" (2006) 29(4) *World Competition*, 511.

the development of standards in high-technology industries.[14] Although standardization processes tend to vary among SSOs, most SSOs encourage member firms to disclose upfront, that is, prior to the adoption of a standard, the IPR that they consider may be "essential" for its implementation.[15] Once disclosure is made, or contemporaneously with disclosure, IPR owners are typically asked to provide an assurance or commitment that, should their IPR be essential for a standard, they will license it on fair, reasonable, and nondiscriminatory (FRAND) terms to members of the SSO and outsiders.[16]

Once a standard has been formally adopted, manufacturers wishing to implement the standard have to obtain licenses from the firms holding the "essential" patents as otherwise they would take the risk of being sued for patent infringement. As will be seen later, not all licenses are royalty-bearing as, for instance, when firms engaging in license negotiations each hold essential patents to a given standard, they may thus decide to agree on a cross-license with limited or no royalty payment. Cross-licenses may involve royalty payments when the firms' patent portfolios have different values, necessitating a "balancing" payment from one to the other. Essential IP holders not engaged in manufacturing or whose manufacturing activities are limited are typically not (or are less) interested in royalty-free cross-licenses as royalties are their only (or main) source of revenues.

This chapter is divided into three sections. Following this introduction, Section II reviews different hypothetical scenarios, illustrating common misconceptions (or misinformation) regarding the determination of the level of royalties that are paid by standard implementers. This section also shows that the focus of competition authorities should not be so much to control royalty rates mutually agreed between licensors and licensees – a complex task for which competition authorities are not well suited – but rather to ensure that vertically integrated firms do not restrict downstream

---

[14] The European Telecommunications Standards Institute (ETSI), headquartered in Sophia Antipolis, France, was formed in 1988 by the European Conference of Postal and Telecommunications Administrations (CEPT) and is officially recognized by the European Commission as the organization responsible for the standardization of information and communication technologies within Europe. Its mission is to "develop globally applicable deliverables meeting the needs of the Information and Communications Technologies ("ICT") community." See generally Mark Lemley, "Intellectual Property Rights and Standard-Setting Organizations" (2002), 90 *California Law Review*, 1889.

[15] ETSI defines "Essential IPR" as meaning "that it is not possible on technical (but not commercial) grounds, taking into account normal technical practice and the state of the art generally available at the time of standardization, ... [to] comply with a standard without infringing that IPR." ETSI IPR Policy (version of 23 November 2005) at Art. 15.

[16] See Geradin & Rato, supra note 8; Anne Layne-Farrar et al., "Pricing Patents for Licensing in Standard Setting Organizations: Making Sense of FRAND Commitments" (2007) 74 *Antitrust Law Journal*, 671.

competition through anti-competitive licensing practices.[17] Protecting downstream competition will do more for consumer welfare than any form of control of royalty rates. Section III presents some conclusions.

II. Are Royalties too High? A Review of Several Scenarios

While common wisdom among industry actors is that the royalties sought by essential IP holders in high-technology industries are generally "too high," information on the level of royalties that applies to the implementation of a given standard is often misleading. Take the example of the WCDMA (Wideband Code Division Multiple Access) standard applied in the mobile telecommunications industry. While the authors of a case study on the royalty rates applicable to this standard indicated that cumulative royalty levels can be as high as 30 percent,[18] Nokia, the world's leading handset makers, said publicly that it does not pay more than 3 percent royalties for implementing WCDMA.[19] Although the inconsistency between such figures is very puzzling, it can easily be explained by looking at some hypothetical scenarios, which are discussed in the following.

A. Four Hypothetical Scenarios

In high-technology industries, standards often rely on proprietary technologies owned by a number of different firms. As a result, significant differences may occur as to the ownership structure of the IP in question.

Scenario 1: The Essential IP is Held by Five Vertically-Integrated Firms
Let's assume, for the purpose of this scenario, that five vertically integrated firms (A, B, C, D, and E) own all the essential patents for a given standard and have relatively symmetrical holdings (i.e., roughly equally valuable portfolios). Let's also assume that these firms consider that, should it be licensed, their patent portfolio would be worth a royalty rate of 5percent, calculated

---

[17] Of course, specialist firms can have incentives for anticompetitive behaviors as well (strategic nondisclosure and subsequent holdup, for instance), but this potential does not suggest that verticallyintegrated firms are exempt from competition scrutiny. To the contrary, we will see that integration is not a solution to opportunistic licensing but instead offers its own dangers.

[18] See Lemley & Shapiro, supra note 6, at 2026.

[19] See "Nokia WCDMA Handsets" ("Nokia confirmed that until 2007 it has paid less than 3 per cent aggregate license fees on WCDMA handset sales under all its patent license agreements. This number represents Nokia's aggregate gross royalty payments made under all the numerous patent license agreements applicable to its WCDMA handsets"), available at http://www.letsgomobile.org/en/1218/wcdma-handsets/.

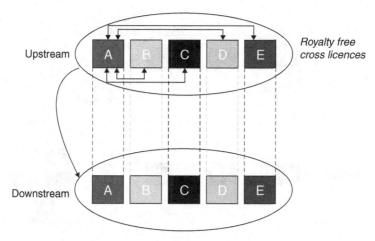

Figure 16.1

on the basis of the sales of the products implementing the standard in question.

In this scenario, the five vertically integrated firms will typically grant each other royalty-free licenses covering their respective essential patents. The reason is that, to implement the standard, they need access to each other's portfolio of essential patents and these portfolios are, for the purpose of this scenario, of comparable value. Pursuant to such cross-licenses, no royalty will be exchanged among these firms. The cumulative royalty rate paid by each of these firms will thus be zero. Figure 16.1 illustrates this scenario.

These vertically integrated firms will then compete on the downstream market for the relevant product. Of course, this scenario does not tell us much about the level of competition that will exist in the downstream market. While A, B, C, D, and E may decide to compete vigorously, they may also choose not to challenge each other and go for a strategy of high prices. That is, they may behave as an oligopoly, with a tacit agreement to avoid price competition.[20]

Alternatively, the vertically integrated firms may decide to charge each other a royalty rate of 5 percent and pass the royalty cost on to downstream customers. This operation would be profitable as each of these firms would have to pay 20 percent royalties (four licenses for each firm, each at 5%), which they would explicitly or tacitly agree to pass on downstream, but each firm would also collect 20 percent royalties, which would directly contribute to their bottom line. A strategy of artificially inflating the price of essential inputs in this fashion would, however, violate competition rules,

---

[20] Tacit collusion is, however, rare in markets for differentiated products.

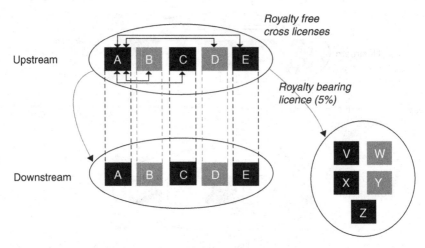

Figure 16.2

as it would be no different than a price-fixing cartel, and it would thus run the risk of being caught by competition authorities. Experience in the mobile communications services industry teaches that this scenario is nevertheless plausible.[21]

Scenario 2: The Essential IP is Held by Five Vertically Integrated Firms, and Five Pure Manufacturers Need a License to Compete Downstream

Scenario 2 differs from scenario 1 in that it not only involves the five vertically integrated firms referred to above, but also five pure manufacturers (V, W, X, Y, and Z), which want to enter the downstream market for the relevant product and compete with the vertically integrated firms. Figure 16.2 illustrates this scenario.

As in scenario 1, vertically integrated firms will typically grant each other royalty-free licenses covering their respective essential patents. By contrast,

---

[21] For some examples, see Notice on the application of the competition rules to access agreements in the telecommunications sector – framework, relevant markets and principles, O.J. 22 August 1998, C 265/02: "There is, however, obvious potential for anti competitive effects of certain access agreements or clauses therein. Access agreements may, for example: (a) serve as a means of coordinating prices"; Revised ERG Common Position on the approach to Appropriate remedies in the ECNS regulatory framework Final Version May 2006, p. 37: "Economic theory suggests that – under certain circumstances – the setting of reciprocal high or low termination charges can be used as an instrument of tacit collusion between networks which are in competition on the retail market." Generally, see Jean-Jacques Laffont & Jean Tirole, *Competition in Telecommunications*, MIT Press (2000), pp. 190–95, and Damien Geradin & Michel Kerf, *Controlling Market Power in Telecommunications – Antitrust vs. Sector Specific Regulation*, Oxford University Press (2003), p. 46.

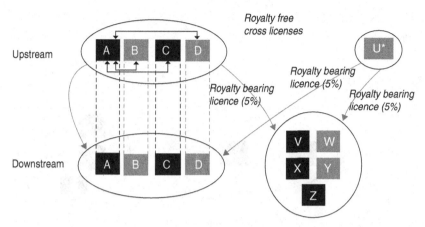

Figure 16.3

these firms will charge a 5 percent royalty to each of the pure manufacturers needing a license covering their essential patents. Such pure manufacturers, which by definition do not hold essential IP, cannot "buy" access to the vertically integrated firms' essential patents through a cross-license. This means that each of these manufacturing firms will face a cumulative royalty burden of 25 percent (five licenses, each at 5%). The average cumulative royalty rate, over all ten firms, will in turn amount to $((0\% \times 5) + (25\% \times 5))/10 = 12.5\%$.

Scenario 3: The Essential IP is Held by Four Vertically Integrated Firms Plus One Pure Upstream Firm, and Five Pure Manufacturers Need a License to Compete Downstream

This scenario is similar to scenario 2, but for one aspect: Assume now that the essential patents for a given standard are shared among four vertically integrated firms (A, B, C, and D) and one upstream-only firm (U*). Let's assume that, like the vertically integrated firms referred to in the first two scenarios, U* considers that its patent portfolio is worth a royalty rate of 5 percent. Figure 16.3 illustrates the scenario.

U* is, not surprisingly, uninterested in concluding a royalty-free cross-license with the vertically integrated firms. Unlike the vertically integrated firms, which make the bulk of their revenues by selling downstream products (i.e., mobile handsets, laptops, etc.), royalties are U*'s main (or only) source of revenues. In this scenario, each of the vertically integrated firms will thus pay a cumulative royalty rate of 5 percent (one licence from U* at 5%), while the nonvertically integrated firms will continue to pay cumulative rate of

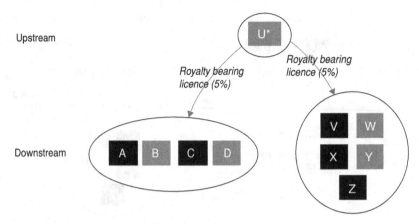

Figure 16.4

25 percent (five licences each at 5%). The average cumulative royalty rate paid by the nine firms willing to implement the standard therefore amounts to $((5\% \times 4) + (25\% \times 5))/9 = 16.11\%$.

However, as will be discussed later, the royalty burden difference between the vertically integrated and the pure manufacturers will be lower than in scenario 2 (20% instead of 25%), which may facilitate downstream competition between these two categories of firms.

Scenario 4: The Essential IP is Held Entirely by a Pure Upstream Firm, and Four Vertically Integrated Firms, and Five Pure Manufacturers Need a License to Compete Downstream

In this scenario, all the essential IP is owned by an upstream firm, which requests a royalty rate of 5 percent to license its IP. Figure 16.4 illustrates the scenario. The vertically integrated firms are in the same situation as the pure manufacturers, despite the fact they engage in R&D, as they do not own any essential IP to the standard in question (either because they focused on technologies relevant to other standards or because their research on the standard in question has been unsuccessful and they do not have any patentable technology). In this case, the average cumulative royalty rate will amount to $(9 \times 5\%)/9 = 5\%$.

B. Discussion

A number of valuable insights can be gained from considering the scenarios in the previous section. First, these scenarios explain the presence of inconsistent reports as to the cumulative royalty rates applicable to firms wishing to implement a given standard and the gross exaggerations often made with respect to the risk of royalty stacking.[22] In fact, vertically integrated firms with significant portfolios of essential patents will, thanks to their ability to cross-license, face a much lower royalty burden than pure manufacturers holding no IP. A distinction thus has to be made between the *minimum* cumulative royalty rate, the *maximum* cumulative royalty rate, and the *average* cumulative royalty rate. Different firms will face these different rates, and thus will have very different views of the reasonableness of the royalties charged.

Consider, for instance, scenario 2, in which the minimum cumulative royalty rate (which applies to the vertically integrated operators) is zero, the maximum cumulative royalty rate (which applies to pure manufacturers) is 25 percent, and the average cumulative royalty (which represents the cumulative royalty rates across all firms active downstream) is 12.5 percent. Those complaining about high cumulative royalty rates must thus refer to the maximum cumulative royalty rate paid by firms with no essential IP, while conveniently ignoring that most standard implementers can significantly lower their cumulative royalty costs through cross-licensing. This omission gives a distorted view of the royalty situation for the implementation of a given standard because it ignores the value of the contributions the licensees make to the standard. The maximum rate thus may be mistakenly used to suggest reforms aimed at reducing what are claimed to be excessively high cumulative royalty rates when in fact they reflect genuine differences in contributions.

Second, scenario 2 shows that vertically integrated firms, which do not pay any royalties, can be at a significant cost advantage compared to pure manufacturers, which face a cumulative royalty rate of 25 percent. Although this royalty cost difference appears to make entry on the downstream market for the relevant product more difficult, it does not in itself amount to an anti-competitive abuse. Since the patent portfolio held by the vertically integrated manufacturers (or, as in scenarios 3 and 4, held by pure upstream firms) generally results from costly research and development (R&D) efforts that need to be adequately compensated, pure downstream firms should pay more to join in a market in whose creation they did not contribute. Allowing firms to freely benefit from the investments of others would have several negative consequences. First, it would encourage inefficient entry. Second,

---

[22] See, for instance, Lemley & Shapiro, supra note 6. But see Damien Geradin et al., "The Complements Problem Within Standard Setting: Assessing the Evidence on Royalty Stacking" (2008), 14 *Boston University Journal of Science & Technology Law*, 144.

the results of such R&D efforts would be expropriated to the benefit of those firms (in this case the pure manufacturers) that would not have undertaken similar efforts. This would negatively impact incentives to invest in R&D.

Moreover, the fact that pure manufacturers have to pay royalty rates to essential IP holders, which can thus place them at a cost disadvantage, should give them an incentive to engage in R&D and develop their own portfolio of essential patents – if only to be in a position to cross-license and thereby lower their royalty payments.[23] Having these firms engaging in R&D would have two main benefits. First, it would likely increase the level of innovation in the relevant sector, which is a socially desirable goal. Second, by reducing their royalty cost disadvantage vis-à-vis vertically integrated firms, these firms would be able to compete more vigorously on the downstream market for the relevant product, thereby putting pressure on end consumer prices and increasing consumer choice.

The fact that royalty payment differences between vertically integrated firms and pure manufacturers may be legitimate does not mean, however, that the licensing strategy of the vertically integrated firms should be left unchecked. These firms often have both the means and the incentives to engage in anticompetitive conduct. First, vertically integrated operators may be tempted to discriminate against pure manufacturers, especially considering that, unlike pure upstream firms, vertically integrated firms take their profit downstream.[24] One way to eliminate downstream competition would be to refuse granting licenses to pure manufacturers, a strategy that is unlikely to be possible in standard-setting contexts since an outright refusal to license would obviously violate FRAND commitments. Vertically integrated firms might, however, foreclose their downstream competitors by imposing un-FRAND royalties, which would amount to a constructive refusal to supply. Foreclosure strategies based on the selling of necessary inputs at prohibitive (and/or discriminatory) prices have, for instance, been observed in network industries.[25]

Alternatively, the vertically integrated firms might charge rates that allow pure downstream firms to operate, but which soften price competition dramatically, allowing the vertically integrated firms to earn considerable margins. Moreover, vertically integrated firms could engage in a margin

---

[23] Alternatively, these firms could decide to maintain their focus on manufacturing but associate strategically with a design shop. This approach is common in the chip industry, where "fabless" design firms having their chips manufactured by foundries can be an efficient division of labour.

[24] See Swanson & Baumol, supra note 6.

[25] See generally, Geradin & Kerf, supra note 18.

squeeze by combining high royalty rates with aggressively low prices for the relevant downstream product.[26] Finally, as was discussed in the context of the first scenario, cross-payments of royalties among vertically integrated firms may be a strategy to engage in price-fixing cartels. Vertically integrated firms may thus adopt licensing strategies that hurt pure manufacturers since vigorous downstream competition is likely to negatively affect their profit margins.

Third, these scenarios lead to the counterintuitive observation that there may be a negative correlation between the cumulative level of royalties and the degree of competition in the downstream market. In scenario 1, the average cumulative royalty rate amounts to zero since none of the vertically integrated firms pay any royalty. In this scenario, the downstream market for the relevant product is, however, limited to five players, and thus the downstream market is characterized by oligopolistic features.[27] For reasons that have been abundantly discussed in the economic literature, oligopolistic markets may not be competitive.[28] In scenario 2, the average cumulative royalty rate is higher than in scenario 1 since it amounts to 12.5 percent. Yet, if the pure manufacturers manage to overcome their 25 percent royalty cost disadvantage by being particularly cost efficient, the downstream market will count ten players and thus will likely be much more competitive, with positive consequences in terms of prices, consumer choice, and innovation.

As the economic literature also points out, whether an input cost increase, such as higher royalty rates, is passed on to end consumers in the form of higher prices depends on the level of downstream competition and consumers' elasticity of demand.[29] Higher average cumulative royalty rates do not necessarily translate in higher end consumer prices. These rates are due to the fact that some manufacturers of standard compatible products do not own essential IP. The presence of these firms will, however, stimulate downstream competition, thereby putting pressure on end consumer prices.

---

[26] See Damien Geradin & Robert O'Donoghue, "The Concurrent Application of Competition Law and Regulation: The Case of Margin Squeeze Abuses in the Telecommunications Sector" (2005), 2 *Journal of Competition Law and Economics*, 355.

[27] "An oligopoly is a market characterized by a small number of firms who realize they are interdependent in their pricing and output policies. The number of firms is small enough to give each firm some market power." See *Glossary of Industrial Organisation Economics and Competition Law*, compiled by Shyam Khemani and Daniel Shapiro, commissioned by the Directorate for Financial, Fiscal and Enterprise Affairs, OECD, 1993.

[28] See Kip Viscusi, John Vernon, & Joseph Harrington, Jr., *Economics of Regulation and Antitrust*, Third Edition, Cambridge (2000), p. 135.

[29] See, for example, Luke Froeb, Steven Tschantz, & Gregory J. Werden, "Pass-Through Rates and the Price Effects of Mergers" (2005), 23 *International Journal of Industrial Organization*.

This observation is confirmed by extending the second scenario. If, for instance, three of the five pure manufacturers were not able to address their royalty cost disadvantage and thus were forced to exit the downstream market, this would translate into a significant decrease in the average cumulative royalty rate from 12.5 percent to 5 percent $((0\% \times 5 + (25\% \times 2))/10)$. Yet, the downstream market would be less competitive, limited now to seven players. This would in turn likely have a negative effect on consumer prices and choice, and innovation. After all, consumer welfare is much more likely to be positively affected by vigorous downstream competition than by minor price adjustments on intermediary inputs (in this case, essential patents).

This observation is important because it is often argued that high cumulative royalty rates negatively affect end consumers and that, as a consequence, measures should be taken to reduce such rates. This claim, however, would be true only if such high royalty rates were paid by the majority of firms (not a minority of pure downstream entities), if the cost savings realized from lower royalty rates were to a very large extent passed on to end consumers, and if the royalty rates were extremely high so that they had a measurable effect on downstream prices.

Fourth, the scenarios show that the so-called royalty stacking problem,[30] whereby essential patents are spread across a large number of firms so that the royalties may stack on top of each other and make the standard very costly to implement, is significantly attenuated through cross-licensing. Thus, in scenarios 1 and 2, the cumulative royalty rate paid by the vertically-integrated firms is equal to zero. Scenario 3, however, shows that even vertically integrated firms will have to pay royalties to a pure upstream firm, which, because royalties represent its only source of revenues, will not be satisfied with a royalty-free cross-licensing agreement.

But will these royalty payments necessarily lead to higher consumer prices as vertically integrated firms are likely to claim? The answer is negative for the following reasons. First, the prices of the relevant product will not depend solely on the costs faced by vertically integrated firms, but on the degree of competition in the downstream market. Except in perfectly competitive markets, sellers may not necessarily fully reflect input price increases in their selling prices. In some circumstances, input cost changes may induce firms to engage in price-fixing cartels designed to agree on the level of cost passed on

---

[30] See Lemley & Shapiro, supra note 6; Damien Geradin et al., "The Complements Problem within Standard Setting: Assessing the Evidence on Royalty Stacking" forthcoming 14 *Boston University Journal of Science & Technology Law* 144–76 (2008).

in price increases to the customers.[31] When manufacturers earn substantial profit margins, increased input prices can often represent a transfer across firms with no impact on consumer prices at all. That is, the upstream firm captures more of the overall market rents, so that the manufacturer's margin is reduced but consumer prices remain unchanged. Moreover, the 25 percent royalty cost advantage enjoyed by vertically integrated firms over pure manufacturers in scenario 2 is reduced to 20 percent in scenario 3 when the upstream specialist enters, thereby making it easier for pure manufacturers to compete on the downstream market. This could translate into lower prices as more downstream firms are able to enter and compete.

Finally, scenario 4 significantly differs from scenarios 2 and 3 because the essential IP is entirely owned by upstream firm U*. This scenario allows stronger competition in the downstream market for the relevant product since the pure manufacturers do not suffer any royalty cost disadvantage compared to vertically integrated firms, which, for the sake of implementing this standard, lose the benefit of their vertical integration. Moreover, the risk of distorted competition is also limited in this case because the upstream innovator has no incentives to discriminate among its various licensees, regardless of whether they are vertically integrated or not.[32] This scenario is also likely to stimulate innovation since the vertically integrated firms will have incentives to engage in R&D with the objective of developing a patent portfolio essential to the standard in question or to develop technologies that will lead to the development and adoption of a new, more advanced standard. The upstream firm will also have strong incentives to continue innovating as this is the only way for them to maintain their royalty revenues over time.

One question remaining, however, is whether the upstream firm is sufficiently price constrained so as to be unable to charge excessive rates. That of course raises the issue of the meaning of the FRAND commitment that essential IP holders typically have to give before their technology is made part of a standard. Several authors interpret FRAND as imposing some upper bound on the royalties that can be charged by essential IP holders.[33] As I have written elsewhere, no IPR policy can be read as suggesting that

---

[31] See BBC News, "BA Accused over Air Cargo Cartel" (reporting that British Airways had been accused of colluding in setting prices of fuel surcharges and other levies in the provision of air freight services), available at http://news.bbc.co.uk/1/hi/business/7158981.stm.

[32] See Damien Geradin & Nicolas Petit, "Price Discrimination under EC Competition Law – Another Doctrine in Search of Limiting Principles?" (2006), 2(3) *Journal of Competition Law and Economics*, 479.

[33] Philippe Chappatte, "Frand Commitments – The Case for Antitrust Intervention" (2009), 5 *European Competition Journal*, 319.

FRAND imposes any specific and concrete obligations on the licensor with regard to the actual level of royalties or any other terms and conditions provided for in licensing agreements.[34] The fact that FRAND is not further defined cannot be viewed as a shortcoming of SSO's IP policies. Much to the contrary, it is the very absence of a definition mechanically translatable into concrete terms that bestows on the FRAND commitment the suppleness required to allow potential licensors and licensees to reach mutually profitable agreements. As this chapter demonstrates, technology licensing is not only about royalties. Licenses may involve other forms of consideration, such as cross-licenses and other forms of "in-kind" payments. Thus, proposals designed to interpret FRAND in a manner that would constrain the ability of essential patent holders to charge royalties by imposing such royalties be calculated mechanically and capped at a certain level have been rejected.[35]

It can, of course, be claimed that pure upstream firms (e.g., innovators that hold essential IP but do not manufacture standard-compatible products) are not constrained by the need to obtain essential IP from other firms. But it does not mean that these firms will not be subject to any constraint. First, as these firms' royalty revenues depend on the ability of their licensees (vertically integrated firms or pure manufacturers) to sell standard-compatible products, it is not in their interest to "kill" the downstream market in charging excessive royalty rates. Moreover, upstream firms will typically face dynamic constraints inherent to the formal standard-setting process. Because standards evolve over time and are superseded by new standards at some stage, attempts to exploit market power gained from the standardization process can be punished in subsequent standardization efforts.[36]

III. Conclusions

The licensing of standardized technologies is a complex subject on which a lot has been written over the last few years. The bulk of the literature suggests that the FRAND regime no longer works and that something needs

---

[34] See Damien Geradin, "Standardization and Technological Innovation: Some Reflections on Ex-ante Licensing, FRAND, and the Proper Means to Reward Innovators" (2006), 29 *World Competition*, 511.

[35] Id.

[36] Dynamic constraints will be particularly effective with respect to innovative firms wishing to play a long-term role in the sector in question and, thus, do not want to be seen as pariahs.

to be done to control royalties, as excessively high royalties threaten the implementation of standards. Royalty stacking is one of the concerns behind the view that something has gone wrong with royalties in high-technology industries.

Standard implementers, who claim that in some sectors cumulative royalty rates can be so high that standards might become too costly to implement, have proposed a variety of reforms. Among the proposals are allowing joint negotiations of licensing terms,[37] encouraging *ex ante* disclosure of such terms,[38] and imposing royalty caps on essential IPRs.[39] Against this background, this chapter has sought to demonstrate that these concerns often reflect a number of misconceptions and a fair amount of misinformation when it comes to evaluating the royalties that are paid by standard implementers. In particular, this chapter makes the following observations.

First, there is a great deal of confusion between the *minimum* cumulative royalty rate, the *maximum* cumulative royalty rate, and the *average* cumulative royalty rate that apply to the implementation of a standard. While scholars, policy makers, and industry officials have referred to royalty rates as high as 30 percent in some sectors, they usually fail to mention that those cumulative rates are not common, but instead apply to implementers that have not technologically contributed to the creation of the standard. Those with essential IP tend pay much lower rates and in some cases do not pay any royalty at all. As we have seen, it is not illegitimate in itself that firms which did not engage in relevant R&D pay two-digit royalty figures to be entitled to implement the technologies developed by others. Risk should, after all, have its rewards. Thus, relying on the highest cumulative royalty rates (e.g., 30%) paid only by a limited number of industry players to argue that royalty rates are generally too high and that reforms are needed to lower them cannot be taken seriously.

Second, there is no automatic connection between the level of cumulative royalty rates and the prices paid by end consumers. This is because the downstream producers' ability to pass on such rates depends on a number

---

[37] See Ohana et al., supra note 7; Skitol, supra note 7.

[38] See, for instance, the DoJ Business Review Letters discussed at note 4.

[39] See, for instance, "Groups push for action on intellectual property," *Financial Times*, 21 November 2005 (reporting that a number of mobile carriers made proposals at ETSI to suggest that IPR terms should be agreed before a standard is even set, and argue in favor of putting a cap on the "maximum royalty payment from individual IPR users to the combined IPR holders"); *The Register*, "Mobile Patents War Shifts to Email," available at http://www.theregister.co.uk/2005/11/29/mobile_email_patents_war/; Andrew Updegrove, "Ex Ante Disclosure: Risks, Rewards, Process and Alternatives" (2006), 5(6) *Consortium Standards Bulletin*, at 13.

of market factors, as we have indicated. More generally, unless cumulative royalties were extremely high, the prices paid by end consumers are much more likely to be influenced by the degree of downstream competition. Thus, high *average* cumulative royalty rates may simply arise from the fact that there are many players on both upstream and downstream markets, and thus a great deal of competition in the market for the relevant product. As end consumer prices must be the focus on competition authorities, one goal should be to ensure that (efficient) pure manufacturers are not excluded from the downstream market.

Third, pure upstream firms and vertically integrated firms do not have similar incentives. While vertically integrated firms compete downstream and can thus have incentives to restrict competition at that level, pure upstream firms have no incentives to reduce downstream competition. Quite the contrary; since royalty rates are their main or only source of revenues, their focus is on increasing downstream output and thereby maximizing royalty payments. Upstream firms not only are lacking incentives to discriminate, but, on the contrary, may adopt strategies designed to encourage or facilitate entry on the relevant downstream market (for instance, by providing technological support and other forms of relevant assistance to new entrants).

Finally, the reforms that have been proposed to modify the FRAND regime should be based on accurate information and should be evaluated to determine that they will not cause problems that are worse than the alleged diseases they offer to treat. Along these lines, competition authorities should refrain from regulating royalties, a complex task that these authorities are not well placed to undertake. Instead, their focus should be to protect and promote downstream competition.

17

Federalism, Substantive Preemption, and Limits on Antitrust

An Application to Patent Holdup

Bruce H. Kobayashi and Joshua D. Wright

I. Introduction

In *Credit Suisse v. Billing*,[1] the Court held that the securities law implicitly precludes the application of the antitrust laws to the conduct alleged in that case. The Court considered several factors, including the availability and competence of other laws to regulate unwanted behavior, and the potential that application of the antitrust laws would result in "unusually serious mistakes." This chapter examines whether similar considerations suggest restraint when applying the antitrust laws to conduct that is normally regulated by state and other federal laws. In particular, we examine the use of the antitrust laws to regulate the problem of patent holdup of members of standard-setting organizations (SSOs). While some have suggested that this conduct illustrates a gap in the current enforcement of the antitrust laws, our analysis finds that such conduct would be better evaluated under the federal patent laws and state contract laws.

The patent holdup problem has become one of the most controversial issues in antitrust policy. The basic economics of patent holdup in the standard-setting context are generally well understood and related to the more general problem of holdup in the presence of relationship-specific

---

[1] *Credit Suisse Sec. (USA) LLC v. Billing*, 127 S. Ct. 2383 (2007).

We thank George Cary, Luke Froeb, John Golden, Willem Hoyng, Mark Lemley, Scott Kieff, Samson Vermont, Greg Werden, and conference participants at the George Mason/Microsoft Conference on the Law and Economics of Innovation and the Tilburg Law and Economics Center Workshop on Innovation, Intellectual Property and Competition Policy for valuable comments. We also are grateful to the Tilburg Law and Economics Center IIPC grant program for financial support. Aubrey Steumpfle and Brandy Wagstaff provided research assistance.

investments:[2] After an SSO has adopted a standard, and investments have been made to commit to the new technology, a patent holder may "hold up" users in a variety of ways that result in more favorable licensing terms than those contracted for *ex ante*. The patent holdup problem has been the subject of a wave of recent Federal Trade Commission (FTC) enforcement actions in *Dell*,[3] *Rambus*,[4] *Unocal*,[5] *N-Data*,[6] private antitrust enforcement,[7] as well as enforcement actions in Europe.

The notion that a patent holder whose technology has been incorporated into a standard can engage in *ex post* holdup has prompted substantial discussion concerning the role that antitrust laws can play in regulating this conduct.[8] Economists and legal scholars have discussed various

---

[2] See Benjamin Klein, Robert G. Crawford & Armen A. Alchian, *Vertical Integration, Appropriable Rents, and the Competitive Contracting Process*, 21 J.L. & Econ. 297 (1978); Oliver E. Williamson, The Economic Institutions Of Capitalsim: Firms, Markets, Relational Contracting 52–56 (1985). Benjamin Klein and others have emphasized the distinction between contract law and antitrust law in resolving holdup by emphasizing that the correct competitive analysis in cases of *ex post* opportunism occurs *ex ante* at the time of contracting. For instance, in the case of *ex post* contractual opportunism by franchisors against franchisees, the opportunism is generally a contract problem and not an antitrust problem because franchisors generally do not have antitrust market power at the time the agreement was entered into. See, e.g., Benjamin Klein, *Market Power in Antitrust: Economic Analysis after Kodak*, 3 Sup. Ct. Econ. Rev. 43, 85 (1993); Benjamin Klein, *Market Power in Franchise Cases in the Wake of Kodak: Applying Post-Contract Hold-Up Analysis to Vertical Relationships*, 67 Antitrust L.J. 283 (1999).

[3] In re Dell Computer Corp., 121 F.T.C. 616 (1995).

[4] In re Rambus, FTC Dkt. No. 9302 (Liability Opinion, July 31, 2006), *rev'd*, Docket Nos. 07–1086, 07–1124 (D.C. Cir. 2007), available at http://pacer.cadc.uscourts.gov/docs/common/opinions/200804/07–1086-1112217.pdf).

[5] In re Union Oil Co. ("Unocal"), 2004 FTC LEXIS 115 (F.T.C. 2004), available at http://www.ftc.gov/os/adjpro/d9305/040706commissionopinion.pdf.

[6] In re Negotiated Data Solutions LLC (N-Data), No. 051–0094 (F.T.C. Jan. 23, 2008) (Majority Statement), available at http://www.ftc.gov/os/caselist/0510094/080122statement.pdf. Chairman Majoras and Commissioner Kovacic dissented from the Commission opinion, available at http://www.ftc.gov/os/caselist/0510094/080122majoras.pdf (Majoras dissent), and http://www.ftc.gov/os/caselist/0510094/080122kovacic.pdf (Kovacic dissent).

[7] *Broadcom Corp. v. Qualcomm Inc.*, 501 F. 3d 297 (3d Cir. 2007).

[8] U.S. Dep't of Justice & Fed. Trade Comm'n, Antitrust Enforcement and Intellectual Property Rights: Promoting Innovation and Competition 33–56 (April 2007) [hereinafter Antitrust/IP Report], available at www.usdoj.gov/atr/public/hearings/ip/222655.pdf; Fed. Trade Comm'n & U.S. Dep't of Justice, Hearings on Section 2 of the Sherman Act: Single-Firm Conduct As Related to Competition: Hearing on Misleading and Deceptive Conduct (December 6, 2006); ABA Section of Antitrust Law, Handbook on the Antitrust Aspects of Standard Setting 60–64 (2004). See also M. Sean Royall, *Standard Setting and Exclusionary Conduct: The Role of Antitrust in Policing Unilateral Abuses of the Standard Setting Processes*, Antitrust, Spring 2004, at 44. The antitrust treatment of *ex ante* efforts to prevent patent holdup has also been the subject of considerable discussion. See, e.g., Antitrust/ IP Report, supra, at 49–56; Letter from Thomas O. Barnett,

aspects of the patent holdup problem but have largely emphasized antitrust moments that arise out of the collaborative setting of standards,[9] the use of *ex ante* auctions to identify and mitigate *ex post* opportunism problems,[10] and patent reform.[11] In sum, the patent holdup literature has generally assumed that opportunism in the standard-setting process is an antitrust problem.

We approach the patent holdup problem from a different perspective, applying insights from the economics of federalism and inspired by the Supreme Court's decisions in *Credit Suisse* and *NYNEX v. Discon*, which encourage a careful evaluation of the comparative advantages of regulatory alternatives. In the patent holdup context, this analytical approach calls for an examination of the strengths and weaknesses of antitrust enforcement relative to federal patent law and state contract and tort law.

Section II examines the economics of federalism and discusses the relationship between jurisdictional competition between the states and substantive limits on antitrust. We review the Supreme Court's highly related recognition of the limits of antitrust enforcement when alternative state and federal options are available to regulate the relevant behavior *and* antitrust enforcement is likely to trigger "serious" errors. Further, we discuss *Kodak*

Assistant Attorney Gen., U.S. Dep't of Justice, to Robert A. Skitol, Esq. (Oct. 30, 2006) (business review letter), available at http://www.usdoj.gov/atr/public/busreview/219380 .htm; Letter from Thomas O. Barnett, Assistant Attorney Gen., U.S. Dep't of Justice, to Michael A. Lindsay, Esq. (Apr. 30, 2007) (business review letter), available at http://www .usdoj.gov/atr/public/busreview/222978.htm.

[9] See, e.g., J. Gregory Sidak, Patent Holdup and Oligopsonistic Collusion in Standard Setting Organizations (Jan. 8, 2008) (working paper), available at http://ssrn.com/abstract= 1081997; Robert Skitol, *Concerted Buyer Power: Its Potential for Addressing the Patent Hold-up Problem in Standard Setting*, 72 ANTITRUST L.J. 727 (2005).

[10] Daniel Swanson & William Baumol, *Reasonable and Nondiscriminatory (FRAND) Royalties, Standards Selection, and Control of Market Power*, 73 ANTITRUST L.J. (2005); Joseph Farrell et al., *Standard Setting, Patents, and Hold-Up*, 74 ANTITRUST L.J. 603 (2007); Damien Geradin & Anne Layne-Farrar, *The Logic and Limits of Ex Ante Competition in a Standard Setting Environment*, 3 COMPETITION POL'Y INT'L 79 (2007); Damien Geradin & Miguel Rato, Can Standard Setting Lead to Exploitative Abuse? A Dissonant View on Patent Holdup, Royalty Stacking, and the Meaning of FRAND (Apr. 2006), available at http://www.ssrn.com/abstract=946792; Damien Geradin, Anne Layne-Farrar & A. Jorge Padilla, *The Ex Ante Auction Model for the Control of Market Power in Standard Setting Organizations* (CEMFI Working Paper No. 0703, 2007).

[11] Mark A. Lemley & Carl Shapiro, *Patent Holdup and Royalty Stacking*, 85 TEX. L. REV. 1991 (2007); Mark A. Lemley & Carl Shapiro, *Reply: Patent Holdup and Royalty Stacking*, 85 TEX. L. REV. 2163 (2007); Mark A Lemley, *Ten Things to Do About Patent Holdup of Standards (And One Not To)*, 48 B.C. L. REV. 149 (2007); John M. Golden, *Patent Trolls and Patent Remedies*, 85 TEX. L. REV. 2111 (2007); J. Gregory Sidak, *Holdup, Royalty Stacking, and the Presumption of Injunctive Relief for Patent Infringement: A Reply to Lemley and Shapiro*, 92 MINN. L. REV. 713 (2008).

and its aftermath as an example of the implied repeal of antitrust enforcement and the recognition of substantive limits on antitrust.

Section III reviews theories of patent holdup. In particular, we consider two anticompetitive theories: (1) patent holdup involving deception, and (2) patent holdup involving the breach or renegotiation of a FRAND commitment made in good faith. We review the strengths and weaknesses of each theory in light of current law, including the D.C. Circuit's recent *Rambus* decision, as well as recent applications of these theories in agency enforcement actions.

Section IV commences our affirmative case that the marginal benefit of antitrust enforcement in the patent holdup context is slight, and possibly negative if error and administrative costs are taken into account. Our argument begins with an application of the principles espoused in *Credit Suisse*, arguing that a strong case can be made for limiting antitrust enforcement of patent holdup based on the comparative advantages offered by these alternative institutions relative to antitrust. This implied rescission of antitrust by another area of federal law is a natural extension of the Court's jurisprudence in *Credit Suisse*, where federal securities law resulted in the implied repeal of antitrust.

In Section V, we extend our analysis to consider the case in favor of the implied repeal of antitrust in favor of state contract and tort law. In particular, contract law offers a promising alternative to antitrust enforcement in the case of patent holdup involving breach of modification or FRAND commitments made in good faith as contract doctrine provides tools designed to identify and distinguish holdup from good faith modifications of long-term contracts.

Section VI concludes with our call for an implied repeal of antitrust regulation of patent holdup by federal courts so as to exploit the substantive doctrinal advantages in state common law, along with the associated benefits of jurisdictional competition, while avoiding the social welfare costs associated with erroneous application of the antitrust laws in this setting.

II. Antitrust and the Economics of Federalism Revisited

A. The Supreme Court Has Recognized the Limits of Antitrust Where Alternative Regulatory Institutions Are Available

Recently, the Supreme Court antitrust jurisprudence has emphasized the limits of antitrust due to the possibility of false positives and the social welfare losses associated with them.[12] In *Brooke Group*,[13] for example, the Supreme Court upheld the dismissal of a $148.8 million jury award. The Court held that plaintiffs alleging that volume discounts amount to predatory pricing under Section 2 of the Sherman Act must demonstrate both that that prices are "below an appropriate measure of cost" and that the defendant had a dangerous probability of recouping its investment in below-cost prices. Importantly, the Court noted that the appropriate liability rule for generally pro-competitive discounting conduct was shaped in significant part by error cost considerations. In assessing the possibility that above-cost prices might exclude rivals, the Court noted that any potentially exclusionary effect "reflects the lower cost structure of the alleged predator, and so represents competition on the merits, or is beyond the practical ability of a judicial tribunal to control without courting intolerable risks of chilling legitimate price cutting." The critical point is that the Court endorsed the proposition that, stated in terms of the error costs, the test for predatory pricing should decrease the probability of a type I error, at a cost of tolerating a higher cost of type II error. Such a standard would make economic sense when the expected costs of type II errors are small relative to the costs of type I errors. This is likely to be the case if successful predation is rare, or when the broader application of the antitrust laws would cause widespread deterrence of pro-competitive behavior.[14]

As a general matter, the error cost framework suggests that socially optimal antitrust rules will underdeter. This result obtains in part because the false positives in antitrust are not self-correcting and are felt by many firms when some conduct is condemned. It is also the case that the error-cost framework requires that the optimal liability rule be a function of the "best" estimate of the potential anticompetitive effects associated with the

---

[12] See generally David S. Evans & A. Jorge Padilla, *Designing Antitrust Rules for Assessing Unilateral Practices: A Neo-Chicago Approach*, 72 U. CHI. L. REV. 27 (2005) (discussing application of the error-cost approach). In the antitrust context, false positives are the erroneous condemnation of pro-competitive business conduct and are also known as type I errors. False negatives, or type II errors, refer to the mistaken failure to condemn anticompetitive behavior.

[13] *Brooke Group v. Brown & Williamson Tobacco Corp.*, 509 U.S. 209 (1993).

[14] Id. at 220–24. See also Bruce H. Kobayashi, *The Law and Economics of Predatory Pricing*, in THE LAW AND ECONOMICS OF ANTITRUST (K. Hylton ed., v.2 Encyclopedia of Law and Economics, 2d ed., Edward Elgar Pub, 2010); Frank Easterbrook, *Predatory Strategies and Counterstrategies*, 48 U. CHI. L. REV. 263 (1981); John R. Lott, Jr., ARE PREDATORY COMMITMENTS CREDIBLE? WHO SHOULD THE COURTS BELIEVE? (1999); John S. McGee, *Predatory Price Cutting: The* Standard Oil *(N.J.) Case*, 1 J.L. & ECON. 137 (1958); John S. McGee, *Predatory Pricing Revisited*, 23 J.L. & ECON. 289 (1980).

conduct at issue. Generally, the theoretical and empirical literature examining conduct such as predatory pricing, but also vertical restraints such as resale price maintenance, have demonstrated that these practices generally benefit consumers while producing a competitive threat only in rare instances.[15] In addition, to the extent that competitive threats have been identified, the development of antitrust standards that would address these threats without simultaneously threatening the pro-competitive conduct has been elusive. Given the current state of economic theory and empirical evidence, it follows that the social costs associated with false positives in antitrust will be high, as will the judicial error rate. Indeed, the error-cost concerns that motivated the Court's design of the predatory pricing standard in *Brooke Group* have been a constant theme in the Court's modern antitrust jurisprudence. For example, social welfare losses associated with false positives also motivated the Court's imposition of antitrust limits on Section 2 in *Trinko*, predatory buying claims in *Weyerhaueser*,[16] refusals to deal in *NYNEX*,[17] the elimination of per se treatment of minimum resale price maintenance in *Leegin*,[18] and stricter pleading requirements under Section 1 of the Sherman Act in *Twombly*.[19] Related to this emphasis on error costs has been the Supreme Court's increasing reliance on economic analysis to inform its opinions. As Brannon and Ginsburg note, this increased reliance on economic learning has resulted in a trend of more wins for defendants, greater consensus among the Justices, and convergence between the opinions of the Solicitor General and the Supreme Court.[20]

While the Supreme Court has consistently understood the relationship between false positives and limits on antitrust, *Credit Suisse* represents an application of this analysis in the case of overlapping regulations. Specifically, *Credit Suisse* recognizes the value of limiting antitrust enforcement under circumstances where an alternative and competent regulatory apparatus is available *and* antitrust enforcement is likely to result in little additional

---

[15] See, e.g., James Cooper et al., *Vertical Restrictions and Antitrust Policy: What About the Evidence?*, 1 COMPETITION POL'Y INT'L 45 (2005); Francine Lafontaine & Margaret Slade, *Exclusive Contracts and Vertical Restraints: Empirical Evidence and Public Policy*, in HANDBOOK OF ANTITRUST ECONOMICS, X (Paola Buccirossi ed., 2006).

[16] 127 S. Ct. 1069, 1078 (2007).

[17] *NYNEX Corp. v. Discon, Inc.*, 525 U.S. 128 (1998).

[18] *Leegin Creative Leather Prods., Inc. v. PSKS, Inc.*, 127 S. Ct. 2705 (2007).

[19] *Bell Atlantic Corp. v. Twombly*, 127 S. Ct. 1955 (2007). On error-cost analysis as a feature of the Roberts Court's antitrust jurisprudence, see Joshua D. Wright, *The Roberts Court and the Chicago School of Antitrust: The 2006 Term and Beyond*, 3 COMPETITION POL'Y INT'L 24 (2007).

[20] Leah Brannon & Douglas H. Ginsburg, *Antitrust Decisions of the U.S. Supreme Court 1967–2007*, 3 COMPETITION POL'Y INT'L 3 (2007).

social value because of the potential for welfare-reducing errors. As noted previously, the effect of error costs is a common factor in many of the Court's recent antitrust decisions that served to limit the application of the antitrust laws. In *Credit Suisse*, the Court's analysis explicitly recognizes that the existence of an alternative and competent regulatory apparatus further tips the cost-benefit calculus in favor of antitrust limits because the marginal benefits of applying the antitrust laws on top of this regulatory structure are small. The Court also explicitly endorses a similar analysis in *NYNEX v. Discon*, another modern case discussing unilateral conduct and the scope of monopolization liability. In this section, we establish the legal underpinnings for our claim that the Supreme Court's antitrust jurisprudence supports pragmatic, judicially imposed limits on the application of antitrust law to patent holdup so as to exploit the advantages of jurisdictional competition between the states and avoid the likely consumer welfare consequences of antitrust false positives.

Before we examine *Credit Suisse* and *NYNEX*, we begin by repeating the basis for and scope of our claim. We concede that there is no controversy that the antitrust laws can peacefully co-exist with a federal law, state law, and a variety of regulatory structures. For instance, we do not claim that certain conduct cannot be simultaneously a violation of state tort law and federal antitrust law. Similarly, it is obviously possible that a monopolist who sets fire to a rival's plant can simultaneously and appropriately be held to violate both arson and antitrust laws. The appropriate question is not simply whether the two sets of laws can co-exist when some conduct might violate each set. We believe this is the wrong question because it mistakenly presumes that the scope and effectiveness of the alternative set of regulations is and should be independent of defining the appropriate scope of antitrust liability rules. However, the Supreme Court's antitrust jurisprudence is consistent with the proposition that the extension of antitrust liability to conduct that is adequately regulated by alternative legal rules and institutions is appropriately limited when the marginal benefit of antitrust enforcement is low or negative. In this section we establish this principle. The remainder of the chapter turns to applying the principle by analyzing the marginal benefit of antitrust enforcement in the patent holdup context relative to federal and state alternatives.

The Supreme Court's strongest endorsement of this "marginal analysis" principle appears in *Credit Suisse v. Billing*.[21] In *Credit Suisse*, the Court dismissed a variety of antitrust claims brought by investors against

---

[21] *Credit Suisse Sec. (USA) LLC v. Billing*, 127 S. Ct. 2383 (2007).

underwriters from whom they had purchased securities. More specifically, the plaintiff class alleged that leading underwriting firms had conspired to manipulate the collective initial public offering (IPO) process by driving up the price of less attractive shares in the aftermarket in violation of Section 1 of the Sherman Act. The investment bank defendants argued that the complaint should be dismissed on the grounds that the federal securities laws impliedly precluded application of the antitrust laws. The district court granted the defendants' motion to dismiss on the grounds that the securities laws impliedly repealed federal antitrust laws. The Second Circuit reversed, finding that Congress had not expressly or impliedly demonstrated its intent to immunize the conduct at issue and that the enforcement of the securities laws was not sufficient to trigger immunity from antitrust liability.[22]

The Supreme Court reversed and agreed with the investment banks. In a 7–1 decision, Justice Breyer's majority opinion held that the antitrust claims against the investment banks arising from the underwriting transactions were impliedly preempted under a "clear incompatibility" standard.[23] The court noted that three of the four "critical" factors underlying the clear incompatibility standard were obviously satisfied: (1) the existence of regulatory authority under the securities law to supervise the activities in question; (2) evidence that the responsible regulatory entities exercise that authority; and (3) whether the affected practices lie squarely within an area of financial market activity that the securities law seeks to regulate. According to the Court, the only factor at issue was the third factor, the existence of a risk that the securities and antitrust laws, if both applicable, would produce conflicting guidance, requirements, duties, privileges, or standards of conduct.

The Court's prior holdings in this area focused on the conflicting goals of the antitrust laws and securities laws, specifically the incompatibility of the securities law with the antitrust law's focus on competition, when

---

[22] *Billing v. Credit Suisse First Boston Ltd.*, 426 F.3d 130 (2d Cir. 2005).

[23] *Credit Suisse*, 127 S. Ct. at 2387, 2389–92 (citing *Gordon v. New York Stock Exch., Inc.*, 422 U.S. 659, 682 (1975); *United States v. Nat'l Ass'n of Sec. Dealers, Inc.*, 422 U.S. 694 (1975); *Silver v. N.Y. Stock Exch.*, 373 U.S. 341 (1963)). Justice Stevens concurred in the judgment on the grounds that the defendants' alleged conduct would not violate the antitrust laws, but did not join the majority with respect to its finding of implied repeal. Justice Thomas dissented on the grounds that the savings clause in Section 16 of the Securities Act of 1933 and Section 28 of the 1934 Act preserves antitrust remedies. Justice Thomas therefore would not reach the issue of reconciling any conflict between antitrust and securities regulation. Justice Kennedy did not participate in the decision.

assessing this last factor.[24] In contrast, the Court in *Credit Suisse* focused instead on the actual operation of the antitrust law, highlighting the role that error costs play in limiting the usefulness of the antitrust laws. Thus, the Court's analysis of this third factor is heavily motivated by the concern that the benefits of antitrust enforcement may not outweigh its costs in this setting. The Court relied on a number of factors in concluding that the need for antitrust enforcement in this setting is "unusually small," the prospect for mistakes "unusually likely," and the likely result of overlapping liability would cause "serious harm to the efficient functioning of the securities markets."[25] With respect to the negligible benefits of antitrust enforcement, the Court emphasized the availability of competent alterative regulatory institutions: SEC enforcement as well as actions for damages under the securities law.[26]

In *Credit Suisse*, Justice Breyer notes the potential for antitrust liability in addition to securities regulation to generate large social welfare losses:

[W]here conduct at the core of the marketing of new securities is at issue; where securities regulators proceed with great care to distinguish the encouraged and permissible from the forbidden; where the threat of antitrust lawsuits, through error and disincentive, could seriously alter underwriter conduct in undesirable ways, to allow an antitrust lawsuit would threaten serious harm to the efficient functioning of the securities market.[27]

The message from the Court in *Credit Suisse* is that caution and modesty are warranted in considering an expansion of antitrust liability when there is a competent alternative regulatory structure in place and the risks of false positives is significant.[28] The Court determined that the benefits of

---

[24] Different standards are likely to result because "the sole aim of antitrust legislation is to protect competition, whereas the SEC must consider, in addition, the economic health of the investors, the exchanges, and the securities industry." *Gordon,* 422 U.S. at 689.

[25] *Credit Suisse,* 127 S. Ct. at 2396.

[26] Id. Justice Breyer's analysis of the marginal benefit of antitrust enforcement in *Credit Suisse* is consistent with Justice Scalia's assessment of the "slight benefits of antitrust intervention" in *Trinko.* Justice Scalia explicitly calls for an evaluation of these benefits against "a realistic assessment of its costs," noting that "one factor of particular importance is the existence of a regulatory structure designed to deter and remedy anticompetitive harm," and relying upon error-cost analysis to determine the appropriate scope of antitrust laws. *Verizon Commc'ns Inc. v. Law Offices of Curtis V. Trinko, LLP,* 540 U.S. 398, 412 (2004).

[27] *Credit Suisse Sec. (USA) LLC v. Billing,* 127 S. Ct. 2383 (2007).

[28] The premise of the error-cost framework is that it is socially optimal to adopt the legal rule that minimizes the expected social cost of false acquittals, false convictions, and administrative costs. See generally Frank Easterbrook, *The Limits of Antitrust,* 65 TEX. L. REV. 1 (1984). Subsequently, several commentators have adopted this framework as

expanded liability on the margin were simply too slight to justify the costs associated with the use of the blunt instrument of antitrust enforcement.

A second Supreme Court decision predating *Credit Suisse*, *NYNEX v. Discon*,[29] reinforces this message. There, the Court considered whether "an antitrust court considering an agreement by a buyer to purchase goods or services from one supplier rather than another should (after examining the buyer's reasons or justifications) apply the per se rule if it finds no legitimate business reason for that purchasing decision."[30] More specifically, the Court concluded that the defendant (NYNEX) had not engaged in a per se illegal boycott by switching its purchases from the plaintiff (Discon) to a rival provider of "removal services" (AT&T).[31]

What makes *NYNEX* particularly interesting for our purposes is that the plaintiffs alleged that NYNEX's decision to switch its purchases to AT&T was motivated by an attempt to commit regulatory fraud that would prevent the regulatory agency from controlling New York Telephone's exercise of its monopoly power.[32] As we will discuss in greater detail in Section III.C, *NYNEX* can be reasonably interpreted to exclude expansion of the Sherman Act to those patent holdup cases involving *ex post* opportunism in the form of renegotiation or breach of contractual commitments made in good faith and in the absence of fraud or deception. Specifically, the Court unanimously held that the exercise of lawfully acquired monopoly power to harm consumers, even where the exercise takes the form of a fraud designed to evade regulatory constraints on pricing power, is not within

a useful tool for understanding the design of antitrust rules. See, e.g., David Evans & Jorge Padilla, *Designing Antitrust Rules for Assessing Unilateral Practices: A Neo-Chicago Approach*, 72 U. CHI. L. REV. 73, 98 (2005); C. Frederick Beckner III & Steven C. Salop, *Decision Theory and Antitrust Rules*, 67 ANTITRUST L.J. 41 (1999); Keith N. Hylton & Michael Salinger, *Tying Law and Policy: A Decision-Theoretic Approach*, 69 ANTITRUST L.J. 469 (2001); Luke Froeb et al., *Vertical Antitrust Policy as a Problem of Inference*, 23 INT'L J. INDUS. ORG. 639 (2005).

[29] *NYNEX Corp. v. Discon, Inc.*, 525 U.S. 128 (1998).
[30] Id. at 135.
[31] While the Court's decision primarily addresses whether NYNEX's conduct constituted a per se violation of the antitrust laws under the Court's boycott jurisprudence in *Klor's, Inc. v. Broadway-Hale Stores, Inc.*, 359 U. S. 207, (1959), the Court also held that the same conduct would not violate Section 2 unless Discon could prevail on its Section 1 claim, which was remanded. On remand, the district court agreed that such an increase in price did not constitute an adverse "effect on competition" that could support a violation of Section 2. 86 F. Supp. 2d 154, 163–64 (W.D.N.Y. 2000). For our purposes, the critical feature of *NYNEX* is that the Court suggests that the conduct, evasion of a pricing constraint through regulatory fraud, was outside the scope of the antitrust laws. We believe *NYNEX* is properly interpreted to apply to antitrust analysis of unilateral conduct under Section 2. *Accord* Rambus, supra note 4.
[32] *NYNEX Corp.*, 525 U.S. at 135.

the scope of the antitrust laws. For our purposes, it suffices to note that the same error-cost concerns motivating the Court's analysis in *Credit Suisse* are important factors in Justice Breyer's opinion that expanding antitrust liability in this instance would "transform cases involving business behavior that is improper for various reasons, say, cases involving nepotism or personal pique, into treble damage antitrust cases."[33] Similarly, in dicta, Justice Breyer recognizes the role of alternative regulatory structures, including state law, in defining the appropriate limits to antitrust liability, noting the availability of remedies from "unfair competition laws, business tort laws, or regulatory laws."[34]

B. Federalism and Antitrust Limits

The Supreme Court's recent antitrust jurisprudence has recognized that the benefits of antitrust enforcement are limited when they conflict with other specific laws regulating the same areas and are vulnerable to a high risk of false positives. In *Credit Suisse* and *NYNEX*, the Court's antitrust analysis incorporates these concerns and responds by limiting application of the Sherman Act to the conduct in question. The overarching principle that emerges from these cases with respect to antitrust enforcement is modesty. Where the Court demonstrates little marginal benefit of antitrust enforcement on top of some alternative regulatory structure, the Court has concluded that antitrust should have limited application because of the large expected social costs associated with its enforcement apparatus. Rather than rely on antitrust enforcement in these instances, it is appropriate to rely on the alternative regulatory structure, which may include other federal laws and regulations. In this section, we argue that the same pragmatic considerations apply equally to state laws and regulations. This "reverse preemption principle" can be usefully applied to the patent holdup doctrine. We argue that application of this principle, and the substantive superiority of state contract and tort law relative to antitrust law in the patent holdup context, provide the basis for a similar constraint on antitrust enforcement.

It is important to recognize that we are not asserting that state contract and tort law actually preempt federal law. Rather, we have demonstrated only that the Court's antitrust jurisprudences have been sensitive to the risk that the marginal benefit of antitrust enforcement in the presence of alternative forms of regulation might be outweighed by its costs in some

---

[33] Id. at 137.
[34] Id.

instances, and that the Court has curtailed the scope of the antitrust laws in favor of relying on these alternative structures in those instances. One may question as too aggressive our interpretation that *Credit Suisse* and *NYNEX* invite an analysis of the marginal benefits of antitrust enforcement and demands an understanding of the potentially heavy error and administrative costs associated with its application in all settings. However, even the most conservative interpretation of these cases must allow for the Court's insistence that these considerations of overlapping regulations and error costs should inform the Court's decisions with respect to defining the scope and substance of federal antitrust law.[35]

Indeed, the Court has chosen to limit the application of the antitrust law in other settings, including its broad immunity for petitioning activity under the *Noerr-Pennington* doctrine.[36] And while conflicts between state and federal laws are generally resolved in favor of federal law, the Court has in some cases limited the application of federal antitrust laws to activity regulated under state law through the Court's state action doctrine.[37] Applying general principles of federalism, the Court has attempted to set out conditions under which the federal antitrust laws must defer to states' regulatory choices. Easterbrook notes that in many of the Court's state action cases, the state statutes in question seek to supplant competition, and thus they are facially inconsistent with the antitrust laws.[38] Under the Court's state action doctrine, states' conscious acts to replace competition with regulation will not be subject to antitrust scrutiny as long as the state actively supervises the implementation of its policy.[39]

While our thesis does not question and indeed supports in a broad sense the Court's choice to set limits on the application of antitrust law under the state action doctrine, we do question the one particular aspect of the way in which the Court has defined the scope this doctrine.[40] Under the

---

[35] Indeed, a similar issue is generated by the existence of multiple antitrust laws that apply to the same transaction or conduct. These include duplicate state and federal enforcement of the antitrust laws, and the simultaneous and uncoordinated enforcement of the antitrust laws of different countries. For an analysis of the problem of overlapping and duplicative enforcement of the antitrust laws, see COMPETITION LAWS IN CONFLICT: ANTITRUST JURISDICTION IN THE GLOBAL ECONOMY (Richard A. Epstein & Michael S. Greve eds., AEI Press 2004).

[36] *E. R. R. Presidents Conference v. Noerr Motor Freight, Inc.*, 365 U.S. 127 (1961).

[37] *Parker v. Brown*, 317 U.S. 341 (1943).

[38] See generally Frank H. Easterbrook, *Antitrust and the Economics of Federalism*, 26 J.L. & ECON. 23, 26 (1983).

[39] Easterbrook, supra note 38, at 26.

[40] For a more general discussion of the state action doctrine, see Easterbrook, supra note 38.

assumption that the antitrust laws serve to increase welfare through promoting competition, to condition antitrust immunity for activity regulated by state law on the existence of active supervision by the state is an economic puzzle. If state regulations are anticompetitive schemes to reward politically powerful interest groups, it is far from clear why one would base antitrust immunity on the existence of active supervision by the state, which created the anticompetitive scheme in the first place.[41] Further, active supervision by the state can be an especially costly form of regulation compared with other forms of less supervised regulation, or no regulation at all. That is, compared with alternative mechanisms of regulation, active supervision may be worse for consumers and regulated firms.[42] Thus, the Court's choice of the particular form under which state action immunity from antitrust liability is allowed seems pathological, unless one argues that this scheme is a type of penalty option that serves to suppress the overall demand for anticompetitive state legislation in the first place.[43]

Indeed, a similar a critique can be aimed at the Court's holdings discussed in part A of this section that base, in part, the implied repeal of the antitrust laws on the active supervision and enforcement of the conflicting federal law by a federal regulatory agency. Congress and federal regulators are subject to many of the same public choice influences as state legislators and regulators. Thus, the requirement that the alternative federal regulatory apparatus be "actively supervised" does not seem to make sense from an economic standpoint for the reasons just noted. Moreover, if jurisdictional competition provides an effective constraint on state legislators and regulators, one can argue that such public choice problems are likely to be worse at the federal level than at the state level.[44] Thus, the case for court-imposed antitrust limits based on the risk that "antitrust courts are likely to make unusually serious mistakes" may be more compelling when applied to conflicts with nonactively supervised state laws than to conflicts with actively supervised federal laws.

---

[41] Timothy Brennan, Trinko v. Baxter: *The Demise of* U.S. v. AT&T, 50 ANTITRUST BULL. 635 (2006).

[42] Easterbrook, supra note 38, at 29–33.

[43] Id. at 33 (noting argument and positing that such an all-or-noting choice would result in more costly regulation on net).

[44] Furthermore, the fact that Congress has the power to explicitly preempt or limit the application of the federal antitrust laws, while the states do not, also makes the marginal benefits of court-imposed antitrust limits for firms subject to alternative state regulations greater than for firms subject to alternative federal regulations. See, e.g., the antitrust exemption for labor contained in the Clayton Act, and the insurance antitrust exemption contained in the McCarran-Ferguson Act.

Previous authors have examined how the principles of federalism and the potential for jurisdictional competition affect the choice to limit the application of the federal antitrust laws. Easterbrook examined the Court's state action doctrine under such a framework, and found that the Court's rulings in this area were misguided, as they had in fact served to reduce the extent and effectiveness of competition between the states. For example, Easterbrook found that the Court's rulings in this area increased the cost of exit, limited the states to a particularly inefficient form of regulation, and were indifferent to whether the effects of the regulation are internalized by the regulating state.[45] Easterbrook would replace the Court's approach with a rule that could capture the benefits of federalism and jurisdictional competition by allowing states and local jurisdictions to adopt any regulations they choose, subject to a requirement that any adverse effects of the regulation are internalized by residents of that state.

The benefits of federalism also have been used to advocate restraint in applying the federal antitrust laws to areas traditionally regulated by the states. Meese examined the case for federal antitrust regulation of franchisor opportunism and concluded that competition between the states was more likely to generate efficient rules and institutions governing this area.[46] These include state contract law,[47] and also specific state statutory regulations of the franchisor/franchisee relationship.[48] Meese argues against displacing or augmenting the system of state rules regulating franchisor opportunism, which are influenced by jurisdictional competition, with federal antitrust regulation, which is not.

The hypothetical use of antitrust law to regulate franchisor opportunism indeed illustrates the potential benefits of antitrust limits flowing from avoiding the erroneous application of the antitrust laws. To see this, consider how the application of antitrust to franchisor opportunism would affect the existing system of state by state regulation. Advocates of using antitrust to address franchisor opportunism cite franchise tying, encroachment, and maximum resale price maintenance, enforced through the threat

---

[45] For a discussion of the conditions under which competitive federalism is effective, see Charles M. Tiebout, *A Pure Theory of Local Expenditures*, 64 J. POL. ECON. 416 (1956).

[46] Alan J. Meese, *Regulation of Franchisor Opportunism and Production of the Institutional Framework: Federal Monopoly or Competition between the States?* 23 HARV. J.L. & PUB. POL'Y 61 (1999).

[47] Id.

[48] For a recent discussion of state regulatory statutes, see Jonathan Klick, Bruce H. Kobayashi & Larry E. Ribstein, *The Effect of Contract Regulation: The Case of Franchising* (George Mason Law & Economics Research Paper No. 07–03, 2006), available at SSRN: http://ssrn. com/abstract=951464.

of termination of the franchisee, as examples of franchisor opportunism that could be addressed through the antitrust laws.[49] Moreover, under the Court's decision in *Kodak*,[50] the antitrust laws could be applied to cases of opportunism that do not involve market power in either the sale of franchise opportunities or the sale of the good or service.

There are many reasons that the application of the antitrust laws to address franchisor opportunism in this setting is likely to result in errors.[51] The Court's opinion in *Kodak* has been widely criticized for confusing the issue of a single firm's power over its own price, and the proper concept of antitrust market power that requires the firm to have the power to control market prices.[52] The former concept can exist in competitive markets where sellers sell differentiated products, or in cases where parties make relationship-specific investments that are subject to opportunistic holdup, and it does not require that individual firms in these industries have power over the market price. Thus, one cannot equate power over a firm's own product's price, which occurs frequently within competitive industries, with the ability to affect the market price, which is the proper concern for antitrust policy. Application of the antitrust laws in the absence of antitrust market power will result in frequent type I errors, as the generation of harm to competition from the use of tying, RPM (resale price maintenance) or the franchisor's choice of new outlet locations is implausible in the absence of antitrust market power. Indeed, as is discussed later, the lower courts have almost uniformly rejected the theory that contractual lock-in creates antitrust market power.[53]

Furthermore, there is widespread evidence that the regulation of franchisor opportunism can be costly. Evidence regarding state laws aimed at regulating franchisor opportunism suggests that such laws are inefficient.

---

[49] See Warren Grimes, *Antitrust Remedies for Franchisor Opportunism*, 65 ANTITRUST L.J. 105 (1996).

[50] *Eastman Kodak Co. v. Image Technical Servs., Inc.*, 504 U.S. 45 (1992).

[51] See Roger D. Blair & Jill Boylston Herndon, *The Misapplication of Kodak In Franchise Tying Suits*, 14 J. BUS. VENTURING 397 (1999).

[52] See Joshua D. Wright, *Missed Opportunities in* Independent Ink, 5 CATO SUP. CT. REV. 333 (2006); Bruce H. Kobayashi, *Spilled Ink or Economic Progress? The Supreme Court's Decision in* Illinois Tool Works v. Independent Ink, 53 ANTITRUST BULL. 5 (2008); Herbert Hovenkamp, *Market Power in Aftermarkets: Antitrust Policy and the Kodak Case*, 40 UCLA L. REV. 1447, 1451–52 (1993); Benjamin Klein & John Shepard Wiley, *Competitive Price Discrimination as an Antitrust Justification for Intellectual Property Refusals to Deal*, 70 ANTITRUST L.J. 599 (2003); Benjamin Klein, *Market Power in Antitrust: Economic Analysis after Kodak*, 3 SUP. CT. ECON. REV. 43 (1993); Carl Shapiro, *Aftermarkets and Consumer Welfare: Making Sense of Kodak*, 63 ANTITRUST L.J. 483 (1995).

[53] See infra Section II.C.

For example, empirical studies of automobile dealer regulations found that attempts to regulate franchisor opportunism, including restrictions on encroachment, produced anticompetitive results, decreasing sales and increasing prices.[54] And evidence on the effect of general franchise regulation statutes finds that such statutes interfere with attempts by franchisors to address agency costs and other forms of franchisee opportunism, and cause a reduction in the overall activity level in franchise industries.[55]

In contrast to the factual setting in the Court's state action cases, where the antitrust laws would be used to attack inefficient state laws, use of the antitrust laws to address franchisor opportunism would be to support rather than disable an inefficient regulatory scheme. More importantly, the potential use of federal antitrust law can serve to disable the desirable effect of regulatory competition in this area. First, outside of regulations directed at automobile dealerships and petroleum marketing, the majority of states do not have statutes that specifically regulate opportunism in franchise contracts. Rather, most states rely on general contract law principles to regulate opportunism.[56] Thus, the use of federal antitrust law to either supplement or fill gaps in state law may serve to extend the effect of these inefficient regulations to nonregulating states.

More importantly, the availability of federal antitrust law may negate the significant effect of jurisdictional competition that has operated in this area. Franchisors have used contractual choice of law and forum clauses to facilitate exit from the application of franchise regulations to contracts with franchisees located in the regulating states. In *Burger King v. Rudzewicz*, the Supreme Court enforced a clause in a franchise agreement by which a Michigan franchisee consented to jurisdiction in Florida.[57] The Court held that the franchisee had established "minimum contacts" with Florida, and had agreed to a contract that had "substantial connections with the forum state," including a provision that provided for application of Florida law. As a result of the Court's holding, the Michigan Franchise Investment Law, which required cause for termination, and also gave the franchisee a right to cure any violations of its franchise contract, did not govern the relationship between Burger King and its franchisees located in Michigan.

---

[54] Richard L. Smith II, *Franchise Regulation: An Economic Analysis of State Restrictions on Automobile Distribution.*25 J.L. & Econ. 125 (1982); E. W. Eckard, Jr., *The Effects of State Automobile Dealer Entry Regulation on New Car Prices,* 23 Econ. Inq. 223 (1985).

[55] Klick et al., supra note 48 (listing statutes regulating franchisor opportunism).

[56] Timothy J. Muris, *Opportunistic Behavior and the Law of Contracts,* 65 Minn. L. Rev. 521 (1981).

[57] *Burger King v. Rudzewicz,* 471 U.S. 462 (1985).

Based on empirical evidence that regulations like those contained in the Michigan Franchise Investment law interfere with the franchisor's ability to efficiently prevent franchisee shirking, an important effect of permitting and enforcing free choice of law and forum by contracting parties is to allow parties to escape such inefficient regulations.[58] Contracting parties can exercise effectively and at low cost their exit rights, which are critical to facilitating competitive federalism.[59] This will, in turn, improve lawmaking by reducing interest group incentives to promote inefficient laws. The importance of this effect is demonstrated by Klick et al.[60] In response to the Court's *Burger King* decision, as well as lower court decisions enforcing choice of law and choice of form agreements, some of the regulating states responded by enacting explicit restrictions on using choice of law or choice of forum clauses to escape the effects of franchise regulations. When the effects of such restrictions on contractual exit are taken into account, Klick et al. find significant negative marginal effects on franchise activity in those states that enacted restrictions on contractual exit over regulating states that did not restrict exit.[61] Moreover, the negative effects of franchise regulation statutes become small and statistically insignificant in the absence of such restrictions.[62] Thus, the evidence suggests that firms have used contractual choice of law to escape the effects of this inefficient regulation. If federal antitrust law is allowed to fill the gaps in state-by-state regulation of franchise opportunism, this important escape value will be negated by opportunistic franchisees.

C. The *Kodak* Example

The primary thesis advanced in this chapter is that the Supreme Court has endorsed the consideration of competent alternative regulatory institutions and the potential for significant error costs in designing antitrust rules, and that contract and patent law are superior regulatory institutions for dealing with the problems associated with patent holdup. Of course, we do not contend that lower courts are *compelled* to conclude that the antitrust laws are preempted by the presence of alternative state or federal laws. Rather, we note that the Supreme Court has encouraged the consideration

---

[58] Klick, et al., supra note 48.
[59] Richard A. Epstein, *Exit Rights Under Federalism*, 55 L. & Contemporary Prob. 147 (1992).
[60] Klick et al., supra note 48.
[61] Klick et al., supra note 48.
[62] Id.

of these other factors and that these factors militate against the application of antitrust laws to patent holdup. In essence, we argue that our framework provides an analytical backdrop that counsels extreme caution in applying the antitrust laws to this particular problem in favor of allowing operation of state contract and patent law.

There is some precedent for this type of implied substantive repeal. After the Supreme Court's decision in *Kodak,* which arguably opened the door to the application of monopolization liability to aftermarket holdup in franchise and other settings, lower courts have all but entirely overturned aftermarket holdup theories in favor of relying on state law. Goldfine and Vorrasi conducted a survey of all lower court opinions in which the plaintiff alleged a *Kodak* aftermarket lock-in claim, between 1992 and 2003.[63] Goldfine and Vorrasi found that courts have limited *Kodak* in two ways: (1) to situations involving a change in policy; and (2) by focusing on the relevant product definition.[64] Based on their survey of lower court opinions analyzing the *Kodak* opinion, Goldfine and Vorrasi conclude that the lower courts have effectively overruled the Supreme Court's decision by limiting application of the aftermarket holdup theory.[65]

We have updated the Goldfine and Vorrasi analysis of all federal district and appellate court decisions citing *Kodak* through January 31, 2008.[66] (See Table 17.1.) We found twenty-two cases citing *Kodak* as authority for an aftermarket lock-in claim from 2001 to 2008.[67] Of these twenty-two cases,

---

[63] David A.J. Goldfine & Vorrasi, Kenneth M., *The Fall of Kodak Aftermarket Doctrine: Dying a Slow Death in the Lower Courts,* 72 Antitrust L.J. 209 (2004).

[64] Id. at 220–22.

[65] Id. at 230–31.

[66] Between January 1, 2000, and January 31, 2008, *Kodak* has been cited 7,305 times and examined or discussed 2,290 of these times. All results were obtained using Westlaw's list of citing references to the Supreme Court opinion.

[67] The 22 cases include both lower court opinions and the appellate decisions. Therefore, a case may be counted twice, once at the trial level and again on appeal. See *Schlotzsky's, Ltd. v. Sterling Purchasing & Nat'l Distrib. Co.,* 520 F.3d 393 (5th Cir. 2008); *Newcal Indus., Inc. v. IKON Office Solutions, Inc.,* 513 F.3d 1038 (9th Cir. 2008); *Harrison Aire, Inc. v. Aerostar Int'l, Inc.,* 423 F.3d 374 (3d Cir. 2005); *Maris Distrib. Co. v. Anheuser-Busch, Inc.,* 302 F.3d 1207 (11th Cir. 2002); *Hack v. President & Fellows of Yale College,* 237 F.3d 81 (2d Cir. 2000); *Westerfield v. Quizno's Franchise Co.,* 527 F. Supp. 2d 840 (E.D. Wisc. 2007); *Delta Kappa Epsilon Alumni Corp v. Colgate Coll.,* 492 F. Supp. 2d 106 (N.D.N.Y. 2007); *Static Control Component, Inc. v. Leximark Int'l, Inc.,* 487 F. Supp. 2d 861 (E.D. Ky. 2007); *Mumford v. GNC Franchising, LLC,* 437 F. Supp. 2d 344 (W.D. Pa. 2006); *Subsolutions, Inc. v. Doctor's Assoc., Inc.,* 426 F. Supp. 2d 348 (D. Conn. 2006); *Newcal Indus., Inc. v. IKON Office Solutions, Inc.,* No. C 04–2776, 2005 WL 1156028 (N.D. Cal. 2005); *Strawflower Electronics, Inc. v. Radioshack Corp.,* No. C-05–0747, 2005 WL 2290314 (N.D. Cal. 2005); *Newcal Indus., Inc. v. IKON Office Solutions, Inc.,* No. C04–2776 FMS, 2004 WL 3017002 (N.D. Cal. 2004); *Harrison Aire, Inc. v. Aerostar Int'l, Inc.,* 316 F. Supp. 2d 186 (E.D. Pa. 2004); *McLaughlin Equip. Co. v. Newcourt Credit Group, Inc.,* No. IP98–0127, 2004 WL

Table 17.1. *The death of aftermarket holdup claims*

Description	1992–2000	2001–2008	Total
Decisions citing *Kodak*	737	985	1,722
Number of *Kodak* Aftermarket Claims	24	22	46
Defendant Wins	22	20	42
Plaintiff Survives Summary Judgment/Mtn to Dismiss	2	2	4
Defendant Win Percentage (%)	91.7%	90.9%	91.3%

twenty were decided for the defendant on a motion to dismiss, motion for summary judgment, or post-trial motion for judgment as a matter of law. Plaintiffs alleging *Kodak* aftermarket tie-in claims prevailed in one motion to dismiss and one defeated a single motion for summary judgment.[68]

III. Antitrust Theories of Patent Holdup

We claim that the conditions for limits on the antitrust laws identified in *Credit Suisse* and more generally by the Supreme Court's recent antitrust jurisprudence are satisfied in the case of patent holdup. Specifically, we find that the application of the antitrust laws to patent holdup will provide little marginal benefit over and conflict with other specific laws regulating the same area, and also will generate high risk for errors in application of the antitrust laws. Further, the potential benefits of jurisdictional competition between the states, especially with respect to contract law and the regulation of patent holdup, also favor substantive antitrust limits that would favor contract law treatment of this issue. In the remainder of this chapter, we analyze the current state of antitrust regulation of patent holdup, the strengths and weaknesses of this approach from a legal and economic perspective, and finally turn to the affirmative case for reliance on federal patent law and state law alternatives to antitrust.

1629603 (S.D. Ind. 2004); *George Lussier Enterprises, Inc. v. Subaru of New England*, 286 F. Supp. 2d 86 (D.N.H. 2003); *Commercial Data Servers, Inc. v. Int'l Bus. Mach., Corp.*, 262 F. Supp. 2d 50 (S.D.N.Y. 2003); *ID Sec. Sys. Can. v. Checkpoint Sys.*, 249 F. Supp. 2d 622 (E.D. Pa. 2003); *Commercial Data Servers, Inc. v. Int'l Bus. Mach.*, No. 00CIV5008, 2002 WL 1205740 (S.D.N.Y. 2002); *Universal Avionics Sys. Corp. v. Rockwell Int'l Corp.*, 184 F. Supp. 2d 947 (D. Az. 2001); *Subsolutions, Inc. v. Doctor's Assoc., Inc.*, No. 3:98-CV-470, 2001 WL 1860382 (D. Conn. 2001); *O'Dell v. General Motors Corp.*, 122 F. Supp. 2d 721 (E.D. Tex. 2000).

[68] See *Newcal Indus., Inc. v. IKON Office Solutions, Inc.*, 513 F.3d 1038 (9th Cir. 2008); *Static Control Component, Inc. v. Leximark Int'l, Inc.*, 487 F. Supp. 2d 861 (E.D. Kent 2007).

The basic patent holdup problem is well known and related to the conventional *ex post* opportunism discussed in the economic literature.[69] The basic notion is the patent holder, once its technology has been adopted by the SSO and relationship-specific investments have been made, holds up licensees for higher royalty rates than would have otherwise prevailed because there are fewer effective substitutes *ex post* after the technology is chosen. These higher royalty rates, in turn, are passed on to consumers in the form of higher prices. The Antitrust/IP Report describes the holdup problem as follows:

> [A]fter a standard has been adopted and switching to an alternative standard would require significant additional costs, the holder of a patent that covers technology needed to implement the standard can force users of the technology to choose between two unpleasant options: "You either don't make the standard or you accede to the – I don't want to say blackmail, but that's [what it] tends to be in that environment." Anointing a patented technology as the standard improves the bargaining position of the owner of the needed technology in licensing negotiations because "[i]f you are the owner of one of the rights to one of those many equally valuable [technologies], then it is the standard-setting process that will reduce the substitution, possibly eliminate the substitutes, and elevate your technology to [be] the most valuable."[70]

But what distinguishes patent holdup from other types of conventional contractual opportunism that result in higher prices but are not generally considered antitrust problems? For example, consider a landlord who signs an initial lease with a tenant under highly competitive conditions that are reflected in the terms. After the tenant has become "locked in," the landlord takes advantage of the incompleteness of the contract to impose a new "parking fee" against the tenant, effectively raising the price. Most would agree this is not and should not be actionable *antitrust* conduct, even if it is a breach of contract. In this situation, the fact that the landlord "evaded a contractual restraint on pricing" is not a sufficient condition for the existence of an antitrust problem. Without more, it demonstrates the existence of neither market power nor exclusionary conduct. The most obvious distinction that can be drawn in the case of the landlord example versus the patent holder negotiating with the SSO is that the former might be described as akin to a landlord having preexisting market power through control over some large percentage of available leases. Even assuming the existence of antitrust relevant market power, the landlord's breach of the agreements or demand for modification in favor of higher prices would

---

[69] See supra note 2.
[70] Antitrust/ IP Report, supra note 8, at 37–38.

not establish an antitrust violation *without more*. As we will discuss, the Supreme Court has routinely rejected the proposition that raising prices is equivalent to exclusionary conduct. Defining exclusionary conduct as a "breach" that raises the price is a thinly veiled attempt to circumvent the Supreme Court's rulings to the contrary.

Some have argued that the special competitive concerns surrounding the risk of collusion in the standard-setting process justify stricter antitrust scrutiny of patent holdup. Yet, the Sherman Act does not proscribe all conduct by monopolists that results in higher prices. To the contrary, *NYNEX* and *Trinko* make clear that the monopolist is entitled to engage in optimal pricing without fear of antitrust liability so long as its monopoly power has been obtained lawfully. The key challenge facing any antitrust relevant theory of patent holdup is to identify conditions that result in the *unlawful* acquisition of monopoly power as the result of exclusionary conduct rather than the mere exercise of that power once lawfully obtained.

It is useful to start by distinguishing two lines of cases involving two unique theories of patent holdup as an antitrust problem. The first line of cases involves allegations that the patent holder employs deception or fraud in order to have technology incorporated into the standard and acquire the power to raise price. FTC enforcement actions against *Dell* and *Rambus* both involve allegations of the unlawful acquisition of monopoly power resulting from deception in the form of intentionally failing to disclose relevant patents. Importantly, *Rambus* also created the possibility that deceptive conduct in the standard-setting process could constitute "exclusionary conduct" for the purposes of Section 2 of the Sherman Act. The Third Circuit's *Qualcomm* decision also fits this description, allowing Broadcom's complaint to survive because it alleged, among other things, that Qualcomm made and broke an "intentionally false promise to license essential proprietary technology on FRAND terms."[71]

The "deception" cases are often heralded as examples of "cheap exclusion," involving conduct capable of imposing significant competitive risks without any redeeming pro-competitive virtues at minimal cost.[72] While is it certainly not a sufficient condition for antitrust liability, the notion that deception or misrepresentation can potentially constitute exclusionary conduct for a monopolization claim is not controversial. Antitrust law has traditionally recognized that fraud, tortious conduct, or misrepresentation can violate the Sherman Act, though courts have insisted on requiring that

---

[71] *Broadcom Corp. v. Qualcomm Inc.*, 501 F. 3d 297, 314 (3d Cir. 2007).
[72] Susan A. Creighton et al., *Cheap Exclusion*, 72 ANTITRUST L.J. 795 (2005).

plaintiffs demonstrate "a preliminary showing of significant and more than temporary harmful effects on competition (and not merely upon a competitor or customer) before considering a tort as an exclusionary practice."[73] Merely describing some fraudulent conduct or misrepresentation as "cheap exclusion" is not a formula for antitrust liability without a separate showing that the competitive process has been harmed. While it is true that deceptive conduct lacks pro-competitive virtue and therefore mitigates some of the concerns about error costs and favors enforcement when all else is equal, it goes too far to argue that the presence of such conduct eliminates those concerns or demonstrates that the benefits of enforcement outweighs its associated administrative and error costs.

A second line of cases and recent scholarly commentary would significantly expand the role of antitrust in policing *ex post* opportunism in the standard-setting context. This view contemplates patent holdup, defined as any deviation from the *ex ante* contractual commitments, as a sufficient condition for an antitrust violation. Deception or other exclusionary conduct would not be required. In *N-Data*, the FTC successfully extracted a consent decree under Section 5 of the FTC Act from a patent holder who acquired its monopoly power lawfully and made its *ex ante* contractual commitments in good faith, but attempted to increase royalty rates several years later. In a recent article in the *Antitrust Law Journal*, Farrell et al. argue that virtually any breach of an *ex ante* commitment to the SSO that results in consumer harm either does or should violate the antitrust laws.[74] We discuss each of these theories, how they have fared in recent decisions, as well as their application by the enforcement agencies in the following subsections.

A. Patent Holdup with Deception

Patent holdup involving deception forms the basis for the majority of recent cases involving opportunism against SSOs. For example, intentional deception of the SSO with respect to a royalty commitment formed the basis of the allegations upheld in *Broadcom*. In *Rambus*, the FTC found Rambus liable for intentionally concealing a patent and relevant applications from the SSO, although the D.C. Circuit ultimately overturned the FTC's decision. In *Unocal*, the FTC found a patent holder liable for affirmative misrepresentations. In each of these cases, allegations that deceptive conduct caused

---

[73] See 3A Philip Areeda & Donald F. Turner, ANTITRUST LAW, ¶ 782a. See generally Joshua D. Wright, *Antitrust Analysis of Category Management: Conwood Co. v. United States Tobacco*, 17 SUP. CT. ECON. REV. 311 (2009).

[74] Joseph Farrell et al., *Standard Setting, Patents, and Hold-Up*, 74 ANTITRUST L.J. 603 (2007).

the selection of a proprietary technology by the SSO were the crux of the antitrust claim. Recently, the Third Circuit held in *Broadcom* that intentionally deceiving the SSO with respect to a royalty commitment could constitute a monopolization cause of action under the following conditions:

(1) in a consensus-oriented private standard setting environment, (2) a patent holder's intentionally false promise to license essential proprietary technology on FRAND terms, (3) coupled with a [Standard Determining Organization's] reliance on that promise when including the technology in a standard, and (4) the patent holder's subsequent breach of that promise, is actionable anticompetitive conduct.[75]

Broadcom relies heavily on the FTC's analysis in *Rambus*, emphasizing the notion that deception is a traditional and conventional antitrust concern,[76] and equating the intentional creation of deceptive FRAND commitments with deceptive nondisclosure of intellectual property rights.

Consider the argument in favor of liability in the case of patent holdup raised by the FTC and Broadcom. The anticompetitive theory is fairly straightforward: (1) *Ex ante* deception allows the patent holder to acquire monopoly power unlawfully; (2) rival technology holders are excluded as a result of this conduct; and (3) consumer welfare is harmed as the monopolist is able to extract supra-competitive royalties. *Broadcom* and *N-Data* endorse the view that *ex post* opportunism against SSOs in the form of *ex ante* and intentional deception (*Broadcom*), or even *ex post* breach or modification of FRAND commitments made in good faith (*N-Data*), are antitrust problems because higher royalty rates to the SSO are passed on to the ultimate consumers. In short, conduct that results in monopoly power and harm to consumers is anticompetitive, exclusionary, and actionable.

The Court's holding in *NYNEX* appears to be fatal to these arguments as price increasing conduct by a *lawful monopolist*, even when post-acquisition conduct involves fraud or deceit, is not exclusionary. However, *NYNEX* does not appear to exclude the possibility of patent holdup claims involving allegations that the patent holder acquired monopoly power as a *consequence* of the deceptive conduct. The D.C. Circuit apparently disagrees with this interpretation, as it appears to hold that *NYNEX* applies with equal force to deception-based claims, concluding that "an otherwise lawful monopolist's use of deception simply to obtain higher prices normally has no particular tendency to exclude rivals and thus to diminish competition." *Rambus* is

---

[75] *Broadcom*, 501 F.3d at 314.

[76] Id. at 311–12, 314 ("The FTC likened the deception of an SDO to the type of deceptive conduct that the D.C. Circuit found to violate § 2 of the Sherman Act in *Microsoft*" and such a claim "follows directly from established principles of antitrust law.").

thus orthogonal to *Broadcom* on this point. Indeed, the D.C. Circuit is explicit in its suggestion that *Broadcom* did not adequately address *NYNEX*:

While the [FTC's] brief doesn't mention NYNEX, much less try to distinguish it, it does cite Broadcom Corp. v. Qualcomm Inc., 501 F.3d 297 (3d Cir. 2007).... To the extent that the ruling (which simply reversed a grant of dismissal) rested on the argument that deceit lured the SSO away from non-proprietary technology, see id., it cannot help the Commission in view of its inability to find that Rambus's behavior caused JEDEC's choice; to the extent that it may have rested on a supposition that there is a cognizable violation of the Sherman Act when a lawful monopolist's deceit has the effect of raising prices (without an effect on competitive structure), it conflicts with NYNEX.

If the FTC's theory depended on the proposition that a lawful monopolist's deceit that raises prices is an antitrust violation, the D.C. Circuit is certainly correct that the proposition conflicts with *NYNEX*. Clearly, conduct by a lawful monopolist that merely results in higher prices is protected under both *NYNEX* and *Trinko*. However, for *NYNEX* to apply to deception claims, it must be the case that the patent holder otherwise is lawfully a monopolist at the time it engages in the deceptive conduct. But this is not the FTC's anticompetitive theory of patent holdup at all. To the extent that the D.C. Circuit argues that *NYNEX* would preclude a claim of misrepresentation or fraud against an SSO as the basis for a monopolization claim, it is mistaken. The D.C. Circuit's statement does not clearly articulate its view concerning the relationship between *NYNEX* and conventional deceptive patent holdup theory – that is, the defendant's deception results in the acquisition of otherwise nonexisting monopoly power and excludes alternative technologies as a consequence. Such theoretical claims, like any others, might fail for factual reasons. Indeed, the D.C. Circuit emphasizes the FTC's "inability to find that Rambus's behavior caused JEDEC's choice." The failure to sustain this particular evidentiary burden is not difficult to understand. However, it is difficult to imagine how *NYNEX* could sweep so broadly across all claims involving *ex ante* deception as a matter of antitrust doctrine.

However, it would be incorrect to read the D.C. Circuit as completely failing to recognize the distinction between patent holdup theories with and without deception and ignoring the related distinction between exclusionary conduct that creates market power and the *ex post* exercise of lawfully obtained market power. The D.C. Circuit concedes that deceptive conduct can constitute actionable Section 2 conduct so long as the conduct also "impaired rivals in a manner tending to bring about or protect a defendant's monopoly power" and does not merely "raise the price secured by a seller." The Court hints at the type of deceptive conduct that it has in mind, citing favorably to its own analysis in *Microsoft* and the Sixth Circuit's analysis in *Conwood*. But the Court also concludes that Rambus's conduct was not sufficient to have such an exclusionary impact and thus falls within the realm of price-raising behavior by an "otherwise lawful" monopolist carved out by *NYNEX*. Therefore, a reasonable interpretation of *Rambus* is that the D.C. Circuit has significantly narrowed, but not completely closed, the window for deception-based Section 2 claims in the SSO context.

One open question after *Rambus* is whether one can reliably identify what distinguishes deception in the standard-setting process, where it is claimed that higher royalty rates are passed through to final consumers, from the deceptive and exclusionary conduct in *Microsoft* and *Conwood*. In other words, precisely what claims involving deceptive conduct in the standard-setting context survive both *NYNEX* and give rise to significant enough potential for harm to the competitive process to qualify as exclusionary conduct?

What are the differences between *Rambus* and, for example, *Conwood*, that justify this different antitrust analysis of deceptive conduct? It cannot be the nature of the conduct at issue or the possibility that the conduct has some pro-competitive element. Wright demonstrates that the widespread characterization of *Conwood* as a case involving *only* "cheap exclusion,"[77] or conduct without any redeeming efficiency qualities and therefore worthy of summary condemnation under the antitrust laws, is incorrect.[78] To be sure, the product destruction allegations involve conduct that is certainly not competition on the merits, can properly be described as "naked exclusion," and can certainly give rise to tort claims and damages. However, the less salacious and infrequently discussed aspects of *Conwood* involved UST's (U.S. Smokeless Tobacco: The Altria Group) efforts to obtain exclusive racks and category management relationships with retailers and also were found

---

[77] Steven C. Salop, *Exclusionary Conduct, Effect on Consumers, and the Flawed Profit-Sacrifice Standard*, 73 ANTITRUST L.J. 311, 317 (2007); A. Douglas Melamed, *Exclusive Dealing Arrangements and Other Exclusionary Conduct – Are There Unifying Principles?*, 73 ANTITRUST L.J. 375, 392 n.48 (2006); Mark Popofsky, *Defining Exclusionary Conduct: Section 2, The Rule of Reason, and the Unifying Principle Underlying Antitrust Rules*, 73 ANTITRUST L.J. 435, 446 (2006); Creighton et al., supra note 71, at 989–990; Jonathan M. Jacobson, *Exclusive Dealing, "Foreclosure," and Consumer Harm*, 70 ANTITRUST L.J. 311, 361 (2002).

[78] Wright, supra note 72.

to violate Section 2. It is clear that at least some substantial fraction of the defendant's conduct in *Conwood* had potential efficiency justifications. It is not clear that this hybrid conduct at issue in *Conwood* would justify greater scrutiny, or is more likely to be anticompetitive than misrepresentation or deception in the standard-setting context.

An alternative distinction is that the D.C. Circuit believes that the conduct in *Microsoft* and *Conwood* was more likely to harm the competitive process than the conduct in *Rambus*. The D.C. Circuit notes that only deception with that potential may be actionable under the antitrust laws. *Broadcom* also recognizes that, while deception is a traditional antitrust concern, it is also the case that conventional antitrust analysis of deception requires a preliminary evidentiary showing that the defendant's deception will result in harm to the competition.[79] The D.C. Circuit found the evidence that Rambus's deception actually resulted in the exclusion of alternative technologies insufficient. However, the evidence in *Conwood* also makes clear that the defendant's misrepresentations to retailers and product destruction were not likely to have the required impact on the competitive process.[80]

Thus, neither distinction is particularly persuasive. The scope of *Rambus*'s application of *NYNEX* to deceptive conduct, and the conditions under which such deception is sufficiently exclusionary to become actionable under Section 2, remains unclear and is sure to be the subject of future litigation. *Rambus* provides an interesting contrast with *Broadcom* and supports our claim that *NYNEX* renders antitrust claims involving deviations from FRAND commitments made in good faith inactionable. However, we emphasize that our argument does not depend on *NYNEX* in any particular way. While *NYNEX* suggests that one class of patent holdup theories is outside the scope of antitrust enforcement, at least as a monopolization problem, our claim is that antitrust regulation of patent holdup provides zero or negative marginal benefit. We claim that a marginal comparative advantage analysis of antitrust versus federal patent law and state law alternatives warrants a limitation of antitrust enforcement in this area, where it will likely generate "unusually serious mistakes" and substantial error costs with little additional benefit for consumers.

---

[79] Areeda & Turner, supra note 72, ¶ 782a ("[T]he antitrust court must, therefore, insist on a preliminary showing of significant and more than temporary harmful effects on competition (and not merely on a competitor or customer) before considering a tort as an exclusionary practice. In the absence of such a preliminary showing, the defendant should win summary judgment.").

[80] Wright, supra note 72.

B. Breach of a FRAND Commitment as an Antitrust
Violation: *FTC v. N-Data*

A second line of patent holdup cases does not involve deception at all. Rather, these cases involve what might be described as "pure" *ex post* contractual opportunism where the patent holder attempts to renegotiate or deviate from the original FRAND commitment made in good faith, and without deception, in favor of higher royalty rates. The FTC's recent enforcement action in *N-Data*,[81] which resulted in a consent decree, as well as recent scholarly commentary,[82] suggest that antitrust liability both does and should extend to this case. The scholarly commentary and the *N-Data* Majority Statement favor a rule that would represent an important deviation from prior patent holdup enforcement actions like *Dell*, *Unocal*, *Rambus*, and the Third Circuit's decision in *Broadcom*, each of which required deception as a precondition for antitrust liability. *N-Data* is significant not only because it assigns antitrust liability without requiring evidence of deception or otherwise exclusionary conduct, but also because it did so with scant evidence of an actual breach of a contractual commitment or of consumer injury. It is also significant that it was brought under Section 5 of the FTC Act rather than Section 2 of the Sherman Act.

We offer two distinct criticisms of the *N-Data* logic, which equates breach of a FRAND commitment to exclusionary conduct under the antitrust laws. The first is specific to *N-Data* itself and relies on publicly available and reported facts, as well as the FTC's decision to apply Section 5 of the FTC Act in the patent holdup setting. We view the application of the Section 5 theory as a significant deviation from the FTC's patent holdup agenda to date, unjustified from a consumer welfare perspective and without limiting principles.[83] Of course, it is often said that hard cases make bad law. And *N-Data* is an especially hard case for the FTC in terms of expanding its traditional patent holdup enforcement agenda because it involves a number

---

[81] In re Negotiated Data Solutions LLC (N-Data), No. 051–0094 (F.T.C. Jan. 23, 2008).

[82] Joseph Farrell et al., *Standard Setting, Patents, and Hold-Up*, 74 ANTITRUST L.J. 603 (2007).

[83] One possible "limiting principle" is that *ex post* breach, renegotiation, or modification of contractual commitments raise antitrust concerns only in the standard-setting context. This does not appear to be much of a limit at all. First, there is a substantial amount of economic activity involving standard setting. Second, to the extent that this limit derives from the view that holdup is likely to result in consumer welfare losses, the proposed limitation conflicts with *NYNEX*, which rejects the extension of Section 2 to conduct evading a "pricing constraint" and similarly resulting in consumer harm. Third, there is nothing in the *N-Data* Majority Statement or the expansion nature of the theory of antitrust harm that suggests such a narrow interpretation was intended.

of hard facts to deal with. Specifically, it is unclear whether any contractual commitments were breached in the first instance. There was also very little evidence of consumer harm. Further, the apparent renegotiation was from a nominal $1,000 commitment to a FRAND commitment, not a FRAND commitment breached in favor of a supra-competitive royalty. However, our more general analysis has little to do with the particulars of the *N-Data* analysis and applies equally to the general theory that an *ex post* breach of a FRAND commitment resulting in higher prices and consumer harm is an antitrust problem.[84]

The second criticism is more general: In *NYNEX*, the Supreme Court considered and rejected the underlying economic foundations of the FTC's theory and, for that matter, any other theory that would assign Section 2 liability for a breach of a FRAND commitment made in good faith and *without* evidence of deception or other exclusionary conduct. The D.C. Circuit's recent analysis in *Rambus* supports our position and substantially weakens any substantive argument in favor of applying Section 5 to similar conduct.

Chairman Majoras' Dissenting Statement in *N-Data* recites the basic facts.[85] In 1994, the IEEE adopted National's N-Way Ethernet auto-negotiation technology in its 802.3u standard. National committed to license the technology for a one-time fee of $1,000. As Chairman Majoras notes, "no one contends that National deceived SSO members at the time of its initial licensing offer in 1994." Indeed, the FTC did not allege that National engaged in any deception, bad faith conduct, or misrepresentation at the time the technology was adopted. In 1998, National assigned its rights to another company, Vertical. When Vertical attempted to deviate from the 1994 commitments in a 2002 proposal to the IEEE by altering the licensing terms of the one-time $1,000 fee to a FRAND commitment, the IEEE did not object and requested and negotiated a number of changes in Vertical's proposal before ultimately posting Vertical's letter on its website along with National's 1994 letter. Vertical assigned its rights to N-Data in 2003.

Remarkably, the FTC Majority Statement for the fractured Commission in support of the issuance of the complaint against N-Data and to accept the consent agreement fails to address the significant deviation of this

---

[84] We also do not consider the case an insignificant outlier and so consider the decision worth criticizing. Indeed, it remains the only case to extend antitrust liability to patent holdup for mere renegotiation of the FRAND commitment without *ex ante* deception in the standard-setting process.

[85] In re Negotiated Data Solutions LLC (N-Data), No. 051–0094 (F.T.C. Jan. 23, 2008) (Majoras dissent), available at http://www.ftc.gov/os/caselist/0510094/080122majoras.pdf.

enforcement action from the prior line of cases involving deception. The Majority Statement, joined by Commissioners Harbour, Leibowitz, and Rosch, characterizes N-Data's conduct as "oppressive" and "coercive" and argues that there is "no doubt that the type of behavior engaged in by N-Data harms consumers." It also asserts that "bad faith or deceptive behavior that undermines the [standard-setting] process may also undermine competition." However, there is no evidence in the record that there was any bad faith or deceptive conduct and the Majority never responds to Chairman Majoras' point that *N-Data* deviates from the deception line of cases and her charge that the Majority must agree that whatever N-Data's conduct, it is not exclusionary for the purposes of Section 2 analysis. There is no doubt that the Majority viewed N-Data's conduct as detrimental to consumers. The Majority goes so far as to claim that N-Data's renegotiation of National's original 1994 commitments allowed it to "increase the price of an Ethernet technology used by almost every American consumer who owns a computer." This is a serious charge. It is also false. Only three companies entered into agreements for the patents, and N-Data had never received royalties on any terms inconsistent with the original 1994 terms.

This last fact suggests a cynical explanation to the puzzle of why the FTC elected to seek liability purely under Section 5 of the FTC Act when the Majority was apparently confident that the conduct at issue would have such dramatic competitive effects and involved the acquisition of monopoly power. The truth is that there was little chance the FTC could have prevailed under the more rigorous Section 2 standard that anchors the liability rule to a demanding standard requiring proof of both exclusionary conduct and competitive harm.[86] One must either accept the proposition that the FTC sought Section 5 liability precisely because there was no evidence of consumer harm or that the FTC believed there was evidence of consumer harm but elected to file the complaint based only on the Section 5 theory to encourage an expansive application of that Section, a position several commissioners joining the Majority Statement have taken in recent years. Neither of these interpretations offers much evidence that *N-Data* is sound as a matter of prosecutorial discretion or antitrust policy.

What is left is the view that the theory in *N-Data* could be extended to any breach of a contractual commitment that might result in increased

---

[86] Chairman Majoras' dissent concludes that the FTC Act Section 5(a) and 5(n) claims should fail because neither theory satisfies the consumer injury requirement.

royalties, or even a good faith modification of a FRAND commitment to the same effect, *always* violates the antitrust laws. Perhaps a showing of market power would be required to succeed on such a theory under Section 2, but not Section 5. But is it worth considering when such a breach or modification would not result in liability under the *N-Data* analysis under either statute? The breach itself is the exclusionary act and evidence of the requisite monopoly power. No evidence of consumer harm is required. An attempt to renegotiate higher royalty rates is all that is needed. This is unsound antitrust policy. A basic lesson of the holdup literature is that the very asset specificity creating the potential for *ex post* opportunism also creates the incentives for parties to build flexibility into their contractual relationships, which allows them to reasonably deal with unanticipated post-contractual shocks. However, even good faith modifications of SSO contractual commitments, whether those commitments relate to pricing or other elements of the agreement, would satisfy the *N-Data* standard for liability.

Thus, there is no principle that would prevent the extension of the *N-Data* theory to the breach of any contractual commitment by a firm resulting in higher prices to some consumers. For example, consider the example of a landlord's opportunistic imposition of a new parking fee against a "locked-in" tenant discussed earlier. While the new "parking fee" against the tenant effectively raises the price above the terms that reflected *ex ante* competitive conditions, most would agree this is not and should not be actionable *antitrust* conduct, even if it is a breach of contract. In this situation, the fact that the landlord "evaded a contractual restraint on pricing" is not a sufficient condition for the existence of an antitrust problem.[87]

---

[87] One could attempt to distinguish this landlord-tenant example on the grounds that the breach does not necessarily involve an increase in market prices, but the price to a single buyer, whereas the breach of an SSO commitment is likely to be passed on to a large number of consumers and therefore produce greater harm. This is similar to the proposed limitation on patent holdup theories, discussed previously, to the SSO context on the grounds that consumer welfare losses are likely to result from holdup. We find such a distinction unsatisfying for a number of reasons. First, we reiterate that *N-Data* discusses no such limitation. To the contrary, *N-Data* assigns liability with little evidence of actual consumer injury, suggesting that the FTC did not consider itself under any such obligation to safeguard against overexpansive application of the theory by ensuring evidence of actual consumer harm. Second, as we have discussed, the Supreme Court has rejected the view that any conduct resulting in consumer welfare harm is an antitrust violation. Rather, the Supreme Court has correctly rejected this view in favor of an underdeterring approach that recognizes that it is difficult to distinguish pro-competitive from anticompetitive and inefficient conduct and that the antitrust enforcement errors have significant potential to harm consumers.

C. Patent Holdup Theories and *NYNEX*

Holding aside the factual issues and disputes in *N-Data*, and the controversy over the application of Section 5 as a stand-alone offense, there is a more fundamental flaw in the view that mere *ex post* opportunism or "renegotiating" an *ex ante* licensing commitment can constitute exclusionary conduct for the purposes of a monopolization claim in the absence of deception, fraud, or misrepresentation. Specifically, the view that *ex post* deviations, breaches, or renegotiations of *ex ante* pricing commitments that result in consumer welfare losses are antitrust violations is based on an erroneous interpretation of the "exclusionary conduct" requirement under Section 2 of the Sherman Act as articulated by the Supreme Court.

The *N-Data* Majority and scholarly commentators such as Farrell et al. implicitly or expressly equate actionable antitrust conduct with the evasion of a pricing constraint that harms consumers.[88] In *N-Data*, the patent holder is alleged to have violated the FTC Act by reneging on its original pricing commitment in favor of a FRAND commitment, thus increasing prices to final consumers. Similarly, Farrell et al. argue that patent holdup violates Section 2 of the Sherman Act, regardless of how the pricing constraint is violated, because opportunism against the SSO members is likely to result in higher prices and harm consumers.[89] The basic proposition is that patent holdup without deception is equivalent to patent holdup with deception under the antitrust laws because it results in the same economic effects. Therefore, a breach or renegotiation of a FRAND commitment in the absence of bad faith or deception of the type considered by the FTC in *N-Data* would violate Section 2 and therefore also necessarily violate Section 5. Three FTC commissioners have also endorsed the related proposition that such conduct is a Section 5 violation and seemed willing to entertain arguments concerning Section 2.[90] They are wrong. The Supreme Court has considered and rejected the "pricing constraint" view of exclusionary conduct, and therefore the "mere breach" variant of the patent holdup theory must be rejected. The D.C. Circuit's analysis in *Rambus* also supports this conclusion.

The Supreme Court has developed a number of principles and analytical guidelines for evaluating conduct under Section 2 over the past several

---

[88] Joseph Farrell et al., *supra* note 81.
[89] Id.
[90] In re Negotiated Data Solutions LLC (N-Data), No. 051–0094 (F.T.C. Jan. 23, 2008) (Majority Statement), available at http://www.ftc.gov/os/caselist/0510094/080122statement.pdf.

decades, but the most directly pertinent to the "evasion of a pricing constraint" theory of monopolization comes from *NYNEX*.[91] In *NYNEX*, the conduct at issue was "a deception worked upon the regulatory agency that prevented the agency from controlling New York Telephone's exercise of its monopoly power." The Court conceded that the evasion of the rate regulation constraint "hurt consumers." But the Court rejected the view that the defendant's conduct violated Section 2 because it did not harm the competitive process.[92] Specifically, the Court distinguished the attempt to evade the pricing constraint from the unlawful acquisition or exercise of monopoly power by pointing out that "consumer injury flowed . . . from the exercise of market power that is lawfully in the hands of a monopolist."[93]

This is a fatal problem for the "evasion of a pricing constraint" monopolization theory of patent holdup based on the renegotiation or modification of *ex ante* contractual commitments made in good faith and in the absence of deception. This theory relies on a consumer welfare conception of the exclusionary conduct standard that the Court has considered and rejected. The Court has similarly rejected the view that any conduct by a monopolist that reduces consumer welfare constitutes exclusionary conduct on the grounds that such a decision rule would result in unacceptable levels of error and administrative costs in *Trinko*, *Weyerhaeuser*, and *Brooke Group*.[94]

Consider the application of *NYNEX* to the theory of patent holdup without deception in *N-Data*. The Commission's theory of antitrust liability was not that N-Data acquired monopoly power when the IEEE adopted its Ethernet technology into its standard, as the contractual commitment entered into between N-Data and the IEEE constrained N-Data's ability to raise prices. Rather, the theory was that N-Data unlawfully acquired monopoly power at the moment that it violated this contractual pricing constraint with its attempt to renegotiate those prior $1,000 licensing commitments. The proponents of this theory cannot argue that monopoly power was acquired at the time the technology was incorporated into the standard because *Trinko* clearly allows the setting of monopoly prices after monopoly power was lawfully obtained. The alternative is to rely on the evasion of pricing constraint theory, which asserts that the exclusionary conduct and acquisition of monopoly power occur at the moment N-Data

---

[91]   *NYNEX Corp. v. Discon, Inc.*, 525 U.S. 128 (1998).

[92]   Id. at 135–37.

[93]   Id. at 129.

[94]   *Verizon Commc'ns Inc. v. Law Offices of Curtis V. Trinko, LLP*, 540 U.S. 398, 414 (2004); *Weyerhaeuser Co. v. Ross-Simmons Hardwood Lumber Co.*, 127 S. Ct. 1069, 1078 (2007); *Brooke Group Ltd. v. Brown & Williamson Tobacco Co.*, 509 U.S. 209, 223 (1993).

attempts to evade its licensing commitments.[95] However, the Court's reasoning in *NYNEX* indicates that it would have concluded that N-Data lawfully obtained monopoly power at the time its technology was included in the standard and would characterize the renegotiation as the *exercise* of that power. Indeed, *NYNEX* concludes that regulatory fraud by a monopolist, conduct far less economically meritorious than breach of contract, which can be efficient, is not exclusionary even when it generates actual harm to consumers. In sum, there should be little doubt that the Court's decision in *NYNEX* compels the conclusion that *ex post* opportunism without deception is not exclusionary conduct and not actionable under Section 2.

The rejection of this theory should not be particularly surprising. It is an application of the well-known and oft-cited language in *Trinko* that monopoly pricing "is not only not unlawful; it is an important element of the free-market system."[96] This statement applies *a fortori* in the patent context, where the creation of quasi-rents that result from such prices serve to give incentives for invention. It is also consistent with the Supreme Court's repeated teaching that antitrust decision rules must be designed in a manner that maximizes consumer welfare, interpreted broadly to include administrative and error costs. While many economists and legal scholars favor a "consumer welfare" test approach to Section 2 liability,[97] critics have noted that the use of such a broad consumer welfare standard as a direct test is inconsistent with Section 2 jurisprudence, which have emphasized the role of administrative and error costs in crafting liability rules.[98] Further, it

[95] One could conjure up a more nuanced version of this theory in an attempt to circumvent *NYNEX* and its progeny. For example, one could argue that the patent holder's single course of conduct from the time the technology was adopted until the time of renegotiation is the actionable exclusionary conduct. See *Continental Ore Co. v. Union Carbide & Carbon Corp.*, 370 U.S. 690, 699 (1962). The only advantage of this "course of conduct" theory would be to recast the *ex post* renegotiation as somehow connected to the acquisition of monopoly power. In addition to the factual problems inherent in connecting two events separated by time, seven years in *N-Data*, this would not be sufficient to transform renegotiation or breach into exclusionary conduct because *NYNEX* still rejects the view that consumer harm is a sufficient condition for such a finding. A simpler solution is to allege that the patent holder intended at the time *ex ante* licensing commitments were made to later breach them. But this allegation also invokes intentional misrepresentation and deception and not commitments made in good faith.

[96] *Trinko*, 540 U.S. at 407.

[97] See, e.g., Steven C. Salop, *Exclusionary Conduct, Effect on Consumers, and the Flawed Profit-Sacrifice Standard*, 73 ANTITRUST L.J. 311 (2006).

[98] See, e.g., Gregory J. Werden, *Identifying Exclusionary Conduct Under Section 2: The "No Economic Sense" Test*, 73 ANTITRUST L.J. 413, 428 ("as interpreted by the Supreme Court, Section 2 simply does not permit" application of the consumer welfare approach); Mark S. Popofsky, *Defining Exclusionary Conduct: Section 2, Rule of Reason, and the Unifying Principle Underlying Antitrust Rules*, 73 ANTITRUST L.J. 435 (consumer welfare approach "cannot be reconciled with certain Section 2 rules").

should be noted that the Supreme Court noted that this style of analysis, which admits some instances of consumer harm that does not violate Section 2, is not inconsistent with an economic approach. The limits on Section 2 carved out by *NYNEX, Brooke Group, Weyerhaeuser,* and *Trinko* are not trivial, nor can they be dismissed as legal technicalities devoid of economic content. To the contrary, the Court has been explicit in its recognition that these rules foster consumer welfare by allowing decision rules that consider both the competitive effects analysis of the business conduct at issue and dynamic consumer welfare considerations such as the chilling of pro-competitive behavior and the burden of administrative costs.

The D.C. Circuit's analysis in *Rambus* also supports this view. While *Rambus* involved allegations of patent holdup with deception rather than mere breach of the FRAND commitment, the Court was mindful of the Supreme Court's teachings in *NYNEX*. The *Rambus* decision takes on precisely the issue of defining exclusionary conduct under Section 2 in the context of patent holdup, noting that the Commission's theory that Rambus's conduct was exclusionary required the Commission to show either that "Rambus's more complete disclosure would have caused JEDEC to adopt a different standard" or, alternatively, that "JEDEC's obtaining assurances from Rambus of FRAND licensing terms, such conduct, alone, could be said to harm competition." The D.C. Circuit found the evidence insufficient to determine whether JEDEC would have adopted an alternative standard and therefore dedicated the bulk of its analysis to the scope of the exclusionary conduct requirement.

The D.C. Circuit relies heavily on *NYNEX* in its analysis and emphasizes its relevance to the patent holdup context. Specifically, the D.C. Circuit notes that, as discussed previously, a unanimous Court recognized that despite the fact that the defendant's conduct resulted in higher prices for consumers, it was outside the scope of Section 2 because the conduct flowed from already lawfully existing monopoly power. Perhaps most significantly to the present problem, the Court distinguishes the Third Circuit's exclusionary conduct analysis in *Broadcom*:

To the extent that the ruling (which simply reversed a grant of dismissal) rested on the argument that deceit lured the SSO away from a proprietary technology, it cannot help the Commission in view of its inability to find that Rambus's behavior caused JEDEC's choice; to the extent that it may have rested on a supposition that there is a cognizable violation of the Sherman Act when a lawful monopolist's deceit has the effect of raising prices (without an effect on the competitive structure), it conflicts with NYNEX.

The D.C. Circuit also recognizes that the possibility of holdup resulting in higher prices is not sufficient to escape *NYNEX*, where the Court also assumed harm to consumers, explicitly rejecting the Commission's contention that "any conduct that permits a monopolist to avoid constraints on the exercise of that power must be anticompetitive" on the grounds that, "as in NYNEX, an otherwise lawful monopolist's end-run around price constraints, even when deceptive or fraudulent, does not alone present a harm to competition in the monopolized market."

The D.C. Circuit's analysis in *Rambus*, like *NYNEX*, appears to require rejection of antitrust claims based on patent holdup, which increases royalties so long as the patent holder was included in the standard without deception or other exclusionary conduct. In short, *Rambus* appears to significantly undermine the Commission's hopes of extending the *N-Data* line of cases under Section 2. To a lesser extent, the D.C. Circuit also undermines the application of Section 5 to patent holdup theories, as it warned the Commission against applying a broad Section 5 theory on remand by noting that it had "serious concerns about [the] strength of the evidence relied on to support some of the Commission's crucial findings regarding the scope of JEDEC's patent disclosure policies and Rambus's alleged violations of those policies."[99]

To summarize, we have thus far argued that theories of patent holdup involving the mere breach of a FRAND commitment made in good faith, and without deception, are fatally flawed insofaras such conduct cannot satisfy the exclusionary conduct requirement of Section 2. While *Rambus* renders more difficult deception- and misrepresentation-based theories of patent holdup, it is also clear that current antitrust jurisprudence allows for the possibility that deception in the standard-setting context might constitute exclusionary conduct. Analyzing the potential for antitrust theories to govern patent holdup, and the weaknesses of those theories, however, is just one element of our "comparative advantage" analytical approach. Our argument is incomplete without a demonstration that the marginal benefit of applying antitrust laws to patent holdup is either zero or, when one

---

[99] More generally, we view the application of Section 5 in cases like *N-Data* involving deviations from *ex ante* commitments made in good faith as a significant expansion of the Commission's patent holdup enforcement agenda, which is without significant limiting principles. Further, if *N-Data* is a representative application of Section 5, it suggests that there is little concern with requiring evidence of harm to the competitive process and consumers or with the fact that the theory does not fill a technical "loophole" in the antitrust laws but extends enforcement to conduct that the Supreme Court has determined is outside the scope of Section 2. See supra III.B.

accounts for potential error costs, negative. This type of analysis requires a more detailed examination of the type invited by the Court in *Credit Suisse*, of the advantages of alternative regulatory institutions such as federal and state law. In Section IV we focus on the federal patent law alternative to antitrust, which is analogous to the situation in *Credit Suisse*, where the Supreme Court placed limits on antitrust in light of federal securities regulation. In Section V we argue that an extension of the principles articulated in *Credit Suisse* would also justify reliance on state law alternatives to antitrust enforcement, such as contract and tort law.

IV. The Limits of Antitrust: Federal Patent Law as an Alternative to Regulate Patent Holdup

A. The "Conflict" between Antitrust and Patent Law with Respect to Patent Holdup

The issue of SSO holdup also implicates conflicts between the federal antitrust laws and the federal patent laws. The patent statute explicitly controls the issues of patentability through the regulation of patentable subject matter,[100] and the requirements of utility,[101] novelty,[102] and nonobviousness.[103] It also regulates the nature and timing of the disclosure of patents and patent applications.[104] Moreover, patents are examined for patentability, a task carried out by the Federal Patent and Trademark Office. There is also a Board of Patent Appeals and Interferences, as well as a specialized Federal Court of Appeals. And there are also the equitable doctrines to control opportunism and anticompetitive behavior within that patent statute. These include the doctrine of laches, the doctrine of equitable estoppel, and the misuse doctrine. The substantive argument regarding the comparative advantage of patent law over antitrust is presented in part B of this section. In this part, we focus on the preliminary question of whether the patent laws should impliedly or explicitly preempt the antitrust laws in the context of this specific set of patent holdup issues.[105] It is important to recognize the limits of our argument. We do not, for example, claim that federal patent laws would explicitly or impliedly preempt application of

---

[100] 35 U.S.C. § 101.
[101] Id. § 101, 112.
[102] Id. § 102.
[103] Id. § 103.
[104] Id. § 122 (confidentiality and publication), id. § 102(b) (on sale bar).
[105] The Court has recently held that federal intellectual property laws can preempt the application of other federal laws. See *Dastar Corp. v. Twentieth Century Fox Film Corp.*, 539 U.S. 23 (2003).

the antitrust laws to collusion between SSO members or other issues. Our argument, motivated on the Court's analysis in *Credit Suisse*, turns on the net marginal benefits of antitrust enforcement in light of specific alternative doctrines that regulate patent holdup problems as well as the potential for "serious mistakes" in this specific setting. A similar analysis applied to problems of collusion or other issues might produce different results.

To the extent one focuses on the four-factor test set out in *Gordon*, the patent laws seem an ideal candidate for implied preemption of application of the antitrust laws to SSO patent holdup issues. While our earlier analysis explicitly criticizes the usefulness of the "active supervision" prong of the *Gordon* test, there is certainly active government supervision and enforcement with respect to the examination and disclosure of patents and their claims. In addition, the issues central to SSO holdup, including the enforcement, licensing, and disclosure obligations of the patentee, lie squarely within the area patent law seeks to regulate. Moreover, under the Court's analysis in *Credit Suisse*, the third factor also seems to be present, as commentators have noted both the apparent conflicts between the goals of patent and antitrust law,[106] and also how the potential for error can result in antitrust liability interfering with the goals of patent law in practice.[107] Thus, a good case can be made that this setting presents "a good candidate for implication of antitrust immunity, to avoid the real possibility of judgments conflicting with the agency's regulatory scheme 'that might be voiced by courts exercising jurisdiction under the antitrust laws.'"[108]

---

[106] See, e.g., Ward S. Bowman, *Patent and Antitrust Law: A Legal and Economic Appraisal*, (1973); Herbert Hovenkamp, Mark D Janis & Mark A. Lemley, IP AND ANTITRUST: AN ANALYSIS OF ANTITRUST PRINCIPLES APPLIED TO INTELLECTUAL PROPERTY LAW 1–10 (Aspen 2007) (noting apparent conflict, and also noting that conflict is illusory once simplifying assumptions are dropped).

[107] See, e.g., Michelle M. Burtis & Bruce Kobayashi, *Intellectual Property and Antitrust Limitations on Contract*, in DYNAMIC COMPETITION AND PUBLIC POLICY: TECHNOLOGY, INNOVATION AND ANTITRUST ISSUES 229–263 (J. Ellig ed., Cambridge University Press 2001) (discussing examples); Hovenkamp et al., supra note 105, at 1–13 (noting tension in means); Bowman, supra note 105 (arguing that while both laws have complementary goals in theory, they often do not in practice).

[108] *Verizon Commc'ns Inc. v. Law Offices of Curtis V. Trinko, LLP*, 540 U.S. 398, 414 (2004) (citing *United States v. Nat'l Ass'n of Sec. Dealers, Inc.*, 422 U.S. 694, 734 (1975), and discussing the applicability of this analysis to the telecommunications laws.) Section 211 of Title 35 contains an antitrust savings clause. However, the clause applies only to the chapter dealing with patent rights in inventions made with federal assistance. For analysis of the effect of an antitrust savings clause, see *Trinko*, 540 U.S. at 406–07 (noting clause in 1996 Telecommunications Act, which states that "nothing in this Act or the amendments made by this Act shall be construed to modify, impair, or supersede the applicability of any of the antitrust laws," and noting the savings clause "does not create new claims that go beyond existing antitrust standards; that would be equally inconsistent with the

Moreover, the cases involving SSO patent holdup illustrate the existence of real conflicts between patent and antitrust law. The DC Circuit's opinion suggests that the FTC's decision in *Rambus* appears to be based on a general duty to disclose that was broader than the requirements explicitly set out by the SSO. Specifically, the FTC's finding that Rambus violated the SSO's disclosure policy requires extending the duty to disclose beyond the scope of the SSO's written policy. Specifically, the SSO's written policy required the disclosure of patents and pending patents relevant to the standard, while the FTC's findings impose an implied duty to also disclose pending applications as well as planned amendments to pending applications. As others have noted, many of the issues in *Rambus* were generated by the SSO's vague and ill-defined disclosure requirements.[109] However, the failure of the SSO to adequately specify or broaden its disclosure requirements is not an invitation to generate a broad implied duty to disclose under the antitrust laws.

Indeed, the creation of such a duty would be inconsistent with existing antitrust law, and would create a conflict with the intellectual property laws. There is no general duty or obligation to predisclose information related to innovation.[110] Such a requirement would be hard to reconcile with the inventor's rights under the intellectual property laws, including the disclosure requirements under the patent laws, and also the right to keep secrets under state trade secret law.[111] One could, in theory, also argue that a firm may be required to share an existing technology that is essential to the operation of a standard under an "essential facilities" doctrine. However, the Court in *Trinko* stated that they "had never recognized" such an essential facilities doctrine, and apparently had limited the use of this doctrine.[112]

This is not to imply that the patent laws cannot be improved. For example, some have argued for earlier and uniform disclosure of patent applications.[113] Lemley suggests numerous patent reforms to lessen the

---

saving clause's mandate that nothing in the Act would "modify, impair, or supersede the applicability of the antitrust laws").

[109] The SSO's disclosure policies were "not a model of clarity." See *Rambus Inc. v. Infineon Techs. AG*, 318 F.3d 1081, 1102 (Fed. Cir. 2003). Indeed, the modification and clarification of SSO IP disclosure and licensing rules may be one of the most important solutions to the patent holdup problem. See Lemley, supra note 11.

[110] *Berkey Photo v. Eastman Kodak*, 603 F.2d 263 (2d Cir. 1979).

[111] Hovenkamp et al., supra note 105, at 12–35.

[112] *Trinko*, 540 U.S. at 410–11; Herbert J. Hovenkamp, *Standards Ownership and Competition Policy*, 48 B.C. L. REV. 87 (2007).

[113] See A PATENT SYSTEM FOR THE 21ST CENTURY (Stephen A. Merrill, Richard C. Levin, and Mark B. Myers, Eds., The National Academies Press 2004) at 128, available online at http://www.nap.edu/catalog/10976.html.

ability of the patent holder to engage in *ex post* opportunism, including limitations on continuation practice to make redrafting patent claims to cover standards more difficult, limiting willfulness and treble damages, limiting the application of injunctive relief, and setting out damages rules in royalty-stacking cases.[114] Moreover, consistent with the thesis of this chapter, he rejects expanded use of the antitrust laws and indeed argues that the role for antitrust be curtailed so that SSOs can find contractual solutions to prevent holdup, including the negotiation of *ex ante* FRAND commitments.

B. Equitable Estoppel Provides a Solution to Patent Holdup with Deception

An additional argument against using antitrust law to address the holdup with deception problem is that an arguably superior solution to this problem current exists within patent law. Again, this suggests that the marginal benefits of applying the antitrust laws, if any, are limited by an existing alternative legal mechanism that would address such problems. Specifically, under the doctrine of equitable estoppel, the patentee that has engaged in deception, including failing to disclose actual or pending patents in violation of SSO disclosure standards, can be barred from obtaining relief from infringement.

The general contours of the equitable estoppel doctrine were set out in *A. C. Aukerman Co. v. R. L. Chaides Construction Co.*[115] In this case, the Federal Circuit, sitting en banc, set out the following factual elements as essential to a claim of equitable estoppel: [1] The actor, who usually must have knowledge of the true facts, communicates something in a misleading way, either by words, conduct, or silence. [2] The other relies upon that communication. [3] And the other would be harmed materially if the actor is later permitted to assert any claim inconsistent with his earlier conduct.[116]

The doctrine has been applied to cases of patent holdup where the patentee engaged in deception.[117] For example, courts have applied equitable estoppel to prevent patentees from enforcing patents in which they misled or were silent regarding patents covering standards adopted by SSOs.[118] The remedy in these cases, the inability to enforce the patent, would adequately cure the potential holdup based on deception problem.

---

[114] Lemley, supra note 11 at 161–9.

[115] *A. C. Aukerman Co. v. R. L. Chaides Construction Co.*, 22 U.S.P.Q. 2d 1321 (1992).

[116] Id. at 1335–36

[117] See Hovenkamp, supra note 111.

[118] See, e.g., *Wang Labs v. Mitsubishi Elecs.*, 103 F.3d 1571, 1578–79 (1997) (finding that implied license existed under doctrine of legal estoppel).

Moreover, use of this doctrine and remedy would be limited to cases where there is both a misleading statement and reliance on the misleading statement. The contours of any duty to disclose would be defined and evaluated by the disclosures required by the SSO, and not by a generalized duty to disclose based on the patentee's superior knowledge. Such an approach would allow SSOs to craft such requirements to maintain incentives for *ex ante* disclosure, yet not suppress incentives for improving on the current standard. Further, this approach would not apply to cases such as *N-Data*, where deception is not involved, and thus would not generate the risk of chilling good faith breaches of FRAND commitments.[119] Nor would use of this doctrine implicate extending or modifying current antitrust law beyond it limits. Antitrust law, therefore, would not have to bend to cover situations where proof of actual exclusion or harm to competition is absent. For these reasons, Hovenkamp suggests that use of equitable estoppel or contract law would be more appropriate than antitrust law for addressing such holdup with deception problems.[120]

V. More Limits on Antitrust: State Law

Thus far, our claim for substantive limits on application of antitrust laws to patent holdup has examined conditions similar to those faced by the Court in *Credit Suisse*. Specifically, our analysis has so far evaluated whether the existence of an alternative federal regulatory scheme warranted an implied repeal of the antitrust laws. However, we argue that the principles articulated in *Credit Suisse* in the context of an implied repeal of antitrust in favor of alternative federal law also support a marginal analysis of the benefits of antitrust enforcement relative to *state law* alternatives.

Our position is not without support in the Supreme Court's antitrust jurisprudence. In *NYNEX*, the Court notes its concern that attaching antitrust liability to all forms of business conduct "would transform cases involving business behavior that is improper for various reasons, say cases involving nepotism or personal pique, into treble-damages antitrust cases."[121] In making its case that the scope of antitrust liability should be a

---

[119] See, e.g., *Symbol Techs., Inc. v. Proxim, Inc.*, No. Civ. 01–801, 2004 WL 1770290 (D. Del. July 28, 2004).

[120] Hovenkamp, supra note 111 at 105–6; Herbert J. Hovenkamp, *Patent Continuations, Patent Deception, and Standard Setting: The* Rambus *and* Broadcom *Decisions* (University of Iowa Legal Studies Research Paper Number 08–25, 2008), available at http://papers.ssrn.com/sol3/papers.cfm?abstract_id=1138002.

[121] *NYNEX Corp. v. Discon, Inc.*, 525 U.S. 128, 136–37 (1998).

function of these error cost concerns, the Court went on to note the importance of alternative regulatory structures. In doing so, the Court concluded that "other laws, for example, 'unfair competition' laws, business tort laws, or regulatory laws, provide remedies for various competitive practices thought to be offensive to proper standards of business morality."[122] For our purposes, the critical point is that the Court's embrace of the principle that limits on antitrust might be appropriate under conditions of potential conflict and substantial error costs does not appear to be limited to federal law.

Two obvious candidates for state regulation of patent holdup are state contract and tort law. As we did with respect to federal patent law, we examine the comparative advantage of regulating the patent holdup problem through these state law alternatives and without antitrust.

A. The Comparative Advantage of Contract Law in Regulating Breach of FRAND Commitments

We first examine the case for use of contract rules as a mechanism to regulate and deter opportunism. In many cases, explicit contracting or use of alternative forms of organization and other forms of self-help will be the least-cost method of avoiding holdup and litigation. These include explicit contract terms, including *ex ante* term adjustment provisions, use of reputational bonding mechanisms, and vertical integration.[123]

However, in other cases, their use can be prohibitively expensive or otherwise ineffective. For example, use of direct and explicit contracting to anticipate all possible forms of opportunism can increase the costs of contracting and decrease the contracting parties' flexibility. Reputational bonding mechanisms, which can be an efficient way to prevent opportunistic behavior when the contracting parties anticipate significant future interaction, will not be effective in the absence of repeated interaction. *Ex ante* term adjustments and vertical integration can be inferior substitutes. The former can result in suboptimal incentives, and the latter form of organization can be costly in the face of organizational diseconomies of scale, or when a firm is forced to take on activities in which it does not have a comparative advantage.

---

[122] Id. (citing 3 Phillip Areeda & Herbert Hovenkamp, ANTITRUST LAW ¶ 651d (1996)).

[123] See, e.g., Benjamin Klein, Robert G. Crawford & Armen A. Alchian, *Vertical Integration, Appropriable Rents, and the Competitive Contracting Process*, 21 J.L. & ECON. 297 (1978); Benjamin Klein & Keith Leffler, *The Role of Market Forces in Assuring Contractual Performance*, 89 J. POL. ECON. 615 (1981).

When self-help is very costly or otherwise unfeasible, legal rules that respond to opportunism by voiding contracts or regulating the terms of contracts through the enforcement of implicit terms can be efficient. By voiding contracts or contract modifications whose terms reflect opportunistic behavior, the benefits from investing in the creation of such opportunistic behavior is reduced. Moreover, potential victims of opportunism can economize on investments in avoiding opportunism, and the threat to deterring potentially valuable contracts will be minimized. Contract law also matters because contracting parties largely accept it as given and do not "opt-out" of all inefficient doctrine, thereby saving significant resource costs by relying on what amounts to an exogenously imposed and impartial set of terms. Because the law matters, efficient contract doctrine sets rules that allow courts to identify terms parties would have adopted when contractual arrangements break down because some unspecified contingency occurs. In other words, efficient contract doctrine should set rules that allow the court to interpret an incomplete contract to reflect the terms the parties would have adopted *ex ante* had they contracted over those contingencies, and voiding contracts or contract modifications involving *ex post* opportunism.

The courts' ability to actually increase welfare by enforcing implicit contracts to control opportunism will depend on the accuracy through which they can distinguish between opportunistic holdup by the patentee and the lawful and desirable exercise of his intellectual property rights. Because of the complexity of the task and the subtleties involved in discerning whether opportunism has occurred, courts may find it difficult to discern reliably between opportunism and the legitimate exercise of the patent holder's property right. If these error rates are high, courts' attempts to enforce implicit terms could, in theory, decrease welfare. High error rates will make it difficult to discern the rule that applies to their transaction and can result in more litigation.

The issue of distinguishing opportunism from efficient adjustment of a relational contract in the presence of asset specificity is one that is well known to the contract literature. It is also precisely the issue raised by the case of *ex post* opportunism against SSOs, and so it is relatively odd that the discussion of patent holdup in the antitrust literature, and cases like *N-Data*, do not attempt to distinguish opportunism from efficient modification. From our perspective, both *Credit Suisse* and the economic principles of federalism provoke the following question: Does contract law outperform antitrust when it comes to the successful identification and regulation of *ex post* opportunism associated with patent holdup? We argue that contract law is better suited for this task in this setting and more likely to reduce transaction costs and welfare losses.[124]

Consider a patentee's attempt to hold up SSO members by renegotiating a FRAND commitment made in good faith and without any deceptive conduct. The most obvious contractual solution is that SSO members may bring a claim for breach of contract against the patentee to enforce the commitment. The first question that must be asked is how courts are to identify opportunistic behavior as opposed to good faith modifications of contract terms or efficient breach. Contract law seeks to identify and enforce the intent of the transacting parties and includes substantive doctrines and rules of interpretation designed to carry out this task. For example, both the Uniform Commercial Code and Restatement (2nd) of Contracts require that the modification be made in "good faith" by the transacting parties, which would include factors such as losses suffered by the parties under the current terms and market changes since the formation of the original agreement.[125] These doctrines can, in principle, be applied to minimize holdup behavior by identifying attempts to hold up a transacting party and preventing parties from using the court to facilitate a holdup. Muris argues that "when viewed as responses to opportunism, many aspects of the law previously regarded as diverse in nature should be recognized as containing a common unifying principle" and that "judges can, and often do, act to lower important costs of transacting."[126]

Consider Uniform Commercial Code (UCC) 2–209,[127] which governs modifications of contracts for the sale of goods. The distinguishing feature of UCC 2–209 is that it eliminates the requirement of consideration in favor of enforcing all modifications that satisfy the duty of good faith imposed by the Code. UCC 2–209's good faith standard allows contract law, in principle, to distinguish between mutually beneficial modifications and holdup in the form of post-contractual opportunism. The comments to UCC 2–209 are

---

[124] On contract law and opportunism generally, see Timothy Muris, *Opportunistic Behavior and the Law of Contracts*, 65 Minn. L. Rev. 521 (1981); Charles J. Goetz & Robert E. Scott, *Principles of Relational Contracts*, 67 Va. L. Rev. 1089 (1981). For an analysis of the contractual issues associated with SSO IP rules, see Mark A. Lemley, *Intellectual Property Rights and Standard Setting Organizations*, 90 Cal. L. Rev. 1889 (2002).

[125] Restatement (Second) of Contracts §§ 89, 175, 176; U.C.C. § 2–209 (cmt. 2). Contract law also includes a covenant of good faith, implied in all contracts, which prevents one party from taking actions that deprive the other party of its legitimate expectations under the agreement. Restatement (Second) of Contracts § 205; U.C.C. § 1–203, 2–103(1)(b). *Photovest Corp. v. Fotomat Corp.*, 606 F.2d 704, 708 (7th Cir. 1979).

[126] Muris, supra note 123, at 589–90.

[127] U.C.C. § 2–209(1).

instructive with respect to what types of obligations satisfy this standard, mentioning specifically "a market shift which makes performance come to involve a loss."[128] The common law takes a similar approach, distinguishing those modifications motivated by unanticipated changes in market circumstances from opportunism. This flexible inquiry enables judges to, as Muris demonstrates, minimize holdup behavior and lower transaction costs.[129]

To be sure, application of contract law is sure to result in some errors in identifying holdup. However, the substantive superiority of contract law is clear. The most obvious advantage is that where antitrust law would find a violation in any modification of a FRAND commitment, with the remedial consequences in private and state follow-on litigation of such a finding, contract law allows for the economic reality that long-term relationships frequently involve modification over time. Further, the error rate under contract law is likely to be much lower than antitrust because substantive antitrust doctrine contains nothing that would allow it to engage in the flexible inquiry invited by contract law. In addition, cases like *N-Data* suggest that antitrust enforcers have little interest in immunizing good faith modifications of SSO commitments from antitrust liability.

Not only is the error rate likely to be significantly higher in antitrust law than under contract law, but the social welfare losses associated with errors are likely to be much larger when antitrust liability is involved. If this were not the case, one might argue that overlapping contract and antitrust liability are appropriate. However, the case for the comparative advantage of contract law is made stronger because antitrust liability threatens to produce social welfare losses in this setting. There are several reasons for this.

First, the conventional argument that breach of contract does not have any efficiency justification and so amounts to "cheap exclusion" is incomplete. Modifications of long-term agreements where asset-specific investments have been made frequently require flexible *ex post* adjustments by the parties to maximize efficiency. Modifications of SSO commitments can be efficient. Further, unlike socially wasteful conduct typically raised as examples of "cheap exclusion," such as setting fire to a rival's plant, breach of contract may be efficient in the sense that it results in greater social welfare.

---

[128] See also Restatement (Second) of Contracts § 89D(a) (modifications are valid if "fair and equitable in view of circumstances not anticipated by the parties when the contract was made" and requiring an "objectively demonstrable reason for seeking" it). See generally Muris, supra note 123, on the operation of U.C.C. § 2–209 and Restatement (Second) of Contracts § 89 in practice to distinguish opportunism from good faith modification motivated by unanticipated changes in market conditions.

[129] Muris, supra note 123.

Second, because modification of breach of FRAND commitments might increase social welfare in some circumstances, efficient conduct might be overdeterred as a result of antitrust liability. Whereas the conventional argument in favor of treble damages is that supercompensatory damages are necessary to compensate for a low probability of detection of the violation, that argument does not make sense in the case of holdup. "Holdup," as the definition suggests, requires the patent holder to announce to the SSO that it is violating the prior terms and "holding up" its members. The likelihood that this conduct would go unnoticed by the SSO members, whether the holdup is successful or otherwise, approximates zero. The case of treble damages for this sort of "open and notorious" conduct is weak. The concerns with overdeterrence are even greater when one considers follow-on private litigation and state remedies. To the contrary, the payment of expectation damages under contract law is not likely to generate these overdeterrence concerns.

Third, to the extent that one accepts the arguments, based on the analysis in *NYNEX* and *Rambus*, that breach of a FRAND commitment made in good faith involves an attempt by a lawful monopolist to raise prices, the Supreme Court has consistently made clear that the Sherman Act does not condemn high prices alone. Rather, as the Supreme Court notes in *Trinko*, the returns to the lawful monopolist are related to the pro-competitive incentive to innovate:

The opportunity to charge monopoly prices – at least for a short period – is what attracts "business acumen" in the first place; it induces risk taking that produces innovation and economic growth. To safeguard the incentive to innovate, the possession of monopoly power will not be found unlawful unless it is accompanied by an element of anticompetitive conduct.

In sum, antitrust enforcement creates the potential for significant error costs, increased transactions costs, and reduced social welfare.

While substantive contract law and contact remedies are better suited to detect patent holdup and distinguish it from good faith modification or efficient breach, it would do little good if there were no appropriate parties to enforce FRAND commitments. Indeed, the debate in the antitrust community has largely ignored the superiority of substantive contract doctrine in favor of an analysis that narrowly focuses on whether a sufficient number of parties could enforce FRAND commitments in a breach of contract action. Commentators have pointed to the fact that standing would be limited to SSO members as a weakness of the contractual approach to regulating patent holdup because losses to nonmembers and, more importantly, consumers would not be actionable.[130] We view this standing critique as incomplete and unpersuasive.

It is incomplete because the discussion largely ignores the question of how much enforcement would be optimal from a social welfare perspective. It is certainly correct as a matter of law that non-SSO members lack standing to enforce the FRAND commitment. Commentators typically argue that contract enforcement is insufficient because injured consumers do not have standing, and thus antitrust enforcement is justified. These arguments typically assume both that: (1) all *ex post* modifications of FRAND commitments are inefficient; and (2) treble damages are required for optimal deterrence of patent holdup. As we have discussed previously, both assumptions are likely incorrect. Some modifications or breaches of FRAND commitments are efficient, and therefore a rule that deters such conduct is likely to result in social welfare losses. Further, because the probability of detecting patent holdup is nearly certain, the case of requiring treble damages and antitrust remedies is weak in this setting. Contract law damages are less likely to overdeter efficient conduct.[131]

Finally, a number of alternative common-law doctrines might allow some recovery for non-SSO members. For example, third parties might be able to recover reliance interests under the doctrine of promissory estoppel where the third party knew of the patent holder's promise to the SSO and the patent holder had reason to know that the third party would have expected to benefit from the promise.[132] In addition, as discussed previously, patent law might grant an "implied license" to third parties on the grounds that the third parties might reasonably assume that they are entitled to use the standard at the FRAND royalty rate.[133]

To be sure, judicial application of these alternative state and federal doctrines is fraught with opportunities for error in distinguishing good faith renegotiation from bad faith holdup, interpreting SSO terms, and identifying breaches of those terms where appropriate. Our claim is not that contract law handles these claims perfectly. Indeed, it is the transacting parties' ability to contract around most contract default rules that mitigates these error costs where they are significant. Rather, we note that the case for

---

[130] Non-SSO members presumably lack standing to bring this claim and are not likely to be considered third-party intended beneficiaries. See Restatement (Second) of Contracts § 302; Mark A. Lemley, supra note 124 at 1914–15.

[131] The conventional damages measure would include what the party injured by the breach expected to gain from performance under the contract.

[132] Lemley, supra note 124, at 1915. Restatement (Second) of Contracts § 90.

[133] See supra Section IV.B (discussing equitable estoppel); Lemley, supra note 124, at 1923–27 (discussing "implied license").

federal antitrust regulation depends on the notion that the welfare losses associated with patent holdup are sufficiently great after accounting for the mitigation of those harms through state law regimes. In our view, the substantive superiority of contract law undermines any potential justification for the application of the heavy and inflexible machinery of antitrust law in the patent holdup context.

The substantive superiority of contract law also provides the basis for rejecting the possibility that the Commission should incorporate the flexible standards of UCC 2–209 into antitrust law, exclusively through the application of Section 5 of the FTC Act and without Section 2 of the Sherman Act, in order to improve its analysis of patent holdup to account for the possibility of good faith modification. While such a development would provide a marginal improvement over the status quo, largely because the threat of private follow-on actions and treble damages would be minimized, any benefits from such a change would be superficial and would come at a significant cost. First, as discussed, it should be noted that *N-Data* suggests that the Commission is not interested in distinguishing good faith modification from opportunism. Rather, *N-Data* appears to adopt the view that any deviation from an *ex ante* FRAND commitment amounts to a violation of the antitrust laws. Second, *N-Data* also suggests that the Commission might be more than willing to apply a monopolization theory under Section 2 in a case with similar facts to *N-Data*, involving only the renegotiation of *ex ante* FRAND commitments made in good faith. The language in the *N-Data* majority to this effect gives us reason to treat with skepticism the argument that the Commission is likely to limit itself to the application of Section 5. Finally, and most importantly from our economics of federalism perspective, such a policy change by the Commission would amount to federalizing contract law and would eliminate any benefits from jurisdictional competition between the states on substantive doctrine.

Thus, while it is clear that the use of such rules to void or modify contract terms can usefully reduce opportunism, the use of such devices must be limited to avoid expropriation of the patent holder, and to maintain incentives for the contracting parties to control these problems *ex ante* through lower cost, alternative mechanisms. These conflicting effects suggest appropriate limits be placed on legal intervention aimed at addressing contractual opportunism. Under contract law, the costs generated by courts' errors in distinguishing between opportunistic and legitimate contracts are mitigated through the use of default rather than mandatory rules. Default contract rules allow the parties to opt out of undesirable or uncertain litigation outcomes by explicitly contracting out of the default rule *ex ante*. If courts choose inefficient default rules, the benefits of implied contract rules will be minimized (that is, such inefficient rules will result in a high rate of contracting around the rule, and as a result will apply to few transactions and have little economizing effect of the cost of contracting). However, if courts enforce contracts that explicitly contract around these inefficient default rules, the cost of error will also be small, as the parties' explicit terms, and not the erroneous default rule, will govern the contractual relationship. Thus, the fact that contract rules are default rules that can be contracted around by the parties and are not mandatory rules that cannot be waived serves as an important way parties limit the application of contract rules.

This analysis can be applied to examine the use of antitrust law to regulate opportunism by patentees. If mandatory contract rules are not appropriate to control contractual opportunism, the use of antitrust law or patent misuse to control opportunism is not appropriate for the same reasons. First, in contrast to default contract rules, antitrust laws, and also the law of patent misuse, cannot be waived or otherwise contracted around by the parties. Thus, the mandatory nature of these rules does not allow parties to avoid the inappropriate or uncertain application of these rules when efficient to do so *ex ante*. Moreover, antitrust laws feature remedies that include treble damages and fee shifting for prevailing plaintiffs, while contract remedies are limited, in large part, to prevent the enforcement of inefficient contracts. Thus, application of the antitrust laws lacks two of the primary safety valves that exist in contract law to control the error costs of erroneous or uncertain enforcement.

Moreover, the erroneous application of mandatory antitrust rules can broadly interfere with the parties' attempts to mitigate opportunism by using explicit contract terms. For example, an antitrust rule that failed to distinguish, for example, between opportunistic and nonopportunistic increases in price will discourage firms from entering into contractual commitments that may be efficient to breach or rescind later. Under contract law, parties can explicitly contract for a fixed or spot price. Moreover, a breach results in contract damages, which are set so that efficient breach is not deterred. Under the antitrust laws, parties are not able to contract around the rule, and damages, including treble damages, are set to deter.[134]

---

[134] For analyses of optimal antitrust damages, see William M. Landes, *Optimal Sanctions for Antitrust Violations*, 50 U. Chi. L. Rev. 652 (1983) (adopting optimal deterrence model); Herbert J. Hovenkamp, *Antitrust's Protected Classes*, 88 Mich. L. Rev. 1 (1989) (arguing for a broader definition of compensable antitrust claims); William H. Page, *Optimal Antitrust Penalties and Competitors' Injury*, 88 Mich. L. Rev. 2151 (1990) (criticizing broader approach).

We argue that, for these reasons, the courts have limited the ability to challenge the enforcement of patent owners for enforcing their patents. For example, the ability to challenge attempts to enforce patents through litigation as an antitrust violation is limited to "objectively baseless" claims under the sham exception to the *Noerr-Pennington* doctrine,[135] and to attempts to enforce patents procured by fraud on the Patent Office under *Walker Process*.[136] Similar considerations underlie the recognition that patentees do not have a duty to deal, and the Court's reluctance to regulate prices or licensing terms through the antitrust laws. These limitations recognize the uncertainty and error costs that would be generated if antitrust lawsuits were not so constrained. In contrast, an antitrust rule that attempted to define opportunism based on the evasion of explicit or implicit contractual price constraints as an antitrust offense would not respect these limits, and would likely intrude on the contracting process and the patentee's intellectual property rights.

B. Tort Law as an Alternative

While patent holdup issues would normally be handled by contract law in suit for breach by the SSO members, tort law offers a backstop as a final state law alternative where contract law is not available. An action in tort against the patent holder has some advantages over antitrust enforcement. While *Rambus* cites *Conwood* favorably as an example of deception rising to the level of exclusionary conduct under Section 2,[137] *Conwood* actually exemplifies some of the pitfalls of antitrust enforcement when applied to deceptive or tortious conduct.[138] Rather than rigorously engaging the qualitative and quantitative evidence to determine whether there was sufficient foreclosure, the Sixth Circuit assumed that UST's aggregate "bad" conduct was sufficiently widespread to create competitive injury. While the record supports Conwood's allegations that UST engaged in at least some intentionally tortious conduct, there is very little evidence to support an inference of harm to competition.[139] Specifically, the Sixth Circuit's failure to distinguish authorized from unauthorized product removal, or systematic

---

[135] *Prof'l Real Estate Investors, Inc. v. Columbia Pictures Indus.*, 508 U.S. 49 (1993) (requiring that those challenging the filing of lawsuits as antitrust violations show the suit to be "objectively baseless" in order to qualify for the sham exception to *Noerr-Pennington* antitrust immunity).

[136] *Walker Process Equip., Inc. v. Food Mach.*, 382 U.S. 172 (1965).

[137] *Rambus Inc. v. FTC*, 522 F.3d 456, 464 (D.C. Cir. 2008).

[138] *Conwood Co. v. U.S. Tobacco Co.*, 290 F.3d 768 (6th Cir. 2002).

[139] Wright, supra note 72.

product destruction from limited, one-time events, allowed harm to a competitor to substitute for evidence of harm to competition. Despite the state of evidence insufficient to support an inference of anticompetitive effect, the Sixth Circuit affirmed a $1.05 billion award, the largest verdict in the history of antitrust law at the time.[140] Consequently, commentators have heavily, and correctly, criticized *Conwood*.[141]

Antitrust claims involving deceptive conduct conventionally require a preliminary showing of harm to competition on the grounds that this type of conduct is rarely egregious enough to exclude rivals and impair the competitive process.[142] However, *Conwood* demonstrates that in cases involving conduct that is perceived to be immoral or tortious, these requirements may be set aside in favor of more lenient standards.[143] For example, the Sixth Circuit did not require the plaintiff to document that the defendant's conduct resulted in substantial foreclosure, to distinguish authorized from presumptively unlawful unauthorized product removal, or that the conduct was causally linked to any alleged antitrust injury.

The lessons of *Conwood* for antitrust enforcement of patent holdup are both clear and related to our primary analytical point. Where the defendant's conduct involves deception and alleged misrepresentation, the potential for assigning antitrust liability without sufficient evidence of harm to competition is substantial and invokes the potential for the "serious mistakes" discussed in *Credit Suisse* in support of creating antitrust limits. When antitrust treble damage remedies are applied to conduct that does not have the potential to create antitrust injury, pro-competitive conduct, such as participation in standards, can be chilled and consumers harmed. Thus, antitrust enforcement of fraudulent or deceptive nondisclosure of

---

[140] Several private follow-on treble damage actions were also filed against the defendant, United States Tobacco.

[141] Herbert Hovenkamp, THE ANTITRUST ENTERPRISE: PRINCLE AND EXECUTION 180 (Cambridge University Press 2005) (describing *Conwood* as "deeply troublesome and offensive to antitrust policy"); Wright, supra note 72.

[142] In the context of false or misleading statements about a rival, a substantial preliminary burden must be satisfied. See *Am. Prof'l Testing Serv., Inc. v. Harcourt Brace Jovanovich Legal & Prof'l Publ'ns, Inc.*, 108 F.3d 1147, 1152 (9th Cir. 1997) ("while false or misleading advertising directed solely at a single competitor may not be competition on the merits, the [conduct] in question must have a significant and enduring adverse impact on competition itself in the relevant markets to rise to the level of an antitrust violation").

[143] The conventional approach to assessing the anticompetitive effects of potentially exclusionary conduct under Section 2 is evident in decisions involving exclusive dealing contracts. See, e.g., *Omega Envtl., Inc. v. Gilbarco Co.*, 127 F.3d 1157, 1163–64 (9th Cir. 1997); *R.J. Reynolds Tobacco Co. v. Philip Morris Inc.*, 199 F. Supp. 2d 362 (M.D.N.C. 2002), *aff'd per curiam*, 67 F. App'x 810 (4th Cir. 2003). See generally Joshua D. Wright, *Antitrust Law and Competition for Distribution*, 23 YALE J. REG. 169 (2006).

intellectual property rights in the standard-setting context can give rise to substantial social welfare losses.

But does antitrust offer any benefits relative to the alternative of common-law tort liability? For instance, a fraud or misrepresentation theory might be applied in settings where the patentee knowingly fails to disclose the existence of an intellectual property right.[144] Such a claim would have the advantage, from the plaintiff's perspective, of avoiding the burden of defining markets or demonstrating harm to competition. On the other hand, standing to bring a fraud claim would likely be limited to SSO members, excluding consumers and non-members. Another important difference is that tort liability would not include treble damages.[145] While commentators have noted that both contract and tort damages are likely to be insufficient to vindicate injuries to consumers, who would not have standing to bring either claim, these arguments seem to assume without justification that more deterrence is always better from a social welfare perspective. As discussed previously, because the probability of detection for this sort of deceptive conduct followed by a rate increase is very high, we are skeptical that treble damages are necessary for optimal deterrence. Because of the possibility of punitive damages in the tort context, however, it is unclear whether fraud damages would be closer to the optimal level than antitrust treble damages *ex ante.* For this reason, equitable estoppel would appear to be a superior approach to fraud claims in the standard-setting context.

While the primary potential advantage of tort-based fraud theories over antitrust is that the former avoids the potential for the type of substantial error costs described in our *Conwood* discussion, the benefits of federalism also weigh in favor of restraining application of antitrust laws to deceptive conduct in the standard-setting context. Courts are especially susceptible to making errors when applying antitrust laws to deceptive conduct because it is perceived as without efficiency justification, immoral, and worthy of condemnation. Applying the antitrust laws to such settings is likely to result in type I errors and social welfare losses. In light of this analysis, we conclude that jurisdictional competition in state contract and tort law is more likely to generate efficient rules and institutions than antitrust.

---

[144] *Rambus, Inc. v. Infineon Tech Corp.*, 318 F.3d 1081 (Fed. Cir. 2003) (finding that Rambus did not have a duty to disclose patent applications, and thus did not commit fraud under Virginia Law). See generally, Lemley, supra note 124, at 1935 (discussing common law fraud claims in the standard-setting context); Richard H. Stern, Rambus v. Infineon: *The Superior Aptness of Common-law Remedies Than Antitrust for Standardisation Skullduggery,* 2001 Eur. Intell. Prop. Rev. 495.

[145] However, fraud allegations classified as intentional torts may give rise to punitive damages which might well exceed antitrust treble damages.

VI. Conclusion

The problem of patent holdup starkly illustrates the potential conflict between the patent and antitrust laws. As Ward Bowman pointed out long ago, a conflict in the goals of antitrust and patent laws is illusory. Patents are not monopolies, and antitrust law and patent law can both be viewed as institutions that seek to maximize consumer welfare. However, in practice, the patent and antitrust laws may generate significant conflicts. Indeed, the Supreme Court's recent holdings on implied preemption of the antitrust laws have recognized the risk of error as a central factor in limiting application of the antitrust laws. In this chapter we argue that these considerations, coupled with the benefits of competitive federalism, suggest that courts and policy makers seriously consider limiting application of federal antitrust laws when a superior state law regime exists. We argue that the issue of patent holdup of SSOs presents such a case and that reliance on state contract and tort law, as well as on provisions of the federal patent laws, would be superior to extending antitrust law to address this problem.

Index

Printed in the United States
By Bookmasters